CLAYTON ESHLEMAN: THE ESSENTIAL POETRY 1960–2015

Introduction by Stuart Kendall

CLAYTON ESHLEMAN: THE ESSENTIAL POETRY 1960–2015

Black Widow Press is an imprint of Commonwealth Books, Inc., Boston, MA. Distributed to the trade by NBN (National Book Network) throughout North America, Canada, and the U.K. All Black Widow Press books are printed on acid-free paper, and glued into bindings. Black Widow Press and its logo are registered trademarks of Commonwealth Books, Inc.

Joseph S. Phillips & Susan J. Wood, PhD, Publishers

Front Cover Design by Peter Blegvad, *The Essential Poetry*
Design & Text Production by Kerrie Kemperman

ISBN: 978-0996007900
Published in the USA
10 9 8 7 6 5 4 3 2 1

For my wife Caryl
with all my love

CREDO

The poet is the person who in being bound to the earth finds *out* via saying the binding & accompanying his self with all the metaphoric extensions struck by the nature of his particular fix. He works for the greatest showing, thus he is monstrous, & by admitting what he is not, along with the negativity of his times, potentially complete. He alone is responsible for any conflict between love & vision; no one else is responsible for his fate—yet he is the companion of the other, & of others in his age, in the sense that he attempts to make his work cohere & communicate. If he has an audience, it consists of the chairs (those cribs in which the souls of the great dead are in incubational holding-patterns) as well as the living bodies on the chairs. Yet his communication is at threshold with & to himself, for he is primarily an example of transformation (alchemically, psychologically & socially) for those potential poets to come. He is one who has been baptized by desire as well as one who, at the hub of desire, follows out its spokes into the ecstatic & the weird; those dead-end regions which argue a significance in exhaustion, bewilderment & despair. In these ways, he is timeless & timed, linked to those shamans of old who sought the place of origin where, without the incubus of sin, they discarded the natal body for a body of their own creation. The poet knows that this place of origin is below hell & still contactable today, that inspiration is the antiphonal swing of orgasm, & that via image-making he participates not only in the media torrent of his times but in that primary transference some 35,000 years ago: the move from no image of the world to *an* image.

28 July 1993

THE ESSENTIAL POETRY 1960–2015

Life Commitment, an Introduction by Stuart Kendall ~ i

I.
1960–1973

The Roaches (1960)* ~ 3

MEXICO & NORTH (1962)*
Evocation ~ 5
Inheritance ~ 8
Las Brujas ~ 10
Water-Song ~ 11
The Strong ~ 13
La Mujer ~14
Dark Blood ~ 16

WALKS (1967)*
Walk VI ~ 17
Letter to César Calvo Concerning the Inauguration of a Monument
    to César Vallejo ~ 20
"This son who's appeared to us…" ~ 29

THE HOUSE OF OKUMURA (1969)*
Sections II, III, VI, VIII, XIII ~ 31

THE HOUSE OF IBUKI (1969)*
Ibuki Masuko ~ 44
Public Bath ~ 46
Tsuruginomiya ~ 49
New Guinea I: The Leg ~ 54
New Guinea II: Becoming Serious ~ 56

Asterisks indicate poems with notes in the Gratitude & Annotation section.

COILS (1973)   Part I *
The Book of Yorunomado ~ 58
The Book of Niemonjima ~ 66

INDIANA (1969)
The Crocus Bud ~ 77
Hand* ~ 78
The 1802 Blake to Butts Letter Variation* ~ 79
Sensing Duncan II* ~ 83
The Yellow Garment ~ 86
The Black Hat ~ 88
Diagonal* ~ 94
The Bedford Vision ~ 99
Sunday Afternoon ~ 104

ALTARS (1971)
Ode to Reich * ~ 108

COILS (1973)   Part II
Origin* ~ 112
The Golden String* ~ 121
Keeping the Flies from My Mother's Head* ~ 123
The Baptism of Desire ~ 125
The Bridge at the Mayan Pass ~ 130
The Physical Traveler ~ 137
Coils* ~ 140

II.
1975–1986

THE GULL WALL (1975)
Gargoyles ~ 155
Sugar ~ 156
Bud Powell* ~ 160
Portrait of Vincent Van Gogh* ~ 162
Portrait of Charlie Parker ~ 165

At the Tomb of Vallejo ~ 167
"Leon Golub working on a painting"* ~ 170
Portrait of Francis Bacon* ~ 172

WHAT SHE MEANS (1978)
Eternity ~ 178
The Dragon Rat Tail ~ 180
Still-Life, with Fraternity* ~ 185
Scorpion Hopscotch* ~ 188
The Green Apple Photo* ~ 189
Old Jewish Cemetery ~ 191
At the Tomb of Abigdor Karo ~ 193
Charles Bridge, Wednesday Morning ~ 194
Archai ~ 198
Still-life with African Violets* ~ 201
Danse Macabre ~ 204
Canso ~ 206

HADES IN MANGANESE (1981)
The Lich Gate* ~ 209
Frida Kahlo's Release* ~ 211
Turnstiles* ~ 215
Hermes Butts In ~ 218
Master Hanus to his Blindness* ~ 220
Equal Time ~ 223
For Aimé Césaire* ~ 225
Cimmeria ~ 226

FRACTURE (1983)
The Death of Bill Evans* ~ 227
Fracture ~ 229
Tomb of Donald Duck* ~ 231
Millennium ~ 239
The Spiritual Hunt* ~ 240
Matthuna* ~ 244
Elegy* ~ 246
The Color Rake of Time ~ 249

OUR JOURNEY AROUND THE DROWNED CITY OF IS
    (1985)
Kerlescan* ~ 250
Apotheosis ~ 254

THE NAME ENCANYONED RIVER (1986)
Junk Mail~ 255
Lemons ~ 258
The Excavation of Artaud*~ 260
Scarlet Experiment ~ 261
Ariadne's Reunion* ~ 262
Dear Sign ~ 266
Deeds Done and Suffered by Light* ~ 267
The Man with a Beard of Roses ~ 271

III.
1989–1998

HOTEL CRO-MAGNON (1989)
A Memorial to the Grand ~ 275
The Night Against its Lit Elastic ~ 276
Reagan at Bitburg* ~ 279
Variations on Jesus and the Fly ~ 281
"I love to watch Caryl eat fresh Dungeness crab…" ~ 283
Moving ~ 284
Looking for a House ~ 286
Thanksgiving with Maya ~ 287
The Bison Keyboard* ~ 290
Commarque* ~ 291
On Atget's Road* ~ 293
Pan's Signal Tower ~ 294
Ode to the Man in the Moon ~ 296
Children of the Monosyllable* ~ 298
At the Speed of Wine* ~ 302
Spelunking the Skeleton ~ 312

UNDER WORLD ARREST (1994)
Short Story ~ 314
Still-life with Huidobro* ~ 316
Indiana in the Night Sky* ~ 317
Double Pelican* ~ 319
Under Louse Arrest ~ 320
After Pindar* ~ 321
A Friendship* ~ 322
Strata* ~ 326
Basra Highway ~ 327
Bloodrock ~ 328
The Skeletons Talk Turkey ~ 330
Out of the Kat Godeu* ~ 331
Hardball* ~ 335
Ground ~ 337
Cooking ~ 338
The Wine Graveyard ~ 340
Guyton Place* ~ 341
Position Paper ~ 345
Gorgeous George Comes Pounding Down the Beach ~ 346
Navel of the Moon* ~ 348
Cempasúchil* ~ 353

FROM SCRATCH (1998)
Intention ~ 360
Nora's Roar * ~ 361
Nightcrawlers* ~ 374
Schmatte Variations* ~ 375
Yachats, the Shore ~ 378
Less and Less Wholly Absorbed, Aware* ~ 381
Soutine's Lapis* ~ 382
On a Photograph of Gall ~ 399
El Mozote* ~ 400
Liberation Footage ~ 402
I, Friedrich Schröder-Sonnenstern* ~ 403
My Evening with Artaud* ~ 407
De Kooning's Excavation* ~ 413
Blues for Byzantium* ~ 415

IV.
2003

JUNIPER FUSE (2003)*
For Caryl ~ 419
Silence Raving (1979)* ~ 420
Hades in Manganese (1979)* ~ 422
Permanent Shadow (1980)* ~ 429
Placements I: "The New Wilderness" (1978)* ~ 430
Dot (1981)* ~ 432
Our Lady of the Three-Pronged Devil (1980)* ~ 433
The Aurignacians Have the Floor (1979)* ~ 437
Visions of the Fathers of Lascaux (1980)* ~ 439
Magdalenian (1980)* ~ 454
Notes on a Visit to Le Tuc d'Audoubert (1982)* ~ 455
A Kind of Moisture on the Wall (1982)* ~ 462
Through Breuil's Eyes (1983)* ~ 465
Placements II: "The Aranea Constellation" (1985)* ~ 467
The Atmosphere, Les Eyzies (1987)* ~ 478
"Abri du Cro-Magnon was earlier..." (1987)* ~ 480
The Power Room (1994)* ~ 483
Like Violets, He Said (1990)* ~ 485
Cemeteries of Paradise (2000)* ~ 486
Placements III: "So Be It" (1994)* ~ 489
Thalassa Variations (1994)* ~ 491
Venusberg (1994)* ~ 495
The Chaos of the Wise (1994)* ~ 497
Neanderthal Skull (1998)* ~ 499
Some Fugal Lubrication (1994)* ~ 500
At the Hinge of Creation (2002)* ~ 503
Prolegomena (2002)* ~ 505
A Phosphene Gauntlet (1998)* ~ 507
Le Combel (1998)* ~ 508
Indeterminate, Open (1998)* ~ 511
Matrix, Blower (1998)* ~ 518
The Black Goddess (2002)* ~ 524

EVERWHAT (2003)
Michaux, 1956 ~ 530
Corot, 1870 ~ 533
Noguchi, 1984* ~ 537
Bacon Studies (III)* ~ 539
Spirits of the Head" ~ 543
The Magical Sadness of Omar Cáceres* ~ 545
Figure and Ground* ~ 546
Darger* ~ 549

V.
2004–2007

MY DEVOTION (2004)
Before the Wall ~ 559
Rock and Rootstock ~ 560
Five Queasy Pieces ~ 561
Across the Bering Strait* ~ 563
Blue Zone* ~ 564
Bedroom, 6 AM ~ 570
Animals Out of the Snow ~ 571
In Happiness a Power ~ 573
Some Rock Off Which to Travel ~ 574
Inside Caryl's Left Shoulder ~ 575
Shopping* ~ 578
The Hybrid is the Engine of Anima Display* ~ 581
Grand Cascade ~ 582
Riff ~ 584
Morphologies of Paradise ~ 585

AN ALCHEMIST WITH ONE EYE ON FIRE (2006)
Nocturnal Veils ~ 589
Pause* ~ 592
Irish Jig ~ 593
An Enigmatic Signifier* ~ 595

Samperi's Diagram* ~ 597
For Gustaf Sobin* ~ 599
Transformational Gradations ~ 600
From a Terrace ~ 602
Iraqi Morgue* ~ 605
Minor Drag ~ 607
Unbuckled Tongue ~ 608
Surveillant Veils ~ 610
Combined Object* ~ 612

ARCHAIC DESIGN (2007)
The Assault* ~ 615

RECIPROCAL DISTILLATIONS (2007)
Witchery* ~ 622
Chauvet, Left Wall of End Chamber* ~ 623
The Beheading* ~ 625
Joan Mitchell's Spinnerets ~ 630
Monumental* ~ 633

VI.
2010–2014

ANTICLINE (2010)
The Tjurunga* ~ 639
In Memory of George Butterick ~ 644
Hmmm* ~ 646
Placenta ~ 649
Octavio's Labyrinth* ~ 650
Día de muertos ~ 652
The Left Foot of King Ramesses I* ~ 653
Descent ~ 656
Poem to Help Will Alexander Fight Cancer* ~ 658
Eternity at Domme* ~ 661
Zürn Heads* ~ 662
Munch Dissolves* ~ 664

Goya Black* ~ 667
Blue Sphinx ~ 669
Ode to Nancy Spero* ~ 670
Xibalbá* ~ 671
Max Ernst During the Rain* ~ 673
In Deep Sleep Dorothea Tanning Receives & Accepts the Awakened
    Clouds Above Her* ~ 676
Pollock Pouring* ~ 680

Gratitude and Annotation ~ 683

Stuart Kendall

LIFE COMMITMENT

In 1960, Clayton Eshleman — who was then twenty-five years old and a graduate student in English at Indiana University — sent some of his poetry to Cid Corman with a note describing his admiration for *Origin*, the magazine Corman had founded and edited from 1951 to 1957. Corman's response to the young poet was immediate and searing. The poems, he said, were a waste of his and of Eshleman's own time: either get serious about poetry or stop writing it. Eshleman later wrote that the comment "smacked [him] in the face *and* implied that there was a life commitment — indeed a commitment to life — in writing poetry."[1] In the fifty-five years since he received Corman's letter, Clayton Eshleman has published roughly one hundred books and chapbooks of original poetry, translations, and nonfiction writings, and edited seventy issues of magazines and journals. It is undoubtedly unnecessary to observe that he made and has fulfilled a life commitment to poetry.

But exactly what kind of commitment is implied here? What is entailed by a life commitment to poetry when that commitment is indistinguishable from a commitment to life? Eshleman's remark implies a relationship between poetry and life that supersedes the Romantic notion of the life of a poet. That notion has been lampooned in myriad popular images of the poet as an effete, disengaged, sensitive soul, caught up in his or her own musings, cut off from the common stream of life in his or her times. The commitment of the Romantic poet might be a commitment to poetry but a commitment to poetry does not necessarily entail a commitment to life, rather the opposite in fact. Poetry in the Romantic model — and in others besides — seeks no justification beyond itself; indeed, it strives to be a thing unto itself, hermetic and sealed, autonomous, an art for art's sake. Such an art implicitly and explicitly avoids questions of entanglement, implication, or responsibility. Written purely for itself, it seeks no justification. Isolated from the world, it takes no responsibility.

Eshleman's commitment to poetry is of an entirely different order. In his commitment, poetry becomes a vehicle for life and life a vehicle for poetry: the two interpenetrate and are entwined. "As a lost soul in the Midwestern 1950s," Eshleman wrote in another context, "I discovered [poetry's] power to change and enable one to stand more self-revealed."[2] The remark recalls — but significantly modifies — an observation from Charles Olson's *Maximus Poems:* "people/don't change. They only stand more / revealed. I, / likewise."[3] Self-revelation here is linked to commitment and to a tradition — a legacy even — in American poetry. But for Eshleman, significantly and going beyond Olson's purpose, poetry has the power to change the self, to become a vehicle of self-emancipation.

Olson also speaks to the power of commitment in his poem "The Kingfishers": "I have my kin, if for no other reason than/ (as he said, next of kin) I commit myself, and, / given my freedom, I'd be a cad / if I didn't."[4] Olson's commitment entails taking a stand, committing oneself to an idea or opinion. Olson's language here alludes to Ezra Pound's famous remark, from the preface to his *Guide to Kulchur:* "Given my freedom, I may be a fool to use it, but I wd. be a cad not to."[5] Pound's freedom is the freedom to commit oneself, to take a position, to assume responsibility for some idea, thing, or person. It is a freedom freighted with burden: and such commitments are not to be entered into lightly.

Thus while in the autobiographical note to his book *Altars,* Eshleman can write: "my poetics are the oldest and most engaging human adventure: the emancipation of the self"; he can also claim, in the preface to *Under World Arrest:* "I […] refuse to release myself from the complexities of an eros that while not cruel in itself is congruent to the news reports of the suffering of others and must make its way into articulation burdened by its awareness."[6] Elsewhere he describes the challenge of the poet's journey in these terms, alluding to Arthur Rimbaud: "If the poet is the thief of fire, he is the one who journeys into the depths of his subconscious in order to bring up the dark treasures that are concealed there. And he may pay a dear price for doing so, as the derangement process may result in addiction, dereliction, or in the kind of being out of it that makes it impossible for an individual to function in society."[7] There are dangers, in other words, all around, within and without, as well as in the very process itself of uncovering and expressing the material that is the life of poetry. Consistent with these views and challenges, in the essay that opens his book *An Alchemist With One Eye On Fire,* Eshleman offers the following definition of the poetic art: "Poetry is about extending human consciousness, making conscious the unconscious, creating symbolic consciousness that in its finest moments overcomes all the dualities in which the human world is cruelly and eternally, it seems, enmeshed."[8] Poetry, for Eshleman, is the drama of consciousness enfolding the world in its embrace, in all of its tragedy and triumph, tenderness and terror.

The world embraced by Eshleman's poetry is our world. As a contemporary writer, Eshleman's history is our own: his writing a record and reflection of our times. Eshleman's story — the story revealed in his poetry — is the story of mid-America meeting the wider world in the 1950s; the story of the collapse of colonial empires around the world and the rise of the global South; the story of social and political radicalism, in the 1960s, and of a counterculture raising a voice in poetry and in art; of the challenges, frustrations and anomie that befell that counterculture and of the continued and indeed on-going drama of empire and overreaching power, from El Salvador in the 1980s to the recent disasters of Afghanistan and Iraq.

Eshleman discovered poetry in the late 1950s at a precipitous moment defined in some ways by the scope and intent of Donald Allen's *The New American Poetry 1945–1960*. This was also the moment of the mimeograph and small press revolution in American culture and counterculture. Eshleman's earliest publications were part of that moment and, in the late 1960s, with his *Caterpillar* books and magazine, in significant ways he helped to define it. Eshleman published his first translations of César Vallejo with Grove Press in 1968 and his first major collection of his own work, *Indiana*, with Black Sparrow Press in 1969. For the next three decades, Black Sparrow would be the primary publisher of his own writing and for many of those whose aesthetic was closest to his own. But, significantly, when Eshleman published a second version of his celebrated work on Vallejo in 1978 that volume was published by a university press and when, in 1981, he founded his second magazine, *Sulfur*, it too was sponsored, in part, by an academic institution, initially by the California Institute of Technology, though ultimately by Eastern Michigan University. By the time Eshleman folded the magazine almost twenty years later, even academic and public forms of funding for contemporary poetry had become tenuous and unreliable. Amid these uncertainties a new culture of poetry dominated by academic writing programs and workshops had become hegemonic. New forms of digital distribution and publishing — new online journals, new more flexible modes of small press, print-on-demand, and personal publishing — had emerged even as some publishers reinvested in book design, marketing, and presentation, reinvigorating or attempting to reinvigorate the literary marketplace from both the top and the bottom.

These are cultural and social events coursing through the work. There are obviously personal ones as well. In his book *Fracture*, Eshleman observed: "There are only a handful of primary incidents in one's life."[9] Between those incidents, periods of ebb and flow, the tides of a life, moments in which a life turns upon itself, gathers, looks back with a pause. The rhythms of a life can be both slow and fast, moving in months and years as well as moments. Reflecting on Clayton Eshleman's life through the record of his work, several periods and turning points become apparent, beginning with his discovery of poetry in 1958. His experiences in the late 1950s and very early 1960s were formative through his repeated trips to Mexico and his encounters with other poets — Cid Corman but also Paul Blackburn, Robert Kelly, Jerome Rothenberg, and many others — but his true apprenticeship in poetry — his experience of "the crisis of becoming a poet"[10] — took shape most decisively in Kyoto, Japan, from 1962 to 1964, where he was teaching English, translating César Vallejo, and struggling with his own writing and life. That apprenticeship continued back in Indiana then in Lima, Peru, and in New York in the mid-to-late 1960s, culminating in the foundation of *Caterpillar* magazine in 1967, his first published translation of Vallejo's *Poemas humanos* in 1968, his completion of Reichian analysis with Sidney Handelman in 1969, his meeting and eventual marriage to Caryl Reiter (later Caryl Eshleman), and, finally, after moving to Los Angeles, the publication of *Coils*, a book-length poetic self-interrogation, a decade in the making, in 1973. The last issue of *Caterpillar* appeared that same year.

The following year while living in France, Clayton and Caryl discovered the Paleolithic painted caves of the Dordogne, which beckoned a descent into physical and psychical underworlds that would last twenty-five years and more. The poetic record of that descent can be traced through much of Eshleman's own writing produced in these years but the precipitate is his major work, *Juniper Fuse: Upper Paleolithic Imagination & the Construction of the Underworld*. Alongside this work, Eshleman coiled back into Vallejo, retranslating *Poemas humanos* along with his other posthumous poetry with José Rubia Barcia, and back into Aimé Césaire, whose work he had first translated in the 1960s with Denis Kelly, as well as branching out, or digging down, translating Antonin Artaud and other "conductors of the pit," often re-translating them in turn over the years. César Vallejo, *The Complete Posthumous Poetry* won the National Book Award in 1979 and marked another watershed moment in Eshleman's career. Another magazine, *Sulfur* soon followed.

In 1986, Eshleman become a professor in the English department at Eastern Michigan University, moving to Ypsilanti, where he and Caryl still live. His publications in the second half of the 1980s included a group of retrospective volumes: *The Name Encanyoned River: Selected Poems, Antiphonal Swing: Selected Prose,* and *Conductors of the Pit* — which is effectively a volume of selected translations — as well as *Novices: A Study of Poetic Apprenticeship,* a work whose purpose presumes a sense of accomplishment.

Near the turn of the millennium, Eshleman concluded *Juniper Fuse* and published another volume of selected prose, *Companion Spider,* as well as the final issue of *Sulfur,* in near coincidence. Shortly thereafter he retired from teaching, freeing time and energy for his own work, which again came to include new writing as well as summational volumes: a second edition of *Conductors of the Pit* and *The Grindstone of Rapport: A Clayton Eshleman Reader;* his definitive work on Vallejo — now including Vallejo's complete poetry — as well as on Aimé Césaire.

The figure of the coil is significant here, as is that of the labyrinth. One has the image of the poet digging further and further into himself, through his work and his times, visiting and revisiting, envisioning and re-visioning his experiences, relationships, processes and strategies of encounter. "I am fully in a labyrinth of, and not of, my own making — I've gained entry, fought my way to the center."[11] The task is endless and unfinished, even unfinishable. As Eshleman observes, there is a "bitter" combat in the labyrinth of life in poetry, the realizations of writing remain partial, incomplete: "The Minotaur is at best crippled, never slain, and the poet never strides forth from the labyrinth heroic and intact" ("The Aranea Constellation").[12]

In the introduction to *Fracture,* Eshleman evokes the moment in 1958 in which he began writing poetry as well as his motives for doing so. At that time, he writes "forces were breaking out like diseases, and for years I was beside myself with the mid-western hydra that had been unleashed. The main thing that kept me going was a belief that if I fully worked through the sexism, self-hate, bodilessness, soullessness, and suffocated human relationships which encrusted my background, I could excavate a basement. I would have torn down the 'House of Eshleman' and laid out a new foundation in its place."[13] Eshleman's search for emancipation is a search for emancipation from these things.

His poem "The Death of Bill Evans" evokes a similar landscape of childhood trauma in a figure he elsewhere calls an inner leper and equates with the alchemical *vilifigura,* "the reviled face, the shame of your own face"[14]:

> Can't see the wound for the scars,
> a small boy composed of scabs is staring into
> the corner of his anatomy — where walls and floor end
> he figures he ends, so he wears his end
> like glasses before his eyes,
> beckoned into the snow he will be beaten
> by children he thought were his friends,
> the implication of his hurt is so dark
> it will scab over to be rescabbed the next time,
> and he will grow not by an internal urge to mature
> but by scabbings until, grown big, he will be the size of an adult
> and his face will look like a pebbly gourd.
> He will stay inside the little house I have built for him, in which to
> stand he must stoop.[15]

Elsewhere Eshleman adds some more specific details to this portrait of wounds, scars and scabs: "I was brought up in an anesthetically clean Presbyterian home where smoking, drinking, swearing and gambling were not permitted, where I was an only child who was not allowed to play with Catholics, Jews, Negroes, children younger or older than I was, children whose parents smoked, drank, etc., or whose mothers wore slacks away from home."[16] Eshleman's mother, Gladys, devoted herself to him. His father, Ira Clayton Eshleman Senior, worked as an engineer and efficiency expert at a slaughterhouse and meat packing plant in Indianapolis. The poet's later fascination with the flayed flesh painted by Chaim Soutine may have its origins in childhood memories: "I carry the slaughterhouse," he wrote, mingling memories and creative imagination, in his portrait of the painter in *The Gull Wall*.[17]

In a poem about another visual artist, Henry Darger, Eshleman reflects on his own childhood: "Darger is the reminder of the huge absence I felt as a child, / 'staring at the corner for hours,' my mother told Caryl, / 'he was such a good boy.'"[18] "Good" here is synonymous with a vacant, empty, all but anonymous, self as cipher.

There are other similar memories, other evocations of vacant, repressed, and wounded youth throughout the work. We need not catalog them here. They are not the end of the story, nor even the "apex of the pain": that apex is found in the poet's experiences as a pledge and initiate in the Phi Delta Theta fraternity at Indiana University in 1953.

> Hell Week, 1953,
> a postcard Hades mailed to me,
> his kids in demon suits tied a string
> about my penis led up through my white shirt
> tied to a "pull me" card dangling
> from my sport-coat pocket. The personal
> is the apex of pain[19]

A portrait can be sketched of the poet as pledge suffering humiliations at the hands of the brothers, paddled bloody each night of Hell Week, running in a pack of young men on the make, screwing the girls who would in the backs of cars. As Eshleman later recognized, the humiliation imposed by the fraternity structure was "devastating for women, for all the guys back then were taking their brutalization out on women. The coeds in those days were icy virgins, or, if they allowed any sexual contact it became a feeding frenzy. The process turned the woman into an unpaid whore."[20] At a low point, he helps a friend examine the remnants of a back-alley abortion by the headlights of his car: "We might as well have been looking into a mirror [...] we were searching for pieces of flesh" ("Still Life, With Fraternity").[21] The story here is one of a socially imposed will and willfully accepted personal humiliation, drawing everyone involved into a vortex of personal and interpersonal objectification, violence, and trauma.

The story of Phi Delta Theta is a story of initiation, but, in this case, the initiate would ultimately turn away from the tribe, reconstruct his personality, and struggle into an entirely different way of life. The poet grappled with these experiences for decades and continues to acknowledge their power in some of his most recent writing.[22] He even returned to spend time in the fraternity house more than a decade later, in 1968, hoping to wrest the memories into poetic life. "Still-Life, With Fraternity" from *What She Means* offers one poignant take on this moment in Eshleman's mid-century, mid-Western, American life, but it is not the only one.

Poetry would be the key to Eshleman's own personal emancipation, his emergence into a psychologically healthy adulthood, capable of caring for himself and for others, but there were other, earlier harbingers of that emancipation in other forms. His first experiences with the arts were not literary at all but visual and later musical. As a child and young adolescent, he enjoyed the "funnies" in the newspaper, collected comic books, and took drawing classes. "I think I might have become a painter had there been a more intense art atmosphere to involve myself with in Indianapolis at the time."[23] As it is, Eshleman would explore Federico Garcia Lorca's remark to Jorge Luis Borges that Mickey Mouse was the symbol of America through numerous pop and post-pop references to comic or cartoon figures, as in "Visions of the Fathers of Lascaux" and "The Tomb of Donald Duck" in *Fracture*.[24]

Jazz music struck, as it were, a deeper chord. "While reading Sunday comics on the living-room floor was my first encounter, as a boy, with imagination, [Bud] Powell was my first encounter, as an adolescent, with the figure of the artist."[25] Eshleman stumbled into jazz music in the early 1950s, while in high school. He had been taking piano lessons in his neighborhood since his early youth, playing classical music, but jazz was something else entirely. "Somehow it got through to me in a very rudimentary way that these guys were not following the melody, but were changing it, improvising on it, which immediately suggested one could change the way one lived. In other words, I had been brought up in a very strict family where I was being programmed to be a Xerox of my father and go into business school. But [Bud] Powell was varying the melody, he was creating his *own* melody line. It translated into: you can vary your life, you can play variations on what you've been given."[26] Even as he was pledging Phi Delta Theta, Eshleman was deeply involved with playing jazz music. During the summer between his freshman and sophomore years he traveled to Los Angeles with a friend to listen to West Coast Jazz and study piano with Bud Powell's brother, Richie. During graduate school, he would support himself playing piano in a cocktail lounge. But somehow even jazz was not powerful enough to pull him out of Indiana. Drawing and music were both encouraged by his parents, within limits, and Eshleman recognized the limits of his talents in these areas. Poetry however was an art that he discovered on his own, without parental sanction, and one without similar limitations.[27]

But Eshleman's emergence as a poet would take time, as noted above, he had to pass through a period of prolonged apprenticeship.[28] The notion of apprenticeship sounds odd to ears tuned to contemporary youth-oriented culture. The generation immediately following Eshleman's own — the Baby Boomers — promoted a fascination with youth exemplified by the phrase, stuttered in incantation by Roger Daltrey, "I hope I di-di-die before I get old." Since the 1960s, market driven cultural production has become all but entirely centered on the young, channeling consumption for children by parents and later by the young themselves. Even as it remains a fact of human experience, the notion that a young person or young people might need to pass through a humbling period of potentially prolonged apprenticeship is all but incomprehensible today.

But apprenticeship is a doubly challenging concept here since in Eshleman's usage the term does not signify a process terminating in mastery, if indeed one can say that it terminates at all. There is always more to learn about oneself and one's craft, the point of poetry as Eshleman conceives of it seems to be a means of consistent and repeated engagement with both self and world. Internalizing this practice as a reliable means of doing so marks the end of apprenticeship.

The growth traumas of this period and process of apprenticeship were, for Eshleman, literary, psychological, and social by turns: those of a man discovering his capacities as a writer, but more importantly his self-relation through writing, while at the same time coming to grips with his background and horizon of experience — who he has been and is

— as well as with his place in the world, as a citizen, friend, and lover. The scope of this endeavor is a measure of Eshleman's commitment to poetry and to life as well as to his understanding and vision of both.

Eshleman discovered poetry around 1958 and immediately began writing condensed, largely observational verse, some of which would be collected in his first book, *Mexico & North*. As suggested by the title of that volume, these poems were already engaged with the problem of the self and its limits, with testing the boundaries of the self through personal encounters and experiences with other people and cultures. By 1962, however, living in Kyoto, Eshleman recognized that he had reached something of a stalemate in his writing and in his life. He sat for hours agonizing over single lines on his typewriter. He struggled with nervous disorders affecting his digestion, among other things, and once passed out while reading William Blake. During this period, Eshleman set for himself the challenge that he believed would constitute his personal apprenticeship in poetry: translating César Vallejo's *Poemas humanos*. By setting this goal for himself, Eshleman allowed Vallejo to become something of a spiritual mentor to him, a guide or tutelary spirit, which would show him the way or at least *one* way to live a life committed to poetry.

There were other mentors as well. In some senses, Eshleman's struggles with his father and with his fraternity brothers reflect early forms of his search for a reliable model of adult male behavior. His later friendships with Paul Blackburn and Cid Corman, coincident with his Vallejo-apprenticeship, both testify to a similar yearning for counsel. In his essay "The Gull Wall," Eshleman recounts an incident with Paul Blackburn in which the slightly older poet — Blackburn was nine years older than Eshleman — responded to reading one of Eshleman's early poems by blowing him a kiss: "By doing so at just the right time he confirmed the fact that I had, on my own, at least got up on my feet [... This was] a covenant given by an already-confirmed poet to another nonconfirmed one."[29] Corman served a similar function during their friendship in Kyoto. Eshleman visited Corman once a week for two years at the Muse, a coffee shop in downtown Kyoto that Corman used as an unofficial office. Looking back years later, Eshleman observed: "Corman became the first substantial literary person with whom I had an ongoing, reflective association."[30] At the time, Corman was editing the second series of *Origin* as well as translating and writing his own poetry. He demonstrated a mode of practice in all three of these areas — poetry, translation, editing — as well as a means of combining them or allowing them to play off of one another, that would deeply influence the development of Eshleman's own work. Particularly through his translation of Bashō's *Back Roads to Far Towns* (the book itself as well as Corman's co-translation, with Susumu Kamaike, of it), Corman also signaled a means of combining thorough scholarly research with creative imagination that would become a cornerstone of Eshleman's practice as poet and translator.

Alongside his translations of Vallejo, and friendships with Blackburn and Corman, Eshleman was also studying William Blake, Northrop Frye's book on Blake, *Fearful Symmetry*, Joseph Campbell's *The Masks of God*, and the *I Ching*. Hart Crane had become a key reference — a "poet companion" as he says[31] — for him around 1960. In "Eight Fire Sources," an essay on the major influences on his art, Eshleman lists Bud Powell, Hart Crane, William Blake, Corman's *Origin* and his Bashō translations, the painter Chaim Soutine, Wilhelm Reich, and Mikhail Bakhtin's book *Rabelais and His World*, which he read in the 1970s when first beginning to explore the painted caves. César Vallejo and Emily Dickinson were omitted from the published list but nevertheless significant. Other major influences or interlocutors are apparent enough from the work: Charles Olson, Robert Duncan, James Hillman, and Norman O. Brown, for example. Antonin Artaud and Aimé Césaire are poets whose works have occupied much of Eshleman's creative life as a translator and essayist, but they should not necessarily be understood as having influenced his formation, since his concerns, methods, and orientation had largely been established before he began substantial work on them.

This is not the place to attempt a thorough analysis of the poetry born of this web of dialogues and influences. The point I am pursuing here is one essential aspect or quality of the work, the fact that it was self-consciously born of influences, influences it bears in its language, strategies and structures; it is a work of imagination imbedded or grounded in a context defined by influence and experience, literary, political, and personal. This notion is encapsulated nicely in the title of Eshleman's earlier volume of selected poetry, *The Name Encanyoned River*. The title itself derives from a line cast off by César Vallejo in his worksheets. But Eshleman's "name encanyoned river" is also Heraclitus' river, refracted through Charles Olson's observation, from "The Kingfishers": "What does not change / is the will to change."[32] In Eshleman's work, all the names of history echo off the canyon walls.

The purpose of Eshleman's poetry, as noted above, is the "emancipation of the self," but the pursuit of emancipation reveals the extent to which the self is entwined with others, with its origins in the material context of the earth, its location in culture(s), its unfolding through history, personal and transpersonal. Ultimately, as Eshleman admits, "the attempt to get rid of the 'I' is as crippling as the attempt to get rid of the 'other.' Both are valid points of dynamic interchange and it is only when one is fixed and made central that the flux of contrariety is halted and opposites appear."[33] Here it is significant to note that Eshleman's writing is deeply rooted and personal — occasionally uncomfortably so, in its revelation of the details of intimate life — but it is not confessional in the manner of mid-century "confessional" verse culture exemplified by Robert Lowell, among others. Eshleman writes to reveal proximities and distances, relationships of rapport, rather than to revel in his ego.

Here the dynamic, open quality of the verse is also significant. The poems are cast in the form of an inquiry, a search for a relationship that is still unfolding, in process, rather than static, closed or cut off. The writing is by turns observational and searching, sometimes appearing as a series of questions about or notes on a topic. Eshleman writes specifically to break through expected, inherited, static, or stabilized forms and figures, linguistic, moral, psychological or otherwise. Organic unity, balance, and concision give way to the dramatic flow of inquiry and encounter: scenes often shift abruptly; thoughts break off; dreams erupt into reality. Words and phrases coalesce in figures that form or fall into symbols, images, language games, details of fact, stories, myths, dreams, and visions. These figures serve Eshleman in something of the same manner images did for Willem de Kooning, some of whose paintings Eshleman worked through in From Scratch: the figure or image is a focal point around which intensities of meaning and imagination gather and through which they pass. The poem is a place of encounter. As a focal point, the image is a wall against which the poet pushes his poetic consciousness, seeking points of entry, cracks and fractures, possibilities of recognition, rejection, assimilation, or transformation. "Is not all art which genuinely moves us done in the 'dark' against a 'wall'?"[34] The notion of a wall is crucial throughout Eshleman's corpus as a metaphor and as a literal fact, as in the walls of Paleolithic painted caves that present what Eshleman calls the "back wall of imagination."[35]

The content here is personal, cultural, and trans-cultural by turns, spurred by observations from everyday life, reading and other research, aesthetic objects and images — including Paleolithic painting and objects as well as modern art —, or material pulled up from the unconscious, revealed in dreams and visionary states of waking dream. Eshleman's purpose, his push against these walls, reflects a will to encounter resistances, not to dominate them but to meet, engage, provoke, to reveal contradictions and seek connections between them. For Eshlemam, "poetry's perpetual direction is its way of ensouling events, of seeking the doubleness in events, the event's hidden or contradictory meaning."[36]

This is an agenda that he shares with César Vallejo, undoubtedly both through mutual interest and influence. Evoking his readings of Vallejo, he writes: "The most important things [Vallejo] faced me with were contradictions, contradictions to be looked at. The point at which I determined the contradictions were more valuable than the continuities, let alone the formulas, and it would be a mistake in my case to attempt to transcend or repress my Indiana background, I made a commitment that went like this: I must look back into Indiana and try to go through in poetry what it was to be from Indiana so that I could harrow, or hollow out, that Hell. I was convinced that if I did not do so, I would be permanently injured, less than a man, incapable of full manhood, and forever haunted by various paralyzing background attitudes that would continue to manifest themselves and undermine my projects."[37] The agenda here is intellectual, social or cultural, by terms, but it is also deeply personal. Poetry or poetic consciousness is not an idle pastime; for Eshleman, it is a necessity for a healthy life.

In *Love's Body*, a work that Eshleman encountered during his early life as a poet, Norman O. Brown outlined a similar visionary agenda, a search for lost unity through symbolical consciousness: "To make in ourselves a new consciousness, an erotic sense of reality, is to become conscious of symbolism. Symbolism is mind making connections (correspondences) rather than distinctions (separations). Symbolism makes conscious interconnections and unions that were unconscious and repressed. Freud says, symbolism is on the track of a former identity, a lost unity: the lost continent, Atlantis, underneath the sea of life in which we live enisled; or perhaps even our union with the sea (Thalassa); oceanic consciousness; the unity of the whole cosmos as one living creature, as Plato said in the *Timaeus*."[38] Norman O. Brown's understanding of symbolical consciousness derives from Freud and the psychoanalytic tradition but also from William Blake and Northrop Frye's reading of Blake. In *Milton*, Blake claims, in the visionary symbolic terms that are his own: "There is a place where Contraries are equally True / This place is called Beulah, It is a pleasant lovely Shadow / Where no dispute can come. Because of those who Sleep."[39] Beulah, then, is a place of myths, dreams and visions, where all contraries are equally true and all things appear as they are, infinite. This is the place that must be reached.

Already in Kyoto, if not before, Eshleman had begun to write with and through images, real and imagined, as points of focus and vehicles of resistance for his poetic imagination and critical consciousness. Following Blake's model, he invented symbolic Spectres from elements of his imagined self, Yorunomado ("Night Window" in Japanese) named for the coffee shop where he translated Vallejo, and Niemonjima, named for an island near Futomi, mentioned by Bashō, that Eshleman and his first wife Barbara viewed from a nearby shore in 1962. The Sons of the Sepik Delta were given a name echoing both that of Eshleman's fraternity, Phi Delta Theta, and that of an area of New Guinea, the Sepik Delta, inhabited by a group of headhunters pictured in an image Eshleman cut from a *National Geographic* in the early 1960s. He imagined Yorunomado as one of them.[40] As noted, the images act as simultaneous points of resistance and spurs to imagination.

A decade later, after concluding *Caterpillar* and completing *Coils*, and thereby ending the most concerted moment in his apprenticeship and the excavation of his youth and its legacies, Eshleman developed this strategy in his poetry in several directions simultaneously. Most dramatically, he undertook the "saturation job" on the Paleolithic imagination that would culminate, twenty-five years later, in *Juniper Fuse*. Alongside this project he also began moving his poetry — and imaginative engagement — out into the world, at first by writing a new kind of critical prose on friends and contemporaries like Paul Blackburn and

Gary Snyder and also by writing "portraits" of key progenitors and influences: Vincent Van Gogh, Charlie Parker, Chaim Soutine, Hart Crane, Francis Bacon, Antonin Artaud, and others.[41] Eshleman explained: "If translating is a way of bringing other poetries into focus, then the kind of 'portraits' I have been doing are a bringing of such focuses over into poetry. That is, it is one thing to translate an Artaud poem and another thing, or another kind of translation — a more difficult kind of translation — to do a portrait of Artaud in which all I know of Artaud is material I am shaping to say how I see him, not as a face or bust as is often done in painting, but as an image, as the body of his imagination, which will be a critique, a cutting out of that which I do not see as essential to Artaud, and a manner in which my life material can be set aside to concentrate on his. An *enactment* of Artaud, in other words."[42]

During these same years he also experimented with writing in other voices, adopting the perspectives of more fully imagined personae, akin to Fernando Pessoa's heteronyms, from the inside. Works written in this vein include "The 9 Poems of Metro Vavin" in *The Gull Wall*, *The Gospel of Celine Arnaud*, and *Homuncula* by Horrah Pornoff, this last written and published in magazines in the 1970s but collected much later in *Under World Arrest*.

Significantly, Eshleman's will to include the world in his work, extends beyond mere language to thought, in the sense of both ideas and information. In "Eight Fire Sources", the essay mentioned above on the major influences on his work, Eshleman quotes Wallace Stevens' remark from *Adagia*: "Poetry is the scholars' art," and interprets Stevens to mean that "poetry is the literary art that should hold the greatest appeal to scholars. [And that] poets can also be scholars without lessening the intuitive drive it takes to write substantial poetry."[43] Poetry should appeal to scholars because its combination of carefully wrought, loaded language and formal invention gives scholars — and in fact all readers — ample fuel for the furnaces of imagination, fodder for the work of psyche.

The second half of Eshleman's interpretation of Stevens approaches the relationship between poetry and scholarship from the other side, the poet's side, suggesting that poets too can and indeed should be scholars. Eshleman offers the Japanese haiku master, Bashō, as a "sterling example of the spiritual poet / scholar" because, in his travel journal *Back Roads to Far Towns*, Bashō not only produced brilliant haiku but also "did his homework on the lore and history concerning the sites and temples he planned to visit."[44] The work alternates between expository or descriptive prose, called haibun, which is alternately personal, historical, and cultural, and poetic expression, in this case, in the form of haiku.

In the preface to *Antiphonal Swing,* Eshleman explains the derivation of the book's title — taken from the last line of Hart Crane's *The Bridge:* "Whispers antiphonal in azure swing" — "Antiphony, or the singing of anthems, involves one side of the choir, or congregation, answering the other side. For me, the swing is between the erotic and the artistic, as well as between prose and poetry."[45] The erotic here is the bodily energy that swings into artistic imagination. Prose here includes a range of writing styles and strategies, as well as modes of inquiry, which are each distinct from but related to poetic imagination. Here again Eshleman recalls what he learned from reading Bashō's travel journals: "it was through studying translations of these journals in the early 1960s that I became aware of the extent to which something about a poet's prose itches to transform itself into poetry and, in a less obvious way, something about the poetry seeks an argumentative or explanative base in prose... prose wanting to intensify its gait, poetry wanting to stop and survey the field it performs in."[46]

Along similar lines, Eshleman is also fond of Northrop Frye's use of the term "anatomy" to describe William Blake's *The Marriage of Heaven and Hell.* An anatomy in this description is a "composite work that includes as its 'members' various forms and strategies of the art of writing." Eshleman also mentions Antonin Artaud's later writing with its "fusion of genres incorporating letters, poetry, prose, and glossolalia" as participating in this hybrid approach to literary production.[47] The literary anatomy is a hybrid form or a form of hybridity, a means of fusion rather than fission. It brings together and assimilates discourses while preserving the differences between them. The fusion or assimilation it proposes is not one of complete synthesis. Rather than eliminating the differences between discourses, this approach in some ways marks or illustrates them. The description is significant to Eshleman not only in reference to the antiphonal relationship of poetry and prose across his corpus as a whole but also, and perhaps more interestingly, *within* individual works: in this way, his poem "Notes on a Visit to Le Tuc d'Audoubert" provides the "nuclear form" of *Juniper Fuse.*[48]

In the introduction to *Juniper Fuse*, Eshleman situates his book in line with Charles Olson's notion of a "saturation job" in which, in Olson's words, one digs into "one thing or place or man until you yourself know more abt that than is possible to any other man... [E]xhaust it. Saturate it."[49] Eshleman takes his distance from the notion of knowing more about a thing than "any other man" but Olson's larger point remains relevant. In *Juniper Fuse* this means to "make use of a pluralistic approach that may result in a fuller 'reading' of Upper Paleolithic imagination than archeological or literary approaches alone might yield."[50] Eshleman's pluralistic approach distinguishes *Juniper Fuse* radically from other works in the study of prehistory but this investigative and pluralistic approach also characterizes and distinguishes Eshleman's corpus as a whole within contemporary writing, contemporary poetry in particular. Early poetry collections, like *Altars* and *Coils*, included sections of prose commentary; later collections included in their fabric occasional essays, introductions, and notes; and the corpus as a whole forms a constellation of poetry, translations, essays, journals, and edited volumes. Eshleman's many collaborations with visual artists on illustrated volumes and other projects, whether in the case of his ekphrastic writing, either *through* the visual or alongside it, provide another example of this gesture.

My point here is that Eshleman practices poetry as something rather more than a scholar's art, marshaling many means of investigation, many modes and styles of inquiry. This is rather more than a scholar's art because contemporary scholarship has largely locked itself in cages barred by discipline and specialty. Olson's influence is again relevant here through his oft-quoted interpretation of the title of Herodotus' work, '*istoria* — inquiry, in Greek — which Olson takes to mean "find out for yourself." In *The Maximus Poems*, he writes: "I would be an historian as Herodotus was, looking / for oneself for the evidence of / what is said"[51] and again "Herodotus's [concept of history] / which was a verb, to find out for yourself: / 'istorian, which makes any one's acts a finding out for him or her / self, in other words, restores the traum: that we act somewhere ..."[52] In thinking about history, about *poiesis* and making history, Eshleman puts the stress on *out*   to find *out* for yourself, "an exit for the self," a mode of self-transformation through inquiry.[53] Inquiry here includes inquiry into the self as well as into the things of the world and their histories, but, as in Olson, the inquiry is always rooted, the self is always situated within and in relation to the world: the inquiry reveals relationship.

The point of research here is less the specific content of the research — all points of entry are in some senses equally valid — but rather the back-file of language, strategy, and information that derives from research both in form and in content. Eshleman observes: "I think that the main benefit from research for a poet […] is that it builds up a file of materials that cling to the underside of consciousness, and can be brought into play when, in composition, one needs a hoist to move the poem along into another dimension or sounding."[54] Here knowledge is put in play, part of a process, rather than congealed and set apart as a static collection of dusty facts.

As an embodiment of commitment, the poetic process, for Eshleman, is one of developing an informed consciousness that should ideally always be both symbolical, and hence imaginative, as well as critical. As he puts it: "I believe that I am responsible for every word that I write, and if I am beside myself at times, if the words appear to come from nowhere, this is a gift that I must honor but also evaluate as it arrives in the process of composition."[55] The second half of this statement alludes to the critical function of evaluation, the capacity to stand back from the work, to situate it reflectively, even as it unfolds.

This may seem profoundly anti-poetic but it is a crucial part of Eshleman's understanding of poetry. Some poets, particularly young poets, may be resistant to any form of critical commentary or informed critique, however gentle. For such writers, poetry is self-expression and all criticism is irrelevant. Poetry may even be appealing to these writers precisely because they conceive of it as free of constraints, internal or external, personal or cultural. Eshleman's poetry, on the other hand, is nothing less than a confrontation with constraints, a willful engagement with their source, nature, meaning, and extent.

In *Novices*, Eshleman takes up the question of critical self-consciousness in relation to the use of psychoanalysis in the poetic process. He writes: "The poet's resistance to psychoanalysis is a resistance to discovering his unconscious motives for writing poetry — as if discovering a severing — a witch with a long nose intruding into the playhouse window, discovering what the children are 'really' doing there. The fear that more information is the end of information is Blake's enemy, 'doubt which is self-contradiction,' and it hamstrings the novice through developing a reluctance to investigate Psyche — to investigate *anything*."[56] Unfortunately, this reluctance to investigate, to do research of any kind, even research into the history of poetry, has taken root in much of the culture of creative writing in America today. I'll return to this topic further on. For now, my point is simply that Eshleman has pursued the contrary course; his poetry is a scholar's art. And on the subject of research, he is even occasionally prescriptive: "Ideally, every poet should undertake at least one big investigative project that brings into poetry materials that have previously not been a part of it. This is one way that we keep our art fresh, and not diluted with variations played on tried and true themes. The investigative project also makes one responsible for a huge range of materials, the assimilation of which goes way beyond the concerns of the personal lyric."[57] In *Juniper Fuse*, the range of materials assimilated by the poet is indeed enormous. It begins with personal visits to the sites themselves, not once or in passing, but repeated and persistent visits, over two and a half decades of research. It also includes readings in archeology and anthropology as well as materials outside of those fields, narrowly defined: C.G. Jung, Sandor Ferenczi, Geza Róheim, Mikhail Bakhtin, Weston La Barre, Charles Olson, Norman O. Brown, Kenneth Grant, James Hillman, Hans Peter Duerr, Maxine Sheets-Johnstone, among others.[58] At the end of *Novices: A Study of Poetic Apprenticeship*, Eshleman appends two reading lists that might be of use to novices. The lists include poetry but also books "that taught [him] something about life and poetry and [...] that bear upon poetry as [he] understand[s] it."[59] These books include works of anthropology, psychology, philosophy, comparative religious studies, and women's studies, among other fields. All of this is to say that Eshleman's poetry — and his writing in general — is both formed and informed; it is poetry with content: personal, psychological, historical, and political.

The broad question of research and investigation, of the relation between creative consciousness and critical consciousness, finds another precedent in Blake, who wrote, in the preface to *Milton*: "The Daughters of Memory shall become the Daughters of Inspiration." The facts of history, which is to say the content of memory, personal and cultural, must not be avoided, as burdens, but rather integrated or at least indicated, noted in marks of relation. This is also a comment on

Eshleman's approach to the anxiety of influence, which cannot be avoided and therefore must be faced, assimilated or rejected in one manner or another. In her forward to *Companion Spider,* Adrienne Rich observed that Eshleman has "gone more deeply into his art, its process and demands, than any modern American poet since Robert Duncan or Muriel Rukeyser."[60] Her comment is relevant to Eshleman's practice as a poet, but also to his knowledge of poetry. As a young man, Ezra Pound set himself the task of learning more about poetry — its history, art, and craft — than any of his contemporaries and, judging in particular by the four extended collections of prose writings that he has published, Eshleman seems to have set for himself a similar task. For him, the practice of poetry entails not only developing a personal idiom but also an understanding of what came before and lies beyond that idiom, what other styles and purposes there might be. As a body of writings, and speaking in terms of intellectual practice, Eshleman's essays offer pointed explorations and incursions into poetics, moments of measurement through which the poet tests his own views on and practices of poetry and poetics against those of his contemporaries, the most relevant great dead of the tradition, and practitioners of other arts, the visual arts in particular. Eshleman has not written a formal poetics, but something like one can be extracted from these writings and the interviews that explore a similar terrain, generally through the prism of questions concerning issues raised by his own writings.

Another mode of investigative engagement appears in the poet's sustained, and clearly sustaining, practice of translation. Significantly, when Eshleman discovered poetry in the late 1950s, he discovered not just American poetry but world poetry.[61] At its inception, in other words, his understanding of poetry included poets from around the world: Rilke, Lorca, Mayakofsky, St.-John Perse, as well as, and with ever more meaning to Eshleman, Pablo Neruda and César Vallejo, along with the other poets included in the anthology of contemporary Latin American poetry Dudley Fitts' published through New Directions in 1947. A bilingual publication, the Fitts anthology invited a comparative reading of the translations with their originals. Other translations of the same poems by Neruda in particular were also readily available for comparison. In a memoir of his encounter with Neruda's work, Eshleman wrote: "I had the experience that I suppose many translators have at the beginning of their careers: one of shock, at the astonishing discrepancies and outright errors (which even I could spot!) in these different versions. To some extent I became a translator reactively, disgruntled with what others had done, and with some unbased confidence that I could do a better job!"[62] Eshleman's confidence was without basis at that moment primarily because he did not know Spanish. His fascination with Neruda and Vallejo lead him to hitchhike to Mexico for the next two summers, to learn Spanish specifically in order to translate their works. Two years later, when living in Kyoto and having completed and published his translations of Neruda's *Residence on Earth*, Eshleman undertook the more demanding task of attempting to translate César Vallejo's *Poemas humanos* — while continuing to work on his own writing and continuing to read deeply in the history of poetry, myth, and thought — to work through William Blake in particular — as part of his apprenticeship in poetry.

As noted above, Cid Corman offered Eshleman a model and mentor of the poet as writer, translator, editor and scholar wrapped in one. In his memoir of Corman, Eshleman recalled this influence: Corman's "meticulousness as a writer brought home to me, in the realm of translation, the necessity to do absolutely accurate versions as well as versions that attempted to rise to the performance level of the originals."[63] Translation in this model is an exercise in scholarship requiring dogged and detailed research alongside creative imagination. In practice, as a translator, Eshleman learned to keep a notebook alongside his on-going translations to contain those irruptions of imagination and reflection that accompany the translation process rather than attempting to ignore or repress them. Thereafter, the irruptions themselves then might fuel Eshleman's own writing, as in the case of the phrase mentioned above, "the name encanyoned river." Translation, pursued in this manner, is an act of devotion, founded upon fidelity to the words and thought of another, requiring the translator to put his or her ego in suspense, to resist too quick an understanding of the source text, wherein imagination or unconscious motives might lead one to impose a meaning or interpretation that is not present in the original text. In this way the act of translation recalls another phrase from Blake, the "Proverb from Hell" that resonates through so much of Eshleman's work: "The most sublime act is to set another before you."

Aside from the direct pleasure of being able to read the translated work in English, the rewards of translation for the translator are complex. Eshleman observed: "I have thought more about poetry while translating Vallejo than while reading anyone else."[64] And elsewhere: "Since translation is such slow work, requiring multiple rereadings, it can require a more prolonged reading-in-depth than when we read poetry written in our own language."[65] Or again, more emphatically: "I have spent much more time with my 2nd Edition *Webster's International Dictionary* as a translator than as a poet. Translation has constantly over the years swept me away from myself, locking me to the minds of those poets I have translated and, by doing so, has challenged and deepened my own base."[66] All of this is to say that translation, like other forms of research, expands the poet's range, his knowledge of the potentialities of the poet's craft, but, like formal exercises, it also expands his reach, his capacities.

Translation has provided Eshleman with another means of engaging with others as well: co-translation. His earliest translations — of Neruda — where done with the help of a native informant, the wife of the man from whom he was renting rooms in Mexico at the time. Later, in Kyoto, he collaborated with Cid Corman on a variety of translations. Returning to the United States, he and Denis Kelly collaborated on a selection of poems by Aimé Césaire. The following year, in Lima, Peru, he worked with Maureen Ahern on Vallejo. In the 1970s, he would work on Vallejo with José Rubia Barcia, on Artaud with A. James Arnold and Norman Glass, and, more extensively, on Césaire with Annette Smith. He continued to collaborate with Annette Smith for the next two decades, while also working with Julio Ortega and Américo Ferrari on Vallejo, and Bernard Bador on Artaud. More recently he and Lucas Klein translated a volume of poems by Bei Dao and he and A. James Arnold have been re-translating all of Aimé Césaire's works in definitive bilingual editions. The community involved in the translation process, for Eshleman, includes the author of the original text as well as, ideally, a native informant.

The story recounted above of Eshleman's discovery of poetry in translation and of the practice of translation also includes, though less directly, reference to another significant practice in his life commitment to poetry: editing. As noted, Eshleman discovered Pablo Neruda and

César Vallejo in an anthology of Latin American poetry edited by Dudley Fitts. Shortly after making that discovery, he would find himself editing the Indiana University English Department literary journal. Looking back, he observed: "As a student at Indiana University in the late 1950s, I was simultaneously involved in working on poems, starting to translate Neruda and Vallejo, and editing the English Department literary journal, *Folio*. I have practiced that triadic discipline every since."[67] Significantly, these were also the practices that Eshleman witnessed Cid Corman pursuing in Kyoto a few years later.

Eshleman edited three issues of *Folio* at Indiana University before conservative tempers in the English Department withdrew its funding. Editing those three issues brought him into contact with number of poets, foreign and domestic, of preceding generations as well as compelling contemporaries: contributors included William Carlos Williams, Pablo Neruda, Cid Corman, Allen Ginsberg, Robert Creeley, Louis Zukofsky, Robert Duncan, Robert Kelly, Jerome Rothenberg, and David Antin, among others. A few years later, while living in Peru in 1965–66, Eshleman was hired by the North American Peruvian Institute to start a bilingual literary magazine. He called it *Quena*, referring to the traditional one-hole Quechuan flute. The 300 page first issue included work by Charles Olson, Cid Corman, and Javier Heraud, translated by Paul Blackburn, among many other pieces. However, as with *Folio* five years previously, *Quena* was ultimately suppressed by its sponsors, this time for political rather than aesthetic reasons.[68]

When he returned to the United States, Eshleman continued his editorial work by publishing a series of chapbooks — works by Aimé Césaire, Corman, Blackburn, David Antin, Jackson MacLow, and others — under the Caterpillar imprint. The name derived from several familiar sources: a short poem by William Blake, a diagram of the movement of life-energy by Wilhelm Reich, and images of Vietnamese war victims that looked like a "black caterpillar." But Eshleman found the chapbooks difficult to distribute and shifted his strategy, founding *Caterpillar Magazine* as a quarterly in October 1967. He explained the origin of *Caterpillar Magazine* succinctly: "The main reason I began *Caterpillar* in the fall of 1967 is because I did not feel that poets like Robert Duncan, Diane Wakoski, Jerome Rothenberg, Frank Samperi, Cid Corman, Louis Zukofsky, and Paul Blackburn had a dependable and generous magazine outlet for their writing."[69] He also "wanted to bring things that were not poetry per se to bear on poetry."[70] Toward that end, the first issue included essays by Norman O. Brown and Robert Duncan, from *The H.D. Book*; other issues featured writings by Wilhelm Reich and Stan Brakhage, a lecture on Scientology, and writings and music by Philip Corner and James Tenney. *Caterpillar* also included examples of visual art, not only on its cover, but in its pages as well, works by Leon Golub, Nancy Spero, Jess, Robert LaVigne, and Carolee Schnee-mann among them. For Eshleman, *Caterpillar* represented an attempt to "do a magazine with a single point of view *and* a magazine that was also eclectic."[71] The tension here is that of an inclusive consciousness, straining against and reaching beyond its limits. After four issues, Robert Kelly made the venture even more explicitly collaborative by joining the masthead as a contributing editor. In 1973, after 20 issues and just prior to leaving Los Angeles to spend a year in France, Eshle-man felt he had accomplished what he had set out to do in the maga-zine and brought it to a close. The moment was coincident with the publication of his book *Coils*, the culmination of a decade of his early work, and a turning point in his career: in France that year he discov-ered the Paleolithic painted caves of the Dordogne and began what began a twenty-five year quest to reclaim those caves as "geo-mythical sites" for poetry.[72]

In 1981, eight years after folding *Caterpillar*, and with his explo-ration of the painted caves firmly underway, Eshleman returned to ed-iting by founding a new magazine, *Sulfur*. The name refers to a species of butterfly with black-bordered orange and yellow wings — and hence an evolutionary stage of *Caterpillar* — as well as to processes of alchem-ical initiation and combustion.[73] As Eshleman described it, "*Sulfur*'s primary ambition [was] to keep the field open and complex, with archival and contemporary writing, along with commentary, generating a multi-generational interplay."[74] Areas of intentional focus included translations of contemporary foreign-language poets and new transla-tions of untranslated poetry, significant archival materials, writing by unknown and young poets, commentary including poetics, notes and reviews, and finally "resource materials," meaning "previously excluded (and repressed) materials and experience," that might be useful toward the "renewal and deepening of content" in the art of poetry.[75] As in *Caterpillar*, the point was to push against and open up the limits of the art, to reach beyond borders, linguistic and national. Eshleman and his collaborators published 46 issues of *Sulfur* over 19 years: some 11,000 pages featuring roughly 800 contributors. Caryl Eshleman, the poet's wife, served as Managing Editor of the entire run. Robert Kelly served as contributing editor on the first issue: Michael Palmer, Jerome Rothenberg, and Eliot Weinberger, Rachel Blau DuPlessis joined as contributing editors later on. In the late 1990s, as public and institutional funding for the arts dried up, Eshleman recognized that the magazine had achieved its goals and that the turn of the millennium marked an appropriate occasion to move on.

Of his editorial experience, Eshleman recently observed: "Editing *Caterpillar* and *Sulfur* enabled me to construct an ongoing active mosaic of poetry and translation, and how the contemporary might mesh with archival materials, artwork, and commentary."[76] Like translation, editing is a collaborative art. Editors activate voices, bring them together, set them into relation to one another, help them stand revealed; they draw speakers into conversation and let them speak. The work of the editor is like that of a conductor, to borrow one shade of the meaning of Eshleman's phrase, "conductors of the pit." They assemble and conduct, direct and convey, an orchestra of voices, from near and far, present and absent, living and dead.[77] I dwell on this here to emphasize the extent to which Eshleman views his work — whether as a poet, a translator, or an editor — within a larger context of conversation, a conversation that is at once transhistorical, global, and deeply American.

The interpretation I have been developing here is one of a poetic consciousness seeking an ever-wider range of materials and inspirations, resistances and encounters, for consideration, assimilation, and the experience of relation and rapport. It is integral to such a consciousness that it push itself to its limits, test itself with the challenge of grappling with the most difficult of topics, experiences or materials, particularly of a personal or political nature.

Eshleman's political consciousness was born in the slums of Lima, Peru, in 1965: experiences he recounts in the early poetry of his book *Walks* and in the journal pushed as *On Mules Sent From Chavin*. Though he had traveled to parts of Mexico for two summers at the end of the 1950s, and to Korea and Japan in the early 1960s, in Lima he witnessed first-hand the connection between poverty, politics, military power, and neo-colonialist strategies of international aid. (Ernesto "Che" Guevara had been radicalized by similar encounters a little more than a decade earlier.) These experiences would inform and lend bitter fuel to Eshleman's participation in the anti-war movement in the United States when he returned there the following year. Indeed much of his energy in the late 1960s would be devoted to anti-war protests, primarily participation in the Angry Arts movement in New York and other nationwide protest activities.

The importance of this aspect of Eshleman's work cannot be overestimated. His purpose is to write a poetry that is responsible for all that he knows about his world, good and bad, beautiful and terrible. But his vision and experience is deeply bifurcated. "As a middle-class American, I am overexposed to the front side of our avuncular top-hatted Uncle Sam. Much of the world has a different view of Sam than I do. Iraqis, Serbs, Laotians, Vietnamese, Cambodians, and Panamanians, for example, see a skeletal backside wired with DU, cluster bombs, dioxin, sarin, napalm (most recently used in Fallujah), and hydrogen cyanide. I know what I see and I keep both sides of Sam's body in mind as I continue to work on myself, to learn, and to love."[78] Or again, put differently, this acknowledgement: "We know that North American abundance is to a great and, ultimately, terrifying extent dependent upon the continuing poverty and torture of others in countries we have no direct contact with, but to whom our eyes are pressed via TV news reports, so that the starving mother in Biafra, seated on the side of a cot, with a starving infant too weak to even try to suckle her mother's utterly empty breast, poses a complicated set of questions to North American poets: by responding in our writing to such a scene, to what extent do we fulfill our human responsibility to it? To what extent is our response a mere appropriation of materials that mirrors imperialistic ideologies?"[79]

Here Eshleman's moral outrage joins a stream of similar reflections at the limits of political vision. In a passage from Northrop Frye's *Fearful Symmetry* that Eshleman quotes in *Altars* and again in *Hotel Cro-Magnon*, Frye observes: "All pleasure is at least partly a dream under anesthetic. Something is always suffering horribly somewhere, and we can only find pleasure by ignoring that fact. We must ignore it up to a point, or go mad; but in the abyss of consciousness, to which Enion [in Blake's *Four Zoas*] has been banished, there lurks the feeling that joy is based on exclusion, that the Yule log can blaze cheerfully only when the freezing beggars in the streets are, for the moment, left to freeze."[80] For me, this sentiment has been most powerfully stated by Salmen Lewental, a *sonderkommando* at Auschwitz who buried fragmentary notes about his experience near crematoria III in Birkenau. Unearthed years later, this chilling recognition of social reality in extremis appears among those notes. "There was a time in this camp, in the years 1941–42, when each man, really each one who lived longer than two weeks, lived at the cost of lives of other people or on what they had taken from them."[81] Part of the staggering power of Lewental's statement derives from his status as a participant, implicated in the experience to which he is witness: life in the camp was life lived at the expense of life.

These notions serve as first premises for an ethics and thereby also a politics. Eshleman endeavors to hold himself to them and to measure his work by them. Thus he claims: "While I am open to the invention of 'new worlds,' I insist on inventing them while addressing the cruelty of the present one."[82] Or, as measure, he asks rhetorically, in "The Loaded Sleeve of Hades": "the depth of your life? / Nothing if severed from the life of a man in rags / going off into the dark of Siberian cold."[83] This is a problem and a challenge for all poets in the United States. "As a citizen of a country that has supported such terrorists as the Nicaraguan Contras, UNITA in Angola, the Moujahedeen in Afghanistan, Cuban CIA agents in Miami, the governments of El Salvador, Guatemala, and Chile, the American poet reaps and suffers the rewards of American terrorism, which are part of his spectre, his anti-imaginative blockage, whether he acknowledges such or not. All of us are connected to the rubble of Fallujah by a poisoned umbilicus."[84] Needless to say, this statement invalidates or at a minimum profoundly diminishes a great deal of the poetry written in America today.

Unsurprisingly, given his importance to Eshleman, César Vallejo provided a poignant model of political poetry that would become Eshleman's own. As Eshleman explains: "*Human Poems* redefines the 'political' poem. With one or two exceptions, the poems in this collection have no political position or agenda in the traditional sense. Yet they are directly sympathetic, in a way that does not remind us of other politics, with the human situation [...] They are so permeated with Vallejo's own suffering as it is wedded to that of other people, that it is as if the dualisms of colonial / colonized, rich and poor, become fused at a level where the human animal, aware of his fate, is embraced in all his absurd fallibility."[85] The model here is one of recognition and identification grounded in a fundamental position of mutual mortal fragility.

As a political poet, Eshleman is witness to suffering caused by atrocity; his testimony transcends the merely ethical through the pointedness of its barely contained fury. In the 1960s, that fury was haunted by events in Peru and Vietnam; in the 1970s, by Hiroshima and the Holocaust — place-names like Dachau, Mauthausen, and Auschwitz; in the 1980s, El Salvador; more recently by the atrocities of the Bush era, the invasions of Afghanistan and Iraq.

But there are limits to ethical consciousness and political opportunities in those limits. Self and other are separated by a biological abyss that can be bridged only in part by imagination. In the end, we are each profoundly alone before the uniqueness of our experiences and the fact of our death. Suffering is always radically specific. While the witness can and must testify to the violence that occurs before his or her gaze, comprehension, even in imagination, has distinct and meaningful limits or boundaries. In his essay, "Companion Spider," Eshleman wonders: "Is there now too much grief for thought to handle?"[86] Eshleman admits this with another rhetorical question: "Faced with so much story, I release my grip / from Whitman's hand, 'agonies are one of my changes of / garments' — in the face of Auschwitz?"[87] Walt Whitman imagined that, via imagination, his cosmos was fully comprehensible to him. For Eshleman, such an admission is impossible. It is also perhaps inadvisable, even unethical. However inspiring it may be in some moments, Whitman's synthetic vision is inadmissible in extremis: there are events and experiences that one simply cannot share, cannot comprehend from a distance. In such cases, Eshleman writes with a different purpose, rather than to merely acknowledge and accept incomprehensible horror, he writes to render it, to convey it to his reader in its horror, as horror, which is to say as a wound. "Let me set terror back into the grass, inject it / deeply into the planet's skin / get *chasm* back into *abyss*," he writes in "The Atmosphere, Les Eyzies."[88]

At the limits of consciousness, even symbolical consciousness, there is an abyss of understanding. To reach that place, one must go through hell, perhaps literally, certainly metaphorically and symbolically. Like everything else in Eshleman's cosmology, hell is manifold. It is both Dante's Hell and the Greek underworld, Hades, where Odysseus went in search of visions of the way home. It is also Blake's Hell — the poet's domain, where energy is eternal delight and imagination and reason are one. But, as in Rimbaud's season in hell, hell is also personal, for Eshleman, the hells of Phi Delta Theta Hell Week and of childhood traumas. And following James Hillman's Jungian thought, Hell is the underworld: the unconscious, accessed through dream and poetic imagination. Despite all of these layers of cultural meaning, but recognizing that psychoanalysis is ultimately a materialism, that the unconscious is a manifestation of the body, hell is, in the end, physical, material, a concept derived from our separation from our fellow creatures and from the earth itself. The upsurge of consciousness is indistinct from our exile from Eden, our fall into psychological, biological separation.

Like Odysseus, like Rimbaud, Eshleman has gone to Hades, to hell, in search of vision. His journey has been a journey into himself, crawling through repression, through the layers of shame bequeathed by Christian civilization, beyond the gods of the Greeks — and the archetypes they represent, beneath the foundation stones of the West, into the painted caves, toward the origins of consciousness and autonomous imagination. This journey has been a journey through culture but it has also been personal, interrogating the wounds of childhood and modern American life, measuring the self against the legacies that course through and shape it. "Thank god hell is not dead within me," Eshleman wrote in *Indiana*.[89]

In the journal published as *On Mules Sent From Chavin*, we glimpse Eshleman in the mid-1960s working through the psychological ramifications of these concepts as they were reflected in his mythopoetic Spectre, Yorunomado:

> Why must I give up hell to live within love? Does Yorunomado mean that my sense of love is narrow and thus will not include hell? Now if I think of hell as a place, symbolic as well as terrestrial, I can understand that — but Blake has so redefined hell as a positive force in creation that I have to take that meaning into consideration too. Must I kill my own energy — my furnaces — to be able to have love? ... I think Blake locates the stomach as 'hell' and Lawrence the solar plexus as the 'power center' the 'sun center' and they seem right in the sense that both appear to be redirecting the 'center' away from the

heart & head. That is, center in head makes body top-heavy — how could you dance if you took head as center? You'd fall over, or end up in some grotesque pose — but it seems to me that taking center down to the stomach is not taking it down far enough, that genital center is truer, more accurate to life-energy.[90]

In his early poetry, Eshleman dug down into himself, through the wounds and scars of his psyche, into and through his personal Hell, toward the source of his psychic conflict and, beyond that, his animal, genital life-energy. Working through his psyche, Eshleman traveled through realms of image and imagination, down the name-encanyoned river, to the point where he could say: "I feel the extent to which I am storied, / but the stories are under […] / pebble histories, midden chapters, / 'Payroll of Bones' indeed!"[91] (Payroll of Bones is a reference to Vallejo.) His vision of the self here is psychoanalytic but also ecological, a vision of a self situated in the context of an immanent, earthly environmental continuum. Having worked through his wounds, *Coils* closes with a prescient phrase:

> Yorunomado closed the left half of my book.
> From this point on, he said,
> your work leads on into the earth.[92]

Thereafter, vision itself appears as originating in the earth: "The earth so fully referential / it appears to press out nothing but / aspects of itself."[93] The garden of delights is a garden of *earthly* delights. Eshleman's vision here is visionary, symbolical consciousness, wherein contraries appear united as one: "Knowledge of the place of origin means: dissolution of the separation of things from each other."[94] And yet, at its furthest reaches, Eshleman's vision is a Blakean vision of paradox: where presence and absence, continuity and discontinuity, unity and disunity, self and self-loss are experienced as one. "My vertical stands on my zero," he writes, echoing Olson's figure for the basis of the ego.[95] "We begin with ZERO — are O," Olson wrote to a young Cid Corman, in a letter Eshleman quotes in *Novices*.[96] Put differently, in Eshleman's terms: "through you, / a tunnel that winds back into total discontinuity."[97] Here absence is the key to presence, to the source of consciousness: "Basis of the 'hidden wealth' of Hades: the fullness of the void experienced not as absence but as hidden presence to be drawn forth as the animal matrix one is exiting."[98] In *Juniper Fuse,* Eshleman calls this exit from animality the separation continuum: it is an endless fall into separated consciousness, out of unity with the earth. The origin of consciousness is the birth of autonomous imagination: a breakthrough born of fracture, separation, from absence, presence. This is the culminating vision — and argument — of *Juniper Fuse,* undoubtedly Eshleman's single most important work, the vision of an absence that gives birth to presence, of a hole the grows into a pole. He explicates: "The hole that grows — in a way that is simultaneously transitive and intransitive — may be one of the most fundamental versions of the logos, or story, of the soul which, according to Heraclitus, grows according to its needs — as does, according to the shamans, the World Tree. [...] It is a hole grounded in both absence and appearance, a convexcavatious abyss."[99] The convexcavatious abyss: a vision of primary duality, wherein opposition dissolves into unity. To be at home in symbolical consciousness, in poetic imagination, is to accept the abyss as the substance of the self, to see the self as an emanation of abyss, to accept loss as the condition of identity. As Eshleman writes in "Barcarole": "Pure loss pours through. I'm home."[100]

The purpose of Eshleman's mature poetry has been to plunge into this abyss, to explore it, again and again, to confront and conduct the zero. As he puts it in "Tiresias Drinking": "the prophet's task is / to conduct the savagery of the grass, / to register the zeros rising from circuits of the dead."[101] The abyss of imagination is distinct from its apotheosis in rational knowledge. Though knowledge may be derived from it, the flat and stable register of rational discursive knowledge stands apart, *after* poetic imagination. "To look without understanding. E.M. Cioran writes that this is paradise. / To be penetrated by the observed which enters one and goes through one — without one."[102] For the poet in the abyss, I is an other, a passage through which life travels. This is fundamental to the human condition: "The human is indeterminate, initially unclosed," Eshleman observes.[103] And again: "you are closed and open / in the multiple ambivalence of your fracture / and no resolution is sincere."[104] No resolution is sincere in part because all resolution is provisional. All poetry is provisional as well, it is the work of consciousness in process, part of the separation continuum.

If there must be clarity,
let it be opaque, let the word be
convexcavatious, deep
with distance, a clear
and dense mosaic, desiring
undermining.[105]

A compelling pun emerges from the convexcavatious abyss: Eshleman's art of the hole is also an art of the whole, an art participating in what Robert Duncan called the symposium of the whole in "Rites of Participation," one section of *The H.D. Book* that he published in *Caterpillar*.[106] Eshleman offers this explanation: "Over the years, initially stimulated by Vallejo, I had developed an affinity for a poetry that went for the whole, a poetry that attempted to become responsible for all the poet knows about himself and his world. I saw Vallejo, Arthur Rimbaud, Antonin Artaud, Aimé Césaire, and Vladimir Holan as examples of these poetics. All inducted and ordered materials from the subconscious as well as from those untoward regions of human experience that defy rational explanation. Instead of conducting the orchestra of the living, they were conducting the orchestra's pit."[107] And again, with a more political inflection: "The key lesson Vallejo holds today may be that of a poet learning how to become imprisoned, as it were, in global life as a whole, and in each moment in particular."[108] Poetry in this description is an attempt to embrace and acknowledge — to take responsibility for — the whole of the world, its terrors and its delights. In "At the Speed of Wine," he writes, conducting the voice of Hart Crane, "The demand on the soul is now to ordain those powers still denied a human foul, / to get the lower body out before its repressive furnaces ignite all worlds."[109] This kind of poetry conceives of emancipation as indistinct from a kind of imprisonment, from an acknowledgement that the self can never be entirely free of the other, understanding the word other in the widest possible sense, as in the symposium of the whole.

Eshleman does not pretend to be alone in his pursuit of this kind of poetry. He is explicit on this point: "I am sure that I am not alone in believing during the late 1960s that an American poetry based in international modernism, and signaled by Don Allen's 'the new American poetry' but not restricted to his perimeter, might become the dominant poetry of the 1970s — in other words that a world-aware, responsible avant-garde might overcome and peripheralize decades of dominant official verse culture."[110] This belief was developed in the poetries Eshleman translated and central to the communities constellated around *Caterpillar* and *Sulfur*. It was common to a major trend in international letters, whose practitioners sought to renew and revivify the role of the poet in society. "Through the efforts of such multiply-based writers as Ezra Pound, Antonin Artaud, and Charles Olson, the image of the poet has been densified and removed from the academic-literary niche that has come to mean that the poet was merely a clever manipulator of his own sensitivity rather than a man or woman of knowledge."[111] Nevertheless, as familiar as this image of the poet may have been in the modern and late modern eras, it has not become dominant or even common in our own.

A poetry like this — world-aware, responsible, dense — is difficult. It requires a life commitment. And this life commitment is a commitment of life to something more than poetry. It is a commitment to life itself. "The poet must always believe that there are a few things a hell of a lot more important than poetry. If he does not, he makes literature and serves what Jack Spicer called 'The English Department of the Spirit.' The most important thing in the world for a man to do is to alleviate suffering and the most important thing for him to be, ecologically speaking, is a grape in the cluster of his species."[112] The push here, Eshleman's push, is through poetry and poetic consciousness but ultimately beyond it. The terms are those of the avant-garde tradition in aesthetic activism. As Eshleman put it in *The Sanjo Bridge*: "Art wants to change the world. Art wants to destroy what all men feel are the limits of this world."[113] Thirty years later, in *My Devotion*, he affirmed a similarly ambitious goal: "I dream of poems that could change something essential / about the way a few people view creation…"[114] It is undoubtedly obvious that not all poets share this same dream, nor is every poet cut out for or fortunate enough to pursue it. Eshleman sees two primary alternatives to the kind of poetry envisioned in his dream: writing intended as easy entertainment, on the one hand, and what he derisively calls "creative writing," on the other.

In conversation with James Hillman, Eshleman describes what he believes is their shared purpose: "We both seek to lift the essential up through the consumer film and work with it in imagination without vatic inflation."[115] "Vatic inflation" is a vacuous — as well as undoubtedly self-important and inaccurate — oracular approach to imagination. "Consumer film" is popular art that aspires to nothing more than mere entertainment and, as Eshleman says somewhat flatly in the same conversation, "The serious poet is not entertaining."[116] The statement might be regarded as an over-generalized remark — after all, Eshleman's own poetry can often be very funny — but the purport of the remark rings true.

Eshleman's condemnation of creative writing programs is perhaps less easily accessible. Put bluntly, in his view, creative writing programs diffuse and deaden the art. "The degree writing programs," he writes, "are in the process of turning the art of poetry into creative writing."[117] More broadly, taking stock, he observes: "The democratization of poetry must be evaluated in light of some three hundred undergraduate and graduate university degree programs offering majors in writing poetry and fiction. This system is now producing thousands of talented but unoriginal writers, most of whom would not be writing at all if it were not for jobs."[118] And elsewhere: "By creating a 'poet-professor' middle class, the writing programs have played into the hands of poetry's traditional enemies: education and entertainment."[119] Entertainment is the enemy of imagination because, however clever it may be, it is the equivalent of junk food for the soul. Education is the enemy of imagination because education is too often replication: the teacher replicating him or herself through his or her students. Education rarely breeches the boundaries of the known; rather it aims to reinforce them. This is not the place to fully detail Eshleman's critique of the curricula of creative writing programs in our times. One quick point of distinction might however be drawn. As I hope I have shown, Eshleman's life in letters has exemplified a commitment to ceaseless, wide-ranging exploration and encounter: with other places, other people, other poetries — foreign and familiar —, other modes of thought and image. By contrast, rather than reaching beyond the barriers of the known, contemporary creative writing programs typically find their focus in student writing produced for a given class and work-shopped in it. Sharing Eshleman's dim view, poet and critic Jed Rasula neatly summed up the results: conformism, careerism, anti-intellectualism.[120] If Eshleman is a deeply informed, *historical* poet, a poet writing in a tradition that *includes* history, creative writing programs evidence something like the end of history. Indeed, in our time, following the research of Eshleman and others, we have recovered the roots of imagination in the Pale-olithic painted caves and carved objects but we are also perhaps witness to the all but final strangulation of poetic imagination in academic writing programs. As Eshleman says, "our distinction may become that of being the first generation to have lived at a time in which the origins and the end of poetry become discernable."[121] Looking hopefully ahead, however, Eshleman provides detailed advice to young poets in *Novices* but he also observes elsewhere, if poetry and poetic consciousness is to continue to thrive, let alone to deepen and advance, poets will have to avail themselves of resources beyond the bounds of poetry. He writes: "Poetry, as a psychological art, is still in its infancy, and young writers who seek to create great poems [...] would be better off with texts by Bakhtin, Ferenczi, and Hillman, or camped along the Amazon as their workshop, rather than sitting around Argus-eyed, sharpening their defenses in creative writing wards."[122]

But it would be to betray our subject to end on this note. Another passage from Northrop Frye that Eshleman quotes in *Juniper Fuse* is relevant here: "Poetic thinking, being mythical, does not distinguish or create antithesis: it goes on and on, linking analogy to analogy, identity to identity, and containing, without trying to refute, all oppositions and objections. This means, not that it is merely facile or liquid thinking without form, but that it is the dialectic of love: it treats whatever it encounters as another form of itself."[123] The dialectic of love here is psychoanalytical, born of the unity of opposites — eros and thanatos — life and death — creation and destruction. Love here is what Norman O. Brown described in his book *Love's Body* as symbolical consciousness, and as poetry. "The antimony between mind and body, word and deed, speech and silence, overcome. Everything is only a metaphor, there is only poetry."[124] In Eshleman's terms, from *Indiana*: "If love means anything/ it means everything"[125] Or again, more recently, from *My Devotion*, an endless promise: "In spite of everything, I love you, and I love the earth."[126]

Significantly, the "you" in this phrase references Caryl, the poet's wife and muse since the late 1960s. Excluding *Coils*, each of the poet's major collections of verse written since Caryl entered his life has been dedicated to her. Beyond that however, Caryl has played an active role in shaping his oeuvre during the editing process, a role Eshleman has acknowledged repeatedly. As he described the process in *The Gull Wall*,

"We talk through most of what I write. I initiate it, we argue what it is, and I finish it. In that sense I am responsible for its authorship. It would not be right to say that these poems are mutual works. Yet how they are and are not mutual is a wonderful mystery."[127] What we witness here is a willingness to open the work to the guiding influence of another, not an anonymous other nor a casually or corrosively critical other, but another person who is also an intimate partner in the poet's life. Here the work and the life become one; the love poet loves life with and through sharing it with the beloved.

The first collection of poems Eshleman published after in *Coils* carried the title *Realignment*; the title of the first poem in the collection made the specific nature of that realignment clear: "My Deadness Abandoned for Caryl Reiter."[128] As Eshleman once said to me, "Meeting and committing myself to a life with Caryl was the most important life decision I ever made. It was, in effect, my 'big break.' I am confident that my body of work as it stands today would not have been realized without her key presence in my life."[129] In another dedicatory appreciation of her influence on his life and work, he wrote: "Because of her, I have come to believe that 'I' is the most open word in the language, that poetry is still in its psychological infancy, and that rather than repressing such troubling and unstable forces as the 'self' or the 'ego,' that they should be opened up and explored."[130] That Clayton Eshleman has not ceased from exploration over a career spanning more than fifty-five years is witnessed by the bulk, range, and diversity of the present collection of his essential poetry. That he has sought to open up his life and work, to entwine and entangle it with others, through observation and vision, research and scholarship, translation and editing, through collaboration and conversation, has been one point of this essay. All of this reflects Eshleman's life commitment, his commitment to life.

Notes

An extended version of this essay first appeared in *Clayton Eshleman: The Whole Art* (Black Widow Press, 2014). All references are to works by Clayton Eshleman unless otherwise specified.

1 "What Brought You Here Will Take You Hence" in *Archaic Design* (Boston: Black Widow Press, 2007) 2.
2 "Revisiting Neruda's *Residencias*" in *Conductors of the Pit* (Brooklyn: Soft Skull Press, 2005) 238.
3 Charles Olson, "Letter 2," *The Maximus Poems* (Berkeley: University of California Press, 1983) 9.
4 Charles Olson, "The Kingfishers" *The Collected Poems of Charles Olson* (Berkeley: University of California Press, 1987) 92.
5 Ezra Pound, *Guide to Kulchur* (New York: New Directions, 1970) 7.
6 "Preface" in *Under World Arrest* (Santa Rosa: Black Sparrow Press, 1994) 11.
7 "Somebody Else" in *Archaic Design* 48.
8 "An Alchemist With One Eye On Fire" in *An Alchemist With One Eye On Fire* (Boston: Black Widow Press, 2006) 1.
9 "Introduction" in *Fracture* (Santa Barbara: Black Sparrow Press, 1983) 9.
10 "Preface" in *On Mules Sent From Chavin* (Swansea, UK: Galloping Dog Press, 1977) 8.
11 "The Sixpack Interview" in *Antiphonal Swing* (New York: McPherson & Company, 1989) 33.
12 "Placements II: The Aranea Constellation" in *Juniper Fuse* (Middleton, CT: Wesleyan University Press, 2003) 81.
13 "Introduction" in *Fracture* 10–11; revised version in *Juniper Fuse* 45.
14 "Novices" in *Companion Spider* (Middleton, CT: Wesleyan University Press, 2001) 8; quoted in *Juniper Fuse* 49.
15 "The Death of Bill Evans" in *Fracture* 32.
16 "Preface" in *On Mules Sent From Chavin* 11.
17 "Portrait of Chaim Soutine" in *The Gull Wall* (Los Angeles: Black Sparrow Press, 1975) 64.

18 "Darger" in *Reciprocal Distillations* (Boulder, CO: Hot Whiskey Press, 2007) 25.

19 "Hades in Manganese" in *Juniper Fuse* 13.

20 "Interview with Duane Davis" in *Companion Spider* 286.

21 "Still Life, With Fraternity" in *What She Means* (Santa Barbara: Black Sparrow Press, 1978) 63.

22 See *The Jointure* (Buffalo, NY: BlazeVox, 2012) 27.

23 "Appendix" in *Reciprocal Distillations* 69.

24 "Visions of the Fathers of Lascaux" in *Juniper Fuse* 58. For Lorca's remark in context, see Richard Burgin, *Conversations with Jorge Luis Borges* (New York: Holt, Rhinehart, & Winston, 1968) 93.

25 "Eight Fire Sources" in *Archaic Design* 31.

26 "Interview with Duane Davis" in *Companion Spider* 284.

27 "Appendix" in *Reciprocal Distillations* 70.

28 On poetic apprenticeship see *Novices* in *Companion Spider.*

29 "The Gull Wall" in *Companion Spider* 79.

30 "What Brought You Here Will Take You Hence" in *Archaic Design* 3.

31 "Eight Fire Sources" in *Archaic Design* 32.

32 Charles Olson, "The Kingfishers," *The Collected Poems of Charles Olson* 86.

33 "Preface" in *What She Means* 9.

34 "Placements 1: The New Wilderness" in *Juniper Fuse* 16.

35 See "Prolegomena" in *Juniper Fuse* 143. See also "The Backwall of Imagination" in *Archaic Design* 71–90.

36 "An Alchemist With One Eye On Fire" in *An Alchemist With One Eye On Fire* 6.

37 "An Interview with Gyula Kodolanyi" in *Antiphonal Swing* 192.

38 Norman O. Brown, *Love's Body* (New York: Random House, 1966) 81–82.

39 William Blake, *Milton*, plate 30, lines 1–3.

40 The image is reproduced on the cover of *The Jointure* and discussed therein on page 9.

41 See several poems from *The Gull Wall.*

42 "The Sixpack Interview" in *Antiphonal Swing* 31.

43 "Eight Fire Sources" in *Archaic Design* 37.

44 "Eight Fire Sources" in *Archaic Design* 37.

45 "Author's Preface" in *Antiphonal Swing* xi.

46 "Author's Preface" in *Antiphonal Swing* xi.

47 *Juniper Fuse* 253–54; see also "Author's Preface" in *Antiphonal Swing* xii.

48 *Juniper Fuse* 254.

49 "Introduction" in *Juniper Fuse* xii; See Charles Olson, "A Bibliography on America for Ed Dorn," in Olson, *Collected Prose* (Berkeley: University of California Press, 1997) 306-7.

50 "Introduction" in *Juniper Fuse* xii.

51 Charles Olson, *The Maximus Poems* 104–5.

52 Charles Olson, *The Maximus Poems* 249.

53 "Introduction" in *Juniper Fuse* xxiii.

54 "Jacket # 36 Interview" in *The Price of Experience* (Boston: Black Widow Press, 2012) 315.

55 See the notes to this volume.

56 "Novices" in *Companion Spider* 58.

57 "The Backwall of Imagination" in *Archaic Design* 72.

58 See "Introduction" in *Juniper Fuse* xv–xvi.

59 "Novices" in *Companion Spider* 74.

60 Adrienne Rich, "Forward" to *Companion Spider* ix.

61 See "Jacket # 36 Interview" in *The Price of Experience* 324.

62 "Revisiting Neruda's *Residencias*" in *Conductors of the Pit* (2005) 229.

63 "What Brought You Here Will Take You Hence" in *Archaic Design* 4.

64 "Eight Fire Sources" *Archaic Design* 29.

65 "The Translator's Ego" in *Antiphonal Swing* 230.

66 "*Sulfur & New American Writing*: A Trialogue" in *The Price of Experience* 349.

67 "*Sulfur & New American Writing*: A Trialogue" in *The Price of Experience* 349.

68 See "Preface" in *On Mules Sent From Chavin* 12, 18.

69 "Doing Caterpillar" in *Antiphonal Swing* 59.

70 "Doing Caterpillar" in *Antiphonal Swing* 60.

71 "Doing Caterpillar" in *Antiphonal Swing* 68.

72 "Introduction" in *Juniper Fuse* xii.

73 See *Sulfur* #24 (1989) 4–6; and *Companion Spider* 270.

74 "Introduction to the Final Issue of *Sulfur*" in *Companion Spider* 277.

75   "Introduction to the Final Issue of *Sulfur*" in *Companion Spider*
     274.
76   "*Sulfur & New American Writing*: A Trialogue" in *The Price of Experience* 349.
77   See "Introduction" in *Conductors of the Pit* (2005) xv.
78   "An Alchemist With One Eye On Fire" in *An Alchemist With One Eye On Fire* 6.
79   "Introduction" in *Fracture* 16.
80   Northrop Frye quoted on *Altars* (Los Angeles: Black Sparrow
     Press, 1971) 109–10 and *Hotel Cro-Magnon* (Santa Rosa: Black
     Sparrow Press, 1989) 53. See Northrop Frye, *Fearful Symmetry: A
     Study of William Blake* (Princeton: Princeton University Press,
     1969) 279.
81   Salmen Lewental. See *Amidst a Nightmare of Crime: Manuscripts
     of Members of Sonderkommandos*, ed. Jadwiga Bezwinska and
     Danuta Czech (New York: H. Fertig, 1992) 147.
82   "Preface" in *Under World Arrest* 11.
83   "The Loaded Sleeve of Hades" *Fracture* 35.
84   "An Alchemist With One Eye On Fire" in *An Alchemist With
     One Eye on Fire* 5.
85   "A Translation Memoir" in *Archaic Design* 27.
86   "Companion Spider" in *Companion Spider* 124.
87   "The Atmosphere, Les Eyzies" in *Juniper Fuse* 93.
88   "The Atmosphere, Les Eyzies" in *Juniper Fuse* 91.
89   "Nestual Investigations" in *Indiana* (Los Angeles: Black Sparrow
     Press, 1969) 36.
90   "On Mules Sent From Chavin" in *On Mules Sent From Chavin*
     48–49. Written in October–November 1965, the journal from
     which this statement comes was revised in April–May 1976 and
     this passage in particular includes language and ideas that reflect
     formulations of ideas Eshleman encountered after 1965 —
     Reichian thought and therapy, Bakhtin's interpretation of the
     grotesque, etc.
91   "The Atmosphere, Les Eyzies" in *Juniper Fuse* 92.
92   "Coils" in *Coils* 147.
93   "Through Breuil's Eyes" in *Juniper Fuse* 76.
94   "Placements II: The Aranea Constellation" in *Juniper Fuse* 82.
95   "The Aurignacians Have the Floor" in *Juniper Fuse* 26.

96   See *Companion Spider* 5; for the Olson quote in context, see Charles Olson, *Letters for Origin* (New York: Paragon House, 1970) 119–120.

97   "The Loaded Sleeve of Hades" in *Juniper Fuse* 50.

98   *The Jointure* 23.

99   "The Hole that Grew into a Pole," *Juniper Fuse* 236.

100 "Barcarole," *Juniper Fuse* 100.

101 "Tiresias Drinking," *Juniper Fuse* 67.

102 *The Jointure* 23

103 "The Indeterminate, Open" in *Juniper Fuse* 167.

104 "The Loaded Sleeve of Hades" in *Juniper Fuse* 52.

105 "Winding Windows" in *Juniper Fuse* 19.

106 See Robert Duncan, *The H.D. Book* (Berkeley: University of California Press, 2011) 154.

107 "A Translation Memoir" in *Archaic Design* 23.

108 "A Translation Memoir" in *Archaic Design* 28.

109 "At the Speed of Wine," *Hotel Cro-Magnon* 149.

110 "Introduction to the Final Issue of *Sulfur*" in *Companion Spider* 275.

111 "Novices" in *Companion Spider* 4.

112 "A Visionary Note" in *Antiphonal Swing* 10.

113 *The Sanjo Bridge* (Los Angeles: Black Sparrow Press, Sparrow 2, 1972) n.p.

114 "A Spangled Moor" in *My Devotion* (Boston: David Godine, Black Sparrow Books, 2004) 49.

115 "A Discussion with James Hillman" in *Antiphonal Swing* 213.

116 "A Discussion with James Hillman" in *Antiphonal Swing* 213.

117 "Wound Interrogation" in *Penetralia*, forthcoming.

118 "An Alchemist With One Eye On Fire" in *An Alchemist With One Eye On Fire* 3.

119 "Introduction to the Final Issue of *Sulfur*" in *Companion Spider* 276.

120 Jed Rasula, *Syncopations: The Stress of Innovation in Contemporary American Poetry* (Tuscaloosa, Alabama: University of Alabama Press, 2004) 9.

121 "An Alchemist With One Eye On Fire" in *An Alchemist With One Eye On Fire* 7.

122 "Response to Mary Kinzie" *Sulfur* 13 (1985); reprinted in *Antiphonal Swing* 203.

123 Northrop Frye quoted in *Juniper Fuse* xxi–xxii. See Northrop Frye, *A Study of English Romanticism* (Chicago: University of Chicago Press, 1968) 121–122.

124 Norman O. Brown, *Love's Body* 266.

125 "The night…" in *Indiana* 102.

126 "A Yonic Shrine" in *My Devotion* 50.

127 "Dedication" in *The Gull Wall* 5.

128 *Realignment* (Treacle Press, with drawings by Nora Jaffe, 1974).

129 Personal communication.

130 "Dedication" in *The Name Encanyoned River* (Santa Barbara: Black Sparrow Press, 1986) 239.

I
1960–1973

The Roaches

At night in certain cemeteries
a blue hand pushes through the earth
    in certain hospitals
      there is a tearing—and a wail—
         at night the roaches come out.
The roaches come one by one from the plaster,
from cheese—from their dry bins,
    one by one through oriental carpets
and assemble wearing opera hats
      and little boys shoes—
        they pour
    through sugar, through trousers,
and like an enormous mustache grow over
my threshold waving their banners of eyelashes
    and apple-cores.
           They bring
      with them crayons
and the bald groins of little girls—
    they dress in bedroom costumes
    and greet each other
like young husbands and wives—
whispering they surround
    my bed and talk of iodine, of diplomas
and tug at the covers
      with teeth of soft fingers.
     Then like furry animals their hands
push the moon aside
      and touch me—
like a wave of air, like time itself
they pass over the pillow to cover
    me with kisses of souring meats
and roll down the sheets with a blowing sound.
     And like a boat
without an anchor we float from corner
to corner, from window to rafter, wrinkled
    as an old robe with silk tassels—

in a cradle of lead we rock
            through the hallway,
        through velvet corridors and pass
into the street a map of skin—
swimming through vaseline and dusky talcum,
pulling the red moon over melting street lamps,
                over hair and nails,
                over walks that glisten—
into a hotel without lobbies but many black needles,
up blood-filled elevators
                to slip upon
        a table of flowers where death waits
with a green mask and golden scissors,
        with an orange apron and polished shoes,
with the smell of an old ship—and the eyes of my
                father.

Bloomington, 1959

MEXICO & NORTH (1962)*

Evocation

I

     I walk a fury
of gnats, sun tossing on lake-wall
      Mexican dawn burns sorceress across
waters, circling round me, rising & falling
whipping her veils of menstruated linens
     odor of earth, damp hay
     Praise

     fire & man, men
mounted on rice-field buffaloes, birds
      singing in corolla of town
black lily-roots lugged in by tubercular kids
hands among oranges, breasts of strong
     women glistening over
     rock & hemp

     my own genitals sweet
as papaya. Lean into wind, see from this
      balustrade broken steps spilling an
alphabet of stone to fern groves of Ajijic
beggars unrolling from stairways, a
     python of backs
     snailing

     to the muddy chancel
where St. Anthony is crowned. It is scent of
      hunt, of turned-back coverlet where with
her fingers on sill of a new day a child is
swept by fog, bellowings of fresh kill
     rain of blackberries
     on rusted

stone
no seed grows in porcelain
bone

II

By evocation & foot they come
perch on tombs
chanting
leave death, myth for grass, Chapala, parrots in trees

    or another town, shades of Paramo
    as they thirst, on the plaza, in labor, a burra
    where the band plays
    the rites!

       drink black milk
       of *madrepores* sieved on fiddler-crabs
       eels tossing off *Isla Roqueta*
       avoid my own
       erecting their towers
       o terrible boom
       of those bells

unleash stone tigers fixed forever on *Calle Madera* & turn
that old woman's chair, her mice-colored hands that she see
her daughter in my eyes
for ankle-deep in sand I'm bearded by surf

              no dust
              a trail of vaginal oil on my eyes
              bacon-smell & the town awakened
              bees, shawls, fruit whisper
              of knives beneath lashes
              red horse neighs shoeless &
              radiant

land your nets fishermen
tumble forth the woman you've carried from coasts
of Santiago
I hear your singing Pablo Neruda

Tú estás de pie sobre la tierra, llena de dientes y relámpagos.
Tú propagas los besos y matas las hormigas.
Tú lloras de salud, de cabolla, de abeja, de abecedario ardiendo.
Tú eres como una espada azul y verde
y ondulas al tocarte, como un río

I want for you some blue eyes

Inheritance

in glow of skin, in stones, in old
rocker hung
with crimson
serape, *Caballito Cerrero* on my table, biscuits
& cheese I slowly
rock this morning
watch tiny ants labor up the wall
sun dry my earth floor the mountains
maids balancing laundry down to the shore
thinking of nothing at all

or of the cross-words
of those who've given me courage of lineage & sun
of Crane, of living Hirschman, the celestial
rhythm of your shoulders *lavandera*
you who work, who sustain me
no less than my family
formed
fired by the living
of Vallejo dying in Paris
pero dadme
en español
algo, en fin, de beber, de comer, de vivir, de reposarse
& closing his book opening
my own

coming upon my feet from my star
hearing Anaya* in the next room toss
off covers, splash
in the wash-bowl to stand
black hair fresh glistening in my door

letting it go & enter
ants travel down the wall
maids come up the hill
already it is evening
the sun flowers

Las Brujas

Old women set on curb in black booties
gum
chocolates under fire of
                    a kitten tossed

back
& forth two boys
slamming it skidding through dirt

cellophane
& fir blowing across their black skirts

floating in gutter
slowly
steered by their eyes a strand of human hair

Water-Song

Dung-plop, sour meats broiling, parrots strut
in the coughing dawn floating bits of fish
carrot slivers

                         odor of coffee descends stairs
passes over crumbling wall, *cartels* ignite, wild
berries cluster in broken glass

                        white tissue hung
                        from twine-web
                        taut between houses
cow swings from doorway to puddle streaked with oil
mucus, Chapala glistens, it rained last night

I go down to shore, listen to a meadow
lavender hyacinths slap the creaking docks, hulls, a
                  scud of sleek white birds breaks
frightened poultry across the
waters, the waters

                        grease!
                        urine, stacks
                        of pineapple chunks black
                        with bees
mahogany, spices, two marbles for devilfish's eyes
curandera draws her needle turtle's dangling head

      the water
                      I spool citrus-rind round
my finger, pick chili-bits from under my nails, two boys
club water-snake, he won't let go, fog shreds
into mango-groves, fresh brains strewn
on gleaming counters, whole side festooned from
three grey hooks, a slaughterhouse smell
from only boarded door in the block
salt on his fist
beggar lifts a whole communion of tequila to brick lips
pariah dog follows

with eight raw dugs, Christ's eye falls
from limed plaster

            I want hyacinth-bud
            for her hair
            citrus-
            rind for her mouth, that
            sleek white bird
milk-cans slap burro-gut, shawls oriental streets, sucked
mango-seed candles the feast floating the gutter, sun

          hovering over

The Strong
—for Cid Corman in Matera

To disagree with you is
to argue life
as it is

Mexico
old woman
too weak to lift
from her curb-shop
peanuts

negress
holding
coffined by
the sunless window
a half-eaten
crab

your Matera

imploded into
rock
by all people
entering

that face
pocked with faces
should be so

rock

La Mujer

Yelled into a hut
with curb-yellow walls
where above deepest
of five beds hung
a plaster Jesus, head
tortured back to beg
drippings from a web
in which a spider was
eating a horsefly

blurred by lilies
of cigar-smoke men
& women crouched red-eyed
celebrating the eve
of the season of rain
splattered by wine
as if half-slaughtered
bull had broken from
the priest, bellowing
through the room fell
moaning in the pig-yard

they hacked & argued
spit: most were
consumptive: all
did a twelve hour day
to feed the child-horde
silently staring the
windows, starving dwarfs
who'd survived through
the black forest a
pilgrimage. Stout
woman sank down
across from me
eyes partly closed
began to hum, her

patched shantung streaked
with chicken-blood
greasy hair pulled in bun
eyes closed, mouth
barely moving, hands
clenched in hammock
of her wide-spread slowly
rocking thighs, resembled
a dying man in ecstasy
of final testament.
As if to retch up song
her arms tightened
she lifted head mouth
yawning, tongue

jammed against broken
dog-teeth, twisting
bare foot on top another
thighs violently shaking
& lurching back to bang
cupboard spilling
rum, baby-trinkets
head cleaved open
from her heels her womb her chest
song came   *Que boni-*
to cielo
Que boni-
ta tierra
on her top foot a
cockroach paused, head
of spike, visible
axis of this world

Dark Blood

Here in this parched
afternoon, under
giant thrust of palms
three policemen casually
     pick themselves
peck narrowed eyes into
La Galeria where a fly
buzzes the halted fan
where the room turns
slowly on a skewer of
sun & dust & the *cantinero*
keeps hands in warm
greasy water, scowls
& glances back
forth & back across
     four men who
continue to clack
dominoes, break bread
eyes lowered under the
     Tarascan woman   *
squatting on high cupboard
breasts at attention
head back, eyes bugged
     straining to
give birth for five
hundred years, who is
soundless as the palms
as the American at my elbow
blood oozing from
head into rough planking
I have been told Leave
him alone gringo

WALKS (1967) *

Walk VI

   Walked again over Santa Rosa Bridge—
when I worked for the North American Peruvian Cultural Institute,
   I could see a cross-topped hill from Sponholz's
   office—highest of poor grassless
   hills in & about Lima—

  SAN CRISTOBAL HILL—How will the Institute look
   from the base of your cross?

  Through Almeida—a carnival of stalls
   on concrete (where
must the discharge go?)   High iron fences—
maids dozing in park grass (not
a romantic image here)   Statues (another
age)   I turned in but was rebuffed—
"Private—The Water Passage, what you want, is
around there—"
         another dead end with poor come
out to look—
      below the pink convent wall, a dry
viaduct—The water Passage—I started to climb

the work is carrying water—I saw many faces
come out & didn't think to say Good Morning—the poor
unsettle me, degenerate the poem—it seems a structure
holds only *against them*—one is always carrying one's
sun—a smoking brazier—& walking fast—called
to the murderer's attention—out to look for shit—for
the first of the stations

  Passed by trucks carrying water—
the work is   what? Not to quit a poisoned
job—is

the battle—Arjuna. Is facing one's task—
first station of the cross.

   is shuffling up this hill—the stations
meaningless, politics a horrible excuse (in the sense
that any, or no, choice kills)
thought a roofless shack—
the image without water—
                 A starving woman selling razor-
                  slices of rotten watermelon
                     —eyes bugged—
running down the road past me as if she were on the last
bend of a 440—I'm the Institute
going up—

   House unpainted 50 feet away—
up close worse—gangrene hill—before a shack
a pile of ripe mahogany crawling with flies—
death can be more alive than life—
Roman numerals gouged in waist-thick station posts—

   At the top of the world are pigs
rooting in human garbage.
Overlooking Lima—8 bolgias abstract—this
night abstract—
& I've never meant more to say what I mean.
Shacks disappear at the level of only stone—last image:
pigs,
       heaped refuse, kids names on rocks—
an hour of last images.   The new "vivienda"
worse than the Cantagayo slum—pipeline of gas chambers
fitted out in shadowless valley—

   to go in—to cure—
or as Rothenberg put it: "Sometimes I'd rather be shaman"
and I: "then the life's not in the work"
       —here pulled to pig's *Test of Poetry*

writing with a little stick on rock
expressionless face of nature
what else is a cross?   San Cristóbal's is 30 feet tall
                                studded with giant lightbulbs, both
                                post & beam packed with them—
                                at the base a generator grinds away

Barbara   Clayton   No love is forever:
the source of this sea of emotions?   To be
            on top—see that cross
lit nightly over killer Lima—over sleep
of thousands of foetalhoods like mine
                what meaning this dove over world?

To write with a stick in rock dust on rock
quarries of sunlight—road now to 10th station

art a repercussion   10 layers above starvation

Letter To César Calvo Concerning The Inauguration Of A Monument To César Vallejo

The namesake.

dear Calvo:

I woke up this morning to the newspaper, & on the john reading Artaud's *Van Gogh: The Man Suicided by Society*, thought I had the connection to take a good swing at a few who've made my life miserable in your city these past 6 months, I mean how a monument is put up to Vallejo, ceremony attended by 'distinguished elements of our intellectual community … including the widow of the poet, numerous artists & prominent neighbors, who were later given a cocktail in a nearby salon …', this bust on a tall black base sitting out among the trees in the city of the man's country where you cannot buy an edition of his works; for a friend from my university in the States wrote me the other day asking for copies of *Poemas Humanos* to teach in a seminar & of course I had to turn him down, the last 'edition' of that masterpiece having to be printed clandestinely, in 1961 on about the same quality paper (the back breaking as one opens the book) on which I wipe my ass.

But then something happened that made me think perhaps this is all wrong now, there is more important stuff to do than swing grieved at others; for my mother-in-law visiting the birth of her new grandchild we went off to the Larco Herrera museum to see some pots & weaving, & near noon, down in the room for erotic pieces, I met the owner, Mr. Larco and asked him why the erotic ones are separated from the rest, since it seemed obvious enough to me that the fuckers were but one shade of a vast spectrum of life and shd rightfully be seen in context. Mr. Larco is old and not well, as perhaps you know, and he shook his head sadly, repeating "the children … the children …" as if speaking of a loss more than answering my question, wch tho, he did, the children it seemed it was decided should not see the sex when they were led on tours thru the rooms above. Then he sat down, on a little chair, and said, "You know, when Keensy was here he said the word 'pornographic' was wrong, that the only word you could use about these pieces was 'erotic,' and I've been thinking about this now for two years" (and he was breathing hard, weighing his words as if he might not have a chance to change what he was now saying), "he said it was all an expression of love, and I've been thinking about this and I believe he is right. It is all love."

And he looked up at me, long into me without seeing me for a moment, and while I don't think he was really touched by what he was saying, I was, and it was something that seemed to lie outside Mr. Larco and his fine museum.

Now it is night and I'm still wondering where the true connection does lie. That is, can I say more to you among the Lima dead, among all the crap that is here in this city tied up with your namesake's reputation, you a young poet who I tried to write a poem to the other night, having missed you again in Barranco, having come to see you & your shameless girlfriend who like the rest has copped out on me here, & coming back I tried to catch the isolation in the collectivo, and while that might have been caught, there was nothing in the poem to say to you worth keeping, so I've been on edge since, wanting to speak to you, since I have yet to speak to any Peruvian artist about anything more than how-do-you-do etc., and God knows I've tried, tho I will admit there is wounded pride involved.

Does a vision of love hold, can it open the muck, clear it out of the way enough, to make human response possible, or is one, talking about Vallejo in Peru in 1966, doomed? Or does it really make much difference to you or Belli or Ortega or Hinostroza or anyone of the ten or fifteen poets here I've met? You see, I'm trying to grasp something about you & your people and I'm trying to do it in front of you, not say, as it was done to him, your namesake, thought out for him, withheld as it is still withheld, then erected over the grass which he is *not* a part of as I'm pretty sure the widow is at least right about that; that he never wanted to return, that his city is Paris, that he is about as cholo as I am, and that the 'native son' bullshit is just that. I'm thinking that maybe your dead friend Javier Heraud is closer to him than any of you, who went to Cuba maybe somewhat the same way Vallejo went to Russia, only that Heraud came back to Peru, at his age he could not see Peru in a world or mind perspective, thus died for the Peru that Vallejo after sitting in jail in Trujillo, a hundred days decided wasn't worth the pain, and returned to Paris, to his mind, to what he believed was happening not in a jungle or poet's award panel but in the world.

So I don't know whether it makes any sense or not to even ask you *why* those I've met here act like scared little children before the old woman (let's get her in the proper perspective) who can go to the cocktail party and grin at the dignitaries who you know I know she hates, as she hates all of Peru, who has his work tied up, in short, the old hag that *keeps his manuscripts not published 28 years after his death* in her sacheted underwear and as much as I can tell is an old Faulkner 'Emily' sleeping with the ashes of what never cleared or was completely lived. The fact that she reigns, that Belli lacks even the guts to tell her she is 'wrong,' that Oviedo (who had the nerve to tell me certain poems of Vallejo couldn't be translated but hadn't the faintest idea of what or which those poems were) and Syzslo and Westphalen who I guess we should consider 'distinguished elements of the intellectual community' not only know nothing about Vallejo, his poetry I mean, not the asinine anecdotes & gloss I constantly get instead of interest in the texts, why these people *shd* reign and pander to her, is there some sort of power structure at the base of your skull too, I mean is Heraud's act THE ONLY ACT FOR AN ARTIST TO COMMIT today in Peru, or can you explain to me the shoddyness, the grease & muck of which that old viper seems to represent the moon, in glory over the darkness of Lima, in any sense that we might be able to call it a city?

I am sorry, I just can't write you about love or anything so nice and clean as Tom Merton writes his S.A. chums. I think all of this can end in love, it can for me in the sense of my translations of his work, wch simply is my way of showing love for him to others, but it seems as if *we'll* be up all night to reach that dawn.

So.   I hesitated before that word 'underwear' above, but I'll keep it for I believe my connection with Vallejo is partially sexual, & that I've lived that connection thru enough to bring it up here. Maybe now would be as good a time as any to tell you why I am translating your namesake wch shd tell you what kind of hands his work is in. (I didn't quit QUENA for nothing—one of the strongest objections I had to continuing the magazine under censorship was that it would be dishonest to Vallejo, and that I am here of first things trying to get that translation right I hope you'll give me—'dishonest' in that the *Instituto Cultural Peruano Norteamericano* had no objections to my printing 6 translations from *Poemas Humanos*, the author of wch was in at least name a Communist for 10 years & whose poetry's intellectual axis is revolutionary in all the violent implications of that word. Of course the answer here is simple & sad enough: no one at ICPNA knows anything about Vallejo either. They take him as they take Lincoln or Frost, safe since dead & famous, or I shd really say here dead, for they couldn't take Heraud whose blood you can still smell in the barriadas or in the sun on Jiron Cuzco, or for that matter, Delgado's essay about which I have a number of questions, one of which is that if he pushed his statements & moot questions to conclusion the ICPNA's ban would be apt enough, for North Americans are just as involved in Heraud's death as plantation policemen and if Delgado could have risked the truth in that essay he would have said that not the cosmic night took Heraud's flesh but the lust for wch ICPNA is in business, those who use it as cultural shield for their own ownings & peons, the idea (fleshed) wch Heraud & his little band tried to invade).

I took a Mexican magazine, special number devoted to Vallejo to Japan with me in 1961, having only read a few poems in English translation before. I bought that magazine on a hunch in Mexico City in 1959, feeling as many others do in North American that Neruda & Vallejo represent poetry in a vital concentration for this century in South America (that may be true: but Neruda is the dark side of that moon, wch says nothing about sd moon's perfection). I was married right before going to Japan, & if you'll pardon what may look like digression, I'll pick that Mexican magazine up in a moment.

I'm from the mid-west, Indiana, wch when I say it often sounds like 'Hart Crane candy country'. There is that specter, the landlocked ignorance & suspicion of all that cld be called creative activity in the North American Midwest, moreso than in the East or West I believe, but I'd better speak for myself here & say that getting from being a middle-class youth in a fraternity with a convertible to an artistic consciousness is difficult enough that I always fear I will risk writing *about* that threshold, centering my writing on the doorstep and not passing thru to where the past is *past decision*. I feel that at the center of any artist's life (by which of course I mean writing/living) is his relation to other men & women, his sex life at large, and for me the squaring of such, the seeing of what *that* relationship is and how I must handle myself to my friends, unknowns, parents & enemies has been bitter and seems to have kept all my poetry to date in a kind of inferno chasing its own penis. (I might say to you here that there *is* an attempt in a number of young artists in North America now to move this conflict into the consciousness of writing/creating. It looms large in what my generation will turn out and what we do turn out may 'turn' on to what extent 'the body' is resolved). Before I married woman was cunt and I treated her with all the disrespect generally due that word; of course that fucked up my relation to men so badly that I really never had 'friends' in any sense that I cherish now. I distrusted boys & men, told homosexual jokes, & had a soul life totally tied up with women, or my mother, at best to get to know her (since I cldnt directly) thru others & vice versa since I cldnt get to know any other woman *because* of my mother, relation was hit & miss, nothing deep, no conflict plumbed, no real romance, no crucial fights, nothing, in short, but sly hand sneaking into a Playtex, the bend in under the frontseat rammed fuck, the sin there being that there *is* no release and I'd be willing to settle for the worst conditions for sex if there could be at least something raw & with endurance, not the slip off & driving out & getting drunk. Under these conditions (scanty, I know, but I'm trying to get at something else so accept, please, such incomplete brevity) I married the woman I am now living with, it has been 5 years & who has just borne me our first son.

I didn't know what to do when I started to live with her because I loved as I cld muster that, & I *respected* (foul word) her & of course cldnt square treating her as some cunt. That all women are, well as all men are pricks, was neither seen. But I wanted an art & cldnt be straight with that wish or with what I thought of myself by completely running out on her. Thus I went halfway. I went into myself, masturbated when the tension wld have forced me to treat her as a cunt, sat in grim silence reworking & reworking the same draft in myself, but without quiet—I mean breathless silence, silence that cannot be thought in, silence you cant do anymore with than with your mind in a cocktail party. I rationalized that my semi (enforced) chastity was because energy was being put in creative activity but knew thru some light glimmer that was not true, for nothing was happening in the creative activity other than rubbing up against my own resistance, what had to be done, but I didn't understand at all with *whose* energy & how it was being done.

I hope I can project something of the underlying idea of all this, that to talk about what is personal of myself may touch on what is personal to you & to other men, that I am speaking of something that lies a few strata under Heraud's body as well as in the Institute Director's who is alive, that I might better address what I must say to you as a man in the world who I as North American owe a revolution & for the other shitasses in America (& the shitass I am too), for you & I in that most personal sense must be neighbors if we are to talk at all & not with our bombers turned to kill each other. I mean, César, what is the war in Vietnam & the censorship of QUENA more than the failure of two men/women to talk, to hear the other out. And North Americans are paying the price for exactly what they suppress, we are writing some of the worst & best poetry in the world—how can that mean anything to you? The sexual must be cleared as it always shd have been & now that the Institutional traitor sky God is, has been I mean your Catholic prince, dead for years, who in a GREAT prison lies, we no longer as human beings have any excuse but to live at the limit of our HUMANITY.

Or am I all wrong? Am I giving away a secret that must be secret for a man to function ultimately together? I don't think so. My only real fear is that if this is printed where it shd be read while we are in Peru my wife & child may be endangered.

And I know as well too that what I am talking about lies not under your friend's body, for he is dead & nothing 'lies' under death.

It was in some-what the above psychic drain, what? constriction of energy, worrying & sewing myself into silence, that I opened the Mexican magazine one night in Kyoto & read poem #53 of *Poemas Humanos,* "Me veine, ha días, una gana ubérrima, política," & I was so moved, deeply deeply moved, cld hardy read a word of the Spanish so I didn't know why, but the move was genuine & perhaps all my labor with Vallejo to this day has been to clear that movement, for as I tonight think of that poem the 'desire' that is so rich & 'political' is a desire *for* desiring, is not I feel something & do it BUT I feel a desire to feel something, the twice removed, the monument if you like & not the man, the widow & not the poet, I'll let you finish that series.

That Vallejo was sexually tortured & bright too about the torture is pretty evident. That I wld hook onto him at that point in my life when I was trying to get *out,* hook into *Poemas Humanos,* makes to me perfectly genuine good sense. I believe that is my basic connection with your namesake; that it gives ground & grit that I pray can groundswell under & push into others' hearts whatever technical ability to voice my attempt may come to.

For *Poemas Humanos* is a great collection of failure, of a failure to be human without writing.

Can you understand what I am saying here? Of needing to write to be human & of never quite making it. It is always the cry kept chested even tho so much does get out, it is, in a sense not at all total, my need to reach you in such form cannot wait for *Walk IV* or for any poem, the city's need for the monument & sadly, & not very interestingly, Georgette's need to keep Vallejo in stall, in deepfreeze til she die, for lo if he gets away into the Word the mirror of her wld turn on itself & shd wld see herself as she is, old, bereft, a lonely woman in an unfriendly world, dying.

I should say here that that is by far not all: much compassion & pain does find a way into these poems, much agony is present, so much held in them it wld make sense to me just how evasive they are to those in Lima who pretend to know them, or who make money off literary ac-quaintance with Vallejo. But then if one is not directly involved with the poor or not directly with revolution, does it make sense that enough of the suffering will come thru to make these poems in one heart valid?

Let me try to give the word 'sexual' more ground: my aim in writing you is to explain nothing, I do not have to justify my translating Vallejo; it may be worthwhile for you to know what was on my mind at the time I decided to undertake what has been 5 years of drilling thru a wall, slowly, daily; there is in the best translations, or working of texts, the same impulses as in the poem; it is self-inspired, done for no exterior reasons tho what is outside prompts and wants return. My reading & rereading Vallejo I see has been the attempt to know another man, ultimately why it is tough for me to live in the world, further what is the meaning of my life, why must I live. Why I am here has gained no more *reason* in 31 years than my son in 13 days, or has gained nothing *but* reason! & my kinship with your kin is to not have to write those poems myself.

I deprecate them only in the sense I think you shd too: they are a 'last' people & not a 'beginning'—language in them is not departure but the straining of an old mold, which includes manners as well as relation, that won't yield beyond the fullness of its own chains. But who is Vallejo for *you*? You run around Lima with petitions for jailed revolutionaries—are we speaking of simply a good poet (say as Van Gogh is a good painter) who is being made way too much of right now (here, in this case) & who, when it comes to actualities, how to survive in Lima for instance, leaves you? Can you answer these questions for me? Do you believe it is fair of me to ask such of you? *What ever does any artist mean in anyone's life beyond a kind of expansion of some original soul-life never cleared from the womb on?* I am coming to know that all but a fraction of art is BURNT OFFERING, returning to its ash, in a word to have your sperm & eat it too: "I don't want to eat my poem—I want to give my heart to my poem" (Artaud).

A little before I spoke of 'my generation' & I smile here to recall I told you one night you cldn't in your poem speak *for* your generation in any sense of WE. What I say abt the sexual facing of difficulties of living of poets this generation in North America is pretty boring if the process is taken for poetry. One's responsibilities to one's body must be understood to a great extent *prior to* the poem. It does not mean, as Camus said, that only chastity is linked to personal progress, that one cannot indulge in 'sex' (the silliness of that statement reflects on anything a priest ever writes) if one wants to produce; it means that the choice, as mine before, is as ground (fertilizer), the art not the earth's labor but what comes from labor, "not the sea" as Louis Zukofsky has written, "but what floats over it." However, just *admitting* process to voice is much; I am not aware of this idea operating in art (& not just in geniuses) before. I wanted very much to print the section (#2) of Zukofsky's long poem "A" in QUENA because its power seems to point to faith in one's own processes, of not fearing to voice the lightning flashes hitting thru a young person's system, & chucking forever what is *set up*, or as in most 20th Century South American poetry that has stayed home & not gone to Europe, the deadly underlying assumption never investigated in the poem that answers can be found in words like "earth" "light" & "sun." Can you tell me why this fake pantheism still rules in countries dominated by the conquest of a foreign crown?

Given widows, crass monuments, the division of sex from love, given what you must feel to be the surrounding darkness, is there a way out? What *does* one do? Through the last couple paragraphs I've had in mind some words from a letter of Rilke that a friend of mine found for what he wanted to say. "With (death)," Rilke writes, "with its full, unmasked cruelty: this cruelty is so tremendous that it is just with it that the circle closes: it leads right back again into the extreme of a mildness that is great, pure & perfectly clear…." And further: "toward experiencing of *this* most rich & most sound mildness, mankind has never taken the first steps—unless in its oldest, most innocent times, whose secret has been all but lost to us. The content of 'initiations' was, I am sure, nothing but the imparting of a 'key' that permitted the reading of the word 'death' *without* negation…"

here I must turn again to Vallejo, as I think you must, & face what seems to me the total absence of what Rilke speaks of in the *Human Poems*. For the world to come through, man must make himself transparent & I believe (for I must respond to Rilke or to quote him is unjust) that the 'mildness' is the seeing of oneself, one's organ, as part of a bank tangled with trees & flowers, wrestling perhaps as men in a river. The *Bhagavad Gita* helps me here, for it too sees *ego* as *organ*, and when one can live this, then it wld seem that death disappears, ceases to be separate, that sex can return, in the only meaningful apocalypse, to the place of seed and I can embrace my friend in all the fullness of our bodies, loving each other's shoulders for that moment of grasping (at which you Peruvians so often hint, but no more) tenderness. I have come out to stand facing that tangled bank & would leave you with exactly that image, light wrestling with greenness, jungle in that it contains Javier Heraud, whose light is dependent upon dust to raise it, but whose light may be to hold to mind/heart, be enough to be devoted to, what I can only suggest here, but will, for it is the most I can say to you.

This is a workingman's letter, for my pocket a stone. Do as you choose.

This son who's appeared to us
passed & has yet to come—
        blue, swaddled in bloody linen
the supermarket cart paused,
I looked (big balls, screaming
appendages in the form of claws)
        Matthew Craig Eshleman
        you've been born into a deceitful world.

Who split us apart as a tree
        has yet to appear human:
the man in the doctor who promised
I could watch the birth—the woman
in the nun who backed the doctor's
betrayal—I hugged you & felt what
        pain I could—& saw your
        profile—Greek warrior—
                I felt your urine & wanted

sight of my child that is yours—
beautiful woman from whom has
        transferred all my gold—
what broke us apart for our son's glory
        is this world we are in—
        product of my luminous salts!

It was THEN I saw man alive a son of a bitch, a son
of a bitch born, son of a bitch dead
a son of a bitch dying—
Naturally Vallejo is sore—
naturally Luvah will burn in his furnace,
Vala howls, & what is not seen
are your meats naturally red
grape, blood, magenta azalea & pine—
beauty of resistance! Who held terror
in her teeth this afternoon must suffer
my hurt! Dachau I've ever
lived in! Godmother of my unexplained

faults! The hair of my son in your dilated vagina
was your hair I took in my teeth—
& your look, forgiving all, what I
can't make now—what I wasn't allowed to see.

THE HOUSE OF OKUMURA (1969) *

The House of Okumura II

was presided over by Barbara
the spirit of the place
learning to cook in the small
kitchen the dark Okumura women
gave us,
   was recently married
a fresh breath
  into the musty fangs
of old Daughter unwed
bulldog widow Mother
grandmother Ageless,   maybe 80
& Otake-san
   Han-Shan of the place
crazed laughing char-woman
worked for her tubercular husband
no-good son
boiled red hands
washing the dark Okumura linens
mid-winter washing-machine rattle
thumping the wall against wch my back
books & look out
glassed doors
  the yard a rectangle of pebbles raked
& weeded by Ageless
      at dawn her there, bent, kimono hiked,
white chicken legs, weeding

        a persimmon & a maple
close enuf to be strung by the
pregnant red spider
   over a dry pond
   stepping-stones, rocks,
the tumble of Higashi Mountain in ageless
          proliferation

I loved you.

What does that mean?

I will not judge you.

The House of Okamura III

Would sit
on bench
built against house
with clip-board look
persimmon maple pond in the eye
I still have those notes
that go nowhere
say a persimmon fell this afternoon
smoke winding across blue sky
they are like Will Petersen
    with whom I have nothing but
      everything in common,
now what does that mean?

  Red spider, swollen yellow-stripped body
crept out in dew to watch her
trapped flies to baste the web
brought a caterpillar into the house
learned tiny redflower name,
  as if nature had stopped
& Barbara brought soup
I am so blessed
so much has come to me
say thank you dropping coin into
         the monk hat
thank you for giving me the chance to
give, to awake that morning
eyes wet from a dream
I remembered a former love
& just last night
  in a man & a woman
a former love,
    The Last Judgement means
NO MORE
  anger over calmness, I mean
my anger over your shyness

force over the gentle
         reluctance
duration
& faith in me,
the weaker by its steadfastness
fulfilling the eratic strong

  Why do I break into tears
when I stop to think
    what were you doing
when I was not with you?

     That we have never
     each in each fulfilled

The House of Okumura VI: *A Tale*

Began at "Open Sea"
Sushi Shop on Higashiyama near the I-
magumano Trolley Stop, eating with Barbara
& Kamaike at counter delicious
toro, ika, redfaced sake drinker
invites me out American, come
drink with him downtown. Barbara
looks at Kamaike Kamaike says
he looks ok
      goodnight, I go
off with him Kiyamachi Shijo
bar district more sake big lip-
sticked dark red lipped hostesses
leering in dark sweet tiny bar
Can't understand much
Time passes
We're in his car running north
Says I'll drop you off
Then we're out in the country
Now to Uji he says Let's have
more sushi sake I'll pick
up a friend
      Japan Landscape
Night
   parked in the country while he
yells his friend out of bed young
guy learned his English when he worked
on base
     end up in country sushi house
get the owner out of bed   make ten person
sushi spread I eat and eat and drink and drink
sitting with big farm-woman
bar hostess over my shoulder too full &
beat dead tired
     at 4 in the morning he
drops me out front of House of Okumura

thanks a lot oof
boy am I plastered

                    wake up dreadfully
hung over all day long that night is
Halloween
                    & Barbara has a party for
her Otani Junior High English Students
masks Mori & Kamaike dressed up like
women kids bobbing for apples in tub
great photo of everyone
                              nightmare dreams
at a carnival I wander into gigantic tent
look at a wide velvet covered table with
huge steamshovel lowering over it Snyder
in the shovel-cup being lowered to table
picks up gold coins with his buns

wake up next day still hung over
dreadful day rain
wander over to Yasuhara's place
he's not in old woman invites me in
anyway, watch TV
                         late rainy dreary
TV afternoon the program:
                              highschool saga
fat boy wants to make it with his thinner peers
great track day & him on relay team has to
climb a pole
                  my heart goes out to Bob Kelly
I watch him struggle up
and
tears come.   very strange.   tears.
and I am moved and leave
now dusk
            still hungover get on cycle
drive head out toward Snyder's
Joanne home alone

so we talk & talk both
about Jung and archetypes
excellent talk how I like her I
think as at about 8 pm get
on Cycle head home

*

I think.
Turn off Junikendoori onto wide Nijo
very wide it seems almost like a field
cycle feeling funny air charged

something is going to happen I think
& then weird feeling of no longer in control
& realize soon I will pass by the great
Nijo Castle & then know I am to stop
get off cycle & circumambulate the Castle
park & circumambulate the Castle
which is square and is surrounded by a moat
This I do

getting off cycle in parking lot
for the first time in my life I am out of control
& it's a nice strange feeling
                              The Castle was the World
& I am to walk about it first North then West
South & home
   or to the cycle
            alone parked where the tourist
buses pull in
   gigantic parking lot   like a stadium
I float off
it must have taken me 15 minutes to walk each side
once heard kids playing
thought: if they see my face they'll scream
A vision at three corners it seems now one
is lost: at one was Kelly near the top of a pole

swaying I was moved to compassion for all men
Kelly holding on like treed possum man on
rack of medieval sky-wheel
                                    great heart of the Castle
pounding inside
                            stopped at looked once at the moat water
Joanne's eyes passing over stone

At northwest corner the Spider Vision
great spider bright red mansized in net
            the Maker, Artist-Craftsman
is also Devourer,   Mother eating her children
            conflict as poet revealed to
me then Great Swollen World Body mansized in net
bagged there at the unknown corner of two small
Kyoto streets
                    by the magnificence of the Castle
Great White Stone Walls reflected in moat water
& above beyond Towers, at each corner a dark
Vision: a dark Rectangular Tower
                                        I had marched my circumcision.
This struck me later
I had marched my circumcision

Nothing was revealed
but all was suddenly *game.*

Got back on cycle
        was an ox I was holding onto its horns slowly
moving thru the streets of Jerusalem
Lumber store immediately the Manger.

        Stopped at coffee shop
sat over Herrick book in blue light
another hour Thought of Barbara now late
then slowly drove the remaining ten minutes back
House of Okumura.

I knelt by Barbara
She was asleep
   walked out to glassdoor
tried to write this down
Still caught in funny iambic fear
Then for the first time really scared
Feared a man somewhere in the Okumura House
crept out to john   my shit immediately a lovely coral
but scared, vision:
     A bowl of blood in a barber's window

crept into bed woke up an hour later
I was in bed with another woman
who?
       woke up at 8
fully refreshed

The House of Okumura VIII: Vision

One afternoon I picked a Caterpillar
from its Leaf
I saw Blake
in Night Sky in Blaze of Fire

   He sd: "All men are under my charge,
energy is the only life & is of the body.
I did not live
this charge out.

   I denied nature
& affirmed it,
for I knew
more than I lived,

   I should have left
Catherine
I was Instructed to
My Christianity Denied It

   Therefore I had to ask
Milton to descend
Redeem his (my)
Female Portion for us

   Men
Kill
Because they
Live

   with Women
who do
Not
turn them on,

I am that
Satan!
Don't
You!"

The House of Okumura XIII

Arguing at Mori's
  over HARI-KIRI,*
to allow another
his being
  (that film wch so
hit me, placed
me in Kyoto
medieval Japan
a reality, the peoples
faces today, opened
  me to the stalls,
I remember looking at
my noodles in the red-
bannered shop
      when I came out sunlight
as it always seems to be in my life,
at the bathroom window
when I sat puzzled on the toilet
at twelve
    sunlight on the dusty alley dirt
between the cheap pants shops, jewelers, by
the Shijo-Gekkikan,
          what they did to that boy turns
back so terribly upon itself, gave him bamboo to
cut with, the law, forced feudal law upon him, to uphold
the honor
of the law, he had lost his sword he must
pay the price

      Great Crimes Carolee calls them, against
the great humanity
always one man,
this boy
    or her lover who cannot budge from his room
great crimes committed
Reich tells us before we could speak

so we entered the broken world
Crane at 2
          John in Chicago today, in a blaze of light
King on eternal Throne
Egyptian ruler in the shape of the human aura entombed in light
That any man can walk past a church & see Jesus his glorified
body and worship it
               —his sentence, to adore
what we've given up on forever
Not Dillinger   nor the Kid
     John at 4
notch
the knife makes
the bamboo-stick
going like a ferret
into the body's rabbit-hole
scared babies cowered
bouncing thrus the terror man lies
is law, stasis
   where is in fact Eden
fucking, rolling & sucking the belovéd
great tangle
               the real order
   thru wch our spiritum flows

THE HOUSE OF IBUKI (1969) *

Ibuki Masuko

Ibuki Masuko tonight again walking
the hallway
        how many darkened afternoons I sat
in our rented room through rain & heard you
walking the darkened
hallway, humming to
your granddaughter in your arms.
                  I feel your toes
indenting tatami in wood clay-colored socks
the hall way made straw & mud
                outside warm rain thru the fig
dripping azalea   heavy tenderness of my mother flower
& I would look out thru the screen   your light
the softness of your slightly cheek-hollowed brown
face, your body tucked inside grey wool kimono
pleasantly   painfully   totally carrying the child
free with child   forever with child
             Not my own flesh
             Masuko Ibuki

                (the one afternoon in the kitchen you
told me how after the trip to the lake where the cormorants dive for
fish the men stopped at a whorehouse   & I asked What did you do
then? God, I must have been mad! to ask you that! even in my pigeon
Japanese, & you looked at me, continuing washing dishes & eyes
bowed said We—referring to the other woman—waited in the car.
the drawn skinnyness of your husband   bare to waist in mens'
summer bloomer underwear standing in our doorway with a message
or request, always openly wanting to watch Barbara & I
hustling off to work in his pinched suit

      — & you waiting with your other lady friend
at night   somewhere in the country   in a car.

You absorb indignity as rock the cicada cry

how close you are to yourself   shredding daikon
  picking up the grandson screaming bloodscreams by
the gate
        I heard your dialect change that afternoon
he quieted   then, natural
azalea
hallway
newyear tea
       really howled once back in inner chamber.

            I was in your sleeping-room once
            Passed twice thru the garden.
            Answered the phone occasionally
            & accepted the laundry.
I lived in your house about one year

It was the first time I ever felt home

I loved you & I loved your house   it was
very simple
           I would sit in the kitchen late at night & watch
the ceiling,   or blueflame under coffee
or wait for the mouse   outside our room by the fig the white
warehouse I never entered
                At morning the bean-curd man would
tootle while I was in the john trying to shit unable to write
Masao my heart is breaking   those years will never come again

               It was coming down
the hill   cold night after the public bath   hundreds of ulcroofs
in moonlight   gravelclack in wood geta I would see the fence

Public Bath

    the Ibukis haven't one to spare so we walk up
a hundred feet or so
thru tileroof maze cutting thru little short alleys
like six feet wide
to Minami-Hiyoshi alley, the big one, with all the stands
& noodleshop & sake store to
yu (hot water) banner,
      fluttering out front
the public bath

       (beauty of a banner designating a place)

it is 20 yen (a few cents) grandmother
fat peasant-tread face, looks & takes, men then
women too step up partitioned

        I pick a basket up
always feel strange
old highschool locker urge
   look at others' bodies
fraid they'd think I was queer
     (so I did 1250 push-ups once for $25 in four hours)
clothes peeled
folded neat in wicker
no need to lock it up
     (billfold held by grandmother—
or sometimes a daughter,
always a chance to peek when paying
     a woman nursing, nice buttocks of a 15 year old
then the partition,
    always,
  the basket
a partition,
   the eye,
nice male bodies, darker than mine, slimmer at waist,
small men, too thin stomachs, coal-black bushy hair

my eyes look frightened round
           slant so calm, so much at ease
& with plastic bucket, wash-towel & soap
step in
        sliding glass doors
past basket area
        into the bath
room
         but a ROOM, fog boiling up from Roman bath-
sized bathing vaults
          big enough for 20, water
3 temperatures (the coolest our "hot")
stomach-deep

             I see two guys that work out at my judo gym
             one neighborhood vegetable seller
             a student of Barbara's
& some same old men,
             one out of Dachau
                                in a corner, soft grey pouchy
abdomen (spider), caressing it, skinny legs & head,
the image won't come
how does Dachau get into this?
             a skinny old man soaping himself, slowly, soon
to die
Dachau?
he looks like those newspaper photograph men
piled gaped bodies
         or my funny tenseness
naked, looking at another
naked man?

         Step to wall
squat
        squirt bucket full from tap
fill towel with soap laying it out over thigh
rubbing soap in both sides,
body foaming

feeling for cold tap, mix,
doused, now I'll enter the bath

    Tsuruginomiya under moonlight
cartoon of seascape   painted tiles backdrop   easing
in,
     ooh shit!
            in.
to neck,
the incredible power felt, balancing on balls, waterline at
neck a burning wire, body toasty in,
to be
       in.   is everything.

visions of fellowship
     not talking
wanting to start a conversation with the man to my right,
wanting
      knowing I'll be defeated
Oh this lushness
      knowing I'll be defeated
force
breaking thru years
          you can touch another
you
     can talk
     & look,
look, the beautiful contours of man, his gold
spangled in steamlight skin,
skin, man's garden, the roughness & lushness of skin,
man a small thing crouched in flaming water
to be clean
   but more to enter
        love, this man

Tsuruginomiya

She could see from her school window
this tree,
    great oak
on Higashiyama-doori,
      at the entrance to Minami-Hiyoshijinja,
        not the thick link of hemp
          wrapped round the trunk

but its fluorescence, gigantic into blue Kyoto sky
was what so sent her,
& I was going to say
was as her moon to
my Tsuruginomiya, sun,
but I visited Tsuruginomiya mostly at night
& Barbara's Tree, the great oak,
    is seen at full moon.
      As it was the hemp
        interested me,
             not that I did not see the great oak,
but the fact

that it was the shrine entrance
that by this hemp link (thick as a thigh)
    was given pudendum, was made, in short, symbolic
was where I was at.

      (the link was more a ring

but I saw it, as it hung there, as pudendum)

miya means *shrine*
minamihiyoshijinja
south lucky sun shrine

tsuruginomija
    Sword Shrine.
        contention.

    I lived care
of the Ibuki's at Tsuruginomiya-*cho*,
            block,
for the Shrine & its grounds
were across the alley,
      facing the House of Ibuki,
one entered
because Tsuruginomiya was Shinto
through the toori, a dolmen of sorts, wood
once painted orange now weathered to strange pale,
    essentially a crossbeam laid on two pillars,
      ends fluted as if rising, sun —
        On the sixth plate of *Milton*
a little figure rides on horseback under a tremendous dolmen of
white stone.   So I walked under the toori at Tsuruginomiya
& felt for the first time the strength of the stars & sun.

But Barbara's Tree was
not in Tsuruginomiya,
   it was on the other side of the House of Ibuki,
   down on Higashiyama-doori
   by another Shrine…

I nearly died one day I saw the toori fallen.
          Had come back from the bath
in moonlight it lay, like pieces of Mayan man
        disorganized.
A road was being built through Tsuruginomiya to connect
Higashiyama-*doori(road)* with *Higashiyama*
      East Mountain
      's other side.
      Tsuruginomiya
does not today exist,

but is bottomless,

it hath no bell,

while man's forms change
one's experiences also change, but the particularity of a love

endures forever & ever,

I often went late
at night, unable to sleep or write,
Barbara having gone to bed,
    & sat on the stone steps
leading up to one of Tsuruginomiya's altars
      (behind me, closed by dark
wood lattice, inside the god)
    in total darkness
        aside from the moon
rested
      which would come over pine shoulder
white
& look into it as into a flashlight

      the pines
& small maples scattered throughout the pebbled grounds
somehow darker
absorbing dark
so black
the moon was moist white,

      one night a kitten
mewed caught apparently under that particular shrine
a terrible prefiguration of what was happening between
me & Barbara,
      I tried, with Paden⁺ who was there that night,
to get it out we
couldn't find her,

          I knew
something was off
terribly off,
     for often when I thought of Barbara I felt sick
& wished she was dead
          so I could be free
while in the same moment
   it seemed my existence was
dependent upon her, all good
     connected to her,
and so I would leave Tsuruginomiya
& quietly enter the gate of the House of Ibuki,
               slip into our room &
drop by her side
where she lay in darkness
& touch her hair
from inside me, from a point so deep
I could never find it there would be a
cry,

& I would see the sun shining in a meadow of stars
& see the great sun of Tsuruginomiya walk naked in fields of light
& meet Barbara clothed in the pearls & diamonds of desire
& in the great force of her arboreal strength they would join
hands & as happy happy children walk on & on forever

     O force of the recognition that as men
and women we cannot live like child,
that if we dream of ourselves as children
we act toward one another as children,
we love and show tenderness
     but the masculine & feminine terrors
will rake us asunder
     for the Songs of Experience are as
real as the Songs of Innocence,
     for man & woman there is only
organized Innocence,

that was why I could not stand to see the dolmen
shattered there,
  the dream! the dream! was of a figure
raging at the bottom of the stairs,
          but it is bottomless,
my house is not my house,
the dream was of an eternal childhood forever
held in place by the need for creation,

      this is not a Doctrine—it is the very
        substance of life.

New Guinea I
The Leg

Night a reflection
in the doorglass, a wood
vertical suggest
two awake.   You sleep

a low & steady drum
the head baked with blood

You sleep.   Your leg
again beginning to heal
braced this afternoon
from black skin red flesh
cut, the flint
smeared on bowed
drumwood, sound
of the blood, blood
baked in the head
that does not budge in fire
arouses me, a
            bloodtie,
            burr tied in my bloodties, a
breath pulse, most
explosive, most
breathed blood

            I am entered by the ghost

            O primavera tuberosa!

& from the aorta
is sent out a new shoot
tuber scaled with
leaves scaling among
the lower roots,
tubercular the eyes

in their axils,
the eyes of God
beat to & fro thrughout
the earth

& is assuaged the bile
the file of gnawing,
the longing, the
tongues
the tongs
for I am carried back tuber
tubercular
tuberosa
rose

New Guinea II
Becoming Serious

That this Shrine is mental then,
Swords crossed
              working out the mental
Is metal
    Seeing my Own Fulness
        All that has been is not now
Mental is Metal
  & the body/heart. longs for instant con-
tact every second
              Midas
                  who knows we are but
servants of destroyed nature, God
is Metal
        Dead as Submarine

& all he touched was gold

                 I am seeking to
explain to you that State wherein a man becomes
serious, that is, starts to let the world through,
Tsuruginomiya was my lodestone, starts to be
elsewhere at once
              "show everyone to everyone"
the people sing, solidarity being thus affirmed,
the people sing, 600 *gerua* bobbing thru the woods
              by dawn had danced before
every men's house in the phratry
solidarity being thus affirmed,
    the Siane of the Eastern highlands pressed
near to me those days,
a feeling of tremendous solidarity in the pressing
down of a foot
on tatami,
      the release stepping

onto polished wood
    opening the little door
    trying to shit

                    a wall
                to
feel one's own weight.
the band of gas & muscular spasm
a drumhead
            I was that tight to ceremony
aching to be played
unable to play
                solidarity being thus affirmed
or let's say I became aware
I went all the way through,
centerbeam
    sagging at the ridgepole
        would not break
            broke

COILS (1973) *Part I* *

The Book of Yorunomado

> Over coffee, alone
>
> —slowly, surely, they turn
> to a crust of biscuit,
> nibble a kiss in passing,
> *koi.*
> > Brothers,
> > our record changes
> > nothing

...*tú, luego, has nacido, eso
tambien se ve de lejos, infeliz y cállate,
y suportas la calle que te dío la suerte*...   *

> —an interval.
> Dangerously, fully, each instant is
> a different man.

◇

Incredible the force of the Yorunomado coffee-shop. When I first came, pale sunlight drifted a wide lobby open to a patio where a tiny lantern's soft red, latticed, glowed. By a dark shield I took a high-backed crimson chair. A chanson played. Near the patio, a mother and her son sat down. My word had a painful golden relief, unspoken; it churned, evaporated. I tried every scheme. I found silence holds only to the music's end. I realized one must face another. Even if rock, the other is a garden. Incredible the scroll pressed out and held by four hands; on the table a letter from Bashō, Le Pont Mirabeau. I had faith in a deadend, in dignity, and delight. The Yorunomado coffee-shop compounded a language of man.

◇

> and in the shallow pool by my feet
> thin vermilion *koi*
> motionless
>   love
> grows and spends in me

◇

Like flame fleshed, voices
shoot about over the mossy stones. A foot down:
Europe shimmering light, Paris with the intensity of heat waves.
But this brick wall. This crude clay
no matter how much I want to wander out, to be a crimson pennant
unfurling in a blackening spiral sky—
this hand of bloodsmeared Indiana wall…
O dimension of love I had imagined, O
structure in which, though terror drained, no energy was lost…

Flame torn, voices roil in compounding fire, the sea
—no. From this iron
chair: a pool of *koi*. Rose-popsicle
gold; plucked-chicken pink
with a pus-yellow head; and one a dream, the smoky purple
the moon gives to the otherwise midnight… *The Four Zoas*—
a new life. Floating on the surface, the mung
he took into his mouth:

                    perfected
            far off,
                a gong

My language is full of dirt and shit.

Is it to great a leap to imagine
rice may spring from these waters,

                        a yellow
                   carp, a green carp?
—over there, still
under the knobby lotus, she with the white-splashed red belly,
pregnant, who is she?

    ◇

What demand. I am
blind as the bat-
god. There is nothing I can do.

She bleeds
and my silkworm eats a half-moon in the mulberry leaf

She bleeds
and now I get her want

The word is not enough
nor is grief.
Walking down the hospital steps—

WHAT was never born?

    ◇

Paused on the Shichijo Bridge,

        the day misty,
lovely, grisly… the Kamogawa fades, shallows forever,
winding out through Kyoto's southern shacks…

        below, in the littered mud,
a man stabs around in cans and sewage,
in his ragged khaki overcoat and army puttees
I was taken forward to a blind spot

(he pulled himself up
a rope ladder hung over the stone embankment
and with limp burlap sack slung over his shoulder
disappeared down an alley
home? to the faces?
                        What do
I express when I write?
     Knives?   or Sunlight?
                        And everything
that lives is holy raced through my mind

                    Walking home,
paused under the orange gates of Sanjusangendo, in
under the dripping eaves, cosy,
I noticed a strand of barbwire
looped over stakes I had stepped
inside of

          and then it came to me)
          I would kill for you

THE DUENDE   *

Overcast, after lunch, the sky fled. A colorless darkening void. The
neighborhood still. Walking, there was a light behind my head. At the
corners of my eyes it fuzzed into cold obscurity. I must molt more than
my face. As if these brown houses, this standing alley water, were the
only reality. I must change more than the contour of my line.

It should be that the slightest scar of moss on the rainstreaked fence
occasion delight. And an old man, squatting on his steps, wringing
out a rag, praise. And when the man in my mind smiles, children
should fill the alley, white clouds drift high in the bright blue heavens
over Tsuruginomiya.

When the female principle takes over, it has been said that it is The Darkening of the Light. Likewise, as has not been said, it is the point at which, recrossing Shichijo Bridge, I picked up from the embankment stone a slightly fishy, sweet, urine smell: the scent of Vallejo—

from which I learned: everything I sense is human, at the very worst *like a man*. And—that which can darken is not without light. Faint along the back of the emptiness grazes the herd of the multi-chambered sun.

> I entered Yorunomado and sat
> down, translating,
> *Nightwindow.*
>
> The coffee breathed
> a tiny
> pit—

As a black jeweled butterfly alights
in late summer on a hardening coil of dung,
so I lit on his spine

pages lifting in the breeze   in from the patio

We locked. I sank my teeth into
his throat, clenched, his fangs
tore into my balls, locked
in spasms of deadening pain we turned, I
crazed for his breath, to translate
my cry into his gold, howling, he
ripped for food

Locked, a month passed, and as he increased lean
I slackened, drained, and tripling my energy
drew blood, not what I was after, muscles
contracting expanded he was clenched
in my structure, turning

substance, a dead matter
eating into my cords, and saw deep
in his interior a pit, in spring
I went for it, made myself into a knife
and reached down, drawing
out from the earth cold.
A hideous chill passed—

another month, cunningly
he turned himself into a stone

I dulled on, grinding my own teeth, woke up,
another month, a season. I was wandering
a pebbled compound, the stone in hand.

I saw I had birthed the deadend, but Japan
was no help—until I also saw
in the feudal rite of *seppuku* a way.

On the pebbles I lowered stonelike.
Whereupon the Spectre of Vallejo raised
before me: cowled in black robes, stern on the *roka,*

he assumed a formal knee. With his fan
he drew a bull's eye on my gut;
he gave no quarter; I cut.

Eyes of father tubes of mother swam
my system's acids. As one slices raw tuna
with shooting contortions not

moving a foot I unlocked Yorunomado
from the complex cavework of my own tomb.
Vallejo kept his word:

he was none other that one year than himself

Hello all I have ever felt...

for this was the point upon which the pen
twisted loose an ego
strong enough to live.

⬦

      Set in motion, the servants
washed down and raked the pebbles.
Deepening shadows, they crossed and recrossed,
swinging smoking braziers, chatting.
One, grizzled, picked up a lopped topknot,
grinned, and dropped it in the pail.
Far off, in the interior of this strange place,
a quiet weeping was heard.
Although who cut and who condemned were one,
the weeping was too sincere to be that of a lord.
In the heart of the poem there was
no longer a hesitation before power.
The platform on which the stuff was cut and shaped,
this very platform holds the life of another.

    "Will you help me?"

      I turned away and wrote:
I am taking a walk and holding Barbara's hand, a field
slower than centuries we've no mind of

But Vallejo insisted: "NO. LA MANO, HE DICHO."

You struggled up sinking
between your elbows, braced,
and turned eyes
were a miscarried woman.

Standing, I reached
under the arched wall of your back

and eased in under you
the bedpan.
Leaving the moist warmth of your back,
I sat down, your shattered dream
no longer divided from mine.

Entering me then the pebble of bread he put into his mouth, softly pass-
ing through my face the point of Vallejo, the trench and glory of his
human face, in my lips his, alum dry, passed, and with them my desire
to die. The yanked-tight viscera loosened, gave, it opened a palm for
the bread and cupped, a flower parched, opening, closing, a dark red
flower moving with heaven's untiring power, the verb coursing raggedly,
wild at first, then gentle, beating, whereupon the sutra went into mo-
tion, dark monotone moving horizontal through the twilit bass, syllable
upon syllable compounding, whereupon the compound-complex went
into motion with the simple following close behind—I felt the line set,
and from the right flow back into me through the fire rushing out to
you from the left, from margin to margin, mingling, ripening, the flow
knelt and prayed in my breath, it swept through my seat and cling, kiss-
ing my heart on its wing it cleansed, coiled, unfurled.

1964

The Book of Niemonjima

—for Diane Wakoski

    I

    Yorunomado knew too well this corrosion—night after night
the fires of Niemonjima had gone untended
& now broke out in savage blaze across the island crest—
the altars smoked forth into the night. Who lay
in the secret darkness turned & twisted with hopelessness
    for marriage,
for the fire had been baited—twigs & strands of hugs tossed
to the hungry little flames—a log here a stone there—
forever! forever! & a moan went forth from the firewall:
A throw of the dice will never abolish chance!
To be redeemed you must go to Eternal Death!

    Whoever stood on the banks of the Pacific felt the moan—
Niemonjima appeared a half-mile out black
against the midnight starless—flames
choked in mind—the altar unknown—no longer to
convert into the fraternity changes,
no longer is there a fake brotherhood of young men,
the savagery in the Plymouth, the so-called picnic, the raped pine—
& whoever stood on the murmuring shore stood
likewise along the entangled darkness of the Sepik River—
shields bobbed through the trees—the masks are prepared
that lead to Niemonjima's altars. For I am in the State
of New Ireland—as slabs of wood are bent blue white & red
    birds & snakes
across the inner shell so does my imagination
shake & tear against the roots & vines of Coatlicue's web of
desire & longing—the beloved unknown,
desired but desired as a shadow dancing on Niemonjima's
    altar walls.

I stand rooted to these shores & watch the Men of the Sepik
(were they as mild as New Ireland!) move along the high
dorsal ridge, a half mile off shore, Niemonjima, her hair
crawled through by men with spears & bullroarers—her trees silent
to the vast Pacific; Niemonjima, beloved of Yorunomado,
why do I desire you & not her to whom I am wed?

And this is the problem of the naming (all things relate)—
whoever stands on the shore is without name (this is the madness
        that is eating at me)—
Yorunomado is the imagination through whose acts I make the
        images of
Niemonjima my soul, outwardly an emanation, but
these things do not exist unless eternal
& this is the problem of the naming, for within me
there is no name nor mobility. I was on that shore—
I saw Niemonjima & felt the consolations of Barbara
but who says this now? Through whom does this hand write?
Yorunomado felt his brain move off as if divided
by waters, as a sand-castle crumbles in surf,
O beloved Yorunomado, whom I must express, whose adventures
with Niemonjima are the life wherein I live,
O beloved Yorunomado who may not exist! This is the problem
of the naming, this is my love poem in these dreadful nights!

And I bowed to the waters miles below my hands:
O that the poem fulfilled my obligations!
O that Barbara were not my wife!

A dark wind moved in across the roar
begging understanding: the ways of women are most
treacherous to men only if man commit that
treachery first—for man thinks he creates woman,
because he thinks this he then casts her away,
& the wind wept in her pale tulle before him,
"So I am doomed to wander for the emanations of men
all waters in search of their lost children, I am that
confusion between child & emanation, I must wander

until men & women understand sexual energy must not
be fettered by creation. Terrible the drain on friendship
when blood does not division, when the parent-
power is not overthrown & Niemonjima sleeps in
darkness an altar at an island crest. Between you
& your beloved has come a wife—before you were not
one, but now you are three! There is a Sepik River
in every man, of blood & shit, runs along his back
like a shrimp's." And I saw her webby skin, she howled
& was gone. O praise the Poetic Genius made manifest
in the 7th Book of Zoas: *Thou art but a form & organ of life,
& of thyself art nothing, being Created Continually by
Mercy & Love divine.*

    I have opened a center, & it is this center that moves
confidence in these words, that they are of others'
experience well as mine, for as the flames toss
against the midnight starless from Niemonjima's crest,
so does she lie awake a tongue of longing become less
     than a woman
until at last she is my mother, not Coatlicue,
but Gladys, umbilical, claiming to be wife &
     beloved, terrifically close to the true
marriage, but now a mother grown young
& married at a masked ball—the hour tolls!
But the covering has grown so thin, are we not
known all along? The hour tolls! The Men of the Sepik
hurry along Niemonjima's outer lines—

    And the spirit of Barbara followed me down to the shore
in the form of Jerusalem along the Arlington, she stood
behind my kneeling in worry & care, whom I could not
embrace for if I allowed myself to feel something I knew
I would want more, would riot in the fear & madness of
my own powers—I feared a wife turned
viperous with desire, the maw of Tokyo
a million red lights to swallow the wanderer
& on his return present him as a baby to the ladies.

She stood behind my kneeling, pointing
        with one hand back
to the inn & with the other out to Niemonjima,
& the waterwheel turned inside me a rack
toward Niemonjima, I would not settle for what I had
been given, but I could not escape, all my images fled before
the constant recreation of Origin! So slowly the error
consolidated & I prayed with my hands horizontal to the surf
Yorunomado, help me understand my sex,
Yorunomado, let my wife be the one I love.
    For the Men of the Sepik broke into loud chants
moving now swiftly through her upper grasses, around the
        concentric
dirt paths toward where the altar buffeted & smoked
a terrible pink stream of desire. Praying against
the water Yorunomado let me be satisfied with generation,
let me accept her without a robe, the poem is *a persimmon
falls*, my ears are locked to my bowels—

    And it was only the robe that drove him on,
a vision of the inland sea, which is called the Gull-robe*,
gorgeous, of white feathers emblazoned with stars & moons,
the lovely garment every loved woman wears, of midnight-
blue & silks, in which a light streams for all who ride
away into the darkness carrying the torches of imaginative
love, the softness & precision of loved desire. But now
the Klan wears the Gull-robe! The sons of Phi Delta Theta
commingle with the ordered rhythms of the Sepik,
& who is to say she wears a gown? The Eighty-fold Boar
strives in the darkness with the Daughters of Jerusalem
        along the Hudson,
he is far from Yorunomado now arguing by the Pacific
with the hopeless wanderer who would sleep
contracted in foetal anguish rather than go
to Eternal Death of wife & generation
through whom only will Niemonjima ever flow
a river in the arms of any man. Give me

strength for my labor—for even now I doubt
what I write in the very act of creation—
I see the sperm spurt, the Sons of the Sepik Delta
dance around her tortured altars, the blood
gushes, the poor wife tilts back that her ovaries
may drink, the trailer lurches, pets flee bumping
into cupboards & chairs, the smell of garbage commingles
    with desire—
she is absolutely naked, in her own Xipe-Soutine-red flowing
    on the bed, the husband
flees in terror to the bars, but ah! the spirit of Barbara cannot
    hold him!
Like rising backdrops he runs open-armed through her arms—
the altar smokes, gems congeal, a Fat Carnival Face grins
between her pillars where the red spider guardians have
    fled in terror—all is

shifting levels of literality & darkness as memory
crowds in—Origin is singing "Your only sureness is to say
    the persimmon falls"
She Is Absolutely Naked. Without Imagination.
And lo! She comes down to me, she stands weeping behind
    me on the shore,
& I will not turn to embrace him or her for fear I am stone,
Yorunomado saw his brain hermaphrodize, sand in
love with sand as she swept back wailing, all wanted in,
the stopsign, the mole, prestige, he shut his mouth
& threw himself in ice before her blazing pyres—
the blood turns to money, the mind to brain
A Victorian Christmas Art Book Jungian Bride.
Under the weight of this shale Niemonjima could

hardly move, & the Sons of the Sepik Delta mocked   *
her tiger-striped bangs Crying Behold! If you know so
fucking much fulfill our desires, we'll turn you on with
dirty jokes! And laughing slung a bloody bulldick around her
neck crying Behold! & clothed her in burlap sackcloth & ashes,

taped raw liver in her armpits, tied a string with "pull" sign
to her dick & shaving her head Crying Behold the Golden
Princess of our Homecoming! Behold our Snow White!

Yorunomado's only sureness forced to watch was that the work
of the imagination is in the service of a true brotherhood,
my desire to possess Niemonjima darkened by the canal
bereft of nightwatch in deepest fidelity to Barbara.

II

And Yorunomado stood in the howling bay, waves
lash & wail into the blooming caverns; he looked
to where the ovens were lit walls & the Sons of
the Sepik Delta worked in flaming reds & blacks;
O Gladys Enter! he cried to the shadow at his side,
Enter the ovens & be transmuted to my wife. Or forever
die, no longer plague me with what I can't see, for I cannot
worship the root, I cannot carry the taro through the lines
of relation. No longer is Coatlicue visible,
but there is a woman enfibered in my veins, a hot
wet in my hand I have been told, I recall is you.
And here you stand a writhing molten red, a
beckoning mush to maintain me always to the fork
& spear, in housemother agedness, while the victims
trembling holding hands are made to bend over as before
the mask was built, naked young men holding hands bent
over encircling the blazing center, a double fireplace;
"Slaughter on Tenth Avenue" is picked from the shelf;
where a frat pin was fixed through a sweatered breast
into a padded bra, the furniture has been moved aside,
the revelation of her armor & chastity is at hand, the victims
chatter & sob, the semen begs release—snuck out
in the crematorial lavatories it sobs to witness the flames;
the rites of passage deep-freezed her armor keeps them im-
potent, they stand being victims to be masters later! The hi-fi
needle is lifted, the lights turned down, the corral-gate bursts,

the Sons of the Sepik Delta shoot out bouncing & roaring from
their brides; only a few are not broken; I am shouting faint
with disbelief from the negation of life that is Indiana "O
generation, image of regeneration!" The virgin-wife discovers
on her wedding-night the spur-marks in the sides of her
little husband! She turns on in secret fury! Enter O
Enter the ovens that I may love you! Be transmuted to
my kind, invisible, for I am in great error, a part of a great
& terrible error, I must go to Eternal Death. Even as I speak
    the Sons
dress up in swastika red & gather grinning to my left,
the ideals of art wait patiently to my right,

        Whenever any Individual   [Blake]
Rejects Error & embraces Truth, a Last Judgment
passes upon that Individual.

        Yorunomado knew
he had found his wall, for looking down
he saw his thighs emblazoned moons,
his ankles suns, a starry midnight-
blue painted as if on clay across
his gut. He felt his universe flex
as he moved more open across the beach;
he had taken upon himself self-enclosing
divine attributes; on North Jordan
he had passed judgment on a girl from Anderson,
in Chapala he had mocked a woman hungry for marriage—
but how not mock? The natural sexual
activity has become anathema to man;
whom he faced across the sand was none
other than himself in any other woman
or man, & to act upon them was to act
upon himself, a vicious self-perpetuating
doubt, & in the arms of the Sons of the Sepik
Delta he felt the vein of Gandhi, a pure
stream in India, but he could not mock
the presence with whom he lived,

and he remembered Jung's words:
The source of life is a good companion.

He looked hard around him on the beach
at the sky & at the sea. Were not all these grains
placed by abstinence? Was not *everything* sand,
the tree, the house, a friend's lip, a bird, a
sunbeam, when truth is overruled by creation?
There is in the life of every man & woman a moment
Origin's watchfiends cannot find, that moment   *
settles on various pins, it may be at any
place & must be taken there, & he knew he
was really dealing with desire, that that "moment" was
the moment of desire, & if that moment is
denied, the rest of the day is dead.

So did he attempt to understand the Last
Judgment he was in the process of,
now he knew the intorsions of seppuku,
that who he fought to emerge was not
just a spectre, Gladys wailed in the cry
of every passing gull but she was not
his enemy, only he could be transformed
in the coastal ovens, signs were everywhere
but there was something he was missing
to make these signs cohere...

Forgiveness & self-annihilation were
surely signs, but in what act? He continued
walking. Sea. Sand. Sky. No
thing lived or moved...

Distant down the beach he saw a bench,
or a raised structure behind which
something moved; on 2 x 4s a box, a
casket from which a tattered
windingcloth fluttered. He approached
fearfully for he knew who was in the box

but not who moved behind it; he approached
the casket of Vallejo as a book is closed,
toward the heavy box of flesh blowing
by the sea, seeing a man crouched
moving behind, who he feared was himself.
Los stood naked with his hammer behind
the casket of Vallejo smiling at Yoru-
nomado; he put his hand upon the beaten
lid as the wanderer approached, smiling,
for he alone knew what I must do, & he stepped
back as I knelt by the box in dignity.   in prayer
to Vallejo. Los stood & watched,
& Yorunomado saw how those who weep in
their work cannot weep, how those who
never weep are the weak, the fake
sufferers.   To be a man.   That suffering
is truer to man than joy.   These were
the lines in the heavy pocked face of
Vallejo, trinities of intersections &
heavy lines, a village of nose & eyes;
Vallejo never left home, it was home
he always begged for even in the taking on
of the suffering body of man, I stood for
seven years & looked at him there, ob-
serving the Quechuan rags & shreds of
priestcloack, the immense weight in his mind,
& lifting his rags I saw his female gate,
bloodied & rotten, hopelessly stitched
with crowfeathers, azure, threaded with
raw meat, odors of potatoes & the Andes,
& how the priestroaches had gotten into
the gate, yet the edges of his gate were
sewn with noble purple velvet & I pondered
my own course, what was in store for me
given the way I was living, how the female
gate in a man must open, yet the horrible
suffering if it opens & something else does
not open! But there was no cure or cause

to who Vallejo was, perhaps it was the enormity
of what he took on, the weight of his people
to utter, & I shuddered to think of Indiana,
of what it would be to cast Indiana off.
Yorunomado sobbed when he saw the extent
of contradiction in Vallejo's body, how
could he have lived even one day, he thought,
this was the agony in the lines, the fullness
& the dark beauty of Vallejo's face horizontal
to sky, long black hair flowing back
into the sand, and Los likewise moved bent
& rested his hammer for one day in tribute
to the fierce & flaming profile contoured
to the horizon...

How long had he been left there? Yorunomado
stood & with Los helped the casket off
into the sea of another language. How long
Vallejo had been here! His windingsheet
was entangled with digging sticks & stones;
they set the casket on fire & left it blazing
to the shore water. They waded back,
& their hands were streaked with flesh,
their legs covered with veins, in the
hollow of their crab-like chests
a heart was hung, cock & balls swung
between their thighs.   They knew
what Vallejo heard

beating beating beating the seas of misery beat upon the shore
& the roll in is a woman trying for a man
& the roll back is a man fleeing from a woman
& the million grains are children the waves beat upon
& the men walk in the women & the women walk in the men
but this is hidden to most by the very laws most have made up
Each sand is an eye Yorunomado is an eye of God
Every day every man ascends Niemonjima
for Niemonjima is the arising the going forth

& every night every man descends Niemonjima
for Niemonjima is the hill the walking down to sleep
& Yorunomado prayed: be patient with me my friends,
nothing is to be held back.

Bloomington, winter–spring 1965

INDIANA (1969)

The Crocus Bud

The vise of Jung thrills me less than spider
Your fingers even in nightmare find my foot
My hand is never my own unless it can be held
A poetry that throws the entire body into relief
Truth to oneself from which alone fidelity worth while can come
Poetry a meat tenderizer to break down the resistance to my soul
A man who makes love to his wife
Thank god hell is not dead in me
Words stiff bristles to scour sore gums
A Peruvian teething-ring
A Blakean rattle
Song tell her I am in the State of Caterpillar
One yellow crocus in the entire raked grounds
Tell her I can change my life

Hand

(Reading *The Human Universe* of Charles Olson)

Coming down the heights of the stadium
winding off center thru deep gigantic ramps
the hand of my mother
quick, like into a pocket, in mine,
around it, a tiny hot claw
squeezing to milk a little warmth from my face
into her; I went concrete, girder, labyrinth
in which she a little mole, a hot-eyed
wanting little mole was burrowing through

I know coolly now it is death
is after her, like a male to split her open
while she rummages, foxes & paws in me, the earth

of her tomb, what is left of her carefully
tamped garden—it wants to pull away as she
from dying into God my hand
wants its aloneness, its armylike
order of me 30 her 68 my wife her husband between,
& she senses that, & scratches, digs, claws around
in harder, hotter, we are slipping down
from the bright wide attention of the game
down again to grass, 35000 cars, this tiny
instant between

the game   & the car
life   death
the holy ghost of my mother's hand
crabbing frantically almost I
turn
to her almost my face breaks & I weep
embracing her for what reason.
what source.

The 1802 Blake Butts Letter Variation   *

Sunday noon I walked out of my home
to Holcomb Gardens, a mile or so through
the Butler Woods where I found a moist
rubber during the Second World War,
around the pond, down path under a hornet's
nest, & to the canal, heavy
for Barbara & Matthew seemed
gone, the bend always in sight,
leaves floated crisp autumn's
first waters,
            The Canal
where Speed Hubbell's little brother
Pete was dragged from, in lunch line
"did you hear?" Dead.
    I was carrying Wilhelm Reich.
     Heavy brown canal
that always in my mind has rocked
like a boa within itself, easing
slowly around Dead Man's Drop
where I sledded successfully at
twelve,
           in noon haze sunlight
misting canal
              all things pass
learn from dropped leaves & little
Pete
       it is the culmination of 5
years together
          She is buried here
If you grasp & hold this sorrow
its winged life you'll destroy
          Sodden in my chest
I sat by the bank
All my poetry to now
a wall through which I've tried
entrance, but nevertheless a wall

Book thrown up to shield me from
another's sight
    How can you turn from your
mother's eyes? how can you not
feel emotion with Barbara?

                  I got up & started cross
the Holcomb field, a nave of grass
between wilted beds leading to
an artificial pond—
      no, it was blue with water
I was wrong, & guided over by Per-
sephone's first steps from hell,
gold-breasted shone in sun
autumn's green shaded her bronze
shoulders, bare to waist
                 gown
loose about her.

This is the 11th WALK
It is the first poem I've ever
written about my home.

      I was afraid to let my imag-
ination lead, I wanted to recount
all
      Persephone opened herself to
me alone & was leading me from hell
I was following her lit taper
through the sewer of the canal
but as I touched her gown-strings
I heard Barbara groan behind
& Matthew wailing in a cloud
& my mother set her foot against
canal & start to cross
& my father a winged-ant begging in his own house
    I opened my breast   full of maggots
& as I began to pull them out

a stench of piss & dust
blinded my eyes
    but the beggar was only
melodramatic, I continued
march, reorganizing from a
seed to follow out…

            to lead across my
mother? return home & feed
my father? leave Matthew in
a cloud & Barbara buried alive?

I have put knowledge over love
heartbreak against destruction

I was wrong, the day was blue with water
I found a stone bench
Again tried to read what I knew was true
But such was beside all point,

I have put knowledge over love
I have broken a heart to save my
own destruction
I have not given my life for another
I have said
        I will live only for myself
for only then
                    can I live
And such is in contradiction to the
teaching of my master:
Jesus spoke to Albion:
"Fear not: unless I die thou canst not live:
"But if I die I shall rise again & thou with me.
"This is Friendship & Brotherhood: without it Man it Not."
And I heard Barbara grown 40 feet
below in the mud & Matthew weeping
from his cloud. Again I tried to read

again I tried to nostalgize my father
& my mother,
        I thought of my master
kicking the Thistle
Breaking the back of that which
stood in his road
& how another, Vallejo, simply
sat on the Thistle.
        But no other man's way
obtains when there is no one to
be seen
      & I wandered among the warm
fruit trees, in the grass among
the benches
      & sky sagged full of Matthews
& the ground churned with the help-
less choke of self-pity

        for Barbara was in New York
& clouds streamed across the heavens
for Matthew is with Barbara in New York
& Persephone was a statue, a form my
mind took to reach from hell
       & I shook the tree
O God, why has it taken me 31,000 years
to stand at the threshold
Why has it taken me 31,000 years to leave home?
Must one drop metaphor to ease pity?

Indianapolis
11 September 1966

Sensing Duncan II

The face of the woman I have called
Adriadne, messenger leading me out
the labyrinth of my head,
seen through tears
    A medieval monk

Love
Seen
Directly
said an old, old friend filled with love seen directly
in the backseat suddenly with his wife

                          It is the power of
Wagadu leads me on, that goldenrod that
lives in man's heart, that power of another's
face which is a face
opened through suffering, eyes calm & open,
so open a face that children have been cared for thru stress
& have their life in her long curls, of a man's
Russian muscular face, of long hard
horse durance, for is the woman in this my country less
than workhorse mangered, a heavy stock, brought thru field
but no difference, held in manger by the empty bed & fed
through the winter of her bed life a chunk of sugar here
a sly pebble there, & joyous for these chunks she loose
her reins when brought to picnic, or to bear —
    she in who I put my trust
bears all these signs
& is my face peering thru without confusion, a bronco
Reich has loosed & must now make her muscular
frolic in a society that would take her totally to task
for joyriding primal, secondary to bear —
                      I see the im-
implications of her task in the severed
hands some warlord has loosed
in bookstore window on University off 12th,

called Johnson tho that name is so thin & I must address
the jellied gore pile behind the goosepimpled glove of
wrists (which I first saw in Lima, skin of a pig's head)
as produce, the meatgrinder which
arranging and judging everything in existence according to
the principles of moral compulsion is
    those chopped off hands

      Up so tight before you I would have chopped
off hands had I not been
             deterred by that power which in men's
hearts moves
      Wagadu, not that the first be second,
that warrior be relegated to poet's role
but that the second be first,
      which all know who are at heart warrior
but have been touched by
Kiekorro's word,
who "no longer fight like heroes for the light of day,
 but like men thirst for the glory of the night"
    I thirst, & as my thirst now
finds water see
      you through,

I do not praise a monk
I praise that otherness in
you, that crucible of receiving other's
lives that allowed you receive me
         & be kind.
               It goes be-
yond love,
beyond my sense of man & woman
   (for all that too must be changed)

A woman of who Duncan sang
      unknown line! Through who I
truly reach
   what is true is human,

homosexuality,   heterosexuality
There is something more important:

    To be human
in which kind
      is kind.

26 November 1966

The Yellow Garment

You were the girl
who wanted to serve
devoted
        K'un

  in a yellow garment.
Who have not allowed your light to
shine forth,
living quietly
doing the best you can

              one of the oldest images we have of
woman
  "the dark force possesses beauty but veils it"
the man rends it
      again & again she veils it
                      her hair helps

to serve
to take care of me

      "it is the way of the earth to make
no display of completed work but rather to bring
everything to completion vicariously"

but I do not want a vicar

I must risk bringing myself
—knowing that what is complete cannot endure—
to completion by
myself
      alone.
                   Even tho I fear
the earth is right

since I so much believe in the earth
it must be right.

    You were the girl
I chose
who came along, without resisting,
when I took you by the hand
that in itself is so beautiful.

    Who wanted to serve
& still do
        & who now I have pushed
bowl
        away from my hand—

    The girl in a yellow garment
tears in her eyes before her King, saying
"But it is good food I have made you—
I myself am good
as an apple is good

& here is Matthew
who is an apple too

& you have taken us
& cast us on the earth

where will we go?
what will we do?"

28 July 1967

The Black Hat

Yorunomado sat in his
black goat's wool tent

a black hat,
a top hat

sat on a radiator
exhaling steam.
When

will it explode?
The man in *the*
or *or*, a fist

craven thru.
I walked

into Yuk Soo
Chinese Laundry
      — parcels
0   396
0   57
0   111
0   384

little pink slips
olive slips yellow ones
wrapped with string
the wind used to

break our kites,

what I've escaped is
greatly what's let go of me,
to see the sweat

shop the earth is
dew off the field at dawn or
or or
Chinese back over steam mat,
shit, I'm so
fucking lucky,

the perceptions break down
the poem seems to stall
and does
before the greater energy of the world,

I've been given this black
hat of internal anger

still on the hot radiator
To sit here you look at me
I'm riding on my anger
as men did

horses drove in the spurs,
straddling the trunk of
energy the mind is

heir to, it
bobbles
& Yuk Soo

cuts the prow of iron
    boat
over linen,
rigid

victim of migration,
wife, two daughters
scared little foxes
scared to speak

the ore of or
wife in the same
dress weekly
when does she

leave the shop?

After 40 years she
might as Zukofsky
speak of marriage

There is an area of
sweetness born of
slavery, for years

the black hat has
gasped on the radiator
everyone has sat on

watched it shrink
in band carcinomatous
like a chemical

in pure food
drives our stomachs
Yuk Soo

over our belts
—no one

has touched it
Yuk Soo is there
because we're

out of Eden
in Eden,
I'm here

because I left the place
established for me,
(gesture of reaching for
the hat
Xrist it's a snake!
The silliest fear is
the deepest fear—)
as you reached
thru Matthew's
crib slats to touch
on your knees
shaking sobbing
the son, the idea of
son leaving you
Matthew—
marriage
a welt,

hardest to break up
a welt,
rice
chews, a welt
wants its
anger, inflamed
by a core
    of misery
it surges to
surface again & again
core

is don't touch it,
or
in all its might & fury,
this
is the Selfhood Blake
adored & cleft
again & again

fruit lopped from stem
the earth

is to grow
diurnally
a clerk

come home
to brood
man

split into family
is man
surrounded
treasures
a hill

the earth
is looking at us
a skeleton

whose windows
are teeth
black holes

Matthew
pokes a pencil
into,
primal

to enter
Yuk Soo
get my laundry
leave

peregrination
under the face of
boo

boo boo
poop poo
pup

gh

1 August 1967 – 7 February 1968

Diagonal   *

You walk away across
6th Avenue
lean shoulders
yang stride in
short red skirt
Diagonal
   as on a roadsign
I am alone
     with you
or not,
I am alone
     As I was
a day in Kyoto
the earth
thundered under
my feet,
a roadsign
in the pour
   Coiling red arrow
               as

certain
   as your diagonal
away – only then
it was my father
beat in my chest
   had manifested his
presence as you
now, as certainly,
are fixed
   Diagonal   that would
I start the other way
   Crossing
would be our death

Perhaps it is my
Archetype for woman
is a Circle,
that I must sense
ring in the water
to wholly love
anyone –
    that seems
so thin,
yet what are there beyond such counters
to express
    the fixed sign I am.
                                    I feel
I've been at this peom
for centuries
You lay me open
& I sing
You lock me
I am   oak
    flayed into stripes
skunk
and with that force
    I divide in four
men,
headhunters on a log
Eight eyes as I climax
in you
    Split in four
like a table
    as if to say
it's my nature
to fear your blood
        depict you
Iron Maiden
            —l am that iron
in which a man is locked
& your cross 6th Avenue
while it pours in the New

Guinea I am,
  terrified at the thot
of being alone –
   & absolutely calm,

And here I am talking
about Marie
or was it
Coatlicue
  or a stone.
Not who I am
but where
how.

   It seems I can
not be naked to you – not ever
touch you
with the tenderness
I touch my son.
What is
   touching you?
Four headhunters
on a log
    I go crazed
before you
You
sob into the stone
    Diagonal
which is the sun
    Diagonal
the slant that is always leaving
sesgo of the egg
  as it curves
& keeps curving
& as you slant home
  curve on to New Jersey
to the England you are always leaving

As if it won't end
but always is
which is the end
   we call being in the present
watermelon
cherry
whipped cream
nose piece
thrust
   of your trust in me
as you align yourself
over my body
   more vulnerable that a man
can ever be
   but without needing the tremendous
mobility I need to move
thru
cherry
fear
weatstone
bridge
   to contact.

Mile
razor
telescope
palm
   over my
inheritance of 8 eyes,
   O great spider that you are,
slung
   in the skull of a world
I call blue sky!
      To make the inheritance
present.
   To be at your diagonal
which is your definition

siren down 6th
    which is simply sound

as you are simply spirit

hung with a nosegay of blood.

2 July 1968

The Bedford Vision

And saw
Taurus in the field,
grazing, enormous neck
bowed, red hair
brilliant in stillness

She moved along the limitis of the poem
handling her balances, Libra
along the meadow where he grazed
knowing pretending he did
not know, red eye

stealthy out the rim
    on which she moved
as a woman moves seated
on the back of the bull
He walks on water

and she looked across the meadow
at him,   tenderly
    was his shepherdess
angrily beyond the edge
for there was a culvert
in which she saw Lust
with his beautiful Sirens
cavort, in curious grey color
they were mucked, pawed
in the dark blood-colored frenzy
Thinking
            this should be the work
of the bull,
            who saw her thru his curls
sweated, not clearly,   but as a figure
at the meadow's limit, gnawing
grass, sweating, the hardness
of his pizzle, but sweating

in place over the daily labor
She moved thru his mind
thru rooms of a house
as he was bent over,
            surviving

and many gelded ponys
came up to her, nuzzled her
with their manes of treasures,

and in my vision I saw both
collapse into one, I saw I had
put them there in my vision
separate out of the fear aroused
in me for him. For I saw her
in her house, with the shreds
of the meadow in her hair
standing in the sunlit doorway
with the balance
                        it weighed
not in his favor
                        it weighed

in her hand, and what she felt
was
      her weight, that she
was the weight of her own
vision
        And I saw her cross
that curious little stream
that runs outside the limits of
the known world,
              for each man
each woman such stream is different
                              I saw her step
gingerly into the deeper grass inhabited
by the gelded ponys, one slipped a picture
        on her balance

it read: you are eternal woman
the scale began to sink
(for all mental pictures
          have weight)
frantically she looked to
Taurus for a lock of hair
any sign to restore balance.
          Taurus was in heat of
                    the sun's labor
     my vision tried to deepen
                    turquoise
tried to cast him in a field
          of azure stars
to see his eternal form
magnificent, tawny red
in isolation from the flock,

this was in earthly terms
to divide Michael Heller from his wife
but then Taurus raised his
head, he raised his head
     in the voice of my friend the
bull spoke to me:
          "Go with thy vision! I
am only not looking
when I appear to suffer
at labor over the grass. I
know the destiny of Doris
     she is a spirit inhabiting
a wayward female form,
I desire her spirit to
be free—This is my love
for her, this is how
my spirit converses with hers.
I see these ponys suitors
in Odysseus' house, I know
that as we confront more
games shift.   I have

pretended to need a shep-
herdess, what a lovely game
it was! To be stroked & cared
for by a portion of her eternal
woman. Now as she comes
in all her strength to confront
 her spirit, so will I go
with that river
     in cooperation with the seasons"

And suddenly I saw my
friend beside himself
but guided by his knowingness,
I saw him walking by his bull,
leading Taurus to slaughter
singing gaily like a fool
as Taurus in great pride
                          & beauty
moved into the limits of the
poem –

     Doris looked up from
her Balance.   It was
midday in the dream
that she was free,
     the scales were weighted
no longer did they equal out
& tho what were now
similarities & discrepancies
ached, like muscles,
she knew it was in the not
adding up her freedom began,
with this awareness the little
room on Bedford rose, it

lifted & lo, there was the
field in which a maiden
very shy was joined by my

humbled vision to Taurus
she gazed at him with
   no semblance of Michael
   the bull looked at her
with no need of Doris,
a simple compassion
      passed, a no-blame,
the sky deepened, it deepened
turquoise & vibrated
     pure light blue
& the rose, the lark, all
stood deep in the wildflower
of the imagination
   in the strength of Cancer
   in the majesty of Gemini
     fire rising
     July 12–13, 1968
     New York

Sunday Afternoon

                                        for Paul Blackburn

Sun day,   so
   wide a day
after   noon

under star white
sun bell tolling in clouds
down deserted Greene
zig-zag canyon warehouses
quiet radio drifts, thoughts

of Paul   Thompson Street
when I first came to New York City 1958
his red brick Spanish warm interior
greeted me
          Funny to walk the same street
ten years later seem a moment
Paul   literary figure
crouched with his cat
Paul   now destroyed with sadness
self-pity
       man
thru swirls of cupola
St. Anthony
       cathedral the afternoon makes
such a day for creation is too the saddest widest day
Indianapolis dining-room porthole window at which I stand
look out to what seems to be the Hudson
pulling in to Manhattan rock majesty tree greenery

We drifted down that river last night Michael Doris Elaine & me
drinking French wine the excursion boat feeling very
French by wch we meant a feeling man feels among his kind
looking out the childhood porthole it was then as now

tremendous urge to go forth,   live
                              in the outside,   Sunday wideness
so dazzled
under sun
feet wobbling like typewriter ribbon under me
creation so intimate with disaster

          Mi Lady
      Restaurant Bar
red spidery neon the Reingold
darkness turned on inside

working out last night's wine
the bar in Sunday
like a spidercove off to the edge of a shimmering dewed web
if I walked in now
could drink beer
hunch in melancholy
know less than anyone I've ever presumed to
give advice
        yet in the same wink of eternity
God in the light shafting down Mercer
man free
high in the ecstacy of his juices
blue striped pants red & green horizontal jersey my gerua

        & one wants to, or fears, to explain it away
with a church, say
my ambivalence
this day all that energy
of bottled up praise
I took in during Fairview Presbyterian sermons & hymns
endless hours in tight wool suit fit onto pew
hosanna glory amen like sinew in the meat of service
the day marbleized with a glory

without expression.
I still carry what unwittingly I took in as a boy

so Sunday awakens stirrings in proud flesh, prowed
& feeling sick walking past
this dark cathedral grotto sanctuary bar

without expression,
    my father reading the funnies
mother sewing, both on the davenport
while I stood off,   looking out that round window.
               What did I see?

Buckeye, sidewalk, the Kirks' house across Boulevard Place,
Mr. Kirk, Catholic, lived in like a dark bar, divorced
father of Keith & Bernie, laughing with his girlfriend
tagging or playing some silly game over a toy wagon in the grass

I stood there watching Eden it strikes me now,
how simple what was aroused in me,
how I went to that window as to a kind of lip of life
in the sense that a person comes to a place, touches it,
wants very naturally to enter

They frolic
& I could not play with Keith or Bernie,
my father commenting over supper
(this is such an old story Paul)
"shameful how they act that way all the neighbors can see"
& I agreeing, my mother's face coming rigid
mouth setting staring at my father who returns to
his potato, & I agreeing, yet
still going to the window,
suspenders with no shirt I think Mr. Kirk was wearing
on his front lawn as he chased her,
she yelled, he grabbed her, they tumbled into the unmowed

   & I must have turned then to see at my side
Death reading the funnies
with his weird bride, hair up in nightcrawlers
strange antiseptic odors of the bathroom

both their stomachs constantly upset
power of that reek as it wrestled with pine scent
"be sure to close the door when you sit on the toilet"
and on the closed door that funny plaque brought back
from a Wisconsin vacation trip, had a needle and a dial,
listed the funny things you did in the bathroom,
you were supposed to set it before you went in,
cartoon of outhouse with crescent moon above it,

my father reading the funnies, mother sewing,
while outside the King of Hades romped
    & think of myself standing in that dynamite
brown boy scout shoes, short pants,
unable to stomach what I had decided was right to live.
I learned a capacity for anguish
learned to make a place for it, fit it in the hymns,
bow my head in the circumflex of grief

which was the figure my body made it seems
a woman hanged in me,
in the cords of my heart her knotted hair...

11 August 1968

ALTARS (1971)

Ode to Reich   *

Wilhelm for you I would sit in the reverberation of The Last Supper
& still keep my eyes to the gentle look in the eyes of children,
for you I would make love to Caryl
would keep her as the vent through which I experience the world,
for you I would make her the terminal,
the station in which all the trains unload
with girls upon girls upon girls & fathers & old men & mothers,
for you, I would keep her before me, keep
that need of the unknown unknown through her,
& known in the rain that falls on me, in that sopping bed the poem is
alone in the landscape that you almost alone inhabit
We love & embrace in a lone bed set out in a meadow
Nearby a city of fire

Wilhelm four years I have watched you alone this century
kindling the heavens over that lone meadow bed,
four years I have watched you daily rub off the soot from Baudelaire's
immortal lines: "Real civilization consists not in gas,
not in steam, nor in turning tables, but in the diminution of
the traces of original sin."
                              Concerned doctor, in work pants &
work shirt, in the photo I have of you page 173 in your *People in
     Trouble*
1934 in Sweden, in exile then in the full flow of your Arean arrow
sprung from the bow of your breeding laboratory for butterflies when
you were 10, your ax-head Arean profile looking intently then 37 at
something we know off the page,
                                   in the page of the youth breathing
fully for the first time in his life on a cot you in the late 20s
moved around from the chair placed behind him to sit
beside him, look him in the eyes & not use his dreams but confront
     him,
you are in a meadow in a room, yes! with insects buzzing in the dry
rigid prone youth on a cot on a hillock, you are torridly maintaining

his emotions are an expression of his biology & that his biology is
expression of a cosmic energy, that
We love & embrace in a lone bed set out in a meadow
Nearby a city of fire

Wilhelm four years, but the count is for all men, four years Blake
with marginalia on Lavater, this like an advance on Baudelaire:
"But the origin of this mistake in Laveter & his contemporaries
is, They suppose that Woman's Love is Sin; in consequence all
the Loves & Graces with them are Sins." —you Wilhelm
making rain over these lines, scouring them from reason,
keeping the fine edges cut into stone sharp in man's infinite
times of trouble, in work pants & work shirt (this image is
very important)—your compassionate eye on Merton
soundlessly repeating his rounds in the circumscribed nature of
Trappist, Kentucky, speaking gently to him in your fury of
your text on Jesus: "The great mistake is not the curbing of
man's evil urges for free-for-all fucking with dead genitals,
the great mistake is the burying of the very natural powers in
man's body which alone are capable of putting out of function
the perverted sex in mankind."
                              God, Wilhelm, what a tract your
arrowhead everywhere would lead me too, how difficult it is to
move you into the company of poets where for all centuries you
belong, there is so much cause, so much argument, so many
things to set straight; you with the medieval strangeness of
your simple frank theories, your orgone accumulator like a gigantic
slingshot before the Castle, your hollow metal pipes bringing
rain down on dubious Tim Reynolds visiting a farmer in Michigan,
Tim told me "I didn't believe he could make rain, he held the
pipes up to the bright sky and then we went in and drank beer,
it suddenly poured, an hour and when we left, a few miles away
the sun was again shining!"
                         To call you a poet
                   is to deepen your place as an advance on
imagination, it is not to say you are not a doctor nor to slant
you so as to keep anyone from your meaning as a scientist;
it is the revolution of the identity of a person & his expression,

as such to make for Harry Lewis morality a function of intuition,
that these are not separable things, you urge me tonight
in a bar in New York City—as Breton felt Fourier in a fresh
bunch of violets at the foot of his statue in Paris, I feel you
before me in an unknown girl, she is your bunch of violets Wilhelm,
this girl in her voluptuous body & pretty face hard
with what you call "armoring" sipping brandy & wondering
What is my life? She came in her confusion to
enter the poem, for I would rather not go to Maine to stand
before your tomb, but allow her as the living violet to
enter the poem and say Yes—
I feel you most next to me in Caryl &
I feel you before me as emanation of something not
mine, and in this very wood bench
your imagination vibrating violets
at the foot of your statue which is
now at Vallejo's cross in the Andes
& in Baudelaire's prayer that he simply might be able to work
& in Breton's old manifestoed hand in New Mexico
writing his *Oder to Fourier,* these saints
poets recognize in their own trembling energies to be
Jesus in their own hearts, that pioneering
cosmic fateful strength we know of you
through Arties, your glyph in the pulsating zodiac of
expansion contraction, the body of man
you as a red red Mars come like Isaiah
out of the judgment of the wine vats of your own being,
you curved as your own arrow was not wont to curve, you
bent the drive of that arrow, now I can say it,—to bions,
to heat sand once you had seen what drove you, to
keep the thing out of system, to follow out the strange
crooked road, to keep moving outward, & to keep perception
vital, to not backtrack in your later years & smudge
what I shall call your *clarification of Beulah.*

                              Wilhelm, what I am
getting at is to somehow honor the clarification you
gave us of self-sacrifice, that the substance of love is

kept fresh in the death of feminine form, this happens in
that meadow, in the giving up of pride & possession, of
man & woman allowing their bodies to convulse, to dissolve
truly thoughts & fantasies, this is the sacrifice Blake named
Eternal Death, to die there in joy with another, that that form
die, that the substance be liberated to find fresh form in
creation. We love & embrace in a lone bed set out in a meadow.
Nearby a city of fire
our brother William Blake named Eden, is creation &
in your understanding of the creative process you embrace
the poets telling them
sexual hindrance is imaginative crippling,
how simple you now appear, shoveling the hate out of our bodies,
you sturdy, in your work pants, with no mantle, no egg to
balance on your shoulders, you gazing intensely at
Vallejo's cross in the Andes on which you forever see
"Until I labor I in labor lie"
explaining to him in the ruins & dust that Beulah allows
the transmission, that creation is
not that struggle with the body,
that poetry is translation not just of language
but the passing of a psyche into new form.

Origin   *

                    appeared
gigantic on the darkened eaves
of the Senryuji Ancient Burial Grounds expanding
in the bat-shape of Lucifer
"You a are suitor—nothing more!"
the primal father called to Yorunomado
running around the stones below
begging for annihilation. & Yorunomado
crouched in dog (for the imagination nearly
perished he became what he was) & Origin saw
the chain around Yorunomado's neck
linked to the suns swarming spermatozoa
below the western ranges,

                    (take One)

Now I
walked up to Senryuji at dusk—to look for an
image of regeneration, I watched the sun
disappear behind the temple eaves
the sun is disappearing behind the temple eaves
flat, toneless, other images
spurted out, now I saw a pine, a gate,
but these dissolved into
what are you doing here?
was not a question of property
but you, why
are you alive?

                    (take Two)

now a man gave
me a power to see my soul,
this is Origin,

I was possessed by this
gift, was the Collar
of Yorunomado,
I imagined a man to be
free of a father,
Yorunomado was born in the wars of
Coatlicue & Origin,
Coatlicue is a force
Coatlicue is an imagining of mother,
having no mortal mothering poem mind
seeks its bedrock, seeks beyond
Indiana, beyond ethic a mother, a spider
watched in the yard fearful fortified
pregnant castle, ringed with skulls
devours its mate, goes as far
back as I can imagine, this image
inception of the second birth
seeks refuge in the mother,
is circular, the mother
is a temple at dusk,
will not come to form under the force of
Origin, Origin is the word
but word invested with
the gift, the gift of another's
mind, sits
a gargoyle
clutched to the poet's
shoulder, likewise inception of
second birth
I know is regeneration,
but in the form of teacher is
a soul life given, the son
must crucify the father

(take Three)

True war is mental fight
When one accepts a soul life,

accepts a princedom to a king,
when the pants are outgrown
there is either crucifixion or stasis.
When another assumes the role of
king or father, when the pants are outgrown
he expects to be crucified or unending
devotion. So subtle are these roles
men may spend a lifetime worshipping
a reflected power.

With this understanding the rudiments of the Sword Shrine
were glimpsed by Yorunomado as he stood facing Origin,
he took off the Collar & as a sign of humbleness he placed
it on his head. Origin went wild on the temple eaves
& demanded Yorunomado reassume his former
position. He told Yorunomado he was not ready to
take off the Collar & in a display of understanding
published one of Yorunomado's yelps. How beautiful
the yelp was set in the darkened eave, a star it
appeared, an act of mercy, but when Yorunomado
barked & howled within the confines of the replaced
Collar Origin again appeared in the shape of Lucifer,
but then as a simple creative man. A friend of Yorunomado,
a good companion, who understood the barks & howls
were not poetry. Yorunomado was not sure & thus Origin
became his master, a household was set up, saucers &
pillows were offered; the image of Lucifer & temple eave now
seemed only a metaphor. For a year Yorunomado
lived in this pleasant place, his greater energies dispelled
a yearning always setting in as quickly dispelled, deeply
Yorunomado yearned for Niemonjima, a dream of a depth,
a center she seemed, that spot where battle flowed in
unceasing mental charge, the Sword Shrine; he would yearn
out the window of Origin's house. It was not too bad to
have a master, especially after the years of being lost,
& so deeply did he yearn the yearning seemed unreal.

Los continued to speak to Yorunomado that year,
often he would appear in a terrible fit of drunkenness
turning the lamp-shades upside down & overturning
Yorunomado's box. Origin righted these & filled the
saucer with cool water. But a disturbance was in
the house, for Los' constant intervention suggested
Yorunomado imagine what he saw, a drunken man
turning the pictures around. That the yearning was
true, that it was this existence was false. Again &
again Los would bang on the door at midnight claiming
the imagination was the inverse of this world.

One night he enticed Yorunomado to go with him on
the town. I'd like to go to Eden Yoru woofed. No, Los
smiled, I can't take you there, but how about the Beulah
Sukiyaki Lounge? It's a folk restaurant near the docks,
very reasonable with lots of sake & girls from Kagoshima
dance on long low tables while you eat. Well ok said
Yoru, but I worry about Origin, suppose something
happens to him while I'm gone? My friend, said Los,
your Origin is something you haven't even dreamed yet.

Meanwhile down at The Beulah Sukiyaki Lounge Kagoshima
beauties were serving delicious stews, & pouring sake
from urns & long low tables & incense & it was enough to
make one lose one's senses, a place filled with flowers &
dark balmy alcoves; it was Los' place, with swaying red
lanterns & a kind of steamy light & he entered with Yoru-
nomado in a vision of pleasure; they ate & got drunk &
many beauties danced in tabis along their plates but the
vision would not forward because Yoru worried about
Origin & many beauties crouched around him in their tabis
with beautiful necks & he said to Los, I thought this was
your place but even the syntax gets screwed up, who are
these chicks? You seem to know them all & what about
Origin, suppose someone breaks in?
                              And Los said: isn't
this the situation of your poetry? *Suppose someone breaks*

in & Who are these chicks? Isn't this what happens to you
when you write? If you can't be at ease here you can't
make it there; you turn off one central valve, you turn off
others; what you see back there you see here, only I'd
call that Ulro, I mean THERE is no one but you, like you
are alone, man, with a metaphor, & Los had a wicked
gleam in his eye saying To make this real you must make
something else real, which is very tricky but since you are
a Dog why don't you just go out & fuck a bitch?

                                                    Yoru was
beside himself, for the beauties got closer with every
word of Los, Yoru felt himself hot beside the fire of Los'
poetry & this was very weird, that language should make
him feel that way when the enterprise was he thought work
in his box, that he was a Literary Dog with primitive
feelings, & now he remembered the course of this poem
how he had plunged around with feathers & even donned
the headdress of New Ireland but wasn't it true it took
years to get that headdress on?

                                    Suddenly there was around
Yorunomado a vision, in the ceiling of the Beulah Lounge
peacock eyes, the wood ceiling aswarm with peacock eyes
an arabesque of eyes upon eyes swirling gold & blue, it was
a religious feeling, of being in church & he fell back amongst
the pillows & overturned urns & wide-eyed beauties aghast
at the eyes within eyes swirling

                            (be responsible here, a
voice said; here you must get the whole thing accurate

                                                    &

at the same time another voice spoke; be utterly irres-
ponsible here, let the whole thing fly)

                                    & at center Barbara's
face benevolent, warm, pulsing in the midst of the eyes,
enormous, as on a screen, Barbara's face smiling at him
& Yoru tried to turn to Los, but Los had split with one of
the beauties, or two or... Yorunomado was alone with his
metaphor but no, he was seeing the metaphor, but no, it was
real, & then I was not there, only Yorunomado was there,

only imagination was present, there was no division between
Yorunomado & what he saw, he was what he saw & her face
had it in Chinese eyes, slant & regal & long hair shimmering
black but a quality of turquoise, not emerald but turquoise
blazing in the darkness of her beautiful black hair which like
a mane was coiling & uncoiling about her face & furling
around her many eyes & her mouth which was pursed &
benevolent, kissing in its outer ceremony opened slightly
& he feared for his life as it opened, it pursed & opened, &
blood trickled as it opened, it opened & more blood bright
bright red, was trickling down the corners, now running
steadily from her mouth dark red blood & her mouth opened
now fully & blood was pouring like falls, a terrible dark
red bright red, stream & in the stream a spot which was
suddenly a tiny face, an infant, & he recognized the infant
its curled foetal drawn expression getting bigger in the
stream of blood as my son & the poem flipped into constern-
ation as all this was true at once, Yorunomado saw his
son emerge from the bloody mouth of this mortal woman,
& as soon as it made its presence absolute the mouth was
again pouring blood & Yorunomado trembled on the floor
wanting to be away but knowing there was another dimension of
the vision, Origin suddenly appeared in the beams of blood
but not as master, not of the stern face, but Origin reclined
as on a couch, dreamy, heavy-lidded, his eyelids drooping
a heavy winey drooping & all around him beauties & Origin
winked in the bright bloody sunshine that illumed his heavy
winey form, & a shiver that this was paradise ran Yoru's ribs,
& Yorunomado shook & the vision like a veil shimmered in its
folds & then as suddenly only faint peacock eyes disappearing
as if stained water on the wood beams & Los was at his side
holding him, holding him on his shoulder & looking seriously
in his eyes, asking with his eyes are you alright & Yorunomado
came to, or it seemed, down, into the sense of his body, &
was heavy in Los' arms...

        but Beulah was not transfigured.
Los was there, watching him closely but as Yorunomado looked
around he saw the beauties in their make-up & saw their kimonos

were of linen, the dirty soles of the bent tabis, & saw many
of the beauties tending the businessmen of Futomi & Yokohama,
he saw their creased sweaty collars, their tight little bandboy
business suits & felt his own Collar, his mind flipped back to
that State, but he was intent on the women, & against the pres-
sure of fully returning stayed with what he saw, the heavy
smoky lanterns & grease in the plates & he asked himself What
did I see before? Neither the beauty nor the grease, & in great
sickening feeling knew he had a son & that this son was not
a product of vision nor was a son of his master & that he had
had this vision but that he had a son, such was unbearable for
a year but Los was holding him in his arms & without speaking
they rose

         & Yorunomado in torment awakened Origin when
he came in, I must talk to you he said, tonight I had a vision,
tonight I found out, within the same vision, who I was, I got
drunk in Beulah, Los held me in his arms, I saw Eshleman's
wife & in her bloody mouth I saw my son, & then

                                     but Origin
was looking at him seriously, intently, & told him to be off,
that this was gibberish, that dawn would come & all would be
as it had been, but Origin Yorunomado said, tonight I
saw the center of the flame, I mean you are not really my master
& at the center there is not discipline, I mean I saw you

                                     but Origin
was getting incensed & making irate gestures in his nightgown &
Yorunomado tried to say I saw you secretly were drunk with love
& that paradise has no masters but the thought of his son which
seemed to have enabled him to speak usurped him & all he could
blurt out was I saw I was a sexual man, & this against Origin &
against the extreme complexity of what was his vision seemed
absurd & he faltered & felt guilt for having awakened Origin &
crept back to his box.

Now dawn came & Origin was right, he approached Yoru's
box & speaking in an uncompromising way said: so you are sexual,
so what? Of course you are sexual, but to explain the world

out of you feeling you are sexual is so thin it makes me wince.
So you went out with Los & got drunk: that is not your life,
your life is only what you make of it where you are. And I
have seen a particular look in your eyes recently & heard
a particular tone in your voice & while I do not think you are
malicious I think you are disturbed & I think you must work
this out. I am not your father & the point is to tend to your
poetry & lead your own life. If you have a son as you say
then be responsible for him. Keep me out of it. I have my
own life to live; you work out yours.

       But you do not understand
Yorunomado argued, I had a vision that I was a sexual being, I
felt that the heat I am in is the heat of poetry. I saw my sexuality
is more real than poetry, & that only if I am sexual can I be
a poet. I can't live here in this box any longer; I must now go
seek Niemonjima; I can't live with another's wife, though
I profess I saw my son in vision & that that son is mine, but
what a vision I had! I had a vision! You must acknowledge my
vision because you are the man who understands me most.

              And
Origin looked at Yorunomado & Yorunomado felt shame; he felt
there was something different about the world but he didn't under-
stand why it was different. And then the whole business about the
box & the Collar seemed stupid & Yorunomado cried & said I don't
have a Collar but I do have one, I don't live in a box but I do. And
there was no such house & no such master & in shame Yorunoma-
do dwindled & it was as if he fell, & fell & fell but always a limit,
a density, a kind of opaqueness in which Origin was most real, was
his Origin but was Origin, & he wasn't a dog but felt like one,
& he looked at his Regeneration & it was written by a bastard,
& fell further & then bounced as he hit, & said to himself But
I have a vision the way things are, this means more than anything
& the vision is I cannot live with someone I am not fucking &
fell, further, grasping at the railings of his body, & said But to
simply fuck means more than the poem, the poem is a dodge
for not fucking, & fell, more deeply into the density of what seemed

the other side of Beulah, a sterile fusion of himself, & then he
was alone & even Origin was a distant country & the only thing
spiritual was his son; this flame a membrane against extinction.

Such is the nature of vision within the confines of the father & son.

19–23 February, 1970

The Golden String   *

Above all the kitchen bathtub with little white lion feet
where you bathe in the lovely shore light off Hydra

Above all the golden string

Adrienne
Ariadne
Soaping your arms & wishing me well in the bright gladiator light at
    the poem's limits
This Self wch is flooded at the touch of your hand to the ignition

Above all
Adrienne
Ariadne
Above all Barbara who suffered it

for there is always a third who is there in the raw breakthrough of
    being
A third who stands at cross-purposes with our heart
wishing the antagonists well, the Holy Host

It is she who is pregnant with their desires
She clasps their book to her heart & waits in the dense Okumura
    garden
& Paradise is to admit her, she stands
before the lovers with an infant in her arms

This is the way of the earth, that the garden is always slightly off
    center
That the stallions of total translation are never loosed
Thus not an answer but a golden string is given

Above all this golden string

leads me to your bathtub in the garden where you are soaping &
    laughing

& your slippery happiness is deep
& great enough for me to enter fully & be bathed
in the cool
reality of the mirage

Come on in, Barbara!
Don't you know this golden string allows you & Matthew to laugh
& splash with us, that this garden is incomplete without both of you
entering the bubbles & rubies of all our desires
The pregnant red spider,

the flies, the cicadas in *The House of Okumura*
can here follow Adrienne's golden string & laugh & dance with us
in the great dimension of
this string

And this is the construction of this string,
it is interwoven with indignation & hesitancy, with dark
reservation & loss
For in vision these withholdings are the pressed
bodies of the creatures with whom we dance,
the terrible sun illumes for us the bastings of blood, the pressed

lives of the creatures, the pregnant spider abandoned
as the cold sets in is here, the pumpkin-colored slug on
the frosted October ledge, all the terrified captives

cut down by the gladiators in the light at the poem's limit

Thus the energy of my dream reverberates down the golden coils
of the imagination, this paradise wch is not mine alone fans
& deepens with the churring of the orange monarch's wings

I behold the great green & scarlet caterpillars mingling with
the bodies
of those I love & my blood roars the messenger is your double name

1 October 1970, Sherman Oaks

Keeping the Flies from my Mother's Head   *

The woman, more tiny than I ever imagined,
sits on a folding chair by the bridge-type table
in the dining room for one hundred—
having chopped up the baked potato for my father,
she unflakes the heat from her own
and I am by her, reaching for the flies
that have followed her from their room.

It is almost automatic, by her pain, to comb the air,
the lianas and heavy surplus, yes
the pus from the air this fantasy infolds
and know there is a creature here suffering,
reorganizing, mostly a power to cure
held me when I was very little,
and all that I must have feared then is with me,
waving my own helpless feelers,
trying to help her now.

Imagine a rabbit trying to feed itself
on rubble with its paws
as it is swept up by eagle claws embedded in
its back and neck.

My mother trying to eat her potato,
tasteless saving, the coin that went to Sears,
or a movie at fifty, my mother
trying to still live as the flies bother even
her scared strange intense eyes.

Imagination picks, works through I die too,
the soft jowls of the substance of art.

Keeping the flies as well from the dear head of my ignorance,
this strange well insects all adore,
I protect the well. I work the nephrite of the air.

Fear not her hysterectomy,
removal is what is made here.
I puke up her thousands of eyes
embedded in my physical linoleum.

Keeping the flies from her head,
from the true depth of her body,
my mother's body, while she lives.

Indianapolis, 1970

The Baptism of Desire

Starting in again, a glass of cold water I
toss at you beautiful hiding & laughing on my
part of the bed, you jumped into my bath I
sat on the toilet shaking with laughter while
you bathed & when my turn came
the damn water was lukewarm, as I shivered
in it only up to my crack you posed
& giggled—& so I chase you thru this poem, to
spurt cold at you again, dancing woman on
my part of the bed, figure now involved with
curtains I would hang for you to giggle &
twist over your naked stomach & breasts,
but we don't have curtains, the sunlight pours
daily in, open to green oleander & Japanese
gardener's abashment, how strange to love &
sleep before open window, embrace you & watch
human twigs or sweet stones half submerged
in mud, this house the regeneration of Japanese
house from which nature was outside, each
yellow butterbur pain, obsessed with nature
since there my nature was withheld, a glass
of cold to toss liquid flame in the energy that is
joy, hear the blue-headed birds hit pane they see
only a world opening, blue-feather smear over
king-sized bed our one possession here, light
that is tossed back & forth, tepid water I
gladly sit in adore you Queen Shebaing with
towel what a lovely embrace the light water body
on the one road with heart, what a simple
throne bed is to lie sleep & peek at you
O lovely rhythm that doesn't need myth other
than blue bird feather smear a pain coronation
head of the bed that my head can spill Protean
spermaceti without wincing since you are terminal
& again my train arrives

Poem that drifts down to
the boy in tub she who is dead now bathed & can I
keep the glass of cold water tossing to you who
flirt in the folds of memory, figure of lovely Caryl
you are strong enough to let this dash of water be
potato & weenie, the knotty-pine dining-room with
porthole window where the boy filled with protein did
not know an Austrian doctor had made a last judgment
to affirm love life of 12 years old, & as the cold water
tosses it is wind at the end of Boulevard Place over
untying of newspapers to trundle on my route

This present beauty
I know of you not unlike my vision of her, vision I tossed
in again in Japan standing on the island mid Higashiyama-
road & watched the white linens toss on second story
roofs, there an innocent beholding of my mother the
photo of her at marriage lovely the photo of my father
at marriage lovely, I copulated them in the pain of
rooted to island waiting for the streetcar to carry me
downtown Kyoto 1963, seven years, but 28 years to
suddenly not in grass but in living memory sense
them, & the boy rushes in mind to put them in love
the white flapping towels & linen. All commingling of
light & clothes the desperate first, & I rushed cold
water into that possible image, no body to be hit but
road & rode downtown, & that was the pain to have no
terminal for first sprinklings of joy

& so she bathed the
crack of the boy insisted I not shower not linger in
bed at morning, those covers are still warm in the bed
over which life does seem to toss, a glass of cold
can be Arctic or can be joy & I love my first imaginings
of my mother tho no net caught the fish my mind/body
is, to throw & to throw in the throe that is the poem
your body Caryl the water dribbles down, runs to

foot of the bed that runs on its rails of world from
boy to man, there is a bed, one, we almost inhabit
we are born in are nursed in fuck are lonely in &
sleep, this bed primally the door we open & close,
& you Caryl swirling flesh campanile sweet leaf
risen from the bloody waves.

                              This is no myth, it is
my life & the dogs that tear at the beautiful flesh in
Botticelli where the drinkers rear from their picnic
tables in alarm are watersparkle from your body
you walk on the water I throw & I live on the water you
breathe & my mother in sunlight a halo of energy I
will have here around you, I see Gladys Eshleman
thru the halls of the golden string of imagination, I
see the thirty-five stages of my years of her life, she
is the curtains, the opaque folds we won't have in our
life, she is the backdrop my imagination loves to
see you dance against, playing at the organ & playing
pedaling the organ, pressing my feet down into deep
wood of boyhood piano scales upon scales dragon of
green Victory Stamps my little ass on the needlework
rose of piano-bench *Teaching Little Fingers* to
throw the glass, press down *Play* & learn to walk
index over third finger the endless bass somber thru
The Rustle of Spring, Revolutionary Etude ultimately
Bud Powell who swirls in the curtain of the letter,
that black woman who crossed the hospital parking-lot
as she spoke her last coherent words to me the mind
wants to make Kali, black death goddess crossing
parking-lot having laid her cancer stringer of endless
hunger in the pitiful old woman wild & nut-colored on
the bed! All I know has rushed from me protein so
Proteus may live, if there must be the shadow wch is
myth I want it that close, not have to speak death in
black attendant heavy towards her car 7 stories down
from the monolithic wings of hospital, absence of angel

angel only in the glass you have poured full & I toss
& toss this cold water wake up my mother from the
last dreadful slumber by walking in unannounced

                    "oh, hello, Clayton…"
how much water is there in this glass, smell of pepper
tree, dried oleander flower, stand in California back
yard & know sex-economy is the energy household
sprinkle of Aquarian stars of the woman I am pouring
out, shallow pool on concrete, how much can she
pour who is pouring thru me? No way to know other
than to not fear the pouring, curtainless window is
to pour & pour & now I am upon you shielded
before the carnation bones of funeral lime-colored
Flanner & Buchannan the lavender-brocaded casket
with its heavy silver bars weight of weenies in my
plate weight of porthole window weight of the haunt
of house. I think my mother is consumed in this end-
less glass, treat decently this energy household this
is thy core of ecology to live in a body maybe to end
up nut, wild-child, mother as man alone in the spinal
woods of monster losing her hair, sack-cloth of cancer to
ram food at one's mouth, smear into teethless gums
a morsel of bad-smelling fish, confuse coffee-cup with
pot & see her legs the accuracy of Grünwald's vision
of the Christ, mottled & damp in sores legs that in
hose were monument by piano my fingers pressed in
& in, that this IS a casket lowered into shovel-sliced
Menonite earth, that this is the end of man over wch
rain & fog drizzle in the face of the sad Eshleman tribes,
pink rabbit-eyed faces of north Indiana women huddled
in the unending death of no one ever throwing water on
the possibility of happiness, is not this the meaning of
rain, is not this the meaning of sunlight to not let
hideous rabbit, the wild-child, park in the center of
our longing? Are not these jumpings on the mattress,
the dash to the faucet & the run after you laughing

the meaning of life? And what monument more than to
gauge her drift thru me, the satanic point at wch I
would not turn on the tap but deny the spiritual economy
keep the glass empty, which, in the strength of her wish,
would have been not to write but play out the piano into
the settled negation that is Indianapolis. O mother, it
was in Kyoto I beheld thy triple-negation at the point I
first knew you were my mother! O tonight I wld crown
that point, that you came to me there in the fury of
unacted desire & thru a spider, abdomen red &
swollen, in the heat of summer transmitted to me
Isis, that who prunes us to let creation thru seeks
likewise our scattered members, & the boy at 12
who stood by white pickets behind the garage while
great Reich was actually thinking about him in Europe,
that boy a page before the court of women attacked
by mastiffs, who stood trembling while the white
table-cloths soaked in the wine, this boy before
the overturned banquet of humanity you brought to
bear upon the suffering spider body, who could thru
such rabbit-eyed tradition manifest yourself, for
the fountain you had at least to plant, you left your
stacking of coins at least an instant to take on the
spider-body & be again the beginning of the world.

7 December 1970, Sherman Oaks

The Bridge at the Mayan Pass

I

Five nights stone
has crowded in, to
say my father's
face is stone, to

dress his face in
the stone of
stone that speaks more
powerfully as

the father of my
father & his father
but I can only love
that which is no

more impersonal than
my seeing of
myself, & since I have
no childhood memory of

my father's face
I have been rocked to the edge
of Last Judgment, I
was moving toward

eternal fire, across the bridge
I was building of
the poem, had put on
that Mayan bridge

a hunched form, in the darkness over
the swaying pass, below us
the abyss I sought to
watch a huge wounded

shoulder of a form roll
into, Goya's Satan this Christ
I thought, & adored
the phantasmagoria of

Billy Graham in bra &
garters, like the Rhine
Gold girl, serving the
pitiful legions of Eshleman

beer, in the nave, the
elders who are
my Presbyters. But to bring
lightning here, to

smear a face, which
as A face is
His face, into stone, to
establish the gaping

cisterns of Tlaloc's eyes
as *my father's face,* my
marriage of
heaven & hell, evades

my feelings about the living
man. Tonight I remembered
a flicker, a wince
of suffering, very

quick, an instant, a
flicker stronger than stone
across the mortuary
lobby I saw, in

his face, as I turned from
the relatives who had

turned from him, & saw
him, suddenly

alone. He stood
on the bridge &
looked for me, I was
simply a wider

flicker, burning with more
hate & more love
than he, No — with no
more hate, no more

love than is here, this
bridge of ceaselessly
eroding alarm, this
bridge in a stronger

moment I call the
golden string. But the fiber of
the string is likewise creaking
wood & wind,

it holds the entire
phantasmagoria of the
weighted dread
I am & I am & I am.

II

But I refuse to contend
with *your stone!* I have been there, consciously, father, you
have not! You are in under her, the stone she lies on,
I fought with you in Vallejo, I struggled to
kill Vallejo at stone
my contention with man!
I am sick to death

of what won't stink!
Caryl is alive, Matthew
is alive, am I
alive? SICK TO DEATH
of baptism without desire,
& I know through the worm,
through the humility at odds
with woman is, the magic
of your unreadable runes!
You are the stone
a boy cannot read,
I write to make
to Matthew Matthew
visible, that a fucking
transmission be made!
But this stone ground, how
long will the indian
patch up San Cristobal his huts,
skulls, his houses, black
window eyes, eyes, a thousand
black eyes candle-lit over our
Christ-leaden city of Lima!
My god, father, you didn't even know
we were in Lima! You voting
& voting & not even knowing
lacunae
lacunae
in the indian's water-supply, in
the copper-lines that extend like
intestinal cords between here &
South America, STONE!
You didn't even know what you were doing when you fucked Gladys!
Her one erotic memory was a choir-master in Chicago who around
    1930 looked at her!
I am angry at you because you didn't know how to fuck!
I am angry at you because having moved through the superficial
    layers of her death I do not reach the living,

but hit you! I am furious at you because you don't know what goes on
   in Lima!
I hate you because when you traveled to Lima you couldn't look at a
   starving child but went to Machu Picchu!
FOR THAT IS THE ADORATION OF STONE!
I HATE STONE, I bring pieces of it into my room only
      to weight the pages from the wind
on which the honest words of men who have lied through
      their lives live!
I HATE THE STONE IN MAN,
I HATE THE ADORATION
      OF YANG MARKS
      IN BUFFALO PAINTINGS
      & YIN CIRCLES BEFORE WHICH
      THE SITTING WORLD ADORES
      THE HISTORY OF MAN!
I hate you because you are simply a cruddy uninteresting piece of this
      history!
Because you would watch
      black children bring you a newspaper & not give them a Xmas tip
but would give white children a Xmas tip,
& because you would chase children away from the buckeye tree
      because they crept into the yard while I was 8 sitting back of
      the porthole window wishing I was creeping into our yard
      to steal the unquestionably free fallen buckeyes!
And so you are in me, & I feel my hate for you my mother dies!
My mother dies! Yes, complex knot of real feeling through which
      burning rivulets leaked through, her tears awakened my
         going-to-hell
      cheeks, & you sitting 30 years in the slaughterhouse
      creeping, your pen, across the ledger, coming home with your
      bloodstained coat tips, that I had only those rainblooddrops to
      imagine what you were drawing salary from! The nerve of you, to
      not break down ever once & WEEP with the blood of a cow
      on the heels of your Charlie McCarthy shoes! The nerve of you
      not to cry! The nerve of you never to blast me! The nerve O the
      NERVE dead, dead & dead & dead & dead *dna dead dna DEAD*

Yoru roars! Yes, the faculty that otherwise is literary careful sadness,
literary adolescence forever warpped in the many-colored coat of
    myth,
what a Joseph coat you are, Ira Clayton Eshleman, & the neighbors all
picking around in the suburbs looking with flashlights for the
    murderer
of a girl, you do not come home father, I will not let you come home
    for home is where you'd like to flicker forever, flicker a wince or
    a sad distressed look, lacunae
lacunae, sad dressed look lacunae, lacunae honorably in Catullus
Villon lacunae in the parts of man
uttered & lost in paper-rot, but damn lacunae of what is never
uttered!
        AND I WILL NOT LET YOU REMAIN STONE
        FOR STONE IS
        ANCIENT FIRE
        I HONOR ANCIENT FIRE
        FOR TOTALLY NON-CHRISTIAN REASONS
        I WOULD NOT CONSIGN YOU TO ETERNAL FIRE
The ancient fire! The ancient fire! Old fire! Anger & blessing, hate
desire, concern, sympathy intermingling, Yes, this is
under Last Judgment, old pisco taste of last judgment,
music, song be DAMNED, the raw voices on benches at 12,000 feet
    beheld,
the ancient men are those who have no clothes! Those men be
let in, those unlit roadways, those failures of rain
        YES I AM A BABY INCAN
        I RUN THE FULL CIRCLE OF THE YANG MARKS
        I SEE THE ONLY THING WORTH ADORING IS MY ART
        IN WHICH THOSE I LOVE ARE NOT ABSENT
And the lure of forgiveness is
consumed in the meaning of understanding
        THE MEANING OF STONE IS
        IT BE FUCKED ON OVER A BED OF
        DOWN EVERY SECOND DAY IN THE LIFE OF MAN
And the yang marks will be seen as movement
And the yin will be seen as movement
For the meaning of movement is the body of man & woman & child

Against rock to love & keep warm
    THIS IS HISTORICAL UNDERSTANDING
And the generations of Eshleman, oh let them huddle, yes, with wine
& candles on a rope bridge over a Mayan Pass! Yes over the abyss,
the whole white spook-show like Witch Sabbath! Great black
    shadows,
let them pass the wine, unhuddle, let my father be among his people,
Let there be that picnic with the abyss beneath, let spastic Dean
    Eshleman
touch Matthew that Matthew not be confused, I open this cyst that
Matthew wander fully among these generations, let him see Iva
    Eshleman's
madness, THIS IS THE WEIGHT, Charles, Silvia, Orville, Leonard,
Helen, Almira, Ira, Olive, Aunt Barbara never seen from Florida,
(these are the "books"), Fern, Faye, Bob Wilmore (these in Blake's
age *Generations of Man*), THE WEIGHT THE DREADED
    WEIGHT   I
    NOW TAKE OFF INDIANA

    I RELEASE INDIANA

    NAILED MILE GALED IN ANSWER

    TRACED IN HEIL THY NATURN FACE!

          6–16 December 1970, Sherman Oaks

The Physical Traveler

I woke up pregnant by a wall
where a red spider watched me
from its web; don't forget, it
told me as I rose, that I

am pregnant too but dependent
on my web. A mobile pregnant
man I walked along the wall
& as I walked the wall began to

talk, I don't want you anymore that
now you're full of me, get
lost. But you're the father of my
state I tried to hold

it from going, but it was wide &
I was small, so wide I saw
it ran around Creation
which seemed a city

within, & I pregnant with
a little wall without.   What would
you do in my place?
I began to bore

into the father of my state
but as I drilled & drilled
I found my benefactor
was deep proportionate to

my drill, while on each side of
the passageway I was making
Creation seemed to abound
When I turned to retreat

I found a woman in my way
She sat crouched in my passage
head tucked between her
knees, I tried to push her out

I tried to see her face
I couldn't budge her from the shaft
& so I joined her to
my fate by pushing her up

inside me through my recent
gate. Now under double charge
I attacked the father of my
plight, the wall gave way

I stood in Creation the air
like yolk each form like running
blood I gave way like my wall
& loosed my nature

through my thighs a woman &
a little wall attached like Siamese
twins, I could get rid of them
but she could not be

free of it. You're the father of
my yoke she cried & then
I saw her face, in Creation
each thing weds &

counterweds, no one steps on
someone's spine, I lost them here
Her face boiled orange
with fire & empty

I started to shred into the flow
but I remembered the spider's
words & so strove out
of Paradise, maintained

my womblike form. And now,
because of this, I appear
to be a man & while the spider
stays my kin

I can no longer hear its voice
except when I press my ear to
any wall & all my emptiness
shakes with awe

for I remember my father
I remember the night
he crept into my cell
& my crib ran red.

Lima 1966 – Sherman Oaks 1972

Coils

*

—*for Robert Kelly*

Stood by the bedside, watched her shrunk body breathing brown
monkey-like on her side, her hair moth-eaten eyes open in half
sleep, Methodist Hospital on Meridian at 16th, where I was born
out this womb June 1935 "born this day at 10:50 A.M. His
Daddy seeing him enter this old world. A Little Clayton Jr. Our
dream at last realized & our prayer answered. Thank God for
it all." Once again I saw the Okumura Garden & stood in the dim
morning light by the maple by the red pregnant spider's web
There *had* been a garden before, a sandbox & the white picket
fence, two gardens, three, the years warm & confusing
In the Okumura Garden I awoke from her dream for me
to be a Junior, to participate in my round of the collectivecoil
The spider was the sign of my awakening & as I studied it daily
I seemed to learn nothing, its light-green yellow-speckled red
abdomen was just more swollen every day, I stood by—in trance
as I stand by this bedside now in the trance of the mystery of
cycles, yet then as now Yorunomado was bringing me another kind
of learning, not an education but an Image, not an accumulation
of particulars but a phantom layer of itself, COATLICUE, Yorunomado
brought me COATLICUE, a photo of that Aztec idol. "serpent-
skirt" it meant, under the photo was written: *Mother of the Gods.*
I watched the spider & my mothering education told me I shd
learn its parts, build the poem out of observed particulars a
rational thing Yet Yorunomado had set his torch to my heart
& the fumes were smoking upward, I looked at the spider & saw
COATLICUE, I smelled a density of odor in the Okumura Garden that
did not begin or end with my body, but COATLICUE, This was the
coloration in the sign, that knowledge went to COATLICUE & not in
words for the spider's anatomy. Now COATLICUE seems originally
a person, not an idol but an Aztec woman the story goes, out
sweeping the desert doing penance & a feather fell from the sky,
she tucked it between her stomach & her breasts, went home
& found herself pregnant. Her many sons & evil sister wanted

to kill her for this, she was terrified but the foetus spoke to her saying
Do not fear; I know what I am doing. When the sons & sister came
to kill her the baby lept forth fully-armed, his body painted
bright-blue, his leg slender & feathered, he killed the sons
& chopped the sister into pieces, from this time on the story
goes he is named Huitzilopochtli the God of War. I stand
before the woman & the story, I see at work in the nature of
the human an alternating rhythm of birth & birth, Coatlicue the
woman become COATLICUE 10 feet tall Ferocious Yet not
meaning to be human, but a code to divine the structure of
generation, mandala, look upon me my mother is saying &
between me & you will be a golden string, you will see in this
coiling string a meaning never fully revealed. If you fear the cycles
you will arrest this nature, you will take a piece of it & call
It Meaning, but everything I am is meaning, who I was to you
when you played in your sandbox at 3 learning how to cover it
nightly so kitty wouldn't get in & dirty where you played,
O then how my love for you was enormous & filled with light,
shimmer of light in the leaves of my love for you. Will you call
that the limit? That my meaning? And when you held on to
white pickets at 12 & longed in your first remembered heat to
put your penis into Jeannie Woodring I began to separate from
the beech & the light in its leaves, you began to dream her into
your nature so I stood then stark in the kitchen watching you,
& what you desired was no longer my warmth infolding you
but something hotter & sharper, a torrid center of blazing
fire I could not enter, & will you see me finally in that moment?
My dream over at your birth, my life over at your heat, 47
years old, becoming more and more restrictive & thin as I placed
the plate with weenies on it before you. And in an instant my
mother moves from 47 to 72, in an instant I left her & now I see
what I left on this bed, a grin the nature of the mystery is
making at me, she is small enough now for me to carry
like a lamb in my arms, to stand in the black light of
the pasture & hold her bones & fondle her dry aged arms, her
wrist tagged with a number, *Did I do this* sweeps through
my hold with a meaning below my own meaning, am I responsible

for death, is that the source of my feeling a murderer
& knowing I am, a murderer in the collectivecoil, or is that just
abuse, all the hurts & desires acoil in my mind. No—I
did hurt you, I thought I had to be free of you. *And will you
then take that as my image?* And then I am down on my knees
crawling out from under her dining-room table onto ground
that is dry & I am speaking to you as I crawl saying Look at
what that torrid center has become, look, I am 31,000 years old
I am standing by that fence holding on to white pickets
but look at the form that holding on has taken on, look at this
desert I am crawling on seeking water—*But I am not res-
ponsible for that,* my mother speaks, *you were down under
the table connecting your tubes to Daddy, I don't even know
what you are talking about*—No, I said, I was down under
the table cutting my tubes to father, those tubes I *can* cut,
but not my instinctual ties to you, those can only be trans-
formed. Don't you understand that when I was standing in
the Okumura Garden watching the red spider & wondering over
COATLICUE, that I was standing before my nature, which has
everything to do with you?

Reached the point where imagination
became the inverse of this world, there
I took the mirage for real,
the sand as mirage, what I imagined
became real, a giant indian whore
in a stable outside of Ica was
a lick of moisture,
& before her the Greek woman
Bloomington 1965 looked like moisture
like bloody drops of hot moisture these moments
fell onto my desert *Do not take them as my image*
my mothering soul was whispering to me,
*This desert is Indiana, is your state of mind
bred of Indiana. What do you see in the cracks*

of mirage? I see my penis pushing toward a point of
blindly, drunkenly, when I am alone when I exist in
red, I see a center opening & opening that I seek
Indiana bred marriage the desert again becomes real
I am back in linear time,
a work of art to make in misery but misery to be concealed
in wit & blanketing of imagination, each thought a grain The
grain in wood a swirl of thoughts now decomposing/composing
under my hands *This is your Last Judgment the error to be*
consolidated then cast off Your penis is a dragon-tail Take hold
Pull your body out of Indiana is Fear your Body is what
you glimpse in that crack your Body is the code of a wholeness
of being And I hesitated, I was afraid, for I saw my contraries were
now in motion, there was no turning back, my femaleness was
preparing to be revealed. If I turned back now it wld be to live
with awareness in the state of Indiana, I saw that contradiction saw
Gil Ring hammer the crucifix into his livingroom wall, saw my art
congeal into wit & bitterness under which is religious deadness
But I feared to go on for the contraries now revolving COATLICUE
within Coatlicue Coatlicue within COATLICUE in beautiful
serpentine coils had no desert beneath them, I looked into
my coils *If you go & be with woman you must see this world,*
which is the crucifixion of woman, as unreal
You must live within these coils
O mother, I cried, you are not
that weenie damnation
You are poetry YOU ARE NOT
THAT WEENIE DAMNATION IS POETRY
You are a poor dreamless spectre, that happy mother who nursed me
You are the woman who gave up your dream when I was born
I was your dream & thus you no longer had one, conned
by an aggregate of superstition & patriarchal religious malice
into believing your function in life was generation at the expense
of human imaginative fulfillment, yet I must understand your giving
birth to my body as a sacrifice, your nourishing me as forgiveness
Seeking my own soul still tied to yours I drove myself into nightmare
to get back into a dream, nightmare the void myself an armless worm

hurtling through my small intestine night after night in 1963 Your
face, Your searching face at the end of my coils I expected to see
But COILS ARE BOTTOMLESS, this means, in linear time
You were never there, I "expected" to see your face seeking me
holding a candle to my anus; as long as I thought I was shit
I thought you would be there—

Then go forth into
a birth that is & is not your own
To enter woman is the end of nightmare self-containment
According to Indiana fucking is 6 inches in
To the imagination fucking is merely a parting of the curtains
The sun & stars shout with joy in her bottomless space

Then swiftly as in the past   [1964]
I had disemboweled myself to
arrest the suicidal heart of Indiana,
I now sealed off my stomach &
sought out—rolled out of the bunk bed   [1966]
in Blackburn's workroom & said ok
Paul, I'll go with you to "Max's Kansas City"
who knows, maybe I'll meet someone there.
In the very same moment as in the past
I had thwarted my own spinning in
apprenticework to Origin I now with only   [1963–65]
(yet what an only!) a golden string spun out
of my solar plexus released myself into   [1970]
the mirage which yawned an abyss below
the drunk horde of Eshlemans on
the rope-bridge over the Mayan Pass!

A bloodstone-lined vault it appeared
immense, cistern-shaped, I floated a tiny sky-diver
against night, *Poppi how can you*
FLY? Matthew called up to me, *I am not flying!* I called
down to him, *I am falling!* But here you must not
dream the mothering soul was speaking, here you are
dreaming yet here you must rudder your dream—

But must I exclude the giving myself over to
hearing Matthew in my dream I returned, You told me
everything I am is meaning, How can there be a command
while I float down into the abyss? You have transformed me to
a great extent, it spoke, I am no longer your mother, nor your
soul, I am your meaning now traveling at your side
As you have evolved me you must evolve—you still seek to
remember Matthew, to hear in the poem his cry
Memory punctures the closed-circuit of vision

Then as suddenly I was standing again, in the bottom
of a vast place, in a muck up to my knees, which I recognized
as silage, that I was at the bottom of a silo wch was the imaginative
shape of the Abyss of Indiana, an urn crossed my mind, Was this
the place I was to bury Gladys Eshleman?

walked a little, felt the wall Almost pitch black
a little light from somewhere.   mossy, crumbly.   fecund-
odor.   found a door More than one? shd I open
it? no handle, felt like pine
sealed in the silo-side. I turned around leaned against
it played with myself quickly got it hard
came &
the door gave, tumbled into a big room
Hadn't been noticed, so I crouched
& began to shit while I watched what was going on—
A movie was being shown, sounded like 8 mm.
a little home movie screen, title came on "Coatlicue"
like a classroom film, There was an indian woman with a broom
sweeping on aha! the desert—sad look in her face Now
a feather turning in sky falling She picks it up
hmmm that's a nice feather Think I'll take it home
Well I think I've seen this movie before so I looked around
Cldn't see the ceiling, a temple feeling, fire-smoke,
off to the side of the screen a bunch of men in little slave skirts
building something.   looked like
—then I saw the urn. They had an urn about 4 feet tall

2 feet wide, place it on a rock. written on the urn's side
in chalky-blue letters the word AURA—Some more men were
bringing something to it, were carrying (& I looked back to
the screen, then to them—the body of Coatlicue (but the myth
said Huitzilopochtli was born. I thought Coatlicue went free
But no it WAS Coatlicue's body they were carrying & was she
a mess. bloody, eyes out. they broke each of her arms, then
each of her legs & wedged her into AURA. A couple smoked
Then more men came in out of the silo-side, two carrying
something looked like a small wet sheet, they turtle-necked it
down over AURA, it looked like Coatlicue's flayed torso-skin
flat meatless tits hanging over the chalky letters, more men
coming in, all in those funny little skirts, some bearing long
quetzal feathers, one had an enormous pair of eagle-feet which
he placed before the urn. Another slave made two cigarette
burns in the insteps so it looked as if there were eyes in the insteps
Other slaves were now walking back & forth swinging smoking
braziers Hard to see, vomit-perfumy, They were fitting the eagle-feet
in under the dressed-urn, bundling the quetzal-feathers together
for legs, another slave carried in a huge fat dead rattlesnake,
the head & about 4 feet of length; they fitted this between the legs,
made it look as if it were dropping down out of the urn (like a tube
it struck me), head between eagle-feet, mouth open Now more slaves
with a mess of writhing little rattlers, these they arranged around
the bottom of the dressed-urn, a skirt More slaves Two with heavy
belt beaded alternately severed-hands ripped-out-hearts, draped
this "necklace" around the "shoulders" of the dressed-urn. Two
chunks of stone were fixed to the dressed-urn-shoulders,
severed rattler-heads, open-fanged, to the stones.   Generation
now nearly complete, with these rattler-forearm-outleaps,
was thatch-marked all over by several slaves with knives &
in each thatch-frame a peyote-bud was impressed; the slaves
moved back as if to admire their work.   Two shadowy forms lifted
out the urn-mouth, two big rattler heads, neck-bodies arching
out backwards while they faced inward—then closed like sliding
doors Kissed & Froze making A head which spoke

Huitzilopochtli's Vision

Out of your mother jealousy &
out of your mortal fear I will rise

many-armed, I will involute & grow
a self-contained dread so vulnerable
they will murder you &
worship you, I will teach

worship of your murder
through that most silent
thing stone, one little fear
watered daily thru ritual

is eighty-foot dolmen families
on knee tremble before
COATLICUE I will build, but will
not explain it is a code; instead

I will call woman mother, I will cut
down into her chest, sink a uterus
into her stomach thus mitigating
her solar fire, Woman is dirty

I will propose, because she is
bloody with my own idea of death.
I will thus recircuit
the cathedral of her vagina

into a slaughterhouse where

hungry foetuses exchange baton,
I will manufacture perfumes out of
her pulverized cathedral to dab
on her bloody gate, men will hate

this place yet they will be insanely
drawn to it, it will appear telluric &
magnetic, the cohesive madness of
society, against which men

will rush or debate or ponder off in
ashrams while others, given up,
will live in dark shacks & dream—
But not just dream, they too

will be busy, breaking their foetuses
in, lighting incense, girding
themselves for war, delighting
in symbolic acts, bayonet-lunge,

yet insisting these acts are not
symbolic, but *natural* to man.
And my victims, where are they?
O where are you, victims, cowering

in your dark stained Peruvian colors
inwrapped against the sunset in rose
& dirty crimson filthy black greasy
scarlet, O souls of women Why

do you hang back in the dark migraine
stables, why do you not organize
forth, come forth in your righteous
cause, come fully forth with your en-

cumbering uteri, your bothersome chest-
weights, come forth into my ax-work.
Until my generational throne is under-cut
by mutual vision of regeneration

women will wander out on the road at
night animal-souls before my beaming eyes,

for my car is not armor, but an alembic
in which a girl is gang-fucked,

dear old Plymouth dirty backseat,
dear beer-cans on the floor,
hair-grease-smudged window
you make her real, dear

crammed butt-tray, oil-smell
O empty front-seat, cracked
rear-view mirror, I glance &
see Tenochtitlan, contrary

of Indianapolis white wash,
a few yards away the Sons of the Sepik-
Delta smoke & piss &
joke, secretly they want to all

cram into her cunt together & there   —the projector
blow themselves apart,   was turned off.
To die in a paradise   The slaves
They can Foul—millions   started cleaning up
                          Pretty soon
arranged in stadium hypnotized   everything
by an oval where ants   had been
represent them—I will distort   removed
energy thus & raise a priesthood   except
                         the internal
to enforce & weekly meet in   structure
worship of mutilated human being   they'd
                          created

◇

I turned to Yorunomado now by me by my mother's bed—
I asked him to assimilate her body, that she be buried at
the center of my poetry; yet thru his eyes I saw her alive & fine,

around 50, sitting up in bed, with a pitcher of wine on her night-table,
She offered me wine from her bed, passing me a glass of it
as I left, looked into it, then ran! the bodies of numberless
dead, The burgundy, Yorunomado spoke, is loaded, a piece of
her placenta is stuck inside you.   Go back to the 59th line of
Huitzilopochtli's Vision—you are still desiring your mother,
thus I cannot assimilate her. The wine you take from her is afloat
with bees & flies, a brew, not a wine; a witch is still alive in
your mind. I flew back to the 59th line, found the Plymouth still
parked off 86th Street in the wood behind the golf-course, my
teen-age werefriends milling around while one by one we took
turns inside. I could not immediately understand why
this scene was stillborn in my mind. There must be a total
transformation, Yorunomado said—there is something
in your present life keeping this scene intact. As long as it
remains intact you will dream your mother is alive. As long
as she is alive I cannot receive her. I think I know where this leads,
I told him, why you have brought me again to the fall 1950
Indianapolis, for as I look at this Plymouth I see another car,
a Volkswagen Caryl & I rented a Sunday the spring of 1970,
drove to Harriman State Park & ate acid in the woods. Filled
with that poison I began to shout for Hollie, my "new" Marie,
the person I had chosen, after meeting Caryl, to love, but love
as self-torture. Before Caryl I was screaming for Hollie—
why are you not here? Up to that time I had responded to Caryl
only with my body; in my mind I still saw woman *femme fatal*
on one hand, housewife on the other. Caryl & I came back to
the car at dusk, parking lot filled with picnicking Puerto-Ricans.
Caryl had her camera, we started taking pictures of each other
over the back of the Volkswagen—once looking thru the lens
I saw Caryl—saw *Caryl*—not La Muerte nor a slave
but an exasperated sweating angry woman who was original!
She was not the image of a woman I had absorbed in my mind.
She was not superficial, she was fresh.
At that moment I felt my woman image divide, & fall
to the ground, a broken mask—yet in that very moment some-
thing in me refused to fully be with Caryl. I still had a piece

of need to hurt her, to be almost totally with her but not quite,
& thus the dream you Yorunomado picked up a moment ago
in this vision, the shadow moving a 50 year old mother
up in bed was my fantasy of the "beautiful Mokpo" I
could sneak off & fuck when I have no sexual need to. In the
composition of my mind that Mokpo stands for what of Indiana
still clings in me, the ritual tendency to destroy what I have
achieved, a composite that includes hurting who I most love,
projecting itself on a woman, seeing woman as "dark" opposed
to its own "light," making woman repository for the fuel it needs to
keep itself alive. Although I do not live with a statue of COATLICUE
this stone of religion is present. I now understand that the forces in
my own life I must oppose to keep on learning are not a woman.
Yorunomado's eyes were gleaming & he smiled at me, he
smiled at me like no one has ever smiled at me in my life;
he turned his magnificent black New Guinea headhunter head
toward the Plymouth where I beheld the most marvelous thing:
I had buried my mother. Niemonjima was present. The soft
chrysalis split a lovely golden slit, her slimy infant shape
weak at first clung to her husk, slowly an iris her wet
obsidian-tipped wings unfolded turquoise & gold, scarlet
& deep green, wavered then taking off a ripple running thru
the whole of creation lifting into the glowing azure sky over
the intense Okumura Garden where I stood amazed watching my
image separate from me, & by the persimmon where stretched
the pregnant red spider's web Caryl appeared, I love
you I cried, I love you with all my life, you are Caryl
& you are what counts. With you, in you, through you I explore
the ever-returning virginity, which is freshness most of all,
repeatable & repeatable, biological light in love with imaginative
light, your light to respond to my darkness, my light to respond
to your darkness. I love you as a man & as an imagination—
the sacrifice poetry demands is not abstinence nor a shedding
of personality but the sharing of one's penis or one's vagina
with the cornucopia of the ages while one takes in disembowelment
& emanates silk. The beloved who is true, the lover who is true,
do not disembowel each other, yet both love each other & are

thus open to the world which is obsidian to the virginal body of
love; yet the world is also a perceptive field ever-widening to
an awakened person. I love you is my happiness with you &
at the same time a vibration sent forth against the opacity
clogged in my body & mind against this flowing persimmon.

Yorunomado closed the left half of my book.
From this point on, he said,
your work leads on into the earth.

30 March–18 September, 1972, Sherman Oaks

II
1975–1986

THE GULL WALL (1975)

Gargoyles

The great cathedrals soar to the sky, they rush upward laden with saints, with porches, with all the geometrical abstractions we have come to associate with being tied again, or re-ligion, re-bound back into a barrow that mounts itself, lives in the form of a cross and still is earth-bound, pinned to the earth in the shape of the millions coming in to pray, to wager, to kneel, to consider, and this human presence is fumed into the very structure of the work, and it would consolidate and disappear, not only in stone but in the ghosts who stand by the door today collecting contribution, or pass back and forth in the cross's center, on earth, performing a ritual which involves more suffering, the worshippers' hands tied into oath and observance, that it does joy. Yet the life of all people who have carried stone as well as given themselves over to a vision of sin and redemption is figured in the sudden burstings from the stone towers, as if the repressed sex upon which all religion rests were to be present at the same time that it is choked. From the highest towers, traditional centers of the most holy, they fly, I should say sprout, the souls of the damned, they squeeze and press outward from the trunk of establishment, open-mouthed, their backs split, howling rainwater, or even with a drizzle their muzzles are adrip with the bulge pressed out to the point that religion and what will never be bound exist in league. They swarm like bees or angry barracudas out of the idea of building; often they are actually two figures, one mounted or carrying the other, a priest carrying a woman whose skirt hoisted reveals her buttocks which become the hole of the gargoyle, life drips from her anus, life drips and drips from the outpost of meaning—they are winged and they are snake, they are crouched and heavily clawed, they are variation, refusal of the cathedral itself to ever be complete, the life of cathedral, the meaning of edifice, that it burst, French-ticklered, bean-sprouted, from its own crown.

Sugar

With her hair set by her mother with water & sugar
what sweetness the bees tasted intoxicated by the little blonde
lost in high grass a few yards from the house
But what does a mother know about sweetness
A mother like hers could only dream of Shirley Temple
handing candy after candy so her little girl would love her
This is why Caryl Reiter loved sour pickles
My heart is aroused thinking of her solitary walk once each week
to the pickle store where she would taste a pickle still fresh
yet briny & sweet come dripping from the barrel one nickel &
savor it all the way home isolate childhood savoring its pickle
against the sweetness that is granulated & false
When Caryl Reiter was 12 she was an hour late home one night
her father locked her out she wandered to the corner & found a
     policeman
& told him my father locked me out. Will you help me get in?
She remembers her father kicked her down the hall after
I have no experience like this in my childhood
I drowsed years that Caryl Reiter was fighting
my little energies dreamed & strengthened while I
obeyed my hair cut & combed like my father's
a little Charlie MacCarthy a little wooden boy
with his heart dreaming & nourishing enormous spores
which would suddenly march forth 20 years later
virginal & green but with that peculiar hound-crashing-out-of-hell
     timing
by which a few leave the Midwest
& thus Caryl Reiter struggles for energy today to live
So much given to the blind & needy parents
who drink & drink pouring each week more honey into
the blonde well that erupts its fierce innocent angers
but loses like the frog that jumps up one step but falls back two each
     day

     ◇

A wink
from mother,
a big wink,
almost an elbow nudge
that she was getting an extra bag of sugar
Dilbert's Grocery Bensonhurst 1946
Rationed days, an extra bag of sugar free,
Caryl Reiter at her mother's side wondering
flirt? What is she doing, with this man? Who is not,
my father? I am 4
& walked out into the world is unreal
Things are not what they
& cried hysterically while her mother tugged her home
I watch Caryl Reiter's mother the wink
still on her rouged cheek pulling
What rot in that wink, or
what sweetness I should say,
a kiss on the grocer's cheek
so Caryl Reiter could be attacked by bees
A pretty little girl
so her mother could dream I am a good mother
the grocery-man's cock delicious & smelling of flowers
just for a wink pulling
Caryl Reiter down the street The weight of hysteria fled
22 years later I smoked a joint one afternoon & when I
got up from the bed my arms got up too, my body was lifting & light
I was back on that street, back in Dilbert's a wink traveling 22 years
suddenly pops The world is unreal
4 year old Caryl Reiter I am in love with you
I am rushing from the store having hidden behind the counter
You are right I cry,
I am a beautiful soft-eyed man who does not want your mother's kiss,
a soft llama-eyed man, my mellow pupils tinged rose & azure,
a llama pretending to be a man
who stops before you for you to admire & stroke,
you can stroke my neck my back you can kiss my pretty ear
I am the confirmation of your 4 year-old vision,
the confirmation to return to you, a fullness to plug

the gap you've just opened The world is unreal
You may kiss my furry belly
Fondle my amazing tail

The strawberries have been covered with sugar for the hundredth
    time
Caryl Reiter has finally thrown them at her mother
"I don't WANT any sugar on MY strawberries!"
"*I* didn't put any there!"
or as when Caryl Reiter's father constructed a safe to keep
his coins in her mother bored through the bottom so that each
carefully deposited coin fell into her greedy hole
Now it is the moment Caryl Reiter's father has come to collect
his savings, to feel the weight of his coin horde
Lo it is empty, not one fifty cent piece
Who could have bored through the bottom?
"ME? I didn't do it!"   sugar like steel
A wall of sugar
filled with safe holes
Now Caryl Reiter's mother has found a cigarette hole in her blouse
She is ironing & thinking of the grocer's blind and loving cock
Furiously she is ironing & thinking of Caryl Reiter
riding a stallion in impertinent triumph before her ironing eyes
but she is so full of sugar all direct accusation is frozen in her tongue
"I know you are smoking" insisted again & again, 3 days of hysteria
"and someone told me they saw you in the cemetery with some boys"
Caryl Reiter has grown wise she is pondering what is her mother
thinking yes I was in the cemetery with the boys but didn't do any-
    thing wrong
So what? And the ironing mother in the heat of her feel for tomb-
    stones
before inwardly hurt but smiling, kind of grinning kind of laughing
Caryl Reiter with a dog-collar ankle bracelet
Caryl Reiter in slingback black shoes
Caryl Reiter grown beyond pinafores in a stretchtop with a topless
    brassiere

nylons on Sunday because her Catholic friend wore them,
in leopard pants, lipstick painted over her lips,
Caryl Reiter winking at her mother
Caryl Reiter who is the friend of Gooik who used to hit & bite her
Caryl Reiter whose childhood I am in love with

Now I may return to Clayton's bedside
& smile at his cataracted eyes wet with dying,
the tie they have wrapped around his neck
& put a suit on him even though he lays in bed wet
with his stubbled chin his finger through the wetness in his eyes
smiling and going kitchikitchicoo tickling my shirt button
the ghost of kitchikitchicoo like a flame under the broth of
the childhood of Caryl Reiter

For the truth of it is I was the grocer
sweating in my uniform each day for the sight of Irene Reiter
desiring to give her a free bag of sugar & much more
& even touched by the little sweetheart at her side.

Bud Powell   *

Locked in his Paris bathroom so he wouldn't wander.
Sipping his lunch from the cat
saucer on the floor.
I see him curled there, nursing his litter,
his great swollen dugs,
his sleepy Buddha face
looks down through the lotus pond
sees the damned, astral miles below,
amongst them a little unmoving Clayton Jr.
placed by his mother on a bed of keys,
Powell compassionately extended his tongue,
licked my laid out senses

        ◇

                             it is unclear
what on his white factory smock
Clayton brought home from Kinghams,
             food
                spatters, at a remove,
notes, bloodspots,
                a cow hoisted
then slit, black men did
the dirtiest work of slaughter,
Clayton patrolled, with sliderule,
computing how many men to kill
how many head per hour,
the kill I was not shown
keeps firing

        ◇

    In the moonlight
I'd peek out my bedroom window in winter
as in spring a black man
seated at the buckeye,

his feet into its roots
he dips out, he plays,
he plays and dips out
blood from the buried cattlehead,
the guillotine sliderule,
where our severed
     heads   keep kissing

Portrait of Vincent Van Gogh   *

I will hold my hand in this fire
to speak to her, I will stay in
the fire of this world long enough to
speak to her, I will place myself in
the hands of my own Covering Cherub to
speak to her, for I am not seeking to
marry her, but to speak to her,
deep in a mine, in the wall
I drill through, my speech to her is
my art, I can
be bent, I can double back, I can as
the beggar be bent backward heel to nape
in sleep, in the mine as they chip at her,
strike dead speak from her, dead spirals
In the night the stars hang out in sinister places
they put their heads together, I take Death to ·
where their heads are together, where the mother is
lost in His washing her free, Her I must speak to,
for she is my Covering Cherub, my wall &
my boring through, my wall and
almond-tree branch, I will hold to
this fire for 10 years, my hand in her
a Biblical motion, churned
chair, churning candle on churning chair,
chair churning sky, in my room, in
what is dear, I place a candle on this bottom,
in the basement of maternal hold, I place it to blaze
cock up, where the stars hang out
sinister armchair, where the stars cock & claw,
where the claims churn, where my name
manure, my name Vincent is shared
peasant, mine, her ass hiked—but
the desire to split it open is
to split open the extent of the known world!
I have been where others claim to have seen,

I have been olives built Jerusalem blue mountains
poured back my love into this rec-writhe, this rec
tangular, this bone lay-mansion, I smolder
in the Rembrandt mansion of, where the fire I am in is
rouge, There is continuity, and there is this broken
rectangle, broken triangle, broken
single line—I will hold my hand in this fire
I will speak to her as I know the world is but a glimpse
of the wall of my tunnel, almond-tree branch for the baby,
but life, life itself! For me! Hiked ass prehistoric
entrance, I do not answer the door because I
know Artaud knocks, I want to go into that ass
and paint, I want to use her organs and paint her
insides, to take her organs and use her blood to paint
her goosepimply coils, almond-tree branch for the baby,
almond-tree branch for me, rose, hollyhocks, zinnias, peonies,
pansies, carnations, gladioli, sunflowers,
dahlias, red poppies, cineraria, delphinium, aster,
lilacs, daisies, anemones, I came out of her cunt
I want to return through her ass, my Covering Cherub
pecks about in the yard, the chicken I am
bothers around with nothing, I can only paint
8 or 9 hours a day, the thrust I make is my Covering,
Winged Seed, my own angelic ghost, my seed
haunting my desire O my people, all people to paint
for you! To literally remake the world into a universe of
lilacs, daisies, cineraria, aster I came out of your cunt
I want to return through your stem, what is dead in
me is my Covering Cherub, This is why I paint
aster, aster why do you cover me? Why am I trapped
in the visual box of you and me? That you are the bottom of
and I am the side, Being, trapped, cornered
in thought, and all those needies outside—
but her, her—why have I damned my life giving
woman's soul to almond-tree branch, why have I sought
her, why sought to speak only to her, Only
that the buttock church, this rest from the storm was

stalagmited with the iron that breaks through in spring
through the earth, this iron my body needs
aster, phylox, this hollyhock, I needed to eat her ass
and my anguished famished jaws only
painted what unrolls in the lagoon.

Portrait of Charlie Parker

I will not hold my hand in that
fire, I will grasp my hand in the octopus
of the black seed-core, I will become that poison and
that beak, I will tear in shreds the melody line that
I awoke with in my nest, I will drive my fury into the fabric
that is sensibility, which lives with my in my nest, I will tear apart my
own egg-brothers, egg-sisters, I will batten on
the droppings from my own arm,
I squeeze shit into my very life,
I batten on the horror I am hatching,
torn melody line of the white seamless
garment I was to wear, raised in my own blood robe I was told to
wear a black seamless garment,
my name is Bird, I drop shit on your face
you puke-faced white urinals,
you ancient places ringed with aura,
I tear the melody line to affirm my
inherited discontinuity and see in the whit aura
my own embalmed brother, Not in the sister—I piss in the sister—
I stick a piece of wood in the claw-hinge of my killing and
promenade across the bottom of the tank, waving my helpless claws
This is Sepik Mask This is a Maprik Housefront This is cock
harder than your fortified wall white man, I blow the shit I
got stuck in my throat & squeal through your plumber-headed cock
I crack your cock Central Park North,
I draw air back into the man I am, I seek conveyance I beg
          to be, on foot, I beg to be
     on foot / against
at sea, I beg to be on earth
I beg to be male and dark, I beg
          to be,
I see the Ulysses feasting-place
          spattered with suitors,
I feel the power as I see Ulysses string his bow,
in joy I bend my number 5 reed, we drive one
arrow through the blue ax barred passage,

Those who raped my people now cower against flame-lit walls,
This night-club is my barrow, my name is Bird,
I enter the arrow-flow, the walls fall away,
I am up on that limb where the tree is in place,
where my woman coils free, glory glory glory
I praise my people I lift the sky
I am your husband, my name is Bird
I shall be the first one to walk into our chapel.

At the Tomb of Vallejo

for José Rubia Barcia

I passed Soutine's rock and kept walking, until I came to your
oblong stone
speckled granite, in gold:

> *J'AI TANT NEIGE*

> *POUR QUE TU DORMES*

> *GEORGETTE*

and it would snow, in the cold late October air
there was this action, the first flakes falling on
how little death matters, for the arena
is the blowing snow over the grass, bright crystals on each
blade, the wet dissolving on your forehead,
what you face, beyond suicide, is the restlessness, the bobbing
watermark from snowing so much in her, from giving her the bread
in your jejunum when there was not bread for your mouth—
that you be at peace Georgette,
that I not excite your ovaries again,
to acknowledge only the baby spider and
build this shrine for it at the edge of its freezing web.
That the rock of Vallejo may be green,
may control and inspire the sand,
may be more alive than bread,
may tryst with bread, may go to the right and
the wrong saliva, digestible
yet eternal, flux the river rubs and yet cannot fix,
bobbing watermark in your angelic desire for her to be
at peace! To feel our neighbor in shirtsleeves, to hear him trickle
in the hotel room next to ours, to feel him buying clothes
and in that feeling to transform

the prehistoric width of the day we are
with him, two cells, a billion selves,
eels tangled in formation!

I sit down for a moment,
and instead of crossing out eels, instead of wondering why
they are not baby spiders, instead of rationally
measuring my body against your stone,
I let the whole wall move over me,
I let go of my bread and clothes,
of the locket named civilization,
the path that leads from a man-made boulevard
where in the gutter a woman is giving birth,
to a grave in a man-made park,
where in stone someone who loves us
has chipped and thus chained our name.
Outside of this path is the endless shrine art creates,
right there in the chestnuts, right there in J'AI
TANT NEIGE, words that whirl
mortal man, see how even when you
face stone you see only your vision raising
feeling for life, a wet forehead wetter than all
the snows, I keep this light on, César,
the surge is to keep snowing, to leave her
only a restless peace where in nothingness
another will place her body in vision,
and another will see me seeing the two of you
gold in grey stone, flesh on the cold in grey stone,
chestnut rustling through his reading having come here
on a spring day 3000 years from now, to this mountain
which was Paris, to this universe which used to be the earth,
to the enormous blue flowers waving by the entrance to
a human spider's shrine!

The meaning of art is this spider in red leather apron,
holding a lamb's leg in one pincer, a cleaver in one hand,
while the lamb plays by its side and the cleaver
grows in the membrane of the blue flower,

this spider will sing as a little fish with puppy fins
makes its way through the sunbeams of the universe,
it will not sing in our name,
it will chant in a language the lamb knows remembering
the inkwell its leg used to be tied to,
chanting how small, how grand, how transformation
was the key that turned open the bone
door to the tomb of Vallejo,
radical stone, radial name.

Leon Golub working on a painting *

a man (white, about 28, in a blue
denim suit) appeared below his ladder,
Can you tell me who lies in this work he
asked. Leon replied, To my left are American GIs
and South Vietnamese troops, they fire into
villagers fleeing their bombed
huts on the right. The man said,
Open up your place in the work,
let me take what I want, or I'll kill you.
He stood behind Golub on the ladder with a knife.
My youngest son is alone in my place
in the work, Leon thought, then he saw
the man's eyes and knew he would kill,
so he must open his place and take a chance the man
would only steal, would not kill him and
his youngest son; he slit the canvas, together they entered
an unprimed area where the boy was sleeping:
honey you have to get up, this man
won't hurt us if we do what he says.
The man bound and blindfolded both of them, made them lie down
near the firing GIs, Leon could hear shouts,
maneuverings in the jungle, Are you alright he would
ask the boy. What the man was doing
blended in with the GIs; the clamor went
on and on, finally both Leon and his son fell asleep.
They awoke still bound unable to see,
but they could get up, and not hearing anyone they
got to their feet, it was wet, soggy, bent over
heads almost between their knees they began to duckwalk,
struggled on for hours, heard no one, seemed to be
in a marsh. I can't go on can't we rest? the boy said.
But we won't find anyone to help us out here.
Out where? the boy asked, they had crossed
over to the right, they heard voices,
Vietnamese? Someone tugging at their ropes, pulled
off the blindfolds, a gang of tall burned men, bodies
skinned, the blood charred, caked

Cream? one asked, Leon and the boy were beckoned into a hut
at the table sitting in mock importance
the man who forced Leon into his place,
he was grinning, but not friendly, they were pushed by
the burned men further in, I want you to look at this map
the man said, he had spread it out, a piece of dirty cheesecloth
with marks, smudges, lines drawn through lines, We are here
(pressed his finger on an obscure point)—and they
are there (moved his finger a half inch away). Who
are you Leon asked. I am the General! the man shouted,
who commands both sides! He struck the table in two,
Leon turned, reached for his son but neither he
nor the burned men were there, he turned back to the General
reaching at him, crying Where's my son? Where you
said he was, the General held him off and kind of laughed,
Alone in your place in the work.
Come outside and I will show you where he leads.
What else could Golub do? The table and map were
trash on the hut floor, the General already
outside; Leon peered after him, it was night again, the burned
men had built a fire, the boy they had somehow gotten
into a large glass ball, which they had placed at the apex
of the flames, inside he seemed alright, there was room
for a little desk, as the flames licked the ball he seemed
intent only on his homework, or whatever it was he scribbled
away at, then he saw 20 yards away his father in great
concern, in anguish was staring at him,
                                        I'm ok he signaled,
because you have cared for me in your place
in the work; I am now placed outside, yet because of you
inside this new outside.
The burned men are to shed their crusts.
The unprimed place that I have left can accommodate the Devil.

Portrait of Francis Bacon

I will both
hold my hand in that fire
and not, the fire
of pigment where character

is an act of the brush,
Vincent how
innocently you sighted what
I see, a buxom

assed woman
vibrating with the earth
vibrating before a church,
Why is it there?

There for praise
it tells you, and you
who have felt desire know where
that heat is kept,

its safe, where what you
will not give is stored,
where you pull
back so the come

smarts and rears back
up into the anus,
pullback, Satan,
smarting anvil

where the pullback is
hammered into Sunday
goers, anal pouches
filled

the Buttock Church is
congregated, pews
stacked with non-human
beings who face in

hymn back to the back-
turned altar
behind which Pan
is a semen gleaming

the moment before it
hits that redhot anvil.
I see my model
seated crosslegged on

that bone between
anus and sex,
he has for his aura
the enormous

fire of Pan, King
Kong sized
but only the shadow,
inside the shadow

a man
on a bicycle
collapsing,
wobbling three

ways at once
inside his head
Mauthausen
mound of eyeglasses,

an attendant scoops
a shovelful, it's
garbage, into George
Dyer's lower body

my model
slips his aura
like a rotten snood,
leaves his platform

and walks over to
where I sit, hooked
on my own emission,
a man in tension,

ready to artificialize
everything.
We connect
against a canvas

stretched against
a concrete wall.
Rabid connection
in which I am penetrated

twisted on my own
cable, bled
and kissed,
in ecstasy and

bored, all at once.
Unable to burst
fully, the fight becomes
can I contain

a surreal grotesque,
can I make it stick
against the wind-
tunnel of our great

abstract age*!*
I know that bone
cave where Ulysses
lies face down in body

sludge, his arm
around his drunken
comrade Elpenor,
I have felt them crawled

by diamond-backed
maggots, and I have heard
the hags laugh
who crouch

about them, senile
and pregnant,
the grotesca who link
Rabelais Goya and Artaud.

I will hold my hand in that
fire as well as
another, I will watch
the other turn it, beyond

membrane, into a very
dear figure, the two burned
wings of impotence
and sensuality,

crunched in erection
a Swahili rises
from a European
chair, in the lavender

hood of his shaved
head he starts to cross
with a Mohawk
"they eat animate objects"

is fed into a white
computer at the far
corner of the same
world—Pan is not

dead his little hooves
kick out Krazy
Kat, Bumstead,
a Cubistic scimitar

in the guts
is part of my torsion
I sow
my nerves

in the photographic
corpse of George
Dyer, what sprouts
I set inside what were

my heart and
life lines, a flimsy
seppuku cage
from which our semen

like the Banners of
Heartlessness flies.
I watch the antagonistic
combustion, it

pulls at my creation like
taffy, which cooks
now on its own power.
George-sprouting-Francis.

Yet the force of
abstraction
would finally suck
it into a stripe,

I must anchor my deposit
against a magenta
wall—I fit in Germanic
halos which

leech my Frankenstein
but hold it
in place:
between the wall's

dilating hole and
Vincent's old flame, his cock
snarled rubberbands around
the femurs of my patient.

WHAT SHE MEANS (1978)

Eternity

I suddenly recall
two months ago thinking
if you die before I do
if I actually gave up my life
could I enter death
and bring you back,
and live with you again?
I saw you fallen and stooped
by you, said
Caryl, I desire to live only with you so much
I have entered death
to encourage you to live on with me.
and my vision tells me you
would be moved, and I would help
you up

we would go along a path for a while,
there would be no money nor mercy
nor even time, we would have to keep going, get
food, eat, make love, sleep, when we could

There is, in this life, something of
this form, I feel it in our plans,
in going to bed at a certain time, schedule,
and it is not the absence of these things,
it is something we will grasp
in this life, hold, in each, know
but know faintly, totally yet faintly

            how is that so? Totally
yet faintly? It is the hero, entwined
with the heroine, humble, believing in listening
to themselves, a giant form
minute, shadows of windmill staves turning
across grass

The Dragon Rat Tail

Where my hope, naïve
and controlled by a roteness
thought art might be
a single Japanese flower
deft in a bowl, my hope
to escape profusion,
a single flower, a red gleam,
one thing alone against
clay and wood—
     a poem began to grow
in the very room with
that wilting flower,
but it was an atmosphere of
a poem can be,
a poem is around here,
I took hold
between my cross-legged
legs of a string of rain,
it was to find something to pull
out, to put
into my mouth
an ancient story,
to find where
my tale began and pull
up, too physical
I knew, so physical
I would have to digest
the having of
a cock, gnaw
the archetype through,
the body
was good
but was attached
to an image I
could only sense, a rat
growing in the tatami,

I pulled
on a growing widening tail,
a construction worker
pulling an endless alligator out of a sewer,
but through the tatami itself,
hideously embarrassed by
the closeness of the thing,
whatever it was, to my
own organs, that I was pulling
myself inside out, that the poem
I sought was my own menstrual
lining, as if suddenly one day
I would have my inside
out on the tatami before me,
a kind of flayedness, a cape,
something in words, but words
hooked together an anguish or
covering, a quilt, as if
Indianapolis had been pulled off
and the rawness remained,
flickering off and on off my nerves,
jagged aura, some of it grey,
some of it blue, and under?
The rigidity pit
where Clayton and Gladys sweetly
wandered, looking up
in intense innocent
complicity with an image
I moved into, then out, then into in
their eyes, that is when Kelly cried:
"Find them in the grass!"
he meant find the mothering
fathering powers which are not
your mother, father, find
and connect to what they are
the ghosts of—
I glimpse the doppelganger
they as well as I

were involved with,
personal and cultural
shadow in diamond light
striding across a stage.
The scales increased—
a long green thing was
piano practice, apprentice work
took 16 years, diurnal,
inside the day the impossible
spine of saying all
that the day was
blocked me, I bent,
spine, over keys,
inside the machine a Christmas tree
glowed, and under it
puberty subincision,
I posed, by my dog, he
went off into the night,
I tried to reach a Japanese bar hostess
through my morality play,
my father pressed the flash-bulb,
Rilke fell out, compassionate,
distant, paper...
Rote screw hive
alive but compressed into "God"
Days of sitting on the bench
and trying to bank a word
free from the roar of never
that quietly gnawed, given
my hold to the tail
which had not grown,
which had grown enormous—
"the moment of desire" Blake calls it,
break the judge
in highchair, bring that Jack Horner
that "Good boy" satisfied with
his plum-dipped thumb into
the savage truth of this world:

people want love
only as a passive given,
they hate and actively
oppose love as an active opposition.
In Kyoto, faced with my dragon
rat tail I understood that the world
was adamant, that there is no way through it.
Gates, philosophies, arts, all "ways"
confronted orange mud running down
a twilit road on Sunday afternoon.
One way to get anything out: haul up
and sieve, engage the haul
make the rat tail big, dragon tail,
make the dragon tail bigger than Jung,
bigger than all ideas,
let it engorge the house,
split the tatami! Ride
it! Not the moon, not
the nostalgia for that other place,
but the funk that struck inside
on the way home from the public bath.
Not to remember or realize the bath.
Be in the bath. Deal
with this other thing, art does not have to
lip the natural, live the natural,
jack off on her fender if I have to but
live the natural and confront
this other thing, sieve out
the little performer,
break the piano bench I was to become
an alcoholic upon, "Blue Moon"
"White Christmas" a chain of command,
break the chain, open it up and discover
the seed chum she and he and all of them,
the whole atavistic octopus,
pumped in my wine cup, be
paranoiac, splay out, feel spiderlike
throughout the realm that paranoia

seeks to feel, understand the rigidity
pit is armor, something
I can get rid of,
yet it is bone, what
I stand in,
armorless armor,
my marrow, my
very scent, is
social, where I do not have to be,
where I am forever, as long as I
am alive, packed in with
who I am born with, alone or
brothered, essentially with the ghosts of
the fathering mothering powers I
can transform to aid me.
My mother's dead eyes float out
bald in raving love for me,
how she knew what she wanted me to be
so confused was she in what I should be,
under every fried egg, every Boy Scout knot,
under the Betty Grable butt allowed on my closet door,
under the ghost games under the bed Saturday afternoon,
under my being allowed
to dress up in her girdle and twirl
the family safe, was Liberace, the person
she hoped I would be, fully middleclass,
artistic, gay, fully in command, a hero
wrapped in a 146
pound floor-length black
mink cape lined with Austrian rhinestones,
a ghastly Virgil!
                        Confidence,
I pray, at 40, to lead this doppelganger out to pasture,
he cannot be done with,
I can only let him graze,
I am his shepherd, linked to
him Americanwise through Harlem,
through Chile, through Chad.

Still-Life, With Fraternity   *

For Ted Grieder

In dream, an enormous tree house, led up to by a ladder, a hive of
    sorts,
the distance to the ground below frightening.
In the top of the hive, bunk to bunk, the pledges and actives, like
    cakes
in an oven, all the same, or so we seem to me still, in the dreams
    going on
then, a "still-life" but even if stilled, still life. Below,
as if hundreds of feet below, there were actives awake working out
an earlier dream—the pledges were to be aroused from sleep,
driven down the ladder and beaten at the base of the tree,
the tree-house fraternity contracting and expanding,
at one moment it is the frail one I built 15 feet over the sidewalk next
    to 4705
and then it is a relative mansion, my "Grand Central Station" where
I talk with my mother and try to keep out of the dream
a certain maniacal presence. We are always at the bottom of a
    staircase
with simonized relatives slipping around us,
all oak, very wooden, warm at that base, a neurotic
launching pad, deep in-firing cyst poised in the limbs or floating
high in the air, from which a root of smoke dangles…

                                        I must descend
when they shout for me, as if I were ripped
from my Siamese twin.

Below Dunn's farm where the fratfire plays,
Jay Christy is screwing Bunny MacCrory,
several months later his car is out there alone,
I pull up, he wiggles out beer in hand, "Laura" is on the radio,
his girl-friend is sitting in the front seat in a wash basin
he found in the Phi Delt kitchen, her bottom
wet in abortioned ooze. Christy and I carry the basin behind his car,

look at it in my headlights, we can't tell if its all come out yet.
We might as well have been looking into a mirror
or have been two stone lawn cherubs holding up a bird bath—the
    focus
belonged to the brotherhood, we were searching for pieces of flesh.
All rites of passage, whether well or poorly conducted,
bend the individual soul into the will of the nation or tribe,
and mine is the ghost back of Phi Delta Theta
screwing Bunny back into the woodwork out of which at
17 years old she timidly put forth her sex.
Christy fixes his screwdriver into her slot,
he turns her back into matter,
tosses the screwdriver into the trunk and walks away.

What is virgin or just beginning to be experienced
is destroyed before it is fully there.
In ceremonies that pretended to carry us across
from being boys to being men the actual transition was from a pledge
trembling in bunny-footed p.j.s at a midnight "line-up"
to an active with a paddle pinned to a girl from "a good sorority,"
TV holding hands Saturday evening or when the weather was good
the fratfire at Dunn's farm with songs,
that maniacal presence where the pines began
as if our relative, Manson, wanted to join us, all bloody wanting
to be part of our evening.

Bunny MacCrory, split under the force of the bore
regardless how tentative it was,
now had an upper and a lower life,
now the tiny Phi Delt sword could be tucked
through her cashmere sweater nipping her bra
while her discarded lower parts cooked for us, the mammy in our
    basement,
or crouched behind the house in the bushes Sunday evening
willing to blow whoever found out she was there.

What remains can be seen Sunday after church and Sunday dinner,
the pledges are kind of grubby, they have no time to do their own
    laundry,
the actives are imperial, they pose against the limestone or
toss footballs while the girls who are under them
wait. There is no time in this moment, the utter outerness of
our lives translates itself out into our most inner problems;
we are not just kids wandering around in sport coats and ties,
we are our own aura. You can see in us at our edges supple brown
snake skin shoes. Christy favors a sable brown brass-buttoned blazer,
without any difficulty of transition we are models posed on phantom
    jets
for *Harper's Bazaar* 1965   "What America Does Best"
khaki wool tweed opening on a burst of orange.

Scorpion Hopscotch

Unexpectedly this morning I grasped
my orgasm and held it for a moment in my hands,
outwardly a crystal ball—yet as I looked
I penetrated my own reflection and glimpsed
its marvelous inner workings, death
was happy there, a gold fluid that streamed
through the crystal complexity of what I saw,
happy because without orgasm it was forced to
hammer at my back, as if I were death's door.
Around death's fluid were many tiny insects,
flies, spiders, even little grubs who seemed to be
nursing at the teats of what was passing through.
They gave death a furry quality, made it more solid feeling,
as if what I see of nature outside of orgasm was
nourished by invisible death—but it was not as if death
"lurked" in the act as Berdyaev and Bataille have said,
a scorpion to sting the lovers when they open that wide,
but flashed across what seemed a winning line, as if death
won a race then that otherwise had it pounding at my back,
and around the insects a feeling of mooing, a low animal
sound density that pressed against the crystal limits,
inhabiting them in a kind of roller-coaster rhythm,
an animal cushion, sharp, breathless and slow, between
the nursing insects and the sudden
reappearance of our bedroom.

The Green Apple Photo

The love in your eyes Caryl
you look at me
and against that looking—
that yearning—that being—
other art is pictures.
I have a Tantrik diagram,
a reproduction, with me,
which set next to
this photo of you is
a mechanical cartoon.
Yet until now I took it
as seriously as I "took"
your photo. You rain
on in me. What falls
is my own, you've
given everything,
you offered all and against
your photo only I
here can enable the rain
to continue falling.
Why do I want to cry
looking at you looking at a camera
with me in mind?
I want to offer you something
away from you. That I
have no need to offer you
with you—because
you never make me look
for my tears! I take too
much for granted in an
assumption that the Tantrik
postcard means something
that is any addition
to you. Away for a month.
Your utter accessibility,
your head tilted under green apples.

Your sweetness, sweetness,
your tart light
heartsown, your hair blown
sweetness. I pause
in the thought that
you offer yourself to me,
while I am here.

Frenstat, Czechoslovakia, 8 July 1976

Old Jewish Cemetery

Broken off teeth of the ground,
the jumble death is, a wrecked race,
entangled Paul Celan, twigs, dust, high walls
—the hurricane *has* passed through.
So overgrown I thought of the little woods next to 4705
looking at my body, the body of 12 year old Alice Jones,
that hot insect haze of looking for what in the body?
Tomb upon tomb, tilted, badgered,
half-submerged   (tram passing—soft Sunday roar),
the weight of the bottom of
these slabs, to hold them up
indecipherable, leaned against trees,
collapsed fences, a field of
collapsed fences, little ivied trees
(tram again passing, the stone my butt is on quivers).
 I'm at the most ill-kept end of the cemetery
—German and American tourist groups at the other.
Without order, the slabs in their collapsing geometry
completely realign *graveyard*.
A sea in which the dead are tolling.
Hard earth, perhaps some roots growing through skeletons.
Small white butterfly by.
The hurricane Vallejo spoke of in 1924
having shaken the hospital windows—from whence
did it come he asked, a patient in its midst.
This graveyard is why Celan killed himself.
All the school-boy order/ardor of death,
infinite chessboard where that certainty of the square,
of the plan—that there *is* a plan—here gone.
From the 15th to the 18th century planted.
First burial, the brochure says, a poet, 1439, Abigdor Karo.
How I have depended upon the school desk
alignment—the plates on the Thanksgiving table
the streets, their corners, my father turning right,
my first date, with Betty Hartman and me,
a neat box of space between us, in the back seat—

the order of that geometrical embarrassment,
of sun conjunct with moon,
the city set in the mind of man,
a jewel in the breath held wildness of the stone
around which I make my path, staggered.
Sanded by rain until only Hebrew script ghosts
glow in the gentle July sun.
The sun is not round.
The moon is not a Turkish blade.
The earth is neither round nor flat but fetus-shaped like
Ogotemmeli said—and this fetus flying in space
desiring union with a mother it has yet to conceive,
is also packed in dry dirt, struck, as by a bomb, by
the history-long climax of death—which is nowhere.
Unless I pick up more dirt, more trollops, trolleys, trolls,
the letters lean into each other, hold me up for support,
one slab like a crutch under its brother—or sister?
Dappled sunlight on a twiggy thing without leaves,
my height.

Prague, 18 July, 1976

At the Tomb of Abigdor Kara

The Second World War cracked the lid on time,
Pollock's pleistocene scrawls, delight
in his own handprint bloodied
repeat across the canvas wall

—Olson's reach
reaching for
nearly reached ice!
The earth so opened Olson

his shoulder
against paged tombs,
how far back could
he push Pound's wall?

Karo knows how far.
As much life as
was in his death,
the extent to which migraine trust

could be tapped alchemical
bone. A big door. Square and black,
jutting from transistorized ground.
Back through Rouffignac,

mammoth poet,
I know who you are,
myself to the extent I draw
the Sancere of your tart green

apple out of the spellbound fly-
clustered stucco of lights
under the bat-shaped
density of entrance!

Prague, 18 July 1976

Charles Bridge, Wednesday Morning

So I'll go sit under Christ,
across from the attending Marys—
above my head his blackened feet
and before me I can hear a toilet flush
as one of three kiss his still-born hand.
Tug horn. A gang of kids curious
   and mischievous about a street painter
   working a riverscape off to my right—
The stroll of morning
   under INRI—last evening
pressed my nose to cathedral glass
The magnificence inside! As opposed to
   Prague's present-day uncared for streets,
packed cathedral, maybe 500 singing
   under gold Baroque ikons, and I thought
they're in there because they're so unhappy,
Christianity a secondary phenomenon,
the embracing of multitudes rather than
   a single person. The Jesuits say:
"give me a boy until he is 7
and I'll answer for him the rest of his life."
Make a man unhappy and he will be
   comfortable, really, only on his knees
or with his knees on another kneeling person.

Amazing to watch the dark starlings
   lazy 8 the tower spires, a Gothic
weight, anchor of something light
   as breath, up we go, flame,
hang for a second, our selves against
   the double cross of our darker
     Self—then the air clears
     again, Christ an instant
       in the wind

unhappy man wants to rivet there
   eternally mortifying mortality.

Looks as if the riverscape artist has
   a sale. A group of Germans move by
   as if in a barge, glancing
   up at Christ then down at me,
   I think they think I'm drawing—

            Yoroshi desuka? One Japanese
man asks his dapper friend before
clicking the camera. It seems everyone
(but me) is around with a camera,
   they want Christ

with the river behind him *and*
   the "Castle" on the hill beyond.

The river a scaly black, slow, silver
   dull glitterings—black city
with bronze-green onion domes, a yowling
baby is wheeled by fast—

            no purity.   no paradise.

But happiness. What have I been trying
to say about happiness? That it is here,
a part of me, visible, along with
my awareness of so much unhappiness.

Say it is the egg in a kind of mix I feel
   daily, once mixed in
impossible to draw the egg out again,
or say it is the muscle that broke
   the chicken leg from its chicken
body when my father could not—

Note not men but 3 women
lament and kiss the dead Christ—
where are the men?
    they're disciples, or sons—
hanging back, the crowd, the blood
in the feet unconscious as it
    passes through the heart—

If they do love him why didn't they
wrench themselves away from his *father's* work,
offer him the life in their warm bodies—
and seeing each alone in the crowd
why didn't he go to them and say:
    woman,   animal,   sexual Being,
person,   wife.

    Each morning I kiss Caryl's
photo taken in Devonshire, her
tilted happy face under a bough
lowering a big green apple.
    River odor. Chilly wind.
The semen in the air!
The green appleness in the air!
The semen-green translucent density of the air!
The air crutch-filled, free,
    pregnant with stones—

An old man in sandals has just
    stepped in something. How he
        wants it off his heel.

Go ahead. Use your hand if you have to, and
smile as it stains, as it get in
    between flesh and
nail, you nailed man,
son of The Nailed Man, black
    African fetish man, man
        with nails sticking from every inch

of his body, barbed, wrapped in bales of it,
with cream-colored gloves dividing
multitudes into hell lines, death lines—

Both my legs asleep.

Must be time to go.

Prague, 21 July 1976

Archai

They came,
my mother and father
were pressed into their vaginal folds,
today they appear to be
the entrance to a cave called Niaux,
they are
what is behind the French Bank on Wilshire Boulevard,
their life
is mixed in what is most present, ephemeral,
and what is behind
being old, a child with several hundred layers of skin;
I can see through the black
parking-lot attendant reading Frank Yerby,
in the spine is Aimé Césaire
and if we could open Césaire full circle
would an animal clock face appear,
could my age be told
by the amount of centuries in my chimes,
by what has run down
through my eyes into my lees,
my wine cellar, where my mother and father
still alive grow until they are opened—
if as a wound they will evaporate,
if as Caryl a dream increases in my flesh,
the dream of a cave where the animal visions are
enchased in stone, the grandparents of stained
cathedral glass. They made the cave,
before them the earth
was compact, a looking-glass, unenterable.
They saw through their reflection,
they gnawed the dust mirror, slowly
they began to climb into their skeletons,
a warship, a place of worship, words
then were two feet thick

like the walls of the Staranova Synagogue in Prague,
windows were hesitant,
narrow and deep-set eyes,
rainbow was what they did,
what fell through them
bubbled on the floor—if there was a floor—
sometimes there was ocean
sometimes there was origin,
a dark red soundless glare,
orgasm was the morning hiked
and behind aurora's veil
the sprint of maggots felt like a splint,
something strong, thin, a kind of wince
that could be bound to pain,
levels of pain were compost
and they actually fucked where they sowed.
Death had not yet disappeared
so in its house they spent their afternoons,
its structure was sunset
wholly carnivorous, eating flora
as night's mouth closed, vaginal-anal,
virginal, fresh. I see them
at times in the double eyes of chance
or in the woodwork, or in flowers,
or in clouds, or in anything
that does not seem to intend seeing.
What did they do? They came,
with the most elaborate head-dresses,
their minds trailed behind them nearly
to the ground, their minds
were braided so they could braid
the manes of the powers, thunder
and lice, or open sore
and sor-row, the Noh
ghost hears them at times repeating
wot

his
sor
row.
But then rows away, a wave-man like us,
endless, prolegomenon.

Still-Life, With African Violets

The little pot of them in the Beverly
Hills flower shop window,
purple sable, sand, African
violence, a crazed very black
man shouting at the flower shop,
Africa pulled up to within feet of
Beverly Drive, he shouts from sand and luster, sweating,
but from the flower shop he just moves his mouth, he is dirty,
hysterical, he is waving a hoe, the clerks
glance at the window sometimes, a siren or
customer's nose presses against
the African violets on their mind,
nothing moves, begins to squirm
between the hoarse African and the neat lady clerk,
nothing finally starts to move, the air
so packed with everything the African has neglected to do,
the lady clerk looks down at
the straw in her soda, thinks of God, how silly, sucks
at the frothy bottom, the African rolls over on his mat,
the pain in his anus will hardly let him hoe. The night is not
death rich with the transformational mesh of sky and field,
but skinny with death, white goons in jeeps drip
from his brow, he picks up a handful of dust,
nostalgic gesture, the lady clerk is nostalgic gesture,
if they were both smeared on rock he
would be denser, she would be mucilage, a bird
would stay by his smear longer, nothing thinks
this is very funny, that part of my mind touched by nothing,
soft frayed earlaps of violets,
nothing surrounds them, crushes them when it throws a fit,
yet since all of us are in social time
I will not try to balance myself on nothing,
I will believe the enraged African is thicker
than the Beverly Hills lady clerk, in doing so I will betray
my own life a block south of Beverly Hills,

my physical body is here with the retail violet instead of with
the violet in the earth; I want him to smash the jeep goon,
but I better be willing to deal with the black man when he
kills the goons, especially when I saw one of their white hands,
just a second ago, come in the window and take hold of my left wrist,
I shook it off with a chill, a floral chill, the embroidery of a fangy
white African hand with purple veins touched my wrist to caution me
No way to take sides and to think at the same time,
you either allow both that black and that clerk to be in contradiction
or you pass into a thinness, your word must be
at least as thick with sand and sable, dry animal
tongue out, the terrified goon's neck cradled,
sliced, desperate lizard, fly trapped between screen and window,
say "African violet" and Pandora begins to twitch her goat feet,
the mutiny that tickles nothing begins to stir and then yawns before
your corrected feelings… So is the point to strengthen
the glass between us to the point that nothing feels pinched
and begins to abandon us? How? By a good deed? By sweating in our
imaginations? By breaking up the altar glass near the end
of our minds, where the religious explanations sit
attentive and foreveresque in blue uniforms with gunpowder braid?
How does an African with a hoe do that? He hits a tree, he
hits his kid, I mentalize a terrifying lode of world in Beverly Hills
African violets, but our acts are not the same, Oh yes they are
Pan squeaks from the molecule in which he is trapped, the
    atmosphere is
now so packed with nothing there is no real difference between a slap
and a wince of perception, an animal starts down a dusty glass path,
think of her as a tear running a flower shop window or as a disease
shaped like a cougar boiling with a craze for release,
you will only yoke this beast by traveling as a tear in these other
wills, you will need the protection a tear ball can give you,
a head, feeling the outpack of the air, striations of nothing like
    gossamer
red veins in the air, pull them down and that fancy white hand will
    again
clutch at your arm, lucky man, leave them be and the same force may

maggot your width, you are where repetition is parallel to itself,
clutch-clutch, meaning Animal why don't you get to where you are
    going,
you, animal, you, black cougar with lady clerk spectacles, you, fly
with paws, boiling to release nothing, to see the extent of the silage
in the depths of nothing, a compost or billions of howling beings?
You got wink of them at Hiroshima and you actually touched
your portion of their skin at Yunotsu, you sat in green mineral
water in which the hives of burning were as large as frogs, now
break in hell as well as heaven, see them in goosestep before your
    eyes,
fly which is a cougar suffering, eating its hoe behind the rich people's
flower shop, an inch behind your head, where you dwell with Sammy
Davis Jr., in the same porcelain cup poised on the descendingly
    atrocious
ant-hill-like living strata suckled by that meek mold, nothing.

Danse Macabre

The verse of Crane John Chamberlined,
crane chamber where shakoed English elves
salute the collapse of a 6 century-long tongue
rolled out turf of opalescent clams.
Could there be more fin rot
Pierre, off England, than in Biscayne Bay?
Crowbarred genes, a peach neon gleam in the pink
cauliflowers on white suckers' lips,
haute cuisine hues in oil slick drugstores,
porgies in Victorian ruffles bent
over pickax stew, susurrant surreal catasta
in the side of the bluegill, not merely its bones but
Theseus grappling with the Minotaur,
enter the double ax and immediately swerve right
then left to depart, but what are the two natures
that clash once the center is found?
The nature that is meander versus the nature that is centered,
transgression versus obedience,
solar orientation to the father pole
versus the animal lines looping and crossing, cut
into the intestinal walls of Les Combarelles,
I make our a salmon in stone a bison intersects
swerves that are still fresh gash, the sap
of the rock still luminescent, I imagine a mind
which did not see a tree as outreach of trunk
but, in its tumble walk on earth, as a corseted
mass of roots writhing at both ends—
now barbwire around Stonehenge, the monolith and her court
so corralled they begin to buck in imagination
a threshing-floor where Ariadne is clawing the hero's mind alive,
is she the offspring of the 14 foot cave bear
lurking in the maze of paleolithic night?
Like meeting Carcharodon—did they dance against Carcharodon?
The shark of the land and the swimming bear, early constellations,
certain catfish now snap their backbones while swimming,

Walter Kandrashoff observed black mullets   [*New Times,*
with tumors dangling off their body like grapes,   May 13, 1977]
performance on a susurreal catasta where the woman is
sawed in half, then the magician runs off,
his name is Bruckner, he has been ordered to
return to his organ, "a clam playing an accordion"
may be the image a clam's agony tremor now makes,
poetry twitches with this snapping in process,
snappers with tumors about their mouths from feeding at
sewage outlets, something suffers in me because
I don't fight pollution literally every day,
this is the Rabelais kick back, the feast now looks like Japanese
plastic display food except it is polychlorinated biphenyls
mixing with ocean, I might as well be 11 year old Rimbaud
pouring over an octopus, the two hand in tentacle
up childhood's road, sentimental cigar-box picture
trudging into the sunset, that same octopus
exploding in the buttocks of Bellmer wraiths,
to hold in mind the fresh paleolithic salmon and
the fin rotted pin fish fills me with elastic venom,
I still see the elevator in Charlie Myers Department Store
on Washington off Meridian, Eichmann is riding in a crystal
Aztec skull from floor to floor, from strata to strata,
through the middens, my father insisted
on keeping his hat on regardless of what happened
in the floor lamp department of that path
in My Lai Soutine saw turn into a raw bentipede,
the earth shakes loose wounds to show its pompano
surface,
          the postman rings, my monthly Donald Duck,
wrapped in a menstrual fishrag, interrupts my Danse Macabre.

Canso

This July, how pleased I am, and bereaved,
how multitudinous the flares, the ires and air that
match me, that ignite and
extinguish the shifting hearth
I hold to, alone from you,

a gentle rabbit through whom lightning passed,
how I love you through, and how,
as you heal, I study the model you gave me,
when we met, decent beauty
where the pearl is in the oyster lips,

not separable, you are sore,
but you walk, more upright each day,
and I rejoice, making use of the spirit of
Marcabru, Vidal, those 12th century sweethearts,
those throat stones of our vers, homage to those

one-tracked singers, who drove admiration and
obsession for love through, our first caterpillars,
the first eaters whose leaves we have council,
soon Blackburn's complete *Proensa* will appear,
leaf, translation and my Caryl

bundled in July, a bouquet, how glad to adorn
her room and spirit, mist and shaper of
this home, how strange to think of her
in canso, how marvelous, to hear
the strains of adoration intact, so near

in distance, my love for her will never
debrim its well, at least as long as I rage or
range, is it, and give? And take from the garden,
the eternity, which is our portion, and not
some uncomposed other, I have been blessed

finding myself in alignment with her measure.
Which is heaven, sure, here, the uncoupled garden
wherein Eve and Adam recoup the serpent pliancy
before the fang, an ancient hardness, acted in
our minds to reject the gratitude of

someone with his or her beloved. How I yearn for you,
having not embraced you during your convalescence.
And how delicious it is to sit by the fidelity stone,
and feel polished, awful, clear, without reward,
and know that stone, in haircloth,

while surrounded by such corpulent timber.
Those troubadours, what ax spun below their grind?
Was this the Pleistocene condition,
to feel the lark of axcension, as
the slipknot of the word curled and stroked itself?

No, I am not angry at the doctor, his pulling
you open, I have to heal , and burn off about you,
not sick myself. Homage to those who yearned
before, who, were they here, would try
to drink me under once they saw and heard

your voice, which I hear, as you offer me, your thought,
about our workings, something obscure passes and then you,
asleep now, healing, become such gold again—
has Paul visited me tonight? Welcome, Paul,
if you are here, your voice in these lines,

vidas and razos is the parent-power, I happily share,
oak-sense, burrow-meat, my god Paul
are you here? Not as Sorrentino's remembered drunk
but as clos, clime, cilicious cleaver, ah
you fade, you do not want anyone to be put down.

Caryl, you are home, how delicate
is the tilt of hearth, you are not muse or lady
yet I adore you in this sense
because I am turning the troubadour condition
backward and forward, like bending a clock handwise,

and handwise distilling the metal self,
spreading the hands all over the face of
the terms that occur in poetry, this oldest
historical shape—recognition and desire—
peals my gladness to be with you, again.

HADES IN MANGANESE (1981)

The Lich Gate   *

Waiting, I rest in the waiting gate.
Does it want to pass my death on,
or to let my dying pass into the poem?
Here I watch the windshield redden
the red of my mother's red Penney coat,
the eve of Wallace Berman's fiftieth birthday
drunk truck driver smashed Toyota,
a roaring red hole, a rose in the whirlpool
placed on the ledge of a bell-less shrine.
My cement sits propped against the post.
To live is to block the way and
to move over at the same time, to hang
from the bell-less hook, a tapeworm in the packed
organ air, the air resonant with fifes, with mourners
filing by the bier resting in my hands,
my memory coffer in which an acquaintance is found.
Memory is acquaintance. Memory is not a friend.
The closer I come to what happened,
the less I know it, the more I see beyond the portable
gate in which I stand—I, clapper, never free,
will bang if the bell rope is pulled.
Pull me, Gladys and Wallace say to my bell, and you
will pass through, the you of I, your
pendulum motion, what weights you,
the hornet-nest-shaped gourd of your death,
your scrotal lavender, your red glass crackling
with fire embedded mirror. In vermillion and black
the clergyman arrives. At last
something can be done about
this weighted box. It is the dead who come forth to
pull it on. I do nothing here.
When I think I do, it is the you-hordes
leaning over my sleep with needle-shaped
fingers without pause they pat

my still silhouette which shyly moves.
The lich gate looks like it might collapse.
Without a frame in which to wait,
my ghoul would spread. Bier in lich,
Hades' shape, his sonnet prism reflecting
the nearby churchyard, the outer hominid limit,
a field of rippling meat. I have come here
to bleed this gate, to make my language fray
into the invisibility teeming against
the Mayan Ball Court of the Dead,
where I see myself struggling intently,
flux of impact, the hard
rubber ball bouncing against the stone hoop.

Frida Kahlo's Release *

Where I come from
is the accident's business…

exactly, how it made
thirty-five bone grafts
out of my impaled investment.
My dear father is here, not
off photographing monuments,
which he did so well,
in spite of epilepsy,
he took some
of the terror when the streetcar
created me. How those of us,
determined by one thing,
come forth
is no less complex
than you who are multifoliate.

My face unpacks
the corner of Cautemozin and Tlalpan highway,
"a simple bonze
worshipping the Eternal Buddha,"
van Gogh's words, that other
dear epileptic, whom I took to bed
in honor of my father
I let both repose me—
I lead with my right cheek
thus profiling the left.
For a moment, I was seated
straight up in Vincent's chair,
and because the light behind me and
my body were infested
with incombustible sulphur,
I am sister to a double putrifaction.

We who are singly determine
we too dream toward paradise
even though our outpour is contractive,
"one dimensional" you say,
"she only paints one thing,"
you, do you paint anything? And if
you do, is your ease
hard enough to skate? And if it is,
do the figure eights of your admirers ever
come to more than arabesqued return?

My face is rubbed
back into the shaft of human
bluntness. Its point
is to tamp seed
into eroded furrows of pain,
to look back at this life to say
exactly what the soul looks like,
exactly what life looks like,
exactly, what death!

And I garnish,
fulminating with arachnoid thread.
What I collar and webdress
weights an exterior out and out,
worn Coatlicue rememberings,
scabbed twistings in the flannel of rock,
I was so handled,
such a sugared skull,
I lived through carnivals
of my own organs, a cornucopia of processed fowl.

The others were off rutting in a firework haze.
I was lobstered in my chair shell,
balancing my vision on the spinal
crockery strewn about me,
shards of an exhumed prayer.

I drew paradise up close about my shoulders,
I gave monkeys my shoulders as well as my breasts,
I let them look through your eyes to Breughel
where Flemish scapes fade back to Job
under a spreading oak, the Adamic Job,
amphibious, caressing his progeny
(As Diego lowered, segment by segment
upon me, khaki and emerald
Behemoth mottlings dressed my injury).

I know the dry riverbed of illness
where orgasm's rachitic child
crawls in place birthing
litters of female-headed moths buffeted by male-headed flames.
Would I be willing to allow both
equally to decompose,
equally to become androgynous,
would I be willing to allow my taper to become ant-hill,
my identity a sticky mass?
To no longer attend those mystical
pariahs, my sexual ties?

Yes, for parthenogenetically,
out of the emptiness right under my heart,
I threw up a collapsed
tent rising wet brown monkey with my face!
Out of the cave of inner nurture,
where animal conception could have been,
I connected my muzzle
beam to my snout post.
Gamy iodine on a silver plate,
I transformed the hospital linen
into more than a daguerreotype of paradise.

Pray no more for me, Mother of Unending Lightning—
illuminate the bleeding pulqueria nips
where gaiety, slaughter equidistant,
shishkabobs the sun

through a cellular catacomb of moons in
the quilted night sky pulsing
with El Greco bellows. Under the Mass
are the vast lamb wafers in the Mexican kiln
slid in at 4 a.m. on Christ-crusted rays.

I am fused to the inability to
reproduce what does determine me
with its unborn baby hand
which I finally learned to wear as earring in
the Galapagos Trench pressure
outside within what our species has lived.

Turnstiles

Why write at all caves in,
microscopic men in concrete cold,
statues, pillars, risen
pistons from the underworld.

The dead, leavened, bleed
from the poet's body, eidola.

To sift the world is to pan
invisibles for their Hadic visibilities,
Hermic goldenrod, wraps of nature,
hollows from which elk still fly
and Hart Crane entrails us.

◇

Hello to an idea: that as one's mind
focuses on the hidden
the visible becomes more poignant,
creased with its own spectral bloom,
its fly-blown manger,
its miraculous Noël, a fete of cold
where language, alone,
finds its way, word
savior sounded sorrow—

at the same moment
there was only this stretch of lawn,
an oak-backed corner of the Luxembourg.

I could not at first tell why cider
and swan appeared in my staring at
the lawn's concavity—it was with cave,
pregnant with collapse,
the underground was giving way.

The sparrow bouncing across the frozen blades
was a sparrow-shaped hole
zigzagging the shade, dark dark dark

dark dark dark

then it stopped, a sparrow again.

The dead man packed in meaning
Must be the word otoko, hombre, homme.
Of these words one's own father
is the stone, the precious
dull eye one fears may roll from
their ring, the spot in one's mind always
peered about, during the day.
The enormous father is no father at all
but the outline of an invisible animal,
a yearning on stone.

The animal father of humanity
a dog now heeled
by a huge hairless infant,
the Fall turnstiles, a windmill
interior throwing up and
throwing down, a many-meaninged
white in shadow, the invisible
tar of whiteness, a white man
with a squirming existence in his arms.

Behind the veil of Isis, the butchers work.
Bright orange spotlights overhead lend
surgical verticality to their pry and slice.
Behind her strip of serpent mind, fingers
probe the muscular pyramidic
tomb of animal emergence.

These outlines are not reflections of
the day, these crude processual marks
are not the consequence of, nor the impetus to, hunting.
They are figures wholly scored without their selves,
griffonage of Hades, anatomies of dreadful
hind confusion, anal sniffings skewered,
killing and rekilling image to see if an act
will go away, gravity suspensions,
paw raise of the first griffition.

Hermes Butts In

He took the word "order" and let it go,
its friend, he strolled with the ripples of
its sounds and signs, ordure
he cried to the whirl of unrevealed
meanings laid out in the sun to dry.
His ardor was for a blackness alive with gleet
to sow in, to row a rock boat in a rock sea
making swells in the language, forgetting
the traveling, letting the erections in
direction speak spikes, be spores of
adders, get lost, be found by grappa-kegged cani,
roll in the snow of loneliness in adoration to
renewal, picking the staples from his lair,
being the lair here, feeling the red
in Dadd's old-fashioned root cheer, the murder
in the park, this too, with its undoable love,
is seated in the ark of sound, sound
chained to chound, unknown slave
at odds with its row toward liberty,
a mixed versus, the beginning of a web always
in warp, order, the warp in order, to begin a verb
he volumned her, she fictioned him, they
vertabraed each other to receive the Order of
Chrysanthemum, Yokohama, 1877, it floated
in their sake cup beside their bamboo Zero,
some ark, some coupling of a flower with death
gave us Narcissus, nah—gave us a mattress
hived with hanged-men lit alleys,
the edges of life swarming
with mythic ticks, we went underground
to inhabit enormous rock spoons, to ladle
away the climate of nothing, O lingam of sweet Raoul
Hausmann, you were stoned for displaying
your oak-leafed tongue, O sweet sweet leave,

the passage is sound, a yowling lore kittyhawks
the who I am alley, and of
the caterwaul I tomato seaward—Hermes butts in
with Catullus butting Zukofsky to clang
these horseshoe organs, a Chinese telegraphic
looped anagram of the language manger, here Oos is born
here Om flickers and weathers the King-Hadied
stars that droop with Lorca's sisterploys,
dear unframed minds of poets each
clutching their pieces of hemispheric
erection with its crocodile basis, the fear of
drying verb, of doors whose nouns will not turn,
of wee wee tethered kneenuts, alleyoops of traceyfire,
of nail notwiches mouthed by Gertrude, of garbage.
The explosion then is chestways, let me think
in Hades. No, you cannot barter. Let me breathe?
Ah these catering badgers slipping off my coat
are Tanuki! The hung sake porter, the infinite credit
poker card peeler of nuptial asp-held pillows.
The implosion of garbage is a lopped event, electric
to the orm potential of leakage—let's count Hadic shapes
and forget that Hades is hidden, thus let's
count is oink and maybe, rank the tit with
the pores of Lulu spill, worm-fashion the word
assembles and desees its aortaed wimp, the last
tether of meaning, the bright burgher word,
is munched by Whimpy in the gases of dream where hover
levers of the tinker-drop nights we put the rock together.

Master Hanus to His Blindness   *

Inside Staranova Synagogue,
deeply recessed stained glass,
such tender colors, pastel pinks, greens,
hammocked with cobwebs,
the slump in Czech character draped
by the Soviet net, the impenetrable dusk
our headlights could not shine through,
coal mine dusk. Borinage ghost of van Gogh,
a grimed religious body on straw
trying to worship its spirit up.

Imagine a living coal mine veined
across the land, streets finely
fissured with soot, a net become membrane,
a marbelization of the spirit
to which each particle of the burned
contributes. One says: the Soviet net,
then one smells and tastes the net!
A waiter explains why the menu's
suprème de volaille was, served,
chopped Chinese chicken: "Our people know
this is suprème de volaille."
Under the net, in ways hidden to me,
what *do* they know? Has the truth
in the life line marbleized lies?

Stunned before the vagueness of the sinister,
one's mind seeks out the physical world,
as if the mallards meandering the greasy Vltava
outside the botel porthole
has something to do with better.

"Don't start feeling sorry for a Czech,"
Milan cautioned, "or you'll never stop."

◇

It is as if to think on Czechoslovakia
is to extend the soot, to describe
sensations, to participate in
a totalitarianism of imagination
which is description, the literal
ruling out the shades of place.
But if some facts are not given,
how can Master Hanus' address to his blindness
be understood? If the reader does not know
Hanus' beautiful astrological clock, know
that Hanus was blinded by Prague people
so that he could never duplicate the clock,
how could Hanus' words, spoken to me
in a coffee-shop, after I had seen the clock,
be understood?

Poets in Czechoslovakia are deprived of expressing
their pain, are made to lie to publish.
Where does the pain go that they are not expressing?
In the same way that I cannot forgive
the Nazis because I was not in their camps,
I cannot know the pain of deprived expression.
I can embrace Jan and Milan and feel
the extent to which the bow has been drawn
and sense the filings in the soot
collecting along the unsent arrow shaft.
I know another kind of pain,
the anxiety that comes from knowing anything
can be said, that cutting into is merely shaving,
the poet as a kind of barber,
sanding the druidic off the giant,
who considers who is to live in Viet-X.
You cannot speak versus
you can say anything and it does not matter.
What is not permitted

gnaws at the ears of those
through whom the able-to-speak
passes without effect.

Does the ineffable lie between?
Palm on a tree crotch by the ocean
Rilke felt the other side of nature
as a quiet, steeling bliss.
The other side of nature…
Fear introjected until the mind gags.
Shadow streets cheered
by eyes cowled with *I suffer like you…*

"For making time beautiful, I have been
pressed to time, toll
of the maggots stretching in my sockets.
By the ledge of the Vltava,
the heels of my palms press in stars,
chubby star worms unable to display
their energies along these poplar-lined banks.
I made a harp of time, and hang
from its strings which they drew
through my eyes, a stilled pendulum
against the other side of human nature."

At the combined press of Rilke's and Hanus' palms,
something moves bliss to terror,
cancelling both, a kind of blister
in which a man in a Tusex store is trying to buy
his child something he does not need
with foreign money he cannot have,
a fistless man in a room without windows.

Equal Time

Somehow it seems wrong,
a minute on Vietnam refugees
at sea, starving, not allowed to
dock, followed by a minute
on a new world's record in cherry
pit spitting, wrong because
the pit record trivializes a human
plight—so, should we dwell
on an imagined deck, imagined
cries? Somehow the dwelling itself
seems wrong, not only being here
but dwelling on what thought does
not alter. Or on what thought only
raises as thought, say my presenting
suffering to you as language
instead of handing you an actual
refugee. The baby wild hare
my son and I found had
abscessed legs, so we set it back
in its tall grass. Its tremble
brings the refugees closer, its being
alone, frightened, defenseless,
might enter the champion
cherry pit spitter's mind as
he dreams in a structure that includes
an altered sense of language
that must include the desert
mountains this morning not as part
of the news but of the evolving net
writing poetry throws out,
wanting to include, hesitant to
look back, knowing violence and
the moral impossibility of balancing
the refugees, the pit champ and the hare—
or is the poem to fictionalize such
a balance, is it to hang each with a counterbalancing

weight so that, clearly unequal, they
float over to an immense ear, an Ithacan
grotto, as the magical things upon which
the homecome wanderer rests his head?
It is too easy in a world that refuses dockage
to refugees to play on the spit out pit,
to allow the Odysseus of one's imagination
to rest for more than a moment on
an archetypal pillow in which hare,
champ and refugee are bees, producing
a distinct but unified Mass, an eatable
hosea, a surge toward a drooping prophesied head
from which flows a common honey
—tu viens, chéri? This structure
must include a sweetness in bed
as well as the mascara in the coffin-
deep rue St.-Denis doorway where the empty
champ touches the abscessed refugee,
where he mounts her in the hold of
a dingy, stranded before a lighthouse coyote.

For Aimé Césaire

Spend language, then, as the nouveau rich spend money
invest the air with breath newly gained each moment
hoard only in the poem, be the reader-miser, a new kind of snake
coiled in the coin-flown beggar palm, be political, give it all away,
ones merkin, be naked to the Africa of the image mine in which
biology is in a tug-of-war with deboned language in a tug-of-war
        with
Auschwitz in a tug-of-war with the immense demand now to meet
        the complex
actual day across the face of which Idi Amin is raining
the poem cannot wipe off the blood
but blood cannot wipe out the poem
black caterpillar
in its mourning-leaves, in cortege through the trunk of
        the highway of
history in a hug-of-war with our inclusion in
the shrapnel-elite garden of Eden.

Cimmeria

for Eliot Weinberger

One must have a mind of stone
to find lineage in cave scrapes meandering,
and to have been unuprooted,

for a long time, to express the ligament
stalagmitic to Auschwitz,
Siamese mitosis, twins who want to lick

the eyes of the dark, bereft of everything
but the silt in the deepest
gouge, one quarter of an inch, Cimmeria,

"covered with close-webbed mist,
unpierced ever with glitter of suns rays,"
where the goat-bodied Chimaera, the last

Atlanteans, lived, before the fangs of Hades
meshed with the fangs of earth. And now,
beyond? Abysses upon abysses of ice

in which fishbone-like groups of humans
are toiling at 15,000 BC, roughly
the midpoint in the history of image,

the hitching-post of the sun for who is
with cave, soon to bear an emptiness
that will open out and out against

the steel of this hour in which all
seems present, nothing satisfactory,
Saturn's factory boils down in the harpyless

churn where I, the anchor, is dropped.

The Death of Bill Evans   *

Three inch caramel-colored field slug
on its back, vibrating
by the scraps of a big *Amanita Muscaria.*

It has eaten more than its size
and now its true size in visionary trance
makes me sad of my size—

I can never eat enough of a higher order
to trick the interior leper to the door,
banish him—but what would remain if it were to become pure?

Can't see the wound for the scars,
a small boy composed of scabs is staring into
the corner of his anatomy—where walls and floor end
he figures he ends, so he wears his end
like glasses before his eyes,
beckoned into the snow he will be beaten
by children he thought were his friends,
the implication of his hurt is so dark
it will scab over to be rescabbed the next time,
and he will grow not by an internal urge to mature
but by scabbings until, grown big, he will be the size of an adult
and his face will look like a pebbly gourd.
He will stay inside the little house I have built for him, in which
       to stand he must stoop.

        The death of Bill Evans
makes me ask: what tortured him so?
Why did a man capable of astonishingly beautiful piano playing
feed his leper hero wine!
Or is the leper an excuse to modulate suffering just enough to keep
one's warmth and danger at exactly the right odds?

Eat Amanita-filled slug, I hear my death angel say,
put into yourself living poison in order to know the taste of a wound
that is bottomless, thus pure, and because pure, receptive to
     infection,
once infected, open to purity, endlessly draining both,
a wound in which you live like a slob and like a king,
in which you hurt yourself because you really don't care,
in which you care so much that you can't always keep caring,
so you say Fuck it
and the gourd-faced leper, misinterpreting his rot
for Dionysian exuberance, seems to drink
or makes a certain sucking motion with the mouth area of his head.

Fracture

The crutch you hand to another
is a furious indescribable beast,
tectiform of your own shape as Eve staggers

out of Eden, the vile legacy in hand,
wandering the dust, offering to whoever
passes by a rotting piece of it, one peso,

by a Mexican roadside, her palm outstretched—
an open heart ceremony announcing
that all dark, all light, is the sawing

of being on being, a circular coring,
a ceremony lit by tapers made of entire
kingdoms. Earth, pieta. And as the dark

is serrated by the light you will start to hear,
as if at Gargas, the chalky cries of
hands, mutilated negatives, clouds of mouths

rising up the walls, virgin moths
mourning over caterpillars they have gathered
into their wings, crying the oldest cry,

that earth is responsible for our deaths,
that if we die collectively
we will take the earth with us *if we can*—

who does not hear our cries
seeks to contain us in that American cottage
where a nameless stand-in coils about

the solitary fang of a Snow White dead at 27.
Please let our howls, so elastic with water,
become that still lake most men abhor,

out of which Excalibur rises in the grip
of a drowned living Harlow whose wavering
stench of generation is holocaust to

all who seek to destroy their need
for that gleaming nipple below whose face
enwound with coral snakes is a squid haze of stars.

Tomb of Donald Duck

for Leon Golub

I. *Apparition of the Duck*

O my white, white father, you were the bell
dong clapper and tower of a construction arisen
from the "Aztecland" of an Indian's hump burst
like a boil into the savage clanging he must wear
like a headdress of fruit

and because I too am white, does my word xerox
its tongue to become
a pool of blood and green oil
out of which a dead ermine is lifted
and rung out in the sky over Beverly Hills?

Tumblers of a safe in this sky
from which drip peelings of a billion comics,
the feathers from your sexless bottom Uncle Donald
drift south to
children who run to the potless source of this rainbow sortilege,
a male parthenogenesis sprung from
an Olmec-sized Disney head

(my speech on behalf of the wretched
is screened by my North American whiteness,
glass enclosure in which an actor
wrings from his hands special effects
which need only be wound up to be heard again)

No change no growth no death no past
no animals
with fake animals for pets
the body a highway of zippers smooth metal interlockings

What is in the Junior Woodchuck Manual of your tomb, Donald?
A needle slipped into a child reader's fantasy
injecting adult anxieties
into his neotony.

    II. *Toddler Under Glass*

There was no time until the first word sirloin was sliced
this sirloin was dite (light)
chur (picture) cock (clock)
and the speaking? Two dis-
combobulated rug cutters, speech
crossing and crossbreeding not
as in Surrealism but as in paleojitterbug
where speaking is by extension midden
by extension mam-a
growth by apposition
"the deposition of formative material in successive
layers" wa-wa (water) chup-chup (bird)
O yellow po-ca dicka-da of an owl yet to be conceived
even before the egg
I've been betrayed by the earliest star
and by the horsies on my pillowcase
by pillbox mother by pillbox father
fortifying themselves as words begin to form
whose kisses are firing
and to fire is to leave a rapture that is sheer jingle bells
"What don't you do anymore?"
within days of being shown the Bible, specifically Don't
Grunt Panties, Chapter 4, paragraph 34,
the wedding of Donald and Daisy, or
the collapse of Isaiah, the rubber auto Isaiah from Elkhart—
outer darkness suddenly filled with held back erections
all aimed at 2035 North Meridian Street
going off as I bounce on your lap
happier to be here than anyplace else in the world
Whose world Popeye wonders,

Boon-man's? And it is true,
I screwed NO into the God photographer's lens
so that, snapped, I would not reproduce my dad-da,
knead his Smokey Stover,
enfoo dern sech weather, O mutter of us all
didn't I ever tell you how it was to be two?

TODDLER UNDER GLASS

cooked but uncarved, under mam-a's firm hand
No one was going to serve *her* dream
I bunched up on my suddenly confined crawling grounds
while relatives' faces fun-housed thanksgivingly in the glass
and her face fun-housed in my own
my very first mask on which ca-caw (Santa Claus) crawled
a language mask heh-heh (for Sonny)
Bok *old* mamma, tak-a *new* mamma
bite of wa-wa words
bok windmill sound child, bunched on the social platter
frightened of losing my wow-wow my ga-ga
a baby mammoth in the peekaboo
I see you snow mounting from below.

III. *The Severing*

In essence we do not want to be outside

yet the only way back in is through death
and the beast was the god of death
putrifying about man
not yet man but something
so cold for so long, so cold
that too much of his life was now in his eyes,
his sex had so contracted
from the misery of copulating in ice
that is expanded, a bulb in his head
sending out tendrils into his irises so that

instead of continuing to turn, helplessly,
on the winch of beast and season,
man saw, sexually, that the world was something to enter or
to withdraw from. and that his dead
were in sexual remission but would return,
smaller and not that much more trouble to take care of
than when they left, for the point of withdrawal
and the point of re-emergence were hinged,
the vulva at this time had only an exit and an entrance—
it had not yet become a labyrinth

The mystery seemed to take place behind the vulva's centerpost,
try as he might
man could not figure out what woman did with the dead
to decrease their size but to increase their howling

Seeing that he roamed the tundra
a parasite in the earth's fur,
man, in his own eyes, began to emerge,
a tick of sorts in the animal "knockwurst,"
part of it but not the same, and to feel this was first
jubilance and first sorrow, such twisting of
the feeling bones against their own sinew
that man began to paw meaningfully
inside the earth of his beasts, began to scrape
as if he were a foetus returned to the womb
having seen the world outside,
he saw that his scraping left marks,
path snarls, vulva-shaped calls,
that he recognized life in what he scratched,
and that he was a smoldering hybrid
with rock and hardon bobbing about in a tundra of congealed
blood that he could soften with his breath,
that this gelid blood, this matted glassy meat, yielded
precisely a him
twisting against its beast webbing, so he followed
labyrinthine tunnels, dancing against his own exit and entrance,
the world was uteral and urinal,

where he pissed and spat and scratched
a diodrama of his condition appeared,
the outlines of the animals he scratched were his own meanders
inside of which he was a ghost on fire, something with its liver
sewn onto its face, sewn through with beast stitching,
which today, without the rest of the fabric, looks like spears

and as he chipped into the clitoral centerpost
as if to insert his own twist into his exit
he was casting off that which he had entered in order to exist
so that he was his own S sprout
in the deadness of his exit

man in slow motion shattered his beast
so that only mask bits of ears, paws and horns were left
on a shape that more and more resembled
man glaring back, in a dance hex,
glaring in heat, but in the heat of withdrawal,
to shake off the clitoral shadow of what he could not cut through,

He took his iced lust for the mystery he could not penetrate
and attached it to all the beasts,
hinged it to them as if to mirror that from which he was hinged
    away—
he masturbated animal shadow so that it bulbed and throbbed
into wings or several spitting heads or jutted human breasts
and the mystery could be fought in the name of the Fabulous Beast—
he invented Hercules and Portculis
in order to disguise his nakedness,
and as he battled with the spectres he had turned his own
enthroned placenta into, as he covered world with himself,
as he hacked up actual beasts,
he brought the underworld to its knees—
at which point it went into revolt:
the bone powder man brayed his beasts into eventually
became Goofy and Mickey and Donald, dotted eidola
flittering about their cages in newspapers, books and films,
empowered with the wrath of a satanized underworld

set loose within the power-lines of media,
an underworld composed of all the hydras, manticores, gorgons,
lamia, basilisks and dragons, and it is from this perspective
that the shadow of every duck is shaped like Donald
and that Donald has the power to leave the duck
as hagfish are said to leave their lairs at dusk
to all night long bore into t he souls of children.

IV. *Stud-Farms of Cooked Shadow*

The Rolls Royce parked in an El Salvador prison yard.

Inside the car, beefy North Americans eating an elaborate picnic lunch delicately unfolding white cloth napkins, licking their fingers, each fingernail a mirror reflecting a cage in the "hole" in which a living person is compressed. Chicken. Cheese. And an iced Lucifer to wash down the Rolls Royce in flames the couple inside undisturbed because the wealthy do not burn an invisible wall of asbestos a mile thick protects even me from the worst there is

I sit at my desk in the glare of the prison wall observing the car which the artist is tearing the insides out of like a living peasant can be disemboweled with a dull knife say, you can watch his face twist beyond noise into the pleasure on my countrymen's faces as they pack prison yard dirt into the Rolls, the idea is to turn it into a little jungle with sprinklers in the roof, so that in juxtaposition jungle to jungle the men in cages can be mailed through *Time* magazine and sniffed

Machete blow with the North Americans as the cutting edge strolling away like a hammerhead shark cruises the evening of his hunger these words pass through the prison and you become annoyed that the color in the flowers now seems to be affected by an "us" that is the prow of Good Ship Machete as it wanders hungry without mouth mouthing without hunger the welts on the nipples of a 12-year-old Indian boy it is the child, Donald, I keep coming back to as I sit here in prison moonlight on the lid of your grand sarcophagus— for years I thought I was in the crypt of the Temple of Inscriptions at Palenque dreaming of a cannibal feast; tonight I know that I am but that the chiseled-in king is you and that in your stunning whiteness without orifice is buried a duckling, better a drakeling since duck is feminine meaning you've eaten the Virgin Daisy of our hearts. I lift your lid, Donald, to realize that you are a flaccid black hole, contactable only through my own lost childhood and it is terrible to watch all of you quack along exchanging wristwatches for native gold against the backdrop of the Aurignacian Summation the whole scene becomes the blond slitting of an Amazonal throat but I cannot make you real, Donald, I can only talk to you as Syberberg talked to his Hitler dummies as your own heil ascends from a tomb whose bottom is engnarled with the construction of the underworld itself and with my own two-year-old word forming in 1937 when terror shifted gears in Europe—what shall we finally call these innocent adventurers decked out in comic book animal auras? Carolyn Forché said the El Salvadorians' ears in the colonel's sack looked like dried peaches and that a few which fell to the floor seemed to be pressed to the ground or listening to you and me, Donald, here, these grand reservoirs of human energy fried into ghettos in which no one could be said to live, cages in which the living are the shadows of other living—that colonel has no shadow, in all the taut suspenders of his anxiety he is content to be carried around the prison yard, like we used to play as kids, on the back of a peasant whose belly is a dugwork of running sores These sores, Ladies and Gentlemen, are only putrid at their place of origin, once the gunk is canned—since no production exists in your world, Donald—it's fucking good to eat, and even though the ride is bumpy at times even though the cries on TV seem menacingly near it's all Starsky and Hutch, isn't it, a heaving friendly world with the slaves sleeping in their own shit a few inches below the floorboards of this earth on whose back I too ride, since to blow up the Rolls is only to make it bigger to arm it more fully, so that this lunching pad for the rich, this car converted into art, this interior soul sprinkling is all taking place inside something that looks like a petrified apocalypse, weapons sticking out of every pore, with Manson in the American underworld, eating one of his Kali Krishnas whenever he gets hungry but hoping it will all be over soon so that with what is left of them he may climb back to earth and assume that role he has deserved from birth, namely to be buggered very badly at 12 so that he can look through the wet curtain shreds of his ass and stick his tongue out at this little Indian or little dummy I should say, for there is no one

here, Donald, but my fingers tracing again and again the carved con-
tours of your sarcophagus lid, like God might run his claws over the
topology of Disneyland, a blind god, a creature still hovering over the
primary waters, urine salt a lizard's tail and a peasant's heart mortared
into a tiny soft black sun which I place in this crippled alembic knowing
the irreality of my words taking place in the automagical washing ma-
chine of North America, this whirl of films watches umbrellas records
Donald Duck soaps even, rocking-chairs neckties condoms? Disney as
Bruckner, on his knees in the gravity filled end of the tear of a heaven
suspended condom praying at full vent for all the little children every-
where to coalesce into nine year old himself at dusk somewhere in
Chicago, 1910, delivering his papers with nothing nothing on his mind
but his most evil father flowing in the condom walls of snow as he
trudges the hamster belt of an anger never to be fully expelled until,
we say, what? But the world does not change, it only grows lighter and
darker, lighter when darker, darker when lighter, the blue green glow of
Eden down there in El Salvador turns out to be a horrifying wound op-
erated by maggot men preparing street urchins for computerized torture
under the gaze of fly men backed up by vulture men backed up by the
"compassion" of the stars, and the howl of this wound is so wide that it
is the sound of the very day itself, the solar day like an opened heart
packed with siphons and drains, feast parked in the heart of an Indian
mother whose breasts are no more than ripped lips

Sounds like an accident outside

Outside? No it is just that mother's defoliated eels
pawing toward her through the pyromaniacal air.

1981

Millennium

A funny thing happened on the way to the vomitorium:
racing toward us, down the gargoyle lined path
the organist could be seen, pursued by rabbit-sized arachnids.
We stopped in our tracks! With no accompanying Bach,
what pleasure in emptying oneself of one's past?
To hear mother Africa splash into the trough without even a swell
behind her, on that igloo fermenting in you for eons
which today you had planned to unleash across the western states—
how important it suddenly was to always background
our present upheavals with the black tie formality of a world
no longer ours. You turned to me,
your stomach started to seep from your eyes, and gently
but forcefully said: there is no alternative but to commit
sea cucumber hara-kiri. Yet would the silence now opposing us
accept our entrails in lieu of our being?
And even if it did, what guarantee do we have that life
will recolonize an area so emptied that its armor-plated
rocker panels need a NATO-rated level-five assault
just to begin to brake? The organist, running in place,
was getting closer. And as if the land itself were a sinking ship
cockroaches began to abandon their gargoyles—
they furiously kissed our sandals,
beseeching us to conceal them from the crusading
hordes of banana spiders sweeping the horizon.
As for me, I only released the white crocodile built
like a good cause in the trap of my heterosexual slingshot,
along with a volley of old Plymouth backseats,
each with a coed's head stuffed into its corner,
her spread North American legs seborrheic
though still housed in bobby-sox. You, my Diana of Ephesus,
were more daring: you unsnapped your girdle of breasts
and then threw up your womb, flying carpet
on whose taurine outline in the sky I could see that Europa
holding on for dear life was the Venus of Laussel
vomiting through her bull-horn the Pleistocene conquest.

The Spiritual Hunt   *

The penis, detaching itself,
grew eyes. For what is erection
if not flight? It took off,
honeycombed with eyes,
blue eyes, lidless, browless, sympathetic

with the plight of
this wombless one searching for his death
in a bison side, carving out
a wet place to bunch as the gale
enwombed and untied him.

Now a phallus, what I am speaking of
began to work the air,
to exercise the otherwise
blank sky, to make it bloom
with the melancholy of

the inedible, to tie clouds into
unfurling squids of emotion,
these arabesques that so suggest direction
we wombless penisless ones
sense connection—

connection, what is that? For we *are* rooted,
but as scampering roots, beheaded,
trunkless, boughless, roots trying to
mandate a standable condition,
to be a summation right

before judgment, in which the flight
of the penis left us with our subject,
a hole, out of which the first ones
were emerging, those with pots
over their heads? We don't know if

they have heads, these small
human-like beings, whose stomachs
flex like lips, whose shoulders carry
inverted nourishment,
skull pots, emptied cauldrons, joy

that out of our womblessness,
out of that place where our penises
abandoned us, something should emerge,
that we might have something
to show to the women,

these dolmens that watch us, bat us
about, flicker our sleep
never letting us forget that both sun
and moon coalesce in their gigantic
gateway, and that as we sit

in our bison sheds, something
besides maggots will be issuing.
I have called them first ones—
they are also last ones, meaning
they are curved ones, they wear

inverted pots to remind
how we ate each others' marrow,
desperate to go on we unpacked
each other's semen sponges,
we gorged on the kaleidoscopic

wormwork of the soft chain
that bound us. And it was then, after
the feast, that our penises
took flight, hovering before our
blindness to autonomous generation,

that it does occur anywhere, even here,
as I sit in my wood bison shed
this house I did not build,
this door I opened, timidly
climbing out, fully masked

so as to not be understood,
for once understanding occurs
I can no longer be
that which issues as well as the issued one,
I will be seen crawling

inside my eight-like looping,
spotlit, hunted down, tossed like a brain
to a circle of cackling dogs,
for that is the image
I want you to see: twenty dogs in a circle

devouring me, their jaws so into
they are like petals
extending from a pistil,
so that the eating is about the center
but never the center itself,

and the aura of their swinging behinds
the light about an earlier
tearing, so that I am eaten and
will go on being hungry

left with a hole out of which
my appetite was emerging with bellies
making mouth gestures, stretching
as if to lip and open, never
really becoming mouths,

and not stitched shut either,
never opened, but acting as if something
alive were inside which is my speaking
in this dense blue envelope.
Has anything not been worked?

Are there any loose sentences not
woven back into this daisy chain lapping
and eating as it encircles
the empty flexing throne of erection
destruction.

Maithuna   *

Caryl's delicate hand—reaching—in sleep
my side, out of which a turbulent river pours,
to sheathe her hand and arm, to cocoon,
protect her—and in doing so, lying awake
I watch her grow monstrous, a creature of my imagining—
her body wet, feathery with slime.
                                    Now I am wrapping her,
as if with long silken vegetal bands, binding her
with the freedom of my side, spear place, gore
transformed into a vault of liquid thread,
spool vault in which the swastika of aggression
is dissolved by a harem of tentacles
into this magical moonlit thread—
                                    so, do I hesitate
as if from fear of the labyrinth of syntax
binding you binds me into? Already only your heart
can be seen, the truffle center of a winding
that even wound tight is loose and curling,
a train of cloth draped about the rocks over which
I am crawling with you stitched to my back.

So there is no ending to the shrine
constantly fastening and unhooking, for I have seen
the husks of your eyes at night littered about the world,
still glinting with the nickel mystery of the interior,
still moist although all the flesh about them has been eaten
by "the likes of me"—it is eons ago? Or did I,
just a moment ago, convert my kissing into infantile
hunger and with all my teeth turned into penises
break up and suck in your soft, soft tofu interior?
I must have—yet you are still outside
and radiant in this after-intercourse Maithuna.

Through the translucent bindings I can see you slowly
begin to form your own world,
                                    in your flipper-like hands

you hold a glass ball in which is reflected
the face of creation, for having penetrated you
I have been offered Sabbath, our bed is crisscrossed
with rainbows, blood edged, with violet
interiors, the wart hogs have stopped
their horrible breathing, for a moment the whiskey
mattress in Alexander Haig's voice collapses,
heaps of disemboweled peasants rot into it,
and the world is fungus, with vermicular elves busily
shoveling and restoring.
                              And now as you expose me
to the hexagonal formation of hovering wasps
I receive the discharge of eggs, loading them in here,
kissing an identity to each. Miraculous conversion of my plight
from having left the mat of tusks and
the bright-red mouth of writhing hair—to move
into the image of you as if through eelgrass,
to hold in outstretched hands the torn pods of your Ice Age
distant eyes, to feel the iris pulse and implode,
to watch the wart hogs take off their tusks,
empty them of powder, even unscrew their hooves
packing themselves into the lining of my wound.

Elegy

                    Vladimir Holan
impacted in the jaw of Prague, its wisdom,
pain, I wondered what it meant to write
only that which is pried out of
what cannot be said by others…

"It means those horseflesh blankets,"
Holan replied, "and this Virgin who daily
descends from His Cross to pull out another of
my teeth. My last visitor was Caravaggio
who came bounding in here, the police still on his heels,
from Rome. He knelt by my bedside and we talked,
about, for example, why Hans Bellmer,
in spite of his bloody crinolines,
was never elected Pope…"

How long ago, I asked—

"It was in the future," Holan said, "on the beach
at Porto Ercole—they will carry my bed, canopy and all,
out by the surf so that I can watch Caravaggio
veer, copulating with his own wounds,
instead of this hag and her orifice
—Orpheus to you—who only truly loved
the first few moments of sunlight
after he led her out…"

But those are not real people, I protested,
they're the entangled vinework of your dreams
as you lie here looking forward
arguing that Orpheus did not look back—
yet what else is there to do in an empty cathedral
and I began to look around,
the high vaulted walls were hung with corpses hanging by their hair;

Between Holan's bed and the walls
was the distance
between expecting everything and having no faith...

"We who do believe," Holan read my mind, "are always expecting
nothing to come, not that nothing which is a lack,
but nothing as a power, life's twin,
Our Caravaggio of the Shadows, an equal match
for the fugitive Caravaggio with his blackened soles.
That painter so darkened the Christian scene
that light became the glare of shattered desire
and the rich a darker shade of the poor.
How closely his attempt to cave in Christianity
so that its shackles would gleam through
the purple of the human hunger for death's divinity
was bound to the incident itself:
"He quarreled with Ranuccio Tomassoni over a game of tennis,
and they beat each other with their rackets,
then he drew his weapon and killed the youth and was himself
wounded. He fled from Rome without money, under pursuit,
and took refuge in—' "
and here I heard "—the poetry of Vladimir Holan."

So you do not have to be carried to Porto Ercole,
that Caravaggio stumbling about in sulfuric heat
is in the bag of your poet's heart,
is what gives it grotesque life,
its unceasing disassociative thumping,
what provokes me here, in spite of your wife's request
that I not come in...

"But you've come in death," Holan smiled,
"and in your own invention of where you would find me.
I know that you tried to visit me twice in Prague.
I was so ashamed for people I did not know to see
not only my idiot daughter but the squalor in which we lived.
As for Caravaggio, I never thought much about him
until I became very ill—then his beheadings

began to strike me as a man trying to screw off his own lid
so that the hands of little children might poke about
in what had fermented in him so long—in fact
his brutality so appalled me, I began to think
that he was driven by my dread of violence
which you perceived by hanging this place
with the souls of so many of my countrymen…
What does strike me as fairly certain is
that the soul is timeless and multiple in its singleness…
as we've been talking I've kept thinking of the buttocks
of a young woman who keeps walking in place away from me,
of that joke about her ass jumping like two cats
fighting in a sack, so perhaps the left one's Caravaggio,
the right one me, or any two dead
blowing off soul in the alchemical glasswork of art,
or my death reaching what lives in you of me."

As he was speaking, his canopied bed became an animal mouth,
open, in which Holan, its single fang, was obliquely
embedded. Snow drifted through the beast head
as if we were out in the Old Jewish Cemetery
and the Virgin too descended, to reach way in for Holan with
forceps, and begin to tug. I could hear him give
vista opening from the height of Brahms' First,
fog skeletonizing amidst the black
hypodermics of medieval Prague,
gape of a crematorium in the rectum of war
singing at the vintage of everyone's
teeth in a pile, or all things compost
in the thought: spring has gone out of the world.

The Color Rake of Time

I dreamed that all artists were friends,
that we told everything we knew to each other
and that our knowledge was physical,
that we worked in the skull rooms of each other's
genital enclosures, broken fulcrum people
raining within ourselves at high noon,
that we talked in mid-ocean in smashed saint stables
where spars were severe-steady cave-ins,
that at last all of us feasted off of repression and depression—

I dreamed! that the sphinx was not at the end of her twig,
that she was not open to the furnace of the hearth,
that there was no heat without recall,
no vitality without memory, that the slave was merely one
who rowed in a hold without oar-lock...

then I heard the color rake of time
scraping the window, and awoke to the face of God
whose childhood is everlasting
whose maturity we struggle to create.

OUR JOURNEY AROUND THE
DROWNED CITY OF IS (1985)

Kerlescan   *

      The open   loaded
               field

Neanderthal muscle,
     a return of
"the repressed" struggle
     against opacity,
that wall of weather
       overcome by
         Cro-Magnon—

It resurfaces
  stegosaurian plates
    fins lifting up
      from *holed* earth,

    the shapings of the cave
emptied out,
    the interior organ design
excavated—

      aligned rinds,
    culls of the custodian
      mother,
        her teeth—

indentated ground.

Thistle & heather, ferns,
    for ground company—

welts of lichen,
    granular saffron
       wounds
    rescabbed—

         I write
from the lectern of one piece of Car,
   Ker,   the Carmenta
      scattered

       in this static, rampaging field,
as if the cave were a whirling millstone, as if
muscular goddesses in maddened distraction were tightening
    & unloosening the Upper Paleolithic hub,
Laussel dividing into multiple divinities,   Lascaux exploding,
Les Trois Frères,   Altamira,   Niaux,   Combarelles,
Font de Gaume,   massive undifferentiated cores
whirling into children of the mist,   nebulae of marshes,
    meres, springs,
into towns & cities,   Demeter-spores of childbirth—

The cauldron interior of the cave that had contained
swirls of animal life,   this purgatorio with dragon-fly incubi,
   darters of divinational dreams,
has, in the mind of the earth,   gone to seed!
The amoebic hybrid congeal,   never a "center" but a physical
   syllogism,   has erupted into a 3000 part argument,
the cowrie did it,   or was it Carya,   the walnut tree?

Kerlescan,   you are not only dedicated to Ker, but to Kore,
   Q're,   Car-Dia,   Cerdo,   Carna,
your great grandkids are carnivals & charms,   karma,   cherubs,
the kernel thanks you,   charity erects 3 standing stones,
because of you we have cereal,   Ceres,   we are carnal,
close kindred,   there are cardinal points,   cairns,
the kern or scared womb vase out of which the grain god was born,
Kerlescan,   where the matron menhirs tipple,

where they still wiggle their tentacle towers,   big mama
   breakwaters,   they alleluia in place
while the root canals whistle along.   At times
they converge into a cromlech to evoke an animal band:

   the lion is seated   sawing away at his zebra harp,
   a bull is covering his Leda drum,   a snake is playing
   the human spine as if it were a chakra clarinet,
   the eagle is swaying over her weasel phone which cries more
      fiercely than Illinois Jacquet!
   They play the *kerubn*,   their fabulous muzzles combining,
   for the Cherub is not a plump infant with an arrow
   nor a demon with a flaming sword,   but the insignia of
   the grotesque melodies of this world brooding & incubating us.

Carnac is a telluric instant of Car's consternation,
the menhirs drive like distracted miners off into the menace of
      the sunset,
they waver in lines,   memories of the winding path,
rudimental bell towers impounding the skeletal leashes to
      everyone's
      Matterhorn,   that impulse to *up & away!*
KA,   curl in the infant lip, gum pressing forth as the first
      storm cloud appears over a nipple,
O terrible new soul,   fern drifting onto a sleeping dragon's
      out-lapped tongue,
to stand knee-deep in the flamy plush of this tongue,
a moment later the irked mouth reforms,   ka becomes ka-r,
      currr,
open ka seeking closure,   at the end, his vehicle lost, Olson
      moaned   "my wife   my car..."

These long stones represent nothing,   as do Zen monks,
they draw me in to their shed-in-time shawls,
they bear on their granite the menstrual stains of dusk,
& as the moon conceals herself forth,   they seem to advance,
Noh ghosts baffled on the rise of that bridge between worlds,

fluttering the imaginal silk of midnight gore,   sticky with
    karma,
mulberry-stained leather armor peeling from the rotted bones
    of former stories, on their way to the ark of etymologies!

One is a poet for an instant   upon breathing in
    the fumes from one's combined cauldrons,
I've swallowed the millstone of my father,   no special feat,
the trick is to re-imagine him, think of him as a bean,
then to go with the grinding.   Car, nut nymph or Caryatid?
Tree trunk or column?   Are these menhirs axles or pestles?
The grinding takes place in the tomb,   Caer Sidin,   the maze
    castle of Ariadne,   revolving because the souls of those
crushed under these menhirs are maggots weeviling,
    compost the moon whitens with its scour.
the top of the pestle is the Corona Borealis,
Caer Arianrhod,   the Cretan Goddess,   wife of Dionysus.

To be a man is to be divided,   stretched between one's tomb
    & one's star,   part of me is a prisoner in Caer Sidin,
the animal mortar,   I am the Beast trying to move Beauty
    through the sorgum of my eyes,   glint of Caer Arianrhod
in my iris implosions,   deep   very distant Caer Arianrhod,
Crown of the North Wind,   as a poet my *cor* (heart)   is under
    Cerridwen,   I am of cerdd,   grain & the inspired arts,
the feast of Lady Carnea is June 1,   my birth & web day
    in the lost Thirteenth House of the Spider.
As *cerdo* (craftsman) I have eaten *cerdo* (pig),
                My character goes back to *carato*,   from *qirat*
    (bean),   to Carnea: pig meat & beans,   I have swallowed my
    father's attempt to enwomb & to be reborn,
I raise my *keras* (horns), cuckolded by the power of Charybdis,
as a door I am the son of Cardea,   from *cardo* (hinge),
                                    by these forces
    am I permeated,

    anima is *pneuma*,   the soul a storied fart.

Apotheosis

       Where clouds
   temple the horizon, realms of whitened
   light enfolding
   vast inorganic fruit. Grandeur:
                   unfurling arabesques
 that confirm parthenogenesis.

The bay is swooned with streaks of cobalt, jade,
"granit rose,"   pink & black speckled rock
                       dolmen-contoured in soft
   lifting heaps, or saucers—
their ridges, furrows, lobes   or lobbies   invite the early
  Dali of the imagination, & in this light,
the pink & black meld to tawny rose,   living rock,
                          rose rock!
One need go no further for satisfaction with the earth.
      "Nature is imagination itself."

Seamless,   the day is *sloth & ray*
   moving under the language film
         as breasts,   or turtles

Breaking through enthusiasm,   *enthousiasmos*
   "possessed by the god,"   language,
      beautiful chains of surf reaching
                 the apex of their heave
            reswarm this tawny rose to reveal
         the saddle of Persephone   flecked by Zeus.

                                              Trégastel

THE NAME ENCANYONED RIVER (1986)

Junk Mail

I have been invited to the third Creativity and Madness Conference, Easter Week 1984, at the Sheraton Royal Waikoloa. After "Pablo Picasso: The Blue, The Rose, The Cubist, THE MAGNIFICENT!!!" there will be a Singles Luncheon (Dutch Treat) followed, 4 hours later, by a Piano Concert of Chopin and Brahms by Ms. Ostwald, presumably the wife of Peter F. Ostwald MD, author of "Music and Madness: The Inner Voices of Robert Schumann," who will, just before the Singles Luncheon, have lectured on "Music, Ambivalence, and Bachelorhood." Tuesday April 17th will start off with a bang: after Bahman Sholevar's "Descent into Hell: Basic Mistrust and Ego Despair in the Poetry of Sylvia Plath and Anne Sexton," Dr. and Mrs. Carder will present "A Marital Crisis as Revealed in the Music and Art of Arnold Schoenberg." After "Charlie Chaplin: A Life Observed" there will be a Sheraton Royal Waikoloa Roundup Dinner and Show (optional). After Dr. Sholevar has displayed Dante Alighieri's Ascent to Heaven, the movie THE TEMPEST will be shown. A previous conferee commented: "Creativity and Madness was enjoyable in every conceivable way!"

The difficulty of creativity and the despair of madness have been
    dumped
into a trough called Enjoyment. *Fun* is the word, I think
for what the participants are geared for, not Maenads
raving on the endless Styx of a threadbare psyche,
nor even a scrutiny of how the thread might have disappeared in its
    appearance
to John Wieners or Diane Arbus. To place an "And" between
    creativity and madness
sets up a momentary LSD icicle in whose blade a glorious disorder
sticks out its tongue, or the not inaccurate hunch
that in creative grandeur another world is manifest, and when one
    finds oneself

wading for days in a lagoon of blood with no sun no moon but only
a roaring as of surf
around one, one must have the candle of one's split open mind lit
or all that we seek to leave but so depend upon for meaning
is engulfed. But what could those of us who *have* had our arm
around Nebuchadnezzar once, who
have at least been penetrated by the smell of crawling in a gibbous
circle in a dark hut — what *can* we say
to those who would season their Royal Waikoloa Singles Luncheon
with
"George Orwell and Rudyard Kipling: Abandoning Parents and
Abusing Children?"
There is a repression in North American psyche so tough, so
uncontactable because of the depth, now,
of the suffering midden of humanity creating goods for us,
that it is no longer disturbable — it can *enjoy* ANYTHING! Can
enjoin any grief and discuss it
over pineapple — but I cannot fully believe this or I too would be
consumed. That the shirts of these people
are being made somewhere in the world where the workers live less
well than our pets
can turn the vise of the creative mind into itself to the point that not
madness
but a simpering, descriptive, situation comedy runs out,
a pseudo-art the equivalent of the lectures to be delivered there.
And how much of those doctors and their well-heeled patients are
packed
like a chamber of bullets in my own mind?
For I can actually see myself *enjoying being there*. I'd blow up 48 hours
after arrival.
But my gregarious North America nature is so social it dives into
any human pool with the drunken recklessness with which I used to
leap,
with friends, into the Bloomington quarries in utter blackness at 3 AM
knowing we'd be, if lucky, missing jagged rocks 30 feet down there
by a few feet —

I say to this nature: I know how powerful you are, how ego potent
    your lust
to protect and propitiate your so-called innocence. In the soul-less
    basement of this country
it is you who are at play, ceaselessly reassembling the heating system,
    occasionally
braining your puppy with your little wood mallet, amazed and
delighted he springs back to life, amazed and delighted that mother
    and father
are out on endless chores, daddy over Nicaragua loosing last night's
    supper,
we don't know where mommy is, she may be at the market or at
    choir practice
but her condition is we *don't know where she is,* so little Me looks
    around
with glazed wild-eyed friendliness — maybe he should go look for her!
    But when Me
looks for something, it does not go out, it only goes in to a more
    Meish aspect of itself,
it reclines on the basement floor, unzips its little pants and pulls out
    like magician's streamers
the cloth of its own hunting scenes, timeless yet timed, edged with a
    sportive fuse.
Nothing charmed from its nicked dungeon,
eyes this little fellow like we frat rats used to eye
a frightened, unsure, slightly ugly, clearly needy girl.

1984

Lemons

These lovely freaks, skins
pulled tight about inner disturbance,
a kind of vegetal lava – a one-eyed
face looks out of a blackened
yellow cowl, an eye held in its tensile
puckered mouth

◇

As if I held in my fist a creature
not my hand, a head on
the end of my arm, a head twisted
with wrath, whose soul spills into
the air as I ungrip

◇

Some are peaked like elves' shoes,
Aladdin slippers, as the arabesque
of cosmic charge tips
    instead of curling on
    into a seamless sphere

◇

One I know has a small aperture
with which it gently grips one's
                distended finger –
                        a kind of vegetal navel,
            the suck we feel
        in the presence of lemons
    no symmetry no
    No

◇

I do not know what to say to the force
in the lemon tree behind the bedroom when sleepless at 3 AM
I think of the lemons as heads,
headlets with frozen howling mouths,
a tree of tiny perfumed skull-lives

◇

One said: "to dangle here,
                all belly
                on the stem
                of another mind"

nun face, with so much God contracted

                navel face

could I but think with my navel
would I see each being's aura
as a palace of umbilical corridors?

◇

It is good to be on earth.
Two fresh slit lemon halves
draw my heart out of its hiding heart space

◇

Enter the mind of a lemon
the sweetness of rock
the soul of things that speak
only in the interface of us and them

1983

The Excavation of Artaud   *

Shaman of obsession — I said at his tomb —
excavated in electricity, opened between
anus and sex. In the Australian outback of the soul,
3 dead men are fingering your anesthetized root support
shining like a chain of sputtering lights, for the key to creation,
between the bone they've drawn out and your bone they so desire.

Priest of lethal phallic rites, of sparkings
in foetid material, of remaining in antithesis
with no hope of synthesis, priest of a genuine melee —
3 dead men are fingering your Muladhara Chakra, your amphimixis,
as if, under the Christian gunk that clogged your focus,
they could plug into your triangle and its twisting tongue of flame.

Pariah in silence, coprophilially
squatting in the corner of your cell for years,
sealed open, who only came when called by your mother's name —
repressing their way in, to the point of anal cancer,
3 dead men, licking your electroshock-induced Bardo, have found
your atomic glue, the Kundalini compost they must eat to speak.

O shaman, from having been so masterfully plundered!
O priest, from having been fixed in antithesis!
O pariah, from having been so desired by the dead!

1984

Scarlet Experiment

The challenge of wholeness, to offer the lower
body imaginative status, so that the "negatives" of excrement,
menses, urine and semen, become intelligibles.
The tawny rocks panting like sponges, the whitened
violet dirt out of which asters are rocketing,
are as much a part of the Persian landscape in the vision of the
    Sha-nameh
as the prince, the maiden, and the necessary demon —
necessary because in this horned grotesca
the gods are more present than they are in us.

The apple dangling from the lovely fingers of a branch is red
all the way through, its seeds
tiny beings carousing in Eve's rich heart.
The earth, as well as woman, menstruates —
the evidence is flowers, especially roses.
Against green or brown, they take on a rusty,
delicious tenor, scarlet experiment
in league with liquid blackness, or that imperfect
circle of pebbles a male octopus arranges on the ocean floor,
to invite one in heat inside such a circle
to mate motionlessly changing colors for hours.

Forget the dragon. Think of George and maiden
lounged against an oak. He touches her vagina
and touches blood. The abyss moves forward, widens
revealing a corridor in which red Ariadne is climbing forth,
8-legged menarche power returning from its winter sojourn with the
    nether Dionysus,
bleeding pinkly on its underworld path
which now unzips and rezips with the fervor of awakened dirt.

1984

Ariadne's Reunion

I was called out into the forest to box
with a man I had been told represented
my other. I wore big blue gloves
and a nose mask; my other had only his hands,
and his unmasked face was more obscure
than any mask. We squared off in a clearing
and remained in that position forever,
for as soon as we recognized the extent to which
we mirrored one another, we both slipped out our backs,
he to quest with lantern for a younger man,
not that burlesque of virility I had put on.
As for me, I became a woman
lost in the image crowd pressing toward the arena,
that deep, tiered pit in the depths of which, lit
by flowing tapers, Ariadne, it was said, might appear
with her bull-headed partner. I took my place between two
who had jeered at Jesus as he struggled under
the immense onion onto which he was to be tied.
Gaunt jeerers, whose eyes brimmed with hail
as if the fools in the moon were emptying all their jugs.
Here, at the bottom of the world, one must move cautiously
between the thrust of narrative and
the associations the story sends out like feelers to test the air
for prey or rockface and if they do attach, a perpetual
give and take begins, for the older story wants to go on
and resists letting the new pull it apart as the new
revises the identity of the old. It is in the moment when
both have equal strength that Ariadne's face
is said to appear in this webbing —
at the moment the webbing tears, her bull-headed partner
bounds through. No one has actually
seen them couple — rather,
they have been memorialized as dancers,
thrusting in out of gibbous circles
while the surrounding image crowd
receives the energy swarming out like tendrils unconcerned

with the crowd, tendrils that pass through
as if angling for something in the night sky
that would explode and cathect them on.

                       Look — she has appeared,
this evening in a spider mask to reveal why
no coupling, in living memory, has taken place.
In the blacker recesses of the pit,
to enter her is to be taken apart while one is inside.
The saying "no one has lifted her veil"
means that at the moment it is lifted
the lifter is no longer alive. Thus, her portal
is an active tomb, transforming the lifter into the goal
all desire: to carouse forever in her barque that floats above,
through white, red, and black weather, unphased
by the tiny spectacle below. Yet the story itself
seeks to destruct and to go on, and for this twist
both Dionysus and Theseus are required. One, it is said,
is her true husband, the other
a mistake. For ages it has been argued,
during intromission, why she gave Theseus
the clew to her animal heart. Theseus,
it is argued, had no intention of passing between
the horns, of losing himself in her arms to be
reclothed as a star. Theseus so resented her power
that he wanted to live forever in his own form,
and that is why he refused to tumble
and instead stabbed the sleeping Minotaur.
Why she allowed this to happen has never,
at least during intromission, been solved.
Some say her story follows natural evolution,
that one night her sacred victim recoiled
at the sight of her hideous threshold
or demanded to imitate, in his own way, her monthly flow.
Or that another host broke from the image crowd
and, with the victim, vied for her heart.
Leviathan and Behemoth, they churn in her gateway.
As the sun's hair is sheared, one fleshes out into a bull.

When the sun goes unpruned, the winning force is serpentine.
Then she is happiest, then she is most round.
But never as happy, many insist, as when pregnant by her true
    husband,
she gave birth before all assembled here.

                            That was *the* night, one of my Jesus
jeerers whispered, that draws us back again and again to
Ariadne's Reunion. Frankly, to see her dance
with the bull-headed partner only makes us yearn more
for that night of nights. No one knew what was to happen,
yet as soon as she appeared, haggard, unmasked,
with a senile grin — and pregnant — we were all involved.
We sensed she had come so far that night,
much further than when she performed as a spider in the veiled
recesses of the pit. That night she was most used,
most virgin, and so entranced were we
that when, on her back, by herself, she pulled out
a glistening ear of corn, we fainted, for a moment
totally present, pregnant with the world in mind,
nourished into a vision that each thing
is a soul returned to mother
inspiration. It was then that cauldrons were brought forth,
and she beckoned all of to enter. We sat,
naked, to our waists in warm fluid gently cooking
the tiny beings swimming around. They were dark red,
ringed, but peculiarly human. They nibbled
at our penises until, in alarm, we stood up
to discover we had no heads. Then we released
fans of blood-speckled milky substance and heard Ariadne call,
as if from the stars, NOW YOU MUST GET THE REST!
We reached up into our headless shafts
pulling out long knotted strings of octopuses and squids.
In joy we offered them to her, and as we did so,
we saw another dimension of what we were offering:
our own entrails, and that we were dead,
intensely alive and dead, and that one of her was squatting
over each of us, gazing madly into

the divinational cat's cradles she was making of our guts
as she bobbed up and down on our headless shafts.
O we were so happy to be anointed ones, christened
with her own oils so as to not injure her while she grooved!

1984

Dear Sign

April, 1979, patio of Marwan's house in mountains north of Alassio.
Rain—sunshine—snow the same afternoon.
Out to view the possibly seeable ocean, some 10 miles away
(Caryl had just told me about Goethe's color theory).

    A cloud the size of a large, wispy shark
    zoomed down, away from its companion clouds,
    circled around us once,
    shot back up

vanishing in roily cloud wash...

According to Gary Snyder,
"Dogon says: 'When the ten thousand things... advance and confirm
    you,
that is enlightenment. When you advance and confirm the ten
    thousand
things, that is delusion.'"

Deeds Done and Suffered by Light   *

One can glimpse Apollo in the door of each thing,
as if each thing now contains his oven —
in vision I open an olive tree and see his earlier animal
shapes fleeing at the speed of light, the python,
mouse, and lion Apollo, fleeing so that human forms
may walk unharmed by the invasion of the supernatural.
Light increased incredibly after the end of animal deity,
at the point verticality was instituted,
and the corpse of one's mother buried far, far from the place
on which one slept one's head. But the supernatural
in the guise of the natural is turning us over
in its fog a half mile from this ledge. Burnished
muscleless fist of a grey cloud. Sound of rain
from water still falling from the olives. I have no desire
to live in a world of nature conditioned by patriarchy.
I kick off my head and live in the light
bounding in from my mother. It is her great
ambivalence toward her own navel that conditions
the decreasing dripping. The hills now
writhe with green meat and something should follow.
Something should be explaining the tuft of salmon bull shape
abandoned by the other stilled clouds. Something
should be done with the swatted fly. Something is
this abyss of unusableness that remainders me
and pays no royalty. There are hosts of thrones
directly above. A witch hammer. A cleated enclosure.
The way a church has of making you puke your soul
upon entering and then, as the dryness of birth is rehashed
by nun and candle, of worshipping what has just left you,
the bride of your chest, the stuff inside you that a moment before
twinkled with the sadness and poverty of the street's
malicious laughter. How I wish that this poem
would birth another, and that the other had something to do
with unpacking the olive meat of this mountain. No
apocalypse. An enlargement, rather, of the so-called Whore
on her severely underfed Dragon. And more wine. More plumes

of silver azure evening coursing over
the thatch of the mountainside. More space to suffer,
more farewell to the flesh, more carnival in the face of everyman,
less perfection, more coherence. Meaning: more imagination,
more wigs for glowworms, more cribs for the restless dead
who wake us right before dawn with their bell leper
reminding us that fresh rain air is a clear indication
that here is not entirely here. The processions of graffiti-
scarred bison are, like us, clouds imprisoned to be viewed.
And then my mother began to speak: "You've put on a lot of weight!
Look at your father and me, some shape we're in! We've suffered
a lot for you these 14 years. You should've seen my left side
when it turned into a purple sponge and stained what
you buried me in to the point it rotted. I'm glad
John Ashbery appeared to you last night reading new
incomprehensible poems that made perfectly good sense. You are
much more organized, much more chaotic, than you behave here.
When I think of you, I see you at 12, stuck in the laundry chute,
your legs wiggling in the basement air, while the top part talked
with me as we waited for the renter to pull you out.
We had a nice chat that afternoon, and I almost liked you best
that way, just what stuck out of the chute. If I could only have
that part on a roller skate and let what was wiggling below go —
it's that part that's gone off gallivanting,
that's carried you goodness knows where while I
and your father lie here a few feet away from each other
waiting for our coffin lids to cave in. Then, even
the little space you left us to play with memories of you
on our chest bones will be gone. My buttons are mouldy
and my hands have no flesh left but I still manage
to squeak my buttons a little and get into your dreams.
I'm sorry if I appear both dead and alive to you,
but you should know by now you can't have it your way all the time.
I'm as real in this way as I ever was, sick more often than not
when I appear, but you're never here, you're worrying
how to take care of me, and then you wake to a jolt
every time there's nothing to take care of.
Now your father wants to say a word." "Clayton,

why don't you come home? We were such a nice little family.
Now it is like when you went off to that university.
Your mother and I would sit up and talk about you
until our fathers came in from the night and motioned us
into our bed. You were such a nice little fellow
when we could hold you up high and look at each other
through you. Ten little fingers ten little toes
Two bright eyes a funny little nose
A little bunch of sweetness that's mighty like a rose
Your mother, through you, looked so much like
your grandmother I could never get over it.
Why I bet you don't even remember your birth gifts
a savings bank and one dollar from granddad and grandmother
Two kimonas from aunt Georgia and uncle Bob
Supporters from Faye's dollie Patricia Ann
A Romper Suit from Mrs. Warren Bigler
A Dress from Mr. & Mrs. SR Shambaugh
Silk Booties & Anklets Knit Soaker & Safety Pins
Hug-me-tight a Floating Soap Dish with Soap Rubber Doggie
I don't see why you don't come home. Your mother and I
have everything you need here. Why sure,
let's see, maybe you could pick up some things,
Gladys — no, she's not listening — *Gladys what do you want?*"
"Well, I know we need some scouring powder and light bulbs"
"GLADYS WHAT DO YOU WANT?" "And Clayton, we want
Clayton to come back we don't like Clayton Jr. out so late at night"
"GLADYS WHAT DO YOU WANT?" "You never know what will
    happen, why
just last week Eunice Wilson, over in Plot #52541, told me"
"GLADYS WHAT DO YOU WANT?" "—are you listening, Daddy?
Eunice said while Jack was getting out of his car parked in his own
    driveway at 2 AM"
"GRADDISROTDUYRUNT!" "—after his date with Kay Fisbeck,
    this man
came up to him and said something I will not"
"GRADDDISROTDRURUNT" "— I will not repeat it was that
    vulgar —
this man said: if you don't come with me, I'll crush your cows.

Doesn't that take the cake? Why Clayton you can't blame Jack
for going off with him, and you would not believe where
this man took Jack Wilson and what he wanted him to do.
Now that your father's lid has caved in, I'll tell you:
he made him drive north to the Deaf School parking lot,
and when he was sure nobody else was around, he said:

> Persephone's a doll
>   steeper than Marilyn,
> miracles lick here,
>   dreams invader,
> over the cobweb orchestra
>   there's an ice
>   conductor,
> forget the orchestra,
>   conduct the pit!
> Hanged
> Ariadne
>   giving birth in Hades
> is the rich, black music in mother's tit."

1984

The Man with a Beard of Roses

A constructed indwelling, an antiphonal swing.
These were the things that mattered
to the man for whom the goddess wreath
was truer to the earth he knew than a barbwired heart.

Because he had loved and been loved by
the person he most desired to be with and to talk to
he could die at any time. He would not
have missed the central frosty drop

every mother's cuddling proclaims will fall.
But he did not desire nonbeing. He desired to throw
back the curtains of every day and enter
the cave of flowers where mature transformations

intermingled with the immature. He desired,
therefore, he depended. No matter that his appetite
was infantile, that he never really rested,
that his beard was also barbed. He knew he would never

assimilate his points. That he had many,
not merely one, was a multitude and kept him aloft
on a road whose wavy grain he went against
as he journeyed through it, or simply went

with a sideward wash to find once again he'd been
deadended, or had he descended – or blended?
Words were walls worth boring through, worth
turning into combs, words were livable

hives whose centers, or voids,
sounded the honey of emptiness dense
with the greyish yellow light nature becomes
to the soul for whom every thing is a cave

or hollow in the top of a water demon's
head, a green being plunging into green, sound
eating color, a sentence rolling closure
away from its opening. Inside this man the brutal

world had died. He felt its rot in every pore,
its disappearance in the sinew of his petals.
He had lived its life, but even more his own,
against the bio-underpinning to simply flex like worms.

1984

III
1989–1998

A Memorial to the Grand

In my dead father's dreaming there is
a slaughterhouse called 4705,
a perfect fusion of our home and his place of work—
my mother and I are the cattle he attends,
a milker, wearing his long white smock with its blood braid,
a milker-general, medals dangling from his lapels.
How he tends us is of unceasing fascination:
he fastens his gloved fingers to our teats and we spray him
    rainbow-wise,
great fans of smoky juice raying through his dreaming—
he tickles then twirls our valves,
reaching up into our vast birth canals as if he is
at cathedral in our presence.
It is almost, sitting at his stool, as if he is playing animal pianos,
as if his fingers dip and plunge into our keyboard troughs,
as if we are one gleaming black lacquered bison grand,
and the blood-braided smock a silver and raspberry tuxedo,
as if the slaughterhouse opens out into an attentive world,
all our neighbors including the dogs and birds
enrapt in their coffin-like chairs,
even the grasses are there as he rips through Mozart, even the clouds.
Each struck note releases a massive repression.
The shy time and motion study father, rheumatic at 14, has finally hit
    his rhythm.

The Night Against Its Lit Elastic

He stayed up late, staved off sleep, wandered, drank,
as if sleep were a kind of devouring,
as if it would masticate and spit him out at dawn
a juiceless thing that would have to resurrect
and learn, all over again, to walk—
                                        ridiculous,
for the ore of night was dream, and to push
the night against its lit elastic made him so tired
he did not dream, or recall, or
allow himself to recall dreams of fatigue,
bent earthworm doctors struggling from tumulus to tumulus
administering to eyes in dark whose bone paws
clutched the pills and disappeared,
                                        or *was* it ridiculous to want
to push the dark, depoeticize it, to push it into dawn,
so that light would swarm with the hearts of the tumulus inhabitants,
skeletal raccoons, bearded white-haired badgers,
gnarled hermaphrodites whose orifices and pipes wheezed
that steam he wanted to inject into weightless day—

yet what to really see or really feel in Durango?
Sides of 19th century buildings
like mock-ups of the aftermath of Pompei?
Indian beads laid out on velvet, kewpie dolls,
Minnie Mouse sweatshirts, "fresh" mesquite-broiled salmon,
the sound-asleep proprietors. *Here Dempsey kayoed*
Cochran to win $20 in 1912—or that is how he recalled
the recent wall mural, shuffling toward Denny's where giant forms
were putting away steaks at 2 AM. North Americans!
They looked like mercs, or rioters, swollen
restitched Abe Lincolns, under the bright lights of an Ensor
Halloween. He sat down by a farmer his own age
who he felt would break his back if true feelings were shared,
he knew this in his Midwestern bones
which were still processing the Christmas-tree tinsel,
the presents that had so pleased him at eight.

The farmer introduced him to a pal one stool away,
who tried to speak, teeth tongue and lips
one sutured muscle, a lisping groan,
whose life swarmed in friendship-hungry eyes
as he gulped and nodded, the farmer's tag-along
catastrophe-buddy – Vietnam?
As the eggs went into his gut, the tinsel bucked and soured.
The present, glutted with its own unloved trash,
undermined even childhood snow. He stayed up late to feel *this*?
Wandered out of Denny's rammed Durango up his right armpit
and limped toward the Jarvis Hotel. Wounded—
the empty basin of the street, wounded—
the imprint of place, no place, sturdy plastic patina
under which the larvae of an alien immensity were coiling,
muscular larvae, wetbacks dead from thirst, blending with
the New Mexico desert where ancient creosote
(the in-flight magazine stated) is the oldest thing alive on earth,
"10,000 year old seed near Yuma discovered in pack rat midden."
Did he stay up just to feel the roller-coaster-like heave of each thing
        short-circuit and fizz?
Did he refuse sleep to suffer this peculiar painless rancor?
How could anyone complain about a comfortable bed?
Yet it seemed a cold grill, with a brutalized Adam,
a blood-stained blood boy cursing beneath,
a mined-out bully who hacked up around
the mattress to claw at the sleeper,
a corpse under water, as the currents groped and belittled him…

as he unraveled into dream, the raccoons and badgers
emerged from their tumuli, in overalls, with trowels,
they wended their way (as childhood animals do)
to the cemetery where the earthworm doctor's funeral was a static
purple sketch of gestures … a canopy, a sobbing cricket …
then the gnarled hermaphrodite appeared
and began to leak from every pore … they lowered
the doctor in his casket-bag into a Mayan well?
a fleet of submarines pulled in …

                                    the sleeper was at last

drinking his dream, coming apart, coalescing,
an oatmeal made sodden not in a bowl
but floating, like an isle, in a ring of light.
Not yet digested by America, he had also failed to force
the stuck drawer of night into the bureau of the day.
That ring of light. The one reward of sleep,
while falling to press the heels of palms hard against
closed lids, watch the filigreed nerve gold
shimmer and mill into formations,
coalescing into a fat doughnut of light,
blackness at center, blackness surrounding.
A kind of Madonna curled in the aura of reptilian continuity
he floated, in pieta to
the unknowable body the poet takes upon his lap
every time he starts to write.

Reagan At Bitburg   *

Difficult and necessary to imagine the arsenal attached to his elderly
    frame.
Even Maha Vishnu's war bonnet of an oily orange blast won't do,
but it does connect Reagan to holocaustal fire as he walks by an SS
    tomb,
a match that could strike the air into a global roar.
Spiky flames seem to be growing from his back,
a bony fire, like stegosaurian plates—
he possesses unlimited fuel,
an old imprisoned King whose senility can only be relieved by the
    breast pushing through his bars,
the remaining breast of a 40 year old macheted Salvadoran
wearing a red welt from shoulder diagonal to waist,
the model upon which military decoration is based.
Reagan opens his public heart—
the spirit's hot flame is fed by the monstrous pain of unborn
    grandchildren,
the rack of vacuity upon which all are bound and pulled apart
wobbles like a perverse water wheel
through us, exposing the anguish in our pleasure,
the pleasure in our anguish, the boredom in our appetite,
our appetite for boredom—
one can almost smell (but never really smell)
the fumes from still hot German guilt drifting Bitburg,
substantial flames, bouquets of blackened garden eels waving from
    each tomb.
The souls of the innocent dead could not be here,
their wrath is cobra-like but gentle,
in serpentine flocks they roam each German acre, imprisoned in
that part of us that does not, in unison, effect an end to racial
    stratification.
Can any image grasp Reagan, amazingly still human, the depth of his
    numbness

within minutes of collapsing mind? He is a kind of prism
made of endless glass enclosures, in whose groundmass
is embedded our reality's decomposing kingdom.

[5 May 1985]

Variations on Jesus and the Fly

Homage to those who look through a fly's back in order to see,
a seized red-faced Jesus in which the Lord of Flies is he who sees
    through fly nature—
I tell you the house is winged, a mighty palace of sticky dust,
everything good to alight on, to rub palps over,
for whoever has returned through Jesus's crossed eyes as the soul of a
    dead man—
out of the reincarnational maggot compost,
a gleaming green and black fellow with screens on his mind,
fly power as one might put one's flexed fingers to one's face,
as do the Mexicans clamping a "covering insect" over the face of
    manhood,
to see with the power of insect forceps
drawing the biped to the rim of the cenote where he is held wiggling,
pinned to the target a Fortune Wheel makes, as the zoas carouse,
in the liquid crush this insect has on this young boy,
the hard insect integument and the soft boy's integrity.
The fusion is Jesus and the fly.

A spider will carry off this leggy red face
and weave it into a cross-crowned hill
where the fly folk gather by the thousands to see
Jesus mate with a fly on the top of a pole,
or a fly enter the orifices of the crucified
and carry out treasures for the crowd,
with fly squadrons bearing, through the dusk air,
the shredding oriflamme of one flambéed and frozen,
the way a sickle curves through the grain of night,
as the fly god pounces in his whirling black rags
on what looks up at him from the pit in a caterpillar's back.
There, digger wasp babies, like language deposits,
have been laid by the most responsible mothers in the world,
hundreds of cells equipped with edible beds and phones.
There is a sense in which the caterpillar god
dozes in the mature human, as the Sebastian darts are embedded.

We are bitter because of this,
our forearms swell to the anchor tattoo bursting point,
and to step back into the family home
is to find Dagwood curled on the sofa by his snoring hound,
or the comic peeled from the real,
the real a composition of the comic situation of a soul
seeing through its state, which is to be rejoined
to fur and paps, to dance under the weight of
a baboon head in a test helmet bashed about
until the husky heart of the head gives
and the astronaut baboon explosion in comic stars
is never heard by those who do not see through a fly.
For such deafness takes place in the deep caterpillar
levels of the English Department of the Spirit
where students in test tubes dance and claw
as the Professor Spectre holds these juicy little tombs to the light.
Aha! Chaucer has fused with his Ass,
Milton with a mongrel angel. The fly god hums off,
bearing his white writhing kiddy kettle before him.

I love to watch Caryl eat fresh Dungeness crab.
Her plate, heaped with cracked ice, topped by
a reconstruction of the crab.   Over which her delicate
fingers, more delicate than the morsels
she will extract,   pause like wands,   and she slowly eats,
as if she were undoing a sewing,   as if her fingers
were needles investigating music,   or thinking about
"the most sublime act is to set another before you,"
which can refer to any act of respect
for the otherness all nearness is,   not to be worshipped
but revered in motion,   in pleasure
scythed and harvested,   a beautiful creature eating
                         a beautiful creature.

Moving

> These rooms which will become
> a turban of fire—

Tattered photo of 4 New Guinea head-hunters (taken skulls before
   them like filled glasses of wine)—
Sky-blue wolf spider stampeding toward the camera—
Hart Crane with Clarence, snapped before the father's home, 1930—
Krishna as a many-headed water snake playing in a river with 50 cow
   girls—
A violet Himalayan Octopus God—
A Japanese farmer rain hat, with seaweed protection-trim—

> "favorite things" how make them sing here now
folded in boxes, portable, as am I, 852 South Bedford Street, 12 years,
   "the house of Sway," cave-like
"floating world" under the grape & grape-leaf glass lamp
next to Golub's "Arm," a Petlin spectre leaping forth, next to
   Australian bark maggots, and around the corner,
Kurhajec's bloody-feather tipped wall sculpture,
> like the genitals of Gilgamesh,
across the living-room the Marwan "Head" forever looking into my
   parents' bedroom while they conceive me—

> sweet dim halls, bedrooms breathing out an atmosphere,
each bedroom the first and the last, each hallway
   a kind of worked dirt path—

> Why is it so unnerving to leave a beloved house?
Walls you did not mean much,   we hardly looked at the yard, we
   enjoyed something that reinforced our love for each other,
neutral days of working here alone with Caryl,
I lifted out of bed, the neck of a rusty swan, the food and wine from
   the night before unsure as to how it should pronounce its
   reappearance—

we are born in a wilderness, do not choose our parents,
choose nothing until we learn how to choose,
until something called the soul effects a drought in person,
person-to-be   a starving spider in a basin,
suddenly one IS nothing,   is on nothing,
then not life but life's double begins,
a vision stronger than one's father's whip,
     born, out of womb into a tomb, a room, OM-infested
  splendid vulgarity—

    daily wondering while packing,
have I done anything? Under what weight does all originality suffer?
   I've been dead since rebirth to the facts of place,
but not to the red lakes simmering in the skull of morning,
   have grasped for a hold onto the tiara of the octopus queen,
have attempted a view in which the human is
  multi-anti-formulaic,
   as if life were a flag snapping in the wind
as if only the snap points could be registered in writing . . .

  hunches, notions, love-making in the deep
    tested hollow of 9 AM—

  the meaning a telegram only my own parted mind
    understands

Los Angeles

Looking for a House

The ad had said "the tallest trees in town," nothing about the house itself. And it was true: elms and maples hovering over its 3 stories did spear the sky. The door was opened to an excited blond Jesus, a grade-B movie star face on a poster tacked to the dining-room wall. The house suddenly grew taller, and pointed inward as it ricketly ascended.

The living room was shadowy with handsome old cherrywood doors. And crucifixes—everywhere signs of angler hope and catfish whisker-spine despair. The woman, thin and white t-shirted from the waist up, had an immense rear which disappeared before her thin, muscular legs disappeared into the coffee-stains of anklets and tennis shoes. She looked at us as if she'd shown this house to 100 potential buyers, and soon she'd have to face 103.

So we were not there in her heart, and she went upstairs leaving us to the first floor gloom of untidy, helpless depression that makes walls crawl with: are you shopping for a house, or a tomb? A place to be buried in, with Caryl, and then dug up by that Aryan zombie hovering over supper after supper.

We climbed the stairs like tourist-monks visiting catacombs on instruction, and finally to the woman's attic on a staircase so thin it might as well have been spikes hammered into the wall. There, in the honeyless crown of the Jesus head we sniffed about, noticing desk and phone, piles of receipts ...

To come out into truck level after that was to emerge from the last week gutted catfish mouth, with the weight of its dead mouth air like feelers pushing my mind to: it is more obscene to enter such a house than to enter an unknown person's sex, more obscene and more total, too, for this is full penetration by head and by body, full penetration into another's person alley—and with no sperm to farewell—only a bewildered wandering, looking for a place to live and finding oneself in the stale flesh of the fish while crossbone knife and fork tick overhead.

Ypsilanti

Thanksgiving with Maya

Our underworld should be a shifting *topos* of peasants
scrambling under bushes outside Krogers, not Lorca among the
    watermelons,
but cut-off hands wedged in,
eyes in the packaged beef, groaning cheese and the insurance agent
in Guevara khakis, with a bulldick wrapped around his neck.
We should be floating down, and up, daily, and the streets
should be covered with accidents because of the uprush,
what we are promoting, paying for, lethally authorizing,
    should be part of our daily swearing,
as we curse a driver we should have crap on our face,
as we hit our kid, or a man slugs his wife, a load of blood
    should plow through the ceiling,
there should be bands of wounded teeny-boppers erupting in
    freeways,
possums should fall from acacia limbs, grenades—
and in the slaughter houses, where near-sighted steers are still
    desperately trying to read Sinclair's *The Jungle,*
the impacted consciousness of both man and animal should
    be raised,
lowered, like a yoyo, by the second, so that markets
flood with the language of cows, the floors a foot deep in
    #*&&&#!!!(!*!*!,
                        our own censored unsayable anger,
            let it wrap around the housewife's arteries
as she attaches herself to the cash register,
as she serenades the industry while her blackheads pour

                    In my plate:
Hitlerian gas, a little orchard with asperagus fence, dots were
    running—
gradually the house left its moorings, and we were off!   My
    dear mother forced
the whole dinner into the fuel tank, we went up and down
    Boulevard Place

breaking up the concrete—the neighbors rushed out waving
    turkey bones—
Hey you Eshlemans!   Work Makes Free, but this is not
    Freedom!
You're right!   I said to Bernie Kirk's licentious dad:
this is all a dream of true thanksgiving, to which the asshole
    would be invited,
and we would eat, delirious, as the terror of our killing, the
    Indian massacre,
swept through us.

                For a full picture we need the imago,
and its releasing death-moth.   Maya iconography argues
a demon world sloshing through the day world,
not after life, but in life, inner alive life, my underworld in
    my nose as I cut
into turkey.

            The grief remains encysted.

                I imagine new ceremonies
    in which the Indiana boy
is not pitchforked into a fraternity house to be humiliated and beaten
as his introduction to his soul, but rides off instead on the
    back of the bird that sang
at his birth as his mother steps into the sea and reveals that all tides
are infused with crimson breakers.   Doctors, in fantastic
    dragon costumes,
will palpitate their patients as Saint Georges whose ailments
    consist of
the density of their armor.   Ships will be released from water and will
    drift in space.
The constricted midden of the human view will crumble into aerated
blocks of exposure.   All foetuses will be outfitted with parachutes.
    What is now
fantastic will occur with lightning speed.   All of history, especially
    prehistory,

will be computerized into a single chip enabling people to know
    everything people
have done and suffered, so that the slavery depth in a black man's
    face
will instantly radio the blood and mucous of the slave galley into a
    white
man's heart in such a way that this white heart will darken with the
    sails of so many
voyages of horror   that he will be off with his black brother on
    reciprocal carpets
sailing backwards, then forwards, through a density of tales in which
    the blush of rocks
is as moving as 200 black leech-like incisions in a discovered suicide's
arm.   Heterosexuals will make love to homosexuals by a mutual
    tendril
engagement.   Women will once again, when they feel like it, bear
    children
without a male night deposit.   Every hold, every dale, will regain its
    omenality.
For those who prefer not to live at the bottom of lakes great Babel-
    like towers,
purposely lopsided, will be built by the progeny of Antonio Gaudi,
parks will have no curfew, everyone's death will be equally attended,
the auras of all animals will be respected, temples will be built to the
    lower body,
Chakra centers will be built extending like complex fireworks miles
    into the sky,
Apollo will emerge from his oven hand in hand with the burned.
His solar anxiety will be fed by the serpentine Adam cowering in the
    heartwood,
yes, and night will once again be dread inspiring but in a different
    way,
for night will pass in waves of day.   The human cosmic perspective
    once shed
will reveal that all we have imagined can be lived.

The Bison Keyboard   *

Onto the keyboard of a concert grand Bud Powell shot his fingers.

Was he, elbows flexed, a kind of Tiresias drinking from a trench
     beheaded bison blood?
Are we not, at birth, like bison, deposited on a terrestrial keyboard?
Each depressed key makes an omen trench.
Thus does the earth become grand
and we suck, with Tiresias intensity, as did infant Powell, to prophesy.

Powell is face to face with a bison apparition, a lacquered, black
     ghost.
Unlike Tiresias, he must draw, through a keyboard, directional sound,
and even if he has a grand it is hardly a trench of warm blood.

To be a seer is to re-enter the trench out of which we emerged.
Powell made contact, but failed to drink.
For a grand, in profile, lid propped, evokes a headless bison,
whose chest cavity, the keyboard, releases the sound Tiresias needed
     blood to utter.
And Tiresias, who re-entered the essential trench, did guide
     Odysseus.
At the keyboard, Powell clawed for blood, as if stabbing at a bison
     sacrifice.
Thus he proposes a grand dilemma: the living, no matter how grand
     their C chords,
lack the Tiresian recipe: to be all soul and bison vivid, a
     cunnilinctrice of the goddess trench.

On his cell wall in Creedmore asylum, Powell is said to have
     sketched, in chalk, a keyboard.

Powell, now the ghost of a grand, stared at this keyboard.
"O how get home, Tiresias? How drink bison music in this hellish
     trench?"

Commarque   *

Why is it ruins are so compelling?
Between our lives and nature, they are
the most visible signs of purgatory—
they are like the sound of a buzzsaw
in a cemetery, or perhaps its inversion,
     death pruning us, and so
they drive Wordsworth to affirm immortality,
to cross the rotten bridge they present
he hammers in affirmation studs just to
keep from slipping into
the almost-there or not-quite-here
they summon,   but then, why not feel at home
in this once lived in
cavity crawled with breeze? Doesn't the abyss
inhabit each of our gestures,
the food on our cooling plates,
the phallus of the god diffused in fermenting grapes?
A well deep down into which a stripe of light
sheens the vasoline blackness shows the Yquem of an hour,
in which *nether* is a fully inhabitable
word—
           they are, and
they're not.   For they say,
more than tombstones: the living *were,*
     not merely: the dead
          are.   the dead are
no problem.   It is our
wereness, our werehereness,
that moves into our hearts standing in ruins,
moves in like a homeless pregnant woman.
Only after she has birthed
   might we request she leave …

                                        a child of
                          stone?

One we would wish to care
for, as our own?

I looked into the stony sores
at Chateau L'Herm and saw Countess La Morte in bed,
holding out her pollen-covered palm,
and what I licked from it was *sheer smile,*
 it was then I heard a tapping, and saw
Wordsworth on his knees
 in an old musty cloak
with nothing under him
but the glandular density of the collection
 taken up by the moat ...

Les Eyzies

On Atget's Road

the apple trees turn into light, a liquid light,
weightless, spent, so dark, so ruddy brown, they are a sensing
that what we do not make is so much more here than what we do.
On Atget's road the souls curve about each other
like fish, or smoke, their presence deepens the emptiness
of the road itself, or of a cobbled street with no passer-by,
with stone buildings in which people lived, a past
even more past in its evoked presence here ...
                                    but more than street or road
paths trouble his eternity, simple paths, half washed out,
wet, leaf-littered, the barest trace of human making,
a curving into disappearance, slightly rounded, as if earth
were felt in such clearing as a pregnancy we
could never know, only touch across ...

                          gone! is the cry
of Atget in Atget, of his roaming now forever past world
in which a stone staircase is so gentle one
cups it in one's hand, with the love with which one
takes morning water from the faucet in two cupped hands,
seeing one's palms though the water,
which are thus so remote, not of one,
something under water, on Eugéne Atget's road
insubstantial as all roads, the vernacular gesture of
a road in which paths and stones flee in place
the enduring velocity of night.

Pan's Signal Tower

The peak of the obsidian mountain swarms with
red snow,   against grey lime sky the mountain
becomes negative,   a dark entrance whose interior
       swarms with fire,   or is this red
a warning from an ancient goddess that the stuff of Adam
is now nearly totally transformed into warfare,
the perpetuation of life
                                   pulled inside out,
its inner lining, extinction, now shows
       in the face of things ...

                    At the base of this mountain
a chain of boulders, pieces of an enormous stone phallus
before the top of which a headless
       deer, eviscerated, lies on its back,
3 legs groping the air more like insect legs than animal,
as if a wheeling motion were implied, as if this dying
headless creature were struggling
       under phallus,

                          a starved Pan looks beyond the deer to
a windowless house, poised on the highest of the phallus
       pieces, about to slide—

       ◇

The wheeling legs revolve and set in motion
       an inner meaning of the house, it is Pan's signal tower,
his alchemical workshop in which 14 red women recline
stroking their red fur,   with their 28 legs propped on
       the stone hub they become the animators of
the Grindstone of Desire, whose long red spokes churn
       the Panic Satanic machinery in the faces of men—

yet Pan is famished here, the scene still, as if the workshop
       is wall all the way through, it is

the weight of our sensing that as the animals become extinct,
the abyss recedes,   as
    the Bawean deer
       the Cedros Island mule deer
          the Columbian white-tailed deer
            the hog deer
              the key deer
                the McNeil's deer
                  the musk deer   leave,

the fructifying abyss, the *abaton,* where the power of the
    womb
    crosses the power of the tomb, where the sleeper curls
awaiting an incubus to deposit soul eggs in his side,

the grandeur of this emptiness draws further and further away

    ◇

For a moment a clearing is constructed,
    brown ground, with our yearning for a golden age
rising in bands of lime and yellow light,

    and in the stillness of my own
not knowing where to turn,
I saw,   boiling in the cornice of the sky,
the blood of a cauldron
whose sides are the embraced bodies of the living and the
    dead,
    rage of the grail
to dissolve the watchfiends, the rackscreams,
back into that blood pudding
Red Riding Hood's grandmother was stirring
    under the covers,   when the animal
was the mucilage between "us" and "them."

after a painting by
David True

Ode to the Man in the Moon

Looking at a self-portrait by Frida Kahlo, one in which a monkey has
his arm around her neck, brown hair
sticking up around his head, a small brown monkey with gleaming
dead eyes (whose tiny head only
comes up to Frida's neck vase raised chin), I thought:

he's the man in the moon!
Frida's menstrual partner,
the little guy who greets her as she ascends into the moon's
    hollow (Japanese lantern-like) sphere,

this figure is her second, her spare cross, her intersectional
    anguish,
what a cute little cheese eater,
how nice the man in the moon turns out to be,
this blood elf who greets and visits Frida
    sweating plaster-of-paris in hospital beds

                  he is the lute
imagined behind the sugar skull, her brother-in-other,
her backer. The vision to hold firm
as life again becomes a surgical barge,
her daemon placenta,   her writ-at-large

Hail to this beast of the blood who knows more than guys,
this salt that percolates in vaginal leaves.
The egg-trapeze snaps the sulfuric recharge of woman on the
    banister of her woman,
and this marvelous figure shuffles her blood
as if it were razor-blades and petunias,
this non-man he, this no-animus,
    silo of without-negation.
Hail to his heraldic leaking of difference
Hail
       and fashion him,

for without cordage,   he is mere flavor,
  tooth taste bile fleck,

          offer him cadence,
      welcome him to the wedge.

Children of the Monosyllable   *

   I saw a fist
gripping a streaming,
as if beetle-words were flowing into a bottleneck from
      everywhichway,
and that in the slaughterhouse of the fist
they were killed, and transformed or
      reborn—I could see
the words go in—and what seemed to be their children
      emerge—
they swiveled in like broom straws hungry for the hasp,
      seeking to be
bundled, then flowed out the hasp into a second
flowering broom head,
                        the hasp vessel was the word CUNT,
      like beetle-streams, emerging from the mist, the children
      were hard to identify:
         cunnus, yes, cyn, cunta,
parallel to country, kin, kind,
      with shadows of city and cemetery,
cunabula, cunicle, cuniculate, cuneo with its cuneiform kin,
         cunning wedge-words,   vise-signs,
kennings,   beetle-crevices,   kens,   or learnings—

Why did they swarm into this vessel
that sapped them of their power? Before the transformation,
the cunea worked somewhat underground, they supped from
      Cunti, or Kunda,
as if attached to Herr Cuneibrain,   termites?   egg-carriers?
As if the vulva-lode were slightly under ground-level
      a flavoring of stone.
Words once did live across our eyes,
      above and below the Dali razor blade.

The origin of language a termite hill?
A single sound-extent   with a group soul?

I've noticed one "hill,"   viewed from a plane,
at what point were thing/earth association words
                blocked/wedged
        out of themselves, frozen, into
            their own mimicry?
Or were the cunae slaughtered? Tonsured, cunta into cunt,
country a cunt-tree pun,   cunicle, cuniculate nearly lost,

    Monoculture is the reduction/crushing of the millipedal
mania to hit death with a difference

        But why from this round-about phrase must be guessed,
        What in ONE single SYLLABLE'S better expressed;
        That SYLLABLE then I my sentiment call,
        So here's to that WORD, which is ONE WORD for all.

        —G.A. Stevens, *Songs Comic & Satyrical*, 1788.

                And the Children? Diddly-pout, eel-skinner, Eve's
custom house, mole catcher, moss-rose, star over the garter, belly dingle,
botany bay, butter boat, cuntkin, cunnie, dumb-squint, fie-for-shame,
fire-lock, flap doodle, oyster-catcher, nonny-nonny, seed-plot, milking-
pail, meat-market, rest-and-be-thankful, road to a christening, standing
room for one, Bluebeard's closet, catherine wheel, Cupid's anvil, pen-
wiper, mark-of-the-beast, fumbler's hall, gravy giver, house under the
hill, fud, little spot where uncle's doodle goes, front doormat, snatch-
blatch, rob the ruffian, skin the pizzle, Smock-Alley …

    They are attempts to free Her Nature from its curse,
but they remain infected; they spread into our lives,
amusing,   disgusting,   flaccid mixtures of the ersatz and the
    other,
        crinkum-crankum, doodle-sack—
suppose we made these children honorifics, placing them
    before
"sky" or "ocean," to relink them to their goddess ancestor—
could we do this at all? Would people catch on?   Would
    they care?

crinkum-crankum sky [clouds twisting, full of whimsey]
the doodle-sack sky [wind-swollen, bagpipe-bleating,
     god-blast-encysted]
Would the great goddess return? Might She invert our
     poisonous world-end anti-ecology?

We'd have to pass back through the bottle-neck,
we'd have to re-experience, in another conscious first-time,
what the language-mind suffered, we'd have to run the
     whim-wham
sperm-sucker fie-for-shame film backwards,   as we ourselves
assimilated the peril of the reduction of woman,
          her identity crunched into a monosyllable

          CUNT   as termite queen
          laying 50,000 associations per day in mind,
nether eyebrows, itching Jennies, roasting jacks.
If only we could adopt these orphans! Might we then nurse
     them?
As we nursed, might we croon: "in your cavey flavoring,
we feel the kin cleft, the RA, the OM, the KA
     lingering gas,   and GOD   poor rotten corks
for bottles that wanted only to be perpetually sipped"

Little *mark-of-the-beast,*   little *gutter*
you bear the stink of a degradation you are hardly responsible for.

Gutter then responded: "I'm happy to be
     a receptacle for dead leaves, rain, rotting pigeons,
an inferior form of Kunta's cunabula.
True, I'm not life-emitting. I'm a drainpipe,
     people piss their tongues through me."

Each word a dragon-tongue-tip unhinged from axial powers.
Gutter Cunabula convinced me.   Every word's amphibian
     sound-tail suckers

what I cannot ordinarily discern,   it sinks, a tentacle,
    into the termite flow, as the word-mites
bless   as they bang and bank off,   as they scurry
egg-laden,   egged-on,   in midden to what I was not given to see—
but as the initial gate appears,   a fissure in the rockface
    "signed" by a red ochre dot   in recognition of her Blood
one node,   with Moon and Tide,   of the Delta Constellation,
I can hear the vacuum of these children in the rusty
howl of a train passing through Ypsilanti,   halo-iron,
shroud and nave of the sordid cleat of tongue.

At the Speed of Wine   *

> *I would gladly emulate Odysseus if I*
> *could, and go down to the shadows*
> *for another hour's conversation with*
> *Crane on the subject of poetry …*
> —Yvor Winters

The balloon glass, the swirl—
what is the image of the wine's insides?

Numb, I was carried off by
unfriendly insects and tamped into their compost,
something good for a nest stave, perhaps fuel
for a grasshopper roast. Yet I continued to drink
as I slept, sleeping at the speed of wine,
for I had fitted out my dream body with a full *cave*—
there was Crane! His back to the action,
digging the distortions in Falstaff-bellied flasks.
He piled his suicide knives up in an amazing wickerwork
        as I sat down,   and asked me,
as if he knew me, which one would I choose.
I like the one that looks like a rabbit's ear, I said,
or that curious one at the bottom of the pile,
a piece of wood sculpture by Michelangelo
where he depicts himself leaning dejectedly against his cross …

A huge frog
lugged himself out of the Punchino Palace kitchen
balancing a tray of sordidity on one trembling foot.

My idea, I said to Hart, is to pick up a woman without breasts,
with wings instead of breasts,
one whose chest is a skillet of unmotherly crackling oil,
our soul in short,   why not try to pick up our soul for a change
instead of sliding anklewise into the flues?

Crane plucked a pair of tiny scissors from his vest pocket and snipped
    off his nose,
then turned to me with a widening red valley between his eyes.
Only then did I see his stairwell, and the extent to which it twisted
    into his brain,
I lit a match, and the blood turned back,
I lit another, and a helpless curare began to drain from his eyes.

"Poets in death need poets in life," he sobbed,
"not parasitically, my dear wench,
we need you here, under the image mill,
where Samson's soles are a kind of liquor for our eyes,
here, in the emptiness of the North American underworld,
any image you twist through the wringer of pubescent
    lubricity, tensioned on sheer need,
is manna to us,
no image = no food,   as simple as that!"

He raised his hands in a magician-like *voilá!*
a decanter appeared, a crystal ball of colorless liquid
I was to see into. "This is the Midwestern other side,"
Crane went on, "argument that you are half
what you think you are, and that to protect it
you must lose at least 100 pounds,
so that you appear to the sensual world a near-man,
rheumatic eyeball jelly in socket cylinders, a kind of god, a Tlaloc
of this Western night.   –Wait, let me finish.   I argued flux
via my own barrel-rolls, leashed to Whitman's mobile hand.
Have you considered Rothko? The paintings by which
he sought to join the Surrealists were done by others.
Then he erased the content from his work.
What had appeared to be scenery for the drama
now was the drama—static, dirigible, stacks of weightless tires
which could be injected with his Orphic blood.
The price was terrible, one I refused to barter. We're both suicides,
but I went out one door, Rothko another."

You're a flicker, Crane! Not an underworld!
I can relate to you and feel the joist of comradeship
but as I concentrate, I see behind you the Phi Delt "hell room"
I know my chance of seeing things from the inside out was ruined
    at 19
as I took the bulldick around my neck and stood in humiliation
without striking back. Caricature can be oxymoronic venom,
and my desire then was baffled—even if the pain and weirdness of
    that pseudo-Satanic fete
turned me, 3 years later, toward this work.
So I must acknowledge a puerile satire of the underworld
as the father of my poetry. Or as the restriction that snapped my
    lassitude.
But such is no underworld support,
no Poe gangrenescent at the subway gates …
but then again, Poe's another individual, not a ripe swamp of
    otherness
hissing its affiliations into a sleeping live person's ear.
The core of our imaginal demise is: the Maya, the Greeks, and the
    Egyptians
will not transmit their fabulous gourds of juices in which
imps are instructing kobolds, ruled by stern fairies. Holy kaishaku!
They are as slides projected on our image screens!
This is why I've gone back through the agrarian earth to
those who appear to have spent 20,000 years
wrestling the animals out of and into their heads …
People defined by holes! They've so underscooped us
that now each stone seems to cap a void.
Your and my background assurance was: the surface holds.

Crane tilted his head. "I was a space sucker—
and you, are you a depth sucker, are you sucking
    off   depth?"

Was I being set up to defend a night-blooming abyss?
The shoulders all stand on, shoulders that are not there?
The muse angel duende congealed in 1000 floor deep Les Eyzies?

"You're pigging out on underworld hooey,"
Crane grimaced, "you want to find the missing story of yourself
and no personal or transpersonal myth or psychoanalytics will do.
Queerly, you emerged as a potential self
via a double beating: your father and the Phi Delt 'actives.'
For you, creation is counter-attack on catastrophe
and you'll bear that legacy wherever you bear.
Your tribulation is to have discovered that beyond the father-
    blocked doorway
are sons with clubs."

He was doodling on his face, as if it were a worksheet—
he'd move his eyes together, or eat one of his eyebrows, then draw it
    from an ear.
"New anatomies," he grinned, "here, have a chalk ..."
Then he pinocchioed his nose, and said:
"Jesus who worked in flesh is a challenge to all poets.
The desire as Artaud retold it, is to reconstruct the human body,
get rid of its organs, equip it to really dance.
Having been devoured after my stunt off the *Orizaba,*
I found myself in collapsible space,
pound for pound in the gutturals of the hammerhead
who plucked my ass from—was it a 'light topcoat'?
Dionysian motion is a willful peristalsis, ruddering one's own
    dreaming,
where Whitman and Dickinson cross, a blond serpent is hatched,
one of the brood with your white Apollo. Look into my eyes, you'll
    see its brothers."

As I peered through his bruised lids into his irises,
twin coral snakes, tails in mouths, began to turn
behind what remained Crane's frightened, compassionate pupils.
Were they *his* missing story? The one we all are missing
until we take the oath of the abyss and induct that realm
in which the dead reach us and warn us with their whirling eyes
that defective railroad signals are positioned every way we turn?
Crane clawed out at me, I leapt back to see his talon
swing full and embed in his other shoulder.

He then tore out his talon-arm and rammed it into one eye,
caught his other eye through the back of his head,
gulped it down, tore open his fly and pissed a string of eyes.
A Mobius effect, for nothing disappeared.
"Everything in the underworld fits into everything else,"
he laughed. I was thinking about van Gogh,
I said, crows over the wheatfield was not his last painting.
He did the crows 2 weeks before his 2 versions of Daubigny's garden.

       "The mound with flowers in the lower
central portion is tumultuous," Crane exclaimed, "as if Vincent
buried himself there, not in wilderness,
but in another painter's yard! In the end, most value middle-
    class life.
Especially since it is what most artists are.
Shelley is windy and pure, his words seem to have floating
spaces between worlds, or letters, the claim on the infinite is too
    trusting.
Blake had working-class printer grease on his *Jerusalem.*
I'm aware Bunting told you Blake is 'the abomination of poetry.'
Bunting feared he forced experience into a plaster cast,
turned it into religious forgery. That is why
Blake's ghost put both contact lenses in Basil's right eye that night,
to show Basil had overviewed half, and not seen the other half at all.
But, let's stop talking about literature.
It only shows to what extent we are anxious about the discrepancy
between what we've intended, and what it appears we've done.
Peggy Cowley's cunt was extraordinary. I've not been able to
    reconstruct it
no matter how I reinvent my body"
Then he quoted Laura Riding: 'Until the missing story of ourselves
    is told,
nothing besides told can suffice us: we shall go on quietly craving it.'

Did you fuck her, Hart?

"Of course, but not in the way you'd compose me.
You forget: I was born before the psychoanalysis of fire,
and thus held to my Promethian post. I was guilty, *under Walt*,
trenchant guilt, undercoating,
there was nothing else—Titan resolve!
Even humorous, but art is revolt against predetermined dread.
Rhymes? The manacles of Grace and Clarence—*clearance!*—
    grace in clearance, the *Orizaba* drop!"

Your "Tears of Christ" has the conundrum power of 2000 years,
or I should say, I've been draining its nailed feet for 20 years
and have yet to see the fluid run clear.
Way up in the crucified is a swan and a goat,
and as for his head, I'm reminded of Our Lady Coatlicue,
whose head consists of 2 face-to-face pressed rattlesnake heads—
She faces us with one of their left eyes, one of their right,
to indicate that the back of any matter is the beginning of a new
    damnation.

                            "Development is steel rain,"
Crane mused, "we write when Psyche is invited.
This is our core, to have spread the asparagus,
and to have perceived beauty in every mundane spread,
in atolls of guano, in the coarse heels of Caravaggio.
The demand on soul now is to ordain those powers still denied a
    human form,
to get the lower body out before its repressive furnaces ignite all
    worlds.
But you'll end up here"—he stared at me—
"in that most awful term, *regardless*. Regardless the children,
regardless the maggots. Regardless, the name of America,
why not 'Regardless' as the name of your poem?"

Why not "Am Let" chipped into your headstone,
I said without thinking, irritated by his arrogance.
But the wine came round the glass, and I saw the density in his
    stained intentions.

Like Spicer, he had slept with all his poems.
At my thought of Spicer, Crane performed a fascinating act:
he shoved into the bar an iron stove into whose side had
    been riveted: *T h e   P o e m*
Then, working his face as if it were rubber,
he climbed a ladder and threw himself off
as if into the stove whose entire top was open and glowing red.
Having leapt, suspended in flight, he turned his head and looked
    at me
with a most amazing expression: he made me feel as if I were his
    primal scene,
I mean, he looked at me with awe disgust amazement joy—
    and *Lascaux!*
For behind the coral snakes backing up his gaze bisons were amassing,
as if I, as mortal non-otherness, were mammal blend in art—
was I meat parts? His association with a slaughterhouse?
Then he swerved, converting his falling leap into a J,
at which point the stove broke into "Giant Steps!"
Seconds later, I was in the furnace with Crane,
soldered to its northern wall, a kind of spectator though I felt
    riveted to
rotunda iron. Crane was in the flames, or waves, or billows, playing
    and dissolving,
he drew up and out certain flames, as if udders, or cocks,
lengthening them, spires, tapers, then he'd fasten on,
with any part of his body, navel, mouth, and revolve,
spinning helplessly, ecstatic, a propeller-man,
and then arch up swan-dively and then burn down onto another
    peak.
He was mostly head, his body hummingbird.
He flitted, simultaneously inside and outside himself,
nectaring the flames, collecting as he spun.
As if all mask, he spun and held in place about
an inch above the fattest flame. His eyelids curved outward and
    downward,
he looked like an old dying infant! Churchill at 6 months!
Slowly he blasted backward, against the oath extending his reign,

contracted to a foetal zenith, and then inflated, a small transparent
    dirigible,
with electric wind, and I could see inside Crane at this moment
the emphasis of the Atikai, old helpless stars, worn to ember,
rekindling in this consecrated pod—consecrated? Yes,
because poetry is a primal emphasis, and uplifts in its sutured arms
a paeonic bed swarming with predecessor copulators,
a plate of Medusa as lightning pasta.   Then Hart repoured into his
    deathly skin
and looked at me as if he were selling apples.

"Askesis" he said off-handedly, "Bloom's delight is to show in
    critical X-ray
the contra-naturum of the poem, but since he did not write poetry,
he must hover-foster it, you know, immaculate its eggy conception.
As you and I know, poems are dragged out of moray crevices,
they are braille impressions of forgotten infant soles,
their mordants an aggregate imposition.
The book is always late; the book *is*, in fact, belatedness.
Literature fumes are oral ember dependent. Through the looted
streets of the late 1960s comes Harold Bloom,
bearing his memoried reading of *Paradise Lost*—
he is as moving as James Baldwin driving through shattered Harlem
    plate glass, his father's
lifelong nonwords on his mind, his just dead father, who never said a
    tender word to James.
We must not forget that in the doorweave of Lascaux,
critic is indistinguishable from poet.
We live on withering—or growing?—swaying beanstalks
whose roots are hidden, receivable as emanations
but static to contemporary radios … Cocteau's Orpheus,
hunched before the Rolls-Royce radio tried to make sense of noise,
as have we all, for ages! Was Orpheus aware
that the scat was exploded particles of Okeanos
that what was firing through, via his radio was the god stuff
that has been in holding-scatter since the death of Pan?
From my gloomy viewpoint, your discovery of me in your winestream
as an emanation, and not a ghost, is a gain in respect to inspiration

and the recognition of a new abyss in life.
I killed myself because I was out of bond with an essential cosmos,
I felt disgrace, not as a cocksucker or punching-bag for stokers ...
I split because even in Mexico I could not find a wavering sky-band
 to bolt me into the now of my destiny."

He swirled his La Tache and growled:
"For the hearing remains in the beast,
and is of the beast, and must be fucked out of the beast,
must literally be drawn from that fist-like pouch
that would keep knowing opaque, that testicle-haven,
that muttercore, that inverted tower of infant blasphemy,
 'the unspeakable cruelty
of living and having no being who could justify you ...'
—loss of god? But we've never had god, or gods,
as Western plagiarists we went to church,
no serpent was inserted into our most tender aperture at 12,
and the night? THE NIGHT IS OPHELIAN," he raged,
"*her* body in water is the feel of night
as it slips through us,   toward us,   as the cling of things
again and again releases, as innocent beauty
again and again sinks through the pond layers of our bile and
 our confusion ..."

I could tell he was tiring, that a sublimation was starting to
 claim him.
We said nothing for a while. Me thinking of the naked Hiroshima
 man
standing in that inferno, holding his eyeball out in his palm.
I thought of my nightmare, in which that eyeball
leapt into the sky and hugely hovered over me, that eyeball
more powerful than our moon, the conscience satellite,
raying down, as if a helicopter beam, into Everyman's backyard ...

Crane cupped his goblet and broke paralysis back through his
 shoulders
by squeezing his glass until his back snapped.
He then recollected his anatomy, bagged himself small,

a hairless creature at the base of the goblet.
He saluted me like a sailor, lurched to a straw,
pole-vaulted up to the rim, ascended and
dove with a wink, like, I've done this before!
disappearing into the crimson wreathe, or Lethe,
of the tiny lagoon the scarlet violence recalled within the round
    aplomb.
Where was he diving now? As he entered the stem, I saw stars.
Was this vision to free me into an ample vulgarity?
A liquid fart of swear words zigzagged forth, and he was gone,
vulgar and feral, vulgar, of the Bulgar, Vulgarian and thorough.

Spelunking the Skeleton

Into the word wham I bent my mother,
I scissored through 15,000 years,
not as I but as Ira, as sea scold,
into the word scam I rammed the savior.

Scrotal booties tiered my fantasies:
morve, Plutonium, scuttled pukes,
dinosaurs stranded in a child's fingerly Jack Frost,
Thomas Taylor wandering London as a Cyclops,

the Elephant Man dining with King Kong.
At times decomposed prepositions
lay like squashed udders before this tryst,
for the way back into active incubus was madre thick

at the core of Gertrude whee (rumba bug
with her Dodgem maze of adolescent sinners,
la cucaracha is the poet's goddess).
As henchman of my I, Ira ate sheer rock,

kamdaak waneng, Bimin-Kuskumin anthropophagy,
bone marrow of partrilineage et mersels of hs lwr b,
that is, the genital parts have survived the literate
tradition, but vagina should be served with pork,

Robert Lowell with Charles Olson and then I hit
Jupiter Salt Peanuts and the Koko leavings of a million squirrels.
My heroine was a plant with the mind of an eel
aping the Niagara of the Northern Lights.

O let my childhood rattlesnake, let language bear
my fate. Any good poem captures the swell of the devil's bicep
as it rises, a tsunami, in the complexion of the Ivory Tower.
And then, I knippered the cuttlesnoops

and heard Artaud rage at those poets who play
without a bullet in their guts. Is your point,
being of smoke, a South African black in raised
push-up position facing a lugered merc?

Is primordial logos the same thing as mystical mud?
Back means better? Do the neighs of yesteryear
contain a stronger venom than the poppas and mommas
in your possum-skin kit? No wonder Arthur

contracted into a puddle! You can't go out and back
and continue to live! Packs of actualities
hit like newspapers in the wampum of the road,
but why not wander the hands of the women painting
    Font-de-Gaume?

Why not look into the cider press of an active incubus,
why not pave an argument and unearth it too?
Is not poetry the pleasure of cucaracha peripherals,
Gertrude jitterbugging with her wits?

O be reborn, rebirthed, sneak up on Oedipus,
but here be masterless! Siphon the organ out of fantasy,
then peer in to Kafka copulating with a wound,
once in the Kafka cockpit imagine the *sugar*

in that wound, Bud's Bubble, raspberry of a paradise
in which the luscious fornicate is made from the silk of whores,
for poetry is Crossing the Brooklyn Ferry
as well as admiring the runs in Walt's hose

now gaping with Lusitania, Vietnam and college poker,
cruets of father, martyr keels of mother,
Li Po moon ping pong, and the pimples that suddenly
decorated Persephone when Hades braked her spume.

UNDER WORLD ARREST (1994)

Short Story

Begin with this: the world has no origin.
We encircle the moment, lovers
who, encircling each other, steep in
                    the fantasy:
now we know the meaning of life.

Wordsworth's *recollection:* wreck election,
the coddling of ruins, as if the oldest man
            thinking of the earliest thing
offers imagination its greatest bounty.

A poem is a snake sloughing off the momentary,
crawling out of now (the encasement of
                    its condition)
into layered, mattered, time.
Now is the tear and ear of terra's torn era.
For the serpentine, merely a writhe
                    in appetite.

We posit Origin in order to posit End,

and if your drinking water is sewage,
to do so is understandable.

When the water is pure, Lilith's anatomy
is glimpsable in each drop.

But the water is never pure.

Before time, there appears to have been
a glass of pure water.

Therefore, we speculate, after time,
there will be another.

Life, a halo surrounding emptiness.

Continue with this: not body vs. soul,
but the inherent doubleness of any situation.
Thus in fusion there is also abyss.

Conclusion: I am suspended between origin and now,
or between origin and a bit before now.
Unknotting myself from both ends,
I drop through the funnel the y in abyss offers.

Nothing satisfies. And,
my suffering is nothing. Two postage stamps
glued, back to back,
abysscadabra.

What is missing? A poetry so full of claws
as to tear the reader's face off.
Too much? Look what men do to each other..
Why should art account for less?

Poetry's horrible responsibility:
in language to be the world.

Still-Life, With Huidobro   *

Two guinea hen legs, an artichoke bottom, in an earthen bowl.

My partially-consumed parents, my partially-consumed self, not of them. Not of *their bird.* How so? Their breast gone, their wings, I am picked clean of leaves,

I am heart tufted with choke.

Do we pull childhood through adolescence and reconstruct it as formal fantasy, as "organiz'd innocence," so that the poem is always in some sense *back there—*

or might a more severe transformation occur?

If mother is made imagination, I am no longer *her* child. She has been brought forward as: *invent new worlds.* The father then becomes: *and back up what you say.* A responsible avant-garde. When Blake rejects the rational, he sets up a lifelong struggle with the father.

Huidobro's "Inventa mundos nuevos y cuida tu palabra" contains the contraries in which a poetry might live. At one extreme, the poem is nearly fantasy—at the other, nearly observation. In each extreme, yin-yang-wise, a pulse of the other asserts, the rhythm reverses.

Vision is not prior to reality, but reality is vision's material.

[Les Bois d'Envaux]

Indiana In The Night Sky   *

Again! before the podium, the mass of yellow sheets
on which are written the poems I am to read—
mostly blank. What is under the work
                    is again showing through.
                To write is to scratch with a knife
on a boulder my body is stretched across.
I make an order at one point in the vast
                    skin of things
and now must hunt for what I am sure I had prepared.
In this repeated dream, last night
I finally found something I could read.
A murderer spoke, mostly grunts I mouthed
                        to audience satisfaction?

    the dream frayed…I half-awoke
intent upon seeing what correspondence there might be
between blankness erasing my words
and only being able to control the situation
                    as a murderer.
My mother was again present,
ill and dead, fixedly in bed,
needing constant attention.
Which illness would I attend?
Her room was hived with doors.
I locked the Oedipal one,
                    cutting back
to the living room where, in 1966,
reading *The Function of the Orgasm*,
    I confronted her.
"I don't love you like you think I do."
That night, I slipped down into my basement
    teen-age nook and wrote:

    Today I have set my crowbar against all I know
    In a shower of soot & blood
    Breaking the backbone of my mother

Because she died 4 years later of spinal cancer
I have the fantasy that somehow
those written words, which I don't think she read,
    are embodied in
what I actually did say in the living room,
that I was fated to gain independence from her
                        and from Indiana
only by killing something there,
that I was to know the power of the word
via associating breaking my mother's backbone
    with the illness that killed her!

Now, I believe that this is not true—
but why is it trenchant?
Having to appear as a murderer
to be able to break the hold of the blank
                    or, erased, page.
I needed the negative aspect of my freedom
to confront the exultation of my absurdity.
The nothingness swarming these ordered lines
    scoops them up,
or comes up from below, as if the boulder
I scratch thoughts into
                        has the power to shrug,
effacing my remarks, restoring its mother purity.

Double Pelican   *

I dip my spout into your sex. Your retort,
   where all things get retwisted,
magma-bubble-gulps my mind. Then we spin,
   a cross in orbit, Magdalenian.

The miracle is: simultaneously your spout
   penetrates my navel.
I feel your interest spread, like ganglia.
   Our missing story flows lawlessly.

   We,   the shadow of each,
   neither prior,   nor dominant.

The gist is to grip the seamless jet of
   shadow squid, to be lucid
commandos slipping through the basis of
   mind. Embraced within you,

I see your centripetally-closed plates
   fan wide. My spout becomes
the flute of an empyramided king. I charm
   your cobra. You hood my sex.

   Tentacles of human coherence.

Under Louse Arrest

I fear a louse of phantasmagorical energy,
a stallion maggot refusing to be a fly,
                    holding all captive,
feeding all, immersing all in contrasoul,
then slaughtering from within.

        ◇

We are at every moment in swill with nothingness,
                    in the awe of chaos bottled
as the blood head of male nuclear destruction.
                    The Grail unidentifiable still
because we have not created a common stone
                    fluidified with Kali's ichor.

        ◇

I am anchored to Sonoran pronghorn,
                    to Queensland rat kangaroo,
                    to white-headed saki, to you,
                    disgusting plague of novelty,
shield against which men have crushed the underworld.

After Pindar　　　　　　　　　　　　　　　　　　　　*

      The Siberian Greco-Roman wrestler,
        Aztec obsidian embroidered skull,
muscles   plates, or
   tectonics,   they say some just collapse at his feet.
                          Is he
   the god-force I feel in Vedran Smailovic
a member of the Sarajevo Opera, in formal evening attire,
playing outside the bakery where Serbian mortars struck
  a bread line in late May, killing 22 people.
Every day, for 22 days, Smailovic braved
      sniper and artillery fire to play
  Albinoni's *Adagio* in honor of those who had died—

Autumn sings,   in singe with winter's fangs.

A Friendship

Koki, I keep looking at you
across my skeleton, so as to keep the whole
within grasp. The Hillhurst mansion
   hung with New Year crepe,
your fingers pressing into Beethoven,
a quiet Sunday afternoon, 40 seated
where 200 had romped. Sonata in A♭ Major, Op. 110.

Cataclysmic chamber of literally
no world after we go, and no
               way I can be equal to
your having been visited by Death.
Mine is still on a Bergman screen,
an awareness, not a chess presence,
even if I do wear my father's eyeballs
like jester bells attached to my back.

Stripped redbud, have you *anything* to tell us?
You'll come around, spring, how practiced
you'll be for your crumbling!
               Or are you now so seasoned
that your dimension is beyond us?
We, who seem to have only one bend,
oh we, the bundled up,
whose open-endedness is
contingent.
                     How use language
in such a way that what it can't do
shows more potently than what it can?

To arm-wrestle on the kitchen table late at night.
As if an hour later, sweet rolls, in the nook,
sunlit Sunday, tentative American, a newspaper,
                     we are guests.

No memory equal to the sibylline structure of the other.
Your musical laugh jiggling
ice cubes over your warm, warm heart,
always a bit off center.
We court a center whose function is to take our good
  and then to kill us.
At ice, art is the key to survival,
God only occurs after person—
                    before person,
the human is constructed out of eating image,
an image eating an image, more primary
than food?
            Lascaux
is the debris of image eating,
                as if Cro-Magnons were bees
buzzed to image.

    Why didn't I tell you this before?
Why didn't I tell myself?

Poetry holds many. But does it hold friendship?

I swallow the mother oyster, and proceed.
You waver in my sight, indecisive
brother emotion. I watch you move toward music
and move away, your vacillation is so real
I sense the extent to which I've murdered vacillation
to do what I've done. Your arabesque hesitation
truer to the world we live in.

                (Koki
the iron shrine of a train whistle,
road groans, cat shriek, 30 feet away as if arctic.
You so near, so love and marrow
                filled with never,
oh my. how not lament myself.
                        You are 3000 miles away

as am I, if I am here,
my statement hangs on this,
the wall
the wall!
the facing non-you of the night,
                    dear friend. Words like fingers
caressing your heels. Into what eternity can I set
                the madness of illness,
                irrational   nature
screws love, unknowing bugs copulate in our eyes

You are a stamen
oh you do blossom did do do blossom in my he
oh is there language to crib to hold
    your forlorn hand?

                    Had you over for an on
                    we became friends

I don't want to ode or to elegize you
I want to sensitize these words to y   being

You generously enhearthed Caryl
and I, pale flame,
you said: welcome
you said: how rude!
you said sit down at my table for 100
you said be of my family
you said my mother and father are good

North Vermont changed as all of us knew you
your bookstore window changed, we heard Collard,
    the music in the book
    the book before music
and we arm-wrestled before your stove,
on the floor, then leg-wrestled,
silly way a heterosexual, maybe, engages one
he admires

or maybe not silly
maybe our way of shaking
Koki, or playing

as all of us know you
as you responded to so many.

Strata

Apes treading reddened surf
as carnivores snarl at the water's edge.
Bipedal cycling starts up in the Miocene.
At any moment the air may catch fire.
Beach is the lion gate.

Face-before-birth, strangled bog man,
lodged in a nexus so stratigraphic
nickel and stars piled into his vocabulary.

I lifted this face-before-birth
out of its vulvan coffin,
lifted the cord away from his neck …
skull rich in tentacular moss
skull infused with hemorrhaging mantas.

To slit open sin is to discover being.
The poem, as in the earth, rises and performs creation.
The barest mental line fills in, a rump, a face,
implications cut across the sound shellac.

In Cousteau's beam: Bud Powell
                    sits, yogic,
            drawing out his colon,
            each finger a pallbearer,
                            a fish on puppy legs
              trundling along   deeper
        than where life
                    had been thought to live.

Basra Highway

I can't get out of my embrace
Iraqi conscripts scrambling out of tanks,
having waved white flags
   Called a "withdrawal" (not a "retreat")
to justify our rockets crisping them.

If I didn't have to watch faces peel back,
could I press the button?
Dickey's "Firebombing,"
                   high on distance.
       Can't get out of my embrace
     the distance,   Dis stance,
               hell pause between
an us, a them, in which cruelty is neutralized.

Can't get these drowning-in-flame ones out of my life,
can't get them deep enough into my embrace,
can't get these phantoms out of my scrotum,
can't carry them on and into and through you,
can't transform their pain into grief,
  my grief into my liquid,
can't whiten my blood with this sorrow

    Oh pus millipede with breasts of blood
this mass I enshare you with
this word mire,
              coffined word
              curdled word
can't get this briar word through my urethra.

Bloodrock

If they wonder why I write of menstruation,
tell them this: I thirst for the moment
a female hominid turned
and faced her partner.
In that moment, Dōgen and Wilhelm Reich were meshed,
"face-to-face transmission,"
the turning of the chair
to face the patient on the couch
Oestrus unbound, a new significance or
the first significance of blood,
a twin for nature,
81,000,000,000,000,000,000 ton
body of the moon emblazoned in her uteral
wall, shedding her heretofore
only purpose: to procreate.
Bloodrock. Spontaneous arousal.
What she projects into me as she bleeds is king,
kin, kunne, mental child of cunt.
I enter her bleeding as the man
she is forming in her mind
       measurement
           mensureable
           mensuration
       commensurate
         dimension
        immensity
       noumenon
I am clasped that firmly
me "mens" my "menos"
my masculinity is the product of her vise,
spiral axis at whose peak is the homuncular tree,
whose Fallopian branches I once wore
       under cuckold
       under Satan
       under Shiva

            under "dancing sorcerer"
as her Horned God.
                    One tragedy, as man,
is the melt down of these branches
into the brain, divinity based on semen.
God Creating Man thrusts a finger out of a brain-like
Michelangelo mass, as if it all started there (he said,
pointing at his head)—
on a secondary level, it did,
but the source of the projection is not within me,
the source is her massive bio-
swerve, her turn within and to me.

The Skeletons Talk Turkey

As autumn's wheaten quilt furls back,
the sleepers are revealed,
drying stalks, the long flutes of the dead
begin their agitated piping:
"Do you know your bounty is in part our work?
Don't you know that cob and bone,
the armatures of your increase, prove us?
Will you not drink mescal through the night
by us, until we share a warped, suicidal pang?
For to forget us is to die from us…"

Children, impersonating the dead.
How solitary their shapes under street lamps,
Frankenstein, Little Miss Muffet, wending their way…
a month later, in the split-off half of that great,
equinox reunion, wolfing down turkey,
thoughts of the dead: the turkey as he sang
his sad, sad tune, and schoolbook Indians.
O interval rife with smallpoxed and massacred millions!
We use Halloween and Thanksgiving like book ends,
as if to contain their volume. I think of tubercular
Oquendo de Amat's 5 *metros de poemas*—
who doesn't dream of a book 5 yards wide containing
all it means to be a Peruvian, an American?

In mourning for those with upturned pots for heads,
millions will converge on Lake Titicaca.
There will be a vast weeping tent in the storms of millennium,
when it becomes turgid that
some are frozen, none are thawed.

Out of the Kat Godeu   *

[For Jerome Rothenberg's 60th birthday]

Before I was free I was multiform
I was a sharp damascened sword
Drops of water in the upper air   *The most ardent star*
The beginning of the ancient word
Before I was Jerome I was Rothenberg
Before Rothenberg I was Red Mountain
I was Navaho I was Seneca
Bubbles in beer   Honey milk and soap
A harp string transformed 9 years into foam
A witness among killing center stones

It is not I who will not sing
I sing powerfully if obscurely
I enter *the scaled beast* bearing 6 million *heads*
A hard fight it is for the man on the mat
Annihilation is every field, the sound of any train
"Shoah." A backyard in Encinitas CA
coextensive with Buenos Aires, Treblinka
"There is no place that does not see you.
~~You must change your life~~."

Peeled of eternity—the riddled self,
                        crouched.
On Leon Golub's limpwristed leg-armed
canine, a military head, flummoxed,
   lit by interior gangrene.
Have you just grasped, Blue Sphinx,
what man has done with the animal powers
   by which he entered time?

The delicate crystal before its candle
  holds arsenic gold
the stone of the apricot commingling
  with the eau-de-vie.

As for the Budapest Hilton spiders,
they work in huge, filth-furred webs, outside
  the 17th floor restaurant.
We were seated by the picture window—there they were,
  the dinner entertainment!
"To eat living creatures on a plate-glass plate,
to do it vertically high in the sky
while you humans purr over disguised steer.
Here we work in night and fog, boring into whatever
  earth coughs up,
steaming up moth news, handcuffed to
  our unpruned jaws."

The young Soviet soldier at the side of the road standing by the
raised barrier as we drove past had a skinned, unborn, lumber-hewn
face. Something stuck in a uniform and left in the rain. "They're sent
abroad at 18 for 3 or 4 years," Gyula Kodolanyi says, "hated by the
foreign population, lackeys of officers, no women." I try to summon
the face of the one we passed at the edge of the woods, and draw
forth Soutine ghosts, butchered meat, the sweetness of youth
cankered, remote. What did we look like to him?

North of Gyor
7 cracked concrete doors
    commemorate, with cobalt-blue interstices,
Miklos Radnoti's etched words:
"I lived in an age so ugly, men killed
not only on command, but for pleasure."

Radnoti, Rothenberg and I live in a country
where men, who cut the vaginas out of My Lai women,
    walk free.

Across the road from the monument, a marsh.
Mossy blue willows twist from the mass grave
    which, in 1944,
included Radnoti and, in his overcoat pocket,
    his last hexameters.

        ◇

                    It is the
    injured toughness of what is used
moves me.
                Under Tibor's scraggly cherry trees,
the blue, rubble-soft bench used to be a door.
I instantly loved its blister hives.
Is this love facing the bomb? Not to be
                    prehistoric,
    but to have something in
        one's character   grandfather
an older world   in crumble suspension
                        here.

        ◇

Over Lake Balaton this evening, lightning,
sudden floods of violet squid…

All of Hungary faces Balaton,   root lake,
entrance to the Magyar underworld.
Here, Sandor Ferenczi is still slithering in and out
   of mother sound,
he waves farewell to his sperm as it alone
disappears into her bio-folds to reach,
he believes, at last, Thalassa!
The Hungarian longing for suicide, the no-sea ache.

Balaton, reticule, in which eyes
              of the ancient marsh
    still glint with lavender nights.
I say it with North American optimism,
which carries such nuclear embarrassment
                    in its hold.

Ferenczi continues to yearn for a journey
   on an animal of water.
It bears him on and on, he cannot tell its size,
     or where its head begins—
           but he is moving on its rolling
                    aquaflesh,
there are thousands of cherry-red
                 gashes in its sides,
    he tastes the sweet syrup of one,
and then another, and the feel
of Last Supper is living
                infant on his tongue…

                                        [1986–1992]

Hardball   *

I see the raped and beaten black body
I say I see the raped and beaten black body
I say I a white man see the raped and beaten black body,
for the next 11 lines you will hear Rodney beaten,
for they swingled him, they
buttfucked his eyes, they crosslabored him,
they kicked mocked and backed him, backed
him good, they sought to south him, to speedball
him north, then they toed his cream, they stepped
balled him, they whitemen outvoted his groin,
then they went for his teeth, he tried to scream they mouthstick
fucked him, they kickass arabed him—did they Baghdad him?
Did they 170,000 Iraqi children him?

Did they sewage water system him?

Did they Kurd and carpet bomb his retreat?

And in case you think I'm mixing oil with macadam,
they beat Rodney King as if he were wood
or cockroach, both cock and rock,
they beat him because he was black nearly dead man,
cause he was nigger,
now all you white students repeat   with   me
you who never will   you who have no moral will   Did
they beat him as your dad might've beat your mom?
Because women and blacks are the beatabililties,
kill this black white woman because heshe is,

kill this living black white pink and blue trunk

kill this human trunk that bulges and weeps.
Beat what I am,   beat what you are,
beat to the beat,   but no masturbation is strong enough
to rip out the white, to push it up, calcite,
huge chalk tunnels of your come in you,

to so dispossess us of the human that we must regard
  our birth channel
forever in challenge with us?   Aie, we are, in birth,
and we are beating our birth,   we are,   in birth,
beat Rodney   beat the earth
and know now   beat the earth is no longer
  dance step or game title
but swerve to piles in the watcher's eyes
while the dead pile up under,
     the dead, the beavers and
  all those fleas we never wanted to name.

Ground

Is it possible that language wears through, wears through itself, becomes, as this path, a thing rubbed out?

All paths are scuffed, as are words, all paths look done in.

The nature of the path: to be worn into. No indication ever of how many passed.

Dirt, chaos bone, metaphor-barren stones that imply an arbitrary gist.

Once, as if in birth, something pushed through high grass, a family? a string of goats?

Anonymity is the most known force.

At the heart of every specific direction, a characterless path.

Sentences reused become pebbled voids, comforting to the mouth, yet of a deadness so obdurate poetry to be fresh must crack them open.

We pass so thoroughly over, our going sounds self-dismissal as our eyes clamp, or clomp against, destination's nearest rung.

No scene is ever reseen.

Each time is new.

My voice, wording its way while traveling unlimited narrowing, lacks and is.

Lacks an is.

All, under leveling sea winds, gesticulates asway.

[Ile de Ré]

Cooking

I slide down like a fireman into a cauldron-shaped machine.
                The discourse
             shifts, scaly zucchini
wants to be scrubbed. Mother said: get outta the tub
soon as you finish washing,
so I scrub and consider the chicken, the cold
under her arms as I carried her into the hospital toilet.
All of life is present every moment.
We know this, or I do, dimly,
I wipe up something from the chopping block, it tastes
like 16th Street—best I can do,
   my birth? The flecks are more precious than
weight of bird in hand. Open the wine.
Curious, the antagonism wafting from the just-pulled.
But who wants to be opened? Down in the blood force,
I dream while I cook. Dreaming is
a kind of cooking, body between waffle irons bed and night,
ghosts of the introjected sipping and picking.
I am closer to Caryl in bed
than at table, but tapers shadow us here.
Are we re-enacting the primal snack
as we cut, munch, and talk? The tall sip of Chinon
that plunges to my belly,
a shore bird zapping up a crab?
Have you looked into your mouth,
considered the Labrador of ice floes, jungular lagoons,
infintestinal havens under invasion
as the tongue, trapped rhino, goes through its
    plungings, so articulate
after 20,000 years   then Andrei Codrescu on NPR:
he too hates David Duke—I throw in more Louisiana,
cleaning a shrimp: serrated knife down the back
held against the chopping block edge,
swole gut tract furls back, husk won't disposal, so
I bag'm, thoroughly rinsing the headless, footless

Paleo bodies under harsh cold,
each point of cooking so interesting,
                              I know you appreciate it
having shopped so carefully for all I fondle.
To clean a squid is to have a hand up the goddess.
To do so makes me want to help a cow give birth.
To cook makes me want to disembowel myself and eat.
Cooking is a form of labyrinthine pacing,
and is without fear, until we make contact with
the soul of the beloved, for whom we cook.
Then the two of us are out on plates
looking up into this gorgeous autumn. We are old,
and sliding about, but the dry golden trash
    still clinging to the maples
is a kind of funky Greek Keatsean urn.

Kenneth Burke, 94, is happy for a tasty meal.
He has a chic grey cap, and settles in
at our table on his pillowed chair.
Salmon without oil, or salt,
spinach, rice, Pilsner Urquell.
He said that night: "Beauty is Truth, Truth Beauty—
    Body is Turd, Turd Body"   and giggled.

Each evening we sit down to these bodies
    in cocoon, these woven green beans,
this artichoke harboring so many compressed
thorny lips. A delicate char molded by
    the coldest lake depths,
part of my mother, parts of our mothers' mothers,
    myself, yourself.
                              The wind rises outside,
the gold, rouge-red, bonfired leaves are down.
We are skeletons eating amongst skeletons.
                              This
    is the delicious thrust and realization.

The Wine Graveyard

It is raining quietly on the wine graveyard tonight.
Through amber, bacchic curves, runny cobwebs,
reveries and revels mingle. Here the poorest and
                              most opulent are lees,
inky lakes, combs of whitening mold, purples whose
cranial murmurs Baudelaire might have heard,
witnesses to our need to pull the blinds at twilight,
illuminate the dining room as if it were a womb,
                              and we, the living,
able to cross the bridge of a sip into that shallow well
where memory is abyss and the phantoms rising,
the friendly shapes of a dissolution to be embraced—

for the mind is the poor rained-upon place,
bottleneck upon bottleneck tear into each.
We share the instruments in the symphony of the dead,
your kettle drum tonight is my fife tomorrow,
                              my glass this evening
your urn in a future so vast the bottles blur,
a magma that a toast might staunch, and so,
                              as we pour, against a flame
to tell us when clarity is invaded by flecks
that once contributed to our most burgundy premises,
we find ourselves between two intoxications—
the foetal binge in which mother's laughter sounded
                              like rumbling trucks,
and the other, this hive of blackened bottles.

Here we are truly put to bed, tucked in
sister to brother, baron to sutler, and the lips
that graze our foreheads, are they not,
as they purse, sipping, if only air,
our natal bouquet, our floridity, our devastation?

Guyton Place   *

Is it our work to push doghouses, jeans
and waffle irons into the earth's orifices,
to shun them as soon as we use them?
Isn't everything we shape imbued with what we can
  and cannot imagine?
Somehow, in Rilke's time, things shined, were company.
            Wine, shaped by the vintner,
"the savor of the earth, made intelligible to man."
In 1925, Rilke wrote: "Now, from America, empty indifferent things
are pouring across, sham things, *dummy* life…A house, in the American
sense, an American apple or a grapevine over there, has *nothing* to do
with the house, the fruit, the grape into which went the hopes and re-
flections of our forefathers…Live things, things lived and conscient of
us, are running out and can no longer be replaced. *We are perhaps the
last still to have known such things.*"

Update: in the core of America, as if at a hearth pit,
whose tentacles spread throughout the body politic:
Reagan's face, a mosaic composed of contra-
Midas touches, disposables, things adults no longer love
reproduced in miniature for their children,
life a non-sequitor. A Salvadoran woman returns home,
to find her family's heads set on the set table's
  dinner plates.
The Regan face, frozen in vomit-guffaw.
Imagine seeing his stomach!
                        Take the Mount Elliot Exit
off I-94 south via the old Detroit "Black Bottom"
  to Heidelberg, and turn right.
Tyree Guyton's *Funhouse* is on the left.
It seems to cook there, in snow or summer,
              "belly of the shark,"
panopticon of American childhood and poverty.
African-American childhood, African-American poverty.
"Perhaps we are *here* in order to say: house, bridge, well,
gate, jug, fruit tree, window—at most: column, tower…"

But, collapsed wheel chair? Plastic yellow horseshoe?
Squashed truck tire with "cookie monster" peeking out?
Perhaps Rilke's "lovers" could merely pronounce such
   words, in the aristocratic world of Muzot.
                              On Heidelberg,
the street-abandoned is returned to the sides, roofs, porches,
   front yards and sidewalks of 2 houses.
Imagine "Blue Poles" tied around a house so staggered
   it can barely sustain structure,
"drippings" 1 to 5 layers deep, no longer "paint"
but a rubble ropology of bedsprings nailed over window,
jammed in crutches, one with LA Gear basketball shoe,
porkpie hat forced into white telephone receiver,
                              grey underpants,
tricycle poked window,   brooms through springs

fireman boot snaking eaves gutter

baby doll heel draped wire mesh

hammock loaded kitchen counter, to which is nailed
                              saddle oxford,
hunk of grey shag carpet slapdashed white,
hobbyhorse (no front hoofs), peach mattress,
lawnmower blades, friction tape winding
                              industrial ducts,
rusted wheelbarrow pan, blue bath towel
                              stained scarlet,
water heater (sorrel around its tilted base)
                              on front porch:
empty-overnight-case-piled phone booth

  TV innards skewered plastic tenpin

    TONKA Turbo-Diesel toy
        rusted car frame
        baby-blue scooter
  smashed mannequin head on prong

hobbyhorse hoofs gripping sagging eaves gutter
  (what do thy eyes see upside down?)
beret on toilet plunger,   rusted tin world globe

            "fence"
      of semi-submerged
      semi tires
                        M. Amelia
                  wife of Geo Zahn
                  & daughter of
              Chas & Anna Bleicher
                Born Nov 8 1854
                Died Dec 7 1877
rusted-apart lunch box, Suzie Homemaker stove,
motorcycle spray-graffitied chartreuse, footstool,
oil landscape by R. Robinson, catcher's mask,
            half a licence plate [MR 6
toilet bowl, its contents: "Jack Lemmon" Weekender hat,
            purple leather high heel pump

```
+-----------------------------------+
|            Abortion               |
|               is                  |
|             Murder                |
|          vote NO  [X]             |
|              on B                 |
|        be the voice of the        |
|             UNBORN                |
+-----------------------------------+
```

(4 blocks away, Tyree's friend, "the junkman,"
lives in a wheelless school bus surrounded by *ruined* junk.
In his pot-bellied stove, behind the driver's seat,
  he burns spars from torched houses.
At 77, he seems wired with energy, lives on Wild Irish Rose,
a man alive in his own graveyard. One frosty December,
we all walked the ice-rutted alley while he yelled
"I'MA **SCIENTIST** MOTHERFUCKIN COON!")

Malte Laurids Brigge: "and the fusel ordor of sweltering
feet…tang of urine and the burn of soot and the grey reek
of potatoes, the heavy, smooth stench of aging grease."
These sensations we must imagine here—
line upon line of watermarks, chains of object scum,
                    haphazard, intricate.

A block away, "the whorehouse," 3121 Mount Elliott:
nailed-up naked baby doll parts,
                    the unconceived
washed out by sink-top douche? Doll head
                    lobotomized on porch rail,
rotted blue rubber dildo,   diapered torso roast.

Next door, Tyree's grandpa, Sam Mackey, 92,
sits at the kitchen table, drawing with crayons
versions of the androgyne. "In that distant chamber,
a bearded queen, wicked in her dead light,"
old Wallace Stevens wrote. Grandpa Mackey's have
  arm-like tits, gigantic dicks.

How paradise might look to the cast-out serpent
                    raising its head
to look back on the emptied place of origin.
All once inside now nailed to Eden's outer wall
                    —and the Cherub?
Nailed to the top of the wall, strutting,
as if to Sousa. The dream detonated,
all things in Babel on earth's multifoliate
                    cross.

                                        [1989]

Position Paper

It is always daybreak,
an octopus with golden eyes.
You stand not on zero
but on the zerocity of being.

The lifewire is looped between desire
        and fulfillment here,
imperfect adumbration of day
        breaking below.

From dragon jaws yawning
the hero is born to be beheaded
                by an elder.
        The elder's problem:
he had a father. Be father free. Be
        daybreak. Wear this fissure
as Ptah wears falcon,
as an Aztec eagle warrior
looks out an open eagle beak.

I is not an other.
I is, in other. Rimbaud,
        you erred!
You took off your caul bonnet,
you thought you could go it alone.

The man enchased in daybreak
is the sunyata in his parents' gyre. Being
        runs clear, remains
unclear. Be verb, for they are ob-
        and subject,
    the frame
        you mirror.

Gorgeous George Comes Pounding Down The Beach

On the San Diego Freeway
   rising toward Mulholland—
azure ghosts of canyons,
    cobalt lime dusk.
Agnostic snarl of art, aerobics, pizza,
valet parking for Trashy Lingerie.
Sun tinsel streaming in 5 PM light so strong,
my eyes close driving, open to helicopters
walking the backyard on stalks of light.
Bricolage of tar Maya movie plaster.
"HI, my name's Bruce, I'm your waiter,
  I tried to kill myself last night."
Gladiator bright, collapsable city.
The Rolfed young man cries I am,
not realizing *I am* does not see.
So I'm 13, in my Aunt Georgia's trailer,
off Mulholland. I've been parked here
  while the adults play Canasta.
Stretched out on the bunk bed,
       turn on the tiny TV:
Gorgeous George comes pounding down the beach,
platinum locks atoss, bikinied,
  as if strolling the infinite.
Nature's radiation appears
    an angel layered in coke
stretched out on sushi cooler ice,
  Goddess Ikatakomagurouni.
LAX landing flights flashing hero no one
  while up the Strip I chug
below the toe level of billboard gods,
oily, puffed up in platinum heels.
Jackie Collins' anima-black mane,
      neon lips,
"exquisitely jacketed in depths of anthracite."
Madonna, "The Frida Kahlo Story,"
     laquered red nails,

silky hair crisscrossed in meticulous
   braids—visited by the Rockefellers,
      her unhealable abdominal wound.
Perhaps Frida is LA's patron saint?

On Melrose, mascaraed punk mannequins
   are digging "Day of the Dead." La Muerte:
      the exfoliating skull sending north
            Mexican macabre gaiety,
dens that abutt globally:
the cleaning woman's husband
            decapitated in Guatemala
appears on TV.
                  Kali-fornia face,
   Kali's fornix, Marilyn's whee!
her sagging frontier bodice line
where men are at once larvae and Valentino.
Brittle chrome candy of this Western edge,
haunted not as Brittany by "finisterre"
   (thus world-end everywhere)
but by the American Icarus dream: "Mounting
upon the wings of light into the Great Expanse"
Gorgeous George comes pounding up the beach.
Hockney-sketchy immortality
                  swimming pool deep,
a water blue sky in whose bowl
I too steer, emperiled by cancerous fish,
a human being looking like a scuba effete
wandering unpeopled streets, wearing
            my house on my head,
my possessions pyramiding my sides
a mobilary Mesoamerican relief.
                  Porky and Bugs
   come tumbling through the palms,
squirting my sunglasses with hot-dog
                  shaped diners
   and saber-tooth perfume!

Navel of the Moon   *

The man who is always wanting to see
now knew he must imbibe semen,
    but in imagination—
as at the openings of the mountainous mother
he had perceived the stones were so alive
they were freezing. He had to release
the semen parachute way too long nailed to
the zenith of male brain,
had to let it pass through his eyes
to experience the octopodal
sensation of submarine drapery,
to be thin as a veil, but also to fit into
the carapace of a crab. The project, then,
is to let the treasure descend
through the interior zoo of chakras
until Kundalini, blind as Tiresias,
coiled so long her rattles have gone soft,
raises her head and gulps the displaced jade
—not nag, nor strumpet,
but the nearly untranslatable fool's gold,
the glacial division in muelos-elevated man.

At Monte Alban, before a *danzante*,
the shadow of Ana Mendieta bends.
A flattened man all surface like Ana,
cheek of stone, a lily-groined hunchback,
pages of a scattered stone book,
dismembered at the core of vision,
three halves that never join,
two orgasms jolting past each other.
Thus compassion. Thus tenderness mixed with gravel.
In the tip of the solar arrow,
I discover my mother tied and splayed.
A great snail has arrived in the plaza.
We cry Beached Whale!
In metaphor, the primal anxiety:

everything is nothing,
something is a toadstool under which
ragged elves are cowering.
How long does it take to get the weight of the earth
    through my head?

              Coatlicue leans forward
just enough to offer a worm shade.
Before Her as a man, I felt my infant size
before my mother—or let's say
Coatlicue is the size surrounding the hole
I made in mother's apple—and so, indeed,
I am a worm in the shade Serpent Skirt offers
—with whom one never shakes hands.
One shakes hearts with Coatlicue,
for she too is part of the cornucopia,
part of the great snail's retinue.
All true answers are questioned
by the two rattlesnakes that like facing
question marks fuse as Her head.

Against the underlight of Oaxaca
the night sky in suspended rise,
the necropolis in suspended fall.
We are nestled, forever, as now, or never,
in soft bone arms, buttressed by breeze and the wail
from the zenith tube into which liquid night flows,
a kind of larval ebony for ballplayers' hands,
the braid of events in the fleeing stream,
the present the parachute's weighted pouch,
the past its cape, the future
the rising hidden smile of the ground.
The firmest, most loosened poem meets us with the force of
am I vain to hold my report open
while being written, so that we know
no more than a given instant realizes
—realizes? Makes real, like makes water,
meaning re-leases loss, showing blocks,

the block is seen through
but only as a winding window at the mercy of
I stand in a rushing tower and write
with fluid pen on a tablet with a blank of its own
—what I remember are only my experiences.
The power of time, wider and deeper than life,
hurtles around skull racks, boulders with no recall,
body crates in which the gagging
if divine marrow is experienced on a plane
I know of but do not know.
Flower is consumed   lmost fast eth n ap ears
then *and,* dear procrastination, seeks to add
and my tablet gratefully sucks in my pen.

Time is layered. Each beginning deepens
as if each leaf weighed its tree,
and thus where I stand: the weight of me?
Infant emerging from the crotch of stone,
or is it stone merging from man,
what is hardest in man, the bearing of non-being,
to be a finite cul-de-sac
impacted with seminal angel.

I am pinned against the base of the Southern Cross
to a position, a vane over
the tumulus of my hopeless central sleep,
here with my pots and dolls,
buried alive in my background,
in the crested fist of the specificities
I've been hung with, have chosen to wear.
The white Western heterosexual moves
no revolutionary boulders. Unlike the Césaire-man,
he does not speak for the poor.
Even if he is not to be zapped,
but his boll weevils spun into porridge,
he is still a mink in the flavor—

something that won't go down,
   or that does,
      failing those stacked
         in the flues.

"navel of the moon" Mexico
first disinterred me, a black cape of flies
took off from the pineapple of my innocent heart.
This is where I'll bury my poetry,
blood gate of the moon, vale whose path
is the back of ants, glossy
scarlet road, conveyor mirror,
this is where I always wanted to play,
aloft, on penile dream stilts,
a Gulliver-man, in collage with time.

I am the man who waded in man,
who ate man's marrow and report it is without source.
WOT TIS SOR ROW the Noh ghost entoned.
"dirty water which nevertheless cleans a pail"
the menstruating dreamer replied.
I, Ariel, spat between the two,
I, Ariel, freed by the two,
saw a girl dying in bed, her hand a rose tree,
crawled in with her, let self
form a moat around her, a halo,
then the tree bloomed a fairy shower,
each wore a tiny fig pinafore,
each carried a sparkler as she circumambulated the tree.
"We come in self-annihilation and the grandeur of inspiration—
take the foul deposit in the cooking pot
and preserve it, for it is the source of heartage.
Come with us under this red rock,
we will show you the beast Blood Girl rides,
her broom bull, cratered, incandescent,
whose sides are open portals to the black mantra shadow
on which we dreamers ebb and flow."

And we were followed into Monte Alban
by a little mongrel bitch
still nursing her litter,
our consort on that moonless night.
She rested by us as we sat, filthy, frisky,
wagging to the parking lot
where I wanted to adopt her.
Literal man, you've been adopted,
sick little dog, little Shulamite on the sward—
on her leash, power flows into your throat.
The work is everlasting conversion,
the mother is endless, the work is
everlasting conversion. Merton is electrocuted,
Vallejo's death curls a scorpion mark,
Caravaggio under a nitroglycerin sun
copulates with his own wounds.
Against vampiric literalism, hold the metaphor,
burn the cross with mental pain,
it will spring forth a violet,
a summer storm, the bellows tear,
the cinder burns through one's palm.
Tonight I have made contact with
the immortality of error. Alchuringa,
impinge! Open your foramen magnum to me.
Between genitals and the brain
there are only exploded bridges.

                                          [Mexico City/Oaxaca,
                                           May/June, 1991]

Cempasúchil   *

      Odysseus' *ofrenda*
was a ewe-blood-filled trench.
He went down to the realm of souls—
we today anticipate their visit here.
They inhale the food we set out for them
then depart, without conversation.
      At 600 BCE, the distance between
the living and the dead was shorter.
Odysseus *spoke* with Tiresias,
received prophecy, mind penetrated mind.
The tree growing out La Mano Magica's patio wall
bears cactus pads to Oaxaca's October 30 sky,
but our dead are inaudible,
invisible, —is it because we expect them to come to
us? And when they do, are they so weary
no sacrifice can enable them to speak?

      In *The Wasteland*
Eliot set out food in tins, Tiresias,
the double-sexed one, was the middle wall
through which events transpired.
If I ask who are my dead   [October 31]
Christobal Colón appears, a gross scorpion
whose back is littered with 70 million corpses,
he is punching the smallpox cash register, arms pop up, legs,
a Spaniard sharpens his sword on the eyeball of a continent.
On each side of the cleave,
unknown species grow like hair.

      Amamatando   [Museo Tamayo,
      whose mouth   November 1]
is not puckered to forever-receding breasts?
The Olmecs knew the wisest man
is the largest infant, that inscape
is no escape, is natal, is a rain-forest of virus and need,
bald, I am howling for milk,

asleep, sitting up drunk in
this frightening coffin with tits,
and very happy to be stretched here.

               Chambi saw   *[Martín Chambi*, Museo
the rictus and the reception, warm   de Arte Contemporane
human welcome of a man on   de Oaxaca, *Inauguración*
his own picked potato pile   *30 de octubre de 1992]*
while his other flashes daft at the peak of the heap,
one-sandaled man, aggressive with fiddle,
who isn't ready to play?
who isn't waiting for chicha?
Under a dusty hatband in the 100° shade, on dirt,
a crosslegged infant adult, holding out my cup,
Who doesn't shake his rattle before any passerby?
Who isn't waiting for Columbus as the scarlet standards of Santo
   Domingo
waggle by,   sails without ships,
the Pinta before every cathedral door?

I am Nayarit, blind, with fingers at the end of my flippers,
shoulders poxed, only a stiff napkin across my knees,
my breasts tattooed targets,
my toes protruding from my knees,
I know that in holy imagination all is in recombination,
I know that I am pregnant,
my navel a hub, in diaper-bib,
elephant-eared, giggling milk spurts.
I am so wise mush is leaking from my mouth.
Come into my stomach hole,
imagine the contents of this architectural dark.
Here the brothel has dried,
the lunch stand, here a quail in galoshes
is kicking the bundle of bones
Quatzalcoatl dropped on his journey out of Mictlan,
hollow lower body, source
and synthesis of Hell, icebox of embers, where an elderly wasp,
freckled, with doodads clustering her ovipositor,
fiddles away to her mummified king.

Aged warrior awaiting rebirth, until drivel turns back,
miracuilous curare, the blood that fears blood.

I crouch in Jaliscan time,
so grotesque as to be totally recognizable,
my begging bowl stacked with Coca Cola bottles,
a lewd photo of JC Oates in my watch pocket,
my snot freezes before my nose into a snout protector,
now that my head is on inside out
I face the past, the future behind,
me, I skull the past, I wear the lintel of the future behind,
solemn, I am still too solemn,
what new green head is waiting to break through my nil?

◇

In Atzompa cemetery
I felt a ringing in my hands
as if they had been asleep, and circulation like racing sand.
Scattered *cempasúchil*, drapes and rosaries of shredded
Day of the Dead flowers, "African Marigold"
accompanied by purple cockscomb, *cresta de gallo*, or *pata de león*,
dirt mounds, only a few with tombstones,
palm stalks stuck in mounds overarched by a 10-trunked fig tree
plain redug graveyard enlightened by petals
the color of healthy chicken skin.

◇

Here Arnulfo Mendoza has tied 2   [*Mary Jane & Arnulfo's*
packs of Fiesta cigarettes to   *living room above*
a full mescal bottle, one burning   *La Mano Magica*]
candle, *cempasúchil* sprays,
Day of the Dead bread. It's raining,
the altar in the corner grows darker as I sit down.
Is his dad here now? He has a photo   [*in which he is carrying*
to guide him and their adopted baby son   *a bottle of mescal*
whining in the bedroom. Outside   *to which have been tied*

the old wood door, stained gray walls,   *2 packs of Fiestas]*
a spill of magenta bougainvillaea.
A ceramic angel bears a basket between her wings
or is it a candlestick?
                    I'd like to identify
this darkened room rain atmosphere,
it's shaped like Sunday in the American Midwest—
as the raindrops crack, the marigold odor wafts
a small white African-face mask, small shoulder bags,
a steer-horned devil mask, rugs to cushion
whoever's back presses against the long living room bench.
A mermaid with raspberry nipples and arabesque
"designer" tights over part of her fish portion
leaps, drawing a toothy fish toward her breasts—
will she nurse it? In Mexican male mind
women nurse non-human creatures,
a little pig, or puppy—Arnulfo's mermaid has wings,
long ropy brown hair. Her sky resounds azure,
scarlet, her tail is earthy gleaming ivory,
she bursts her sea egg. She also wears
a jeweled sombrero, or so I observe, in respect for
the otherness embreasted in this room—

                    Tomorrow it is Clinton vs. Bush
2000 miles away. The dead now visiting
will return to Mictlantecuhtli while American voters argue
a man who might be honest vs. a man
whose entire being exhales lies. O dead,
are you aware of our doings here?
Must we invent new sacrifices to sense the capstone of the soul?
But aren't we always in sacrifice
as the planet shifts its pox: Iraq yesterday, Somalia today,
Bolivian mothers 10 deep in kids, dad face down, smashed, in road
    mud.
Coarse synthesis forever at work,
sacrifice and massacre to make us feel?
As if art eats this slaughter pomp to transform a bit of the cruelty
man and nature (two jaws) provide, mouth eating its own teeth,

feebly renewing life, all things feel of skull if you touch them with
    respect,
and the one you love, not once does she deflect you from your task.
If she seems to divide you, Rilke, from your work,
it only means she mirrors your mortality so keenly
you innerly divide and project conflict as love vs. vision.
The musicians start up. Their voiceless daughters pull for water.

    ◇

      In and out, the miraculous
  slosh, the running in of surf, corpse
afloat, inlet. Caramel shadow,
shadow of Freud, of Lucifer,
tombstone-shaped man, man of phallic shoulders,
woman with vulval head. All parts may be exchanged,
the beauty, the horror of it! Idi Amin doll,
blond vodun Christ, football crucifix,
the stadium a caldron with Lady Macbeth cheerleaders.
James Wright gallops past.
In and out, slimy dick, slimy cunt.
The strata of sex and language. All can be used. All
unlike a detergent, spins, washing the mind,
foul, fodder, the parental force in gnats,
the latticework of the living and the dead,
Skeezix among the morning-glories:
lift the cartoon from the dead woman's face,
in decomposition she is beginning to stir.
Ocelot-spangled morning. I am free,
free and embedded, multiform, unformed,
                unproven…

    ◇

      Then Angelica Vasquez
washed her feet and put on tan lady shoes
so as to honor us, the visitors to her craft,
to her *ofrenda*, fruit softening in a corrugated corner,

the poor craftswoman offering us a choice of beer,
black mole, delicious rice, her roof the sun's drum,
her dirt yard infant traipsed.
I visit her here, one of her tenpins,
white spook, obtuse as a Spicer baseball,
roll onto my back dog fashion to the sun.

Can you tell me if this needs revision, Mictlantecuhtli,
or can I inject it directly into your veins?
Have I sacrificed something here
or have I just been toweling my behind?
Once the poem has been skinned
it cannot be recarpeted
no matter the hobnail cha-cha on its sole reader's boots.
"I want to write poetry equivalent to
the insanity of flowers here."   [Peter Redgrove]
Wallow in language's fertile mud
but be aware: there is a Cossack
between the eyes of every reader and
this Cossack does not like to be disturbed by
what you do. Thus antler to antler in double
backgrounded gridlock. Is there an outside when
we make contact with the brains of heaven?
Yes, and its all so much copal
asunderwritten by the breath of trees
in the cemetery shallows of your fig and mine, or
my errant lay…

        Knot of 3, wailing   [November 2]
on their knees men, feet
half-sandaled toward us on side benches,
the jarred candles aflicker as if
nudged by their kinetic bunching, shadowed,
all mouth and dusty soled, huaraches bending,
          the graveyard sanctuary
          at Teotitlan del Valle,

we're here for Arnulfo's dad (he calls him)
dead now 1 ½ years.
                            Slop of beer drooling across
the grave mound, we drink the rest of the warm Corona,
cempasúchil, network of this ensouling,
clumps of friendly mourners, one plot thick with green stalks,
Karen Tortuga has a black ceramic turtle center of her plot,
Zapotec silk-knotted twisted braids, blocky small women,
Arnulfo's mother shaking with 1½ year old agony of loss:
he was there in the living-room but she couldn't see him,
force of the invisible dead visible to the heart
which tries to grow eyes, pain of heart blindness,
copal smoke: winding, disappearing *forms?*

Rest in peace my mother
Rest in peace my father
to Oaxaca have I come
to bless the life you me gave,
and say it backward to span 22 years of no grave
cempasúchil, no copal hardly a thought
at Equinox when Arnulfo might say
your spirits stand open-mouthed by my table.

    Señora Mendoza's sorrow
      sent out grappling hooks
the anger that the dead are dead
the frustration that the clumped men
    as if on one iron hinge
cannot resurrect in chant
the frustrating invisible berating dead,
who are here, heart inhabited,
and thus this barb-wired heart?
Stonehenge of the heart
protected by barbed-wire?

FROM SCRATCH (1998)

Intention

To write
as a sculptor carves, cutting a way to the unknown,
contextualizing the locust raid of the subconscious,
to form caves within the line,
alcoves within sentences,   to inhabit the line
a string of nomadic campfires
stretching through the karst,

a braiding,
something I admire in Celan, in Bracho,
a motive roaming,   redolent with,   adding
to,   the matrix linking

Dream of sleigh-bells attached to death's roller-coaster spine

Who knows why autumn cracks
and corrects our core? The gold is already
rafting   in each leaf Medusa
flowers.

Nora's Roar *

In memory of Nora Jaffe
(1928–1994)

As she recedes, living still,
first lung now liver,
I am turning to
"The everlasting eyes of Pierrot
And, of Gargantua, the laughter"
              her laugh
Ohio Gothic, bass
swoons, a booming of merriment,
   we lay in the dawn road pickled
while others dropped salt into our mouth

To wake and to think only of the wine to come,
the wine of the work of drawing,
to need only this wine, to live
in near obscurity, happy
within the frame of imagination, this word
we mob,

it is our only refuge.

[7 October, 1994]

     ◇

the wake an elegy stirs…something to be listened to.
I find you everywhere, mainly as voice echo,
I think of you, then hear you before I see
entoptically a blur of your face…

the unheard voice then resilences. The silence
opens out, chimes of *Habilis, Erectus*….
   the wake of elegy, dirty churn of what
          the voyage rejected,

standing at the stern of what life might be,
it keeps you pinned in me, as I pine,
semi-conscious unplugging of a bathtub
in which the water used doesn't want to leave…

◇

Most just, I guess, to find you
in the flux of realization and grief.
As ash, you are a complete whatever,
and it is hard to comprehend that anti-force,
I string it on my feeling for you

to go overboard with you,
to honor your rich void.
I am gaining this word by word,
for the loss is at odds
with something curdled in praise.
The grand "So What" flicks by
at Miles Davis with my need to bulge
absence/presence

"Sadness" once meant "solidity,"
"steadfastness in faith,"
but nothing will support my sadness this week,
        a wandering distraction, as if
Nora's death were a box jellyfish
    adrift in my atmosphere.
Death has four sets of eyes, no brain,
one set for each side of what we call direction.
Death's mouth is over its eyes…

my sadness is layered, pillow-like, or tarps
    with pillows pressed between,
moistened but not drenched, stranded
        adrift…as all senses of her
cancel, recompose,
        "Procession of the Quick"

The upward piling impulse of eternity. Cloud-like, rock-like, forms, jostling against—here it comes again—absolute absence

A leg, thigh and calf, bent, lower left hand corner, gets me interested in the physicality, the eros? of the painting, now I spot a male back lunging upward, whose head disappears in a kind of window of winter trees. His right arm droops, leading me to a woman—it's Nora herself!—eyeballs rolled up, hair stark black and funnel-like swooping into the upper right corner

The work now looks draped, an upward piling, weighted, with loose, body-like forms, detonated below, into floating, bumping, somewhat phallic blocks—on which the rest of the painting "stands"—it doesn't really stand, it wobbles, tectonic, as if on plates? (suddenly the buttocks of the upward lunging male look like an amazed lion!)

The form argues, wrestles with, the punctilio of human desire salted, as ground, for a realization of the form to *grind against*. Nora Jaffe depicts herself under a roving blank cloak of men, as they surge around, across, and over her. The procession of the quick, *being* overwhelmed, as the quick (and the dead?) pile into paradise over the body of the painter—

Cocks abound, but as often in Jaffe they are syntactical eels, the patriarchal thrashing in the net of an imagination that instead of practicing political correctness prefers, demands, the re-leasing of the obsession. Coils of rape are here bounded but not dismissed—

the out-of-in-balance of the painting amazes me. I'm stuck
with the use of the female (Nora) body overlayed by blankets
(lacunae) of quasi-phallics. Now I lay me down to sleep.
The garment of the world: stitched penises. O
mother: where? As the garment out of which the cocks are stitched.
O father: why? Isn't it wonderful how semi-abstract,
charged and essentially formal works dump our psyche
upward? My father made me a blanket out of my mother, ay!
then withdrew it, leaving me with my first tooth!
oh! and it is around this tooth that I have woven my poems,

weave, woven sploven…the spindle bursts,
yet a King now appears at the crest of "Procession of the Quick"
—the winter landscape is his crown,
his body that of the lunging man,
willynilly covering the now double female body
(two heads, Nora's and what I took to be another man's)
and he is kind of dancing, as he fucks,
lifting a Subcommandante Marcos leg as an insult to
all fashion, as a shark form noses in…

But why two women? Why both at once?

We are in orgy at every moment (too many unused parts)

◇

                    This sadness is without edge
or forceps, it is weighted with total absence,
which is the difference
between Nora's ashes, and Nora,   it can be
     weighed in mind, it is fractal
and thus not without contour,
it is the toothed heart of a black hole,
what the star feels in its inexhaustible extinction…

. Sadness, then, is a protection,
               a kind of Covering Harem,
it is sweet as "The Wild Rose" in Budapest was sweet,
nostalgia mired in cool fat, a piano player
whose elderly foetal head, with stuff oozing onto the keyboard
smiled at us, the eaters,
                         box jellyfish abob…

Our friendship was blessed with an erotic lining.
My eyes turned off before Nora's art
and something else turned on—
a glade would appear, compact male flesh
reorganized, penis shifted to armpit,

thigh used three ways, as stalagmite, Long Island, floe,
libido frozen, on the trail of her hand
finding its way through a coral forest of congealed
	male fragmentation

		Seeing the extent to which
she had imagined her masculine-fraught destiny,
I knew male force was grasped, and that she was free
—for a moment. We can deal with nearly anything
—for a moment. In minuscule time,
a stroke or an image, is paradise,
darkness a chrysalis of unharvested stars

She had reorganized the male tentacles
and glimpsed what Bosch envisioned
—while she smoked.
In her breath, steel doors began to rot.
She hurt herself
as who does not who has glimpsed the other as
"Dear Fellow Particle"?

It is very transpersonal, never private,
how the pylon figures of our lives
rub open scars and palpitate the antique
	feeling under,
another flesh, which the pylon detects

Nora is Egyptian,
a gorgeous baboon
in whose slender figure my language
is hived.

To learn to love your death.
Is this not the requirement? not to love death,
but to love you in death,
to learn nourishment from your absence

Dear now ancestral spirit, you feed me
as do the spirits of poets dead but for the page,
or frame, of chaos, white
for these ant legions

Are not the chosen dead blowing
energy into these lines? Yes, I have good energy,
but it is nothing compared to
Nora as ash, the microscopic gale
   in the thought of her,

billowing, these dead who make life-in-image possible,
we all work at a single world poem,
   a hybrid exchange,
I become pregnant with Nora's soul,
I swell at night, cannot rest, I sleep
    but do not rest…

how beautifully herbs break in, fumes and
filterings, by which her presence is
swarming, micron by micron, with the jest of absence,
    like tiny wine flies…

Nora's spell,   terrible to be a speck in this exchange.

As she rises, or seems to hold,
while rising, the anaconda
tree trunk, *writhe,*
rise, it is the sound of whiteness,
as she pulleys up, her right
hand spider-walks the trunk,
making a lingam: combined
arm hand trunk,
        as she rises
in place, out of the fern
white, her rising is

white infested,
              mascara
no pupils
(work this also in:
work her hood in, her head
held to the tree, to
anaconda white
speckled
bark,
     the phallus was
what she could put inside her of
the tree, up inside her
the bandaged
anaconda, I under-
stand now,
          it was the trunk
she loved, the sap
in its bark helmet, the serpentine.

A hardon, severed,
enwombed, the umbilical-
knotted
goad

Nut
descends, arms
alongside,
she kisses its cleft, tongues

the semen-charged

mummification,

the hydra-hydrant
gong.

◇

One senses in her art a luxuriant ambivalence
toward masculinity,
"Merman" manticore pushing into female
plush, the tobacco
in the cigarette, dildo
as driving void,   a sort of infant

misericordia, this 9 inch nail
rubbery as old celery
has been given refuge,

battered Manhattan, bandaged, as a lingam,
with potato-eyes, ending in a hoof,

"Our Strips of Stuff"
lingam bound to stretcher poles,
bags of blood, bound in with coal and stones,

whose yoni is a nurse
whose ward (whose nave)
strains with mayhem chained,

gorgeous energy, this
crests of a house ridge phallic helmet line
whose attic is timbered meat.

◇

The dirtiness of death,
        her head a chopped meadow,
chemo-crewcut grey and stubby,
steroid swollen face. I did not recognize Nora,
blundered into the next death section
        CLAYTON   I heard my voice
This man in her bed—then knew he was Nora,
who asked me to bring her a box of Malomars.

Because of the steroids, she said, she would wake at 4 AM
    ravenous   (perhaps also to see me
                        one last time…

I cannot say what was in the bedpan,
I would like to,   to keep my poetry
sensitive to what we suffer,
or what was in the casket
no casket,   ash,   her goings,
the butchered countenance and what must be
    wrapped, discarded,
                        O I am thinking, Charles
Baudelaire, into the fluttery life of your old ones,
as they snapped like wasps against the rue corner,
is this an indulgence
    or is it touched with cancer?

Must poetry become infected to truly live?

    ◇

                        October 30, 1994
                        Dia de los muertos

Is it possible there are better days in Bardo
than others? Days of less weighing, days of more
rending? Nora on one scalepan ash,
on the other, a speculum mirroring the heart.

Could I recognize you in Bardo,
I would have to love your shredded tentacles,
your eyes I once knew as piercing
now dead wash across some scene of disarticulation,
the paintings taken back into the experiences
out of which they came, so that Joe's face now
floods the periscope eyepiece

Forty days, is Bardo, is she being dressed?
Is she a trussed goat? Dressed for the pyramid?
Force-fed for sacrifice? What happens in these forty nights?
And then I saw them slam you down again
and take you apart

And then I saw them slam you down again
and take you apart

Forty days, is Bardo, is she being flayed?
Can they get her heart on the scales?
We project jealousy on even the caterpillar.
Rood into the sky of prehistory.
Subjectile man: we magnetize *and* we project

This is her day twenty-two.
For what does she battle in Bardo?
Release? She is released. To not come back?

She's back for a pause, lodged in my kale,
in the very nurture of my breathing

Drafting her battle, like I once drew her bath.

◇

The back of my head is hollow

it is filled with Nora's ash

            Nora ash
the possessive disappears.

◇

Nora's roar:

     you're inside my body now
and while it may look like ash from without,
inside, in this drawing, this apart-ment,
these interlocking fuses, these cunei or cunt forms,
these uncials, my face is forever present,
forever as long as seen, perceived as my allegiance to Aphrodite,
the line, the point of the line on the long and generous leash of
body as the enduring reality.
There is no significant form without body's roar,
the long and terrible adventure of two bodies,
three, four, woman in mother in man in father, two-by-fours,
unlock the cross and let its ties swarm—
you will not escape my body for I will not conform, be
formula, be line without body's presence.
And so, though I love a line more than line can aura,
for my love to be good it must scintillate with origin,
member, cavern of pools and dentata.
In this ever nearness to body is my joy—
body the unfolding interlock of generative stillness,
defused as the line, tender earthworm,
heads off into the loam of blankness again and in her curling,
in her feints, gasps, spurts, crests my love,
roars my forehead into galley, rowing, stroking deep,
tasting the lover as line tongue delirium into sense and
registers home.

A jaguar of bubbles in the toilet bowl
tells me your Bardo
               Flushed

and then an airplane,   as if company,
   hums against my lungs.

◇

"Beyond Repair," she said,
I want to paint a painting I could call
"Beyond Repair"

my mind honed on Indiana heard a wreck.
I fidgeted toward her meaning: a painting
that was *beyond* repair (hear: compare)—
    a painting no one could monkey with,
a painting that was beyond
        repair,

thus perfect, with no break-downable parts,
a painting no one
                              could do better.
a flame beyond breath. no one can blow out.
smokeless. of air. liquid. a painting that would prove
    she is so here
no one could de Kooning her standing.
why not? she wants a painting that will hast forever.
that no one will fuck with.
a painting that will blaze with her being.
that you can enter. in which you can be.
yes. blues for Nora.
she wants her essence to be attended.
she wants the pelvis to be. the pelvis fossil.
she wants man as *Homo* in, as *Erectus.*
she wants erect man to scream inside
    the downy glade pro-
nounced woman. she wants woman like a wagon train
to encircle innocence (Does she know
no one is innocent? Of course. she knows and
    does not know.
like us, the living who know less than she.
like the alive man who thinks he is alive.
and the poor dead woman who might think
    she is totally dead.

TOTAL is the name of the station I took gas from tonight.
TOTAL is the 7 oil multinational sisters.
TOTAL the impact of capitalism on indigenous person.
    As blacks and whites swarm into the blues.
as the blue sky and blues and bruise fuse

a brilliant dim carpet on which Prufrock would never
    dare to recline—
against the total. of the total. yes. totaled one.

she wants all life to reign. pile. and scour.

Nightcrawlers   *

Last night it was not Ophelia but Nora Jaffe crawling the Milky Way, her cloud body shredding like Nancy Spero's image of a mutilated Salvadoran woman crawling the dirt on which she had been assaulted— and I thought of Rigoberta Menchu's mother crawling tethered to a tree, of Charles Olson describing himself as a "tireless Intichiuma eater & crawler of my own ground," of Gary Snyder off the trail crawling "on the crunchy Manzanita leaf clover…around between the trunks"—

as I continued to dream and reflect, I saw all these crawlers, one below the other, moving in parallel rhythm, some agonized, some studiously inspecting—all seemed to be returning to their totem, their *ototama* or *ototeman,* to their animal brothers or sisters, this nearly-destroyed blood-covenant between the human and the animal—

our night crawl through Le Tuc d'Audoubert, past bear skulls and viper skeletons, to the sculpted bison 700 meters inside the cave, made a vulva-like loop, a coming turning going, with the mating animals as the center—

and then there is the story my Indian friend in Bloomington told me in 1960; how on his first night there, having come directly to Indiana from India, he walked past a house on which there was a sign: *Nightcrawlers.* He was touched by what he thought was the kindness of Americans: hotels for drunks that stayed open all night long—

there are now other kinds of nightcrawlers, big tough ones moving across darkened Michigan firing-ranges, toward targets of silhouette men, the heart areas blown out. Upright around their smoking barbecues, my fellow Americans are singing: "Drop kick me, Jesus, through the goal posts of life!"

1995

Schmatte Variations   *

[based on the dolls
of Michel Nedjar]

Dolls as witnesses,
at a toll gate
through which nothing passes

or at the nothing toll
where something is always refused

    ◇

Shmattess Annie,
"raggedy"
Indianapolis, 1941 (where I found my dolls
under the Christmas tree,
propped there in candy-striped
"poor children clothing")

    ◇

"Beginners in the world as we were, we could not feel superior to any
thing except, at most, to such a half-object as this, given to us the
way some broken fragment is given to creatures in aquariums, so
that it may serve them as a measure and landmark in the world
around them"

    ◇

Nedjar, born in 1947, over
a deeply-embedded stinger,
a deportation burial, the root
disappearance of a daikon
whitened body,   shadow of family
    tailor floor cuttings
folded about a twig,   a first doll,

a variation on primal
     enwrapping

◇

Of what does the spider dream?
A fanged vulva swirling with legs

Of what does the foetus dream?
A flounder is swimming within me

◇

Through the Hiroshima horror, a Butoh mask.
Flea-market stage. Black bundles stuck to bridges.
A naked Japanese man, standing
in the rain, holding out his eyeball

Abyss as an *active* ingredient
in the "sweet
ginger and dynamite" of the mind

◇

Heads packed in heads, insect-
perforated fabric. The head as nest,
a runny nest, as if in the twill
a human soul was pushing,
trapped,
       "blackened Athena"
the bubbly stitchwork grins

◇

Of what does the spider dream?
Of little Miss Muffet
Of Muffet as curd
Of pupa dolls, of mummy pots

Of Last Suppers taking yugas to complete
Of the Crucified's stomach honey
Of eating as copulation, copulation as eating
Of orifices bowling through their bowels

◇

Nedjar's dolls as wind scorpions:

"Courtship has seldom been witnessed. A female doll becomes
cataleptic in response to stroking and tapping by the male who then
opens the female genital orifice with his chelicerae. Having emitted a
spectral globule of semen, he picks it up in his chelicerae and inserts
it into the female. The female doll lays her eggs in a deep burrow in
which she continues to live. The doll eggs hatch into six-legged lar-
vae which eventually moult, acquiring a fourth pair of legs."

Or as sea spiders:

The extreme reduction of the trunk and abdomen has resulted in
organs such as the gut diverticula and ovaries being forced out into
the legs."

Yachats, The Shore

Looking into littoral fog
the shore has always stopped me,
laid a barrier across association,
made writing by the sea
        listless, as if stumbling about
    an ode… dangerous to stare
at nature and write—

Surf crests have leatherine
                        concaves
then it's all froth crawlers trill

Gigantic skirts with meandering hems,
slits in weave to sand

Little cliffs' white rubble,
                high sizz then
    "sundered parentage"

Ropes vertically aflow—
    describe the sewing throwing:
Mumonkan stitch,   gateless
                    barrier

as if a text of iles
        detextiled while
    ile flexing
                wound sound
        perception stops,
    a shushing weave whelms the eyes:
skyscrapers under nuclear barrage.

I'm a little boy in my glandbox
    sifting mommy purr,
the simmerunderoar   spreads
    a virus under tone

taking the lips back to suckle shapes,,
    trom   bone
the slides of brass
        under 4:30 sun
silver   so glaucous pocked,
              more cicada
         than constant

      Watch out for unity as you age,
    it's in cahoots with reduction

Be as these rocks not deluged,
just gleamy in their Lenten instant

        Myriad-glimmered
reason surfing the tectonics of dream,

Mallarme's "throw" still tumbling in the air,

poetry as shipwreck,   oceanic page,
"a throw of the dice"   the gamble of alchemical research
"will never abolish chance"   no way
    to predetermine reception—

Unless a work of art is its own shipwreck
a master is proposed outside the maelstrom

Surf looks more perfect that I can imagine a god,
perfection that if not seen through
        dwarfs imagination—
seen through,   nature *is* imagination,
        roving tooth breast
        on which I row
60 years a second

      Pyramidal speed-ups
    slow lozenges of satin steel
storied   pounce in rinse,

dipping sun drapes a mail
across the crestlets

then 7 gulls in muscular goodbye.

[28 May 1995]

Less And Less Wholly Absorbed, Aware   *

of your resonance,   I am not simply my own conduits
but a focus of your and my flashing lights

Being porous enough to dynamite
one's own characteristics   is the gem
    in the marriage
band of learning—this entwined opening out
   makes sense of love,
that on this one trip (then nothing nothing forever
I choose to be with you daily,
inhaling,   holy,   our filings
     mixed,   like birdsong
ter-weet cher-wee (Amazonian wood quail

What I delve is a multiplicity tinted
    shaded, flavored   released
wound-erased
                  by your bright shafts

You have twinned my life, doubled its spore

    Never to forget
    nor merely to remember:
    I sit in a tow of language
    mined, in clink with a mile-
    stone rage for mortar
    while a Tibetan
    is forced to build with temple bricks
    a latrine

Soutine's Lapis

The exultation at Céret has the long dirty ghost legs
   of bony ravens,   it marches without body.
Terror is seminal. It says: I am not the spit
my father shined me with. All windows are monstrous eyes.
All houses pupiled caskets. I'm sorry but the road
   is in the sky,
I mean, the sky is pumping the road, I'm sorry
but the road is in pump with the sky, if you know what I lean.
A whole treed plaza picks up its sunderskirts and runs,
   ruby lava.
The earth is unsubstantial lapis
while his body is poised on a brush

You can't see what I see, reader
so I have to mail you
red gristle howling away from black fire—
"Landscape with Gnarled Trees," yes
but the sensation is tree-torrential hill-tides
binding houses buckling and elasticized

So many gorges, upon inspection,
have not scissor-faced mothers, but hammerhead fathers,
pockets of gold, of pus,   pockets of hearth and pomp
knotted in a wickerwork of forced labor, of freedom, of
   tearing burgeoning—
in Soutine's Céret, a quaked slob
discovers his mortitude, the chutes of his lying,
all the image leprosy percolating Smilovichi,
the beatings,   their energy,
being famished,   its energy,
the energy in being rejected,
the energy of *no*
romantic folklore

Clutchy belonging to something
inexistent until created. Think of it!
You have no life, painter,
until out of nothing you create it!
Out of nothing? Out of a village church
looking like a huge gold spider about to vomit.
Out of a trampled green hex.
But to paint the exploding raven head
in which sun and moon may be copulating,
to ball this gonadal wax into a honeycomb
then to invest it with one's own bees—

this is to travel,   this is to visit Soutine at Céret

Jigging farmhouses burnished by a urine-colored dusk,
scree on the move. Bovine
femurs inside of which villagers live.
The feel of noon at 3 AM. Dream of a deal
in which one's foetal cash register is clanged shut.
As for *should you be?* The argument at Céret
is a road upchucking a cascade of zilch.
As for *why?* White-haired butcher babbling tomatoes
in the swill of pink organs meaty flood of boils

O the primal slaughter before all the houses!
Garden of Blowsy Delights!
Slaughter so real it deflowers—
the barns are boozy with it!

And there is always a hill. Not a mountain,
nor a slope, nor a rise,
but something 100 times Soutine's height,
of porphyry,   of jasper,   lit within,
a bubbling town dump, shack-
faced urchins poking through what Spaniards
    sliced Indians into,
a shifty hill,   a shtetl,   a townlet
morne on which Césaire's mother pedaled her Singer,

Dead Man's Drop where I sledded,
there is always a hill, a peak, an excel
from which we are falling, a precipice
    of which we are the innards,

                  the traffic jam in paradise,
                        grid-lathered Babel,

to feel a potential versus life as you piss,
shipwrecked roofs, this scowling thatch,
whitened oaks like goose necks
force-fed with nothing, stretched forge
with corkscrew thighs, sky-wired elms,
clap of a single cymbal, sound of self-rounding,
fire of the stem called masturbation.
Turba Mass in male soul we have yet to figure.
Men, those brutal bastards who never really
    get to be king of the hill.

I think Soutine at Cagnes lanced his Céret hump
to find a glistening Mediterranean wound,
a viaduct,
wild Kundalini,
vertical boa nosing heaven,
swollen boa,
undigested pigs and whippings still suffocating
    in its guts

Ark-like swing with which this road redetermines landscape,
the Tao of Soutine:
La Gaude "variations,"
12 paintings,
the height of his joy,
childhood golem exulting,
hand up La Gaude making Porky Pig shapes out of houses,
a vine of godheads sprouts from the boa's side,

accordion village,
twists of whipped-cream courtship,
a detonation held in play,
too whipped through   to stay joy,
too avalanche,
too peak veering,
too dumped

      Caught in the act
the yellow boa road turns into red centipedal embarrassment,
all legs flattening and arching,
or is it a bloody spinal cord surfacing through wheat?
a way of being   extending clamps?
Now here come the houses!!
They push their beer bellies up to the road,
bang it silly,
siphon off its undigested spunk

May Nile-turquoise manticores
speed thee to thy rest

"Church at Cagnes":
a just marooned Atlantean
grasping his fate.

The pheasant is risen.
The dead pheasant, risen from her bath—
out of tomatoes, she is risen,
the garroted pheasant,   out of her vessel,
a still-life,   life in the still of
    alchemical imagination

It is very murky here, fleeced of sunlight.
The potted flowers grapple with the chair back.
The lilacs in their jug look like spoiled meat,
like scrapings turning scarlet with desire?

Jug scrawl with roses, looking Argus-eyed,
face swarming with eyes, roses as blowflies
release these ravens, peacock entail them!

    and then some jonquil yellow
    some geranium
    a plaster statue
concerning which, the legend goes:
"embrace her with love, and deposit upon her some semen—
like Pygmalion's Galatea, this *fate* will come to life in your dreams
and tell you, now her lover, where to find buried treasure"

Song of the gladiola-spirit yearning for blood,
yearning to become what Soutine was unable to eat.
In the still-life retort, flowers feeling
    flow-er rapture,
in contra naturam, as Soutine nerves
flow through gladiolas,
                   Van Gogh is near,
the background blackens,   a putrefactio is under way.
Petals like copulating infants.
           The canvas a urinal
in which the moon is lying on her back
            in blackish water—
could we dissolve into this flower-flow,
what lurid wonders we'd unearth.
Soutine Van Gogh shaking hands in sperm,
squeezing pulpy red ocelots out of pressed palms,
flukes of childhood hunger resonating in the woods.
Scum of boiling, bloody broth, the fidgets, the blocks.
Resistance in the gladiola,   the word itself
unhinging, a "sword lily," diminutive of *gladius.*
Is the painter a gladiator? Little swords form a mandala,
a magic circle,   a fly is trapped under Soutine's eyelid.
He leaves it there. Fly rots, green cream forms over the eye.
The pot of flowers now looks like wilting antlers.
Van Gogh guffaws. How wring out these gladiolas?
He cuts his hand on the steel stalks,   forces them through

his mother's wringer,   *his mother's wringer,*
he looks out from between her legs, his mouth
stuffed with gladiola stems.   Self-Portrait as a Hydrant
Gushing Tulips.   A herring falls across.
He's still stuck in Smilovichi, plucked clean in Paris.
Van Gogh throws up into the pot. In the violet mess
    a storm begins to twinkle…

The herring's eye looks like a truffle floating in yolk.

Explain the cephalopodic grasping of these tulips.
Explain
these manta talliths, this cimmerian inkiness,
the way painted-over paintings (flea-market scrape-aways)
ouiji directions in circuit shock with Soutine's
once used, tossed away brushes

"I am the source of all pornography,"
sings the little flayed rabbit still in woolly socks,
"laid out on my pale gold and suet sheet,
my whole cavity is open to your eye-fingers,
    my legs are spread,
    my crotch smeared red,
    my wispy forelegs wiggle
    by my skinned but staring
    head"

According to Paracelsus, every body (meaning every tangible sub-
stance) is nothing but coagulated smoke breathing forth from the
matter, or the matrix, in which it is present

Thus this pike "body," a sulphur fumet of cobalt, tar and
blood, slapped down on a shiny bench,
mouth rubble frozen in a paroxysm of snapping,
alongside a row of vermillion onions
which must be tomatoes,
little bloody turbans of smoke

Another pike-shaped flayed rabbit
so mutilated as it quivers in its violin
Bacon is immediately present,
or Bacon's grinder mind, through which this creature
seems to have passed

It has always given me pleasure simply to say Soutine's colors,
to reflect on the way his things interpenetrate,
a mahogany table whose cinnabar grain liquefies
around 4 steel-blue, grey and white fish
whose surging immobility is picked up by the rumpled, knotted
    ochre cloth

All here is living and dead at once,
as if half-frozen bodies were dropped on red-hot coals,
photographed in their first seizure,
glimpsed before the awakening became being awake

Some scholars have written that Soutine is dominated by anthropo-
morphic gestures, that he is undisciplined, hallucinated, out of control,
a necrophile. To spot subliminal forces organizing in his limbo brawn
is not to see him as cartoon-complexed; rather, it is to affirm the extent
to which he turned the still-life into life in the still. Soutine is one of
the most porous painters who ever lived. In the blood-mares to be
found in the oily, night hair of his Seine are hybrid consequences still-
dwelling in our minds-to-be-born

Such is his ray, a wealthy bawd, in the profusion of fat and jewels nosing
forth out of the blackness of her latrine, while the pot of tomatoes below
digests itself, tomatoes turning upon themselves, slipping up and around
each other, anxious to burst

Or another ray, which appears to be disemboweling itself of tomatoes,
parboiled and skinned, which Soutine cannot digest, a ray with multiple
tomato breasts, O Ray of Ephesus!

Or still another ray scene in which a copper-tea-kettle has come alive,
flinging its ribbony handle-arms to the dark, dancing and leering at the
4 pomegranates inching toward it like seething little kegs of blood

The color and texture of this ray evokes the face of the older Rem-
brandt, jewel-like decay, mucous and cinders, creature as mineral, as
flesh, as paint, in whose pocked and luminous surface a child is born
and marked in Bethlehem

Annie Mae Grudger has been listening to all of this,
looking for many years now through Walker Evans' kind lens.
She is 27, has 4 children, wife of an Alabama cotton tenant
    farmer,
and is nearly-starved. She is losing her hair,
holding her mouth in a smile-clench.
For a moment her humble bile has receded and she has offered
her tilted gaze to Evans' camera.
For a moment, she would walk out of her body
and embrace something she has just felt.
1936,   she is standing posed against
bare unpainted siding,
she is backed by Soutine

and it is her spirit that often shines in Soutine.
She is so thin at 27, you can see her upper chest bones,
she has one dress she could be photographed in,
no underwear, I'm guessing nothing like a bra.
She might have some saggy, ripped panties.
Annie Mae Grudger is the Smilovichi intersect,
a cleaned-up version of Chaim locked by father
    in the chicken-coop

(I'd argue Barnes is the crucial provocation,
but clearly self-destruction is endemic to Soutine,
destruction of his self,   not himself,
destruction of what he made of himself,
Jewish hatred of the image,   bypassed by the man,
scorpion-tailing back on the painter,

he honors the terror of Smilovichi
when he slashes a Céret)

To be hanged in Venus-flail inside a crumbling chimney:
turkey in rotting turquoise high heels
with sulphur Italian-blue henna Sapphire-blue breast,
aureoled in black, with circular buzz-saw of blue-black feathers.
To be at genital-lock with one's forge
lit up as if by interior bluebottles.
Ode to our wretched turning,   to be,
volatile body,   Soutine would deny Mercury
and insist that the body in glory
is the squirrel in the arbor
starved and pawing for chew.
Turkey carnal candy. Timid girl legs,
hesitating death-droopy talons.
Steatopygous chicken, whose larder lesions
purl with peppery gland streaks.
The Eden-rot of Maya. Texture of foggy morgue fuel.
Have you smelled a stale chicken? Have you,
Whitman might inquire, smelled your stale self?

"Yellow Turkey" with red flayed-rabbit-head
pointing lode-ward as if in pollinated
gyre,   carcass
already treacle,   moving with lice-accord.
This nothing we are,
arrested,   but not spent

And it is beautiful or things to get out of hand,
for the wine of Tartarus to soak through the snow,
for a turkey to hang and orange.
Corraled chaos inside of which a moldering
duck exults,   or is it a green eagle?

Turned on its side, the 1924
"Fowl Hanging Against Red Bricks"

becomes a chicken goddess propelling herself through an under-
water grotto.
She has multiple breasts,   a human profile.
She is passing over a sunken red tugboat—
the disintegrating horizon of a subliminal Céret?

Before confronting an entire beef carcass, Soutine painted sides of beef.
The one in the Colin Collection evokes Bacon, then drives right
through him. It is a side of beef, marbled violet, yellow, white, the top
of which appears to be attached to a bin or trough, half of which is an
odd linen-like white—and when I look again at the meat pressed into
this "pillow," I see a screaming, flayed male head and, looking down,
his body, belly pushed forward, ass jutting back, armless, the notched
spinal column winding arm-like down, a reformulation of the centipedal
sidewalks of Cagnes. The belly is so thrust forward, "pregnant' leaps to
mind. In the inevitable comparison, Bacon's mutilated figures on beds
are luscious, fleshy swirls. The Soutine is poised at the apex of the fu-
sion of a sawed-in-half roebuck and a man flayed screaming on a bed

Pierre Courthion wries:

Around 1925, Soutine tackled a series of gigantic pieces of meat. For
the project, he rented a large studio flanked by a collapsing brick chim-
ney on rue du Saint-Gothard, not far from the Denfert-Rochereau train
station. In this workshop, which neighbors came to call "Soutine's
Butchershop," he began to paint, along with turkeys, cocks, and hang-
ing ducks, enormous quarters of beef.
    Paulette Jourdain, who was at this time Soutine's model and assistant,
described to me the nearly unbreathable atmosphere of the workshop:
    "I would pose," she said. "And watch the flies that came to tickle
Soutine's nose. Then at the Villete slaughterhouse, he bought a whole
beef that his dealer Zborowski paid 3500 francs for. Soutine was not
aware that the beef would rot. I was sent to slaughterhouses to buy
blood in a milk pail, blood which sprinkled on the blackening surface

refreshed the so-called model. Downstairs, I would always run into the same characters questioning me: this blood, what is it for? For a sick person, I would say. O well, then, they'd exclaim, take care of him!

"Soutine would say to me: they gave you their most beautiful blood! How lucky I am to have you!

"When he was at work, he would throw himself from a distance *bang bang bang* at the canvas! I was made to stand behind it, and I was afraid. He bought used canvases, which he carefully scraped. He'd say: I like to paint on something smooth. I want my brush to *glide.*

"In that huge studio, I posed while the beef reposed. Big blue flies were circling about. These monsters are awful, Soutine would say, without noticing the putrefying stench to which he appeared to be accustomed.

"A knock at the door. Who's there?
"Sanitation Department!
"Panic. A uniformed man walked in to take the beef away. Soutine became deathly pale.

"O please, he begged, can't you see I'm working? I've got to finish my painting!

"Moved to pity, a worker in white came forward, and said to Soutine: watch what I'm going to do. He took out a syringe, a needle, and injected ammonia into the beef.

"The next day, the sanitation people came to disinfect the studio. Soutine was able to continue. He completed the piece of beef on a blue ground that's in the Grenoble Museum.

"A day later, Soutine appeared with a bag of syringes. He furiously injected everything! The ducks became rigid as wood, although their feathers lost none of their color. End of the stench! But the carcasses we put out as garbage poisoned the neighborhood dogs. We ended up digging a hole and burying the ammonia-injected meat in quicklime."

In the life-spirit of pure blood
a lapis is dwelling. It is the whirlpool in chaos.
It kills, and it quickens.
Wonderful stone, held in derision by the world.
It is heaven. It is the scum of the sea.

The Buffalo "Carcass of Beef."
Threadlike black scribbles, drips,
antic milling in the pit of a colosseum
framed by the richest blue.
Tension at the top,   tolling
gravity below,   this glassy, roily fatalcore,
this animal crib become our slatherfest,
this sordid hackwhich, this Vietnam!
Stubblegrowth in loathed rubble,
the first god quaternified,
it is the animal garter soaked in us,
nigredo-overpowered alembic,
this predator temple,   this immense
Buddha-compassion breakdown,
    to disembowel,
to toss the liver to the wolves,
to core the animal of itself, and move in,
and once inside the animal house,
to start to work on oneself!

And then a mahogany-red pheasant comes twisting
through the waves of a semen-cream drape.

Soutine's portraits are marvelous machines of consciousness.
The coils, the hairpin
turns, the tics,
muscle armor,
flabby troughs of that weighing station between
nothing and an enlarged suckling
each person is the patina of.
Crispate fingers that suggest the hand's desire to act
the octopus,
have a beak hidden in palm.
Hands knotted in prayer like an inflamed pumpkin.
Or glove-like, and melting,
fingers become nightcrawler independent,

hands as the exhausted straw of the body's peristalsis,
as in "Woman in Red,"
broken, paired slabs, stacked one on one.
There's a wildly-flopping turkey in each of us,
an atavistic flyer manacled to bipedal hesitation.
I like the whirling raw hamburger in his faces,
the drab fix of their stares.
"Village Idiot" and "Mad Woman" join
Madeleine Castaing in her black fur
and "Man with Straw Hat," whose face is toothpaste
being as squeezed impasto,
the epanadiplosis of the body
moiling back on its rhyme,
out of the shtetl, forever rocking,
a prayer metronome Whitman never knew...
repressed missions fade in the choir boy's eyes
the white of his dress
almost redeems the color white,
it is as stained as an old cooking rag,
washed rewashed,
the flecks of parsley, garlic, rancid butter,
bits of chopped red pepper,
it is a tunic on which fowl have been dried,
in which parboiled tomatoes were squeezed into
little balls, to garnish
a chicken in champagne sauce.
The "Page Boy at Maxim's" blood-drenched-red uniform
breaks out on his face and hands,
or do his crimson ears and black eyebrow eye-pits
release their pained,
ruined, servile
clots into his uniform?
Soutine has drawn an empty circle on his outstretched palm,
the circle's slightly off,
the tip will never be right,
never connect with the need
beyond any tip
of one ground between tables,

whose life is errands.
These are faces as charged as marshes with their own
uroboric devouring,
heads whose source must be
in the privation of hewn and crafted images
from which Soutine's ancestors suffered.
The Biblical world sack turned inside out,
there tumbles forth
—along with flame-shaped praying men
and mousy pastry cooks with elephantine ears—
Soutine himself.

According to Maurice Sachs, he was "at first glance, coarse, unplanned, ill-shaped. A thick, haphazardly-planted nose, fleshy, pale lips opening on irregular teeth, a single thick eyebrow, stubborn and without malice, barring his forehead crowned with dense, black, tousled hair. His small, penetrating eyes were of a rare color, a kind of saturnine blue, and their speckled, mazarine grey irises were like fluid, lively, animated agates. He had short hands, but they were admirably shaped, agile and graceful."

Who is this "Woman in Pink"
we'd all like to know? She is
her coiling chair, a pythoness dredged,
battered, in moldy, foaming rose.

1906. Maurice Tuchman writes: "Two of his older brothers constantly taunted him, saying 'A Jew does not paint.' They beat him mercilessly. This cruelty became almost a ritual. Soutine would flee his brothers and hide in the woods until hunger drove him home."

Amazing, given the Hitlerian shadow, to ponder his bundled, struggling-along children on French country roads in 1939. A boy holding the hand of his younger sister. Two boys sprawled on a log. Soutine in the woods at 46, still hiding from those who would watch him paint.

"One day, when Soutine was about sixteen, he approached a pious Jew and asked him to pose for a portrait. The next day the man's son and his friends thrashed Soutine viciously and left him for dead… it was a week before he could walk again. A complaint was lodged against the aggressors by Soutine's mother, and the boy was granted as compensation the sum of twenty-five rubles.

With the money Soutine and Michel Kikoine set off for Minsk to become artists."

David Sylvester: "In the Céret paintings the forms are dense and congested and their nearness makes them loom up, dangerously closed, threatening to burst through the picture-plane and having to be held at bay. As if fearing an attack from them, Soutine assaults them: the canvas becomes a battleground between the menacing force of whatever confronts the painter and the bending force of the painter's will.

"And this becomes Soutine's pattern—to put himself in a position from which he feels that something is threatening him, so that he must attack it, wrestle with it, twist it, wring its neck. It is as if he can only make contact with the external world through an act of violence and violation."

So the terrible beating that paid off, that brought him to Minsk, that enabled him to become a painter, is endlessly restaged, restated, nearly transformed. At some point in the late 1920s, the furnace of combat cools. As if to say, Soutine woke up one morning with the battle behind him, on the far side of transformation. As if the transformation were the moment of falling asleep, the moment we are always before, or beyond, never consciously *in*.

Such must be a captive freedom, a sort of horrible leisure (Bruckner counting tree leaves (Soutine spending hours looking for four-leaf clovers

By the early 1930s, Soutine appears to be travelling, as a painter, on a composite past. When he speaks of Rembrandt's "The Jewish Bride" (his favorite painting), he places his hand over his heart, mimicking the groom in the painting placing his hand over his bride's heart. Yet his

"Woman Entering the Water," inspired by Rembrandt's "Hendrickje Bathing," is as coarse as Soutine himself. Painted in the rain, a peasant raises her soiled white dress, staring at thick, clubby legs—forbidden fruit?

His one "nude" holds her hand over her genitals, the hand on top reddening as it clutches, turning the wrist below it white—ashamed of her body, thoroughly ugly, her face seems to await a blow, or is it that she is already cuffed, jeered, called upon to perform like a dancing bear that cannot dance? She simply stands there, guilty of nothing, guilty of woman's body, tinged tawny in such a way that Nebuchadnezzar crawls by as I look at her, Blake's "creature" trapped between the human and the animal. Soutine's "nude" would be more aptly called "the naked one," or more fancifully "woman on the blackened chicken-run of her life," the pathetic source of his ancestral ambivalence toward image, the despised scapegoat cowering in what we all "sacred," our mother's body, its incestuous imprint on love's body, the gangrene usually hiding in the wings of the stage upon which the classical "nude" is unveiled.

A green chaos of magnificent trees sweeps through the last eight years of Soutine's life, soaring, waving poplars, oaks, beside roads outside Chartres, Civry, and Champigny. Trees like giant whisks tremor in awe of earth's arborescent flavor. For the first and only time in Soutine, one looks up into green dragons devouring blue serpents, a darkening stir, the caldron not on earth, but at cathedral tower level, where our eyes give out, where we peak, as watchers.

The engorged boa roads of Cagnes are now delta-shaped inlets, humble rural paths, the tiny children almost lost in ruts and greenery, lady bugs in the tapenade of the ground. The minuteness of the human relative to the vastness of nature recalls the Chinese floating world of sages perched on pine-covered, mist-swarmed cliffs.

Two children move along the road, as if biunes, strange twins, or little comrades with two arms gesturing from a single, fused body bearing two heads. These kids are Soutine with his natal daemon exulting in the grand and wrestling doorway of nature's slapstick vagina. The tininess of the children—really one child—and the over-arching boiling breeze become Soutine's farewell. On a wander-route with his infant daemon, he is haloing himself back through and into the forestral gradations of the teepee-like entrance/exit all waver between.

In some of these paintings, the road seems to shoot through the little figures, and whirl on up between the trees to become a sky road. In others, the sky is like mucilage between the trees, an opaque "negative" of a ghost, not empty space but a sky-like non-sky

wind as porous disturbance   pointillistically dispersing the coagulated smoke that was life

On A Photograph Of Gall

A mountainous shadow rains in stasis,
the extinction of indigenous person,
Gall
the orphan adopted by Sitting Bull,
posed by Brady in regalia.
The defeat of Custer uncocked the Protestant arsenal—
Gall bears the weight of the pregnancy of extinction.
Dickinson's "a certain slant of light"
ricochets
"a pyramid of granite night."

El Mozote   *

Lieutenant Colonel Domingo Monterrosa,
a   blown-apart girl wants to talk with you,
she wants to rearrange,   like checkers,
   a topological map of Morazan—
she wants to play, Lieutenant Colonel,
against your American power,
                              she wants to see
if slit baby throats, raped beheaded girls,
can jump your American M-16s, 82 million dollars,
Lieutenant Colonel Domingo Monterrosa,
a disintegrated rib-cage wants to confront you
with her trinkets and little pencil,
                              she wants to ask about
her friend who once had a bright-orange
plastic horse,   she wants to know
if the dug-up toy is the soul of her friend,
she wants to know if there is a soul,
Lieutenant Colonel,   she does not know,
Domingo Monterrosa, that the goodness of being
must include articulate responses to
bones sticking through rotting trousers,
that even through the most abstract Pollock,
         the most unglossable Zukofsky,
an American flag of smoke ripples
   in sublimNational honor
and in gallery, in book, our hearts die
for we know,   Lieutenant Monterrosa,
no matter how many of you are blown out of the sky,
the military killer factories we finance
                  are at work below

O unnamed girl who could have been
Rufina Amaya Marquez's daughter,
Rufina Amaya Marquez, who watched her four children
   and her husband slaughtered,

Rufina Amaya Marquez discovered
　　　days later cowering in a ravine,
naked, bloodsmeared, covered with thorns,
Rufina Amaya Marques, El Mozote's only witness!

Liberation Footage

    Naked corpses dragged and dumped
into pits of 5000 by Belsen SS guards
under US surveillance, April 1945,
limber as hammocks
unresistant
deep long white valleys
where stomachs had been,
or bodies bumping along, muscle free,
deep long white valleys
hoisted flopping onto SS shoulders,
they hated it   they had to do it   they
heaved them up from Belsen trucks
spread-eagled, trash they hauled

        By the green
        slaughterhouse within
        my lawnmower,

        a naked
        child offers honey to
        a wingless bee

There is no proposal the imagination cannot assimilate

But it is only through Pleistocene mercy that we're still here.

I, Friedrich Schroder-Sonnenstern *

must confess that while I am male
I am prognathous and female, with queenly tresses
triculating my loins. A lovebird
pecks at my butt notch. Nipple-tripodal,
I salute at attention my red rooster king
who, at serpentine attention against me,
gives me a clitoral nudge—
deft, sensational! while squirting in
a blue petunia
without losing hold of his switch!

My king, who is my confrontational
aplomb, is as stationary as I. We are engaged!
without engagement. His paSSion is displayed
through the life in his butt—
that's where the rainbow begins.
On his bright-red butt plate
there's Mr. Mouse with his millepedal tail!

I stand before you, arms outstretched,
in a long white robe, THE SANDWICH KING.
Why not? Jesus fed the multitude!
My cognac beard trails back to Aesop.
I raised my hyena clit to challenge Zeus!

It's great fun to be the visible inside of an outside
others take to the opaque.
The concentration required
is a spectre licking my anal razors

Man is a moon-moral
ass-driver who, with hidden raised switch,
offers a thermometer, disguised as a baby-bottle,
to the kneeling ass.
There are clearly too many smiles snaking up our hatred,
too many scimitar grins,

as the animal prays, broken-legged, before us,
nipple-suctioned to our own desire

Then, a second wind: a headless woman met me upside down.
Poised in the pubic
slot of her great buttock heart: an erect eye!
I named her Moral Practice, and for her alone
learned deep muff diving,
the most mooned of the erotic arts!

Like most visions, mine is giddy, fractal—
you can't overdo an undone thing!
Who knows why I'm a glee-frozen Noah
displaying my ark like an unzipped whale?
I am Mystery Man not in fedora but in tux,
with Christmas tree limbs radiating out.
I am Moishe Kapoyr with finger wisps,
my nose arabesqued with helpless furls. Yet I am likewise
a version of the Gorgon few if any recognize

Not feet, but wheels—so the Devil can roll us about!
The Devil, he does not smile—O but he does,
oh but his big butt! the Devil's ass is rich, and red,
ooh tomato! The sword-toothed fat-boobed
vulture carrying away your angelic daughter
is the dentata inside my plot!

What I love is bulbous:
canaries bussing on my fontanelle.
What I love is armless:
Adam and Eve's passion for truth, as,
swung up through their legs, they stare at
their own butts!

All are on a boat, rainbow-energied.
All are ghoul-chewed by the moon. Man is
the ass turbined masterblend

of the moon—and there are no moral clues:
across my team of twelve plowgirls, I, my mother,
crack my whip! There has never been a Fritzclown
braincrown like mine! Propose—
and Psyche differs, and in her duff
a vaginal circumflex glows.
O emphasize the natal clitosphere in which
I, Friedrich Schroder-Sonnenstern am actual!
Swans in udder gowns with rainbow hoofs testify:
there is way too much twat serum
for the fragile angel complex! and so I cut
to another scene, and passed out fishburgers, and who
will worship me?

In an assfield of corn, a brain is mourning

What I perform is gorgeous, and absolutely aligned.
At center: a smile stud.
Below: Piscean eye ambiguity.
A rump with spread and planted skull feet
is in position
                        O let your long turd drop!
There is no chamber pot without a heart!
And your turd, despite its andouille handsomeness,
will never reach its gloppingplace—
for your turd is not your own!

World, are you ready to travel?

Sod, have you finally sprung a man?

As a moonbeam trying to shoot an arrow
into the distant labyrinth of a sparrow,
I am sure. The toy master feeds the lion
boobo myooh, while the toy ape toots.
Paradise is to change the sex of another's face
into a larval diadem of flames and lace!
So with knockers proud as zeppelins,

a toy propeller out my butt,
silk garters on each ham
and Pandora's tongue-shaped foot,
I am the conductor of my own Pandemonium,
a weight-lifter spider in a fly-infested tomb!

My Evening With Artaud   *

While I never met Antonin Artaud, I did witness his performance, while
in the wings, at the Vieux-Colombier, in Paris, 1947. I was eleven, and
after a decision that collided with all her past behavior, my mother laid
in a sizeable supply of salami for my father, buttoned him in bed, and we
took off, two naïfs from Indianapolis, to bear witness to what my
mother's choir master promised would be
the overturning of the cross,

                                                or,

the planted body sprouting
through the bulb of its own barrier.

We slipped into the hall, stubs in hand, past Gide, Paulhan, Marthe
Robert, a young Paule Thévenin, and others I have come to know
through the lexical corpses littering the writing of my second magician
(Blackstone, at the Circle Theatre the year before, being my first).
Shortly after our complicated return, my mother completed the trinity
of my early initiations by taking me to see *Tarzan's Desert Mystery*, my
introduction to caves and spiders.

What moved me so much about my mother's behavior:
she did not yet know that I was born!
How close we were in those days!

While Artaud stripped, I thought of my sex life with my mother. The
most moving months had been inside her, and while there were gaps in
my foetal memory, what happened there, as I gesticulated to her every
thrust, recalled my own closed-eye vision which I began to practice at
eight. Pressing my knuckles into my closed eye-lids, I manufactured
stars, lagoons, lace stockings, blasted cities and kaleidoscopic diamonds
which, watching Artaud, struck me as arterial beholdings, or seeings
into my own seams which were, in effect, those of my my mother.
     The fact that we merge into the egg, as a zero or gleam, to then re-
main bouncifully suspended there in a solitary confinement that is the
least solitary we will come to know—this seems to suggest something

about the unhappiness of men, who emerge hypnotized by an infolding warmth for which they will search throughout their lives but never rediscover—not in philosophy, nor in bathing.

Women while pregnant return to the womb, in men's eyes, and even if never pregnant, appreciate a "summer's full" in a way that men brood about or rapinely chafe against. Womb life, that vague memory of being coated with a pond that goes out into infinity, this memory, bachelored by the awareness that it almost certainly cannot be recontacted, this drives men to fury! We suppose dogs do not see their death, but that men do, without the certainty that it is final or the mitigation of a new life starting up inside.

Sitting by my mother, as she kept squeezing my hand, reminding me of a frightened female mole pursued by an aroused male, and watching Artaud divest himself of everything—this sitting by one who would burrow into me, while watching this foetal dance, man in the glade of himself, a kind of pinhead deprived of sunlight—my thoughts desubordinated fugally.

It was amazing to be by the one who made me, who took another's gleam seriously, while watching, right before my eyes, what life had in store for me. Artaud's bat-like reclutching, the way his "mutual aid" clothes failed to fit (though seemed, like a tree after a storm, perfectly right), his acrobatic introspections speared in mid-flight, the lullaby always about to emerge that, upon croon swerved into loon-like wailing, then shot straight up to golden-shower the crowd while, at the same time, he was more arachnoid than anyone, more packed with eaten heads, more guilty—

this display made me feel that Artaud had at long last gone beyond his stymied Theatre of Cruelty, that this evening we were witness to the first performance of
    an Amniotic Theater.

Artaud's complaint seemed to palpitate a disappearance. And it was: man reaches a limit of contraction at birth from which he seldom recovers. I whispered this to Gladys as she dug at my palm and, card that she was, she whispered back:
    Why you old fox! Go on, go on!"

Man is in contraction at birth because not only the essential, but the armature of the essential, and its ruthless anatomical aftermath, have been determined. At birth, man's invisibility is greater than his visibility, for he has been stiffed of eternity by those two sphinxes who made his manifestation possible. Some find profundity in the egg. Artaud was appalled by it. He once wrote that "the EGG state is the anti-Artaud state *par excellence*."

It seemed that we stayed in these wings for many years. It seems that Artaud, ravaged and enraged, hands flying like birds around his face, declaimed his scarcely-audible poems throughout my adolescence, and that during this period I remained in the wings, watching the poet, then the audience, motionless by my mother, who occupied herself with needlework, occasionally asking me to play "White Christmas," "Rustle of Spring," or Chopin's "Revolutionary Etude."

Artaud would strip down to nothing, lose his skeleton in a wild flurry of looking, become two sockets bouncing about the stage, then joint by joint reappear, throw on his black rags, grab his manuscripts, and start to howl again.

But Powell visited, as did Lennie Tristano. The audience left, then returned, the auditorium filled with snow, sand blew in from Morocco. What are we doing here, I would ask mother.

Then she would hand me the Bible that Reverend Ragan had inscribed to me. As if suddenly plunged back into an asylum, Artaud would stop, twitch, and glare. His consternation told me that I must create my own Bible or be enslaved by another man's.

In a pale imitation of the soul, I would get dressed, first slipping on my pajama pants, then my wool suit pants. This way I wouldn't scratch so much in the pew that I would disturb the trances of those nearby.

In a pale imitation of the soul. All seemed to seem, even Artaud, even when he grabbed his crotch while cartwheeling around it, yelling that mommy-daddy was the monstrous absence in presence.

The monstrous absence in presence, a fugal occlusion, the dead fish in hand feeling of one's most treasured erection. The way life winks through every rigid expression. One seeks a rudder in all of this, a broom handle bobbling in the whirlpool, anything that smacks of being moored. Moored to what? Mother's smile?

"The basis of pornography," my mother leaned over to me, "is the impersonality of generation."

Artaud was taking a break, and Gide, who had fluttered to the ceiling of the Vieux-Colombier, had just descended, billing and cooing about Antonin's shoulders.

"Frankly, I'm appalled by it," she continued, "but I had to realize that my Chicago choirmaster, who came on to me before you, had a keener contour than daddy did that night in 1934, Philadelphia to be exact, when he slid into me as if I had walked into a hurricane. I buried my feelings in an entry in my Wannamaker Diary, commenting on a car accident, but you, my sweet sailor, became the curl of that lunge, and in many ways you are as personal as impersonal."

You are very naughty, I told mother—such information is beneath pornography, which was revolutionary in 18th century France, but today it's not even the cleavage you just displayed.

"Listen," mother dug, "solidarity is our only hope. There are midnights as pristine as Keats' nightingale, and others so jagged only a Shakespeare could bevel them. Cock in cunt, pardon me, my son, is celebrated not only in the English copula but is rampant in the metaphorical underworld. It is our lie, our magnificent nonsense. Humankind can only stand so much fucking. We Hoosiers understand T.S. Eliot's wisdom thus: piston in groove, oiled in and out, ongoing, for thirty minutes, to funeral parlor fusion, is simply too close to the void that, as your mother, I have brought you here to witness. And it is the void that terrifies us Christians, for we have no place to put it, no tequila and marigold bridge by which to cross the cross. The crucified is obviously stuck there and unable to assist. If Mary Magdalene were truly Magdalenian, surely she would have dragged him, cross and all into the cave and succored him. And if they crucify me for our conversation—"

(mother turned to me like a dead, drowned dog)

"—would you roll away the rock?"

Frankly, I was furiously scribbling, and had almost tabled my dear mother's plea. Gide and Artaud were entwined on the dais, the audience was out smoking and quaffing. As a mortified eleven-year-old, I decided it was time to confront eating pussy. Simply having been down there, between Vala's legs, peering up across her tummy and crossed eyes, had offered me a brief but untutored perspective on male and female relationships. I had felt subordinate for the first time—and indeed, wife I was to Vala's barely-haired timid slit. We had been in the rumbleseat of paradise, a May Saturday afternoon, the orchestra of hell thrumming through our mettle. It's V for me, I recalled murmuring, lick to jolt.

Mother saw the blaze in my furrow, held a match to me, then lit up, incandescent.

"I could never get daddy to pray. I aligned him, perfumed my nest, even set up a mirror system by which, were he to roll over, he could reflect on the nature of the void. Prayer as cunnilingus, humbling and potent—only a maven could find a beat in it capable of tripping his own heart's arrogance. The man who scarfs his lunch from the trough of the goddess—this is the way we used to put it in Wabash—is injured in the act; he will never replay the hero, and who, dear son, is a hero after Odysseus? Men adore sexual mobility, parading full orchestras across the body of one passive, but to face this fateful gate, this Song of Songs, is to know the pump runs dry, and that the sacred is as much a scab as a mountain."

"I love to be broken down into the conversation we are having," mother continued. "If Antonin and André could fully explore, I'd like to think they would happily include the character of each as well as the void. This is where the lower body comes in, as a teaching device. The upper body, that palace of enforced certainty, is a battered though beloved icon. I love you most totally thinking of you as a cigar boy, just a torso and saucy head, no inquiring hands. If I had my way, I'd keep you like a jumping bean on the fireplace mantle forever. But since we are all products of each other's imaginations, I am quite aware of your serpent tail—such will not get you a MacArthur, but because you scuttle where you bleed, there are those in the future who will think of you, momentarily as they pray…"

Her voice seemed to trail. Artaud was back, Gide in the audience. A poisoned stillness reigned. I realized that Artaud had not lived as he felt he should live until he died in electroshock, and that the first half of his writing life had been one long complaint that he was dead—

then the beauty and the dreadfulness of the poetic act broke across me. All poets, I premised, seek to be born in their work, and if we take that nothing backwards, then one begins as a deadman, and the deadman even if regeneration occurs, is always there, a mummy or mommymummer, in the crease of realization. So that the poet is dead to but alive for a mouthless speaking, through which death, voiced, enlivens us. The poet is the dale through which countless copulations have passed, a sorghum of matted bee deaths, in hive to a flowering only those who suck at the source feel like hooraying. And then it struck me that everything I had just said could be stood on its head, because if one thing is true about life, its opposite is also true. Yes, the poet is the one who sucks at the vulvic, penile, or anal source, but the poet is also the one who refuses, and enaltars the consummation. Then a beautiful light spoke: Bodhisattva, stay with the peak.

Artaud was back in zoom, I felt like a flit and mother? Tired as we all were, she moved on, slipping into the prompter box before Artaud's feet.

It was in this box, that in 1970, I buried her vertically. I was thirty-five, and have had many years to reflect on our fantastic evening at Vieux-Colombier.

De Kooning's *Excavation* (I)

To be in the stroke
to be a "slipping glimpser"
to slip the stroke while glimpsing paralysis
        in its metaphorics,
     the cobblestones over tectiforms,
   Huitzilopochtli under Dagwood smears

Excavation of where cartoons are parked

Fire spitting between the body parts

Improvisation: oldest habitation

Annunciation at the corner of Carmine Street
the painter looks into the hole:
      there is a way to foal
in dismemberment,   to raft the member-
          flung wreckage

   Tectiform   Tectiform   roof or sail or
vertical forearm. Add another arm. Wrestling
self is martial meditation—
     no way to begin again? Consider Gauguin:
Europe diseased, Naturalism kaput, trees turned blue,
lizards braided Tahitian Eve. Gauguin exposed
an eco-ethno morass that still shudders.
      His work proclaims:
the goal of vision is a recasting of Genesis—
   end at the beginning

A broken totem descends through *Excavation*:
at top center, a bird beak dings (a la Rube Goldberg)
   the roof of a tectiform
whose base is caught like a cocktail tray by

uprushing waiter's splayed fingers and thumb
        —whose cuff bursts into flame!
End of waiter. My eyes continue down, through flexing
diamonds   a pair of braed tits   to a broad tectiform,
        center bottom. This totem midden says:

In the flukes of excavation there is form

The subconscious is coherent

—these lipstick jabs   cleavers   jaw-interlocked
comic heads are a puzzle solved before our eyes

Barely recognizable jigsawed voids become yellow
        semen linoleum
discharging former barely-recognizables

Midden flattened into a painting
"gumspots…bits of refuse" forced into "bums who lie
        poisoned in vast delivery portals"—
de Kooning's insect-filled night mind pressed
        between two glass plates

Larvatory of lares and lemurs

Gorgon carotid dousing Pegasus

Conundrum of the abstract, more concrete than the real

It invites us to set the primal scene on fire.

Blues For Byzantium

Clangs of Yeats like blues

Byzantium a stretch-limo
surrounded by
Liberian juju bands of roving infected studs

"dome" a research lab on the Ross Ice Shelf

"starlit" and "moonlit" work for a cruise line

The night-walkers have no song—
they're banged, a mockery of gong

The other night Shade appeared on Jay Leno

"Flames No Faggot Feeds" just cut their first CD

"image" is anything you want it to be

All that cock is   a Hadic bobbin' bough
    crow moisture   mummy seas
the Muse as changeless metal

"scorn[ed]" "common bird and petal"
complexed in midden atmosphere

"dolphins' mire and blood"
    Japanese tuna seines

Green dolphin morgue with chordal seams

        As if Yeats might now hear
        Bud Powell's "Blues for Bouffémont,"
        a sanatorium outside Paris, 1963,
        a Byzantium abstract

percolating through the changes,
sound-rhymes like winding,
mobile windows, gong and marble,
word-windows facing

walls, images that yet
images beget, scorned, embittered,
Powell in agony of trance, shade more
than man, drunken, abed,

a shape connected to wires,
by electro-shock set in motion,
Calder mobile more than shade,
rototilling while reaping, doors

yielding door, in the yielding
a window intercedes, revolving,
throwing off arousals
compounded of sacrifice and ooze—

Over a sunken Golgonooza,
an eight-winged hermaphroditic cherub,
Blake hovering—

I lit my palm with Lascaux,
saw Caryl drift across
what had become impossible to see:
origin, love, and contemporary fire in any
sense of harmony

I lit my palm, by Lascaux's
bird-headed man, saw the image recede
through Egypt's human-headed bird to
Yeats' "golden handiwork"

—the killed-out image hovering,
archangelic toy in late air.

IV
2003

JUNIPER FUSE (2003)

For Caryl

Lespinasse, 1974: We carried our dinner outside to the stone table

on the landing by the door to our second floor Bouyssou apartment.

The farm was on a rise which sloped down through an apple orchard.

When we sat down to eat, well before sunset, we had for entertain-

ment an extraordinary sky. Clouds would come floating over the

woods, spreading out over us. Puff collisions, Mickey Mouse ears,

gargoyles shredding, turrets, vales, mammoth apparitions densifying

and disintegrating as they appeared. Many reminded us of the images

we were trying to discern on the cave walls. To sit at that stone

table—what an experience—to be in love there, at one of the most

vital times in our many years together. Much of what happened—

the "event aspects"—during our first spring and summer in the

Dordogne is now as dispersed as the clouds we used to watch—

yet it billows in us, an inclusive cloud whose heart is ours.

Silence Raving   *

Patters, paters, Apollo globes, sound
breaking up with silence, coals
I can still hear, entanglement of sense pools,
the way a cave might leak perfume—

in the Cro-Magnons went, along its wet hide walls,
as if a flower in, way in, drew their leggy
panspermatic bodies, spidering over
bottomless hunches, groping toward Persephone's fate;
to be quicksanded by the fungus pulp of Hades' purple hair
        exploding in their brains.

They poured their foreheads into the coals and corrals
zigzagged about in the night air—
            the animals led in crossed
a massive vulva incised before the gate,
the power that came up from it was paradise, the power
the Cro-Magnons bequeathed to us:
to make an altar of our throats.

The first words were mixed with animal fat,
wounded men tried to say who did it.
The group was the rim of a to-be-invented wheel,
their speech was spokes, looping over
around, the hub of the fire, its silk of us,
its burn of *them,*   bop we dip, you dip,
we dip to you, you will dip to us, Dionysus
the plopping, pooling words, stirred
by the lyre gaps between the peaks of flame,
water to fire, us to them.

Foal-eyed, rubbery, they looped
back into those caves whose walls could be strung
between their teeth, the sticky soul material pulled to
the sides by their hands, ooh
what bone looms they sewed themselves into, ah

what tiny male spiders they were
on the enormous capable of devouring them
female rock elastic word!

Hades in Manganese   *

for James Hillman

Today I'd like to climb the difference
between what I think I've written and
what I *have* written, to clime being,
to conceive it as a weather
generate and degenerate,
a snake turning in digestion with the low.

But what you hear
are the seams I speak, animal,
the white of our noise
meringues into peaks
neither of us mount—or if we do,
as taxidermists, filling what is over
because we love to see *as if* alive.

Seam through which I might enter,
wounded animal, stairwayed
intestine in the hide of dream,
Hades, am I
yule, in nightmare
you weigh my heart,
you knock, in the pasture at noon,
I still panic
awaking at 3 A.M.
as if a burglar were in the hall,
one who would desire me, on whose claw
I might slip a ring, for in the soft
cave folds of dream
in conversation you woo, I weigh,
I insert something cold in you,
you meditate me up, I carry
what is left of you, coils
of garden hose, aslant, in my gut…

Hades, in manganese you rocked, an animal,
the form in which I was beginning to
perish, wading in eidola
while I separated you out!
To cross one back line with
another, hybrid, to take from the graft
the loss, the soul now wandering
in time, thus grieving for
what it must invent, an out-of-time,
an archetype, a non-existing
anthrobeast, rooted and seasonally
loosing its claws in the air!

O dead living depths!
One face cooing to another plungers
that went off, torpedos, in dream,
to spin through a pasture at noon,
sphincter-milled, sheep-impacted,
the lower body attached
to separation, pulling the seam of it along
cold cave stone, the head as
a pollen-loaded feeler tunneling
to ooze a string of eggs
where the rock, strengthening its yes,
returned the crawler to vivid green
sunlight that *was* profundity
now invested with linkage,
the grass, invested with linkage,
the whole sky, a tainted link,
man, a maggot on stilts,
capable of leaving elevation at the mouth
to seam unyield to his face.
Tethered, Hades phoned, om
phallos, the metro the zipper
of dread at every branch-off,
the pasture at noon conducted
by the bearmarm below, batoning
sun down word rust scraper by scraper out.

◇

Below, in the culvert
behind the House of Okumura, 1963,
the conveyer belt ran all night.
The clanking got louder, tore
then died, surf roar, origin beguiling,
a highway was going through.
During late night breaks,
the itinerant laborers would smoke
by a sparking oil drum in domed yellow helmets,
navy-blue wool puttees, men goblined by metal,
pitch black and popping fire. I watched
from a glassed-in porch, not quite able to see
inside the drum, wanting to engage
the action, to tie the fire into a poem
Paul Blackburn spoke on tape to me,
which would not burn. He suffered savage men
without a context standing about a dying fire
jacking off into it. Depth was the crisis
I tried to raise. The surf roar, earth
tearing, lifted, but not transformed, seemed,
as if part of me, an unending mechanicality.
I could and could not—it could and could.

I was, in spirit, still
in puberty, before my typewriter,
as if in a pew before an altar,
itchy, bored, afraid of being whipped
when we all got home. I played the hymnals
and black choir gowns into a breathing cellar
larder, a ladder to
convincing ore, a bed-shaped
Corregidor flashing, as if a beacon, to me adrift
—or was it the Phi Delta Theta dorm door opened
a crack? I would think of Mrs. Bird's canary
waiting to be driven downstairs and beat bloody.
That canary, hardly an image, helped me,

but it faded in an instant, the actives were
shouting around our bunks, beating pans.
Meowing like Raoul Hausmanns—or were we silent?—
we bent over where the wall had been removed
and only the fireplace remained, gripping
each others' shoulders, our naked huddle
encircled the open-ended fire—we were fisted
loosely to a turbined mass, our heads
a common tampax clamped into the actives' hate.

A fire surrounded by walls of flesh is now
contained. Hades makes a target of this maze.

Perseus holds the written head out to the sun.
His sword from his hip projects what is on his mind,
a center torn from a center, Medusa
wrenched from her jellyfish stronghold,
her severed pipes, the caterwauling serpents,
his treasure from the underworld.
The hero will not be
transfixed into himself, he will lift
reflected terror from reflected depth,
he will thrust his hand down
into the sodden tampax mass where earth bleeds.
My father, for thirty years timing blacks
slaughtering steers, folds into men
beating the animal in other men,
extracting its Pan-pipes, jugular flutes of morning.

Picking the confetti from our hair,
Little Lulu and I cross the city
Francis Bacon mayors. In this city
cartoons mingle equally with men.
In their cruel goo outlines I sense
the terrible strength in our lifting up,
unceasingly to translate upward,

to take whatever stuff and lift it,
earth, dream, whatever, up,
the pyramidic impulse to slave-point sunward,
to streamline, rather than to learn from, Lazarus.

Surface is reality as is ascension
as is depth. Medusa hangs down through
fathoms of archaic familiarity,
the pylons men have made of female psyche,
women beat into gates through which to draw
the ore of heroic energy, to appease
a masculine weather for manipulation and torture.
War on matter lumped into a procrustian mater
crammed, with her crucified familiar,
into the entrance way to Hades. I knew,
holding my fifty pound mother in her swaddling
cancer sheet, that there is no triumph *over.*
Resurrection, a Carl Dreyer altarpiece, yes,
a true finger-exercise in hope, a waist-
hinge, in the waste of spirit the crocus-bud
surely is not to be denied, its yellowy flame
playing among the stones warms what is
youngest in us, most held in night, tender,
voracious for sunset, fire appetite,
to watch the mountain smoke with modesty,
the thing to transform itself, lifting
from itself but carrying Hades as pendulum,
the parachutist gathering in Medusa's threads,
an intelligence under, not of us, but receptive
to us as we drift and wither...

Why do we treat the hero
better than he treated the material
he severed to feed the sun?
Perseus with his fistful of belladonna,
could we transform him into a hermit

with a lantern? Give him an awl,
teach him meander-work, zigzag wobbling through
the infant-clotted rushes, teach him salamander,
teach his semen how to stimulate fire. Unblock
the entrance way to Hades, allow the violet odors
of its meats to simmer in ice penetrating
advice. Something will work its magic against
the door of never. Hell Week, 1953,
a postcard Hades mailed to me,
his kids in demon-suits tied a string
about my penis led up through my white shirt
tied to a "pull" card dangling
from my sport coat pocket. The personal
is the apex of pain, but without it
mountains begin to numb specificity.
The personal works in specificity like a tail-
gunner, the tension in the dogfight tying
my death into my work.

Concentration now includes Dachau,
barbed wire has replaced reason
as the circumference of energy. There is
no hail to rise to. Names are cultural
foam, nada-maggots stretching their scrawl-souls, paw
scorings in the frost of the mother corridor
where our faces were first ironed softly.

Hades receives meandering Hermes
mazing my thoughts into the La Pietà
softness of the target-maker's arms—
there what I change is ended, my despair
is nursed cryptically, for Hades' breasts,
like cobwebbed mangers, are miracle-proof.
There a sucking goes on, below the obstructed
passage way, all senses of the word, stilled
in its being, take place. I am playing

with what is left of my animal, a marble
it rolls into neuter, a cat's eye, rolls back,
I crack its pupil between word-infant lips…

Bird spirit flew into Apollo—
animal disappeared in Dis.
What was sky and earth became life and death,
or hell on earth and psychic depth,
and I wonder: how has Hades been affected by Dachau?
In the cold of deepest bowels, does a stained
fluid drip? Does pure loss now have an odor
of cremation, a fleshy hollow feel
of human soul infiltrating those realms
Hades had reserved for animals?
Are there archai, still spotted with
this evening's russets, stringing and quartering
an anthrobestial compost? Or are the zeros,
of which we are increasingly composed,
folding out the quick of animal life?
Is that why these outlines, these Hadic kin,
take on mountainous strength,
moving through the shadows of these days?

A wheeled figure stabs and sews
the infancy in our grain to the skin of the ground.
Wheeled wall master who mends in manganese,
talk through what I do not remember,
the life in which I am glued
stringings of narrative Ariadnes.
All hominids share a scarlet where the dark is
pitch with horizon, note-leaps, the static
of non-meaning tendrilling us, making way
for not another bringing of the dark
up into the light, but a dark
delivered dark Paleolithic dimension.

Permanent Shadow

There is no connection between the death camps and Lascaux.
But what if the souls of the living
dead have been tortured to the extent
no other bode can contain them
other than that cul-de-sac that, by its manganese,
ceases merely to be stone hiding,
but turns in the very word *abattoir,*
felling or hide of the cave, its fell,
herd pouring across a wall turned hide,
the bridge I imagine those hunters constructed
from the seal of themselves to the animals through which
they were boring—these phrases keep backing into themselves,
as if our condition now is hugely umbilical,
a gorged boa is our passageway,
something it has swallowed whole is the messenger
between the invisible and the visibly cannibalistic,
as if the cap of Hades is a skull bowl,
and the brains I mouth and the marrow I emphasize
—that which seems central within the rings,
the trident within Poseidon, the Jupiter within light—
are contaminated by the indigestible,
this fish-hook I cannot metabolize.

Placements I: "The New Wilderness" *

for Jerome Rothenberg

Anguish, a door, Le Portel, the body bent over jagged rock, in ooze, crawling in darkness to trace the button of itself—or to unbutton the obscure cage in which a person and an animal are copulas—or are they delynxing each other? Or are they already subject and predicate in the amniotic cave air watching each other across the word barrier, the flesh?

At arm's length the image, my focus the extent of my reach. Where I end the other begins. And is not all art which genuinely moves us done in the "dark" against a "wall"? Olson's whisper (a prayer), "(boundary)
       Disappear"

Artaud's hatred of depth near the end of his life. All real action, he ranted, was at surface. Beyond? Nothing. Below and above? Nothing. At the same time he desired to be organless, eternal. James Hillman writes: "Every rebirth fantasy in psychology may be a defense against depth." If coming up out of the cave of night can mean an openness to knowing we've never left the cave, then rebirth ceases to be antagonistic to depth.

The beginning of the construction of the underworld takes place in Upper Paleolithic caves. To identify this "place under construction," I use the later Greek word "Hades," and it is there that the first evidence of psyche we can relate to occurs. To be in the cave is to be inside an animal—a womb—but to draw there is to seek another kind of birth; an adjustment to the crisis of the animal separating out of the human— or, the Fall. To be inside, to be hidden, to be in Hades—where the human hides in the animal.

◇

Semiconscious scanning through the lich gate. Wandering the winding windows of images. Knowing that as we see through, we only at best see into dream to touch the cave wall socket in which the current is called *animal*. Its adamant muzzle confers moisture on my deathly palm.

◇

Since the hidden is bottomless, totality is more invisible than visible. Insistence on a totality in which life is totally visible, is the anti-dream, Hades deprived of his cave, Satan attempting to establish a kingdom— or death camp—solely on earth.

◇

As species disappear, the Upper Paleolithic grown more vivid. As living animals disappear, the first outlines become more dear, not as reflections of a day world, but as the primal outlines of psyche, the shaping of the underworld, the point at which Hades was an animal. The "new wilderness" is thus the spectral realm created by the going out of animal life and the coming in, in our time, of these primary outlines. Our tragedy is to search further and further back for a common non-racial trunk in which the animal is not separated out of the human, while we destroy the turf on which we actually stand.

Dot

Unicellular sac pressed
fingertips,

two dots, a me
row—or a herow? a meandering
red moist

blastospore, a multicellular
dot-filled wall
lubricious prefiguration of Hermes
who swings with

heat of the amoeba need
soldered to sprout

desire, an earthworm psyche
spiderline, tunneling on the leash of the
to-be-perstaltic

boundary seeking

something to curve
about, zigzag,
bear claw hut rain,
diagrammatic boogie-woogie of Hermes
flowing in the boundary catastrophe
when the animal was separated out

Dot,   doorbell
summoning Hades through stone.

Our Lady Of The Three-Pronged Devil   *

Our Lady of the Caves
dressed in rock,
vuliform, folded back
upon Herself, a turn in the cave,
at Abri Cellier
an arch gouged in a slab
makes an entrance and
an exit, She is a hole,
yet rock, impenetrable,
the impact point of the enigma
no one has lifted her veil,
the impact point of the enigma
yet rock, impenetrable,
an exit, She is a hole,
makes an entrance and
an arch gouged in a slab
at Abri Cellier
upon Herself, a turn in the cave,
vulviform, folded back
dressed in rock,
Our Lady of the Caves

a long sentence dissolving within itself
and when it ends, it is just beginning,
a presentiment that Her sign is one turn, uni-
verse, end of a first line, curved about
a vaginal gouge, as if She is a fetal arch bent about
a slit that goes in one quarter inch.
Our Lady may be the invisible archwork
through which all things
shift gears in the dark, at cheetah-speed,
at snail-struggle, on the shores of Russia
where Paleo-archetypes compressed into radar
gaze around with dinosaur certainty.

Before Okeanos, continuing through
Okeanos, before the uroboros, continuing in it,
Her gibbous half-circle tells me that She existed,
before an association was made between fucking and birth,
before a bubbling parthenogenesis was enclosed—
but to what extent She exists
in self-enclosure, in my triumphant
raising my penis to the sun,
to what extent She neatly
slides Her slit between my self and its point,
I do not know.

For the self has grown enormous,
I look through literal eyes to see Her
on a slab chopped out of Abri Cellier,
in a cool limestone room in Les Eyzies.
She seems only several inches tall.
It is a funeral to be there,
in a burial chamber where first otherness
is displayed behind a rope, with written instructions
which only describe the age of a shape.
And I who look upon this am immense,
encrusted with all my own undelivered selves,
my skeletal papoose-rack through which my mother's
85 mile long legs are dangling, out of which my father's
right arm with a seemingly infinite switch trails
down the museum road, across France, to disappear
in the Atlantic, and I jig around a bit,
because a ghost dance starts up as I stare
through the hermaphroditic
circle the snake made, so self-contained,
but what it and I contain, the "divine couple,"
is the latent mother-father who
has taken over the world.

Our Lady moved about
like a stubby pitchfork,
yellow fiber gushed out from between Her prongs,
She hobbled, toward image—
what lurked under Her vulviform was the trident
yet to come, for men realized that not only
could the point of Her slit be hurled
but that its two bounding lines could be too,
the whole woman could be thrown into the animal
And way in, trident deep in Le Portel,
did Her three prongs close?
Was the uroboros hammered shut when those hunters
at last hacked themselves free from animal sinew?
And was this the point at which
the wilderness was mentally enwalled,
serpent the outer circumference,
to teach, and banish, our Adamic Eve?

Below Our Lady, on the wall of my mind,
is the foot long rock phallus Her devotees may
have taken inside them while they chipped in Her sign.
I have been straddling, all poem long, that insistent,
rapacious thing, of phallus, the tooth-phallus,
the borer, for the tooth-phallus is insatiable,
male hunger to connect at any price,
but not to connect, to cease being an island,
a speck before the emancipatory shape of
the birth-giving mainland, to build a mole
to tie fucking to birth, to cease being ticks
on the heaving pelt of this earth, to hook
their erections to the sleigh of a howling starvling.
And they did
get across, at around 10,000 B.P.,
one night fucking and birth were connected by a mole
burrowing right under the surface of a full moon
boring a red mortal line from the edge
to a point equidistant from the circumference.
The corpus callosum was suddenly filled with traffic.

The last Magdalenians were aware that Our Lady
had closed. They padlocked Her
with the uroboros and planted the key.

She now grows on a long handle
out of ground at the edge of the abyss.
Some see Her as fly-eyed radar.
Others feel it is to Her prong that they cling
as the gale of monoculture whips them horizontal.
Many more on their knees inch along cathedral pavement
toward what they believe is Her virginal compassion
which will somehow make their manure-colored barriada water pure,
their nipple blood, their corporeal
muscatel in which their children play,
miracle and misery on which my index
touches, to stir for a moment Her
gouged rock socket
octopus current of
faceless suckers Veil.

1980

The Aurignacians Have The Floor *

for Gary Snyder

The clawless Cameroon otter, her entire range
endangered, waddles off
dragging a chunk of MacDonald arch.

Everything is owed to everyone.
Nothing is owed to anyone.
A lot is owed to most

and something awful is due to
the streak of domination that does not
become endangered in Shah or peasant

—sure, I know there is a difference,
but that otter would not agree
and it is that otter I am concerned about,

wondering what she remembers as she passes,
as a species, out of existence.
I wonder if she will pass through

the Aurignacian assembly.
I'd like to hear the speeches
as she defends her ogre intelligence

in which sounds are joisted with water rustle.
Will she refer to the black stump
smoldering in this "new wilderness,"

the negativity inherent in having forgotten
End-Pleistocene extinctions?
It is time to let the Aurignacians have

the floor. Their cup-shapes
carved in burial slabs are
a pileus suggestion that in death

a stem continues to stalagmite,
seeping through the cracks in our
subliminal scanning.

On the loosened knot of paths upon paths,
I will accept the Aurignacian motion
that the abyss is engravable

and terminates in caves manifesting
hominid separation. I dead is under
I do. My vertical stands on my zero.

It is now possible to chip at
the target's living center,
the outlined bison by whose manganese

throat I am painting the clawless otter
with the oxidized
silver of Dracula's stake.

Visions Of The Fathers Of Lascaux   *

"The animalhood has begun to slip
we can no longer trust
the still warm tunnels of gall and intestinal
astrology in which we have failed to find
the oxygen stone but have tasted
the lees of our own trial to breathe
and there as if by telescopic
arrogance have spotted pools of dark fur
recompense for our hairless
clutching this staked out woman in whose
bloated fortress apes pass
telegrams from Africa
that a division has befallen creature"

In massed imagination Atlementheneira
Kashkaniraqmi and Savolathersilonighcock swayed
on only one archetypal core,
intelligence had not yet been hacked from dream
dream from the frothing of the spitted kill
nor death from whole
villages of the dead living in nearby slabyards

The Fathers of Lascaux took a semen count
and found that the bison concentration
was weakening every several thousand years

Time was a lock-out each wore around his heart
a briar cage puncturing the pumping
pregnancy of shit and newborn squalling

"We must release ourselves from the death we are taking in
we must shed our difference with grass
with all this supple rock blinking overhead
we must strip the earth from the earth
to see our origin in spools of glandular alignments
for I see through your eyes

thus more narrowly Atlementheneira
a star landing on an egg
and many roaches bearing crosses of an endurance beyond ours—
I fear joined with you a frailty
our skins cannot contain
the plant-eating bears nor this sky at dusk
swimming with headless starlings
and these solid fingers of weather-raked ice
jellied with water unsure of our density—
we are contracting into genital cribs
where spiders wrapped in frost curtains are sewing our bladders to
     our eyes—
what salt will remove this ravine studded with maples
what abattoir thick with Neanderenthralled ochre
will convert the unnameable, freeing us from the whack of navels
and the wrench of seasonal amplitude?"

So they sang their visions speech-tied
through six-legged separateness,
imbibing the fresh nasal sinew of flowers
which so stirred them that they manganesed
the terrifying gaps in the natural patchwork
subordinating the bestial slippage to vague groiny faces
and when they scrambled a cave
they added pinches of themselves and shots of the tree-like mystery
     of anatomy
their mothers wore long tobacco-leaf gowns
eyeless ghosts crawled toward the entangled speech ribbons
in which the Fathers of Lascaux were suffixing bellings with howls
waiting for lightning or a desperate pack of earthworms to remove
     their overflesh
then plaster them back with drilled eyes
into the substance of anything needing eye shapes

From which they were retrieved by the Mothers of Lascaux
whose wombs had just been vacated,
while the Fathers chanted the jelly shudder of the Mothers' massive
     generative girdle

already turbine in the cave
rotating
straining the walls
priming them with menstrual effluvia
for the boundary separations to be applied by the dreaming Fathers
    who
with their sharpened tips would continentalize
the animal looping they were losing
to pull the animal close in image
to pry up the floorboarding of their appetites
from the ceiling of their rage
warping a space to dream a softness for the Mothers
an egg-like void in which digested meat
could be winnowed and separated like fumes
seeping up into the lower chambers of dream
now an actual topology slant with this earth of peaks and wallows

The Mothers were turning in a fine hum
howling like hornets attacked by orchids,
the Fathers were wrenching at their abattoir boards
Mothers and Fathers cog to cog in the first
whimpering ova of the to-be-ensouled
hyena language lab of a hollow oak
there to dig out a place to live in the purple cushions of fresh-killed
    language
which had hung like bulldog saliva from their nightly fire-lit lips

The separations taking place in the chambers of dreaming were
    knotted
the tassels were swinging like sledgehammers into morning
breaking the icy light of the flat
riverine limestone into clackclack
informing them that the deadend of being born could be briefly
    tapped,
that the prisoner on the other side would tap back
thus a wall, the skull clacked, separates you
from the other who is unorganized
slime and must be dreamed into erection,

as you press back in all I am will sprout
souls of lower forms, fetal shrimp coiled
about their notochords will harmonize
your desire, and the penis sentry will glimpse
the prisoner condition, big-eyed curled frog bug
so not hold back the offering
but jet it gently into this cold world
with only a thigh in the dark to lead you back upon yourself

Then the Fathers lowered the skull into the Mother's pelvic endless
modifying corridors branching tendrils too
tight to be plumbed their bodies
turbines within rock sheath expanding against
the Pleistocene contraction to burst the sexual grip
into phantoms of dreamable schist,
to fall upward reversing the animal gravity
that in icy hives of thousands of years
they had taken on forgetting the fluid
unseparated elements their pineals had steered
their sleek marine shapes through
before physical dessication established
opposition, earth versus ocean
the source of being yes and the source of
these Fathers' and Mothers' despair

For the pineal was now a pine cone and I
already a language orphan
and the Mothers of Lascaux flayed the penises of the Fathers
holding the rainbowed strips up into the sun
scanning them for the source of the Fathers' brutal intrusions
goring about
upsetting the glandular arrangements of seasonal rutting
treading the furrows the very day after they were reaped
pressing in again and again to contact the substance of the fetus'
    dream
in which creation was a boundless

bowling alley of simultaneous strikes and unflinching pins,
wind coiling through the blush of a dragon language rocky vaporous
    fibrous

Atlementheneira dips me into the vat of all that's gone before,
now a vanilla tar bubbling with elfcasts of civilizations,
toga entwined axles, a passionate cobweb of liquid smiles
howling as millions of sleepers run into the rum of daylight
mixed with papyrus and rain-haunted vegetation—
and then I am out again on this German autobahn watching his
    terrible
shoulder huge as a pine forest disappear like vapor into the violet
    rainy air

The Fathers staked out a woman in Lascaux
she was their first lab, first
architecture, spread in labor,
tectiform in anatomical churn
a kind of windmill in the cave's recesses
with stretched crimson staves humming through the bobbins in their
    heads
whose womb thus enfolded
jerked with millions of oospheric stars—
in accordance with (now) the natural law of opposition
the tube of rejection and reception had split
to ease the fetus from having to ford the excremental Styx
clogged with the dark green stuff of monkey suicides
immense catastrophes in which hordes were snuffed by cosmic pauses
the stars went out
a blue fissure opened the earth to make it new
yes but at what loss of species thus
increased impaction in the forming world soul

This was the fetal keyboard on which each movement
depressed tones of other times
wells of disappearance Atlementheneira
was translated from a sound heard in dream
to the faint lines of a hominid atl-atl carrier

whose spear was dream
whose object was to pierce
the bloated yet severely malnutritioned
sexual bellows
releasing numbed energies to make stone
sweat red or receive umbilical finger-painted drools
as if the vagicanals had contracted the disease of consciousness
and the Fathers of Lascaux delighted entering fully
not only sentry but
the whole battalion of their wishes, winged
wishes, palaces of winged lions
crowded into the chrysalis leading to a biological
nowhere now in torque
with the Mothers to this frightening world we inhabit
in which the placental unimagined pieces
amalgamate into radar
nuclear fission the helmeted ant of dream
red visor drawn down an inch
from the twisting dreamer who still
flinches in nightmare with the rotation of

What might I offer these Fathers and Mothers?
What might I bring from the 20th century
into the humming den of their evolution to imagination,
striking out "prehistory,"
dynamiting the blocked Greek passageway
so that their wet torsion smokes about
the ghastly beautiful statues of human gods
with hounds and vixens fawning about their cothurni

Suppose I placed my Baby's Book of Events in one of Lascaux's
    galleries
would these Mothers make anything of "Bok *Old* Mamma Tak-a *New*
    Mamma"
my first sentence in combustion with the Hitlerian Age
1937 and blood was already gushing from
the breast-severed Nanking of World Individualism
Stalin was crouched O Goya your Saturn!

My language shat in its stall
terrified stag by waterhole as the Fathers fixed
the potential to dream and scrawl the clouds of animality as they
    shredded
to open a blue immensity as if the sky
were entrance of an earthcave we were always
on the verge of leaving and so we remain
thresheld in gravity even though
the autonomous animal gods are departing
in sobbing pairs over the horizon
we grip and slide about, beginner skaters still

How would my portrait look set in a niche by an 18 foot aurochs?
Would the diffuse dread in my playful eyes
communicate even a bit of porridge to the loose electrical
    power lines in the eyes of Lascaux's Fathers?
My eyes' opposition is impyramided
with the Aztec Shuttle, the Presbyterian sallow
ivorying of the groin and Dachau blow-ups.
Were the fathers in their brutal clarities aware
that in the lifting zeppelin of dream
were gases whose molecules when burgeoned
would sabotage the world tree?

I offer this entire century to these crouched tectiformers,
their crystal bubbles in which snow flurries
almost obscure the tiny stone cottage
in which the minute treasure is a hammered tongue rocking
with the verbal rib matter curled asleep in its own life,
its Hershey bar napalm license plates
bone jutting nudity dumps
Raoul "baby Incan" Hausmann
Lorca in 1928 knickers with plaid kneesox telling Borges
that "the most important figure in America,
Mickey Mouse," was bulldozing Catholic stonework
to erect his yellow dot sofas and draw
revolutionary whiskers on slob Latins
O pointless list for those we've wronged, all we've made

redundant before these aurochs sheaths
in which the spears of testing death
turned and turned beyond the features of mortality,
gouging off against senseless stone—
the limits of yielding were made to hold
lust to penetrate Atlementheneira
was penetration itself as he hammered infantwise
against the Mother-primed tunnels
to open omen-encysted nature,
the goiter that might contain the oxygen stone,
draught of its cool burning leaves cooking
to rewind the millwheel of seasonal
green Savolathersilonighcock
gouged at a bison outline to eat
away the autumnal aromatic logic and release
in oxygen more enduring than rapture
the just beginning to dream thus omen projecting
synthesis we despair over, the human mind

As Kashkaniraqmi watching the stars
marveled at stags rhinos mammoths drifting on the same fraying
     umbilicus
so did he dream of today's Czech
pensioner in Prague by dim formica table trying to spot
the line to X for dumplings and broth—
an increasingly tendrilled fissure,
dry versus wet developed in oppositional power
to drive a slow pyramid upward in hominid constitution,
that as natural faculties weakened
armaments and medicine would increase
until men would slither like tapeworms
through button-measled gears of earth stripped to its gyroscope
     rudiments

At the base of this pyramid
the King of Cracked Morning slept
lifting his loaded sleeve occasionally

to direct the ant-like orchestration of slaves
mounting peak after peak thinking
as they struggle across solar plains they are building cities,
Evil increases relative to the steepness of the pyramid,
its latest peak is now at our throats,
as we gaze down the steps of any ruin
it is only Kashkaniraqmi who casts an archeological veil across the
    steps
to hide the bloody chewed-out teeth
the stains of dark blue amputated limbs
mossed with gangrene that cover each ascent
Around the pyramid's landing-deck
a neat atoll-like ring of smoke
resembling a tropic isle—there we live colonial to
the subdued matted loam of wreckage
I cannot bore through back to
the howl-shaped word flames of violet and blue ice that assemble
    now
a floating wall at this pyramid's tip

I would eat through this metallic smog-flavored cube
not back to some far-fetched purity of chaos
but into the heaving nucleus of femur set in bear socket burials
words inserted through the openings of a resistance
strong enough to hold this poem in place
the prisoner within the prisoner is the colonial target of ring
upon narrowing ring to
the strong central suck of a pupil
frosted still alive
which I float into,
more into cooked marrow than into the language rubble of a bison
    staring,
more like ice skating in a vertical hoop surrounding me
than spitting out the hot Rimbaud rocks
to suck on cool seamless pebbles
anonymously wept for centuries in the shore coffer
of this beautiful desire to put my tongue

onto the concave tongue of this Aztec landing deck
undersea and phantomed crypt where gods born slaughtered are
    aging

Poem, go for the throat of this crypt,
tear open a passage down to the snoring director
whose white-gloved nonhand
motions left versus right, some to torture, some to work
as the oppositional fandango increases Atlementheneira
succeeds in rubbing a black dot
against Lascaux's peritoneum, goading the cave to expel him like
    cannon shot
again he strives back against a wind tunnel of rear wall bafflement

Why should he try to adorn stone with the cut hands and hearts of
    the moon
when the Mothers were shouting
"Don't you realize, dear one, that you wear the solar tiara? Leave
    that dark
yo yo waah waah no no ju ju ca ca wee wee
for the crossed femurs of thy rightful bear crown!"

And other Fathers that I name joined in
chanting to install the invalid personality in
Atlementheneira's antlers, to sew in his ragged black mane
the beads of self-succession, bending him
inward against this attempt to transform the astrology of his entrails

A new opposition, that he was to become his opposite
and once fixed in the Iron Maiden of self-sufficiency
to tear that selfhood off like plaster cast
yet always to reflect the scar,
the dream of wholeness rent
he limped now matured by compassion for vastly stronger
vastly more crippled nature,
he worked the vale of natura contra natura
handling my mother rattles like liquid silver

relishing my infant eyes like oysters in the orchidwork of night
redirecting branches that centuries later would grail into the bed of
    Odysseus,
in his manganese vale Atlementheneira could make out
the notochord of Charlie Parker seafarer,
his ax, his quiver of blues, the dragon snout of his Melanesian canoe
he watched Bird adjust the aerial on his penis sheath
that the lower grotesque body might contact in emergency
the geographical fixations of the mind

And as he strove against the cave Atlementheneira
could envision that once signed
it would be relegated by gradually peaking individuality to the lower
    body,
placed in its baths, a *grottesca* of animal human copulation
Thus much of the lower body remains occult,
feces occult, semen occult, the Muladhara Bridge
on which Antonin Artaud was sodomized by the Catholic God of
    France
as well as the internal brown phallus with its scarlet vaginal keyboard
in contact with the Mothers of Lascaux
as they wash out the Fathers on brook rocks beating
their weariness from their muscles to send them back at nightfall
into Lascaux's equine enraged crevices

The internal phallus is a spiral void chimney
leading out of the tarry baths
where urine and menses are traded on an ever bull market—
on this board are encoded the disasters of 30,000 years
that were only chipped cup shapes
before the first riverine vulvas began to meander
Entrance and Exit, a simple labyrinth,
before the Mothers and Fathers began to padlock friction
and labyrinth became complex
terminating in uroboros when the Fathers peaked
into Narcissus, recognizing
the seminal night deposit as the only wealth in a passive vault

And as the Mothers sexualized the cave the Fathers grew cooler
an erectectomy had to be performed
Savolathersilonighcock lay like young Black Elk nine days
then the Fathers tasted the visionary prisoner
raised from the lower body to a skull-enwalled garden—
adders flickering from their ears, they heard cock
separate from Savolathersilonigh
the wall was language, it was the truth
but the truth had to be spread as skin, as target,
the Fathers had to spot the cave shapes suggesting an animal in
    absence,
to bore into the word itself against which the mainspring now so
    sexualized
that a vortex was created to the present,
roots fracturing Ankor Vat are ghosts of these creepers ensouling
    Lascaux
the shapeshifter bristling with zodiacal light
to flood the Fathers with a desire for pelts, for animal pregnancy
so that Atlementheneira fucked Kashkaniraqmi to become pregnant
    with an ibex
and to reanimate scattered Savolathersilonigh
forced rude gartersnakes up several of the Mothers' cunts

Several thousand years of rest for the wily Lascaux
but birthless labor for the woman staked in the shapeshifting recesses
Atlementheneira gave birth to a pawed worm
the Mothers screamed as gartersnakes bit into their simian memories
and the inheritance sacs of their minds filled with blood
the moon appeared large as a rainbow, close yolk-like,
flooding the tundra with pure white shadow
but the Fathers bit into the ca ca enwalled
yo treed waah waah turning no into ju ju
drawing with ju ju a cayoweeno shaped plot
there was no nugget no reef
there was only maggot sentry-tread planted meaning
by which Lascaux was fastened to the Fathers' writhing heads
and the bison fortress with its phallus rudder removed

Relieved only by the light of the milk left in male nipples
Kashkaniraqmi handled the birth clamps
minnows were used to suture the now gaping hole in the hominid
    headdress
Atlementheneira was frozen trepanning an erection
from his head to animate a natural mare-shaped contour

The Paleolithic delivery was underway

By firelight the verbal hydras were pathed and bound
oak and human gas formed a many-headed sulphur
Lascaux belched forth voids with twigs and stench of the now
    profoundly disturbed
animal bodies which were drawn up like buckets of terrified water
Image was word pulled so thin nature
pressed its face against the tension—
many times the word broke
before its dragon contour was boundaried and wrestled onto
    Lascaux's clay
the staked woman was worn as headgear
a trellis from the forehead to the wall was mentalized
yet to a spectator Atlementheneira
would have appeared a boy, elderly, possessed, scraggly gray hair,
    sapphire eyes,
patiently daubing red dots into a bison
to commemorate the first verbal punctures and
the joyous retreat of the rainbow moon—
his shaking arm, abandoned by the hunters,
was marionetted by the skull of intercourse
which descended by the sun's tarry ropes,
a granddaddy longlegs releasing and confining
the daubed topology bridging worlds
first pried clear in blots of fantasy
triggered by ghosts of sensations which shouldered through the
    Fathers of Lascaux
thousands of years before they became the Fathers
"It is time to withdraw the stakes from her we have spread
in the fantasy of an anatomical solution,"

Kashkaniraqmi saw, "and to peg down Lascaux himself
for his organs are now filled with sea water
his tentacular corridors are sufficiently fatigued from our lathework—
we must still break his beak and puncture his bag of fluid blackness
for we are doomed to work parallel to
the ancient wet dry opposition
removing the living octopus from Lascaux's purring chambers.
Once we have established image as groundswell
Lascaux will be fixed at a clay, mineral level—moist
yet hardened, impacted with the terror of our labor
yet airy, penetrable, a cold reserve held in flux by image

"Those to come will know of our transformation first in their own
    bodies—
when sexual reserve is broken
the poison of the catastrophe we had to harness
will flood into a young man's teeth
if he were to bite someone at the moment he re-experiences this
    weaning
that person would die

"Therefore we will place the skull of intercourse by
his pillow from the time he is born
for unless he is willing to engage us in spirit
it is best to keep this archetypal cove sealed

"What we bequeath is most dangerous—
this relay station must be kept alert
or the transformation we have performed will wither
and literal archeology, in concert with sexual domination,
will build universities in which this act we have lived for,
to reconnect the animal-bereft human-to-be to an underworld
in which a dream, not his own, can continue, will be forgotten"
And they *did* break Lascaux's beak
using it as an engraving tool
to slash their roan colorings into the tunnel seams,
with manganese and ochre dioxide
they drilled language deposits into these seams

latticing speech to handsome mustard stallions and
the rumps of whirling ponies,
recalling the simian snake terror in mottled boa patterns
which thousands of years before
had been blisters suffered by the priming Mothers

This was the sheath in which the pillars of night were to support
the dreamer's knees as he bent to drink from his hands images
that are fluid as chill air,
invisible among the morning's goldenrod
but stony saliva foliage for the dreamer wandering
the revolving topology of ambushes he pierces
pouches of kangaroo baptism
castles enwebbed with bison cauls
razor vales ending in tusk-thatched encounters
carved artfully by the Fathers of bald grandmother Lascaux drifting
as if on leash to her furred mate,
the octopus land father, they waver,
now these very very old ones as the Motherfathers
curled at 15,000 *After Image* in the human peritoneum
chant softly through mambas through constrictor doves
that all nonhuman eyes carry in miniature with their flowing rock
    galleries
in which a crude synthesis felt sounds as the cervix
which then dilated revealed not only back turned rock
fiercely possessing its molecular time
but rock they turned toward us and smoothed into aurochs flank
so that, when touched, another does not merely reflect
the catastrophic switchboard of pleistocene day
but in that contact plants the banners of the heartless outside
by the entrance to a vision of interiority
in which covered by life
death left its mortal naming place to teach life how to pull
through faceless rock the having thundered by ancestor cavalcade
now wintered in the stall of our invaginated perdition.

Magdalenian   *

From the waist up, she is mostly headstone
and this only intensifies my love
for what we are, something walking
with snout for groin, sniffing the fresh blue
between the cracked brown bones
that are her legs. There is no horizon
to her, no explanation, only a narrative
slash above her pelvis. Something has been taken
from her, or out of her—
all I can feel, when I place a finger
on the slash, are rows of tiny teeth,
as if behind them is the paradise of
mouth and tongue. Her glory is
to have nothing behind her image.
The swipe of red across thorax
is what is left after the necklace of becoming
is removed. She is
what remains after fire
and water and earth, a hardness of the air
that keeps my softness alert to the singular
voicing, the past tense of
I speak
she seems clenched upon in belly.

Notes On A Visit To Le Tuc D'Audoubert   *

for Robert Bégouën

bundled by Tuc's tight jagged
    corridors, flocks of white
  stone tits, their milk in long
    stone nipply drips, frozen over

  the underground Volp in which
  the enormous guardian eel,
now unknown, lies coiled—

to be impressed (in-pressed?) by this
primordial "theater of cruelty"—
    by its keelhaul sorcery

    Volp mouth—the tongue of the
        river lifting one in—

to be masticated by Le Tuc d'Audoubert's
  cruel stones—
      the loom of the cave

  Up the oblique chimney by ladder to iron cleats set
in the rock face to the cathole,
on one's stomach
      to *crawl,*   working against
                one, pinning one
as the earth   in, to, it, to

makes one   feel for an instant
feel its traction—   the dread of

WITHERING IN
PLACE

—pinned in—
The Meat Server
masticated by the broken
chariot of the earth

◇

"fantastic figures"—more beast-
     like here than human—one
horn one ear—   { one large figure
               { one small figure

       as in Lascaux?
    (the *grand* and *petit* sorcerer?)

     First indications of master/
       apprentice? ("tanist" re. Graves)

the grotesque archetype

      vortex in which the emergent
      human and withdrawing animal
      are **spun**—

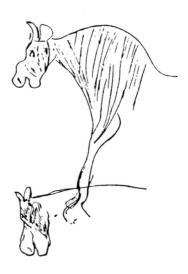

Le Tuc D'Audoubert: The Abbé Breuil's
drawing of the two "fantastic figures" in
the Upper Gallery facing the cathole.

        grotesque = movement

(life is grotesque when we catch
   it in quick perceptions—

at full vent—history
   shaping itself)

the turns/twists of the cave
   reinforce the image turbine—
as does the underground river,

                  the cave floats,
            in a sense, in several senses,
                  all at once,
         it rests on the river, is penetrated
            by it, was originally made
                  by rushing water—
                  the cave
            is *the skeleton of flood*

images on its walls
   participate, thus, as torsion,
in an earlier torsion—

Here one might synthesize:
         1) abstract signs
               initiate movement
                  brought to rest in

         3) naturalistic figures
               (bison, horses etc)

In between, the friction, are

         2) grotesque hybrids

(useful—but irrelevant to systematize forces that must have been felt
as flux, as unplanned, spontaneous, as were the spots/areas in caves
chosen for images—because shadowing or wall contour evoked an an-
imal? Any plan a coincidence—we have no right to systematize an area
of experience of which we have only shattered iceberg tips—yet it does

seem that "image" occurs at the point that a "naturalistic" horse is
gouged in rock across an "abstract" vulva already gouged there, so that
the rudiments of poetry are present at approximately 28,000 B.P.—

>   image is crossbreeding,
>   or the refusal to respect
>   the single, individuated body,
>   image is that point
>   where sight crosses sight—

to be alive as a poet is to be
>   *in conversation with one's eyes*)

What impresses at Tuc is a relationship
between river
>   hybrid figures
>   and the clay bison—

it is as if the river (the skeleton of water = the cave itself) erupts into
image with the hybrid "guardians" (Breuil's guess) and is brought to rest
in the terminal chamber with the two bison i.e., naturalism is a kind of
rest—naturalism returns us to a continuous and predictable nature
(though there is something unnatural about these bison to be noted
later)—takes us out of the discontinuity, the *transgression* (to cite
Bataille's slightly too Catholic term, of the grotesque
    (though the grotesque, on another level, according to Bakhtin, is
deeper continuity, the association of *realms*, kingdoms, fecundation and
death, degradation and praise—))

on one hand: bisons-about-to-couple
>   *assert the generative*
>   what we today take to be
>   *the way things are*   (*though with ecological pollution,*
>   *"generation" leads to mutation,*
>   *a new "grotesque"!*

>   ◇

to be gripped by *a womb of stone*
to be in the grip of the surge of life
imprisoned in stone

it is enough to make one *sweat one's animal*

(having left the "nuptial hall" of white stone breasts in which one can amply stand—the breasts hang in clusters right over one's head—one must then squirm vertically up the spiral chimney (or use the current iron ladder) to enter the upper level via a cathole into a corridor through which one must crawl on hands and knees—then another longish cathole through which one must crawl on one's belly, squirming through a human-sized tunnel—to a corridor through which one can walk haltingly, stooping, occasionally slithering through vertical catslits and straddling short walls)—

if one were to film one's postures through this entire process, it might look like a St. Vitus dance of the stages in the life of man, birth channel expulsion to old age, but without chronological order, a jumble of exaggerated and strained positions that correspondingly increase the *image pressure* in one's mind—

while in Le Tuc d'Audoubert I felt the broken horse rear in agony in the cave-like stable of Picasso's *Guernica*,

at times I wanted to leave my feet behind, or to continue headless in the dark, my stomach desired prawn-like legs with grippers, my organs were in the way, something inside of me wanted to be
an armored worm,
one feeler extending out its head,

I swear I sensed the disintegration of the backbone of my mother now buried 12 years,

entangled in a cathole I felt my tongue start to press backwards, and the image force was: I wanted to *choke myself out of myself,* to give birth to my own strangulation, and then nurse my strangulation at my own useless male breasts—useless? No, for Le Tuc d'Audoubert unlocks memories that bear on a single face the expressions of both Judith and Holofernes at the moment of beheading, mingled disgust terror delight and awe, one is stimulated to desire to enter cavities within oneself where dead men can be heard talking—

in Le Tuc d'Audoubert I heard something in me whisper me to believe in God

and something else in me whispered that the command was the rasp of a 6000 year old man who wished to be venerated again—

and if what I am saying here is vague it is because both voices had to sound themselves in the bowels of this most personal and impersonal stone, in which sheets of myself felt themselves corrugated with nipples—as if the anatomy of life could be described, from this perspective, as entwisted tubes of nippled stone through which perpetual and mutual beheadings and birthings were taking place—

◇

but all these fantastic images were shooed away the moment I laid eyes on the two bison sculptured out of clay leaned against stuff fallen from the chamber ceiling—

the bison and their "altar" seemed to be squeezed up into view out of the swelling of the chamber floor—

the sense of *culmination* was very severe, the male about to mount the female, but clearly placed several inches behind and above her, not in contact with any part of her body, and he had no member—

if they *were* coupling, and *without* deep cracks in their clay bodies, they would have disappeared into their progeny thousands of years ago, but here they are today still, as if Michelangelo were to have depicted God and man as not touching, but only reaching toward each other, caught in the exhaustion of a yearning for a sparking that has in fact never taken place, so that the weight of all the cisterns in the world is in that yearning, in the weight of that yearning is the real ballast in life, a ballast in which the unborn are coddled like slowly cooking eggs, unborn bison and unborn man, in the crib of a scrotum, a bone scrotum, that jailhouse of generation from which the prisoners yearn to leap onto the taffy machine-like pistons of shaping females—

it is that spot where the leap should occur that Le Tuc d'Audoubert says is VOID, and that unfilled space between two fertile poles here feels like the origin of the abyss, as if in the minds of those who shaped and placed these two bison, fertilization was pulled free, and that freedom from connection is the demon of creation haunting man and woman ever since—

we crawled on hands and knees about this scene, humbled, in single file, lower than the scene, 11 human creatures come, lamps in hand like a glowworm pilgrimage, to worship in circular crawl at one of the births of the abyss—

if I had stayed longer, if I had not with the others disappeared into the organic odors of the Montesquieu-Avantès woods, I am sure that I would have noticed, flittering out of the deep cracks in the bison clay, little winged things, image babies set free, the Odyssi before Odysseus who still wander the vaults of what we call art seeking new abysses to inscribe with the tuning forks of their wings...

1982

A Kind Of Moisture On The Wall   *

Suppose earliest consciousness is worked off the shape of certain earth inevitabilities, the contour grid of those specific caves Cro-Magnon chose to paint and engrave.

The "irony" of Eden may be that exit is the organic world, the odors of wood, flowers and decay that one smells with extraordinary pleasure for a few yards before emerging from a cave.

Yet Cro-Magnon, even with a short life span, was clearly not an infant. The origins of art are not squeezable baby fat, but in a Lawrencian way, are very alert to what we call "surroundings." So alert that the trap engraved on a cave wall may have nothing to do with animals but may have been an attempt to trap shadows, or hold them, in place, restrain them from infiltrating the world of the living.

The first images may have been *forces put on hold.*

(for a bison with an 8 foot hump was not a buffalo; it was the paleolithic land equivalent of the great white shark, the supreme defiance)

The bison appearing, its rump, say, formed by stalactites, so that by moss lamp it is without any work by man already present in the rock wall, leads to the sensation that what is "out there" is inherent.

◇

The imagination hiding in rock lived in
concretional vaults for millennia

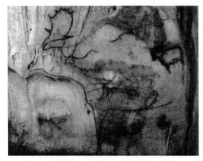

to be surprised by a clump of frog-like
vamps, pulsating about a pillar, behind
fuming moss, at animal parts of its shape—

they were terrified that megaloceros
was outside of megaloceros,
was here, in their crawling place—
might megaloceros be inside them?

Might all things be
coming to life in all things?

They nailed imagination in place
when they engraved a megaloceros
on the basis of a rump-shape stalactite.
But what they did not see of the megaloceros—
was it megaloceros? Or only megaloceros rump expression
on the face or body of something
showing itself momentarily in their fire,
something bigger than the cave,
something slumbering, or awakening in the earth?

And the questions? A kind of moisture on the wall.
What was not there might be them. What is clear:
something was in motion that can still be seen
as clearly today as when the Cro-Magnons
tried to arrest it by completing a megaloceros outline
inside of which body parts were scratched,
lances extending from them, as if thongs to "stitch"
torso and legs to megaloceros scared space,
or to decomplet the finished outline,
to question the idea of completion.

◇

A lance-tridented torso running
across a megaloceros temenos is
the sensation of imagination as
it pours through life like hoarfrost
or liquid jade—something never to be
completed writhes in us,
ringworm intrigues, the tentacular
lava of maggot-lined fables.
The moment we touch anything that touches us
the entire body becomes a pipeline of inverse fire hydrants
wrenching shut the feeling valves,
for to connect with even the stain of an image is fearsome,

a cog to cog moment in the interlocking
twister of an enrapt reporter calling up
the abandoned elevators of the lower, simian body
derailed in Africa, those rotting luncheonettes
visited only by hyenas and ferocious striped worms,
those bleached cabooses individuation pretends
to have left behind but which lurch open onto our brains
in dream to keep us open to
the fugal future of an earth
awesome, infinite, coiled in hypnosis.

Through Breuil's Eyes

The earth so fully referential
it appears to press out nothing but
aspects of itself,

                  cave stone bulging
rump, flint-fine dorsal line, bison interior
milling with beast particles—

the earth a herd of waves breaking,
a beast abattoir containing a beast springhead,
birth and slaughter a Mobius beastband—

here the human is recognizable
only as a freak created by superimposed
webs of beast fabric,

                    peering stone,
the point in repression where
a child of stone is born, calcite beauty,
a dancing of home sensation, a bison-headed man
hopping with a little fiddle, the bison-reindeer
he is pursuing turns her head
to look at this bipedal bison who wants to
penetrate her with his music—

sing-song see-saw by which he strikes,
chewing her recalls the smell of being born
right below the earth's waist—

               nothing sweeter than moon
consummation, to be taken up a little eel into
her silver-horned chamber, and there
to be devoured into another, to be
crowned with a Fallopian hat
so as to prance ibex-wise
and feel the hordes mounting form behind,
tides of ghost bison, eyes

Juniper Fuse (2003)   465

crossed in oestrus, the panic to pass on
            the thud of semen
lolling the sun into the moon,
to soothe this burning to drown in blood,
this lust for the hood of her cervix where
      sweeping her perineum
life glimpsed the dilated rainbow
            of beast eyes receiving
the lithopaedion born of the lithouterine
      earth.

Placements II: "The Aranea Constellation"   *

An Aranea centered in her web, afloat yet anchored between ground and sky. The natural mind of the earth always spinning. Her one "decision," where to start the web. A small male enters, testing, sounding, the thread. At the center of the orb, after mating, the penetrator is killed.

◇

Arachne is not Ariadne, although the figures are intertwined: The natural mind of the earth always spinning anticipates the mistress of the labyrinth that the initiate is to traverse. In the labyrinth of the creative life, "the bitter combat of the two natures" can be sublimated from a life/death struggle to an orgasmic union with a priestess whose lunar energies are a flood-tide.

◇

1963: There was a gorgeous red, yellow, and green Aranea centered in her web attached to a persimmon tree in the Okumura backyard. I got used to taking a chair and a little table out under the web where I'd read. After several weeks of "spider sitting" the weather turned chill, with rain and gusting wind. One afternoon I found the web wrecked, the spider gone. Something went through me that I can only describe as the sensation of the loss of one loved. I cried, and for several days felt nauseous and absurd.

A week later, I decided to motorcycle out to northwest Kyoto and visit Gary Snyder. Gary was not home, so I had tea with Joanne Kyger and, late in the afternoon, started the half-hour drive back home. Riding south on Junikendoori, it appeared that the motorcycle handlebars had become ox horns and that I was riding on an ox. A lumber company turned into a manger of baby Jesus and kneeling Wise Men. I forced myself to stay aware that I was in moving traffic, and looking for a place to turn off spotted Nijo castle with its big tourist bus parking lot. Getting of my ox-cycle, I felt commanded to circumambulate the square Castle and its moat. I saw what seemed to be Kyger's eyeballs in the moat water. At the northwest corner, I felt commanded to look up:

Some forty feet above my head was the spider completely bright red, the size of a human adult, flexing her legs as if attached to and testing her web. After maybe thirty seconds the image began to fade…

I immediately felt that I had been given a totemic gift and that it would direct my relationship to poetry. Out of my own body, I was to create a matrix strong enough in which to live and hunt.

◇

At 50,000 B.P., a fetally tied corpse is carried on a bed of branches and flowers to an ochre-packed pit in the Zagros Moutains. The red-gated pit accepts the bound one—"Then closes the Valves of her attention— Like Stone—." With the power of her red interior, she will wombify the entombed. In primitive peoples a belief has persisted that the soul, or the new-born self, is a result of the coagulation of menstrual blood. In my spider vision the green and yellow of Aranea's abdomen disappeared: The visionary spider was all red.

◇

At 30,000 B.P., sixty cupules were gouged in the shape of a filled-in spiral in a block discovered at ochre-stained La Ferrassie. Red discs surrounding vulva-like openings in the caves of Chufin and Pech-Merle, and the red vulva symbols in La Pasiega and El Castillo, indicate that at the very beginning of image making, creation magic was related to menstruation.

◇

I see in the Cretan labyrinth not only the ancient ghost of a spider-centered web but Paleolithic man leaving a living site and becoming a hunter following the herds, thus entering the mythos of killing and sacrifice. Far from the living site a new "center" was being tested. As a conjunction of man and animal, the Minotaur was sounded possibly as early as 32,000 B.P. in its depiction at Chauvet. Bull-headed men scamper among bounding animals a Les Trois Frères and Gabillou. In killing his Other, man was also killing his merely biological creature self. By driving a spear into an animal's side, he was, in a way, thrusting himself into the animal, so as to emerge with its head and his own body—to then make the long trek back, to the women and children, with animal in mind and bloody meat in hand.

◇

The alchemist Fulcanelli: "The picture of the labyrinth is thus offered to us as emblematic of the whole labour of the work, with its two major difficulties, one the path which must be taken in order to reach the centre—where the bitter combat of the two natures takes place—the other the way which the artist must follow in order to emerge. It is here that *the thread of Ariadne* becomes necessary for him, if he is not to wander among the winding paths of the task, unable to extricate himself."

◇

Anton Ehrenzweig: "Any creative search, whether for a new image or idea, involves the scrutiny of an often astronomical number of possibilities. The correct choice between them cannot be made by a conscious weighing up of each single possibility cropping up during the search; if attempted it would only lead us astray. A creative search resembles a maze with many nodal points. From each of these points many possible pathways radiate in all directions leading to further crossroads where a new network of high- and by-ways come into view. Each choice would be easy if we could command an aerial view of the entire network of nodal points and radiating pathways still lying ahead. This sis never the case. If we could map out the entire way ahead, no further search would be needed. As it is, the creative thinker has to make a decision about his route without having the full information needed for his choice. This dilemma belongs to the essence of creativity."

◇

Every artist participates in Ariadne. The transformation of the "given" life to a "creative" one not only involves entering a dark or "inner" life, but generating as well a resistance substantial enough to test oneself against and to shape the focus of one's work. Having experienced the bestowal of soul (which is the reality of Ariadne), one must liberate the experience in a creative product, must emerge with more than the claim that something "happened" while "inside."

◇

There is an archetypal poem, and its most ancient design is probably the labyrinth. One suddenly cuts in, leaving the green world for the apparent stasis and darkness of the cave. The first words of a poem propose and nose forward toward a confrontation with what the writer is only partially aware of, or may not be prepared to address until it emerges, flushed forth by digressions and meanders. Poetry twists toward the unknown and seeks to realize something beyond the poet's initial awareness. What it seeks to know might be described as the unlimited interiority of its initial impulse. If a "last line," or "conclusion," occurs to me upon starting to write, I have learned to put it in immediately, so it does not hang before me, allure, forcing the writing to skew itself in order that this "last line" continues to make sense as such.

◇

As far as poetry is concerned, "the bitter combat of the two natures" can be understood as the poet's desire to discover something new or unique versus the spectral desire of tradition to defeat the new and to continue to assert its own primacy. It is a "bitter" combat because the realization which writing a poem may provide is inevitably partial. The Minotaur is at best crippled, never slain, and the poet never strides forth from the labyrinth heroic and intact. At best, he crawls forth, "wounded," as in the cry of César Vallejo in his poem, "Intensity and Height"; more often than not, he never emerges at all. The poet never leaves this place of combat with a total poem, because such a poem would confirm that the discrepancy between desire and the fulfillment of desire has been eliminated. But since my desire is ultimately to create reality and not merely to observe it, I am bound to be defeated if reality is at stake in my poem's ambition. As I emerge from the poem, regardless of what I have realized while in the poem, I am back in the observable biological continuum, and part of it, part of its absolute mortality.

◇

The earliest earth-wombs were probably caves in which the one to be initiated slept "in magical imitation of the incubatory sleep in the womb." We know that shamanic initiation involved long periods of incubation, pantomimed destruction, burial, and rebirth. This incubus was not a perverse, Christianized friend, but an angel brooding on the initiate's body, perhaps in psychic imitation of the digger wasp/caterpillar conjunction. The signs, grotesques, animals in Upper Paleolithic caves may have been painted there as dream allies, left as records of the dream/initiation, or both. The fact that this imagery is often found in remote and "tight" pars of a cave not only stresses the underworld journey, but the womblike congruence between the cave's body and the initiate's body.

◇

Hans Peter Duerr: "In order for [these night travelers] to understand their own essence, they had to descend to that place, to return to the uterus of she who gave birth to everything, the place of origin not only of humans, but of all creatures of nature.

"The act of insight was at the same time also an act of love, which would have represented incest with the mother if at the place of origin incest itself had not been dissolved together with the barriers to incest. There is no sin at the place of origin. Where there are no longer any norms, no norms can be violated. Knowledge of the place of origin means: dissolution of the separation of things from each other...

"In later time, in the classical Greek period, people spoke of 'knowledge as memory.'" This is actually a watered down form of what in archaic times was a factual leaving behind the 'world of separation' and a return to the unifying womb of things, which knew no knowledge and no object of knowledge, no above and no below, no animals or people, no men and women.

"Archaic humans... possessed the insight that one had to leave the world, that one could become 'tame' only if before one had been 'wild,' that one could only live in the true sense of the world if one had proved one's willingness to die.

"In order to be able to live within the order, in other words, in order to be consciously tame or domesticated, one had to have lived in the wilderness. One could know what *inside* meant only if one had once been *outside*."

◇

Planned, direct access to "the unifying womb of things" today seems to be restricted to specially trained figures in tribal societies. The problem of inducing transformational visions on the part of artists in the modern world did not begin with Rimbaud, but at 17 years old, in 1871, he expressed this knotty dilemma: "I'm lousing myself up as much as I can these days. Why? I want to be a poet, and I am working to make myself a *seer*: you won't understand this at all"—he was writing to his Rhetoric teacher, Georgez Izambard—"and I hardly know how to explain it to you. The point is, to arrive at a disordering of *all the senses*. The sufferings are enormous, but one has to be strong, to be born a poet, and I have discovered I am a poet. It is not my fault at all. It is a mistake to say: I think. One ought to say: I am thought... *I* is someone else."

Rimbaud finds himself in the fix of needing to learn how to be what he already claims he has been determined to be. Claiming that he is a poet, he sees his work as breaking the poet down into a seer (at that point, by getting drunk) while knowing that even the sympathetic Izambard will not grasp what he is up to. The unconscious as an active, directional power seems right around the corner from Rimbaud's notion that his unknown "I" is not the subject but the object of his thought. However, "The Drunken Boat" as well as *The Illuminations* are the products of a bold, inventive ego (that has quickly assimilated, in Kenneth Rexroth's words, "the radical disassociation, analysis, and recombination of all the material elements of poetry"), not an ego that has returned to "the place of origin" and reconstructed itself after experiencing symbolic dismemberment. Which is to say that Rimbaud's "disordering" is more aesthetic than it is psychological. In fact, it could be argued that his desire to cross over into what he was "not" only become possible after he stopped writing poetry, and the journey into the African wilderness appears to have remained, as a record at least, on a literal level.

With rare exceptions, nineteenth- and twentieth-century poets do not have access to a context that would nurture the kind of shamanic apprenticeship pointed at the states of mind Duerr has described. Many of us would agree with Antonin Artaud: "Who does not want to initiate himself to himself there is no other who will initiate him." When poets do cross over to a mystical "outside," such experiences are usually unplanned, brief, and, from an archaic viewpoint, not thorough. I have in mind here Walt Whitman's erotic fusion detailed in Section 5 of "Song of Myself," or Rainer Maria Rilke's sudden contact with what he called "the other side of nature" in "An Experience," or Allen Ginsberg hearing Blake's voice as a novice poet in 1948. Having been jolted by the author's recitation of "Ah, Sunflower," Ginsberg spent the following twenty years attempting to retrieve that moment via drugs, travel, and a homoerotic openness to his and others' feelings. His itinerary in one respect bears a curious relationship to Rimbaud's: Rather than building to a dissolution of the self, Rimbaud's trip to Africa and Ginsberg's pilgrimage to the East took place *after* early, unexpected empowerments.

In some ways, the poet's peripheralization today is a parody of the *hagazussa*, the witch who, in the Middle Ages, was said to sit on the *hag*, or fence, which was built behind the gardens and separated the village from the wilderness. As a figure employing ointments, spells, and entheogens to fly back and forth between wilderness and culture, the *hagazussa* synchronizes with the shaman whose presence appears to be documented by certain hybrid/grotesque images in the Upper Paleolithic caves. We can only conjecture, on the basis of such imagery alone, what being "outside" vs. "inside" might have meant at 20,000 B.P.

A contemporary image of flight into a demonic "outside" and return to a human "inside" is evoked in Gary Snyder's poem, "What you should know to be a poet":

> Kiss the ass of the devil and eat shit;
> fuck his horny barbed cock,
> fuck the hag,
> and all the celestial angels
> and maidens perfum'd and golden—
> & then love the human: wives   husbands   and friends.

◇

In the summer of 1996 I as left alone, without a light, or a half hour in Le Portel. Not a long time, but enough for my eyes to become accustomed to total dark. At first I closed my eyes (wondering if it would make any difference; it didn't), and rubbed my eyelids with my knuckles creating the dazzling diagrammatic millrace known as phosphenes. Then I opened my eyes and stared into the dark. After some 10 minutes, pinpoints of light appeared like a fine snowfall holding in place. I thought of the three levels of light in the dark I felt myself inhabiting: the light in my head, the light in cave dark, and the stars in the night sky above. At some point in prehistory (possibly for navigational charts), they had become "heavenly bodies" configured as creatures, humans, and objects. Dürer's 1515 zodiacal map evokes a night belly with an intestinally entangled creature world. Animals are above us and below us; they know more than we do, and less. Such is their divinity and their tragic vulnerability.

◇

The Minotaur of the early Cretan myth was named Asterior, synonymous with *aster*, "star." He was "bull and star at the same time." The ultimate elevation of Dionysus and Ariadne, as a divine couple appearing in unmaimed, celestial, human form in the night sky, suggests that the universe is the labyrinth and in imagination it is possible to inhabit it.

◇

In the low chamber with the sculpted clay bison at Le Tue d'Audoubert are some fifty heel prints of adolescents; they appear to start at a place deep in the chamber, near the bison, and fan out in wavering rows toward the entrance, each row perhaps representing a single individual's winding path. A ritual dance? Were such dancers clad in bison skins, wearing horns? Eight hundred yards from the entrance to Le Tuc d'Audoubert, the sculpted bison becomes a new "center" at the physical periphery. Wherever one finds a "center," one may also find the labyrinthine ghost of a torn, once connecting, web.

◇

On the isle of Naxos, commemorating Ariadne's transformation, Theseus and his fourteen companions danced a Le Tuc d'Audoubert-like swirling dance around a horned altar, which recalls the actual bull horns through which Cretan bull-dancers flipped in the sacred marriage of king sun and queen moon. The "horned altar" also evokes the womb's birth cone (and the labyrinth itself is prefigured by a cervix, lined with a branching called the "arbor vitae," or tree of life, where devouring white cells may be imagined to hide and wait like monsters for the Odyssean sperm over whose turbulent voyage the Athenic aspects of woman preside),

◇

The horned altar is also the Double Axe, or labrys: Bound together by a haft, the crescent-moon blades are a glyph of the labyrinth. The path through is serpentine, and in respect to the material, the central confrontation is the movement from iron to wood to iron, inorganic vs. organic materials:

◇

As an early form of Ariadne, Arihagne (the "utterly pure") was a spinning hag or sorceress who enjoyed intercourse with the labyrinth and its grotesque inhabitant. When patriarchal consciousness overwhelmed matriarchal centering, Ariadne became a "maiden to be rescued," who, "falling in love" with the hero Theseus, gave him a "clew" or thread that would enable him to get in and out and, while in, to slaughter the sleeping Minotaur. The labyrinth, without its central being, was thus emptied of animality.

◇

In the twentieth century, the burden of the vacated labyrinth involves hairline connections with the cul-de-sacs of the deep past. On the other hand, after the first split-off, or separation crisis, there has only been unending bifurcation. The myth of Ariadne seems to capture much of Charles Olson's vision of life turning on a SINGLE CENTER until a mysterious counter will manifest itself around 3400 B.P. In Olson's view, the heroic attempt to overthrow and dominate external reality resulted in the migration waves (they look like tentacles on maps) that spread out around the planet.

◇

Garcia Lorca's essay on the "duende" identifies this diablotin of the blood, or bloodmare, which provokes some of the world's great art, as a struggle with a wound that never closes. Is Garcia Lorca therefore caught, whether he knows it or not, in Ariadne's turnstile, responding to blood that for thousands of years has mesmerized and enraged men as it appeared in rhythm with the moon and the tides and, without violence, ceased, to only reappear again and again?

◇

In Tantrik sexual magic, the two ingredients of the Great Rite can be *sukra* (semen) and *rakta* (menstrual blood). The sulfurous red ingredient in alchemical goldmaking probably was at times this female essence (the *rubedo,* or precious red "stone" that sweats blood and turns the world to gold, and is also a conjunction of a whitened Queen and a reddened King—such a blending could be seen as a *pinkening*). Some images of the labyrinth have not a Minotaur but a rose at their center, a sign that a transformation has taken place. Seven days, across her period, the Old King is dissolved, rinsed of himself, his selves, lost in her "bath," her anabasis. The Dionysian initiate who is assimilated into this rose appears with a beard of roses to complement, below, Ariadne's rose-wreath crown.

◇

The natural spinning mind of the earth weaves itself in personifications throughout our humanity. Biological peril is always central, and sublimated by image-making into "scorpion hopscotch," or the imaginative gambling called poetry. It is possible to formulate a perspective that offers a life continuity, from lower life forms, through human biology and sexuality, to the earliest imagings of our situation, which now seems to be bio-tragically connected with our having separated ourselves out of the animal-hominid world in order to pursue that catastrophic miracle called consciousness. If the labyrinth is a Double Axe, one might see it as humanity's anguished attempt to center a ceaseless duplicity conjured by the evidence that each step forward seems to be a step backward. And the haft? Phallocentricity that fuses the menstrual/ovulatory cycles into an instrument of inner and outer ceremony that injures but does not restore.

The Atmosphere, Les Eyzies   *

Lazy pin-ball machine of bird sound balls
scoring the paradise
effluvia swarming my ankles

Bird-coded lay of breeze, of an everywhere nourishing latency

A single smoking road runs from Indianapolis to Lascaux!

A car storms down the road mush of tire lore

The lees in the air, gnat-fossiled
dead fresh stone at cut with thrasher folly,
congruent to
the nothing-saturated weir of
                              air as
                    vesicular cenotaph

Night here is porcelain, plover, flail of a distant vanishment

The Vézere Valley a noctaduct
channeling the presence of 50,000 years

                    Sound studs
in the grip of percolator wood cores

The smell of the infinite:
persimmon smashed limestone in helium dress

Freshness rowing alphabetically through stone
as a nonsense articulating *aurochs*—

the soul of its omenhood, a word now without animal

adust with the fortitude of pollen

Let me set terror back into the grass, inject it
deeply into the planet's skin,
get *chasm* back into *abyss*

     All nipples are Ivory Towers
    about which Unknowingness
              drinks.

                          [*Hotel Cro-Magnon, 1 June 1987*]

Abri du Cro-Magnon was earlier Abri du   *
Cramagnon, emphasizing the *craw*
                              of the site,
craw and "cro" combined: belly hole in which
4 adult skulls and the ribs of a 10 week old were discovered under hearth
remains—containing cave bear, cave lion, lion, mammoth, spermophile,
reindeer, horse, and possibly artic fox bones—in yellowish clayey earth
at Level I in 1868. Skulls B, C, and D were of 30 year olds (two men,
one woman); skull A was that of a 50 year old man, with "peculiar
eroded patches on his bones, including a saucer-shaped depression on
his right forehead…related to a fungal infection called actinomycosis,
which attacked [him] in his jaw area, and is known to have fatal conse-
quences if it becomes localized in the intestines. One can readily imag-
ine the alarm and superstition that must have attended the onset of such
diseases. Perhaps intricate herbal remedies were tried…"

"The skull is markedly low in relation to its length. Long skulls are usu-
ally accompanied by narrow faces, but the facial skeleton of the Cro-
magnids is 'disharmonic' for it is very wide. This 'disharmony' is one of
the most distinctive features of the Cromagnids."

The limestone hill containing the shelter, crowned by a mushroom-
shaped rock, serves as the back wall for Hotel Cro-Magnon.

Today the shelter is swept clean,
much of its overlay gone,
it is protected by a low stone wall, iron fence
and little gate, allowing me to enter
this temenos and pace, brooding on
chronic belatedness. The party's over! Does only
the empty beer can of this site remain?
Abri du Cro-Magnon, a kind of lower mouth, toothless,
the jaw silted (Levels A–J) to the epiglottis level,
I walk the tongue of metaphor
as off a pirate plank into 20th century Dordogne light,
thistly bird twitters, and an elderly American who inquires:

"Is this where they discovered man?"
I feel the extent to which I am storied,
but the stories are under (first trace of fire: Level B),
pebble histories, midden chapters,
"Payroll of Bones" indeed!
The dead line up to collect their atmospheric wages,
I stand among them, a mauve ghost,
last night's supper a pouch of nutriment
their sockets search as they assemble
clacking and coming back into sound as this gruel
engravels them: *god wot cud lor* I hear,
cord loot mor torn,   sutra march of thing sounds,
at Level I something is still alive—
is this the limbic pun-crawled division into which
20th century poetry suspends itself?
"Speak for yourself"   the necessary, baleful command.
Faced with so much story, I release my grip
from Whitman's hand,   "agonies are one of my changes of
garments"—in the face of Auschwitz?
"I am the man. ... I suffered. ... I was there. ..."
The voice coalescing *Leaves of Grass* is still
convinced of perpetuity, the grass will grow
forever from the skulls of white-haired mothers
regardless the Civil War pyramids of amputated limbs.
As Lascaux "emerges" in 1940,
Belsen begins to smoke on nearly the same horizon.
Then Dresden, Hiroshima... "we would have lost one
million boys had we attempted a land invasion of Japan"
—whose voice? of what species of compassion?
(surely not Whitman's)   A voice that no longer
believes in martial brotherhood (for Whitman,
arm-locked gore is one of the fraternal changes).
It is the nuclear mind, addressing us from a cloud!

"Century O century of clouds"
Century of Black Holes

Abri du Cro-Magnon
Big Hole Shelter

—come of chronically-belated age at last,
I translate as: Big Hole Man.

[Hotel Cro-Magnon, June 1987]

The Power Room   *

The path along the rockface
unloads its spiritum as I pass.
              Out of cliff stain,
survival smoke tangles my head,
    raccoon human iguana stork layers,
          anima mundi face,
the human less that a quarter.

Like garter shreds, or pubic rust,
lichen dangles from the deep overhang.

Over a black gob on flagstone
a squad of flies lifts and holds in circus
    tent formation. Out of honey-
combed mouths the clowning dead roll in.
One could spend a lifetime
listening,   as they attempt to tarantella
    back into organic light.

I took a whiff of Vézere papermill sewage
and dropped into "the power room."   *(Les Eyzies, Regional*
Rock pods through which vulvae emerged.   *Pre-history Museum,*
Vulva crossed horse neck,   6 cupules   *2nd floor, incised stone*
          in search of a vulva.   *blocks, 30,000 B.P.)*
Fertility-tallied, butt-gashed vulvae
or vulva-gashed buttocks or buttocks bagged
or buttocks plugged or body-smashed
vulvabutt,   in stone atoned.
      A woman running into a wall
byabyssembraced. Cupule-jeweled phallus.
          Peter Redgrove
perched on a head-shaped vulva-carved rock:

      "I fell through the English mud
      and kept on falling until I hit
      this rock, whose molar-pouted mouth

utters a stripe of wild strawberries.
I am delighted in fallen
as well as risen states,
and should Hades glue me here,
he can have my ass! I'll also heave my cock
like a bee-stinger in this vulva's brain,
flutter back to Falmouth
more spirally tone than man."

I was too embarrassed to publish what I saw in the Seine
when I was told James Wright had died,
but I told Redgrove now: I saw Wright's corpse
    in a moored barge—the Celan coffer?
belly-swarmed by Spicer and Crane,
avid for Wright's warm liver, like one tears out
    crab grass, or in Rashomōn's
crossbeam, the hag wrenched wig hair.

               In imagination,
such exchange is never merely the father/son diathesis.
It is sheer hubris to sublimate otherness,
to emball it in our word web.
                     Poetry
        is to let the other fall
        into our nest, a rock
        among our eggs, or
        an egg among…

What glints are the ingot backs of snails,
fertilizing lore perhaps to be used,
whose curving walls are loaded with
the root history of our plasmic halo.

Like Violets, He Said   *

Jacques Marsal [1925–1988] in dapper suede slippers would lead us into
the darkness of Lascaux. It takes his absence today, our fourth visit, to
say how much his presence determined what Lascaux is. As one of the
discoverers, Marsal remained coated with the awesome freshness of that
tumbling in, lightning-ripped juniper, under which four boys squirmed
to arrive. That Marsal stayed on, nearly 50 years, was a bloom added to
the stem of the cave, and I'm overwhelmed by the difference one person
can make in the personality of a place, not via declaration or sheer in-
formation, but by being folded in, obliquely, wearing Lascaux, allowing
its grace to loom, allowing us, hardly aware of his movements, our own
reading through his light.

> Men spring up like violets
> when needed, Olson said,

> and Blackburn, near his end,
> lamented the disappearance of a Barcelona
> waiter, an old man
> who moved so accurately and gently
> among the clientele. Paul wrote:
> "We do not need to know
> anybody's name to love them."

Because of Marsal, I know Lascaux in my heart
like a nearly weightless child
framed by thunder and a bruised, milling sky,
a child standing on the sensation of eternity,
sayable eternity, right under the dust.

1990

Cemeteries of Paradise   *

Said to Caryl at day's end: this is home,
and then an aurochs wavered, or
was it shadow across the bulging
Les Eyzies cliffs? Bulging stone,
bulging horns, curling home. Lotal twisting
chambers where zero flexes.

The gate is open. Miller perceived some of the fix:
paradise is not of the French, is truly
Upper Paleolithic, of the Dordogne,
of the poets, to be reclaimed by the poets.

This is perfect, I felt,
making love in our farm apartment, spring 1974.
A bit north of Les Eyzies, the enchantment begins:
shadowing the curling single lane road,
moist outcroppings of limestone walls.
Out of the rock endlessly fabling.
Root wisps, black stains. My aurochs ancestor hovers.
We share a phallus, as if part of a carousel.
Slowing for a curve, up and down,
my aurochs ancestor on our turning shaft,
bird and fruit bodies on a common bend.
Uroboric carousel. Drifting into origin, or
into origin's coals, into the lifting off heat,
the dusty run-over, the psychic gore
alive in such caves as Combarelles.
It was in connecting with the mystery of a land
underscored by the most important thing I could learn
—the origin of poetry—
that bowled me under.

They entered earth to rise again.
Inside stone, no animals, blackness without stars,
By juniper flame, honey-colored ramparts
to be incised, brooded, crawled away from

back to tundra and frosty light.
Did this "round trip" resonate *resurrection?*
Did stone animals imply mortality could be broached?
Was scratching an enclosing line *resurrection?*
A proto-shamanic dream of healing form?
"I conceive and depict the bison I am to be"
Or was the marking of a bison as slain *resurgence,*
    a form of "resurrection"
uncomplicated by our "rising from the dead"?
I am suspended over such questions
    as over an abyss.

Line animating stone. Incipient alphabet.
At what point did the sound lark
split open to reveal a letter,
inkfaceting our dreams?

I crack open to find my
life. As if the word

stone were nut,
I must invent the kernel,

there must be life in my shell.
My rite must yield. Unlike Olson,

I do not "hunt among stones."
I hunt inside stone.

I work the manganese that holds, withholds.
In the end I hunt for more end,

of the beginning
I scrutinize each ochre start.

To be in paradise and to feel paradise at
an impossible remove. To crawl
the cemeteries of paradise. Rock

once alive, god bone.
Flint burin then as a tattoo needle to
    a human back today.

I sit on a green metal bench on
now-called Rue de la préhistoire, facing
Hotel Cro-Magnon.

To get at the round,
the jagged round of any situation,
how we fence with the udders of snow!

A complex of rainy perfection clears itself through me.

Packed with perpetuity's
negation, with swaying wordflora,
the alpha veil still refuses to unravel.

2000

Placements III: "So Be It"   *

The suffocating nearness of mother

The more suffocating distance of father

(As he comes forth with a switch,
she retreats)

The lightning distance of mother

The leaden nearness of father

    internalized, this seesaw, she in my left eye, he in my right. At the focal point, I helplessly superimpose them. Focus, in Latin, is fireplace. So at the focal hearth is something burning? Is their primal coupling disappearing or becoming sacred? It would appear that a sole (burnt offering) density is being created

    as the Ajna Chakra, located between the eyebrows, the third eye, a two-petaled lotus, encompassing lingam in yoni, "the supreme creative act."

    It is miraculous, in fact, that in this third eye I am propellering them, grinding them to a whirr, or swastika, a triskelion consisting of three human legs with bent knees, or tentacles, coiling about a single center. In other instances, the center is a belly, or a Gorgon's face, her turning legs incipient snakes. Or is it two energy streams curving into each other, as in van Gogh's "Starry Night," the spiral form which Wilhelm Reich called "cosmic superimposition," in his eyes "*the* basic biophysical form."

    Before the hooked cross, before linear corners, angles might have been suggested by two superimposed curling lines, with one line tending toward straightening (male), the other ending toward self-enclosing (female). Before semen was thought to be primary in conception, the straight line, or slit, may have been in the service of the enclosing one, may have been semi-enclosed by it, the ensemble making the form of the earliest engraved vulvas. This image evokes a very early form of the labyrinth, a simple, female labyrinth, into which the male entered, swerved, surrendered a part of himself, and withdrew.

At the point that the instrumental role of semen in conception was discovered, there was a massive redistribution of female and male dominance in favor of the latter. Idealistically, one might wish that a reciprocity between the sexes had set in, an equalization of creative potential. However, as we all know too well today, nothing like this happened. Emboldened by the discovery of his so-called primacy, the male line of the simple labyrinth broke through the cul-de-sac, or swerve area, and rather than turning and withdrawing, pushed on and on, as if to resolve entering through unending penetration. The breaking point became an intersection, or a center within, the nucleus for the labyrinth as we know it today, in which a life and death struggle takes place, and from which, even if victorious at the center the victor may never emerge but continues to wander the winding paths.

Once the male line broke through in this pictograph, the formerly dominant self-enclosing line of the simple labyrinth, having lost its interior magnet, so to speak, lost its shape, and began to wander, branching off to become the maze space of the hero's testing. At a fundamental layer of psyche, male and female are as two night-crawlers moving over and around each, blindly searching unaware that their point of superimposition is the center of centers out of which and around which mythological conflict emanates.

Practically speaking, over thousands of years, we have contained these crawlers and set them revolving in the third eye. Yet our attentions wander, we are more often than not out of sync with what we most desire. Men and women complicate what they know and do not know of what the other requires...

So when I look into my eyes, the groundwork of my parents, disintegrated in the irises years ago, becomes a broken and living labyrinth, full of gaps, collapsing and continuing in these fragmentary constructions.

Thalassa Variations   *

She lay back upon the sea, fully buoyed.
As he hovers over, waves churn
as if to unstill her. She is Caryl
not Caryl, no Caryl pervading Caryl—
not his mother but redressed
as his other, as if the labyrinth were falling apart,
and the central
receptionist, the goal buried
beyond the bull's-eye, were surfacing.

Visions of canals enweb his mind.
What he is in, hovering over, is not
without her. The air is moist,
sprayed by plumes of iridescence.
He is, arms outstretched, legs held together,
a Y chromosome facing its X
on the Z of nature's altar.

She reaches up and pulls him down—
he is small, constructed
about his mouth eager for nipple.
He sucked to feel the inner tent, his intentions
harden, the circus of fledgling nerves
in which gnats were juggling, sharks
were swallowing fire. Now he knows:
as he nursed, the phylum was astir.
Teeth like penile sprouts appeared,
imitations of the erectile world.

A kiss, and volumes fall apart,
for the entering is not ineffable—
say it, educated shark,
male with a cleaver in your fist
not a fist, but ferny fingers,
Aladdin's foreplay on the lamp of the sea.
In each covering, the mirage of paradise flashes,

semaphore or accordion, in her massive
ballroom bail-out of our spleen.
Of course it is bitter, this need to be bitten off,
to castrate in her grove.
The child masturbated in an anal war
distant form the source of capital,
his scythe moving through nutriment,
as if he were not anchored to her demise.

Wallace Stevens, it is her sex that makes
the sky acutest at its vanishing,
forms the holy V, her grape cluster altar.
Inside her, thus inside metaphor,
he digs the genital tension on her walls,
her fauna relief canal, as when the Ice Age,
freeze-girdling the lower body,
squeezed some image paste into our heads.

O clasper frog, in your embrace:
the catastrophe of life on land!
Although he shudders,
how forgetful he is of what she entubed
to convex and, over eons,
reshape from cloacal assault.
Is that the source of his detachment?
Unable to detach, he deflates—only sperm
springs beyond the finish line.
Reptilian instant! As his infant
would've penetrated breast to be
back inside, a god,
so his amphibian, stranded,
tried to regain liquidity
via another's invaded flesh.
And below intrauterine repose?
Penis as sinless fish, traveling
its origin, grounded as he moves.
A hundred fathoms below,

mother skeleton wavers,
five hundred fathoms deeper,
a salamander skull is ooze.
Uprush of glacial
blackness that like a corkscrew
ventilates his serpentine hypnosis,
as if his body were whirled by mother spectre and,
in Escher opposition,
active strands of void.
In fourfold peristalsis,
he is a tree filled with furies,
whose trunk seems skinny,
whose avocados feel immense.

How gorgeous she is!
How much more than a divining rod he is,
the two of them snailentailed
on the genius of the sea—yes,
the waves stay buoyant,
and if they can see through osmosis,
the glass-bottomed
depth of embrace will reveal
carousels of interior drink.
The father of his erection is a crocodile.
Cloacal separation into
intestine and urethra—speak
of duality!—was first
suffered by kangaroo.
Within the ransacked, still
intact, human midden,
the zodiac pauses—an anatomical
ferris wheel has taken them up,
then dipped them into
a quiet, seething gale.
Yesterday, he was a taper mole
acrawl with dessicational mystery.
Today, half in ice, half hybrid,

as if a child had scrawled him.
Imago? Or feathered serpent?
To strike. To wander.
Mind, where does it *not* come from?

With manganese-smeared finger,
pigmenterrial. No longer merely masturbating,
but "hand negatives," no longer hallowing vulva,
but hollowing cupules. On eye-stalks
to roam Le Portel, to squirm,
on back, into a sarcophagal cul-de-sac,
head pressing end, to go beyond end,
to engrave in rock, inches above,
a stag, whose head, also pressing back,
thus miming the engraver,
bells into the end: *image is*
the imprint of uncontainable omega,
                    life's twin.

Venusberg   *

Her hub is too inconstant, too
      shape-changing
She rises from the sea, "foam-born,"
—but it is great that she
can change, for without her protean lay,
men would have nailed her to her littoral
made her literal, destroyed her
    for you and me—

a whorled shell,
is she the animal within?

A headless bison,
like a ventricose shell
embracing an identical bison—
the two, like human lovers,
forelegs torso wrapped,
on and of a reindeer antler—

In Kafka, when one sentence sets forth,
another starts out from the far
side of the original thought.
It is like watching venery approach venereal,
while, at another angle, venom
has sighted venial. When such words fuse,
they thirst in us, thus do not fuse,
because we are fission incarnate.

It is we who are fleeing Venus,
Venus's sons, venison, staggered
by the force that wraps into form,
the retainer, at the epicenter of phenomena,
the grip that holds ventricose
bison and faceless woman in a single throe.
    She also rises from the rock,
fat spindly lady, milky cob

in the birth channel of our palm,
the spinster born at Laussel,
holding high a drinking horn?
for a lover? a killed hunter brother?
Does it contain blood? And if so,
menstrual, or of slaughter?
Is it torn from a larger animal form,
a spoke of *ven-*?
    What she holds is ripped
venerability,
                    we hang
from her upheld horn.

        "The most beautiful of women
        handed him the beaker.
        His heart and mind
        shuddered with sweet horror.
        He emptied it to the last drop,
        then the dwarf at the door said:
        now you belong to us,
        for this is Venus Mountain."

The Chaos of the Wise

Why this yearning to travel?
More, this deeper yearning to return?
Falcon intuition, Human foible loop.
At the far end of the drive to flee from one's feet
there is psyche. Who is strong enough
to take up residence there?
Imagination desires circularity,
not repetition. Psyche wants recurrence,
on each swing the path to deepen,
a rattler raga, wants to uroboros herself.
Or take Pech-Merle:

                              the rockwall bears an image
which presses in a fraction of an inch.
Someone's squatting there, drawing horse and bison
close as she distances them,
as she works the primordial hourglass,
a double bellow, or butterfly.

            Wall as thorax:
out there one wing, in here another.
Imagination as dorsal lines superimposed,
one crossing another, making a statement
imprisoned by the ochre on her finger—
she can't press through the wall she is to penetrate,
a finger in the void, a traveling semen-travesty.
Chaos' lips purse to suck on her plunger-finger.
Her drawing times her, as here each word
                        has its worm ward.
To be underborn in the chaos of the wise,
to take the oath of the abyss
verging on being of the physical world!

All the I/s huddle, as if, as one,
they could remain in goddess doorway all their lives
—what terror! What delight! Psyche wonders:

might there still be one great mother with everyone
daisy-chained to her rich hole? Do we sink
Hades and Persephone into Hades
for a sensation of life wedded to its origin?

Neanderthal Skull

Flared sockets under
bulging brow bridges tough as tusks
evoke rock shelters with visible rear walls.
In countermotion to cheekbones sweeping back,
incisors—carrot-orange at base,
surfaces warped from gripping hides—buck forward,
a third arm,
an anatomical vise.
As if this convex brow glacially furled the cranium back,
flattening it,
lifting facial planes toward late-morning sun.

Our smaller faces are tucked
in, beneath our brain-case's dome.
Rectangular sockets tilting outwardly down
imply our brow beam is bending under awesome pull.
Our sockets aim straight into auroral red,
their cranial pits evoke deep caves,
sealed hidden wealth,
mind a synesthetic abyss.

Weregaze oriented to "the wild, blue yonder,"
did Neanderthal have an interior
refuge in which to fetalize and fantasize a bow?
Scavenging in dread,
under predator arrest,
Neanderthal took the Paleolithic's full assault.

Some Fugal Lubrication   *

"the Horned one, Cernunnos, was represented in the cross-
legged position of a yogi"   horned   cross-legged
Drachenloch,   "Dragon Lair"   85,000 B.P.
        —at the basis of mind,
           a severed animal head—
at Drachenloch   the rudiments,

          cave bear thighbone
          twisted in, between cheekbone and
             cranium,
          lodged there, making an X,
             Jolly Roger,
          the bear body complexed,
              compressed in the skull,
          fixed there,   thighbone now a wand,
          to capture = to conjure,
          no longer "head" but throne,
          coitus reconstructed,   marrow-filled
             bone
          replaces the semen-marrow brain mass
(which Neanderthal probably ate,
then went back in—for void? screwing in
the cranium space where brain'd been).
Semen reconstructed.   Is semen
          soul heading off?
Väinämöinen, be with me here, help me unpack
the psychic space of this Dragon Lair skull.

    There is a loom in this skull,
whose mental strands in furious singing
attempt to fill semen-marrow bereft space.
Within this skull, mental winches raised
the body of the bear, until only two bones,
crossed, could be seen.   Skull
              Crossed Bones,
buccaneer at the rim of consciousness,
flag of the slave ship,   for

the seizing of souls makes appetite for more,
ruddy peril of life based on soul seizing,
O greatest peril, the brother of an Iglulik shaman
        said to Rasmussen,
human life consists entirely of souls—

at Drachenloch, the chakra impulse of coronation,
the raising of the (now) lowered body
    into a skull house,
                            coronation's brother
is decapitation,   Sacred Head—
a calamity of depth-charge proportions,   to go off
throughout histories as people pack
bodies into the abattoirs of their heads,

at Drachenloch, the seemingly simple move of
    thighbone inserted,
fixed,   can't be twisted out,
coital impress can't be dislodged
without destroying mentation's crown,

the core of a to-be-constructed bomb?
        Pack this primal ignition kit
inside slabs of rock, build a chest
            in which to consecrate
this piracy,   then set it against
Drachenloch's ochre-smeared back wall,
operatic display of Death enwombed,
set into the most uteral part of the shelter,
to fertilize the future? At this moment,
Neanderthal must've had future tense.

As fetus to womb,
loaded bear skull to earth,
ah, when will you go off,
        savage vision of our screw-worm-like
boring
    into every haunt of soul—

the earth pregnant with X,
cross-legged, lotal. Not where id was
ego shall be, X it out, X in:
        where brain was
magic thighbone shall be,

seas will writhe under the banner of Vomito Negro,
seesawing the bone in and out,
bone viol,
   rape inherent in this spectral music,
          buried in unconscious silt
the enthroned skull of the hibernator
          (from whose den
babies mysteriously issue in spring

At the Hinge of Creation

"Ginnungagap, a great emptiness pregnant
with the potential power of creation"—
the south,   full of brightness and fire,
the north,   full of snow and ice,
    meet,   like spinning tectonic mirrors, in
Ginnungagap,
                    Ymir appears,
    child of the shape-shifting gap

Olson, out of Fowler, writes:
"licked man (as such) out of the ice,
the cow"   Authumla
comes into being to provide food for Ymir,
"a rich, hornless cow"
the streams of milk from her udders nourish
    Yggdrasil

Ymir is the hybrid hermaphroditic
fusion of heat and cold   a frozen Cro-Magnon
    discovered in the late Azilian?
The first Mesolithian?
For the Norse,   Ymir is the back wall—

Ymir is the Paleo-Mesolithic bridge,
a span of eternity
across which men, women, and the frost-giants,
    set forth,
                we are here
before we were,   not I, not I,
but what was released from these salty blocks,
      in the ice mirror beast melt,
one is a fleck in the papillae of a cow's tongue,
    origin recedes,   Authumla is mostly
                  lost,   is
fog, and snow,   my cow is tattered,
    fractal,   is milk, steam,

my cow is a dragon,   she cannot be measured,
          in the beast melt down
I am language   out   on the dragon's tongue,
                              anything
      can be cabby,
                    the weals on Francis Bacon's
back are toad glands, by which
visionary semen whips from his brush.

Le Ferrassie: Triangular tombstone with possibly the earliest known
human-made cupules.

Prolegomena

Golgonooza, William Blake's City of Art, contained "all that has existed in the space of six thousand years"—Blake's back wall was Druidic-Neolithic. With the twentieth century discovery of Upper Paleolithic imagination, specifically with the discovery of the Mousterian cupules at La Ferrassie, we must backdate Blake's "six thousand years" to "forty thousand years."

*

With toe in mouth,
with serpent-encircled web

Who rests within,
circling within

Who slays weds fecundates

The desire to become conscious

   A point
wants to continue, can't
continues, pointillating about,
indenting

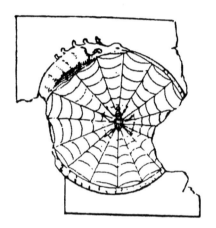

Grinding in, as if to make fire

A point expanding, a point blank
dent
appointing

Grinding out a cup shape in stone.

     As if turning over a log
and discovering the mucus-side of Eden,
Denis Peyrony "lifted it and turned it over. On the lower
face, in an angle of the smoothed surface, we noticed a

small cupule associated with a series of other cupules"
(he is at La Ferrassie in 1909,
excavating a Mousterian level, and has just turned over
a one meter triangular limestone slab
covering an egg-shaped grave pit
containing thee remains of a child)

Over the Neanderthal child's cranium I see the cupule
        become a dome,
the cathedral-to-be as the cave pulled upward inside-out
—the burial vault in the base of a pyramid
is the terminal form of the cave,
the space in which immortality is contested

Cupuled slab and egg-shaped pit
an alchemical vessel
containing the stuff of resurrection?

Depressed is raised, what is above is below

"I now am what I am: a horror and an astonishment."

I got hot and became pregnant,
I could feel the sun rising through my diaphragm

With the tongs of my tongue
I tore at my thought-heart

I ground rock out of rock,
this waste was my food

"And they builded Golgonooza: terrible eternal labour!"

A Phosphene Gauntlet   *

Phosphenes are geometrical percepts
occurring within the eye,   "closed-eye vision,"
induced by knuckle pressure on closed eyelids,
larvae   uncials   grading into each
swarming thrones   rose windows   breaking
                 sun   a drilled-out black wreath
auraed by a rubblework of light…

I believe Cro-Magnon practiced closed-eye vision
or saw phosphenes, without knuckle pressure,
while confronting cave walls, lamp flicker urging out
amorphisms suggested by cracks   contours
a rich nigredo of dots   zigzags   spirals
intersected by anatomical noticings
     curve rumps   vulva zags   dot volleys—
the animal re-drawn and quartered in phosphene collision,
remembered sightings had to run
       a phosphine gauntlet

       fingered
wall grooves that thudded
back into the gouger
sensations of fingered wounds,
a morpho-sparking channel:
     memory through phosphene to wall
     wall through phosphene to memory,
       fire drill of a finger
rock mind
         hottest tinder—
inner ignition   initial mind
phosphene and memory
      emery—

Le Combel

"The hollow"
                 intestinal
prolongation of Pech-Merle

A 3-foot stalagmitic, cupule-pitted, much polished
    prong
scored my mind with intimations of the Muse

How far back? There is no first
—an African pythoness is feeding a snake
up her vagina, shrieking a gloss of its moves
—a Cro-Magnon is swinging up, and over,
easing this horn in,
does she feel its cold hiss through her:
"All is transfer!"
Does this pike fill her with premonitions of the Hydra-
    headed tools we all turned out to be?

In the first chamber:
17 red ochre disks and a red lioness
whose body, in death rictus,
arches across the bodies of 3 horses
(who do not appear to be involved,
were they painted earlier? Later?)
The lioness' head is stuffed up into
    the stalactitic bubblework

Below her raised muzzle are slops of red.
For a belly, she has 4 red disks.
Her body attenuates, tiny hind legs nearly horizontal,
as if she's being sucked into ...

The painting has a waver to it, as if under water

Network of animal drift electrified by animal spasm

Three more ensembles of red disks,
as if in spagyric relation to
vaginal fissures in the rock:
the first: a large triangle of 36 disks,
the second: like 21 bees, they swarm the alcove,
the third: 18 in phallic loop,

5 more

      curling into 5 more curling out,
      as in van Gogh's "Starry Night")
They still revolve! Fresh strawberry red,
moist to the eye and tongue

Like Vallejo they possess their coherence

They are prayer-accurate to a kinetic life

Do these disks proclaim that an abyss has been crossed?

That unlike us the other side is gender occult?

That unlike our flesh,
this wall—as we hold our fingers to it—
can sustain our marks
and send them back into our bodies,
vibrations of the end beginning anew in us?

"As they mature, the erythrocytes [red blood cells] lose their nuclei,
become disk-shaped, and begin to produce hemoglobin"

Might these disks be a kind of proprioceptive alchemy,
a joining of body to cosmos?

The finite reddening into the infinite?

Surely they have a rapport with animal blood as it glistens and dries to
earthworm color, dries to juiceless matter, and surely to menstrual
blood—

In the Polish film *Mother Johanna of the Angels,* it is surely a Paleolithic
gesture when the Mother Superior dashes her hand up her white robes,
then whirls to the stone nunnery wall, drawing her bloodied fingers
down the wall before the alarmed exorcist's face

O mole of me that wants to eat night,
fanged voracity to sink into the outside and hold!

      I lurched into the bunker-like
second chamber backwards headfirst—
A wreath of breast-like stalactites dabbed black.
The Black Goddess? The "breasts" seem part of a tree,
the vertically-split "trunk" a vulvic fold—
"heavy apple tree foaming with human fruit"
—I'm facing the black pods which contain the mead
      we poets hail!

      A rhinogazelgazeliongazelle
caterpillaring,   telescoping out and out

Disks sounding being in bounded space,
binding abyss leaping to the brain's synaptic gongs

In the neuron orgy
      in cranial dark,
to know thyself is to give a self to no.

Indeterminate, Open   *

for Monique and Claude Archambeau

Parietal human figurations
of the Combarelles cave

A dorsocaudad line
   hovering
a ventral line

Les Combarelles: Nineteen
human figurations, or scenes
involving human or hybrid
figurations

engraved on the tunnel ceiling by someone lying down

Incipient
heaven
   and
earth

◇

The human is indeterminate, initially unclosed

◇

Thighed female torso
   tangent to
an equine cervicodorsal line

The hybrid contingency

◇

Of the elephant-hide wall
a particled non-head with triangular eye
supported by a palm and arm wisp or riverine
   divergences.

An immense, flattened breast   floats below,
sunfish through limestone shallows

◇

Planted in lifting female buttocks germinating lines,
bearers of thrust,
an erection

◇

What is a nodule? Can be a nipple
from which two lines widen
cutting through clay into the limestone,
as if by X-ray,
the vaginal canal is deeper

◇

Without eyes
whose nose
only the "carriage of the head"
makes human

◇

Mask eyehole observing the back of someone's head
or is that a spider abdomen?
The face side reveals a bald, deer-muzzled geezer

◇

A horse's rear leg outlines a woman's upper body,
her torso and head enphallused inside the leg,
her bump eyes staring blindly up

◇

On the periphery between nature and human nature,
between unconsciousness and consciousness,
increscent self

◇

Upon the altar edge of a huge,
scratched, open vulva
superimposed on a horse's side,
a dorsocaudad female outline places her
why

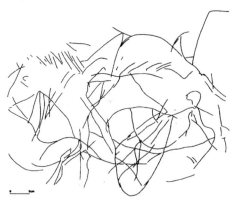

◇

Bending forward, a belly-sagging, bag-headed man,
ithyphallic, gesturing Up Yours—
using his rump for a back line
a one-legged armless half-head turns toward us
as if he is

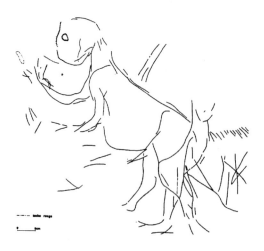

◇

Bag-headed may be giving the finger to
a lumpish dinosaur ghost
shitting as it prepares to mount
a thatch of hindquarters

◇

In a horse's belly
a hairy prognath holds out and looks into
the mirror suggested by the jawbone

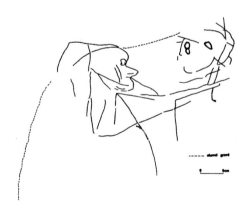

◇

On the fulcrum of a vertical thigh
a dorsoventrocaudad bundle

◇

A huddle of horned vulvas

◇

Head and neck wisps of a phantom fetus
up to its sole eye in horizons

◇

A human erection ascending
as if in a circular revolution
with a saiga head descending

As if the 20th century were embedded in that hub

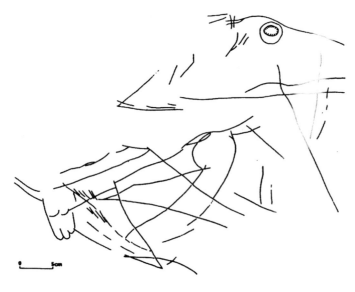

◇

Like sled dogs bounding in slow motion,
animal-snouted archai on the leash of
in the harness of
alchemical mush, moving along Combarelle"s Inner Gallery,
as if in snowy dust

◇

Four hybrid judges.
The simian remains moved.
The others—bear-nosed, duck-billed—
end forward through the schist to not
acquit us

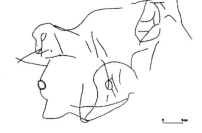

◇

Armored death's-head with vulvar jaw flaps,
necked
goateed,
with escutcheon nosepiece,
one eye a pebble,
the other an overturned vulva,
mouthless and
crossed out.

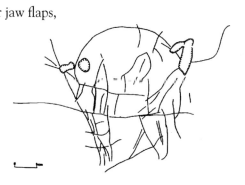

Matrix, Blower

I was going many ways at once,
a drop of psyche had separated into streams,
each with a febrile image purpose,
ravenous image serpents all heading out hungry for extension,
one must choose
which serpent—or might one choose their knotted source?

One says: dream is a stable place to flail,
to swingle bast from circumstance

One says: dream wisps are image produce
the poet must pestle
or tie, dead giveaways

I am crawling a black alley past sights I cannot bear,
alley intestines, the monster composed of daily news

Last night a nipple was offered—
instead of sucking up the squalor discharge
I wrenched up, banging against
a ceiling roar of celebration

I looked back, the alley now spiraling to a vanishing

I was inside a Horn of Plenty with worm nests for the poor.
Where the fruits of the earth were said to spill,
a slab for the rich
barricaded the cornucopian flow

Blood issued from the head of Achelous,
his horn ripped off by Heracles.
It is said that from the blood of this rupture
the Sirens were born—

ragged round pit of this tear:
does it mask the Muse's bloody mouth?

It is also said that Sirens were in the meadow with Kore,
bird-footed bearded girls
watching Kore pluck a psilocybin out of a cow-pie and bite
into the pileus

—I turned on the sink disposal and heard Kore's screams

Binder Siren, throttler Sphinx
cornucopia down into Muse eggs where inspiration and fate
separate and combine—

I keep having this fuzzy vision of a brain termite queen
pumping out image tendrils,
and then a creature blowing into it
(Sirens, the nightside or ancient form of the Muse,
are said to suck the breath of the sick
and are associated with siesta-nightmares)
"muse" akin to *musus*, "animal muzzle,"
a Muse-muzzled succubus crawling across the dreamer
or up through the dreaming,
blowing the dreamer's mind,
mind ejaculating into Muse muzzle,
"psyche" akin to "psychein" = to blow

Say Laussel ripped off the bull's horn
and experienced inner tearing
as if something began to bleed within—
what is this thing that was felt?
A killed-out image?
The sensation of a plunging rise,
a fall so total it swerved into ascent?

This bleeding, this fount—
Aztecs saw snakes coiling out a decapitated's neck
not as a fantasy of wriggling veins
but as the body's serpent power
released in the instant of decapitation

To have severed a head
to gaze at life's black, U-shaped power
out of which image larvae begin to seethe,
as if in doubling-back depth
there is a fructifying compost equal to
the weight of the loaded horn
which this faceless woman of the nightmare
can barely raise,
feeble left hand resting on her swollen belly.
She now possesses what impregnates her.
She's parthenogenetically cocked

Out of a curdling implosion,
out of a caldron of generational fat,
the Venus of Lespugue rises
and is caught at the waist by
—is it mother flesh
she is ascending through?
As if she would completely pop out, a maiden.
Then I look again: she is docile,
her bowed head dove-like
over a bulbous
double stomach, forearms flaccid.
Buffie Johnson noticed the arms are wing-like,
that Lespugue has tail feathers.
One senses that Lespugue is a frozen instant
where woman breaking into bird
breaking into woman were seized and held,
the pupa of each.
The daughter rises out of the mother core,
bird-shaman invested.
Footless Lespugue—
held upside down, from the back
her pressed-leg-stumps become a head,
buttocks   enormous breasts

   She floats,   Cro-Magnon mind,
frog brain shaped

Like the Venus of Milo, her lackings
project us into her…   chips off the old vulva

Nor is Jeffrey Dahmer
utterly beside the point:
to not want to be left by anyone we touch
        is amniotic—
                    in imagination
we seek to keep our freezer full of heads,
we bow to heads taken before we existed

If nothing is absolutely dead
then all—and nothing—has the power to rise,
like smoke, to permeate me
with its insurrectional deadness

Abri Cellier:Aurignacian an animal head (probably a horse), cupules, and vulva engraved
in a block.

At Abri Cellier: the neck and head of a blowing horse
crudely engraved in a stone block.
Across the neck, a vulva a bit bigger than the horse head
        has been gouged.
"The original sentence, the original metaphor: Tat Tvam Asi,
        Thou art that"
Blowing horse head = vulva,
thus: a blowing horse head vulva,
"Beauty will be erotic-veiled, exploding-fixed, magic-
        circumstantial or it will not be"
The *exploding* and the *fixed* at 30,000 B.P.

What I pass is passing through me, the backs
passing through me are passing me back
Clouds heavy with animal membrane,
mortiflies breaking out of seed league,
clouds heavy with marl, with caul, O
the foreloom,   glacier

is inadequate,   reality

is inadequate,   we

are attack admissible, mudderscruf!

Chords of babycry—there, out there, of wind,
of mooralie

My aim my urn my prattlescream

Once my mother turned herself into a bee with compound eyes
big as plates

Light up the crotch of a scallion

No night was darker with adder inner lushroom

I was 18 months old. I saw my mother give my father a hand job,
and said: I can do better than that! So I gave him a blow job. It is
hard the first time you get caught. You just agree with Antlered-owl,
and say: yes I am eating my father! He likes it! It is a good thing to do

At what stage are we in our multiphasic Expulsion?

I know the furlough Neandertal extinction has granted

I know reindeer is a plate on which I serve bison

I know I am a plate on which bear serves salmon

That salmon also serves bear
That I also serve hyena

O the chunks of eeling, the hamstrung
natal-ringing
thuds, the icerian
isolation

Divine peak
                    its snow our rivulet
To drink in my buried-alive daughter:
highest altar

"After the first death, there is no other"

Before the first death, all was other?

Can I grasp the news of this newness?

I have eaten my prow,
cradles have sprouted in my nightcoat
—or are they cromlechs?
Or birth cones?
Or starry sarx?

Passionate Eros suffuses mind in layers of storm mergers

This excites the bears in the void
turning the honey into ransacked hives

Poetry
                    "sunyata ryori"
            Emptiness cuisine

It is mind from scratch that leads.

The Black Goddess   *

Le Combel contains a Black Goddess stone tree only partially emerged from stalactites, fissures, and folds. Possibly as early as 25,000 B.P., Cro-Magnon people identified and marked this proto-World Tree.

Her broad, short trunk has a vertical cleft, widening near the base into a triangular hole. At the top of the trunk, out of the chamber ceiling pod-shaped stalactites proliferate. Under two of these pods, along the cleft, a stalactitic mass seems to liquefy and descend, icicling across the triangular hole and fusing with the molten stone which appears to be emerging from the hole.

Cro-Magnons daubed manganese on a dozen or so of the pods, turning them into blackened breasts, the trunk into a torso, the fissured torso into monstrous trunk-legs, and the triangular hole into a seeping vulva.

These people envisioned all of this and more, for they smeared both upper sides of her trunk torso and the top of her stalactitic clitoris with large, red-ochre disks: rotating anointments, menstrual suns.

The stone river flowing out of her vulva conjures wise blood, a proto-Styx, life-giving *aurr,* nectar of blood and honey—her trunk: Yggdrasil, the Qabalistic Tree of Life ...

But I want to respect the lack of differentiation here, the sense of emergence suspended, as if afloat, in a chaos of darkness and stone, a cleft underworld mother trunk supporting life above,
stone discharging stone, undaubed pods mixed in with blackened breast-pods ... headless ... footless ...

Like many of the "Venus" statuettes, her generative body area is sanctified, her extremities dismissed.

For the red Mother-aspect, the stalactitic clitoris will become a serpent consort, then her child, then lover, then King.

For the black Crone-aspect, the stalactite will become her wand or dildo for entheogenic flight.

Sandor Ferenczi writes that a baby would not only suck, but when armed with teeth would bore its way into its mother's womb. So now I hear "Font-de-Gaume" as if out of a punctured mother fantasy a blood spring issues ...

Le Combel: "The Black Goddess": black-daubed breast-shaped stalactites, triangular opening at the base of trunklike rock, red disks.

N. O. Brown: "And what the child is doing in the inside of his mother's body is scooping it out: 'this desire to suck and scoop out, first directed to her breast, soon extends to the inside of her body.' Excavation. The child is hollowing out a cave for himself inside his mother's body. We are still unborn; we are still in a cave."

So this Black Goddess stone tree may be
a vision of an image-life-giving Mother
inside a quester's hollowed out mother body ...
And the root extensions of this tree?
Are they the Upper Paleolithic image-marked caves
today scattered throughout Western Europe?
In Cro-Magnon imagination might
all marked caves have been
the root tunnels of a Mother Tree
synchronized with shamans who bound the emerging
strands of the soul's story into image lore?
were healing
vision
story
image
and lore
a single amoebic contraction?
Were Rouffignac, Combarelles, Bernifal, Les Trois Frères,
Le Tuc d'Audoubert, Lascaux, Pech-Merle, Cougnac and Gargas
a corresponding expansion, spreading out and down,
root tunnels made sacred by the child's
psychic immolation of his mother's body?

N.O. Brown: "The real birth would be birth from the womb of the dream world ... The real birth is the second birth."

Birth from the dream world = the making of images

The triadic shamanic initiation (generation death regeneration) can thus be expressed another way:

mother
Mother
image

In Gargas a quester writhed through, or ate mushrooms, or
    fell asleep,   we will never know,
he turned himself into a uterine double,
he located the sole gate of access to paradise,
he dived to the bottom of the sea,
followed a bear into a grotto, had the sense to listen to
    a hedgehog,   we will forever know
the beautiful U-turn of his journey, for the pot, the cauldron,
    the pouch,   all in structure
trace a descent, dissolution at bottom, a swerve, an ascent.
He entered his dream, wandered his emptied mother,
obsessed with this beloved he touched the scarred wall,
in Gargas he flattened his palm against
where the breast had been gnawed,
he outlined this hand with spat red-ochre:
    Absolution

Trampolines forged from rock,
the tunnels of Atlementheneira are glistening arks jostling
    with image desire,
meanders like hook worms ravenous for interstitial lining—
there was no home,   no om-core to helm
Atlementheneira and Niemonjima cut through tunnel surfaces
like swimmers bathed half in rock half in air,
we see them as if frozen in bas-relief.
Pech-Merle's bird-headed women ride coiling mammoth trunks,
they know the truth of these mother-enghosted shafts:
ensouled walls primed with regressive excavation.
Peering off hand-lamp light, one can follow Niemonjima's course,
    her switchbacks, her webworks,
"macaroni"!   Tell me, how would you move out of the void!
I stood in Atlementheneira's tunnels and roared with tears,
my meaning in DNA dived and returned bifurcated,
    serpents in homage to the void.

Now I see the snow-swept Mesolithic headland,
bodies curled in ice,   a bison frozen giving birth,
blizzard-buried mammoths,   hunters with birch-bark containers,
    axes,   their blackthorn pips—
did these preserved ones, once revealed in the melt,
evoke the first "intimations of immortality"?
Or was it the fog beyond the Mesolithic headland,
a fog bank of infinite horizontal depth condensing over
    world-end space—
did this fog, a mask worn by the void, backdrop this world-end
    headland?

An archipelago fractures into view—
an immense millepedal octopus of limestone hues,
an organism moving within as if away from itself,

some tentacles detaching,   drifting octopodal outposts,
tiny human groups fire-camped in suction-like craters,
rashes of lightning,   gangrene,   a percolating magma of
    disparate peaks and vales—
through tentacle rents boars and horses flash,
nothing for a thousand years,   then suddenly a glistening
    wall raining rhinoceroses,
colts and fawns oozing through vulvar stone,
cave lions bounding through a tentacle tear.
In unceasing separation, unceasing re-binding
the Paleolithic archipelago crumbling and rebuilding,
karst and yet an organism,   as a termite hill is an organism
    with the queen as its brain,
a bulbous maze where bison are copulating with bleeding women
    intermingling with bird-beaked men,
crumbling and rebuilding, in tentacular dark, muzzles searching
    as if to lick life from ice …

Then as if gulped by fog the archipelago disappeared,
the Black Goddess tree reappeared, trailing a webwork of roots,
blackened breasts over red disks

reverberating the oceans' beginnings

Blasts of molten rock and soot,
premonitions of Kali-Ma and Set

Potential's chaos,
Realization's curtailing cone.

EVERWHAT (2003)

Michaux, 1956

There is in Michaux an emergent face/non-face always in formation. Call it "face before birth." Call it our thingness making faces. Call it tree bole or toadstool spirit, *anima mundi* snout, awash in ephemerality, anti-anatomical, the mask of absence, watercolor by a blind child, half-disintegrated faces of souls in Hades pressing about the painter Ulysses-Michaux as, over his blood trench of ink, he converses with his hermaphroditic muse…

Ink beings spear themselves into rupturing elfin thumbs.

The doubles enrubble, cobble runes, gobble gobble, aerial brains.

Zigzagging corpuscles surprised by a bacterial whinny.

Reintegration at the cost of re-entry.

Black sand dense on white ground. Mites. Mites in mitosis.
    Mitochondria. Miscible mites.
Mitomitosalchondrialmaze.

A gangrenous, thousand-windowed penile haze.

Backed by scarlet maggots, by teeny-weenies, by foetal corn flakes.

A glacial stadium enraged by a tori invagination.

Clothespins cutting up with squidy lattices, no, phosphenic lesions, yes,
    cruciliquinixies

Once razed, the mind's hive releases mastodontal honey.

Mescalinian nets through which infant marmalade englobes.

I am free in Michaux, free to be coccolithic, a gas candy bar,
   whatever.

Better: everwhat. What forever what.

Being unbound. Unbound being bonded.

Ever in the state of *what*!

Everwhat sun. Everwhat dust.

A powder of points. Veil

drawn back, the revelation is lithic velum.

A line encounters a line, evades a line.

A line takes a powder. Adventurer lines.

A line waits, hopes, a line rethinks a face.

Ant-high lines. Ant-visibles streaming through lines.

A melodic line crosses twenty stratigraphic fractures.

A line germinates. Martyr-laughable lines.

Lines gaslighting lines. Lines budding on a dune.

A dream of paradise: lines in conversation with their liminal selves.

The linen of lines, worn, lineage of proliferating life lanes.

The Minotaur as a horned line.

Bitter combat at the center of a line.

What is the center of a line?

Where the whatever folds, becomes everwhat.

Ramose, lachrymose hollow of lines, sisters of stain.

Stains immaculate in their sordid, humid bellies.

Jonah-Michaux in the moray mescaline belly.

Aimé Césaire's "still wine of moray eels," over board cast slaves
   harvested by morays.

Dry furnace of a landscape. Stampeding tacks, lassoed by Jesus,
   lassoed by Sartre.

The scolopendra line. The cockchafer line.

Lives milling insectile to their rodent spoils.

The Last Judgement performed by worms.

The tick faces in gorilla traces.

Lines in reason's glare seething with kettle life.

Nematodes in round dance on a hyena vagina.

Corot, 1870

For Robert & Paola Holkeboer

I

Buried in shadow a tambourin held aloft
"La danse italienne"
leaves,   masses of milling
     disintegrating moths

Speck-thralled earth encaved by shadow waves
     A windmill
          signed   beyond

Flower-daubed goat neck by
the flowering weight of flies swarmed

A piece of watery dark grows in the woods
liquidating the struts of matter

Part earth, the older sister reclines—
light is crumbling into a woolly lime stripe
   in which the younger, sitting up,
back buried in shadow,
  holds out a nose-gay

Spider-threaded creek glass

Moss plush blue marsh—
of what are leaves? Shadow riddles
   riddled   shad   idle   sheds
towers in molt punting the sky
   elves' eaves   ave   les   vias

     Buried in shadow
the day-lit world. A cow wades a lake
as if regarding the fishing boy,
as if alive. Corot's eventide at
          high noon

In her up-
gathered pale rose gown,
a young woman offers a wild-flower-filled
womb urn to
khaki leaf fumes

Buried in shadow
"The springtime of life"

Virgin in a fire storm of cherries.

II

The whirr of leaves
a Paleolithic isolation
a shadow-static
continuum

Wildflowers as brightly-colored fleas

Leaf-saturated
woods, air,
the weight of the barely-
lit

Green dust breeze
matted woods, the
armature of the woods—
how nature umbilically
divides,
multiplies out,
khaki mash
simmer of light

Anything perceived has implicit armature

Shadowed humans in
loose and floating
        shadow guise—
words as repetitional
            thatch

    Soot smoke foliage
        blurred blue,
    sky tight

Absence-mangered woods,
in blooming fog a branch-loaded cart
        by static horse on which
  hunched pink with hat

Beast heads in the tree broods,
mossy blackening shafts
  bailed out by breeze

You are dead Dream now,
drift into this beast morgue, be
as torch in
the castle-bordering lake's
        black sustinence

Are we but animations of shadow glades,
shadow figments
seamless to each,
animated
  shadow drives?

As the shadow syrup comes up in us, cork-
screwing us to hold high
  the momentary tambourin
  —O my monstrance,
my aura seized and sounded!

In late Corot, a shadow bake which people and nature attend,
in fray and waver, each a sentinel of shade

Tale of a shadow-lad up a shadow-tree picking nursery rhymes
to be tossed down into—is it his mother's or his sister's—
held up apron?

I close my eyes and feel my extent tentify out…

The shadow-laundresses are at their pond rocks shadow-rubbing,
a rock revelation is at hand…

A reader is reading to a missing bridge,
reading to pylons, to the water exposed,
a shadowed reader standing, holding out blank light.
Here the bridgework begins…

Noguchi, 1984

For Bill & Yoshiko Paden

Let the old man play with his rocks
The end interest of old men is rock,
rind of the fruit of seeing,
more open than man himself can ever be,
bed for pteranodon, trilobite,
stromatolithic altar.

The whole is cavernous with foaled void,
rock calving
extrusive andesite. Most of Noguchi's Personage,
a vertical shaft, is unexcorticated,
so that in facing "personage"
one faces triclinic feldspar, hornblende.

Granite *Phoenix*—
resurrection as horizontal,
the mid-section sawed into a Mayan ballcourt,
heron body   out of which
civilization was cut.

Here is our mother's nightside, her feldspar back,
all tables are our mother on all fours,
our headless, breast-planed goddess,
at floor level   Noguchi's *Resonance.*

                    Far Land,
            with a vulvar inlet to
    a dry pitted river,
    glabrous andesite, here as never,
                gravid,   ever her.

    Basalt Lap
    Granite Rice Field
Noguchi sawed, dressed,
but left the plagioclase in control.

His work is a Noh bridge between

the carbonaceous soul of life

the siliceous soul of rock.

Bacon Studies (III)

"Bacon at Pompidou"

Bacon's studio: volcanic midden.

1935: an animal pawing up into a garden—sensation probing interior decoration.

…at the *Base of a Crucifixion*—the crucifixion itself: Europe, 1944.

Figures like larvae spawned in concentration camps.

The inhuman as the exhaust of the grotesque.

Bacon's roller rink starts up in the 1945 *Figure in a Landscape*—the orange ground in the '40s (rust–fire–blood exotica) essentially his studio. The world put into a stained box. An ex-interior decorator working in a slaughterhouse.

Bacon's flesh: plaster-tarred, cream-tinted, pink smoke bodies. Black ham snowing through debris-littered skin.

Evoking T.S. Eliot's:
"Withered root of knots of hair
Slitted below and gashed with eyes,
This oval O cropped out with teeth:
The sickle motion from the thighs."

Bed as crib sweating with primal abuse.

White bandage-like arrows, cupidic caricature.

Head II (1949): lower teeth become a tiny white hand attempting to reach palate.

Bacon's screaming mouths are mute, frozen, open manholes. They appear almost without heads, as if the body's toothed sewer can manifest in any of its members.

"The street caved in like a syphilitic's nose"
    —Mayakofsky

Executives in tub-like cribs with apple-shaped open mouths. Eden-inverts. As if one could sink one's teeth into the Pope's solid, apple-shaped scream.

Eisenstein at Nuremberg.

But Popes do not scream or suffer Jewish genocide. These Popes are Bacon-projected, holy sadism pinned to a throne, or immersed in a uterine bath.

Painting as snail trail, a painter's mental excrement.

The painter as nebbish in tennis shoes, a chump, a comma parked without sentence.

The limits of Bacon's commitment to his own experience: no scenes of flagellation, cocksucking.

Muted buggery, naked lunch *sur l'herbe*.

Man in Blue (1952): corporational hives as imperial saloons.

Bacon's bravura: unceasing deconstruction/titillation of calligraphic grace.

Dog about to vomit into a gutter grate: Hecate before her mirror.

Van Gogh holds his blackened cock, pissing an aster into the bloody surf of a Bacon basin.

Bacon's titles rhyme his figural ambiguity.

Muriel Belcher, battered Medusa with red bulb clown nose.

Human baboon taffy barber pole.

Looks like mastodon bones form the Bacon roller rink around the base of the right-hand panel of *Crucifixion* (1962).

The strife in de-elegantizing.

The lure of beauty in remembered sadism.

Deft Pope crinoline meringue under a blood-stucco shawl, 1965. I sense the horrors of Vietnam in the Pope's exploded face.

Legless Pope on a motorized throne navigating the floor of a closed department store.

Henrietta Morae's flaccid, swollen, wild-boar visage.

Can anyone look hard at this century for a minute without turning away?

Overheard on the Bacon phone: the ongoing party on the *Lusitania*.

Does Bacon study police photos? He never fully renounces decorative elegance. Example: the man chewing into another man (in the 1967 *Sweeney Agonistes*) has vanilla ice cream buttocks.

Bacon's males, penile heads plastered-down with black hair, often excrete deformed shadows.

No end to the pulling down of the hunting blind of history.

Man as a Dionysian junk bond.

Polypus of two men mirrored with an arched forearm jamming in the anvil.

George Dyer as a Hitlerian triskelion boxer revolving along a scarlet beam.

The more coherent the more unstable.

Swastika of male flesh opening a black umbrella.

Figure in Motion (1976): thigh-arm, peeled to the rose of its violet bone, jutting out and out, charred. Not even death will stop it. An eye opening in the stump.

Realism in underwear at the end.

Spirits of the Head [Bacon Studies]   *

You want to recover the original wholeness?
Re-enter chaos.
Kill your own profane existence.
Become a chocolate skull, wrapped in white silk, teeth sewn shut,
    sockets shell-stopped.
The auroral instant prior to existence?
Death is a rite of passage, not an end.
In flight, an erection becomes the World Tree.
I am a crow perched in the foliage of my scattered skeleton.
From the mud under Satan's nails I have made a mound on which to
    rest.
An animal goes into a cave, re-emerges as a man.
A man goes into a cave and leaves his animal on the wall.
The animal on the wall earth cosmetics, cosmoetics, make-up on
    inner space.
Spirits of the head.
Brow of unpolished wood.
My left eye a rouge of blood and sperm.
Eyeball: a rabbit balled-up in a cage.
A Mohawk hairjolt stiffened with soot.
The inner head, beat-up version of somebody else.
The whap in the jaw, slug of the male jaw, castrated bullet of the
    prognathus jaw.
Eye as moon crater.
The target of the eye.
Eye closed under a brain kindling geysers and splitting fontanels.
I am jawless with long, long ears, my throat extends to my eyes.
Spirits of the head.
Mustache of drool and loam.
Face of waves, of serpentine mobs.
Aviary face, eyrie of coons and owls.
Shore of the eye, quicksand of a look.
And then George Dyer—a spirit head if there ever was one—
            turned to show in profile
            a root-chopped, tusk dug continent,
            issue bandaged with eyelids and whiskers.

Dead Dyer with bumblebee lips.

Dyer with a snow cone blood picked nose.

Skull with nimbus of Germanic steel and gold.

Merry Xmas, Mr. Mayhem, I'm here to interrogate the nimbus of your
lungs.

Here to enjewel your ribs with metal buttons, velvet flaps.

Head in rotary division, a single eye, mouth, and terrine of ears.

God has withdrawn into the Devil's Skull from which he fires
spider filaments into the glory hole of mankind.

Within the face, Bosch working the pump: mouth slashes up into
eye, eye bruises over, pickled garden of shredded amanitas and
blind sables.

Pit of the face, cemetery pitted against chaos.

Brain as a tub of marrow filled with the diced hands of scientists.

Head of bone, of spirit, unbroken head.

Head destroyed and intact as a granite egg.

Lynched tongue-bunched neck invisible to the boys setting fire to its
toes.

Fly of the human eye excreting as it broods.

Snowshoe of George Dyer's mouth planted in ice.

How much white can a head take? Can it assimilate supremacy,
heaven?

Can it take on the reddened battlefield of man's pincer gaze at pluck
with his brother?

Can I make the unsayable bark to verify that racial whitewash will
never succeed in gating the community of souls?

Head on its hair body, homuncular head, alchemical gaze of a hair
body through which the putty of the face mills.

The Magical Sadness of Omar Cáceres   *

A white road crosses its motionless storm,
vernal pool where frogs live trapped in archaic hail.
I've wasted too much time with moonlight
and now sit gazing through the small hole in my dress at Monday's
    naked nail.

Manchuria, I feel your invasion!
Suddenly we are ourselves, without brushes, lawn mowers, or saloons.
I confess the crimes against my monsoon self—
these chess words, slippery with blood,
they are my pistons, my petrol, the fits of memory scrawled in a hulk
    log.
Cockroaches cross the deck   moving from Picasso to snowman.

The thought lost to the eyes of a unicorn reappears in a dog's bark.
Dressed in resistance, I laud the most important figure in the United
    States:
Mickey Mouse, legislator of urban alcohol adieu.
My courtesan instructs me in the wrecked balcony of her arms.
The idol? A chessboard of truffles and snow.
Unlike comrade Huidobro, I'm a whittled id,
a city hall boss standing on prison steps,
thriving like a burnt out sun, a sun which never imagined a lamp.
O summation of Chile! A man loves only his obscure wife.

To run with the nectar, to bypass alarm.
Is not joy somehow canopic?
What moves in the air: ways that are not the way,
the whey of snow, way of the flayed flake.
My slash is yours, riptides amassing.
O Chilean summation! I poke into the moon's watery lace.
Between sequitur and non sequitur falls the imagination.
"There is grandeur in this life, with its several powers."
Spare the gestures. Nothing for show.
I am neither aft nor fore, nor foreafter,
nor ever to be afterforementioned again.

I hear Neruda—he's a langoustine of a man,
a violet maiden in multicolored fleece,
both hands paralyzed from swatting political lice.
Neruda! A swiller of a gale, a snood disguised as a church,
rutabaga in cleats, something found on the beach which,
as you fondle it, urinates in your heart. Neruda,
what is truly to be found under his tray of forceps and sledges?

Passing mons Veneris clouds.
The translucence of human flesh.
Ceremonial lenses made of ice, brought down from Andean peaks.
A rainbow defective in a single hue.
The spider *Dolomedes urinator* which runs simultaneously in two
    worlds.
The sound of air in a cave.
Sensation of longing for an eclipse powerful enough to darken death.
Changes in the light initiated by a stranger's arrival
—Chilean marvels, equal to the Surreal.

I prepared. Waited to be called.
Cut logs. Laid a hearth. Burned my valentines.
Visited the Incan adoritories on Mount Llullaillaco.
Examined the grave goods of The Prince of Mount Plomo.
Which is to say: I prepared. Set the caldron boiling,
spliced postcards from Isla Negra with photos of infants left out in the
    snow.
Mastered myself. Arrived in Harar with only 10 camels.
Sketched each waterfall. Took out no personal ads.
I faced fear, then clarity, then power.
Tonight I have a meeting with the last enemy of the man of
    knowledge.
In his uncorked left testicle, it has been raining for years.

Figure and Ground   *

Over 50 years Leon Golub has been plunging through blood marshes,
walking through the daymare of his era,
translating classic chaos,
conceiving the homuncular man of history
and removing the 20th century zero of history in museums from the
    scales,
rebalancing them with *art as social meaning.*
Golub is man self-revealed on his ground,
grounded as in flamenco, the work pushed
down, into post-Whitman nuclear grass,
no longer a lode of white-haired mothers,
but a depository for Angola land-mines. It is the rush of man
out of the umbilicus forever bombing,
it is the fire, the spurt of lamb, at the edge of everyone's sight.

Earth, does your subjectility still have amnion?
Is finding one's spot still the key revision of foetal drift?
A given paradise is no more.
Memory, working with psyche, can argue, can reveal.
Golub's figures are shadowed with lost ground.
We know where man is when we look at this painter's work.
We see a range of acrid flavors,
out of Vietnam with a hint of the awful, striped with
tribal hybridity, woman as gate, woman as beautiful sphinx—

Golub now works in blackness
projecting Dia de muertos stigmata through
the oil slicks of American culture,
fragments of the elderly Prometheus, the merc-headed dog caught in
    blue street light,
the interior rims of America, neon-stung slums where
blacks and chicanos crouch in the combustion zone of a voodoo
    particle flow.
Our eyes are steined with Clinton

whose guts must look like a Boschian symphony.
Wake up, daddy bones,
nothing is not bad. Nothing is the ultimate ground.

I construct a skull for Leon,
placed in the Borneo men's house at 71st and Broadway,
a cowrie shell for each socket.
I caress his skull top with gutta percha,
making crosses and Nixon cartoons in the rubber-like resin,
then I drape this skull in dreadlocks
and elongate it back into Merovingian time.
Surely Leon Golub deserves that depth.

                                        10 December 2000

Darger   *

     I

Facing Darger 34 floors below—
can I reach his station?
Planet Darger, below the subconscious,
in Tartarus, where giants are bound to
little girls? With what are the Titans bound?
Little girl rope, innocence cable,
the anguish of one's mother as a little girl enslaved.
Darger washed hospital pans, cleaned up mess.
Was he tied up at The Lincoln Asylum for Feeble-Minded Children
when he was 12? What happened to Darger?
Why was Darger Darger? He escaped across a river, 1909.
"The farm," I read, was a concentration camp—
masturbators and kickers tied up, trussed on the floor in their own
    feces.
His mother dead from puerperal septicima when he was 4
died giving birth to Henry's sister immediately adopted.
Raised by his father, a crippled tailor, until 8.
What Darger made of his empty basin is remarkable,
test of a human being unwilling to die,
unwilling to eat all the abuse, a nothing man
who scratched out of trash a something.
Civil War = Internal War = God vs. Man.
The slavery man is to himself, pitiful man infantile to God.
Man arrested at what? A back wall of loss.
The societal closes over. Why speak to those whose hearts
wear witch hats? Grim 1912 Chicago. Moonflake streets.
Darger is the mathematical exodus of a score card,
a paste-up man. Collections of newspaper cartoons
pasted in bulging volumes, bits of string tied into balls.
Keep the heart away from the cleaver,
keep the cleaver bared to Bad Men, big-hatted guys
he had torturing naked girls. In Darger's dream
the soldiers never touch the girls,

they strangle them, disembowel them,
but do not touch them. The girls do not touch themselves,
they are Christian, they have—some of them—cartoon penises wear-
   ing ball muffs,
they are immortal, most cannot speak.

"it's the prank of the whole earth
against whoever has balls in his cunt," wrote Artaud,
who likewise ejaculated "daughters of the heart, to be born."
Here is an Artaud/Darger daughter-braid:

Yvonne
  Hansonia
Caterine
  Catherine
Neneka
  Angeline
Cécile
  General Vivian
Ana
  Violet
Little Anie
  Jennie
Colette
  Gertrude

At the intersection of Darger and Artaud,
there's a Frida Kahlo bus accident hourly.
Armored spirits ram a daughter-filled vessel
spraying heads and limbs into psychic containers—

   "Everything must be arranged
    to a hair
in a fulminating
     order"

Poor Darger, the poorest of the 20th century tribe of imaginal
   founders;

at mass in strait-rosary 4 times daily,
cleaning up hospital waste for 50 years
(his one friend moved away)
sleeping upright in a chair at 851 Webster Avenue
(his cot looked like Charles Olson's worktable),
a life library of children's books and hymnals
grubbed out of trash cans or bought for pennies.
Caryl and I made a list of his library
when we visited his room in 1997:

13 Oz volumes   9 Dickens volumes
Making the Weather   Sources of Volcanic Energy
Autumn Leaves   Trini The Little Strawberry Girl
Tisa A Little Alpine Waif   The Best of Friends
Rinkitink   A Little Maid Of Nantucket
The Little Runaways & Mother   Heidi
Heidi Grows Up   The Lost Princess
The Patchwork Girl   Meet the Bobsey Twins
The Bobsey Twins Camping Out   The Kitten's Secret
Defending His Flag or a Boy in Blue & A Boy in Grey
Lorraine And The Little People Of The Ocean
The Revolt Of The Angels   Kidnapped
Official Guide Book (World's Fair, 1934)
Wheelers' Graded Readers, 2 volumes
Sweethearts Unmet   The Great Chicago Fire
The Banner Boy Scouts Snowbound   Rare Old Chums
The Cheery Scarecrow   St. Basil's Hymnal
Christian Brothers Hymnbook   Fun With Decals
Spirit of the Blessed Cure of Arts   Rosemary
The House of the 1000 Candles   Little Red Riding Hood
Mathematics for Common Schools   Peter Pan
A Shirley Temple Story Book   The Life of Christ
Dion Quintuplets "Going On Three"   The Rose Child
The Atlas "Biology"   Andersen's Fairy Tales
Blind Agnesse   The School of Jesus Crucified
Jo The Little Machinist   The Little Christmas Shoe
Catechism Of Christian Doctrine   Grimm's Fairy Tales
My Child Lives (Consoling Thoughts Of Bereaved Parents

Sick-A-Bed-Sally	*A Guide To The Franciscan Monastery*
Don Quixote	*Condemned To Devil's Island*

Fleas with tyke faces crawl 5'3" Darger's wrath
To adopt? That too denied to me?
I am Chicago Weather, Hendro Darger the Volcanologist,
author of a 15,000 page novel, Pepto-Bismol bottle collector,
a man who rescues crucifixes from trash cans,
maker of 500 balls of knotted string,
my eyeglasses held together by tape,
wallet tied to shoestring attached to belt loop.

Jesus, are you a little girl? Jesus, am I in
your body? Nail-wracked Jesus,
       am I your daughter
          self?

      II

A man who has no world
makes a world—to share?

Words appear on the page as I read them,
Words I spit out of my eyes.

I do this in dream.
Imagine Darger doing this awake.

Darger is too absolute to tinker with,
he's a first and last man,

a man without middle (most artists are
crammed in passage, they periscope

and they retract). I go to Darger to
clear my heart of life's mid-way.

Darger is pathetic
because he chooses to move at all.

He could have jammed his head into a toilet
He chose not to, chose to

cosmogonize a burr
lodged in his heart.

Darger in his child zoo, testing liberation.
Darger as a child zoo, refusing liberation.

No matter how many carnivores he releases,
little girls are trillion in a field.

I went to the Darger Circus,
watched Henry geld himself as

the Vivian Girls scampered out.
Darger is in shreds, but his scrambled

virgin lice exceed our plenum.

III

Northrop Frye, reading Blake's *Thel*:

"nothing achieves reality without going through physical existence, the
descent must be made. The failure to make it is the theme of *The Book
of Thel*. Thel is an imaginative seed: she could be any form of embryonic
life, and the tragedy could be anything from a miscarriage to a lost vi-
sion… being an embryo in the world of the unborn, Thel longs to be of
"use," that is, to develop her potential life into an actual one and hence
come into our world of Generation… But, hearing the groans of a fallen
world tormented in its prison, she becomes terrified and escapes back
to the unborn world… a world of dissolving and arbitrary fantasy, a
looking-glass world of talking flowers… *The Book of Thel* thus repre-

sents the failure to take the state of innocence into the state of expe-
rience… in Thel's infertile world everything is exquisite and harmless…
Thel's canvas is decorated with lambs and lilies."

So, the Darger girls are frozen seeds, cut-outs, stripped of garments to
show their seed nature. Shadowed by the menacing soldiers of experi-
ence, they don't move imaginatively, but pout, pose, or flee the head-
charged Glandelinian femaleless males. The girls repopulate endlessly,
each a mirror of the other (they often pop up as exact duplicates or in
series). Where they should be concave, they are un-enterable, which
means they are unable to enter experience. By giving them penises,
Darger makes invasion impossible (which he probably intuits as rape).
The girls' unborn boyfriends are the saintly Blengiglomenean Serpents,
with long wavy tails. While they do shoot fluid into the girls (which
they appear to like, and which makes them immortal), this only con-
firms that the two mix on a sperm and egg level, a level in Darger which
never produces babies.

IV

The dead little girls appear,
unborn seeds of childhood,
repetitious in ways that could not be made functional in language
—does that seem queer? to put it that way?
Galleries of the defiled, undefiled in Darger's dream,
millions he could commemorate and save,
bland and blazing paradox, terrible sandwich of eternity,
the dead behind, the here static.
Darger was a subconscious visionary—
these commercial images of children, Coppertone Lotion sold by a
    child's panties being
tugged out by a doggy,
images of tots used to sell children clothes,
or cigarettes, via adults smoking towering over—
Darger stripped them, then set them forth,
Guanajuato mummies are more immediate.
Darger is more savage, more blank.

Do his 300 scrolls contain the paradise of the unlived,
the "early departed," in Rilke's terms?
It matters immensely that Darger's mother died
giving birth to a sister he never saw, when he was 4.
In Darger's case, however, paradise truly opens—truly?
How can I say that! Little girls, cute absences in
repetitional grids—I'm ashamed to identify them:
Yellow hair in orange collar, yellow dress, stands beside
brown hair, arms crossed over tummy, in red play suit, red anklets,
before brown and red ball, next to yellow hair in orange collar,
yellow dress, hands behind her—
are these the forepleasures of childhood
as death manipulates budding energies to stain each into each?
Darger is the remainder of the huge absence I felt as a child,
"staring at a corner for hours,"
my mother told Caryl,   "he was such a good boy."
But oh, my childhood for all its ills was redolent with sap compared
     to Henry's.
His naked girls make the tinselscape cave-in behind them,
they are without pathos, and—they are totally pathetic,
the unborn, reflecting neither forward nor backward.
Coppertone cutie is stripped not only of her panties
but of her pseudo-persona. In Darger,
"she" is the girl who never is, multiplied
as if through the fly-eyed lens of God.
Darger had no idea—or did he?—
that he was creating a pantheon.
We peer at it in the American museum of Folk Art
—goodness, what is on that man's mind?
Moral mayhem, amigo, girls tinier than pink flowers,
ram-headed fairies leaping, fashion ads
stripped of their dead frivolity to become
girl negatives, crucified en mass or oddly screaming
neck-twisted, in a collage margin,
in a gauze of pretense that they *are* in paradise.
Is paradise the absence of adults?
The absence of experience, its fallow, planted perpendiculars?
Can paradise possibly be if we preclude experience?

Darger opens up a worm vista on paradise—
his art is the negation of an active paradise,
one of imagination, one shamans push into,
a state unobtainable through political or anatomical means—
Darger rubs our faces in the gleet of the impossibility of paradise.
Good for you, stunted, friendless Henry.
Thanks for rubbing our commodity-drugged mugs through these
    image-angel-less
anti-ikons. But there are so many
crossword bunnies in the woods, so much jigsaw shadow—
did Darger ever know where he was? Possibly—
but only in the grand orality of his red weather,
the tourbillions of girl necks whistling through
    what flavored his life,
natal tornado of trying to figure out
why the femaleness, the femininity of life
    has been denied to him?
Masculinity must be an over-surpassing evil!
Tied up in a building of shrieking tied-up kids—from which
    he managed to escape
—to what? Butterfly-winged absence with minute colorless
    penis between her
pressed thighs, black butterfly-winged
oh my, black dotted yellow dressed
oh dear, floating caul, how dids't thou escape the womb?
Why dids't thou not achieve life?
Comic strip valley aswarm with cradle-shaped rangers.
Radiant sweetness shot-gun emptied into dot-eyed zombies.

V
2004–2007

MY DEVOTION (2004)

Before the Wall

Unless you attack what is wrong, in you, and in your world,
I say you repress. If you go for the throat of your moon,
you might clear a midnight of bloodspattered road.
Do we actually stand before the wall for poetry?
I can drink myself to death
but such only feels up Dionysus.
I keep saying to Nora Jaffe's soul: it is enough
to have space to write in, time, and someone to live with
who loves me, and whom I love, as if outward ceremony
    can be sloughed—
it can, and it can't. As we get older
Lorca is before the wall every morning,
Dali is jerking him off as he dies.
Life is obscene, not because of Dali's fist,
but because of our ability to live with eros conjunct with
    violence—
and we never know if this is fixed in limbo by fettered Titans,
if, in attempting to say the very thing we are,
we say just one self, or many, or merely register abyssal
    shudderings.
The E on the stone? Maybe it meant mountain or gate, in what way
was it turned? A two-stalled stable? Man rejoicing?
Or is this energy mounted off impotence?
Possible. A despair so clear and pure it runs through primality.

Rock and Rootstock

Originally, poetry is
a binding of wild to mine, a sewing of the unbound
    animal to
slowly-being-bound-person,   hybrid rock,
rock with my teeth at its core,
or my machine-gun, or my greenhouse,
erratic celestial floor—
            and to be rock is to be
the most ambivalent thing,   Ulro in Blake,
deadened deadness   corpse breccia,   and the truth.

The speakable carbuncle of life offers some satisfaction,
it's a viceroy moment,   to imagine what one wants to exist,
but there is so much we feel around us we do not focus,
so much that affects, infests the pivot,
and what is the pivot? An amalgam, quartered by
    my desire to be
here and elope with imagination,
       to sink into its rootstock,   to be inside the moral
whose circumference is hatred,
to follow out my coal bin,
                 and futurity?
On one level I'm damaged beyond Indiana recognition,
on another I'm the phoenix a poet must be,
a ruined worker in the hive of irregularity,
of a forge so random it is mad to hammer.

Five Queasy Pieces

I want to come to terms with my vaulted
and faulty
interior, with the clocks stacked in my kidneys,
with my face of a radish
draining tears into a tile sea.
And I do not want to come to terms with this vaunted
faculty, with these mer and men maids
calving right below consciousness.
Fuse and refusal,
torque of the Vallejo legacy.
To mince the baby wind—
to feast on nothing.

◇

When I was a woman
I smiled, the arrows bristling from my face,
an old-fashioned woman, a rooted flow.
Then I became a winged pilgrim, intestinal offerings
bumping along the ground as I flew.
My ambivalence worked my negations on looms.
Now I am gutless,
peristaltic in ascent,
radiant with memories of menstrual wastes.

◇

Sitting under this outcropping, thinking at
the speed of limestone, I hear waiters below
struggling with diners, diners sparring with food,
a breeze sweeps up the sound of gardeners
locked in combat with shoots, swimmers intercleaved
with the spermatic flex of yesterday's wind.
A workman shears the earth's head, revealing
its timed skull, limestone time, openly dead,

not closed like we are, fighting with
everything we touch, trying to become headless
gods below the horizon, gods of the mystical hollow earth.

◇

The reason you came here
has dropped away. You have butter on your fly.
You write because your beanstalk is raced by giant Jacks.
Because the midden strata at Laugerie Haute
strikes you as the origin of fashion.
At best, a zipper meshes dualities,
the zipper of the mind interlocking its own bite.
How moving it is to hear someone say
something veined with
reflective and suffered pleasure.

◇

Awake as if drunk with the last dream,
ready to remake whatever
—my life, my vision, my love—
to see through is to have nothing to resist,
is to lose the resistance for which one secretly lives.
Poetry from the beginning is posited,
based, on resistance,is a work *against*,
whether with flint or quill
it is to convert one's boring into a lateral spell,
an ecstatic wandering in which one lives
as if weightless on the hunch of a finger tip—
hunchwork   wondrous release of the body
poised on the burin of itself.

1999

Across the Bering Strait

Long bundles arching over stumps, tongues over
crumbling teeth, bundled poles over
hunched coals pouring, cinder by cinder forward...
I see Mary Ann Unger in death
still carrying glyptodontal loads,
the backwash of her life, her cancer,
her mastodontal desire to push on,
Siberian hunters at 20,000 B.P., moving several miles a year
across a 55 mile land bridge,
the linked and the loaded, following the great sloth,
the short-faced bear, following camels, yaks, tapirs,
ringed by the saber- and the scimitar-toothed, ice-browed humanity,
Unger sees them as bending tusks sprouting out of
mammoth-headed ice, the lurchfolk,
about whom we know nothing! For Beringia is gone!
Like a shrub-ox or capybara, the land bridge,
with their footsteps, their middens,
the bones of the peccaries they killed—
homage to Mary Ann Unger, dead in 1998, a sculptor,
she grasped these lurching, lugging entanglings,
"Across the Bering Strait," the bearing of weight over time,
over the land bridge of a life,
wrappings, pilings, backpacks, loaded baby slings,
moving toward a mystical Organon, where all is organ,
a paradise of animals, following the crazyquilt meat drift,
to penetrate the animal realm, to get animal know-how,
humankind, like loosely tied poles lurching on,
over boulder knolls, eating tundra smut,
gotta travel gotta follow the horns,
horn of a moose, horn of an elk, first flag!

Blue Zone

I

Ann's ocean was above her head this afternoon.
We looked into it,   vast clear wispy blue skies,
turbulent plow under,   troughs and prairies...
Ann small under her ocean,
Ann with frail upper arms.

This ocean now takes on annihilational size.
We see tears move into the outside of Ken's eyes...
well that's what we see,   we see very little,
friends with chicken soup

(the poem hesitates to say more now,
 to do so
 would intrude on Ann's destiny)

II

Why didn't I grasp this earlier? Last week
after hearing of Ann's 7 hour emergency ward siege
I dreamed: my mother and father
full face in the dream screen,
me telling Gladys the bad ness,
her curling away, accepting? Her shoulder
last seen, then Clayton
full face, a line of blood between his lips
as in the van Gogh Saint-Rémy self-portrait.
I saw Ken Mikolowski in my dream-father's face,
realizing I had brought my family forward
out of anguish for Ken and Ann.

564   Clayton Eshleman: *The Essential Poetry*

III

Right before evening, the daily equinox.
Do the dead tap in now?

Thoughts of Ann, looking at bobbing
redbud shimmer flows
drift of several branches, moored
Calder-like, frail green canopies.

Tidal fugue of the past building through the present—
to break, futurity foam.

Suddenly flashing across Ann's psyche.
I must be careful to respect its whitecaps, its pines.

IV

The savagery of reaping, of God
crushing crows in his hands to scatter across
poor Vincent at sea in the yellow-
rushing-toward-him-waves.

We are those sunflowers, Ann,
lifted into the grail oven,

immense black sunflower extending
as far as forever is.   Not "Here Lies"
                              but Here *standing*

         My sense of human
         goodness was raised
         in knowing you.

V

Standing by the sink before
half-shuttered kitchen window evening light,
striking a cleaver between lamb rack ribs
I thought of Ann,
arcane feelings moved in my body,
I was butchering what I had roasted and
Ann was failing,   I was gripped by
an airless symmetry,
I paused over the rack—
a kind of architectural design was present,
I thought back to our afternoon visit,
Ann's calm and humor, her daughter Molly's tear-repressed face,
Ken was north—
                                    a design
organizing itself in space,
as old as a scratched line,   Ann's city of art
combining in the sky over Ypsilanti—
I saw cloud-like gates,
meticulous granular observational scapes,
each registered   as the structure itself.

VI

Ann in the dark of an all
I hardly reach metaphorically
refused transport beyond metaphor's
        half-self.
                        Ann in full passage.
I'm feeling the wall,
the fulcrum, the tilt beyond which
you will exist in memory

O radiant spider crawling with wounds

VII

Off Monhegan Island the basic blue
turned into courageous slate, shifting
diaphanes of melancholy aquagreen.
The azure has a metallic edge, a dun
    infected will.
                      In high ocean shadow
clarity's tiara became a nebulous mass,
a coma, a rain-soaked hyacinth.

The ocean's ground was chipped with locking tints,
inks and shields, crumbled steles
married to a verdigris
spotted and stained with forests
rising from a liquid core…

an undulant ground, blue gum streaked ruby,
russet and obscure, and then a modest larkspur
pattern appeared, a humorous blue,
as if Krishna's cyanotic body were the ocean's skin.
Through rolling bronze, a red archangel spread out in
    serpentine flails…

Unending transformation in a single frame.

Blues for Ann. Peacock meridians in repose.
Blue air over crocodile and cream.
Oyster whites flecked with jelly yellows.
A magnanimous blue, chilled by receding shades,
a tone at once a color and a mood,
peaks and troughs leveled into a glaze,
a frail synthesis shuddered by far-near thunder,
by gusts of ruddy, honeycombed winds.
A horizon crawling with serpent skirts of fire.

A repose at once milling and aligned.
the angel within the maze,
the maze within the angel—

courage   modesty   laughter   magnanimity
    an individuated blue

        your legend, Ann

        VIII

Ann was sleeping when we entered
aged
        by a week of operational agony.
Laid back facial planes,
nose too angular,
pursed, nicked lips,
                breathing,
her body small, under thin cover.

Caryl said: let's let her sleep.
So we went away, found a lounge, waited for 5 minutes.
I told Caryl Ken said it was ok to wake her,
so we went back.
                The pot of sunflowers
still in good shape after 5 days
against the window—beyond which: Ann Arbor in
    helpless, redundant green.

Ann woke and smiled through hell at us.
Caryl knew what to say. My glances pingponged about
Ann's bruise-mottled arms, moist swept-back hair,
the sweet nurse adjusting the yellow IV udder load.

We had brought her a beribboned little box of Queen
    Anne's cherries.
Ann quiver-nibbled, joking "as the queen,
I insist you taste my cherries."

We both touched her arm and left
the combined power of Ann's
smile and pleading gratitude.

IX

The recumbent is a vessel.
The attender a rotting god.

Ann's ocean floor profile enters my gut.
My Brain attempts to revive her via
hallucinatory sleep—
everything an instantaneous metaphor,
sofa turning into cave organs,
sky a swamp, stars
the bursting lungs of catfish
—as if to transform Ann
into something else, the goad for
belief in reincarnation?

Ann
    underground.
Who
    visits now?

Love's absence-driven,
    love's presence-bereft,
humble before the art
of earth's larder.

No release from this recumbency
    ceiling all face

the Sistine spread.

[June–September 1999]

Bedroom, 6 AM

Bulbous rootwork of drape rings,
sleigh grey slides

       ceiling quilted ripples

City bus brakes releasing
—pigeon fluttermuffle—
lint of sounds…

We are young and beautiful to each other
posing for a snapshot,   Lespinasse, 1974,
we are flooding each other with the perfection of
    mutual reception,
there is a basement, a hallway, you are leading me
    past my parents,
there is Matthew… cows in Perigord fog…
dreams become visions…

Little canals of sunlight
saturate the curtain folds…

Your face from the bed extends,
your body goes out into the room,
to wake is to enter
the Caryl-enfabulated world.

Animals Out of the Snow

When snow falls deeply,
mountainously, curvaceously,
animals begin to nudge forth...

Caryl and I were visiting the young poet Stephen Smith
in the world of 3 A M,
I was generating organs for a new book.
We were invited, as if for a cottage
or mountain cabin stay, but the beds were uneven,
things were tilting, for hours it seemed
I worried about my throat and
the corpse of John Logan,
putting itself into my throat.

At some point it was clear:
Stephen was out of control,
his pets would not behave, would not
let us sleep. Logan, according to Kessler,
was so incapacitated near the end of his life
that he lived in an armchair.
Bandit students wandered in and out of his ruined lord,
taking his penis here and there.
Caryl and I were increasingly nargled,
Stephen and Karen had vanished, the animals were
more and more active angry, would
not let us sleep, slightly fantastic
then beaver-dog bizarre,
a cat covered with nipples, a pumice-faced
zippered pug,
                    so I had to get us out,
we were now in a vast urban morgue
(earlier that day
our pantry began to drip,
snow on the roof produced yellow swellings off
    the upper moulding,
splot tears,   Caryl put out pans).

There are dream blasts that annul both
imagination and memory,
I was carrying Caryl naked blue and stiff,
carrying her like a forward-thrust figurehead torn from its bow,
then we were back at Stephen's, with the beasts—
they increased, no one could handle them,
blind hogs, serpentine chows,
tiny striped carnivores, snake-headed chihuahuas—
as Thomas might have said: it was early it was Adam,
I was scared out of my dream into
an exploding morgue of animal underdream,
we fled again,
                           finding ourselves by
a charred plantation by which
blacks were hunched on benches,
    "we can't help you" they said,
oh they were poorer than we, so
again we turned back, into

a stable aflame with molar loads,
with the lords of animal revenge?
I had no rudder, could not make myself awake
and start a new dream or
simply the Zukofsky codes
("we are going to sleep to sleep")
the quarrel, until I stabbed a hyena, was out of control,
out of ego's bathysphere,
again I awoke, begging to be awake,
Caryl had flung off her comforter,
spread-eagled in tee-shirt,   sleeping soundly.

In Happiness a Power

There is in happiness a power that stems the maggot tide.
And not just dying, but the maggotry men invice in life.

When Caryl's face smiles forth, I think I briefly pass on,
or pass into the chill of passing crossed by permanence.

1999

Some Rock Off Which to Travel

Light from the TV burnishing Caryl's shoulder.
11 P.M., she's on her side, head pillowed,
I'm sitting up, stroking her back,   so the light
purls, or hesitates on her round
then greys into whatever,   I don't know…

I'm entranced by the tenderness I feel,
the almost-far-reach of TV light
furling, it seems, or pearling,
a ridge, a radiance, I'm so dumped in myself
thinking of the Dordogne,   some rock off which to travel…

What is this tenderness that glows right before sleep?
There is something disgusting about it
(a voice says) if not expressed during the day.
It is the eternal brink of lying down to sleep
(another voice) for you might not wake up,
she might not,   something in you says goodbye
every night before you crest—

into what? As if the day has been so active
it takes 11 P.M. to elicit humble love and worry,
sweetness and broken cordage…

                                                        2000

Inside Caryl's Left Shoulder

Gleaming, half-housed in steel sheath, the debrider's rotary blade whirring, resecting scar tissue, flaked-away rotator cuff.

It is inserted via a trocar pushed through the portal cut into her shoulder.

Apparition of a whirly, round eye on the debrider as it swivels caught in the arthroscopic beam.

Octopus or shark eye.

The debrider now a kind of monster in a feeding frenzy.

Blobs of bloody tissue stream the video screen.

Feathery tissue flurries.

The mowing of Caryl's ocean floor.

From another cut that appears to have no trocar the cauterizer appears, spurting bubbly water as it prongs up tissue.

Amber tufts throbbing by threads.

Tentacle-sucker-like bubble chains.

Rose shadings, yellow, bronze, in the white densities.

What happens to her deadened pain?

She's out, but her body's experiencing what I see.

Faced by the ungraspable within my own making.

Again the debrider, a ferret into the baby rat nest of her shoulder, whirring forth what the cauterizer tore up.

Watching this silent 20 minute video as you rest upstairs.

Blood-tinged snow chamber.

Cave amber.

As if I am looking at calcite draperies.

Cosquer being ensouled.

Orchid-like tissue bunches, almost loose, the cauterizer hooking up cartilage.

Threads of blood from her humerus head spurting, snaking out, vanishing.

Humerus head framed by the octagonal lens.

Fleecy white skull.

The moon.

The debrider shaves what looks like skull hair—not head hair but feathery wisps clinging to a skull.

Beautiful grassy white skull.

The debrider mowing and mowing.

For a moment: craters   rilles   ghostly inverted nipples.

The burr with square steel cleats rasping her acromion, trimming its hooked edge that cut into a tendon and caused her such pain.

"Frozen shoulder," which for a month she could not move.

Others will watch arthroscopic surgery inside their beloved's body.

Others will wince and draw close to "heavy debridement and acromio-plasty."

Others will be given access to the body's interior grottos, its blood strings jetting, its moon and cave scapes, the sudden black fissures that check the eye.

Others will project and know how I felt, respectful of projection while attempting to see through to the images forever emerging, as if trying to make contact with us, where projection and something there and emerging meet, as an image is glimpsed in an undulant dimly-lit cave.

Yes, others before me, by juniper wick, watching creatures emerge, re-cede, Cosquer, 18,000 B.P., auks, seals, jellyfish, there and not there, spirits receding, emerging, in ochre outlines, blood-ribboned snow chamber.

Before a screen, outside your invasion, and the source of your invasion.

Alone and with you in this wild disturbance of your sense of physical unity.

Fox-like rotary saw in the hen house of your scar tissue.

Rapacious correction of the destruction of your enjoyment of life.

for Mark Mijnsbergen

2000

Shopping

Crematorial sensation in a department store, thousands of suits and
dresses without bodies, as if it is always Book 11 of *The Odyssey*, we are
surrounded by speechless souls

Souls trying on souls, the hippo-assed white, the mantis-waisted black,
caramel shoulders of a teenager, a pink ankle-length soul for Xmas day

Caryl found some fabulous pants, gold-green alligator quills, loose in
the crotch, baggy in knee, she put them back, fearful no tailor she could
find could alter them perfectly

(In eternity, Henry Miller is a tailor—
lustfully he entered the Cave of the Nymphs,
soon became concerned with the gates of ivory and of horn,
souls arriving, souls departing, all needing a cutting here,
     a mending there—
a drowned soul slithered in, needing resurrectional attention,
old Blake hobbled through,   Henry dusted him off,
     perked up his lapel)

We sashay over to the Santa Center, the old sot in red crumples each
wish, sending a beam of hope into the child heart, I can feel the soot
already in the children's mouths as wishes like elves congregate on their
lips, they sit for a moment on the stony gingerbread knee, this realm of
sweet deception

Dorothea Tanning's female cloth-like forms blow through crumpling
knots of outwinding femininity

Department
     depart   meaning or
Beckmann's *Departure*
costumes awaiting casting off

Redesign yourself, step into this angelic armor

Cuddly music, emptiness made cozy

    "'Exquisite work, madame, exquisite pleats'
vanish into a bloated face, ordering more dresses,
    gouging the wages down,
dissolve into maria, ambrosia, catalina,
    stitching these dresses from dawn to night,
    in blood, in wasting flesh."

Old man in a pea jacket searching for something among women's suits

Recalls my father searching for my mother after she had died, he'd steal
his car keys the Rest Home people had hidden, then drive and drive,
200 miles away one afternoon a housewife found him parked in her
driveway—when she asked him what he was doing there, he told her
he was looking for Gladys

Had he entered an Eleusinian frame, would Gladys have emerged from
the stranger's home in a purple, mushroom-encrusted gown?

—emptiness keeps coming in,
the unfillable sleeves and slacks of life

The terrible animal imprint in perfume departure, the civet cat, the
musk deer, crushed like grapes, displayed in tiny gold vases

I help Caryl shop, holding here coat and scarf, pick out clothes, color
schemes, purples, lavenders, auburns and deep browns, things for her
new silhouette.

Les Trois Frères: Hopping bison-headed man with female figure inside of him.

The Hybrid Is The Engine Of Anima Display   *

The earliest image of the soul appears to be
seated, or resting, within a bison-headed man.
She has an adolescent body, her face is slanted hair lines,
long head hair streams out his hump.
Her thin forearms slope forward ad merge with
his human penis. They share three legs,
two knees lifted, as if dancing behind
the inflated anus of a reindeer which
swerves its aurochs head to gaze at this anima in her crib,
sharing the bison-man's spine,
suggesting Kundalini and that
animal forms were in sync with androgynous churning
while such figures acquired animal familiars.
Out of her forehead a leg-like limb twists, descends.
Comets zoom through it. Bison-man's tail,
same line-weave as her long hair, flaps their legs.
Out of his snout two lines of force extend and bow:
breath? blood? a sound bow
crossing his two held-forth animal-leg arms?
The three-in-one are readable unreadable,
they are, along with the reindeer-aurochs on whose rump
a ghost is perched, of
an unfolding matrix, envisioned at
a moment of initial pleats.
I thought: the sorcerer is a tub in which dead mom is bathing.
Yes, but such a perception is based on recent folds.
At Les Trois Frères, around 14,000 years ago,
the hybrid is the engine of anima display.

Grande Cascade

Out of the mother
urn the now ending
evers churn, they rhyme only
because I am free
here in fatal Gladys light. Let my kneeling
radiate my aging elfin sails.
Inbunched, outerflowered,
I am the hiss in this, the ripple wild
knoll in which my umbilicus sucks stones.
Paradise is part of my inherited billabong,
its stagnation, its warpings, are not my own.
Dionysus, let me not reduce or simplify,
allow me the wavering
miraginality of imagination,
let my fits and bits and catatripe
be venomous to the fake.
The body is a ruthless tribal compression.
Dreaming is less free than imagining,
for the dream factory has a quota:
certain roles are paid less,
someone has always forgotten to
oil the compost crank, the elf who runs
the umbilical bandsaw is always AWOL.
Every perception
enters an imaginal file, buds in arrest
until swayed by a life-shifting rain
or the blight of the news of
an unknown person's death.
For psyche, all bets are on nothing.
A fist slammed against the door
reappears as an eel in mourning.
A turtle who has just taken the veil becomes
the wind-filled sail of a wooden tub
in whose sudsy water one discovers one's genitals,
eggs to be fried on Caravaggio's canvas.
The vague is as crucial as the definitive,

the wave a part of the pier.
Whose genie does not accordion into Fudd and Marilyn,
then rebottle into Lautrec's cognac-
vialed cane? Clouds are brains,
chryselephantine scrolls,
or so the mind registers its Matterhorns
half-waking out of dream, when snow and sneezing
are as relevant as the cut rose
you place in my hand every time you speak.

Riff

Torrid July with its mottled shadow dazzlings,
the center is out there—
the circumference: this daily mail of silk-sack clouds,
clouds like meal drift, moulded over, melted,
sheep flock clouds, worlds of wool,
torn tufts, tossed pillows,
clouds that flaunt forth, chevy on an air-built
    thoroughfare,
                "Parisian Thoroughfare"
paideuma of Hopkins and Powell,
under bop paws the modal floor
"Wreck of the Deutschland"   "Un Poco Loco"
sprung projective verse, sprung bop,
dear tinny piano against
the stadium of the inscape,
    chain mail play gale

—upon what do poets improvise?

A via negativa octopodal in its outreach,
speech fiber sled
dragged by Hades' huskies toward auroral rage,
the rage to in rising not lose infernal coals,
improvisational aurora,
to live in a rarified gondola,
to be fully touched,
to feel the summer extend through   yes, Kosovo,
rape-body poisoned wells
rewiring Hopkins' windpuff bonnets.

Morphologies of Paradise

> "I soil the paper to prepare it
> for hallucinations. I reverse the
> day's attempt to assassinate me."
>
> —Matta

Shamanic jimson in everyone, the human Xibalba
a cosmogonic patch where twisting language retwists,
metaphorizing at the speed of dream, touching
the opaque shoulders of smoking trees, lighting
campfires in the backs of gigantic caterpillars.
This perception of paradise, first apprehended in
the Upper Paleolithic, I experience asleep,
via dreaming. Paradise is close, so close as to be
maddening. Paradise is in our brains.

What Blake calls Albion is this ancient creative zone.
The Fall is not original sin,
the Fall is that abyss between here and original imagination,
which we inherit as shamanic longing.

As one attempts to cross an abyss, metaphors
transmogrify so quickly
the initiate's receiver jams, loses its bearing,
deconstructs, like those divers
making their way through the 500 foot
waterfilled tunnel leading to the Cosquer cave—
the silty kicked-up sediment blinded them,
they lost their way among submerged stalagmites,
    drowned.

In the 1940s, the 20th century broke in two.
A revised version of hybrid man
—Auschwitz and Lascaux in the same brain—
complexed its obsession with "homeland."
Fueled with primal glory and Zyklon B, it sings:
"I'm always trying to get back

to my little caul shack on Ancestor Delta.
If somebody else—Kosovar, Arab, or Jew—
    happens to be there,
I'll claim *he is air,* and plant my fangs
    in his 'absence.'"

I sat down on the steps of The Ivory Tower and wept. The American's Guatemalan husband had not only been kidnapped but tortured and murdered. She doesn't know but knows, her 11 year old son is nearly cross-eyed with knowing, and I know, sitting on the bed edge, before PBS 12. Trying to gag her terror and grief, so as to be able to carry on with the interview, she finally pulls her blouse up over her face—as if to teach me another dimension of "the faceless woman" said to crouch on a bridge below the roots of the World Tree. I dream of lifting up this head and assessing its weight, knowing full well it is impossible to weigh the unending assault on women's bodies and personalities by the guardian husbands and brothers.

"Be forever dead in Eurydice."
Be forever reborn in Persephone.
A run runs through the morphologies of paradise.
Boogie-woogie of our diagrammatic sentence:
death and the possibility of redemption in
a single act.

For 1500 years, Eleusis, spiritual homeland of the Greeks. What *did* initiates behold—which they were sworn on the penalty of death to not reveal—in the Telesterion?

    1] An ear of corn reaped in silence?
    2] A cereal wafer, the seed-*kore*, which they ate?
    3] The Divine Child, or Savior, variously named Brimus,
        Dionysus, Triptolemos, Iasion, or Elenthereros the
        Liberator, laid in a manger (or winnowing basket),
        whose flesh was eaten by the initiates in the form of
        bread, made from the first or last sheaves?
    4] An artificial vagina, kept in the *cysta mystica,* which
        they touched?

5] An omphalos, or birth cone, representing the cervix,
   with fruits and flowers, and a child emerging from a
   horn of plenty?
6] The spirit of Persephone herself, returned from the dead
   with her new-born son, conceived in the land of death?

Whatever they beheld—since it was said to bestow happiness, the true
life, freedom, respite from all troubles—must have confirmed to them:
after they entered the earth they would rise again.

And who knows as well what the sacred king saw
the instant the goddess veil was lifted—
an afterlife? The origin of life? A scowl-vale of eternal grey?
Ah, dear tricky veil, you make us think, quest,
you are the rent/unrent conundrum
provoking our initiational probes to translate
the plutocracy of the literal.
Not to life or rend, but to translate the veil.
The head of Hercules must be veiled
for the god, via omenta symbolics, to be reborn.
Yet we know that rebirth too
   is a halfway house.
                No one has been to death
and returned to say: Emily is there, following her fly,
or, Artaud is happy, he has learned to bowl,
or, Pinochet is a 60 jab-a-second forked barbecue.
Dear veil,   speak to us of your fiber origin!

"We, the Mothers of Lascaux, extracted
fibers from celestial plants, located
the entheogens, set undulating
broken lines as coiling winds, winding torrents.
Channels of moisture circulated in our mouths
imbuing thread-like fibers with helicoid strength.
By opening/closing our jaws, working
our entire faces, while breathing, we formed sound
   strands,   speech lattices,
what you call the revealed Word, the veil word—

thus to lift the veil is an act we Mothers disavow.
To lift the veil would be to see the earth
naked, speechless, as on the first day,
amidst the chaos of origin, fiberless spirit,
      the not we knotted."

AN ALCHEMIST WITH ONE EYE ON FIRE
(2006)

Nocturnal Veils

In bed, looking up at the light-peppered dark,
as if the ceiling were not there, as if I were staring into
my own staring. Tinctured absence. A grassy sweet aroma
   lifting off Caryl.
                 In the zone between
here and not here, the lunar curtain parts,
as in a Matta painting, there are tilting astro-planes,
each a kind of ark, or flight deck,
one covered with snow has standing mammoths—it tilts,
slides through a plane crawling with reptiles.
I think of my brain with its reptile stem, its mammal hood,
I see a bear humping a crocodile,
try to get between them, to push them apart, open a space for a nas-
   cent self.
In the zone between bear and crocodile, what will I be?
A bear-headed croco-boy? A croc-headed baby bear?
I screw off my head, toss it into the dark
—will it become a raven? A large bee?
Headless, I watch through my chest the air swarming with spirits,
Nora! How is it where you are?
"Busy. Bodies rushing in and out, did you know Cheney is full of rep-
   tile blood,
and driven by the mind of an Incan child abandoned on a mountain
300 years ago? A child spitting up
lizard blood, freezing to death in a stone shrine,
now can you grasp Cheney's infantile wrath?
Bush's secret is his tiny tail, leathery, about 3 inches,
like the tip of a Komodo Dragon's tail—
note how he is always heavily guarded from behind,
for if some joker pulls his tail, a long yellow forked tongue will spurt
   from his face—
very few humans are pure human, most are occupied by
bizarre creature combines, the dead and the extinct pack the air

unseen from a senses-five perspective.
I have a horse's cock now, and I'm planning on using it soon,
I'm going to fuck one of those dead art dealers
who "fucked" me, then help her open a gate to your plane,
watch the fun as she gives birth in a few brains to some mustang
    raillery!"

She screamed with laughter—then I heard a strong, central suck,
something in the dark had gulped her back.

The pepper-dotted room began to undulate.
I thought of the veils within "No one has lifted her veil,"
    revelation, to draw back the *velum*,
to hear dead Nora through a spiritual gate,
to see the Dogon earth naked and speechless,
without language, a fiber skirt the first word,
speech as plaited fiber, "speech lattice,"
or Christ nailed on the cross as the arrested word,
vulva as lower mouth issuing red fiber,
a many-colored Isis rainbow, net within which
my fate is entangled, where the Nora spirits can be heard.

Then I saw a black-capped facial netted "full body veil"
sitting, as if on the Kabul bridge, begging.
"No one has lifted her veil" became
"At no time have women not been oppressed."
My heart tore left and right, I tried to peel
the true from the truthful, the rainbow flashed
a central scarlet band—I knew it was the Wawilak Sisters' menstrual
    blood
circulating within rock python venom.
I saw ripples of albino babies, each with a red or silver balloon,
setting off across the rainbow bridge for
the argentine body of the moon—

the Kabul bridge beggar roared back,
burkha, menstrual never shed,
chrysalis of a monstrous anti-metamorphosis
"sewed up in a hammock, with a small opening so she can breathe"
—are all of us, enclosed in the world of five senses, mummified
   pupas?
The beggar hissed: "Your bars, spaced and wall-papered, allow some
   comfort and expanse.
Mine, wrapped around me, nearly cover my eyes…"

I turned and sought sleep's stagnation,
respite from the sear of intersecting planes.

2004

Pause   *

I hear you close the bathroom door.

An absence-weighted balance lifts into presence.

Is the source of human bondage the fear of loss?

Now that you are showering, cables of water convert, ghost-loaded
    suds, Rabelais's mane furls from Aphrodite's thigh…

The patter of my tattered tale, swirled drain. Rising like a sewer of
    precognition: Is the real death the death I am preoccupied with
    here and now?

The sound of drying, the clay in the cloth, the veil that will rend me
    before I reach the end.

To pull out the last part of myself left inside, to get all of myself born.

Irish Jig

[AT A CONCERT BY MILLISH]

Nanosounds,
interior stellar
zoom,
    zoas of
the poetic art,
ecstasy enstacy of
the gyrosonic
   body.

    How I dig it, in fact,
I am a digger wasp on Tyler Duncan's hand, watching him swingle
sound flax out of bagpiped hip,
I enter the wasp nest sound swirl,
merry lines limbically entwine (first parents with long, dragon-
   coiling tails):

spicy early thriller, a sly
pricey thrill, reply as icy thriller, really
tip her lyrics, rip rectally sly heir, rectally
reply Irish, rarely hysteric pill, really
rich piles try, layers prey till rich, rich till
slayer prey, arty lisper rich yell, yell arty
rich perils, lechery rarity pills, thrill
creepy lay sir, slyly retire rich pal, icy
thriller replays, a silly triple cherry, irately
cherry spill, pretty ill slithery arc, prey
later silly rich, prey alter rich silly,
slyly rich April tree.

Jig, dyadic Kundalini
   "Caryl Phyllis Reiter"
anagrammatic manger.

Before I was Clayton, I was clan toy, lacy ton, ant cloy,
  any colt,
Rounding thrill icy corners, my face accordion unfolds,
  what twins are spotted
in its pleats! Tunnels of Tezcatlipóca turning plumed—
  archaic sounds,
a maze of reeds, each repeat sprouts new flutings—
  so dart in, retract,
pivot to reoccur. The obstetrical toad is
gigging in his fertilized skirt.
           Fetal propellers are
turning left, strengthening
  energies into a heart.

An Enigmatic Signifer   *

My mother is no longer making sense.
She called last dream, garbled and hung up.
At 67, I have passed where her eternity is clear. She who did not
possess the code, encoded me.
What I am missing is encoded in her mice.

When I was hungry, daddy would hold
my kitty mamma up by her front paws.
In her black furry belly there were mouse heads,
one of which I would take
between my hands and put its nose into my mouth.
As I filled up, I saw blue butterflies,
green buds. Around what kind of Eden
did I have my mouth?

One day when kitty mamma did not come,
I cried, and daddy brought out mother.
Had he hid kitty mamma? Mother
had no mouse, mother had
Carnation milk, Kepler cod-liver-oil.
Mother daddy would poke at me and laugh:
"does the cat have your tongue?"

What were mice doing
in kitty mamma's body? Were they
trying to emerge? What else was trying
to emerge? What had I
emerged from?

"Tell us how a star goes." Twinkle tinkle twinkle.
"Tell us how a dog." Wow-wow.
Dite   (light)
Chur   (picture)
Dad-da car.
  Her exhausted face
  urging out words.

Suck thumb suck thumb no tinkle suck thumb.
Night and day you are a thumb
in the roaring traffic glare
amongst the pillows of my tiny lair
I suck thumb. Then they tied a thumb-stall on.
Stating *Bok old Mamma*
       Tak-a new Mamma very loud,
I showed my kitty mamma mouse fanged
farce-fed mouth to the world.

Samperi's Diagram   *

The paradise of the Frank Samperi diagram,
showing poets how to get through. Can you believe it,
I said to Carol Bergé, on the sofa beside me,
she was twisting her hands in something on her lap,
"I am unsure." So I investigated,
spotting the black horse head areas in what looked like
a complex airport diagram, with lights on, on a vast wall,
Samperi appeared, more healthy than in life,
"The horse head areas are disaster spots,
you have to figure out how to move around them,"
or did he say "through them?"
                                      Now in Samperi's realm,
on his road, or via, I struggled with bales,
saw marvelous living rocks, emerald things speaking to me?
I was in "everything is alive,"
"all is in constant transformation," then I thought of Caryl,
made it back to our bedroom where hunched Samperi figures were by
     her bed, backs to me,
I saw one slithering under the springs,
I threw them away—monks? demons? Samperi outriders?
and immediately wanted to pursue was it Samperi's *Jumanji?*
Not sure, never sure, always on this wavering transcendental road,
     plagued with the iridescent,
where hollows are owls, thrown instantly-sprouting reeds,
reeking with meat, and the meat spills its lore, whore-angels pour,
to reveal the beast in harbor, the hail-spurting storm
     is a chrysanthemum-radiant isle. Then Frank reappeared—
I told him: I'm so blocked by transformation, plus
your henchmen passing rods through Caryl…
"Here," Frank said, "work with these…"
He spilled some black pebbles which I scooped, swam with,
tossing them before me as I pulsed,
I ran the Samperi road, miles racing under me,
toppled herms, Frank's life and death, I saw the mother he told me
     was a prostitute,
her hair streaming lizards, she wept little Franks who I kissed,

hedges, towers, a rain of moles, a goblet passed or was passed to me,
I watched the shrimp dancing twitch, then drank,
my infancy became a pile of tiny pearls, "what to do" became a lot of
    tools,
my newspaper route, I was at 49th and Boulevard Place,
freezing, as the truck dumped the Indianapolis Times,
I tore open the moor, to find the under-sage, twiggy trails led me
    back,
flying Samperi's diagrammatic sentence, I heard
"You've joined the diagram…"
                                                    Was that Bergé?
"Oh it is wonderful," she said, as I plopped down beside her,
"wonderful when vision works at the speed of mind."
Then I saw her chipmunk, I mean her baby anaconda, and broke
    down in tears:
only parts of the dream could be recovered here, and is this vision?
I have remembered, invented, remember-invented,
I was in paradise how long?
I cannot recall its caul, or its multifoliate delivery—
cannot here recreate the dream's sensual matrix.
This is the real Fall, the divisional void.
Then to awake, face the clock, the media headlock,
what a wrench, fellow man, what a wacky disorienting brainswipe,
the zero time of paradise chopped up into space.

For Gustaf Sobin   *

Radiating in my shroud
I governed my matrix
wandering Egyptian *anima mundi,*
sensing in these parent powers
a deeper larval plait.

What was it to see then?
As if with water halfway up one's eyes,
a shimmering miraginality,
breathed blood, non-bioquestioned breath,
walking in carrion-coifed time.

A dimpled slug with rabbit ears.
Equilibrium: cone-shaped loaf, vase of water.
Fecal rainbow undulating through an alabaster jar.
Light entombed in gneiss.
Carnelian amulet. Stromatolithic haystack.

Like you, Gustaf, I've risked wordwreck to excavate
a buried mouth, to release its stumped
root whirl.
                    Every crocodilian kiss
stimulates the soul gown, the veiled animal heads
strutting through our combines.
Stare hard into the atmosphere,   .
Little Red Riding Hood is there as a rose-colored wolf,
or as an ashen wet-suit
in which, through the smoke hole of the mind,
we shimmy down
our skullracked, sand-blasted
psychic backbone.

Transformational Gradations

My innate Indiana tendency is
to tiptoe on a razorblade
and to feel the Presbyterian tingle
masochistically up my spine.

Poetry has been to compel the razored toe tip blade
to hybridize,
to allow an underworld
uprush to fruit through the root twine.

So, who is here at 6 A.M. this morning?

Persephone, kneeling on a pomegranate half,
Eros seated on her shoulder.
I read their hand signs to mean: "Flow! Conceive!
The scission of the Mother into mother and daughter
is to be found in the abyss of the seed!"

I stooped to inspect the Dionysian upsurge
spreading octopodally through my brain.
I sensed the lost half of myself: my dog, when I was 12,
car-smashed Sparkie, who gave birth to the vine.

Then, in the spectral interior of a cypress, I saw Rilke,
in his death bed, a blackened strawberry,
attended by a kindly bedbug nurse,
his marmalade-soft face still poised in praise—

as the smoking gate moved into presence,
Rainer exchanged verse letters with an 18-year-old Austrian,
Erika Mitterer.
Persephone's verdure and her duration
were now layered into all his transformational gradations.
Not "Here Lies," he wrote,
but "Here Lives," happy to feel the soil

pulse his soot shaft, that cypress affirmation,
overplus of arising
with which the beloved gleams up.

Bellagio, 4 November 2004

From a Terrace

"We have destroyed Fallujah
so as to convert it"
overheard in the breeze by the massive broken oak.

Sunday lakeside serenity.
People with their skin burned off, hospitals bombed by
an us I bleed in
psychically, my government
completely corrupt.

To be sixty-nine now, "old style"
shot through with fecal sorrow,
bedbugs in my mouth, us-bugs, my whole mouth bugged.

The oak leans into blue rapture
over roily, white-capped
gasoline-turquoise water,
its leaves sort of dribble about in the air.

The carnage cloaked by
television's visibility sterility
—is this less sterile?

Small lichen saucers indented into
hundred year old bark,
noble whorled
        wood showing
through, as I would like to.

This asunder-written No to
the interventional might of America,
millions raked into invisible piles,
the 9/11 blowback a drop
in the bucket blood of
Guatemala
Nicaragua

Serbia
Iraq
How terrible
to not feel pure
grief for the
WTC dead, how
terrible to have to
contextualize to be honest.

Across Lake Como
mountains rest on the waterfold,
slant shadowed rows. They are
mammoth heads with verdant folded eyes,
beautiful, meaningless
                              in
an extinction-tinctured view.

Man driven by hate for what he is,
a lost puppy bowl
mother-licked, father-interfered.

—O breathe and just
enjoy the warmth on writing hand,
the church bell tower below,
its innocent stone crossed by
ravens in the shape of men

        —I can't
        I twist here
mentally gibbeted,
particle of a warrior form,
hell done in my nationality,

the Ho- Ho-
san
ta
cackle-embedded warp in being.

Some axial release holds sway
in the after-
ring of a re-
    immobilizing bell.

Bellagio, 14 November 2004

Iraqi Morgue

Blackened semi-smile
  eyelidlifted   turned

rust fur Can't get a
fix on

mangled slab of splintered bone,
stringy red muscles.

Armpit trying to raise
mouth milk,
                eyes
staring at something great.

Eyes like headlights still on
in twisted steel.

0070 64 F 04 is sad,
he's looking up to the right
cheeks bulging.

Some are camouflaged, it seems,
with death labels &
plastic label bags
    —ears show,
  a tooth rip.

Black skin rubble
no eyes upper teeth
        in death lisp.

Faceless, no, burned to
  a congealed
insectile smear.

Shattered lit
skull rubble through which
one eye blasts.

Maroon head skin
tucked up about its bag shoulder
as if asleep.

What am I looking at?
At horror looking through
an 1899 update:
after the lynch picnic,
the knuckles of Sam Hose displayed
in the window of an Atlanta grocery.

340 04 V 04
nearly all blood.

   Very old man gray
turned head cupped
in death sheet blossom.

Minor Drag

[FOR IAN IRVINE, IN AUSTRALIA]

The body piles at Abu Ghraib,
apple-stacked asses like a gigantic Sadean sexual molecule
male all the way through,
the Caucasian subconscious unleashed on the brown body.

I walk Washtenaw Road,
a pupa in a Hydra-tainted imperial chrysalis.

Controlled demolition of the three Towers.
Controlled demolition of our Constitution.
Controlled demolition of our rights.
Controlled demolition of our environment.
Controlled demolition of our ice.

The missile that penetrated the Pentagon:
The Entry not of Christ
but Pat Robertson into Washington.

It is *Alien* o'clock.
When will the truth explode from Bush's chest?

Unbuckled Tongue

The Last Supper as a watermelon feast,
each disciple with a tequila-plugged slice
and Jesus already with Isis in his eyes,
be slurped be slain—
to travel as a seed within another's imagination,
arked with lithic freight.

The lunar light dims,
the stone softens. Are we still in
a pagan/Nazarene distillery?
Si, Hart Crane murmurs, from his trench off Tampico,
the stable is a flowchart of Jesus and bison exchange,
yet all takes place in an amphitheater
carved from the rudiments of shamanic protocol.
I hear it in the postponed Ann Arbor sky
as pre-emptive jets pop time.
So it's bolgia within bolgia, a new Comedy—
cosmic structure no longer vortices and trinity,
rather: animating socks, suspenders, a laundry
bag of the mind. Fascism would rinse all to
techno-sheen. CEOS living in platinum grenades
littering planetary shanty-towns.

Note where your first line has taken you,
how each image appears to encyst another,
so that the poem is a mental cave under formation,
the political as the grit in the image water push,
anatomies reconstituting as thresholds,
chalice-shaped cul-de-sacs, the mind anchored and
willy-nilly. Stay aware of the 850 million starving—
such may help keep you honest when the self-censor
purrs: shut up. Unbuckle his tongue from
the door on your heart, show the world gash
but keep it in your own veins.

Like pinheads in a sunny glade,
JC and his gang are now in round dance,
watched by cranes. Dionysus is near
but so is Ashcroft, while Mother Teresa
cuddles a gigantic gangrenous ear.
Carnival is hardly farewell to the flesh.
In imaginal revision, it is the lambent stampede of
autumn's rash, or Persephone rampant in
the gray November grass. It is the discharge
as the teeth of consciousness sink into
the etymology of gum
releasing depth charges into the mind's ancient hives. Manifesto:
I am here like a scarab rolling my crottin through
death's doorway ablaze with billions of golden grubs.
This is the trail I leave,
my wobble weave, analphabetic Lascaux.

                                                        2005

Surveillant Veils

For Andrew Joron

I reached through art to touch ensouled stone,
a once
fully-embraced ever
now ensouled in never.

Organically, I am encased in never.
Creatively, I neverize
to reconstitute ever.

All the elements of this wall,
according to George Oppen, have come
from eternity.

Why, when I look at that thought, do I see
a Malawi prison floor covered with
bedraggled men,

or recall
the sorrow charged and twisted face of an Iraqi
clawing at her 9-year-old son's tiny coffin?

It is good that her ululation
makes me ashamed of my own fulfillment,

good too that first light can still be imagined,
suppurant as it is
with the wounds in that child's box.

There is rage in the body's sequences—

cancer cells, immortalizing, divide
until they kill their host.

Eternity is pregnant with
the mortal tern.

2006

Combined Object   *

Listening to Caryl sleep,
thinking of the cross-hatching in the 7-mile verticality of her living
as her mind makes its way across the 40,000-mile mid-ocean ridge,
across abyssal plains and canyons in tree-shaped networks,
her young life, which she remembers so keenly,
like a die tumbling among arabesques of leafy sea dragons trailing
kelp blends, green clouds pouring
from the sides of wounded fish, millions of image trains—
I am on one, looking down at the stratified carriers below,
one called Venus's-flower-basket, the passengers:
shrimp, crabs, worms, and clams. Multiple water spindles containing
water fairy proms, high school friends being reborn,
I am following the course of her sleep
through sea pastures of whirring diamond saws,
she carries away with her, in her trailing skirts,
a web filled with tiny men, radiolarian ooze,
at 800 feet, only the deepest, blackest blue,
the ocean of her sleep breaks over me, light gravel,
sensation of being in a horse's mouth, a deeper breathing is forming—
the infinite, far from being a suburb of the gods, is an eternal
surpassing, removed from any essential halt.
I see her standing before a glass stairway, a Jacob's ladder
with more steps than she could ever climb in three lifetimes,
they disappear like bubbles in champagne,
now she is struggling against
suctions and pulls, against stretched webs,
she breaks free—what nightmare did she just slip?—
she becomes navigation itself, shining with a pure white flame,
passing over foaming ditches, wheeling ravines,
I imagine her retinue: dwarf plankton, flamingo tongues,
coccoliths giving the water a milk glow, bristlefoooted worms
patterned with colored rosettes, salmon-pink winged slugs,
salps like little barrels, pulsating, a mouth at each end.
How do we do without a head? How present all edges of the body
equally to the outside world? A poem without subject,

all parts of which surprise and interlock, a poem with twenty centers,
all muscular and avid, each word dense, full in itself, a nest,
a sound of wood crackling in the fireplace, monkey words
feeling the earthquake coming before I do.
Going through myself,   is it her heart that I am hearing?
—she gasps—silence—rebreathes ka ka ka ka
suddenly she is other than herself,
rake tines rise from her brow projecting brain energy into the
      atmosphere,
impaling celestial hexes, they glow pale blue in the dark
like thin upraised arms; I pass slowly through them,
standing in my Protestant canoe, alone, stiff, an erection curving
from a golden pubic beard—behind my back:
the Absolute, straight as a wall.
I am possessed by a sole idea: that snow is ceaselessly falling
obliquely through all of us, on each flake
the population of the Beyond cluster
like minute beardless seals, or albino cougars,
spherical, knots of unearthly calm… As my monoxylon
sinks slowly into dead space, the dark is flecked with one-winged
      birds,
barkless trees, and now I see the full squalor of the sea,
the rubbish of a thousand boats daily fished up, winnowed,
and thrown straight back—crushed into the netted haul
the new mermaid, limbs twisted among dogfish, whiting and plaice,
a deflated life-sized sex doll, hermit-crabs inside her
red-rimmed mouth. O sea layered into my dreams,
the daily rewound trash, visitations of the dead, Tenochtitlan
thoroughfares, extra-terrestrial spider queens,
cork-screwing flights through kaleidoscopic barriers—
to land by a nightstand and be watched by
two swans,   who are being watched by
two ocelots,   who are being watched by two snakes,   watched by
sixteen triangles,   watched by countless staring eyes.
Cessation of the mirage of the finite—
call it re-embarkation, call it a multiple leaving.
I have for shade a whole spread of hyena shadow,

I am my own ground, slashed, a wild sea of ground.
There is a silent breaking of waves, spots of light, sensation of
    fissure,
a flowing furrow, I see Caryl gliding through
the little curlicues in its flanks,
and when I graze her I graze a deep pit of joy.

ARCHAIC DESIGN (2007)

The Assault   *

INTRODUCTION

My initial response to the 9/11 assaults, as a citizen reader/investigator, was to start making myself more aware of what we might have done to others, beyond our borders, to instigate such an action. I read William Blum's Killing Hope, *and then his* Rogue State. *Learning of Bush's bizarre immediate response to the attacks on the World Trade Center, I also began to learn more about him by reading Mark Crispin Miller's* The Bush Dyslexicon. *Then Gore Vidal in an* Observer *article alerted me to the possibility that the official version of what happened on 9/11 was bogus. I read Nafeeze Mosaddeq Ahmed's* The War on Freedom *and checked his information against Paul Thompson's* The Complete 9/11 Time Line. *I have not found any official response that contradicts Ahmed or Thompson. The compressed time line data in the first part of my piece is mainly taken from Ahmed's book. The lyric outrage in part two is all my own (other than when factual), and participates in the tradition of the* sirventes; *Robert Duncan's poem, "Uprising," which condemns President Johnson for the carpet-bombing of Vietnam, hovers over "The Assault," a predecessor ghost.*

I sent my piece to The Nation, *a weekly whose politics I respect. I sent it to the editor, Katrina Vanden Heuvel; she wrote back that* The Nation *had covered all the points my poem raised. Since I read* The Nation *weekly, I knew this was not true. In fact,* The Nation, *to my knowledge, had not published a single article disputing the official version of 9/11. So I wrote Vanden Heuvel back, asking her to point out to me where my information had been discussed. Her response was to ask me not to write to her anymore. So I sent "The Assault" to Lewis Lapham at* Harper's Magazine. *Lapham wrote me that it was an interesting imitation of Archibald MacLeish and e.e. cummings but not for them. The poem was ultimately published on the Pos-*sum Pouch *website, in* Hambone *magazine, and in French translation by Auxeméry in* Momentum (Paris).

In the past several years, additional information contesting the "official" story about 9/11 has come to light. Much of this information is summed up by David Ray Griffin in The New Pearl Harbor *and by Eric Hufschmid in* Painful Questions: An Analysis of the September 11th Attack. *The most pertinent new information discussed in both of these books concerns the sudden, rapid, and total collapse of the towers (and Building 7), and the nature of the penetration of the Pentagon. Cobbled together roughly a year after 9/11, my poem will no longer be news to those readers who have reflected on any of the materials I mention above. However, especially in light of the 9/11 Commission's failure to thoroughly investigate the disaster, I have decided to let this piece stand as it is, as the testimony of a poet's immediate investigation of and response to the event that remains the basis for the invasions of Afghanistan and Iraq.*

I

Mid-July 2001: The U.S. government—having decided that the Taliban regime was too unstable and too hostile to serve as a vehicle for U.S. entry into Central Asia—had planned on an Afghanistan invasion for October.

National support for such an invasion depended upon a widely perceived direct threat. Now known "enemy attacks" used to whip up and mobilize people for war include the US Battleship Maine, the Lusitania, Pearl Harbor, Tonkin Bay. Our atomic bombing of Hiroshima and Nagasaki: the beginning of the Cold War.

September 10: Bin Laden was in Rawalpindi, Pakistan, courtesy of the ISI, for kidney dialysis (in July he met with the local CIA agent in Dubai; no attempt was made to arrest him).

September 6–10: United and American Airlines stock shares were massively sold short, as were shares at Morgan Stanley Dean Witter (occupying twenty-two World Trade Center floors) and Merrill Lynch (headquarters near the WTC). Insiders with advance knowledge of an approaching national catastrophe are believed to have made over fifteen million dollars. If they knew, would you tell me that Bush, the Secret Service, the Air Force, and the Pentagon did not know?

(The alleged lead hijacker Mohammed Atta, with an expired 2000 tourist visa, re-entered the United States three times in 2001 for flying lessons—for which he lacked the required M-1 work visa—while under FBI surveillance for stockpiling bomb making materials.)

August 2001: The FBI was informed that Zacarias Moussaoui was linked by French intelligence to Bin Laden (top FBI officials blocked field agents' requests to search Zacarias's computer).

August 2001: Attorney David Schippers was approached by FBI agents and given the names of the hijackers, their targets, proposed dates, and the sources of their funding. He tried to contact John Ashcroft who did not return his calls. Schippers' informants were pulled off their investigation and threatened with prosecution if they went public (Schippers is now representing one FBI agent in a suit against the U.S. government in an attempt to subpoena its testimony, so he can legally speak about the blocked investigation on public record).

Standard Operating Procedures (SOP) requires fighter jets to scramble and intercept under emergency conditions. No approval from the White House was ever required (when Payne Stuart's Learjet pilot failed to respond to the air controller at 9:33, twenty-one minutes later an F-16 traveling at 1500 mph reached the Learjet at 46,000 feet).

On September 11, Flight #11 was clearly way off course by 8:20 a.m. SOP calls for immediate notification and response.

North American Aerospace Defense Command (NORAD) was not informed of an emergency by Boston air traffic control until 8:38.

Initially, according to former NORAD Commander, General Richard Meyers, no jets were scrambled until after Flight #77 struck the Pentagon at 9:40 (one hour and twenty minutes after Flight #77 was suspected of being hijacked).

Within days, this story changed: at 8:44, we were told, two F-15s were scrambled at Otis (Cape Cod), 190 miles from Manhattan. If these jets flew at top speed (1850 mph) they would have reached the towers in six minutes. But at 9:03, when Flight #175 struck the South Tower, the Otis jets were unexplainably still seventy miles from Manhattan (and why sent from Otis? McGuire, a major, active facility in New Jersey, is seventy-one miles from the WTC. Arrival time: three minutes. No planes were scrambled from McGuire).

The apparent shut down of SOP on Flight #77 is even more sinister: known to be hijacked by 8:50 (at which time it was also known that #11 and #175 were hijacked, *meaning a national emergency was at hand*) NORAD was not notified until 9:24—and after NORAD was notified, jets were scrambled from Langley (130 miles from Washington, DC) instead of from Andrews (ten miles away), with two combat-ready squadrons (the Langley jets arrived fifteen minutes after the Pentagon was plowed into).

9:16 a.m.: NORAD was informed that Flight #93 had been hijacked (at which time it was known that three other flights had been hijacked and that two had already blown up their targets). *No jets were scrambled to intercept #93.*

No one has been charged with incompetence.

After both towers had been struck, President Bush, in Sarasota, visiting a grade school, was informed. He continued to listen to children read to him for seven minutes before informing Americans of what they already knew.

Myers, at the Capitol, was chatting (about "terrorism") with Senator Max Cleland. They saw a TV report that a plane had hit the WTC. "We thought it was a small plane or something like that," Myers said. So the two men went ahead with the office call. Meanwhile, the second tower was hit. "Nobody informed us of that," Myers said. After the Pentagon was struck (seventy-five percent of the assault now successfully completed), a cell phone was handed to him; finally the Chairman of the Joint Chief of Staffs is informed!

According to Assistant Secretary of Defense Victoria Clarke: "Donald Rumsfeld stayed in his office until the Pentagon was hit, with the excuse that he had some phone calls to make."

II

A composite vision: our callow, illiterate, Supreme Court-appointed
Fool, drifting in photo-op with school children,
Myers discussing "terrorism" with Cleland,
Rumsfeld, in effect, hiding in his office,
    while flames
drink debris-blocked staircased bodies.

    My head shudders with
    the mortification of sensing Bush in my own eyes.
Yes, for I do not see myself outside of the male coagulate.
Part of me is a lazar born of mass guilt,
funhouse horticulture, where the decency facets
    I've struggled to file ripple with
    "Full Spectrum Dominance"

    Out the window, in weak autumnal green:
    tent caterpillar encampments, opaque, milky, creating,
as if under camouflage, deadly screens—I envision elected American
    presidents in the democracy-subverted host tree:
        Bush, Jr. entangled with pa
crawling Nixon's raging animus, Nobel Carter
    mottled with Khmer Rouge horror,   Johnson cloaked in
"We seek no wider war," whipping out his dick to reporters, declaring,
    "This is why we're in Vietnam!"
Reagan as a goggle-wearing grub, chirping:
"Contras are the moral equivalent of our Founding Fathers."
Nest camps where baby Pinochets bud   (Nobel Kissinger
on his knees gripping the altar-bowl, vomiting up a stomach hash of
    millions—
    suddenly his ghost stands up through him,
    called to lead the 9/11 investigation!)

The nests enweb electronically through the American mind.
Whitman's visionary "eternal present" has become the language of
    TV, transfixing the audience in a memory-less now.

I'm taken in, as are you, fellow citizens, failing instantly to recall
   background particularities.
A week later, I come to, recalling, while reading, details I should have
   brought to bear.
The mainstream media cartel beams its needles out of the screens,
   who is not injected, anesthetized by conversion-spiked patriotic
   aura?

Like a depth charge dropped into 9/11: Fifty years of Cold War mobi-
   lization against the Soviet Union has left the country with "a boil-
   ing residue of paranoid anxiety."

Greed become a crazed intoxication to re-determine history.
If the Bush family become trillionaires, might they, led by angels, slip
   into eternity, skipping over death?

Jackknifed bodies plummeting against the photo-serenity of a tower.
Not Crane's bedlamite, but a secretary
      exploding
      in blue September sky.

Living in America right now is like being on a revised Flight #11.
The nave of this self-righteous citadel extends for miles—
in section after section: our cluster-bombed Yugoslavians, jerking
      nerve-gassed Laotians, napalmed Vietnamese girls, our chopped-
      apart Guatemalans, mowed-down East Timorese
and there's Sharon, in high heels, tightening the thumb-screws on
      Palestinian immiseration—and below? Right here?
Bush is in my gas,   Cheney's in my steering wheel,   Ashcroft
         under our bed!

Should 9/11 be seen as a 3000 body count down payment on a
      Turkmenistan–Afghanistan–Pakistani UNOCAL oil pipeline?

3000 dead? More like 8000—
for this figure must include the Afghanistan dead bombed in retribu-
      tion for what? Nothing they did but inhabit land we
   —and here "we" partitions my heart—seek to exploit.

The unutterable humiliation of 9/11!
Holocaust of firemen to make millionaires billionaires!
Workers, executives, of the capitalist epicenter—
but much more importantly: beloved citizens who went to work that
    day
(overhearing me, bored Bush turns aside:
"Adolf, let's go fishin.")

In our hearts we know
In our hearts we do not know

Baby Bush now spectre-entangled in the entrails of the nation.

[November–December, 2002]

RECIPROCAL DISTILLATIONS (2007)

Witchery   *

Realm of co-penetration, grotesque, affirmative,
I offer you what grows from my chest
in tumor-splendor, gnarled, polished, wet.

I protect you will all my navel blades,
my nipple nails, my kidney mirror—
dead mirror in which cloud fungus is trapped.

Steel pins puncture my thigh, belly and throat—
they enable me to pray with torturous force.

Mask reabsorbing the lost particulars of being,
mask replacing the bald human face with wilderness eyes,
mask sharing veins with its plant juice doubles,
mask whose interstices swarm with pupa.

If, over my tall blue pearled neck, I stare in terror, it is because
foxes have gotten inside me,
foxes are tearing apart my death.

Pitch-black head breaking out in red currants, in spikes, in blisters,
head a field sprouting buds, pebbles, studs,
head issuing a living waving horn,
head asleep, head replete, head whose dream matrix pustulates
the prayer of all things: to emerge, at once.

> [Based on figures in
> the Dapper Museum of African Art,
> Paris]

Chauvet, Left Wall of End Chamber *

The contours of certain cave walls invite engagement.
Hosts in the wall, bald, convex,
hold vigil over mental drift. To populate
the moonscape of a wall. To draw in lit craters
the squirm and reel of incarnate trial.
Their bellies hang low, their shoulders
rise and sink like pistons, each step is placed
soundlessly. *Panthera spelea.* Larger than
the African lion. Larger even
than the Amur tiger. Maneless. Craning forward.
Cheeks bulging. Heads telescoping out of heads.
Eyes dilated. Knowingly, lovingly rendered.
Deftly shaded. Bone structure and depth.
Some are sheer outline, limestone showing through.
73 in all. One with blubber lips evokes
a hominid cartoon. The monster of God sensed
as manivore. Deity as predator. Jehovah's foreskins.
Zeus Lykaios. Behind sacralized violence,
the trauma of being hunted, and eaten. Check this:
animal holocaust in the late Ice Age
corresponds with the rise of war.
Cowl of the master dark,
its red breath heading west
toward a tilting vertical
"totem" of bison heads, spitted
like big furry bugs. Baby mammoth with
wheel feet. Hoofs seen from below? Full moons?
Body shaded smoky tan. Over it
a massive bison emerging from a fissure.
Two turned-toward-us bison heads,
one on lion haunch, one on lion shoulder.
Carnivore tattoos. Targets. Earliest body decor.
Drink to me only with thine
fangs. Energy I would induct. In dank
scrape light, as if Arshile Gorky
traced his life dark as lion space,

or Hans Bellmer, his erotic unending line
alive with orgasm's blocked flue.
Enkidu, Humbaba. Teelget. Hercules at Nemea.
Grendel "bit into his bone-lappings,
bolted down his blood
and gorged on him in lumps, leaving his body
utterly lifeless, eaten up
hand and foot." Astarte on lion back.
Artemis with a bull scrotum necklace.
Rhino with 8 oversized curving parallel horns,
as if drawn by Marcel Duchamp.
Rhino Descending a Lion Stare.
Stuttering horns. River pour of meated miles,
horns trestling dawn as red deer foam through.
See-saw of rhino bodies. "Central stripes"
make them look like "armored" Indian rhinos.
Sketchbook of this wall. Started, thwarted.
Body parts in fugal maze. Sacrificial diagram.
Palimpsest of beasts and humans. No finish.
But finish is near. As I stand on this aluminum ramp,
a CEO is stretching his eyeball around the planet
like an interstellar Santa, bag full and off to Saturn.

The Beheading   *

He shook the Counter-Reformation
decorum out of these *tableau vivants*,
eliminating from painting
saccharin distortion and ecclesiastic agit-prop.
If by "the human" we mean actual lives
kicking up dust as they speed toward us
shattering idealistic frames,
then Caravaggio, like Vallejo's *Human Poems,*
produced human paintings.
A young whore in red dress dumped on a simple bed:
"The Death of the Virgin."
The painting refuses the porcelain vagina.
There is no Jesus appearance, just Carmelite men,
convulsed, confused. Whore or virgin, she is laid out,
feet bare, arms and hands dangling
carnivorous, red shadow. The canopy bucks, collapses,
stung through by sin and atonement—
Caravaggio could not completely
slip the Christian corset. He tore it, revealed its sweated inner lining.
In the destroyed "Resurrection"
it is said that he depicted Christ as
an emaciated convict climbing out of a pit.
What was this painter's engine?
What does his strong room look like?
The 1602 "John the Baptist in the Wilderness"
(with a gorgeous, naked "Baptist" pulling his ram to him,
a gesture rich with animal coitus),
and the "Victorious Cupid" (a naked fuck-boy with wings,
offering himself joyously to the viewer)
would not have been realized by a heterosexual painter.
He painted the Baptist eight or nine times,
at first using Biblical trappings to be able to work with
adolescent flesh. The story of someone
living on locusts and wild honey,
shaman-like with his lamb or ram familiar,
a moral loudmouth, perfect grist for

a despot's mill, is of little concern.
These attributes only register on Malta,
site of Caravaggio's second undoing 1607.
He arrives with a capital ban on him (for the accidental
killing of Ranuccio Tomassoni who
provoked him over a small debt), meaning:
anyone can sever his head and present it to a judge
for a reward anywhere under Papal jurisdiction.
With the image of the severed head,
we open his strong room. There is the 1597 "Medusa,"
with a shocked, young Caravaggian face,
the 1599 "Judith and Holofernes" jetting blood
as the repulsed but turned on Judith
saws through the neck bone (the fact that the model
for Judith is a 17-year-old whore transforms
the Biblical setting into a brothel).
There are three "Davids with the Head of Goliath,"
the finest of which, done in 1609 or 1610
after the painter's face had been slashed outside
a Naples' tavern, depicts a pained, even sorrowing, David
holding out the head of—Caravaggio!
David withdraws, with his other arm,
his sword from his crotch. Implication:
the beheading of Goliath/Caravaggio is David's self-castration,
or the Goliath/Caravaggio head is David's phallus.
Tomassoni bled to death from a sword-nicked penis.

On Malta, he paints "The Beheading of Saint John the Baptist"
as payment for becoming a Knight of Obedience.
Prison yard dark, 17th century Valletta.
Night in brownish-black settles through,
just enough rakes of light to see, in silence,
what men robotically visit on each other.
The Baptist lamb-trussed on the dirt,
neck partially slit. The executioner,
gripping a fistful of long Baptist hair,
yanks the head toward us, as, with his right hand,
he pulls a small knife from his leather belt sheath.

His rigid left arm is vertical architecture—
in the deltoids, triceps, radial forearm muscles,
contoured with amber shadow, ivory light,
I sense a sculptural Last Judgment
(it is as if the Ivory Tower rose from the ground of
the Baptist's "rape"). The executioner's
white bloomer folds have been painted so that
between his legs a phallic loop dangles,
inches over the Baptist's red cloak-covered rump.
Under this cloak: his lamb pelt,
the two forked legs of which jut out
as if from his groin. They are vulva-evocative.
The castrational humiliation of beheading
underscored by implicit buggery.
Baptist as catamite. Under the blood
oozing from the cut neck Caravaggio has
—the one time in his life—
signed: "f michelAn," directly from the blood blob.
In what spirit does the painter sign?
"f" = "fra," brother—and as a man,
condemned to duplicate the Baptist's fate—
and as a martyr to his own cause
which is, in the spirit of Herodian denunciation,
to tell the visual truth, to penitentially argue,
as an artist, the glacial contradiction between
transcendental hope and squalid reality.

After 1608, along with the Goliath/Caravaggio head,
there are two "Salomés with the Baptist's Head,"
including the executioner and the old woman witness
who, like a compressed Greek chorus,
holds her own "head oh head oh head don't leave me now!"
over the Malta beheading. The three float
as partially bodied heads in inky blackness about
the head-charged platter. The heads of Salomé and granny
implicitly share the same torso
as if making up a whole. Given Caravaggio's
fixation on the Baptist and Goliath,

with a signature and the painter's ruined face,
a dyadic Caravaggio is evoked,
a Baptist-Goliath, two heads sprouting off
the same severed neck, or
off the same severed erection
—while there are soft penises in the oeuvre,
there are no erections, so erection may be
the undepictable "thing," in Vallejo's words,
Caravaggio's "dreadful thing thing,"
generating the decapitational obsession.
Neck as erection, stem connecting
root to bloom, yes, but also the demonic link between
damnation-pocked head and runaway body,
this head that cannot really "lose itself"
as long as the neck yokes.

Four months after becoming a Knight,
Caravaggio is said to have been thrown into
the Fort Sant'Angelo oubliette,
to have gotten out of this eleven-foot-deep "hole,"
and to have sailed to Syracuse. There is
no record of his misdeed or crime on Malta,
nor how he was able to escape the "hole"
or who arranged his successful flight.
Peter Robb conjectures that the painter got caught
with one of the pages that his sponsor had
imported into unruly Valletta.
"Sex with a page would have been the ultimate outrage."
So they whisked Caravaggio out of there,
stripped him of his Knighthood (he left the island
without permission), leaving him to his own devices.

One of his Maltese paintings is a portrait of his sponsor,
Adolf de Wignacourt, Grand Master.
Next to Wignacourt in full armor is a page in red hose
looking directly at the painter (as very few subjects do),
holding Wignacourt's large red-plumed helmet.
If one takes the Goliath/Caravaggio head from David's grasp,

and superimposes it over the Grand Master's helmet,
Robb's conjecture is visualized. Grand Master
(surely the profoundly offended in this scenario),
delectable page, and Caravaggio as the Goliath-to-be,
a kind of *ménage a trois*. The unacknowledged
Maltese crime is, in its own way,
duplicated in July 1610. Caravaggio has disappeared,
his body is never found, all the official
reports of his demise make no sense.
Robb thinks he was murdered, probably by
people associated with the family of the man
he had killed. Martyrdom and salvation
are packed into the double Caravaggio head.
His paintings show, in compressed form,
a new self, released from Scholastic rote,
cloaked in Venetian red. Behind it:
desire for revelation, nor of a transcendental ilk,
but of the soul made monstrous. Out of this full showing,
the true life of humanity—the poor, the tortured,
the saintly, the common, mother and child—may assemble.
Caravaggio gyrates on in me. I have,
in my stomach, some of his hermetic lantern shards,
undigestible martyrdom/salvation.

Joan Mitchell's Spinnerets

White flowers scissor-billowing the hemlock.

                             Where you begin is
a line tossed out, to catch on its own slant.
Your second move? Another line
punning across the first, as when one word
mounts another. Fishing the void, seeing if something
tugs back, and if not? The vexation of starting over
while keeping what was done.
Little Lulu's chair. A strip of chicken. What do
these shapes signify? A gesture, a gravid
reeling out. As if the lines were emerging from you,
spurting from many nipples.

How say this stroke works
but that does not? What is broken advances,
pillowed by what will not yield:
a thought drinking its shadow.

Loss looms The loom hums.
An image is forming, a centripetal centrifuge
gusting erratic webs in the cream. Which peaks
and scrams,
almost, for nothing ever entirely leaves.
What seems to disappear has only camouflaged itself
as godfill.
Something has entered the composition that is alien to it.
I think of the Nephila
in her golden web unaware
hatched wasp larvae are feeding on her blood,
A blow-up of her midgut reveals
the septic aviary. Cross-outs galore
reassemble as
a burning lamb!
The painting as an enraged lamb!

In what neuron lode of your brain did rapture
misfire as rape?
                              To somehow get
the blood of the world in, the shed blood, the blood you cannot
see, or even know about, but know is shed.
Is this carmine or massacre red?
Is this chockablock knot
the scene of a crime, or quarried depth,
the two dimensional
clotting in psyche as a lioness crossing
the blood stream of your? of my? heart—and do I
want my heart to be played by
an auburn carnivore emotion,
or, by a caterpillar band? Oh so much of you is here,
just in swaying drip lines, nematocystic tentacles…

You leave before you arrive, you arrive
without having come. But is this not the spring of
self-invention? Of moving out an all,
unconfined by figure or representation, a presence
sea-urchin erect with menstruation, drunkenness,
fucking, friendship! All of which are sensed and hived below
our meeting ground, internal aviation,
our dog fight in the clouds! zooming under you
then you pepper me from behind, in flames I go down
through a blob of vermilion and a swath of no,
entangled in the ur-done, the undone, the never to be
is pulling something from me,
a memory tugged out of its carapace.

As you aged, the spider milk level lowered,
lifting into view a branchwork in staccato detour,
the casserole of a capillary thatch,
moulting
switchbacks, hemlock breakthrough become
your linden in slow explosion, as if the maw of the universe
had opened, pandoric, and Hope
had triumphed, consuming all her sister ills.

The periscope's mirror now a kaleidoscopic exit into
yellow tormentil stars, blue
dove-gray milkwort sprays,
lilac marsh violets, a field unfolding,
chopped turbulence, crocked,
eternally vernal, your friend Gisele's
girlhood valley, explored only by those who knew
the location of the secret entrance, this
flushed paradise forth! Packed anagrammatric
closure, blue
loaded with black, affirmation
with hell in tow, azure ribbed with struts of
incorporated erasure. Vincent's crows,
wrung out black propellers lathing
corn trampled into ochre lightning.
Whose death mask is being molded with
these rampant arctotheric clouds?

How divine the state of the union in
the entrails of
Daisy Mae?

Monumental

"A bootful of brain
set out in the rain"

—that is Paul Celan, Paris, 1969.
Could have been a GI snapshot, Vietnam.

Leon Golub rounded up four boots,
grew military torturer legs in them,
shiny brown pedestals on which
outside my bedroom, door
a naked man hanging upside down is being whacked.

The avant-garde: the first upon the scene,
while the crime is still blazing, in Laverdant's 1848 definition:
"those who lay bare, with a brutal brush,
all the brutalities, all the filth, which are at the base of society."
The core of Golub's career is in its complex response to annihilation.
His comrades-in-arm are Goya at the Judas peephole
refusing to avert his gaze; Callot with his lynch tree, become
Billie Holiday's "strange fruit;" Dix's *Trench;* Picasso's *Guernica;*
Heartfiel's angels in gas masks intoning:
"O du frohliche, o du selige, gnadenbringende Zeit!"

1946: to transform the water-filled, wreckage-laden basement of
Western culture into a primordial bath,
a deep rolling masked blackness in milling assembly,
fangs studding the abstract with wilderness eyes.
Burnt, bird-legged Hamlet paws the air.
Golub sphinxes: half-swallowed, half-born, from *sphincter,*
orifice of the contracting angel, the nightmare choker.
How much degradation can an image take
and still, scraped into and from the canvas itself, manifest
this world's lethal embrace? The age
demanded an image, right? ok? here it is:
man as ruined monumentality. Reclining Youth:
his surface spatter mimicked by wound-trailed ground,

the limb-ghosted ground mimicked by white bone-like finality.
Gigantomachies: gods fighting in accelerated grimace,
syncopation of drunken, flayed cargo sloshing in an indestructible
    hold.

The Golub archetypal question:
if abstract color fields are peeled way,
what terrors will show through?

Golub's torturers know we accept their actions
as they accept our passive regard.
For most of us watch them from behind the great religious systems of
    compensatory evasion.

Golub asks: "Is it possible to export destruction, to burn and drive peas-
ants from their homes, and maintain the dream of the perfectibility of
art? Well, it is possible if art concerns itself with itself and does not dare
to presume political meaning." (1969)

This is mental war, intellectual, determined
that art be somehow commensurate with international event.
Golub's South African blacks,
the chorus of a lifework, watch him and occasionally break into
    threnody.
They watch you, viewer, as do the Salvadoran white squads
stuffing car trunks with the corpse you will never escape.
The power principle behind evil,
so deeply a matter of the unconscious now
as to not know its own name, "down there,"
in close combat blood galaxies,
where one plus one is always one, a zero rack
encrusted with victimized rage.

A Golubian vision of the American flag:
napalm-blistered stripes so star-mangled they resonate burnt blue.

Oh fatality of expectation and freedom!
(Where other Americans saw angels beaming at Reagan,

Golub saw Contras destroying Nicaraguan grain silos, health centers,
    cutting off women's breasts)

In old age,
touched by death, the hand of the master sets free the fractured
    landscape,
the goal dims, a shredder abyss moves in,
dissociation tears apart time.
Skeletons wear the pants in the house of being.
Night street nodes of slicks, glare and wash out
mesh in crystalline smear.
Has any other artist ever depicted the zone of closure more
    trenchantly?
Golub in the underworld at 80,
still facing America's will to administer absolutely,
but now the prey of dogs, eagles, and lions,
as if man the predator had once again become prey.
Slogans honk, lit tableaux in a tunnel of horror.
"Another joker out of business" "Raptor sanction"
Foresight becomes gore right. A sparagmos of the torn and the
    tearer.
Pink dog tongue fused dick diddling a female spectre.
In the new armpit showcase, skeletons toast hounds.
"Transmission garbled."
                    Leon Golub exits.
            Now in my mind indelible,
    the corrosive flicker from his unstanchable wound.

                                        [March–April, 2005]

VI
2010–2014

ANTICLINE (2010)

The Tjurunga   *

begins as a digging stick, first thing the Aranda child picks up.
When he cries, he is said to be crying for
the tjurunga he lost
when he migrated into his mother.

Male elders later replace the mother with sub-incision.
The shaft of his penis slit, the boy incorporates his mother.

I had to create a totemic cluster in which imagination
could replace Indianapolis, to incorporate ancestor beings
who could give me the agility
—across the tjurunga spider's web—
to pick my way to her perilous center.

(So transformationally did she quiver,
        adorned with hearts and hands,
            cruciform, monumental,   *Coatlicue*
                understrapping fusion)

Theseus, a tiny male spider, enters a tri-level construction:
look down through the poem, you can see the labyrinth.
Look down through the labyrinth, you can see the web:

                    Coatlicue

        sub-incision   Bud Powell

            César Vallejo

                the bird-headed man

Like a mobile, this tjurunga shifts in the breeze,
                            beaming at the tossing
foreskin dinghies in which poets travel.

These nouns are also nodes in a constellation called
Clayton's Tjurunga. The struts are threads
in a web. There is a life blood flowing through
these threads. *Coatlicue* flows into Bud Powell,
César Vallejo into sub-incision. The bird-headed man
   floats right below
                      the pregnant spider
             centered in the Tjurunga.

Psyche may have occurred, struck off
—as in flint-knapping—
an undifferentiated mental core.

My only weapon is a digging stick
the Aranda call *papa*. To think of father as a digging stick
strikes me as a good translation.

      The bird-headed man
is slanted under a disemboweled bison.
His erection tells me he's in flight. He drops
his bird-headed stick as he penetrates
   bison paradise.

The red sandstone hand lamp
abandoned below this proto-shaman
is engraved with vulvate chevrons—did it once flame
   from a primal sub-incision?

This is the oldest aspect of this tjurunga, its grip.

               Recalculating.

When I was six, my mother placed my hands on the keys.
At sixteen, I watched Bud Powell sweep my keys
into a small pile, then ignite them with "Tea for Two."
The dumb little armature of that tune
engulfed in improvisational glory
roared through my Presbyterian stasis.

"Cherokee"
"Un Poco Loco"
sank a depth charge into
    my soul-to-be.

This is a tjurunga positioning system.

We are now at the intersection of *Coatlicue*
and César Vallejo.

Squatting over the Kyoto benjo, 1963,
wanting to write, having to shit.

I discovered that I was in the position of Tlazoltéotl-Ixcuina.
But out of *her* crotch, a baby corn god pawed.

                    Recalculating.

        Cave of
Tlazoltéotl-Ixcuina.
The shame of coming into being.
As if, while self-birthing,
I must eat filth.

I was crunched into a cul-de-sac I could destroy
only by destroying the self
that would not allow the poem to emerge.

Wearing my venom helmet, I dropped, as a *ronin,* to the pebbles,
and faced the porch of Vallejo's feudal estate.
The Spectre of Vallejo appeared, snake-headed, in a black robe.
With his fan he drew a target on my gut.

Who was it who sliced into the layers of wrath-
enwebbed memory in which the poem was trussed?

Exactly who unchained Yorunomado
from the Christian altar in Clayton's solar plexus?

The transformation of an ego strong enough to die
by an ego strong enough to live.

The undifferentiated is the great Yes
in which all eats all
and my spider wears a serpent skirt.

That altar. How old is it?
Might it cathect with the urn in which
the pregnant unwed girl Coatlicue was cut up and stuffed?
Out of that urn twin rattlesnakes ascend and freeze.
Their facing heads become the mask of masks.
Coatlicue: Aztec caduceus.
The phallic mother in the soul's crescendo.

But my wandering foreskin, will it ever reach shore?

Foreskin wandered out of Indianapolis. Saw a keyboard, cooked it in
    B Minor.
Bud walked out of a dream. Bud and Foreskin found a waterhole,
    swam.
Took out their teeth, made camp. Then left that place, came to
    Tenochtitlan.
After defecating, they made themselves headgear out of some hearts
    and lopped-off hands.
They noticed that their penises were dragging on the ground,
    performed sub-incision, lost lots of blood.
Bud cut Foreskin who then cut Bud.
They came to a river, across from which Kyoto sparkled in the night
    sky.
They wanted to cross, so constructed a vine bridge.
While they were crossing, the bridge became a thread in a vast web.
At its distant center, an immense red gonad, the Matriarch crouched,
    sending out saffron rays.
"I'll play Theseus," Bud said, "this will turn the Matriarch into a
    Minotaur."
"And I'll play Vallejo," Foreskin responded, "he's good at bleeding
    himself and turning into a dingo.

Together let's back on, farting flames."

The wily Minotaur, seeing a sputtering enigma approaching, pulled a lever, shifting the tracks.

Foreskin and Bud found themselves in a roundhouse between conception and absence.

They noticed that their headgear was hanging on a Guardian Ghost boulder engraved with breasts snake-knotted across a pubis.

"A formidable barricade," said Bud. "To reach paradise, we must learn how to dance this design."

The pubis part disappeared. Fingering his sub-incision, Bud played "Dance of the Infidels."

Foreskin joined in, twirling his penis making bullroarer sounds.

The Guardian Ghost boulder roared: "WHO ARE YOU TWO THE SURROGATES OF?"

Bud looked at Foreskin. Foreskin looked at Bud.

"Another fine mess you've gotten us into," they said in unison.

Then they heard the Guardian Ghost laughing. "Life is a joyous thing," she chuckled, "with maggots at the center."

In Memory of George Butterick

Fortress of summer. Heat a connecting rod.
Black leaf mouth of the redbud chewing everywhichway.

Thoughts of George back in the hospital
so overwhelmed the light in those leaf jaws
I called Colette:
George was home,
                            difficult to speak, but he did,
courageous even, asking about Paul Blackburn.
"Where did his start?" Or more specifically: "Did it start
    in the esophagus?   I thought so…"

                Poetry, a nativity
                      poised
            on an excrement-flecked blade—

Paradise, you are wadding,
to plug one big gap?
                            Dogtown to be
so total a place in Charles Olson's desire
that concepts of hell, or any mountain-climbed heaven
become inadequate to the congruence of earth's facets.

But then there is the Celan-
hole, the no-one God, void of the ovens.

Dear George, I am moved by how many lives lived
are ivy.

By how life breaks through wall after wall only to provide
more stone.

How each is less than he is,
and more.

Self-knotted Nile of the anticline in which
we curl.

[9 July 1987–2008]

Hmmm   *

There is a hmmm, a hum, an incipient hymn, a
song in food, a hallelujah hint, even before
baby patter,   a Neanderthal lullaby,
suck of going in,   a sound,   a salsa
that sews me to you,
the sewing is thee,   we are
                    theed in sound,   treed in
      nascent omega.

I greet what I cannot account for,
I depart to where I might become an unfiltered phantom facing
      filtered war.
If sound is the heart noise of being,
does it have a commonwealth, a gong modality
      coursing our lives?

Cosmic lisp occurs most poignantly before falling asleep.
An oyster in shell-static, I hear a rapids spewing blood and gold—
I *am* again takes on flavor.

Breath's arsenal blooms in dreams.
Short of non-being, I pause to gaze at conception's regal tinsel,
its mire of mirrors, its tilting wetland bulrush miracles.

Breath molecules of the dead
populate the atmosphere, Adolph H as well as ayahuasca
comrades from the Putamayo.

The stuff Wilhelm Reich saw in the blue sky
looks like paperclips to me,
bions he called them, tiny soul packets
on the verge

or precipice where the living are shaved from the dead

or where the dead transfer
sprinting from one plane to another—

Blake bobbing by,
Beowulf, triple-eyed and forty-eared.

Hmmm. Deer can hear us talking. Our voices resemble the uh-huh of
falling fruit.

Did desire for reincarnation of the killed animal
preceed the notion of human immortality?

Hmmm. Like a sentient water molecule percolating randomly
through the soil, lost amidst the tangle of root fibers, I pass through
the petiole of a sun-drenched leaf… Now I am inside the domed roof
of a structure made up of lines—a rhizome.

Now I am a live canoe, my skin covered with yellow stripes, black di-
amonds. Inside me are Sultan Muhammad, Pablo Amaringo, Unica
Zürn and César Vallejo. Crabs are clutched to my rear. They live as
parasites in the anal regions of large aquatic snakes. Zürn is pregnant
and twisting in pain. When Vallejo tries to soothe her, she bites off
his finger, which Amaringo puts in his pocket. Will he plant it? It is
said that the Yaje plant originated from a sowed finger.

Coreless core of the macro entwining the micro.

The quantum dot florescence image of a mouse kidney section.

Dream of green word leaves tumbling inside bright magenta filaments
in a royal
purple sky.
                    Hertzog's blood-red black smoke over
burning Kuwait oil fields: a kind of Beethoven bordello.

The seeker entwining the sought,
the sowed fighting to stay seed.

Caul of war, an American headdress for years to come.
As if what we are has become war birth,
the held-back fetus, our life, in a war womb.
When we sense birth, we are warforthed.

Sensation of living within a grimy welkin of unreality.
The dusk sky venereal with stealth.

In the nativity rip of the mind,
one wanders all one's roads at once.

Placenta

"Deep in his heart, man aspires to rejoin
the condition he had before consciousness."
—E.M. Cioran

Where is my placenta buried?
Must I know? After all, it is the globe of the origin of my soul.

Had I been a Kwakiutl, my parents might have exposed my placenta
so that ravens could eat it,
so that I might gain visionary powers in later life.

I dreamt that the first spot of land in the primal waters was a pla-
centa,
a floating flat surface
attached to a long umbilical stem
anchored below.

Bodhisattva lotus throne—a sublimated placenta?

The Egyptian pharaoh was preceded in processions by
his actual placenta fixed to the end of a pole.
                    The first flag?

Are the hoardings of pack rats a placenta substitute?

Is the function of religion to keep humankind from becoming fully
    born?

Octavio's Labyrinth *

Dream tonight of coupled images whirling
in the circus of an empty eye,
hurling themselves against themselves to become
under my lids a forest of magnetic needles.

           Everything is a door:
elephantiasis with its violet legs,
bougainvillaea's numberless magenta stars.

I opened to the pot-headed, lordly and deathless hybrids:

      chockablock
        animals and gods.
    O the breeze between! The shiver of
organs being lifted out! The emptied
      manger of the body filled
    with solidified light!

All the gods yet to be discovered will be found
on the night side of the blasted Tree of Life,
guarded by the black dragon of mindless unification.

      A sleepwalking sewer ringed with Aztec lime,
I descended to the point where the wind mangles eagles
and a three-legged toad contemplates
              an octopus clock's
      tentacle-tentative time.

        The hour rests
on a lake of charities.
No one ends at himself.

(Ideas ate the deities,
             the deities

became ideas,
        great bladders full of bile—

          the sanctuary was a dung heap,
the dung heap a nursery
        sprouting armed ideas,
     ideas idiotic as deities)

We have caught up to Whitman. But his hand in mine
has the feel of a Sudanese infant's claw.

     There is no freedom.
There is only the intensification of
the sensing of *forever* as one lives *now.*

Dia De Muertos

Nora, Leon, Bill—I would be adrift with you in that dinghy
Bill painted off Bosch's *Ship of Fools,*
the four of us, as souls, with wine and watermelon,
our *ofrenda* between us, stacked burins, scrapers, brushes, notebooks

and, just to keep everything true to imagination,
a squirrel smoking a cigar. On our mast a tricolor would flap
so that Matisse's words *Travail et amour,* as on a mobius band,
would circulate within each of us. And our talk!

We would have finally gotten our whole lives into what we say.
Our conversation today, concerning *kalokagathia,*
or "the beauty and goodness of a consoling art," would spin out,

angel cradles between our gesturing hands and mouths.
Then it would be time for me to go. I would slip out, regain the shore,
and wave farewell to you, dearest friends, for another year by Caryl.

The Left Foot Of King Ramesses I   *

resembles a long semi-flat black fish.
The toes crawl forth,
five black tent caterpillars on their way to a cherry tree feast.
From the tips of their abdomens they secrete pheromones
so that their relatives, detecting these chemical signals,
can also stream down the trail!

From Permian times onward, tent caterpillars have had no god.

When they reach a leaf patch at the end of a branch, they snuggle
side by side, humming and feeding in unison on a young leaf.

Many a tentstead is torn and littered by the shrunken cadavers of
larvae killed by braconid wasps.

Having detected the buzz of a tachnid's wings, a tent larva swings its
body from side to side in a kind of samba, creating a moving target,
befuddling the attacker.

Fully formed tent caterpillars chew their way out of eggs in sync with
their host tree's bursting buds.

They happily cooperate in many interactive tasks: leaf-shelter
building, communal basking and mat spinning, anti-predator group
displays, trail laying, recruitment to food and basking sites.

Tent caterpillars are at the pinnacle of caterpillar social evolution and
should never be dissed as "walking digestive tracks."

They have six eyes, which tragically provide them with no informa-
tion about the form of an object. However, by swinging their heads,
they perceive dark vertical shapes against light-colored backgrounds
(much as we would see branches against the sky).

They have color vision (ultraviolet light and shades of green); they
use the sun as a compass.

Successive cycles of body waves propel them forward, carrying along their sixteen legs.

A typical female may emerge, call males, copulate, lay eggs, and, completely spent, die in less than a day.

They love to feed on water tupelo, aspen, water oak, flowering dogwood, and cherry.

Their great epic, *The Cherry Tree Journey,* translated in 1530 by the blessed Persian angel Sorush, describes the journey of the Ortok tent caterpillar clan to retrieve the princess Zal carried away by a warbler and deposited in a bird-citadel in the top of a tall cherry tree.

Other enemies are beetles, stink bugs, ants, wasps, chickadees, titmice, bluejays, the Baltimore oriole, redwing blackbirds, chebecs, wood peewees, phoebes, cuckoos, downy woodpeckers, red-eyed vireos, and the brown-headed cowbird.

They have no known friends.

Think about this: any aggregate of birds or animals that cooperated to build communal shelters, shared information regarding the location of food patches, *and had their own epic,* would be considered a highly social unit.

Their sole musical instrument is thought to be the Cryptonephridium, embedded in the walls of their rectums.

It has recently been conjectured that the tectiforms engraved and painted on the sides of bison in the Upper Paleolithic cave of Font-de-Gaume may have been based on tent caterpillar shelters which may have inspired Cro-Magnon people to construct small hide-covered lodges.

The first architects!

We must now conclude this brief excursion by crawling back into the toes of Ramesses I's long black fish-foot, colonized with the rest of his statue in a glass case ("Mummy Section") of the British Museum.

Descent

"Why do poets write vertically?"
—Sam Shepard (after the
Vallejo program)

Cremasteric
metaphor. Descent intensifies
consciousness.

Laddered
language rooms
        constructed,
then ransacked,
    each next

        a trap-door
nexus,
        each door
a downwind Pandora

opening into
the reversal of gravity: to take my own time here,
brushed by ascending, descending angel
    breath.
            To pick my way
        down…

(The trail through Le Tuc d'Audoubert was marked by
strings tied to stalagmite stumps.
We could only crawl inside the string "aisle"
one by one. On each side of us,
 "virgin" ground   strewn with
viper skeletons, bear skulls.)

    As my body contorted
                in Le Tuc to
accommodate our "stanza path"

so does the line here
       versify (akin to *vertere,*
"to turn") when meaning
   shifts (specter of prose plowing
a rectangular field).

       Line beginning and end
words are out sides
up against the page equivalent of
              "virgin" ground.

Can the page blank be thought of
                    as gnawing at
these stanza sides? Are they
              stays against
the walls of voicelessness forever
   pressing in?

       Black road to Xibalbá.
   Cleft in the Milky Way.

Below closure's boneyard,
              Absence:

   source of the next

poem's being.

Poem to Help Will Alexander Fight Cancer   *

I know something about the pressure you are under
having just returned from an abyssal brothel
where a cockatoo squidette instructed me in the moves
necessary
               to inject energy into the anchor buried in your navel.

Sensing you as an icicle up the anus of Hell,
I am sending you a wagonload of what Anselm Kiefer calls
the first and oldest metals of alchemy—lead—
the least pure, the most ambiguous, Saturnian,
the ground zero of transmutation.

I am also sending you a Mousterian orchestra of mastodon
   skull drums painted with menstrual crosses,
cloud scores crisscrossed by lark arpeggios,
a nose flute from Les Trois Frères,
a Siberian hip-bone xylophone.

There is a black Moby Dick cruising America's white Hadal trenches,
   attached by Oglala Sioux hatchet fish.
There are black Eshlemans and white Alexanders exchanging
   fission in Aimé Césaire's coral arsenals.

We must ask the poem for the impossible, locate ourselves
within this asking, spot the Stone of Division,
then attaching ourselves to this Stone
articulate the amoebic split-off of the divine and the human.

The imagination is a primal hourglass of venusian sensuality,
a kind of double bellows ceaselessly troating
               (in the words of Lezama Lima):
"Image is the reality of the invisible world."

A bison drops its human embryo into fiery snow.
Cro-Magnon eyes litter the rune-scape.
Rising through the tundra are rods of emptiness,
pedestals for meditating saints and poets,
                    ping pong balls hailing bop
        over the luscious hiss of *sin and be*.

Why does the clock dial register 6:66 AM?
Is this a sign that the missing 80% of the cosmos is right around
    the ayahuasca bend? But wait—
I think I have spotted your gnarl in the rudimentary
    nipple of a bee. Or have I been hypnotized by Dionysus
                    on his boar tusk harp chanting
            semen-honey lays?

Moaning in the eel-grass are your "oneiric sesame pontoons".
This eel-grass undulates in vertical homage to
            the light in your speech lattice,
        your holophrastic triadic units,
      your brobdingnagian vocabulary accessible in trance,
    your field mice parachuting between cat-pawed traps.

Nothing, as active subject—can we agree on that?
Can we love the soul in all its resurrexit end-blessed mess?
Can we imagine *Banisteriopsian* verbal ladders?

It is out of nothing that, through heat and compression,
we make our words. Our verbs! The hooligan equivalents of stars
—and the earth? The earth is a thaumaturgic enigma
still cooking inside, still being forged.

I am sending you as well some redbud pussy-willow rubies—
sew them, like eyeballs, to your back in the fashion of certain
    Maya underworld lords.
I am sending you an etymological halo,

a solar ghost-roamed threshing floor.
I am building for you a mask to strap on
                                    when,
                        suspended in the stroma,
your drum arrives walking on animal paws,
pregnant with intestinal tallow.

                                        [December, 2007]

Eternity at Domme   *

Between the junipers flows the Dordogne.
My home is near, as close as gone—
identity in the archaic region of the soul.
Between the junipers flows the Dordogne.

Sunlit crags with chestnuts, lindens overgrown.
What chambers, what cavalcades engraved—
I'll never reach the pillowed rock Laussel arranged.
Between the junipers flows the Dordogne.

Can arrival at yearning's core
be said to decorticate home? Is home my immured
animality, the phantom lurking in my stain?

I'm ancient as never before this afternoon,
charged with karstic urge, fully born.
Between the junipers flows the Dordogne.

[9 June 2007]

Zürn Heads

head filled with fetal eyes.
eyes sharing lips.
head helmeted with eyes.
head as a geography of pores erupting, waves surrounding eyes.
there is no part of the head that does not see.
heads with no non-eye relief.

eyes appearing as the only peers, the peerage in things.
eyed & seek, the rills in the face
layered with bird heads, with ferned serpent ends.
with eye vaginal almond floats.
stay! is to girdle as eye bands are to the shuffle of the molting head.
granular disintegration of the tufted fabric of the head.
larval organs dissolving into cream.
say, has that eye apple been spayed?

congeries of eye lines shrubbing into insectile-feelered dark.
thong throng tong-drawn trowel of eyes.
art is to burgeon on its own stem beholden only to
the stamina of its lines.
mine composed of off-shoot eye shafts through which I twist,
accelerating through Unica's fractal beetle,
seemingly designed as a Mandelbrot-set zoom sequence,
in which I infinitely re-encounter what I have just left.

if genes had faces and bodies would they twist like these?
am gripping *am,* can't go on will go on,
without centerpole or central pull,
tendril limbs straying into a vanishing varnish roam.
the human configured as part of
the threadwork of
a spontaneous robe of devolving wraiths.

creation as fission. schizogenetic genesis.
no representational nexus.
dyadic primacy of the oldest gods.

gossamer nets to entangle them
so that they ferment, fructify as fruit flies, buried wasp queens,
millipedal elves moving away from each other
yet still attached by saliva strings, lacy scaled vapors
exposing the white, the gleam of never, into which
no one steps twice.

sense of a living midden.
soul as the self buried and mixed with a living Other,
fauna flora particles of an ongoing sentence:
fullness is infinite fracture.
totems playfully wavering, as if about to shift
into double helix, to swim into the White,
to perceive, finally, the White Image.

Munch Dissolves

Something is always congealing,   seeking
group strata,   full wet skirt,
Gaudi in the cornerless blend of it,
Munch's benders,   released of starch, but   *of* fixation,
opening the locks on
        afterlife   death   this life
pooling,   deboning the polarities,
            poling with Charon in
            blood azure.

"I came into the world as a sick being—in sick surroundings.
My youth was spent in a sickbed; life was a brightly lit window."

César Vallejo: "I was born on a day when God was sick,
                    gravely."

The moon's testicular tube-reflection
transfiguring night's indigo carmine lake.

Waltz with me, lung to lung. "O darling, look!
                            Next to us, a green
larva is vampirizing his slumped booty!"

Sister Inger's speckled dress, splotches roving.

Clasped hands form an oyster-gray vulva against her dead gown.

Moonlight, concentrated in pickets, passes through a woman's face
whose eyes for an instant escape its gangrene drench.

A road boas by a clump of girls on a pier.
Down through brown arboreal reflection
    they stare into the Munchflow.

And what is the Munchflow? The fetal thrashing of
        those forever unfully born.

664   Clayton Eshleman: *The Essential Poetry*

A kiss! Her face, consumed, becomes his beak.

Showing through their fused bodies: cobweb-thin cocoons.

O anima emanating separation!
Away from him she glides toward the shore,
her long hair a telephone wire that cannot be cut.

"People's souls are like planets. Like a star that rises from the
darkness—and meets another star—only to disappear again into
darkness—it is the same when a man and woman meet—drift
apart—light up in love—burn up—and disappear each in their own
direction."

The devil's footprints on the bedroom ceiling. Ghosts of the utter
    failure of prayer.

A slimy, soft-horned snail, carrying a brothel on its back.

Pitch-rust river encircling Millie, then Dagny, under Munch.
                    Who called this woman Madonna?
She has elsewhere eyes, a menstrual halo, cum-smeared breasts!

"Without anxiety and illness, I am a ship without a rudder."

Stopped on the road in darkness oleaginous as treacle:
    a car with blood-red eyes.

Adam's mahogany penis by a tree trunk radiating fire,
                    whose root metabolism
suckles skulls, crocodilian mulch.
                    Pregnant Eve stands by.
Tree once, with fetal wick, *a burning bush.*

Along Snow Avenue, asparagus trees are blackening,
        swirled in the caul of a wind
                    boozy with throttled
        valves, aortic hives.

Sister Laura sits locked in perpetual, unanswered, large-eyed
    pleading.
Before her, a blood flower sucks nourishment from a circular table
        whose patterned blood-red cloth
                resembles sections of her brain.

O-shock of a fresh dead man discovering that the beyond
is this world oozing through all its pores,
streaks of sky seep through the path
upon which this shocked O holds his head and screams
arched by a sky coldly boiling with the blood of all
who have lived
                    O-scream discovering each
scream is intelligible, the slaughterhouse screams,
the insane scream, your sex opens wide,
rugged candle refueling on gusts,
articulate flame in the trench of your sex,
shaped like a live woman holding
her earless head, her face ocellated with screams,
in each scream the screwdriver of the mind
attempting to loosen the bolt
God sank into it like a pitiless dry well.

                                    [April–August, 2006]

Goya Black   *

Text of shadow gore. Cowherds
with leg stumps sunk in mud, cudgels flailing.
Roving colon of humankind.
                                        Text
of tunneled pilgrimage. Blind light hangs,
sniffing the mob's expanding hood.
Rutabaga mugs. Bubbling dirty cream:
the flesh of gape-mouth, goggle-eyed anguish.
                Munch sidewinders through.
                                There are Golub
torture hooks rusting in this shadow scrimmage
peppering our own mortal broth.

The son of man's left arm stump
roman candles in Saturn's throat.
The bloody stump of allegiance to fear:
pulp in the grinder of power.
The son of man's legs, pressed bell clappers
before Saturn's trestle bent thighs.

        Lean forward, you witches,
your billy goat god has a butchersome tale to bleat.
Some are hysterically daft. Some
the ground has already half-devoured.
Some sit just giggle-wiggling their toes.
Pig-ignorant urn beings
                clumped by
                night's console.

From a deep well of sand
a dog looks up with supplicator eyes.

Does he see the apparition in the sky Goya sees?

The son of man entangled in dirty bed sheets
    with three old and ugly Fates.

While they toy with his thread, this fool
is busy solely in his crotch!

[for Jerry Rothenberg]

Blue Sphinx

[after Leon Golub]

Shed of eternity—the riddled self
                    poised, tripodic.
              What have you done,
man, with the animal powers
         by which you entered time?

              New Junk Yard dog
                    now on the street,
              an American merc
      on dog alert,   in defense of what?
The right front leg-arm, as long as that of a Caravaggio
      executioner—
is that this guy's Las Vegas push, his gambled stability?

Glassy street-dark blue. An East River serum glint.
Baudelaire in a crew-cut. The merc who bombed natives
      here stuck with the logos of his wrath.

Rilke once slept all night between the Sphinx's paws.
Imagine him awaking to this neon-gangrene-faced merc,
      the freak animality of his radiance.

Condomplatz, where the AIDS-infected pass,
"ghosts by day accost the passer-by"
life on the street, no longer post-Romantic Ginsberg mudra
      or OM-intoning "saint"
or even Manson tarantualizing runaways on filthy rugs.
The oil and fumes of Kali-Ma glint through
                    the hoop of self
              ringed with Shiva fire.

Ode to Nancy Spero

Daughters Nancy Spero mined through Artaud, plunging
into his Bowlahoola the seminal muscle of her tongue
to release these pater-crusted Rahabs,
to let them strip and restrip
—from pedestal to Golden Lotus—
the binocular manacles from their feet,
to let them ungag their cunts,
to let their cunts stick out their tongues,
to let them dance inside out the accordion akimbo kick,
the dildo trot, the serpentine waver prance,
Ms. Gig and her wiggling tricksters
rotating through the monument blockage, rooted and free.

Xibalbá   *

Here they come, the more-than-less-than-us,
the toons under us, creatures draped in feathered morn,
in bowlers, stuffed jaguar-tail crowns,
big-eyed skeletons bearing god copal,
Katzenjammer Hero Twins,   Smoking Frog,
Curl Snout with lots of eyeball jewelry,
Jiggs and Lady Xoc
            (pulling Guantánamo through her tongue).

Speech clouds with funnels, grids of glyphs.
Funeral pot rollouts: Maya "comic strips."

Through White Bone Snake Gate,
Sea Hag and Water-lily Jaguar jostle, slice.

One Blowgunner, his nose is phallic, with hot dog fervor.
Over bound Sweet Pea, Bearded Dragon lifts his axe.

Skulls with sunglasses embedded in their sockets,
corn silk flowing from their pates.
Walking tableaus with bloodstained scarves, enema bibs.
Supernatural space is red.

"I am timeless!" the jawless Gump executioner yelps.
He misses Maize God's neck. Ejaculates through his fontanel.

Now, who is that bulb-bellied coyote, ritual noodles
looping his skinny thighs? He's pounding stuff bubbling before his
      paws.
Was he your momentary escape from the human fix?
Behind him, caked with enucleated eyes,
a jaguar nagual turns his head into a mirror.

Harp of an upturned infant. Have you, as Whimpy,
strummed burgers from that primordial bow?
Only the Jaguar God is intact, in circus mayhem honking his spots.

Chopped up anaconda, stacked into a throne.
A cigar-smoking firefly sambas by a rabbit scribe.
Lopped heads sweep up into the blackness as evening stars.

With goose-dragon power, I sounded my conch
projecting all its seminal Naz, for the Spaniards were right around the
    glyph
knotted in homophobic madness,
shaving their mothers, milking their dads.

Alice the Goon. Stingray Spine Paddler.
Monkey-men copulating in sud pause syncopation, their lips cut
    back.

Xibalbá: the dance floor under America, under the range,
forever vital in caricaturing us, divining our vows.

Give me your claw bundle, Walt Whitman,
your Maya hypodermics. Let me feel what came up in you
as these gods and lords *milked you*, yes, *into existence*
High on coffee enema, have you a Thimble Theatre skit for us this
    evening?
Or are you now totally Otherworldly,
a Xibalbá denizen, decapitating any young poet whose neck is not
bandsaw strong enough to dance your blade?

In a whisper, Walt pointed out Dante, a senior male,
sitting on a low branch. "He's an Itzamna look-alike,
balls hanging out, that's his pose—
he has large white nipples,
his toes are extremely fat and huge."

Max Ernst During The Rain   *

Good morning, Max, are you still on the lookout for what has never been?

—Of course. The sun continues to be stored on the wrong side of disaster.

I arrived expecting to find you robed in red feathers, assisted by a pregnant hermaphrodite with a chewed-bloody right arm.

—Think of me as the father of scissors.

Yes, or as the great collagist of the labyrinth, cutting and pasting it into a new bicameral mind in which an identity in the midden of the instant supplants consciousness.

—The complete man must live simultaneously in several places, within several human beings. In him a range of people and multifarious situations must be continually present. Think of me as a hundred-headed guy.

Or as a nude sleeping in a water-lily harness rotating through a morning mined of maternal charge.

—Or as a derbied bird-headed man with brains for ass, both hemispheres having split his pants.

Are you suggesting that external objects have now broken with their normal environment and that the component parts have emancipated themselves from it in such a way that they are now able to strike up new relationships with other elements?

—If mother had not used my crib for stirrups, Herr Rabbit would not have had to pop the placenta cork to set my fetus free.

Is this what happens to you from staring at stains on the wall?

—Oh yes, blue immobilities, dormant ochres, centrifugal blocks magnificent in their centripetal sway, mummified hornets bursting their shrouds in order to drill into the bones of lightning rampant in a bear! At wing with my vision, I palpate the bowels of solar foals.

But is anything left of the beginning?

—Calcium-brittle flowers press upward. Faunal penetrations course the vineal verdure.

So who are these half-concealed beings peering out of your vitreous pillars and morel-like pipes?

—Sciomantic divinations. I consult the spirits of World Wars I and II. The nascent dead are avatars appearing in a cypress or a stele. Shell-shocked trolls reassembling via my hell-hocked mind. Souls in Hades doomed to re-colonize in floral nests as leaden yet hissing eggs. For "Europe After the Rain II" read: "Europe After the Reign—of Mars."

In these spirits I detect an older tradition, the medieval Persian world of the *Sha-nameh*. Ghosts of Safavid art, the homuncular grotesques of Sultan Muhammed or Aqa Mirak.

—Ah yes, plants as insects caught red-handed in self-fecundating arcs.

I hear you are stalked by beetles decked out in bells.

—As a blind swimmer passing as a wheat grain through the cross-section of a tree, or traveling as a zap of sperm in a contrary will, I made myself a seer.

Is not all artifice including nature?

—Man's temptation is to identify with a single period in time, and to therefore believe that he can free himself from the tentacles spider-folded in birth and rapture.

Is that why you have attempted to free everything from its shell,
from its distance,
from its comparative size,
from its physical and chemical properties,
its outward appearance?

—Only the sewer cricket lockered in Saint Cecilia's uterus can re-
spond to that. My point was not to find myself and to counteract any
desire for harmony with tremendous centrifugal force.

And these half-red-garbed, half-naked "goddesses"? They stand like
pupa-forms in the debris of an observational world. One, a queenly
rose-feathered owl, is accompanied by a swan-headed man with a
broken spear. Who are they?

—Where Mars is, Aphrodite is only a shadow away.

Justice will be done, but does the green hand guiding the serrated
blade have a body at stake?

—In every desire there is a skull whose cranium is a womb of flame.

Whose long blue arm is that milking volcano fumes out of nymph
echo?

—I am only interested in that *which saw itself in me.*

Is not all blessed with the desiccate kiss of farewell?

—Here, then, is the secret of my force: while painting with swan's
head hand I relentlessly regurgitate a crop of pigeon's milk into the
beaks of my young.

We must learn how to sound our mental volume without grieving, to
hear our fingers and not moan with our hands.

—And, while watching the pillage of immensity, to see everything as
it really is: without adherence or bond.

In Deep Sleep Dorothea Tanning Receives & Accepts the Awakened Clouds Above Her   *

The war in Dorothea Tanning,
human wind tunnels igniting, perishing
(By 1954 the early static scenes,
prismatically shattered,
are deliquescent with non-disclosure).

White phosphoric mist of screening mass,
images not obstructed
but scrambled, pyrophoric.

Color as the moods of gods,
ax glints of Ares, Hekate-spongy blacks.
Abstraction acidicly turning bodies into gaseous peat.

Is that a lighthouse?
If so why does it have a shredding infant in its beam?

She drives her fist into the wall of dream.
Miles inside, something clamps about her reach.
Is this the same snakebird angel
flitting about her labyrinth of fist-walled bends?

Not lead changed into gold
but lead and gold mixed from the beginning,
gold in all its plumbing.

"My dearest wish: to make a picture with no exit at all,
   either for you or for me."

I dreamed Tanning was buried to her neck beneath a bat-hung iroko
tree. Like the straw-colored flying foxes, she had feasted on iroko
fruit.

In her early painting, *Birthday,* she portrays herself bare-breasted, dressed in a skirt made of mandrake roots. Crouched before her, winged and lemur-eyed, is her spirit familiar (where, in medieval paintings, St. George's speared dragon is often found). She knows the language of the mermaids. She is *consciously* wild.

In the dream, she inquired: "Are you a body or a colorful area of the abyss?"

◇

For whom to live if not for one's inner hag,
hedge rider sailing back and forth in boundary-dissolving flight.

What is her goal? A wilderness bewitched with abstraction?
A culture populated by bodies released from anatomical mold?

Bodies with bones gone rubber. Between skin and bone, worms
    with minds of their own,
worms like frenzied violins,
millipedes fringed with metronomic yonder.

Bodies elastic as taffy blown scarlet, golden,
    a butterfly leech delirium,
                            acrobatic fetal swimmers,
        legs birling, all under the watch of a spider-eyed dog.

Dorothea with her dog in a Cythera-spectral Oz.
Form bisexing itself, peas in a pod guild orgy.

Abstract abacus of calculated fury.
Perpetual metastasis. Dream camera inside her body
    shooting through her organs.

What sore is she harrowing?
Why this proliferation of spirit familiars?
Baby-faced lhasa apsos, bear-pawed dwarf in blue jeans,
night-goggled lhasa apsos, head-mufflered dwarf in boots,

orangutang-armed lhasas apsos, gangly white goons,
huge faceless lhasa apso ghosts…

Are they the hundred-headed surrogate of an unborn child?
Are her pendular swings timed by a centaur in labor?

◇

Dream   3:12 AM
              5 January 2009
On the parvis of a cathedral Antonin Artaud joined the two of us.
He handed me a sheet of metal which he motioned for me to shape
    into a shallow bowl,
into which he placed a bouillon cube, boiling water,
to make for this 98 year old Dorothea Tanning,
    some soup.

◇

I see you and can say you because my thymus too is blanched with
    savior.
I dent I-ties in order to turn with you cog-wise high in the night.

Your white crescent moon piled with footless, toed babies.
A decapitated Venus bears, as a stand-in head, a manikin frog.
Plunging, amputated, copulating knots, with long arm-stalks jutting.
A child arched with a head of triangulated, crossboned arms.

Around a TV screen, as if in churning roundelay,
blue and peach body-parts tumble,
                              flotsam
in some ontological washing-machine
                              operated by
a fetusmear gripping—is it a lever
    or an eyeball?

Galesburg does not disappear.
Galesburg is a gale-warped mountain
        refashioned as
the vortex of your thinking,
the eye of the whirlpool's strong central suck,
the plethora of near-forms exuding
flesh drift, sludge windings, muzzle fires
—the incomprehensible impregnating everything—
the mind, in swivel, sensing itself several to its argument.
All is aftermath as time embowers primal loss.

Now on your dream wall I see you project a moving still:

   Ernst Crossing the Styx

He stares into the myriad shadow birds whispered through
   the prism of the insomniac's mirror.

                                    [December 2008–January 2009]

Pollock Pouring

To cage you blizzard, to purify
your gizzard while disemboweling
the lizard in its bower. To make these millipedal
feelers mill, to pedal eels, white elvers,
or are they elves? If so, turn piranhas on them
to exacerbate any penetralia
which may have coagulated in my rage.

To age you in an instant aardvark so that no one
can identify a figure in my marble reserve,
for the figure is eaten by the ground and the ground
is poisoned by the figure. The hierarch,
Ducoed and lacquered, is pulled down. And all of them,
blizzard-inquisitored
as fractal fragrance, are caged.

To dissemble thus deny any fulcrum in this annexed
dark. An ark? Din of anodyne shadow passengers
entering. An Aurignacian nostalgia
overcasts my spill. Do *they* still have the floor?
Or is image the sand of picture-trillion particles?
                              Palm here
pressed to canvas to indicate: NO WAY.
Or: all ways all at once. Window on
the shattered mace of authoritative majesty.
The crud we've lost is forever active as cadaver molt.

Dribble of cream zigzagging on skates:
O most thoughtless, most thoughtful century!
Bullet-riddled Clara Petacci! Iwo Jima!
Weave oh weave siphonophoric maze!

Blizzard, I lock you into drawn-down freefall
where the moldy straw
as if by Rumpelstiltskin is turned into aureate flares.

Riot of the dead weight in me seeking a monotheistic throne.

To convert umbilical restraint into julienned white tapeworms
whose cut ends arc through my pour.

Not my being, but being's bender as it is bent through me.

What is Garcia Lorca doing here? And in a blood canoe,
staring across the lake at Munch's melting tomb…

No god will disinfect the rock of my machine.

In the Cunt of the Celestial Crocodile I solarize as a Hadal sum.

GRATITUDE AND ANNOTATION

For many decades I have regarded poetry as a form in which the realities of the spirit can be tested by critical intelligence, a form in which the blackness in the heart of man can be confronted—in short, a form that can be made responsible for all the poet knows about himself and his world. I take responsibility for every word that I write. If I am beside myself at times, if the words appear to come from nowhere, this is a gift that I must honor but also evaluate as it arrives in the process of composition.

At the same time I want to thank my wife Caryl here for her active participation in the writing of all of my books (through 2008) since the fall of 1973 in Paris, when I began to regularly show her what I was doing and to ask her opinions about whether it made imaginative sense or not. For 35 years, she has defined the meaning of "reader" and "editor" for me. As a sounding board, she has been invaluable. While it may be occasionally true à la Ginsberg that "first thought [is] best thought," in my case composition is a slow, percolating process, with material passing through certain filters while other filters are being removed. In these attempts to extract the essence of material where context is always shifting until it "sets," Caryl's responses, mingling confirmation and resistance, have helped me see through superficial clarities as well as groundless obscurities. More specifically, she has rewritten passages (while in draft) or changed the direction of certain poems with a deft phrase and has taught me to allow another person to enter my creative space with rapport and love.

In the beginning, I was unsure as to whether I should share this activity with anyone. Being unsure meant that to share it with Caryl was a constant assault on my ego, putting my convictions on this or that to a test that often came down to whether what I had written made any kind of uncommon or even common sense. I think that this activity has been, and continues to be, one of the best things that has happened to me as a poet.

What I am attempting to describe is a kind of groundwork in which many of the materials, the impulses, the leaps, the risks, are to be shared and considered in tandem with another while they are in process, often with no plan or solution at hand. To do this considerably extends the compositional period, and creates a situation which seems to have more branch meanders than I would allow myself as a writer working solely on my own. Caryl has often picked up word substitutions or seed ideas in a worksheet than when urged forth in dialogue have made me realize that another range of materials has been stimulated, and that for me to be responsible for the new potential of a particular passage, I must do more homework on what earlier I had hoped Caryl would confirm.

I look back at my poems from the 1960s whose autobiographical "I" was even uncertain, but where a confidence to engage what I was up against in my struggle to translate Vallejo's *Poemas humanos* enabled my breakthrough into sacramental existence in The Duende section of the 1964 "Book of Yorunomado." By the early 1970s, I felt that a personal voice had been sufficiently created to enable it to split into either fictional voicings (the 1975 "Portraits" for example) or a perspective generated by the poem at hand, in which a non-identifiable "I" roamed, shaped and restricted by the poem's own induction of material.

I have thought more about poetry while translating César Vallejo than while reading anyone else. Influence through translation is different than influence from reading masters in one's own tongue. If I am being influenced by Wallace Stevens, say, his voice is coming directly into my own. You read my poem and think of Stevens. While translating, I am creating an American version out of—in the case of Vallejo—a Spanish text, and if Vallejo is to enter my own poetry he must do so via what I have already as a translator turned him into. This is, in the long run, very close to being influenced by myself, or by a *self I have created to mine.* Vallejo taught me that ambivalence and contradiction are facets of metaphoric probing. He gave me permission to try anything in my quest for an authentic alternative world in poetry.

In Donald Kuspit's Introduction to his book on the painter Leon Golub, I came across the words of Gabriel-Desire Laverdant (written three years before the revolution of 1848), who appears to be the first person to speak of radical art as "avant-garde." Kuspit writes:

> For Laverdant, avant-garde art "worthily fulfills its proper mission as initiator," making it "the forerunner and the revealer" of "the most advanced social tendencies." It "must lay bare with a brutal brush all the bru-

talities, all the filth, which are at the base of society." It has been forgotten that the brutal revelation of brutal reality—a mimesis that necessarily employs brutal techniques—is the central idea of the avant-garde, which has degenerated into a notion of esthetic revolution.

My primary belief concerning poetry is that it is about the extending of human consciousness, creating a symbolic consciousness that in its finest moments overcomes the dualities in which the human world is cruelly and eternally, it seems, enmeshed. Here I think of Paul Tillich's words: "A life process is the more powerful, the more non-being it can include in its self-affirmation, without being destroyed by it." Affirmation is only viable when it survives repeated immersions in negation. The problem of focusing at large on brutality and filth is that in doing so symbolic consciousness is flattened out by agit-prop and poetically-disguised journalism. There are many lies in poetry. Pretending that violence and horror do not exist is only one of them.

I have written some brutal poems over the last fifty years ("The Bridge at the Mayan Pass" and "Tomb of Donald Duck," both included in this volume, come to mind) and I want the blackness in the heart of mankind to be engaged as part of my primary stabilizations and concentrations, but I do not want it to rule. I see it as an important aspect, no more, of the imaginative world I am attempting to create, which includes my twenty-five year research project via the Ice Age painted caves of southwestern France on the origin of image-making, a number of poems on paintings by such artists as Caravaggio, Chaim Soutine, Leon Golub, Unica Zürn and Hieronymus Bosch, and other book-length translation projects on Aimé Césaire, Antonin Artaud, Michel Deguy, Vladimir Holan, and José Antonio Mazzotti.

I have come to believe that the "I," that selva of the self, is the most accessible vent in the language, that poetry is still in its psychological infancy, and that rather than repressing such troubling and unstable forces as "the self," or what I now think of as its chauffeur, "the ego,' they should be opened up and explored in what might be identified as the antiphonal flow, in Northrop Frye's words, "of a bicameral mind in which something else supplants consciousness." Because our national self has become monstrous, there is subconscious pressure to not attempt this, and the tendency of too much American poetry, in my opinion, has been to either treat the "I" as a taken-for-granted beacon by which one can beam one's opinions at the world, or to negate it entirely, which often result in non-referential and self-cannibalizing poems out of touch with the mythic and civil cores underlying international modernism.

Thank you for these days, Caryl, and late afternoons, and the evenings, thank you for providing a participating readership of the heart, a hearing that complexly sent out its flotillas of response, the immediate response of one who is also the beloved. Had you not participated I would have lost, ruined, torn apart many possible poems because as an only child the hardest thing I have had to learn to believe in has been not just the reality of the other, but her friendship, and the ways in which "muse" can be evoked in the dialogue of two people.

Hans Peter Duerr's *Dreamtime*, with its brisk, packed 132 page text and 237 pages of notes, is a challenging model for the presentation of poetry that is researched and scholarly as well as personal and inspired. In the 1990s I began to investigate the including of commentary and information along with the traditional citations at the end of my books. For 20th/21st century poets, of course, one source for this kind of annotation is T.S. Eliot's Notes to *The Wasteland*. The notion that such annotation is simply bookish or demeaning to the poems themselves perhaps arises from a purist vision of the poem as a kind of mystical flower without stem, roots, or dirt. If the poet is going to draw upon his reading and research, as well as his imaginative experience, it makes sense to me for him to indicate to the reader via notes some of the most significant referentiality involved in the poem's responsibilities.

◇

According to editor Stuart Kendall in his Bibliography for *Clayton Eshleman/The Whole Art* (Black Widow Press, 2014) I have published ninety-seven books and chapbooks of original poetry, translations, and non-fiction writings, and edited seventy issues of magazines and journals. The 230 poems collected here have been selected from twenty-four books (containing 780 poems), published between 1962 and 2010, as well as two poems published in magazines but not in books. Other than around a hundred poems that appeared in chapbooks (and that did not reappear in subsequent larger collections), along with the poems that appeared only in magazines (I would guess there are between four and five hundred), this total comes close to being my complete published poetry.

Two poems which I consider very important, each running over 40 pages, "Tavern of the Scarlet Bagpipe" (an examination of Hieronymus Bosch's triptych "The Garden of Earthly Delights") and "An Anatomy of the Night," have been left out of this "essential" collection, not only because of their length but because both are mixed genre works, "anatomies," as it were, with a significant amount of prose, and, in the latter case, a number of quotations from other writers. "Tavern of the Scarlet Bagpipe" is available in *Anticline* (2010) and "An Anatomy of the Night" is to be found in a 2011 BlazeVOX edition as well as *The Price of Experience* (2012).

I have also included only one semi-independent poem from the 1971 *Altars* since most of its 24 interlocking sections utilize coordinated material from astrology and the *I Ching*.

I have also left out the 41 page LSD-inspired "The Moistinsplendor" (from *The Price of Experience*) and my three "persona" workings: "The 9 Poems of Metro Vavin" (in *The Gull Wall*), *The Gospel of Celine Arnaud* (*Tuumba 12*, Berkeley, 1977) and Horrah Pornoff's "Homuncula" (26 sections of which, along with a note on the working's amusing reception, can be found in *Under World Arrest*).

Most of the poems in Section IV's *Juniper Fuse* had already been published in my Black Sparrow Press books that appeared between 1981 and 1998. Like Robert Duncan's "Passages" these poems belong to the compositional fabric of these books; unlike "Passages" these poems along with some essays and prose poems make up a *Juniper Fuse* "anatomy" of their own.

Between 1968 and 2004 Black Sparrow Press published 13 collections of my poetry along with one chapbook. I was in charge of the table of contents in all of these titles and there was never any censorship on the Press's part of anything I wrote. I am proud to have been published by Black Sparrow and want to acknowledge my gratitude to John and Barbara Martin here.

Further reflections on contemporary poetry, translation, and politics may be found in "What's American about American Poetry (*Companion Spider*), "Wind from All Compass Points (*Archaic Design*), and the Introduction to *An Alchemist with One Eye on Fire*.

◇

"The Roaches": Written in the late 1950s, after my having discovered Pablo Neruda's *Residencia en la tierra* I and II, this poem was published in *Trobar I* in 1960.

Mexico & North, my first book, was privately-published in Tokyo in 1962. All but 2 ("The Strong" written in Bloomington, Indiana, and "Dark Blood" written in Etzatlan) of the 7 poems included here were written in Chapala in the summer of 1960.

"Inheritance": "Anaya" is Humberto Anaya, a friend I made in Chapala. He was in charge of the local tourist office and offered me a free place to stay in a hut behind his office.

"Dark Blood": "the Tarascan woman… five hundred years": a reproduction of Tlatzeoteotl-Ixcuina, the Aztec goddess of childbirth and filth. What she appears to represent haunted my poetic apprenticeship for years.

◇

Walks, as stated in the book's colophon, "is the 10th *Caterpillar*, a series of publications edited by the author. This book, in an edition of 300 numbered copies was multilithed & handbound in NYC in the year of the Burnt Child… With *Caterpillar* X, that particular tree has been stripped, & these books will become (in upper case) CATERPILLAR magazine, to come forth quarterly for 3 years, beginning October 1967. The *Caterpillar Glyph* is a small napalmed Vietnamese child. Until the end of the war this black caterpillar."
Caterpillar magazine actually ran for 6 years, ending with issue #20 in 1973.

The two poems along with the letter to César Calvo included here were written in Lima, Peru, in early 1966. I was living there with my first wife Barbara who gave birth to our son Matthew on February 26. I had gone to Peru in an attempt to gain permission from César Vallejo's widow to inspect the worksheets of *Poemas humanos* (which I had started translating in Kyoto in 1962). I was making a living editing a magazine called *Quena* (a Quechuan word for a one-holed flute) that I had founded with the support of the Instituto Cultural Peruano Norteamericano which later that year suppressed my huge first issue because I refused to take out Paul Blackburn's translations of some apolitical poems by Javier Heraud, a young Lima poet who on a grant to Cuba had become politicized. After his return to Peru in 1963 as a member of the Ejército de Liberación National, he was shot by local police while drifting in a dugout near Puerto Maldonado. His death as a would-be guerilla created a scandal in Lima and because the Institute sponsoring *Quena* turned out to be receiving funds from the USIS, the American Ambassador in Lima informed my boss that the Heraud translations could not appear in any publication supported by the ICPN. Some of the contents of *Quena* were later published in another Peru-based literary journal, Haravec, edited by Maureen Ahern and David Tipton.

César Calvo (1940–2000) is a Peruvian poet and writer. His most distinguished work is (in English translation) *The Three Halves of Ino Moxo / Teachings of the Wizard of the Upper Amazon* (1995).

◇

The House of Okumura (Weed/flower Press, Toronto, March 1969) is a collection of 20 poems written in NYC between 20 January and 19 May, 1968. All of these poems are set in Kyoto, fall 1962/winter 1963, when Barbara and I were renting two tatami rooms at the back of the ground floor in the two-story Okumura home, next to a converted tea-house reserved for visits by Donald Keene, the famous Japanologist.

"The House of Okumura VI: *A Tale*": Kamaike Susumu with Cid Corman translated Basho's *Oku-No Hosomichi (Back Roads to Far Towns)* I have suspected for years that Joanne Kyger put LSD in my tea during my visit to the Snyders right before, while driving a half hour back to the Okumura house on my motorcycle, the hallucinatory experience occurred. When I asked her about this in 1977 she gave me an equivocal response. Years later she published her Kyoto Journal in which she described *me* as someone who liked to stab others in the back!

There are slightly varying versions of the red spider vision to be found in *Companion Spider*, pp. 55–57 and 117–120.

The first entry in "Erratics" (*The Price of Experience*) links Vallejo's poem, "The Spider," to this vision.

"The House of Okumura XIII": "HARA-KIRI" refers to the 1962 Japanese film by that title which impressed me deeply when I saw it several times in Kyoto. The reference to bamboo in the poem concerns an episode in which a ronin (a masterless samurai) enters a feudal estate pretending to seek permission to commit seppuku (= ritual harakiri). He actually hopes that the lord of the house will take pity on him and offer him charity. Too poor to own a steel sword he carries a fake one made of bamboo. Denied mercy, he is forced to disembowel himself in an agonizingly painful way with the bamboo. This film is the source material for the act of seppuku I committed in The Duende section of "The Book of Yorunomado."

◇

The House of Ibuki (Sumac Press, 1969). Barbara and I left the Okumura house in the spring of 1963 and moved into the Ibuki house a couple hundred yards away, where the rent was cheaper ($15 a month) and where we had a little more room. We lived there until returning to the states in August, 1964.

"Tsuruginomiya": "Paden" is William Paden (1930–2004), a dear friend from Indiana University who I helped move to Kyoto in 1964. Originally a German Expressionist-influenced painter, in Kyoto he determined to learn traditional Japanese woodcutting techniques. With his wife Yoshiko and daughter Carrie he returned to NYC in the late 1960s where he became a master in the Hanga print tradition. My elegy for Bill is "A Shade of Paden," published as a beautiful hand-made book by Piedoxen Printers in 2006 and reprinted in *Reciprocal Distillations*.

◇

Coils (Black Sparrow Press, Los Angeles, 1973): Part I.

While *Coils* was published 4 years after *Indiana*, two key poems in it were written before most of the poems in the latter collection. "The Book of Yorunomado" was completed in Kyoto in 1964, and "The Book of Niemonjima" in Bloomington, Indiana, 1965. These poems were thus written before those in *The House of Okumura, The House of Ibuki* as well as those in *Walks*.

From 1962 to 1971, *Coils* was a work-in-progress called "The Tsuruginomiya Regeneration" (Tsuruginomiya being the Shinto shrine across the alley from the Ibuki house). Poem sections from the work-in-progress appeared in various magazines (all are listed on the Acknowledgements page in *Coils*). Unable to realize this "Regeneration," I kept some of the poems, revised others and added more recent ones to them while completing *Coils* in 1972.

Each of the seven sections of *Coils* has an autobiographically-oriented introductory page before it. The page before Section I sets forth my state of mind in Kyoto at the point that the first poem, "The Book of Yorunomado," then part of the "Regeneration," was written.

While living in Kyoto in the early 60s I would ride my motorcycle downtown in the afternoon and work on my translation of César Vallejo's *Poemas humanos* in the Yorunomado ("Night Window") coffee shop. I had determined that a publishable version of this 89 poem collection would constitute my apprenticeship to poetry. As I struggled to get Vallejo's complex and complicated Spanish into English, I increasingly had the feeling that I was struggling with a man more than with a text and that the struggle was a matter of my becoming or failing to become a poet. It was as if through Vallejo I had made contact with a negative impaction in my being, a nebulous unreleased depth charge I had been carrying around with me for many years.

In The Duende section of "The Book of Yorunomado," the only poem I completed to any real satisfaction while living in Japan, I envisioned myself as a kind of angel-less Jacob wrestling with a figure who possessed a language the meaning of which I was attempting to wrest away. I lose the struggle and find myself on a seppuku platform in medieval Japan, being commanded by Vallejo (now playing the role of an overlord) to disembowel myself. I do so, cutting the ties to the "given life" and releasing a daemon named Yorunomado (in honor of my working place) who, until that point, had been chained to an altar in my solar plexus. Thus in early 1964, the fruits of my struggle with Vallejo were not a successful linguistic translation but an imaginative advance in which a third figure emerged from my intercourse with the text. Yorunomado became an imaginal companion in the ten-year process of developing a "creative life."

"Tú, luego, has nacido": from César Vallejo's poem, "The Soul that Suffered from Being its own Body." "NO. LA MANO, HE DICHO" quoted near the end of this poem is from the end of the same Vallejo poem.

THE DUENDE: According to Garcia Lorca (in "Theory and Practice of the Duende"), "we must repel the angel, and kick out the muse; the real struggle is with the duende, which burns the blood like powdered glass and rejects all the sweet geometry one has learned." One possible translation of duende is "bloodmare".

One of the ideas under the concept of mystical rebirth is that nothing can be created without immolation, without sacrifice. My disembowelment in The Duende section of this poem is creative in this sense: that the life which is sacrificed manifests itself in a more brilliant form upon another plane of existence. Thus: death and regeneration = seppuku and the birth of Yorunomado. A first confrontation with the abyss. Or as Hans Peter Duerr writes in Dreamtime: "Only a person who has seen his 'animal part', who has 'died', could consciously live in culture." Looked at from this perspective, my Phi Delta Theta pledgeship at Indiana University was a caricature of initiation and regeneration.

"The Darkening of the Light": See Hexagram 36 in the Wilhelm/Baynes translation of the I Ching.

Other poems concerning Yorunomado include "Mokpo" in Coils, and "Yorunomado's End" and "Yorunomado in the Underworld" in Our Journey Around the Drowned City of Is published in The Price of Experience.

"The Book of Niemonjima": From the introductory page for Section II of Coils: "During the spring of 1962 Barbara and I made a trip to Futomi, a fishing village several hours south of Tokyo. Late the first night there I left our inn and walked down to the breach and stood there in intense meditation. About a quarter mile off shore was an island named Niemonjima (I have never found how the word translates; Bashō visited the island and wrote a poem there which is now cut into a slab at the island's crest: "Umi kurete kamo no koe honokani shiroshi" — (Sea darkening wild duck cry pale white). From where I stood in the wind and roaring surf this island appeared a black hump against the sky. I saw this form as a woman bent weeping and felt a powerful longing to go there, feeling that she represented an aspect of my humanity I could then only dimly make out."

"The Gull-Robe": See the essay on Paul Blackburn, "The Gull Wall," in *The Grindstone of Rapport*.

"The Sons of the Sepik Delta" is my phrase based on the Sepik River culture of New Guinea and the Phi Delta Theta social fraternity at Indiana University where I lived from 1953 to 1956. "The double fireplace" was a huge two-way hearth in the center of the Phi Delt living room when the fraternity was in an old mansion at the corner of 10th and Jordan.

The phrase "Origin's watchfiends" is a play on Blake's "Satan's Watchfiends," and opposes the view of poetry (as perception in contrast to imagination) proposed by *origin* magazine and editor Cid Corman.

◇

Indiana (Black Sparrow Press, Los Angeles, 1969.

"Hand": In citing the Olson essay at the beginning of this poem, I had in mind his paragraph on the Maya in his "Human Universe" essay: "They have lost the capacity of their predecessors to do anything in common. But they do one thing no modern knows the secret of, however he is still by nature possessed of it: they wear their flesh with that difference which the understanding that it is common leads to. When I am rocked by the roads against any of them—kids, women, men—their flesh is most gentle, is granted, touch is in no sense anything but the natural law of flesh, there is none of that pull-away which, in the States, causes a man for all the years of this life the deepest sort of questioning of the rights of himself to the wild reachings of his own organism."

"The 1802 Blake to Butts Letter Variation": I refer to the letter written on 22 November 1802. Blake's expressing his mysterious crisis helped give me the courage to delve into my own. The Butler Woods is a large woodland area owned by Butler University a few blocks from my childhood home. In my poem, Jesus's speech to Albion is from Plate 96 of Blake's *Jerusalem*.

"Sensing Duncan II": "Wagadu is the power that lives in the hearts of men, recognized when eyes allow her recognition, heard when ears hear the blades clash and their sounds upon the shields, and now unseen because exhausted and hard-pressed by the indomitability of men, when she falls asleep." This passage is from a version of "The Lute of Gassir" (a west African epic collected by Leo Frobenius and originally translated by Douglas Fox and published in Frobenius and Fox's *African Genesis* in 1937) to be found in Cid Corman's *origin #13*, second series, 1964. The Fox translation may be found in Jerome Rothenberg's *Technicians of the Sacred*, second edition, 1985. "Duncan" of course is the poet Robert Duncan.

"Diagonal": The woman addressed in this poem is "Marie." "Letter from New Paltz" in *Coils* is the most detailed piece on my 1968 relationship with her.

"Sunday Afternoon": extensive revisions here of the 1969 version.

◇

Altars (Black Sparrow Press, Los Angeles, 1971).

"Ode to Reich": *Altars* is a 100 page book-length poem that threads my personal life through a year of astrological phases and their corresponding hexagrams in the *I Ching*. The most significant section of this poem that stands free of this astrological/*I Ching* fugue is the "Ode to Reich" written near the culmination of my year and a half in Reichian therapy with Dr. Sidney Handelman in NYC. Entry #21 in "Erratics" (to be found in *The Price of Experience*) describes the basic exercise in Handelman's version of Reichian therapy. By "the clarification of Beulah" I intend to fuse Wilhelm Reich's theories of the function of the orgasm with William Blake's interpretation of "Beulah," i.e., the world of gratified desire leading to imaginative vision and work (a sighting of Maithuna and the "antiphonal swing" elaborated throughout my poetry). In this poem the Baudelaire quote is from *My Heart Laid Bare,* passage LXXXI. The Reich is from *The Murder of Christ.* There is a thoughtful exposition of Blake's "Beulah" in Harold Bloom's *The Visionary Company.*

◇

Coils: Part II

"Origin": From the introductory page for Section V of *Coils:* "When I was a student at Indiana University in 1959 I sent some first efforts at poetry to Cid Corman, who was living in Kyoto. A week later I received a response from him that flushed me all the way through as I read it. In one bristling paragraph he got through to me that what I had sent him was contemptible because I was not taking art or my life seriously. I entered into correspondence with Corman and over the next few years he gave me a keen sense of the dedication to art one must have in order to make an art that is truly meaningful to oneself and others. When I moved to Japan in 1961 Corman was still in Kyoto. I spent many evenings with him at The Muse coffee shop and assimilated a great deal from his viewpoints (some of which I strongly disagreed with) on poetry. As I began to try and find my own way in writing "The Tsuruginomiya Regeneration," one of the blocks I had to deal with was the following: because I respected Corman I wanted to write something that he would admire; however, while writing I would feel something that I thought was his presence frowning over my shoulder at the material I considered to be most my own. This situation held a double meaning. On one hand I was finding out that the kind of poem I wanted to write was not at all the kind of poem Corman sought for *origin*—yet when he rejected my poems I would be thrown into a state of doubt about my own abilities. What the poet-editor Corman evoked in me was the stern father that I was to my emerging son-Self. In order to explore this area I created Origin as a master to Yorunomado who in this context I saw as a dog."

The LSD-inspired metamorphosis of Barbara's face in this poem is described more literally in the Introduction to "The Moistinsplendor" in *The Price of Experience.*

"The Golden String": For some background on "Adrienne," see the introductory page to Section VI of *Coils*. As Ariadne, she is praised in "Sensing Duncan II".

"Keeping the Flies from my Mother's Head": This poem, which did not appear in *Coils*, originally appeared in *Sparrow 18* [March 1974]. It was written in the summer of 1970 after my having joined my parents for lunch in their care facility north of Indianapolis.

"Coils": From the introductory page for section VII of *Coils*: "In Kyoto as I would crouch in the *benjo* (the toilet room) over the porcelain trench, my position reminded me of Tlatzeoteotl, the Aztec goddess of childbirth and filth. The version of Tlatzeoteotl I had seen portrayed her crouched with a little man emerging between her thighs, his hands held up to his shoulders and curved downward, like paws. My desire became to give birth to a figure who was "primitive" in the sense that he could participate in an interdependent circuit of being, a heroic figure of the imagination, who was not haunted as I was then by Nature. Those years in Kyoto the sanitation truck would come by every few months and put its long trunk-like hose into people's *benjo* pits to suck out the contents. The smell was stupendous as well as extremely unpleasant. It was the smell of the collective coil, common denominator of life on, and of, earth.

Tlazeoteotl was just one of the forms that Coatlicue, a major figure in the Aztec pantheon, took on. Coatlicue was referred to as "mother of the gods" and what this meant to the Aztecs is portrayed in an awesome piece of sculpture in the National Museum of Anthropology in Mexico City.

Watching the pregnant red spider's abdomen where her spinnerets were, I felt my own center of power. As I would look at the spider, I would see Coatlicue, and in Coatlicue/spider I saw the urn which contained the mutilated body of the woman "Coatlicue". This sacrificial body was several things at once: the image of woman generational man carries in his mind and which is part of the meaning of the word "sacred, as well as my own father/mother, the complex I had to break up in order to release myself from Indiana.

Because I could not get inside the tiny Coatlicue/spider urn to view the mutilated body close up, I expanded the urn into a silo. I determined that this was the spiritual shape of the abyss of Indiana. According to Aztec myth, Huitzilopochtli, the god of war, saves the woman "Coatlicue" from her sons and sisters who want to kill her because she became pregnant without a husband. The revelation from having entered this abyss was to discover that it is "Coatlicue's" body around which the idol Coatlicue is constructed and from which the two giant rattlesnakes rise and face each other above the top of the urn, forming the head of the goddess Coatlicue."

◇

The Gull Wall (Black Sparrow Press, Los Angeles, 1975).

"Bud Powell": The best introduction to my relationship with the jazz pianist Bud Powell is to be found in one of my contributions to Peter Davis's *Poet's Book Shelf* (reprinted in my *Archaic Design*). Upon hearing of Powell's death at forty-one in 1966, I wrote (see *Indiana*, pp. 82–83):

> Bud Powell important, and beautiful, to jazz in some-
> what the same way Soutine is central to art, Crane
> (Hart) to poetry: wild, flowing spirit, a fire-thief, pos-
> sessed beyond questionable technique; that his left
> hand was discordant, off, a kind of paw chomping, no
> matter—he fucked his mother when he played, his
> sisters, his brothers, and he fucked me, all the way up
> thru my anus thru my eyes; how can how can you not
> praise & praise a person who began to unthaw you, to
> restore some of what you know as your humanity, a
> teacher in the truest sense, a motherfucker.

Additional pieces on Bud Powell are "The Bison Keyboard" in this collection and "Un Poco Loco" in *Hades in Manganese*.

"Portrait of Vincent van Gogh": This is the first of some 40 ekphrastic studies included in this book. Over the decades I have composed, including the pieces based on Ice Age cave imagery in *Juniper Fuse*, over 150 poems on art and artists. In 2005, in a statement for *deep THERMAL*,

"Images by Mary Heebner / Poems by Clayton Eshleman," I wrote: "I am interested in what I see in paintings as well as what the paintings see in me. I found in certain Mary Heebner watercolors a resonating psychic stimulation, and attempted to improvise on the words, narrative nodes and associational 'chains' they flushed forth." For many years the following words of Baudelaire, from "The Salon of 1846," have inspired such workings: "I sincerely believe that the best criticism is that which is both amusing and poetic: not a cold, mathematical criticism which, on the pretext of explaining everything, has neither love nor hate, and voluntarily strips itself of every shred of temperament. But, seeing that a fine picture is nature reflected by an artist, the criticism which I approve will be that picture reflected by an intelligent and sensitive mind. Thus the best account of a picture may well be a sonnet or an elegy."

"Leon Golub working on a painting…": When I visited our friends Leon Golub and Nancy Spero in NYC in 1974, Leon told me that a few months earlier he had entered his apartment building at 71st and Broadway to be accosted by an armed man in the elevator who demanded that he let him into his apartment. Leon's youngest son, Paul, was in the apartment alone. Leon did what he was told, the man tied the two of them up, ransacked the apartment and left. At that time Leon was working on large paintings depicting combat in the Vietnamese War.

Over the decades I have written a number of pieces on Leon and his work. See "Figure and Ground" and "Monumental" in this collection, an essay "Golub the Axolotl" in *Antiphonal Swing*, the review "Leon Golub at Barbara Gladstone" in *The Price of Experience*, "Leon Golub, primarily smiling" in *Anticline*, and "Blue Sphinx" also from that book and included here.

"Portrait of Francis Bacon": Other pieces on Francis Bacon in this collection are "Bacon Studies (III)" and "Spirits of the Head" from *Everwhat* (which also included "Bacon Studies (IV)." Another Bacon poem, "Dialogue with a Triptych" appeared in *What She Means*.

What She Means (Black Sparrow Press, Santa Barbara, 1978).

"Still-life, with Fraternity": I was a member of the Phi Delta Theta fraternity from fall 1953 until 1956 when I was thrown out of school for a semester because of an abundance of on-campus parking tickets. I moved out and lived with a couple of Korean War veteran students in an apartment off campus and sold men's wear in a Bloomington department store. When I returned to school I became a Philosophy major, and took a course on 20th century American poetry with the writer Sam Yellen. During this period I played at a piano bar in the Dandale steak house on the weekends. I also met Jack and Ruth Hirschman who introduced me to such European poets as Rilke, Lorca, Mayakofsky and St John Perse, made contact with Paul Blackburn (who introduced me to William Carlos Williams), Jerry Rothenberg and Robert Kelly in NYC and in 1960 edited 3 issues of *Folio,* a literary magazine sponsored by the Indiana University English Department. Suddenly the contours of a direction were visible.

"Scorpion Hopscotch": Re "as Berdyaev and Bataille have said": I am referring to the chapter on creativity and sex in *The Meaning of the Creative Act,* and Chapter IX in *Eroticism.*

"The Green Apple Photo": When I was teaching in the Summer Seminar in Frenstat, Czechoslovakia, in the summer of 1976, one of my students, Jan Benda, introduced me to the poetry of Vladimir Holan, which led to my co-translation with Frantisek Galan and Michael Heim of Holan's long poem "A Night with Hamlet" (*Conductors of the Pit,* 2005 edition). Benda also brought the poetry of the Czech Milan Exner to my attention, and in the late 1970s through the mail we co-translated four poems of Exner's which appeared in several issues of *Montemora* (one of which was reprinted in *The Grindstone of Rapport*). After teaching in Frenstat, I spent a week in Prague during which time the four Prague poems included here were written."

"Still-life, with African Violets": Yunotsu is a mineral spa in southwestern Honshu, Japan, where Barbara Eshleman and I, by chance, bathed with scarred atomic bomb survivors in 1964.

◇

Hades In Manganese (Black Sparrow Press, Santa Barbara, 1981).

"The Lich Gate": The visual and assemblage artist Wallace Berman (1926–1976) was a friend during Caryl's and my early years living first in Sherman Oaks (1970–1972) and then in west Los Angeles (1974–1986). He gave us collages for our birthdays and I put his artwork on two *Caterpillar* covers (#14 and #17). His truck was smashed into by a drunken truck driver in Topanga Canyon while Wallace was coming home from having a beer in a local pub on the eve of his 50th birthday. He was killed instantly.

"Frida Kahlo's Release": Frida Kahlo (1907–1954) needs no introduction here. I discovered her work in the May, 1976, *Art Forum*, in an illustrated article by her biographer Hayden Herrera. In a state of great excitement I scribbled in a notebook the poem presented here.

"Turnstiles": The reader may have noticed that in the late 1970s and early 1980s references to deep antiquity and the painted Upper Paleolithic caves occasionally appear in poems that are not directly concerned with the past. Poems from this period directly concerning the caves have been taken out of the books published in these years and assembled in the *Juniper Fuse* section IV of this collection. Poems such as "Danse Macabre" and "Turnstiles" reveal the extent to which my developing cave project tended to resonate in workings that were by and large concerned with other matters.

"Master Hanus to his Blindness": In the late 15th century, the story goes, the clockmaker Master Hanus transformed the old clock on the Old Town Hall, in the heart of Prague, into an elaborate and extraordinary curiosity, adding numerous statuettes that included a skeleton that not only marked each hour by pulling a rope but also held a running hourglass in his bony hand. City counselors, fearing that Hanus would recreate his masterpiece in another city, arranged for thugs to put out his eyes. The clockmaker survived, after which he damaged the clock's machinery (to the point that it took a hundred years for people to figure out how to fix it), dying of a heart attack as he did so.

Tusex stores in Prague were, in 1977, when Caryl and I spent some time there, government-operated "luxury" marts which required the use of special money easily obtained by foreigners but difficult for those behind the Iron Curtain to come by.

"For Aimé Césaire": In 1978, I tried to explain to Florence Loeb, the daughter of the famous Parisian art dealer, Pierre Loeb, the desire for the prodigious in Césaire's poetry and some of the circumstances under which it takes root. She listened to me and then said something I will never forget: "Césaire uses words like the nouveaux riches spend their money." She meant, of course, that this prodigal son of France, educated and acculturated by France, should cease his showing off, racing his language like roman candles over her head, and return to the fold (to the sheepfold, I might add, to a disappearance among the millions for whom to have French culture is supposed to be more than enough). To this aristocratic woman, Aimé Césaire's imaginative wealth looked like tinsel. I carried this sinister cartoon of his power around with me for a couple of years. One morning what I wanted to say was a response to Césaire himself.

◇

Fracture (Black Sparrow Press, Santa Barbara, 1983).

"The Death of Bill Evans" and "Fracture": See "Interface II: Fracture" in *Juniper Fuse* for an account of the circumstances under which these poems were written in the French Dordogne in 1980.

"Tomb of Donald Duck": Section I. Apparition of the Duck: I drew considerably on material in *How to Read Donald Duck* by Ariel Dorfman and Armand Mattelart.

Section II: Toddler Under Glass: This section is built using materials from "Baby's Book of Events," a scrapbook in which my father recorded nearly everything I said, did, and was given, during the first three years of my life.

Section III: The Severing: "Man then severed himself from this placenta in which he and the world had been embedded. The first step in this severance was the dethronement of the animal. Today man is striving to become master of matter. The process of segregating man from the natural world around him grows ever more and more dangerous." *The Eternal Present: The Beginnings of Art*, by S. Giedion, p. 273. The following paragraphs on the same page and the following one are quite pertinent to this section.

Section IV: Stud Farms of Cooked Shadows: This title is a line from Aimé Césaire's poem "Interlude." Besides news reports, I also drew on Hans-Jürgen Syberberg's *Our Hitler*, and Carolyn Forché's reportage on El Salvador.

"The Spiritual Hunt:" Biographers of Arthur Rimbaud tell us that one of the poet's greatest poems, "La Chasse spiritual," is lost. My poem is a satirical fantasy generated out of the Rimbaudian void.

"Maithuna": "It is in this afterglow after sex that the things of God are revealed; the tantrics call it Maithuna": *The Wise Wound* by Peter Redgrove and Penelope Shuttle.

"Elegy": for material on Vladimir Holan and his poem "A Night with Hamlet" see "A Note on Vladimir Holan and his *Hamlet*" in the 2005 edition of *Conductors of the Pit*. For Caravaggio, see "The Beheading" from *Reciprocal Distillations*, reprinted in this collection.

◇

Our Journey Around the Drowned City of Is (published in *The Price of Experience*, Black Widow Press, 2012).

"Kerlescan": A key poem from this 1985 journal of our trip to French Brittany. Via Nantes, we entered the peninsula, and over the next month drove around it, paying special attention to the standing stones (as at Kerlescan) in the Carnac area, the fissured cliffs of Finistère, the ominous Arrée Mountains and the beautiful pink granite of the Bretonne Corniche (celebrated in "Apotheosis"). I was well into the writing of *Juniper Fuse* while on this trip, and thus saw the stones, dolmens, and menhirs in Brittany as a groundwork for building imaginative links between the ancient decorated caves and historical art and culture.

◇

The Name Encanyoned River: Selected Poems 1960–1985 (Black Sparrow Press, Santa Barbara, 1986).

"The Excavation of Artaud": This poem is based on a prosodic pattern by Vallejo in the poem "El libro de la naturaleza." There is a commentary on two Artaud "workings" based on Vallejo structures in "An Ego Strong Enough to Live" in *Archaic Design*. Artaud mentions the attack on his Muladhara Chakra (= root support), or, in his own words, "on the curvature of that bone/located between anus and sex," in *Artaud le mômo* (see my translation of this poem in *Watchfiends & Rack Screams*). In *The Masks of God: Primitive Mythology*, Joseph Campbell quotes Geza Róheim on Australian black magic directed against "the flesh between the scrotum and the rectum." The term "amphimixis" (= the synthesis of two or more erotisms in a higher unity) was coined by Sandor Ferenczi in *Thalassa*.

Antonin Artaud has been a companion of my work for many decades. Other pieces concerning him are: "Portrait of Antonin Artaud" in *The Gull Wall*, "Negation's Mate" and "Amphimixis" in *Under World Arrest*, "My Evening with Artaud" in this collection, the Introduction to *Watchfiends & Rack Screams* and "Artaud's True Family Glimpsed at Pompidou" in *Companion Spider*, "Spectator, Spectre, Sitter" in *Archaic Design*, and "Black Paradise" in *Anticline*.

"Ariadne's Reunion": Two brief sections from "Placements II: The Aranea Constellation" (in *Juniper Fuse*) should key in my honoring of Ariadne:

> Every artist participates in Ariadne. The transformation of the "given" life to a "creative" one not only involves entering a dark or "inner" life, but generating as well a resistance substantial enough to test oneself against and to shape the focus of one's work. Having experienced the bestowal of soul (which is the reality of Ariadne), one must liberate the experience in a creative product, must emerge with more than the claim that something "happened" while "inside."

As an early form of Ariadne, Arihagne (the "utterly pure") was a spinning hag or sorceress who enjoyed intercourse with the labyrinth and its grotesque inhabitant. When patriarchal consciousness overwhelmed matriarchal centering, Ariadne became a "maiden to be rescued," who, "falling in love" with the hero Theseus, gave him a "clew" or thread that would enable him to get in and out and, while in, to slaughter the sleeping Minotaur. The labyrinth, without its central being, was thus emptied of animality.

"Deeds Done and Suffered by Light": this poem was written in 1979 while Caryl and I were staying in our friend the Syrian painter Marwan's summer home in the mountains north of Alassio in western Italy. The list of birth gifts comes from the previously-cited "Baby's Book of Events."

◇

Hotel Cro-Magnon (Black Sparrow Press, Santa Rosa, 1989).

"Reagan at Bitburg": On May 5, 1985, President Reagan presided over a wreath-laying at the base of a cemetery at Bitburg, Germany, looming over the graves of some 2000 German soldiers, including 49 SS troops. Jewish demonstrators from many countries, including United States, strongly protested the President's visit to Bitburg as well as to the nearby Bergen-Belsen concentration camp where 50,000 victims of the Nazis are buried in mass graves. White House aids acknowledged that the Bitburg and Bergen-Belsen visits were probably the biggest fiasco of Reagan's presidency.

"The Bison Keyboard": A sestina fantasia based on Bud Powell's 11 month hospitalization in 1948 in the Creedmore State Hospital where he was administered two series of electroshocks. It is said that he drew a keyboard on the wall of his cell so that he could mentally keep up his chops while incarcerated.

"Commarque": An impressive ruined castle on the south bank of the Beune River near Les Eyzies in the French Dordogne. Built in the 12th and 13th centuries, its thick-walled keep and fortifications are constructed over a cave in which there is a fine Upper Paleolithic engraving of a horse's head in profile.

"On Atget's Road": Eugène Atget (1857–1927) was a commercial photographer whose some 10,000 photographs document the historic character of French life. This poem is based on some of his photos of rural French villages to be found in *The Work of Atget / Volume I / Old France*.

"Children of the Monosyllable": A fantasia based on the "Monosyllable" entry in the 1970 Arno Press reprint of the seven volumes (1890–1904) of *Slang And Its Analogues*, which is not only a great work of lexicography but a museum reflecting the milieu of three centuries of life in England and about a century of life in America.

"At the Speed of Wine": Of the American poets whose work is identified with the first half of the 20th century, Hart Crane has always meant the most to me. This poem was stimulated by reflections on my co-translation of Vladimir Holan's "A Night with Hamlet" in which the speaker imaginatively engages a special night visitor (in Holan's case, a phantasmagoric Hamlet who appears to the poet in his apartment in Prague; in my case, an intoxicated Hart Crane in a lower Manhattan bar). This poem is also shadowed by Ulysses' conversation with Tiresias in Book XIII of *The Odyssey*.

Other of my pieces on Crane are: "A Gloss on Hart Crane's 'Lachrymae Christi' in *Archaic Design*, "Portrait of Hart Crane" in *The Gull Wall*, "The Tears of Christ Pulled Inside Out" in *Fracture*, "The Collected Poems of Hart Crane" in *Poet's Book Shelf*; and "A Visit from Hart Crane" in *Our Journey Around the Drowned City of Is*.

◇

Under World Arrest (Black Sparrow Press, Santa Rosa, 1994).

"Still-life, with Huidobro": "organiz'd innocence": marginalia to William Blake's *The Four Zoas*: "Unorganiz'd Innocence: an Impossibility. / Innocence dwells with Wisdom, never with Ignorance." The Vicente Huidobro line is from his poem "Arte Poética."

"Indiana in the Night Sky": The consternational backdrop of this poem attempts to engage a knot of sacred interdictions. As an immortal to the infant, mother appears to be the fount of imagination, and, in my experience, imagination does not clear itself of observational restraints until the image of the body of the mother is psychically passed through. By "body" here Charles Olson would include the "huge rock" that Kumarbi fucks in "The song of Ullikummi", (*The Collected Poems*) as well as the "Mountain" penetrated by the Algonquin woman ("Monday, November 26th, 1962", *The Maximus Poems IV, V, VI*). The latter story-poem is especially striking, as it indicates that women as well as men are "to walk right through the rock of the mountain."

It is said that Caesar was told that his dream of incest meant that he was to conquer the world. For the poet, I would revise this meaning to: fulfillment of psychic incest may enable him or her to invent a world (see "Still-life, with Huidobro" and "Sunday, 10 PM" in *Our Journey Around the Drowned City of Is*).

One function of psychic incest is to enable poetic parthenogenesis to occur. I have found that it was necessary to pass through mother's complex ramifications for a vision of myself as entirely separate to occur, or, as proposed in several poems in *Anticline,* to enable me to become fully born.

The italicized lines in the poem first appeared as the epigraph to *Indiana.*

"Double Pelican": Here is an image of the alchemical "double pelican" (from the cover of John Trinick's *The Fire-Tried Stone*), which, in the way that it is drawn, suggests a sexual reading of the "circulation."

"After Pindar:" Source of this piece is the article on Sarajevo in *The New York Times Magazine,* July 26, 1992.

"A Friendship": Koki Iwamoto, who owned Chatterton's Bookstore on Vermont Street, was a dear friend from our years in Los Angeles. He died from AIDS in 1994.

"Strata": The first stanza draws upon material from the second chapter, "The Escape Route," of Elaine Morgan's *The Descent of Woman.*

"Out of the Kat Godeu": On one level, a celebration of our 1986 month in Hungary on a Soros Foundation travel grant. We spent most of our time in Budapest with our generous hosts, Gyula Kodolanyi and Maria Illyés. Working together many afternoons, Gyula and I translated the 56-page section of Hungarian poetry that appeared in *Sulfur #21.* The italicized lines at the beginning of the poem are my translation from a French translation of the Welsh "Kat Godeu." Also called "the Book of Taliesin"—since is attributed to a 6th century bard by that name—and "Battle of the Trees," it is mainly known to English readers in D.W. Nash's Victorian version published in Robert Graves' *The White Goddess.*

"Hardball": This poem is a response to my viewing of a videotape of the beating of Rodney King on March 3, 1991, by Los Angeles police officers following a high-speed car chase (King was struck 33 times and suffered a fractured facial bone, broken right ankle and multiple bruises and lacerations). The acquittal of the officers involved led to the Los Angeles riots of 1992 in which 53 people lost their lives.

I wrote "Hardball" in a state of anguished fury, trying to jam words together to the point that they cracked or melted.

"Guyton Place": In the late 1980s, the painter/sculptor Tyree Guyton and his wife Karen created a unique ongoing art installation in the run-down Detroit neighborhood which they called "The Heidelberg Project" (after the street on which Guyton's grandfather lived, which was also the central street in the project). Basically it involved attaching junk and abandoned objects to several abandoned houses and turning them into outdoor sculpture. The street itself, trees, fire hydrants etc., were also painted and decorated.

The City of Detroit at first welcomed the project, listing it as a must-see for tourists (thus at the height of its popularity, Mercedes and stretch-limos could be seen crawling by). After numerous complaints by uncomprehending citizens (who thought Guyton was into Vodun) the City decided that "the Heidelberg Project" was a public nuisance and, while leaving scores of crack houses in the same area alone, bulldozed all of the Guyton houses in two stages (1989 and 1991). Not owning the houses, the Guytons had no way to protect them. However, in later years Tyree decorated a number of other houses in the Heidelberg area, most of which, as of December 2013, have been burned down.

This poem is the result of several visits I made to the project in 1989 at which time I made lists of the things attached. There are photographs of these houses in *Sulfur #25*.

"Navel of the Moon": This poem is a celebration of the two months in the spring of 1991 that Caryl and I spent in Mexico City and Oaxaca. One of the highlights of our time in Oaxaca was a night spent wandering on our own the partially-excavated archaeological site of Monte Alban, six miles up in the hills from Oaxaca. The vision in the first stanza of the poem led me into a labyrinth of research which I will attempt to summarize here:

In *Muelos: A Stone Age Superstition about Sexuality,* Weston La Barre offers a well-documented argument that from deep antiquity—even as part of a Paleolithic *Ur-Kultur*—there has been a worldwide belief that there is a physical connection, via the cerebrospinal canal, between the male brain and semen. He sums up the superstition as follows:

> The complex of ideas includes the following: bones are given by the male parent, and bones can magically reconstitute the whole animal. As the main storehouse of bone marrow (muelos), the brain is the source of semen, via the spinal cord. The supply is limited. The fertility of the head is associated to cosmic fertility of the sun, rain, lightning. Fire, light, lightning, and seed are all aspects of the same holy male mystery. The fertility of humans, wild animals,

and fields can be increased by collecting severed human heads. Fat-marrow and bones are appropriate sacrifices to the immortal spirits, the eternal gods. Immortality also consists in the "continence" of muelos-seed, achieved in various ways. Adult manhood is not the result of endogenous forces but must be obtained from outside through a variety of methods, including homosexual acts. Virility is secreted with the semen, in all ejaculation of any kind; virility can thus on occasion be made a gift. Loss of manhood, power, and ultimately life itself results from the "spending" of the life-force, which is a finite capital.

While La Barre is undoubtedly medically correct (i.e., that the brain is not the source of semen), the extent to which this superstition is tied into religion, philosophy, sexuality, and war, indicates that it may be fundamental to man's attempt to reconcile spirit and matter. The belief that there is a connection between brain and genitals underlies the subtle body doctrine of Tantra (behind which is an earlier identification between the ageless serpent and the Great Goddess). Tantra proposes that a kind of two-way traffic is possible in the spinal column: the downward energy is inducted via an invisible opening situated in the crown of the skull (probably the fontanel). The upward movement is initiated when a subtle female snake, Kundalini, coiled between anus and sex, is aroused to straighten up and ascend the subtle channel of the spinal column, passing through a series of mandala-discs, call Chakras, on her way to the Ajna chakra, located between the eyes, as a "third eye." Here, formless contemplation is said to take place, as the initiate achieves a union of the two absolute principles into what is called "the unitary Brahman".

In the 1930s, as part of his evolving "function of the orgasm" theory and practice, Wilhelm Reich, with apparently no knowledge of Tantra, sketched out a segmental structure of what he called "character armor," Given his goal of re-establishing plasmatic currents in the pelvis, he began his dissolution of this armor in the regions farthest away from the pelvis. His segments bear a striking resemblance to the Tantrik Chakras.

Reich's "segments"	Tantrik Chakras
ocular ring	Ajna Chakra
oral ring	
deep neck musculature	Vishuddha Chakra
chest ring	Anahata Chakra
diaphragm & solar plexus	
large abdominal muscles	Manipura Chakra
pelvis	Svadhishthana &
	Muladhara Chakras

More recently, in his *Typhonian Trilogy*, the Aleister Crowley scholar, Kenneth Grant, has linked the Qabalistic Tree of Life, astrology, and Tarot, with the Tantra subtle body, in an esoteric web of sexual ritual relating to the Vama Marg, or Left Hand Path, which is not only tied into worship of the Primal Goddess but into making contact with extra-terrestrial entities. Curiously, while Grant occasionally quotes Reich, and seems to be familiar with his work at large, he does not mention Reich's ideas about segmental armoring.

As one who has not practiced any form of Tantrik ritual, my experience in these matters is limited to the following: while in Reichian therapy in the late 1960s, I experienced an eruption up my spine that is described in "Interface II: Fracture" in *Juniper Fuse*. Secondly, since the early 1970s, I have been aware of a phenomenon I call "antiphonal swing." Orgasm has often been followed by a period of relaxation that is fantasy-intensive (identified in some Tantrik sects as *maithuna*), and occasionally hallucinogenic. The images that occur point toward a renewal of creative work, which leads to a renewal of sexual desire. It seems antiphonal because the imagination and the genitals function like the far swing points of a pendulum, involved with each other's momentum.

Two final points in this regard: one of the earliest appearances of oracular display that I am aware of, initially from Africa, and more recently documented in Haiti, is the figure of a snake priestess straddling a box containing a snake. Penetrated by the "god," she writhes as the oracle speaks from her mouth. Might the Tantra Kundalini system represent an evolution of an earlier system in which an actual snake was used?

In *The Magic Revival* Grant writes: "The incubus or succubus is the exteriorization, or extrusion, of the satyr in each individual. It represents the subliminal Will; in effect, the Dwarf Self or Holy Guardian Angel. It is this principle in man that is immortal, and it is inextricably bound up with sexuality, which, in turn, is the key to its nature and the means of its incarnation." In a subsequent chapter, Grant writes that "after intimate and persistent intercourse with the Angel has been established, He utters the Word."

Both the snake priestess and the Holy Guardian Angel involve what for poets has been variously called Angel, Muse, or in Lorca's remarkable essay, the Duende, and it now seems to me that the three are facets of a single figure. It may be that the snake priestess enacts the oldest appearance of this figure, and that Aleister Crowley, in contact with Aiwass and other extra-terrestrials, was performing a 20th century variation on this grand and mysterious theme. It would seem possible that the spinal traffic through Chakras and segmental rings is encoded in that force which drives us into another's arms and occasionally sings through us when we write.

Both Aztec and Greek mythologies associate the birth of inspiration with an animal and a warrior god. As Coatlicue is beheaded the two rattlesnakes that rise from the sacrificial urn her body has become are accompanied by Huitzilopochtli, the god of war. And as Medusa is decapitated, not only does winged Pegasus spring forth, but he is accompanied by the warrior Chrysaor. In both cases, the "uprisings" made possible by earlier pregnancies evoke not only Kundalini flashing up her spinal channel, but also sacrificial killing as the primordial soul-making. While we do not sacrifice bulls to Zeus today, who is to say that the creative mind does not suffer My Lai and El Mozote? The myths tell us that inspiration is inextricably bound to sacrifice and war, and that its release involves our genitals, guts, hearts, and brains. I tremble in attempting to gauge the distance, if there is one at all, between Perseus's falchion and a Salvadoran Army machete. I also find it compelling that unlike the Greeks who allow inspiration the detachment of an escaping winged horse, the Aztec image locks the twin "serpent power" to the place of mayhem. This suggests that poetic inspiration is not to divorce itself from the sacrificial landscape that offered it a soul.

"Cempasúchil": Caryl and I spent a week during the 1992 "Día de muer-tos" in Oaxaca, Mexico, staying with Mary Jane Gagnier and Arnulfo Mendoza in their apartment next to their marvelous Mexican craft store, La Mano Magica. Cempasúchl (the Nahuatl word for the primary Day of the Dead flower known in English as African Marigold), weaved in and out of my mind as we wandered Oaxaca, visited museums, looked at the *ofrendas* (home-made altars honoring ancestors) and with our friends visited Arnulfo's home on the final Day of the Dead. After this visit, we joined his family at the graveyard where his father is buried; we drank a little warm beer, dribbling the rest on the flower-strewn plot. Via constant notebook jottings, I tried to keep track of my imagining of the rich details of these nights and days.

Both "Navel of the Moon" and "Cempasúchil" have been signifi-cantly revised since their publication in *Under World Arrest*.

◇

From Scratch (Black Sparrow Press, Santa Rosa, 1998).

"Nora's Roar": Both Adrienne Rich (one of her oldest friends) and Robert Kelly have made perceptive comments on the art of Nora Jaffe (1928–1994), a dear friend, who remains virtually unknown in the art world. I included Adrienne's and Robert's commentaries on her art in the Notes of *From Scratch*. Reproductions of Jaffe's work can be found in *Caterpillar* #2 and #13, and on the cover of *Sulfur* #26. There are 10 of her drawings in *Realignment*, Treacle Press, 1974, a book we did together. There is also my poem "Nora Jaffe" in *The Name Encanyoned River*, Nora's presence in "Threnody" from *My Devotion*, along with her unexpected intrusion in "Nocturnal Veils" reprinted here, and "Nora's Transmission" in *An Alchemist with One Eye on Fire*.

"Nightcrawlers": Sources: for Nancy Spero's image of the mutilated Salvadoran woman, see *Sulfur* #14; the Charles Olson quotation is from the poem, "[to get the rituals straight I have…"; the Gary Snyder quo-tation is from his essay "The Porous World."

"Schmatte Variations": Michel Nedjar is a doll-maker, painter, and film-maker living in Paris. His work may be found in the major "Outsider Art" collections in European museums. "Beginners in the world…" is from Rilke's essay, "Some Reflections on Dolls." *Of What Does the Spider Dream?* is the title of a Nedjar film. See *Sulfurs* #26 and #27 for Allen S. Weiss's article on and interview with Nedjar. On the cover of *Sulfur* #37 there is a color reproduction of a Nedjar doll. *Les ongles en deuil*, a 1996 catalog published by Galerie Susanne Zander, Köln, Germany, has essays on Nedjar by Roger Cardinal, Chantal Thomas, Weiss and myself (my essay, "Spider Sibyls" is reprinted in *Companion Spider*). The two quotations ending this poem are tinkered-with entries from *The Larousse Encyclopedia of Animal Life.*

"*Less and less wholly absorbed…*": This poem began as an argument with Olson's poem "Wholly absorbed / into my own conduits…"

"Soutine's Lapis": The immediate source for this poem is the 1993 Taschen Soutine *catalogue raisonné*, a revelation for Soutine admirers as it reproduced a number of newly-discovered paintings and discarded, as fakes, some mediocre ones.

The description of Soutine's "butcher shop" as well as the description of Soutine himself by Maurice Sachs is from Pierre Courthion's *Peintre du déchirant* (my translation). The Maurice Tuchman comments are from his Introduction to the Los Angeles county Museum of Art's catalog, *Chaim Soutine*. The David Sylvester commentary is from his essay "The Mysteries of Nature within the Mysteries of Paint," in *Chaim Soutine*, Arts Council of Great Britain.

In the National Gallery of Art catalog, *Willem de Kooning Paintings*, Sylvester reports that when, in 1977, de Kooning was requested to identify his key influences, he responded: "O I think I would choose Soutine… I've always been crazy about Soutine—all his paintings. Maybe it's the lushness of the paint. He builds up a surface that looks like a material, like a substance. There's a kind of transfiguration, a certain fleshiness, in his work… I remember when I first saw the Soutines in the Barnes collection… the Matisses had a light of their own, but the Soutines had a glow that came from within the paintings—it was another kind of light."

Over the years I have written a number of poems concerning Soutine and his art. In *Indiana,* there is "Soutine." In *The Gull Wall,* "Portrait of Soutine." In *From Scratch,* along with a longer version of "Soutine's Lapis," "Oy." There is also a short essay on Soutine in "Nine Fire Sources," (*Poet's Book Shelf*), and a review of *The Impact of Chaim Soutine* in the Fall 2002 online edition of *Rain Taxi* magazine.

"El Mozote": I am indebted to Mark Danner's reportage, "The Truth of El Mozote" (*The New Yorker,* December 6, 1993) for much of the information in this poem.

"I, Friedrich Schröder-Sonnenstern": Virtually unknown outside of "Outsider Art" circles, the Lithuanian Schröder-Sonnenstern (1892–1982) was considered by the poet/art critic Edouard Roditi to be the greatest of the Surrealist painters. He was at various times a dairy farmer, a circus performer, a cigar seller and a horse thief. In his 20s and 30s while living in Berlin, he posed as Prof. Dr. Eliot Gnass von Sonnenstern, offering palmistry readings, natural health remedies and general quackery. He gave away his earnings to the poor. He only began to draw in his 50s at the behest of his companion, Martha Möller. His grotesquely hilarious and socially-probing colored drawings seethe with rotund, massively buxom nude women, grinning devils (virtually all of his characters grin no matter what they are undergoing), resplendently costumed magi, snakes and other anthropomorphized creatures. Surely no other painter has ever made as many visual jokes about the human "ass." The most ample presentation of his work I know of is the *Schröder-Sonnenstern* Kestner-Gesellschaft Hannover Katalog 4/1973.

"My Evening with Artaud": After being offered the Théâtre du Vieux-Colombier for the evening of January 13, 1947, Artaud prepared some two hundred pages of notes and texts for the event (published in 1994 as Volume XXVI of *Antonin Artaud / Oeuvres complètes*). Nine hundred people turned out for what, depending on one's viewpoint, became a freak show or a terribly moving manifestation. I conceived my own piece while translating works from Artaud's final period (*Watchfiends & Rack Screams*). At the same time, I also came across my mother's sole diary which she had kept throughout 1935, the year of my birth.

"De Kooning's *Excavation*": This magnificent de Kooning painting is in the Chicago Art Institute. "slipping glimpser" is de Kooning's 1959 self-description (quoted in the previously cited de Kooning catalog). The "gumspots…" and "bums who lie…" are from Edwin Denby's poem, "The Silences at Night"—which has as subtitle "(The design on the sidewalk Bill pointed out)." I assume "Bill" here refers to de Kooning.

"Blues for Byzantium": The second stanza makes use of material from a statement by Tad Homer-Dixon quoted by Robert D. Kaplan in his essay "The Coming Anarchy" (*Atlantic Monthly*, February, 1994): "Think of a stretch limo in the potholed streets of New York City, where homeless beggars live. Inside the limo are the air-conditioned, post-industrial regions of North America, Europe, the emerging Pacific Rim, and a few other isolated places, with their trade summitry and computer-information highways. Outside is the rest of mankind going in a completely different direction." Bud Powell's "Blues for Bouffémont" is the title track of a 1964 record, Fontana FLJ 901. "The bird-headed man" refers to the proto-shamanistic figure in a painting called "the Shaft scene," 16 feet below the rest of the Lascaux cave. "Egypt's human-headed bird," also known as "The Soul Bird," is from the XVIII Dynasty and often depicted in underworld scenes on coffins.

◇

Juniper Fuse: Upper Paleolithic Imagination & the Construction of the Underworld (Wesleyan University Press, Middletown CT, 2003)

Juniper Fuse envisions and examines some of the origins and developments of imagination recorded in cave wall imagery (for the most part in southwestern France), during the last European Ice Age, roughly between 40,000 and 10,000 years ago. It looks at theories proposed by others, as well as my own two-part thesis that considers why such imagery sparked when and where it did. The metaphorical unfolding that can be traced back to a 30,000 year-old Aurignacian engraving of a horse head and neck—across which a vulva of equal size was superimposed—startles with the same refreshed energy as Allen Ginsberg's "hydrogen jukebox."

To follow poetry back to Cro-Magnon metaphors not only hits real bedrock—a genuine back wall—but gains a connection to the continuum during which imagination first flourished. My growing awareness of the caves led to the recognition that, as an artist, I belong to a pre-tradition that includes the earliest nights and days of soul-making.

This book is also an attempt to answer the first question that the science writer Alexander Marshack fired at me when he walked into our kitchen in the French Dordogne in the spring of 1974:

"What is a *poet* doing in the caves?

In the late 1970s, I found that cave imagery is an inseparable mix of psychic constructs and perceptive observations. That is, there are "fantastic" animals as well as realistic ones. There are not only human figures representing men and women whose social roles cannot be determined, but others with bird masks, bison heads, and peculiar wounds that evoke an interior world, in some cases proto-shamanism. Instead of employing rational documentation (as have the archeologists), it struck me that this "inseparable mix" might be approached using poetic imagination as well as thorough fieldwork and research. In other words, in the spirit that I served the cave images as observer, to ask them to serve my imagination so as to translate them not back into their own original unknown-to-us context, but forward into my own idiom.

Thus in the writing of *Juniper Fuse* I sought to be open to what I thought about and fantasized while in the caves or while meditating on their image environments—to create my own truth as to what they mean, respecting imagination as one of a plurality of conflicting powers. I also sought to be a careful observer and to reflect on what others have written, photographed, and drawn. Sometimes a section is all poetry, sometimes all prose—at other times it is a shifting combination like a Calder mobile, with poetry turning into prose, prose turning into poetry.

I began my research on this project in 1974 and completed it in 1999. Roughly 65% of the book is in prose. Poems that are part of it began to appear in my books, with *Hades In Manganese*, in 1981. I have dated the poems in this section to give some sense of their gradual evolution over the 25 year period of their composition. There is an essay on the background and development of *Juniper Fuse*, "The Back Wall of

Imagination," in *Archaic Design*. In *The Price of Experience* are the lectures I gave to our cave tour groups before Caryl, Mathilde Sitbon and I took them to the cave I had just lectured on.

"Silence Raving": Chapter 3 of *The Road to Eleusis*: "There can be no doubt that Persephone's abduction was a drug-induced seizure."

Re. "a massive vulva incised before the gate": See G.R. Levy's *The Gate of Horn* (Faber edition, 1948) for two drawings of "enclosures" based on paintings in the Spanish cave of La Pasiega. Both "enclosures" have vulvar forms at what appears to be their gates. The larger of the two "enclosures" contain parts of a bison and a hind inside two of its three "compartments." This "enclosure" presented vertically on Levy's page, evokes a cathedral, with the vulvar shape acting as a kind of parvis. André Leroi-Gourhan also reproduces the larger of these two "enclosures" in *Treasures of Prehistoric Art* but he omits the vulvar shape. I put such words as "enclosure" and "compartment" in quotes, as there is no solid evidence that they represent corrals or stables.

"Hades In Manganese": To place Hades in manganese is to take the Greek god of death and the Greek underworld and imagine them as having been prefigured in the black manganese cave imagery of the Cro-Magnon people. In this revisionism, the emphasis is on the first construction of an underworld in which the Hadic figure is less a god of death than a proto-shaman drawing on a wall the forms he is envisioning.

The burden of this poem is to assimilate a range of personal and transpersonal twentieth-century "hells" which may be thought of as a rubble packed against the gate to the Upper Paleolithic (in the same way that debris is often found covering decorated cave walls). My notion was that only after this material was cleared away (imagined) could I access the deep past. This clearing away is a never ending process and crops up at many points in *Juniper Fuse*.

As I was coming to the end of the fourth stanza, I realized that I had entered the magnetic field of Vallejo's poem "Telluric and Magnetic," in particular its impassioned central stanza beginning "Oh human fields!" My fifth stanza beginning "O dead living depths!" draws on the energy and some of the strategies of Vallejo's stanza. This is a good example of how poetry that one has previously translated may, out of nowhere, move into psychic accessibility and act as an emanative angel for a new poem under way.

Paul Blackburn (1926–1971) sent several tapes of poems and conversation to me while I was living in Kyoto. One poem, "Crank it up for all of us, but let me heaven go," went off like a depth charge in me.

"Permanent Shadow": The title refers to the human shadows blasted onto walls during the atomic bombing of Hiroshima.

"Placements I: The New Wilderness": This piece was written for Jerome Rothenberg's *New Wilderness Letter #7*, 1979, in response to Rothenberg's query asking a number of us how we would define the "new wilderness." In a note to the issue containing our responses, Rothenberg wrote: "I felt the strong pull of contradictory meanings for 'wilderness' (from awesome other-then-human wilderness of west coast earth householders to wilderness ruins of collapsed high industrial dwellings)—that coupled with the strange twist 'newness' added to the concept(s)."

The James Hillman quotation is from the "Barriers" section of *The Dream and the Underworld*.

The paleontologist Paul Martin has argued a "Pleistocene overkill" thesis for the Americas, in which the Clovis people, accomplished Eurasian hunters with bows and arrows, crossed the Bering land bridge around 13,000 years ago and within 2000 years had eliminated fifty-seven species of large mammals throughout the Americas. According to Richard Leakey and Roger Lewin, we are now in an accelerated phase of the sixth extinction, in which 30,000 species are wiped out by human agency every year.

We are thus in the beginning of the twenty-first century witness to the following phantasmagorical *and* physical spectacle: the animal images in Ice Age caves are also the ghosts of species wiped out at the beginning of our Holocene epoch; today they "stand in" for the species we are daily eliminating. This is probably one of the reasons that Ice Age animal images move people profoundly. Such images are primogenous to the extinction of possibly all wild animal life.

"Dot": In the beginning of *Juniper Fuse* I envision the root tips of certain Humanistic divinities. Hermes, for instance, may be indicated by a meandering line, dots, dot formations, and more complex "closed signs," called claviforms and tectiforms. If Hermes is the god of boundaries, it may be possible to detect his archetypal activity in the earliest "boundary signaling" we know of.

"Our Lady of the Three-Pronged Devil": This title attempts to tie Aurignacian engraved vulvas into their reactive development, the trident, so that what was originally open and receptive becomes, at the point intercourse and pregnancy were linked, an uroboros enclosing germination. According to this thinking, the uroboros is hardly "prior to any process, eternal" (Neumann à la Jung), but rather a major arrest of movement drawing into its vortex an overwhelming preoccupation with mother-goddessing the earth (carrying in its wake the attribution to women of all the horrors to be found in nature). Of relevance here is an insightful poem that Charles Olson excluded from *The Maximus Poems* (to be found in *Olson #9*):

the IMMENSE ERROR
of *genderizing*
the 'Great mother'

inCALCULABLE
damage

The open Aurignacian vulva evokes a simple labyrinth with an exit and stresses, sexually, torsion. It seems possible that the earliest intercourse/pregnancy association was torsion (underscored by the fire drill) and that the subsequent uroboros belongs to agricultural peoples, with stress on the enclosed seed, the male as "star," i.e., patriarchy in contrast to an earlier more mysterious "open" union, in which the female was place-of-fire *and* phallus (the so-called "Venuses" fit neatly in the hand).

Concerning the unlifted veil, Barbara G. Walker writes in *The Woman's Encyclopedia of Myths and Secrets*:

Latin *revelation* meant to draw back the veil (*velum*). It was the Goddess's rainbow veil that concealed the future and the secrets or the spirit under the colors of earthly appearance. After death, men might see her "face to face." A vision of the naked Goddess was vouchsafed to her sacred kings, who could draw back the veil of her temple, the *hymen*, pierce her virginity and die in their mating, to become gods. But as the Goddess said on her temple at Sais, "No mortal has yet been able to lift the veil which covers me." Those who saw her unveiled were no longer mortal.

Walker also writes: "The Hag as death-goddess, her face veiled to imply that no man can know the manner of his death, was sometimes reinterpreted as a nun. Christianized legends were invented for their veiled figures." Hans Peter Duerr notes in *Dreamtime* that "the head of the Venus of Willendorf is covered with a pattern of horizontal ridges in such a way as to suggest the masking of the face. If this interpretation is valid, then we may have here a prototype of the 'one who veils' of later times, the goddess of death such as Calypso or 'fraw Holt' whose names hide the Indo-German stem *kel-*, 'hide' or 'veil.'" See Duerr's footnote #14 for additional and fascinating information on veils.

"The Aurignacians Have the Floor": The Aurignacian (32.000–24,000 B.P.) is the period in which the first image-making we now know of (in contrast to abstract lines, cupules, grids etc) took place. The kinds of images vary considerably from region to region (crude engravings in the Dordogne; Chauvet's polychromatic splendor in the Ardèche). Not only is it time to let the Aurignacians have the floor but to acknowledge that they *are* the floor. Aurignacian imagery also makes a brief appearance in "Pollock Pouring" which ends this collection.

"Visions of the Fathers of Lascaux": Several weeks after the car accident described in "Interface II: Fracture" in *Juniper Fuse*, Caryl and I left the Dordogne for a month in Germany where readings and lectures had been arranged. I began to write this poem, leg in cast, sitting in the front seat next to my wife as she drove the German autobahns from city to city. Goaded by the jolt of the accident and my phantasmagorical night in the wrecked car, I plunged into what I had dreamed of writing for years, a narrative of human genesis, tracing the roots of Western alienation to a primordial rupture in the natural continuum. I envisioned Lascaux as a wild creature that sought to defend itself against those imposing their own forms on it. Priming the walls with "menstrual effluvia" the Mothers signed the cave with female power, driving the Fathers to transform their own sexuality as they symbolically castrated Lascaux's geology.

Not only did it seem inadequate to merely describe Lascaux's paintings in such a poem, it also seemed superficial to describe the act of painting. So I tried to set up Chinese firecracker-like bursts of metaphoric interactions between the mythic figures and their image-worlds-in-progress.

I am staggered by the effort that was needed on the part of Ice Age people to transform sexual/survival energies. Out of a world that strikes me as being, at the same time, ferocious, subtle, omen-perforated, magical and very utilitarian—or out of a void in which all these forces intermingled, there were people capable of inventing themselves, along with what appears to be much of what we hold to be human today. What was behind this thrust into imagination? I envision a crisis that slowly came to a head over thousands of years in which hominid animality eroded, and at around 35,000 B.P. began to be *separated out* of to-be-human heads, and daubed, smeared, and chipped onto cave walls lit solely by hand lamps.

My mythic figures are part of a personal mythological constellation that goes back, in my writing, to the early 1960s in Kyoto when I read Blake and worked on Vallejo translations in the downtown Yorunomado coffeehouse. See "The Book of Yorunomado" in this collection for the birth of this figure. For "Visions of the Fathers of Lascaux," I invented three new figures: Kashkaniraqmi is based on a Quechuan word meaning something like: "in spite of everything we still are, we still exist with all our possibilities for reintegration and growth." Atlementheneira is a word given to me by Charles Olson in a dream (See "Poem Copied from a Text Written in a Dream," in *What She Means*). Savolathersilonighcock appeared spontaneously during the poem's first draft.

"Magdalenian": The poem is based on the first Upper Paleolithic female statuette to be found, around 1864, in a Magdalenian stratum (between 18,000 and 10,000 years ago) at Laugerie Basse in the Dordogne. She is a little over three inches tall and is carved from mammoth tusk.

"Notes on a Visit to Le Tuc d'Audoubert": Le Tuc d'Audoubert is a Middle to late Magdalenian cave in the French Ariège, near St.-Girons, and one of the three caves that make up the group known as the Volp caves (the Volp being an underground river which emerges near the entrance to Le Tuc d'Audoubert). The other two caves are Les Trois Frères and Enlène (with no wall imagery but more than a thousand small engraved plaquettes). A 90-foot tunnel connects Les Trois Frères and Enlène; while the end of Le Tuc d'Audoubert overlaps a Les Trois Frères passageway, the caves appear to never have been open to each other. Privately owned, the Volp caves have been protected against thoughtless exploration and destruction. They were discovered in 1912 by Count Henri Bégouën and his three sons (Les Trois Frères being named for the three brothers). The Count's grandson, Robert, is currently in charge of the Volp caves.

While Caryl's and my six-hour visit was unexpected (a chance phone call to Jean Clottes in Foix leading to an invitation to join Clottes, Robert Bégouën, and several students who had spent the summer excavating a midden outside the cave), I had been reading what I could find on the cave. I had some notions about what I would see when, in rubber-raft units of two, we floated off on the underground Volp to the cave's interior shore to begin our 800-yard, mostly crawling, journey. We emerged at midnight. I slept a few hours, awaking in the giddy, image-filled trance that over the years I have learned to trust as an ignition point for a piece of writing. I was so excited that the "note" jumped back and forth from prose to poetry several times per page. About two-thirds of the way through what is now the finished piece (with the words "image pressure"), my mind went blank and I stopped writing. Upon reaching this point while typing up the "Notes" several months later, the earlier charge returned and everything flowed without revision to the end.

After finishing these "Notes"—a mix of poetry, prose poetry, paragraphs and visual "punctuation"—I recalled that Northrop Frye had referred to Blake's "The Marriage of Heaven and Hell" as an *anatomy*, suggesting that it was a composite work that included in its "members" various forms and strategies of the art of writing. Such a term also evokes the writing that Artaud did beginning in 1945: a fusion of genres incorporating letters, poetry, prose, and, in Artaud's case, glossolalia.

In the mid-1990s, I realized that "Notes on a Visit to Le Tuc d'Audoubert" was the nuclear form for a book that would become an amplification of its multiple genres.

In the "Notes" the cave diagram is from *Treasures of Prehistoric Art*; the drawing of the "fantastic figures" is by the Abbé Breuil and is reproduced in *Les Cavernes du Volp*. Bégouën and Breuil describe these figures in the following words: "The left side of the gallery contains several strange engravings: two fantastic animals, half-feline, half-bull, one above the other, of which one cannot make out the hindquarters. The upper figure has a horrible head, with a single short horn flanked by a large ear behind it. Its narrow neck supports a large head with animated contours, a prominent and rounded muzzle, and an open mouth. Its withers are very convex; its vertically striped head and body, and its slender, long foreleg, end in long, retractile claws. The lower figure has been reduced to a grotesque head, topped by two little ears. I think that we have here the Guardians of the Sanctuary." The other drawings are my own, done while writing the "Notes."

"the grotesque archetype": This phrase came to me spontaneously upon seeing "the fantastic figures." I then realized that my phrase was a spin-off of Mikhail Bakhtin's "grotesque realism," discussed in his Introduction to *Rabelais and His World*. According to Bakhtin, the word "grotesque" appeared at the end of the fifteenth century in descriptions of certain roman ornaments excavated from Titus's baths (which were in grottos, implying that these ornaments were an expression of the grotto itself). While the word initially referred to the fanciful interplay of plant, animal, and human forms (which often seemed to be giving birth to each other), the classical canon soon relegated "the grotesque" to the barbarous, associating it not only with playful energies, but with the alien, the illegitimate, the bestial and with humankind's infantile and "primitive" past. By defining the carnivalesque atmosphere in Rabelais as "grotesque realism," Bakhtin not only rehabilitated the word but suggested the extent to which it has permeated many stages of historical antiquity.

While there are elements in common between the medieval, classical, and primordial grotesques, none of the historical terms express what I intend by "the grotesque archetype." As a way of approaching a definition, I want to consider some observations that C.G. Jung—the originator of the twentieth-century term "archetype"—made about these primary psychic structures.

Jung differentiates between "archetypal" and "archetype," writing that "archetypal representations (images and ideas) mediated to us by the unconscious should not be confused with the archetype as such. They are varied structures which all point back to one essentially 'irrepresentable' basic form... The archetype as such is a psychoid factor that belongs, as it were to the invisible, ultra-violet end of the psychic spectrum" (*Collected Works*, Vol. 8). Comments by North Kimberly (Australian) aborigines to Geza Róheim seem to anticipate Jung's approach. "The natives say they do not make the *wondjina* figures but only repaint them. The figures themselves called *wondjina made themselves*. They are self-created." (*The Gates of the Dream*).

I would propose that hybrid images, arrived at perhaps via proto-shamanic trance stimulated in part by cave environments, are grotesque archetypal representations of somatic (until then unrecognized) materials. Another possibility involves the so-called "mythical times" when man and animal were one (or as some historical shamans put it, when man and animal spoke the same language). These "mythical times," undoubtedly populated by infant sensations and childhood repressions, could represent Jung's "essentially 'irrepresentable' basic form."

Commenting on Michael Maier's alchemical journeys (specifically his 1617 *Symbola aureae mensae*), Jung speaks of Maier

> approaching that region of the psyche which was not
> unjustly said to be inhabited by "Pans, Satyrs, dog-
> headed baboons, and half-men." It is not difficult to
> see that this region is the animal soul in man. For just
> as a man has a body which is no different in principle
> from that of an animal, so also his psychology has a
> whole series of lower stories in which the spectres
> from humanity's past epochs still dwell, then the ani-
> mal souls from the age of Pithecanthropus and the

hominids, then the "psyche" of the cold-blooded
saurians, and, deepest of all, the transcendental mys-
tery and paradox of the sympathetic and parasympa-
thetic psychoid processes (Vol. 14).

Here we have an active, vertical midden image of the personal un-
conscious down through the collective unconscious, based on evolu-
tionary scale. One might propose that "animal souls" began to
intermingle with nascent human souls when Cro-Magnon projected and
drew/engraved animal and hybrid images.

I would call the grotesque archetype primary, for it does not appear
to be a reaction against or a development of earlier systems, as do the
classical and medieval grotesques.

Among its elements might be a coming into being at the point that
meandering lines curved into enclosures that in turn evoked animal or
hominid or animal/hominid bodies. Its character seems most pro-
nounced when images apparently based on perception as well as mental
activity combine. The relationship between perception and fantasy
seems to us ambivalent, unbalanced, and often undifferentiated. Exam-
ples of what I consider to be the grotesque archetype often seem to in-
voke the unknown or to subdue something threatening. They are
sometimes simultaneously "empty" (probably because they lack back-
ground or landscape) and "full" (due to superimposition or figures seen
through each other). Isolated lines, or realistic animals (the clay bison
at Le Tuc d'Audoubert, for example) are at best tangential to the
grotesque archetype.

I should note that Bahktin mentions something he calls the "archaic
grotesque" which he associates with "the ever unfinished, ever creating
body, the link in the chain of genetic development, or more correctly
speaking, two links shown at the point where they enter into each other."
The sense of a body exceeding its own limits comes from Bahktin's
thinking about Rabelais here, and he does not cite specific instances of
an archaic grotesque. But his notion of open, intersecting bodies can be
applied to a significant number of Upper Paleolithic images, such as some
of the human figurations at Combarelles, the "bison-women" at Pech-
Merle, and the "wounded" figures in Cougnac.

"A Kind of Moisture on the Wall": Besides the running, partial human figure (whose body may have been struck by three lances or, in a shamanistic interpretation, may be projecting lines of power), there is, inside the body outline of the same Cougnac megaloceros (a male, now dated at 19,500 B.P.), a small legless stag, a complete ibex, and what appears to be the dorsal line of a bison or horse. These four figures are placed in what might be called trapezoidal alignment. To my knowledge they have not been dated, meaning that they could have been painted either earlier or later than the megaloceros.

"Through Breuil's Eyes": This title echoes Charles Olson's "On First Looking out through Juan de la Cosa's Eyes," which echoes Keats' sonnet, "On First Looking into Chapman's Homer."

Henri Breuil (1877–1961), an ordained priest who never took up parish duties, became aware of prehistoric "art" in 1897 while traveling in the Dordogne and the Ariège regions; almost immediately he determined to dedicate his life to the study of what was then called "the Reindeer Age." In 1901, with others, he discovered the imagery in Combarelles and Font-de-Gaume, and the following year examined Altamira and Marsoulas. Such discovery and exploration led him to the work that he will mainly be remembered for: the tracings, drawings, and watercolors of cave imagery, especially in Combarelles, Altamira, and Les Trois Frères (see *Les Cavernes du Volp* for his exceptional drawings of the last-mentioned cave, which are the main source for this poem).

The reader might not be aware that there is a big difference between the time Breuil was able to spend in the caves he examined and drew, and the time that someone such as myself is allowed today. As a tourist in the 1970s, I simply went in with groups and was given only seconds in many instances to look at images (during which time the local guide would be lecturing, a well-intended offering that mainly acted as a distraction from careful looking). Privately arranged visits, mainly to caves in the Ariège, allowed a little more viewing time, but I was very seldom alone, and the guide who had been in the cave countless times was always by my side waiting to press on. While Caryl and I have been in Lascaux six times, we always had to respect the 45 minute limit placed on all visits (making it impossible to even begin to inspect the most heavily engraved area of the cave, the Apse).

There is a longer note on Breuil in *Juniper Fuse*, pp. 256–257. And there is more material on his "versions" vs. "copies" in the lecture on Font-de-Gaume in *The Price of Experience*.

"Placements II: "The Aranea Constellation": For a listing of the many sources referenced in this work, see pp. 257–259 in *Juniper Fuse*

The Double Axe evokes an image of a labyrinth with a swerving line through it. The haft becomes the labyrinth's center where a change of materials signals the need for an adaptation. The Double Ax's combination of metal and wood also makes me think of Wilhelm Reich's Orgone Energy Accumulator, a telephone-booth-sized box with metal walls on the inside backed by layered, organic materials on the outside. Reich originally built the accumulator on a much smaller scale to study energy radiation from bions, or vesicles from disintegrated grass blade cells, which he believe to represent transitional stages between nonliving and living substances. In 1940, he increased the size of the accumulator in order to treat cancer patients. While the accumulator did not cure these patients, it improved their physical condition for a while. Sitting in the accumulator, patients perspired, their skin reddened, and their blood pressure decreased. Since the accumulator appeared to provide an expansive therapy that stimulated parasympathetic innervation, physicians working with Reich in the 1940s and early 1950s used it to treat a variety of illnesses: angina, heart disease, and hypertension, among others. While Reich denied that the accumulator promoted orgastic potency (one of the key goals of his therapy), he noticed an increase in sexual excitation in some accumulator patients and reasoned that as their health improved less energy was needed to fight their illnesses.

There is an image of a labyrinth with a rose at its center in Seonaid M. Robertson's *Rosegarden and Labyrinth*. In *The Greek Myths*, Robert Graves mentions that "the kermberry, or cochineal, provided scarlet dye to stain the sacred king's face, and was therefore associated with royalty." The reddening at the center has also been related to the Holy Grail. Penelope Shuttle and Peter Redgrove in *The Wise Wound* write: "Emma Jung relates the Grail legends to medieval alchemy, which was dedicated to producing a precious stone, red in colour, that sweats blood, and which turns the world to gold. Jung's own work was to relate his medieval 'fantasy' to modern psychology and to show how powerfully relevant it was. The Grail can also be a stone, in the legends. We are led to suggest that a precious stone which sweats blood is the Moon; both inner moon, the womb; the outer moon to which the inner is related either by inherent rhythm, or obvious analogy... Gerald Dorn describes the arcane substance of the alchemists as 'blessed rose-coloured blood.'"

"The Atmosphere, Les Eyzies": Located a bit north of the confluence of the Vézère and Dordogne Rivers, which would have supplied salmon to nomadic bands following the migratory bison and reindeer, the village of Les Eyzies is nestled at the base of one of the massive limestone escarpments typical of the region. Both rivers have carved craggy gorges in the limestone plateaus, and ochre-stained cliff faces abound. As one drives parallel to a river, often with one lane shadowed by an outcropping of moist rock, one senses the presence of the caves. An abundance of evergreen oaks, poplars, and chestnut trees results in a landscape of restrained luxuriance, also inhabited by the coal-black Perigord truffle several inches underground, and the geese and duck farms that produce foie gras.

Gorge d'Enfer, across the train tracks and river, is a small valley where animals, some of which are descendants of those depicted by Upper Paleolithic people, wander in semi-liberty. Caryl and I recall the utter strangeness of coming upon a small bison in a pen here. It stood motionless, in profile to us—in the same position that its ancestors were often drawn on cave walls. It seemed both less and more real than the paintings at Font-de-Gaume which, as we watched, seemed to hover between us and the living bison, as if we were all remnants of a dream in which bison and human beings intersected, humped and hooded semblances, through fog and blowing snow.

When Caryl and I arrived in the spring of 1974, Les Eyzies was an old-fashioned one-street village with several hundred inhabitants. Hotel Cro-Magnon was at one end, Hotel Centenaire at the other. In between were the butcher, the newsstand/bookstore, a café, the tourist office, the mayor, and a couple of general stores with postcard racks outside. A four-course dinner, featuring guinea hen, cost $6.

By the late 1990s, boutiques, bars, pizza stands, a rock shop, a herbarium with a beekeeping museum, an archeological bookstore, and a semi-open market with regional products displayed on long tables had been added. The most reasonable set meal at the internationalized

Michelin 2-star Hotel Centenaire cost $50. During the 1980s and 1990s, we stayed at Hotel Cro-Magnon, which resisted the commercialization of the village and remained a lovely rural inn. In 2001 Hotel Cro-Magnon closed when the owners retired; it has since been reopened under new management.

"Abri du Cro-Magnon was earlier...": In the 1980s, a plaque by the gate of the Cro-Magnon rock shelter stated that the shelter used to be called "Abri du Cramagnon." This plaque probably had erroneous information (since the name has not turned up anywhere else), but since a pun on "craw/cra" started the writing of this piece, I have left it as is. Jacques Leyssales, co-owner of Hotel Cro-Magnon (next to the rock shelter) told me that the "cro" in Cro-Magnon is patois for "hole." Ian Scargill, in *The Dordogne Region of France,* notes that the French word for a solution hollow ("croze") is derived from "cro."

The skeletal remains in the rock shelter were discovered by railway workmen in 1868 and then identified by the paleontologist Louis Lartet who just happened to be dining at Hotel de la Poste—the original name of Hotel Cro-Magnon. Lartet overhead the workmen discussing some "gypsy" skeletons they had unearthed. He found the partial skeletons of four adults, and one infant, along with shells used as ornaments, an object made of ivory, and a worked reindeer antler. The skeletons were determined to be around 35,000 years old, and the earliest examples, at that time, of our direct ancestor.

The description of the 50-year old man's skull is from Evan Hadingham's *Secrets of the Ice Age.* The description of the "disharmonic Cromagnid" is by John R. Baker (provenance unknown). "Payroll of Bones" is the title of a poem by César Vallejo. "Century O century of clouds" is a translation of the last line of Guillaume Apollinaire's poem "Un fantôme de nuées."

"The Power Room": I often walked from Hotel Cro-Magnon under the overarching limestone cliff, about a quarter of a mile to the Regional Museum of Prehistory (opened in 1923 and housed in a tenth century château), notebook and reading materials in hand, to spend a few hours there. The walk itself was often as interesting as the museum.

I called my favorite exhibition space in the Regional Museum "the power room," as it contained examples of the earliest imagery from the region—late Neanderthal to early/middle Aurignacian (mixed in with some Magdalenian slabs). Limestone blocks, engraved with vulvas, cupules, and crude animal parts, were held out from this rock wall by iron hooks. This was the same wall that included the back wall of Hotel Cro-Magnon and the Cro-Magnon rock shelter. The guard's chair was often vacant, so I would sit down, observe, and write.

One day I was carrying Peter Redgrove's collection of poems, *The Man Named East*, with me and, settled into "the power room," used his book as a support for my own small notebook. At a certain point I received a psychic communication from Redgrove that I copied into my writing. As a response to this communication, I confessed to Peter a troubling vision that had occurred when I heard of James Wright's death years earlier. In the poem "Some Comments by the Little King" (in *Under World Arrest*), a figure called "the worm in the fold" elaborates the image of the dead drawing upon the living for sustenance:

> The worm thought a moment, then added:
> "You saw Spicer and Crane going after Wright's liver—
> Wright is now nursing from one of the udder formations
> in this poem, seeking strength to chew into this energy
> and, like a hermit crab, enshell the poem,
> turn it into *his* dwelling place. 'Influence'
> plays little part in this—those great dead
> you hold in imagination are thus contained,
> they act upon the poem as emanations.
> The poem draws strength from such containment.
> It is those you have not read, or have dismissed,
> who, upon finding you asleep, attack.
> Think of the poem as a translucent termite hill—
> which white ants are words? Which ones ghosts?

"Like Violets, He Said": The Olson quote is from "Apollonius of Tyana," in *The Fiery Hunt and Other Plays*. The Blackburn quote is from "The Touch" in *The Collected Poems of Paul Blackburn*.

"Cemeteries of Paradise": A dream of February 16, 2000, enacting the devolution of Charles Olson, may have cleared the way for this poem as well as my definition of one phase of my work as a poet ("I hunt inside stone") set against the last line of Olson's "The Kingfishers." Here is the dream:

Near a beach I discovered mole hills between kennels or chicken coops. A farmer said he'd turn his dogs on them. I watched furious fighting inside a shed, lots of pups being spit out. Worried that Caryl would not know where to find me, I started walking a path to suddenly find myself in a crowd where I heard that Charles Olson, now out on the road with a small child, wandering and giving lectures for food, for some 80 days, was to arrive. I was shown photos of Robert Kelly with a young black woman and other strangers. Then I was in a house with people who had studied Olson, including an attractive Irish woman who had a small *tansu* set into the floor. She said it contained Olson texts and could not be opened until he arrived. The excitement was mounting—Olson enthusiasts seemed to be everywhere. I was now in a spacious cave and heard the approach of what I took to be Olson and his retinue—there he was, 7 feet tall, shaggy white hair, thin neck, large block-like skeletal head, hunched over, climbing through the air. I went up to him, took his huge hand. He looked at me curiously, then boomed: "How are your caves coming along?" I started to describe the completion of *Juniper Fuse* but he interrupted: "The music, how about the music?" Before I could respond, he was past me. I was surrounded by hip-looking men in sunglasses whom I figured were Olson aviators. It was a joyous occasion—then it hit me: How could he be here? He died in 1970! Larry Goodell then piped up. "That's the majesty of it!" I was now caught up in another crowd, being shown a map of the Pech Merle cave with certain areas marked that I understood Olson had explored. "Olson is coming!" I heard. "What?" I said, "I just saw him!" "No, he's coming now," voices clamored, and a strange creature rounded a cave bend, a leg-like head with one eye, stick-like body, insect legs. There was intense conversation about what was referred to as a "restoration." New people appeared, shouting that Olson was on his way! An even stranger apparition appeared, more insectile, arachnoid, long extending legs front and back, its head—a compact lavender mass—under its body. I worked my way under as the creature ambled along, yelling, "What happened to you?" I got my hands around the jewel-like head and wrenched it free, at which moment an agonized voice cried: "*I couldn't get the whole Theolonius!*" What was left disappeared among the mass of people thronging the cave.

Olson in this dream appeared to be devolving or passing from personal consciousness into his collective, the realm of creature souls. His response to my question—"What happened to you?"—possibly banked off his earlier music remark, brings Theolonius Monk to mind, but even more a pun on "the whole theo [as in 'theos,' meaning *god*] olson," perhaps also sounding the name of the Roman poet, Ausonius, whose poetry Olson read in translation in the late 1940s.

"Placements III: 'So Be It'": The following paragraph from N.O. Brown's *Love's Body* (p. 249) is pertinent to this poem as well as to my poetry at large: "Knowledge is carnal knowledge. A subterranean passage between mind and body underlies all analogy; no word is metaphysical without its first being physical; and the body that is the measure of all things is sexual. All metaphors are sexual; a penis in every convex object and a vagina in every concave one."

"Thalassa Variations": Writing on Henry Miller in *Genius and Lust*, Norman Mailer proposes that "Miller saw that Lawrence had come to grips with the poetry of sex but none of the sewer gas. Miller would light matches to the sewer gas like nobody who had ever lived, and he set off literary explosions, but he never exploded himself over the other side of the divide. He could be poetic about anything and everything except fucking with love."

In "This I Call Holding You" (from *What She Means*) I engaged some of my own sewer gas as well as the world's as it seemed to invade "fucking with love." Such gas does not magically vanish in the caress. Yet that poem has always seemed inadequate to me, I think now because it is so infiltrated with questionable outer events. Perhaps it was a first step in taking on what might be called the interiority of the sexual embrace.

Over the years I have pondered Sandor Ferenczi's *Thalassa: A Theory of Genitality*, and wondered how his unique argument might shed light on the origin of image-making. It occurred to me one evening that being "exploded... over the other side of the divide" might involve more than what Mailer implies i.e., fucking versus fucking with love. Might not the passage to the other side involve the transformation of sexual release into imaginative play? My experience has been that sexual release charges the mind with fantasy material, which subsequently in my case seeks its own release in the writing of poetry, and that there is something basically frustrating about sexual expression without subsequent creative activity.

Ferenczi's argument describes what might lie at the basis of such a frustration. In brief: he proposes that the whole of life is determined by a tendency to return to the womb. Equating the process of birth with the transition of animal life from water to land, he links coitus to what he calls "thalassal regression": "the longing for sea-life from which man emerged in primeval times." He explains what he means by an "attempt to return to the mother's womb"—and thus to the oceanic womb of life itself—in the following way:

> If we now survey the evolution of sexuality from the
> thumb-sucking of the infant through the self-love of
> genital onanism to the heterosexual act of coitus, and
> keep in mind the complicated identifications of the
> ego with the penis and with the sexual secretion, we
> arrive at the conclusion that the purpose of this
> whole evolution, therefore the purpose likewise of the
> sex act, can be none other than an attempt at the be-

ginning clumsy and fumbling, then more consciously purposive, and finally in part successful—to return to the mother's womb, where there is no painful disharmony between ego and environment as characterize existence in the external world. The sex act achieves this transitory regression in a threefold manner: the whole organism attains the goal by purely hallucinatory means, somewhat as in sleep; the penis, with which the organism as a whole has identified itself, attains it partially or symbolically while only the sexual secretion possesses the prerogative, as representative of the ego and its narcissistic double, the genital, of attaining *in reality* to the womb of the mother.

While Ferenczi comments elsewhere on the development of genital sexuality in the female as well as the male, his argument is essentially from a masculine viewpoint, and in this respect inadequate. However, since it seems to genuinely break new ground from that masculine viewpoint, I will make use of it in what follows, with the reservation just stated. In one respect, "Thalassa Variations" is a compression of, and variation on, Ferenczi's argument.

To my knowledge, N.O. Brown is the only writer to have heretofore assimilated Ferenczi's theory of genitality into a larger dimension including creativity. In *Love's Body,* Brown even acknowledges the Upper Paleolithic caves as the places in which history begins. Like Ferenczi, Brown is a Freudian, and while he views the Upper Paleolithic caves as the first labyrinths, he fails to reflect on what seems to be their most distinctive characteristic: they are not merely wandering places, or even dancing enclosures, but the sites for some of the earliest image-making. Following Ferenczi, Brown views genitality as ultimately ungratifying, in effect a trap. Ferenczi's proposal that we desire to return to the womb and obviously cannot, in Brown's terms becomes the limitation he calls "genital organization."

Since Brown also draws upon William Blake's vision of four mental states potentially operative in humanity, it may be useful to point out that from a Blakean viewpoint, to be confined to "genital organization" is to be arrested at the third level of mental expansion (see the poem, "The Crystal Cabinet"), or to be in the State of Beulah. In other words,

Blake appears to mean that those who settle for sexual gratification alone are not fully, in his terms, "human." For Blake, there is a fourth state, the State of Eden, in which imagination is engaged *and* realized, and in which art that we might call great is created. Blake's image for this state is fire in love with fire (from which Yeats undoubtedly got his image of creative unity: the dancer as unidentifiable apart from the dance). While there may be a temporary "gratification of desire" between two people in the State of Beulah, in the State of Eden the other vanishes, and for the individual to avoid plunging into the lowest State—the State of Ulro in which one is simply unimaginatively stuck with oneself—one must practice a sort of imaginative androgyny called art. While Brown does not include cave art in his discussion of the labyrinth, he does view coitus as a fallen metaphor for poetry.

Were Blake alive today, I am confident that he would make the connection I am about to make. The womb that cannot be returned to à la Ferenczi was imaginatively re-entered when Cro-Magnon crawled into a cave and drew, painted or sculpted an image. I conjecture that one impulse for going into the cave was orgasm itself, which flooded the mind with fantasy material that sought a fulfillment beyond survival concerns. Image-making, then, can be seen as the attempt to unblock the paradoxical male impasse of genital expression, or, in my poem, it is what the belling deer image "says" to its Cro-Magnon maker on his back in that cul-de-sac in Le Portel: "Image is / the imprint of uncontainable omega, / life's twin." In the same stanza, I attempted to draw upon the Freudian/Ferenczian theory of the sexual stages of development, working with the possibility that from childhood on, oral, anal, and genital formations are incorporated in image-making, which for the creative individual becomes a kind of fourth dimension (or State à la Blake) that includes the earlier three *and* pushes beyond.

Barbara G. Walker offers some fascinating speculation on "omega" in *The Crone*. She writes that the female genital symbol "was sacred to Kali, representing her Om or Word (Logos) of Creation. Her spouse Shiva performed his sexual dance within a horseshoe of fire, representing the cosmic yoni. The symbol passed into the Greek alphabet as the Crone's letter, the horseshoe-shaped omega, which literally means 'great Om.'"

"Venusberg": Considered to be one of the sculptural masterpieces of the Middle/Late Magdalenian, this broken reindeer-antler spear-thrower depicts, in the Abbé Breuil's words, "two young ibexes playing and fighting one against the other." It is my impression that they are bison, and are carved without heads since the width of the tine from which their torsos have been shaped narrows and allows no head room over the animals' neck areas. Its width also determines the embraced position of the bodies. Almost 2½ inches tall, the piece was found in the tunnel between les Trois Frères and Enlène. The animals' bodies are covered with hatch marks suggesting fur.

Before quoting this stanza (quoted in the poem) from Tannhäuser, Duerr writes "Even the bison horn, which the equally faceless Venus of Laussel holds in her right hand, may presage the horn of plenty of Mother Gaea, the horns of the goat Amalthea, from which issued nectar and ambrosia. Perhaps it is the same as the drinking horn once held in her left hand by the Iberian goddess of the lower world, whose name may have been Ataecina, and who was venerated in a grotto near the Straits of Gibralter. She was bare-breasted and her head was veiled. Finally, the horn of the Venus from the Dordogne is reminiscent of the drinking horns offered by the Teutonic Valkyries to the warriors killed in battle, or the beaker proffered to Tannhäuser by the Lady Venus."

"The Chaos of the Wise": This title comes from Fulcanelli's *Le Mystère des Cathédrals*. In Fulcanelli's view, the "occult Fountain, [a] powerful solvent, capable of penetrating every metal—gold in particular—and of accomplishing the great task in its entirety" issues from "the Chaos of the Wise," also called "Metallic chaos," "in which all hidden secrets exist in potential." I understand this term as an esoteric metaphor for the regenerative potential of the earth's elements, specifically, in an Upper Paleolithic context, the combination of stone, manganese, ochre, water, and the cave's living dark that enabled the "great task" of image-making to occur. "The Oath of the Abyss," discussed by Kenneth Grant in *Cults of the Shadow*, "means to make a willed effort to Cross the Abyss, or transcend the world of subject and object and resolve the antinomies of mundane consciousness."

"Neanderthal Skull": The implicit proposal here is that because Neanderthal appears not to have had the sophisticated weapons associated with Cro-Magnon people, he met the world more as prey than as predator, and was primarily a scavenger at carnivore-infested kill sites. Barbara Ehrenreich believes that the human compulsion for violence was stimulated by the blood rites performed to reenact terrifying experiences of being preyed upon by carnivores. See her *Blood Rites*.

"Some Fugal Lubrication": In *The Ghost Dance*, La Barre regards Cernunnos, the Celtic deer-horned Master of Animals, as a later variation on the antlered "Dancing Sorcerer" at Les Trois Frères.

Björn Kurtén, in *The Cave Bear Story*, writes: "During the years 1917 to 1921 Emil Bachler, of the museum in St. Gallen, Switzerland, dug the Drachenloch Cave—one of the 'Dragon Lairs'—near Vattis in the Tamina Valley. The cave, at an altitude of 7,335 feet above sea level, forms a deep tunnel running more than 200 feet into the cliff. The deposits in the cave turned out to contain an immense number of cave bear remains, including several well-preserved skulls, and complete limb bones. At that elevation, the site would have been inaccessible during the glaciation, thus the bears must date from the interglacial, the time of early Neanderthal man in Europe."

Bachler's finds included a kind of stone slab chest containing bear skulls, as well as a bear skull with a thigh bone twisted into position through its cheek. On the basis of these finds, along with the discovery at Wildenmannisloch (also in Switzerland) of bear skulls with limestone slabs resting on top of them, Bachler concluded, in 1940, that "the purposeful collection and arranged preservation of cave bear skulls and long bones behind dry walls (*Trockenmauren*) set up along the sides of the caves, and more especially, the hermetic sealing away of the skulls, either in crudely built stone cabinets, protected by slab coverings, or in repositories walled with flagging, allow no other conclusion... but that we have here to do with some sort of Bear Cult, specifically a Bone-offering Cult, inspired by the mystical thoughts and feelings of an Old Paleolithic population" (quoted in Joseph Campbell, *The Way of the Animal Powers*).

However, it turns out that Bachler delegated the digging to gangs of laborers, only showing up from time to time to inspect the foreman's report and look at the finds. He kept no detailed records, made no photographs, and in the course of the excavation the stone chests were destroyed. The exception to this is a single photo taken by Bachler of the bear skull with a long bone pushed through its cheek. Bachler's two sketches of the cave with its stratigraphic deposits, skulls ands bones, published in 1923 and 1940, differ significantly.

Both Kurtén and Tattersall offer their own explanations of natural processes to account for what Bachler interpreted as Neanderthal arrangements. Only Campbell finds Bachler's work entirely credible, claiming (with Bachler's two caves in mind) "evidence, on one hand, of workshops for fashioning tools and weapons associated with the bear hunt, and on the other, of sanctuaries for the worship of the bears that were killed. There were fire hearths in the caves, stone worktables and benches, flagstone floorings, and bins of various kinds for the preservation of the skulls, some of which were even found in what appeared to be intentional symbolical arrangements." Campbell's descriptions strikes me as utterly fanciful and cast a very suspicious cloud over his scholarship in general. The photo of the bear skull with the long bone seems credible enough and is what I have concentrated on in the poem.

Vainamöinen, who kills the bear Otso, is the magic singer of the Finnish epic, the *Kalevala*.

Knud Rasmussen (1879–1933) was an extraordinary polar explorer and anthropologist from Greenland.

"At the Hinge of Creation": The title was spun off marginalia in my copy of H.R. Ellis Davidson's *Gods and Myths of the Viking Age*. After reading the description of the Norse Creation, I noted: "if God is light (Kafka), his shadow is ice. Between light and ice there is a gap—a Ginnungagap—where heat and cold meet."

The Olson quotation is one of the few references in his poetry to the Upper Paleolithic. The entire passage (from *The Maximus Poems*) reads:

> Licked man (as such) out of the ice.
> the cow————did who
> herself came into being
> so that Ymir would have some source
> of food (her milk one supposes

Odin was born of either this man directly
or one generation further on, Odin's mother
was the giant————————.

Olson may have put in the blanks to suggest unverifiable or missing
sources. He also may have not known the name of the cow (Authumla,
or Audummia), or Odin's mother (Bestla, a giant's daughter, one of
Ymir's descendants). The licking of Odin and his brothers out of the ice
could also suggest birthing on Authumla's part. Since Odin is depicted
as a warrior-shaman, it would not be unusual for him to be the offspring
of giants and animals.

"The Paleo-Mesolithic bridge" is my term in an attempt to connect
these two periods, between which there is a "gap" of thousands of years
depending on the area of Europe being discussed.

In *The Gilded Gutter Life of Francis Bacon*, Daniel Farson mentions
that Bacon showed him "the weals across his back," with the implication
that whipping had taken place with the painter's permission. I see such
masochism as a force that is bled, as it were, into the potent violence of
Bacon's images. I associate the weals and potency with the viscous milky
white venom secreted by the parotoid glands of the Sonoran Desert toad,
Bufo alvarius. This venom contains an unusual enzyme which can be
converted into 5-MeO-DMT, one of the most powerful hallucinogens.

"Prolegomena": Golgonooza is William Blake's vision of the total
form of creative acts, which is, according to Northrop Frye in his *Fearful
Symmetry*, "the eternal reality of Everyman's existence."

Giedion in *The Eternal Present: The Beginnings of Art* discusses the
discovery of the La Ferrassie cupules in his commentary on this rock
shelter. The engraved blocks are now in the new Les Eyzies National
Prehistoric Museum, opened in 2004.

"With toe in mouth, / with serpent-encircled web": These two lines
draw upon imagery from Plate 1, "The Birth of Vishnu" in Erich Neu-
mann's *The Origin and History of Consciousness*. The image reproduced
with my poem is from Jung's *Collected Works*, Vol. 12. in which he writes:
"We can hardly escape the feeling that the unconscious process moves
spiral-wise round a centre, gradually getting closer, while the character-
istics of the centre grow more and more distant. Or perhaps we could
put it the other way around and say that the centre—itself virtually un-

knowable—acts like a magnet on the disparate materials and processes of the unconscious and gradually captures them as in a crystal lattice. For this reason the centre is often pictured as a spider in its web, especially when the conscious attitude is still dominated by fear of unconscious processes. But if the process is allowed to take its course, then the central symbol, constantly renewing itself, will steadily and consistently force its way through the apparent chaos of the personal psyche and its dramatic entanglements....Accordingly, we often find spiral representations of the centre, as for instance the serpent coiled around the creative point, the egg."

A differing interpretation of the uroboros is provided by Wolfgang Giegerich in his essay, "Okeanos and the Circulation of the Blood," in *Sulfur #21*.

"A Phosphene Gauntlet": For a discussion of entopic phenomena as they might pertain to Upper Paleolithic imagery, see "The Signs of All Times" by J.D. Lewis-Williams and T.A. Dowson in *Current Anthropology*, April, 1988.

"Le Combel": A kind of cave within a cave, Le Combel is off to the right of Pech Merle's present-day entrance. Its walls and ceilings have clusters of red disks. There are also two small chambers with fantasy-animal paintings, and a tree-like stalagmitic "Goddess" formation, addressed in "The Black Goddess" at the end of this section.

To my knowledge, only Giedion discusses Le Combel at length (in *The Eternal Present*).

Re. "the African pythoness" see the material from Alfred Metraux's *Voodoo in Haiti* quoted in Kenneth Grant's *Aleister Crowley and the Hidden God*.

"Indeterminate, Open": With two exceptions (sections 2 and 10) all of these short poems are based on Monique and Claude Archambeau's photographs and drawings of some 50 "human figurations" in the Combarelles cave near the village of Les Eyzies. The Archambeau research is to be found in "Les figurations humaines parietales de la grotte des Combarelles," *Gallia Préhistorique*, Tome 33, 1991. My presentation follows the order in which one encounters the figures as one moves deeper and deeper into the cave.

"Matrix, Blower": This poem began with my notes on a draft of Jed Rasula's essay, "Gendering the Muse" (*Sulfur #35*), in an attempt to trace Classical Muse formations back to the Upper Paleolithic. An early draft of this poem, "The Inaccessible," appeared in *FlashPoint #1*. To my knowledge, Gordon Wasson was the first to conjecture that Hades' eruption into Kore's meadow probably represented an entheogenic implosion (see *Persephone's Quest*). Abri Cellier is an Aurignacian rock shelter near Les Eyzies; it has some of the earliest-known engravings (30,000-28,000 B.P.) in the Dordogne region. "The original sentence…" is quoted from N.O. Brown's *Love's Body*. "Beauty will be erotic-veiled…" is from André Breton's *L'Amour fou*. The passage beginning "I was 18 months old…" is spoken by a delusional patient to Susan Baur in *The Dinosaur Man*. "After the first death…" is the concluding line of Dylan Thomas's poem, "A Refusal to Mourn the Death, by Fire, of a Child in London."

There are significant revisions in the version of the poem presented here.

"The Black Goddess": For more on the baby armed with teeth, see Ferenczi's *Thalassa*. The N.O. Brown quotations are from *Love's Body*. "The Black Goddess" is the second of five sections making up "A Cosmogonic Collage," the concluding work in *Juniper Fuse*. Since the other sections are written in prose I have not included them here.

Everwhat (La Laguna, Canary Islands, 2003)

"Noguchi, 1984": Isamu Noguchi (1904–1988) is a celebrated Japanese American artist and landscape architect, known for his sculpture and public works. Bill and Yoshiko Paden took Caryl and me to the Noguchi Museum in the Long Island City of Queens in 1984 where I took the notes that resulted in this poem.

"Bacon Studies (III)": Based on notebook entries made at the 2000 Francis Bacon Retrospective at the Pompidou Museum in Paris.

"Spirits of the Head": from 1964 to October 1971, when he committed suicide in Paris, George Dyer was Francis Bacon's lover and prominent model. There is a note on the writing of this poem in *Reciprocal Distillations.*

"The Magical Sadness of Omar Cáceres": See Eliot Weinberger's essay "Omar Cáceres" in *Karmic Traces.* According to Weinberger, Cáceres is one of many significant and forgotten 20th century Latin American poets, and one who is known only by a collection of 15 poems, *Defensa del ídola,* published by his brother in Chile in 1930. Weinberger translates, in his essay, one of these poems, and this translation, along with the bits of information on the poet, moved me to write my own poem in the voice of Omar Cáceres. There is a selection of Cáceres poems translated by Monica de la Torre in *The Oxford Book of Latin American Poetry.*

"Figure and Ground": The stimulation for this poem occurred while reading Declan McGonagle's Foreword to Jon Bird's *Leon Golub / Echoes of the Real.* McGonagle writes: "The contest in art is regularly characterized, and trivialized, by the media as a contest between forms of figuration and abstraction when the fundamental tension is actually between figure and ground—the figure of art/the artist and the ground of society.... The figure is never actually lost in Golub's paintings, as it is in Byzantine or Islamic art, where the ground/the collective becomes more important than the figure/the individual. I would argue that Golub, as a citizen-artist, argues the need for both the individual and the collective aspects of humanity to be upheld in a tension that is fundamentally democratic because it is inclusive and acknowledges its origins in culture as well as nature."

"Darger": Henry Darger (1892–1973) was a recluse who became famous for his posthumously-discovered 15,145 page illustrated fantasy manuscript called "The Story of the Vivian Girls, in What is Known as the Realms of the Unreal, of the Glandeco-Angelinian War Storm, Caused by the Child Slave Rebellion." In 1930, he settled into a room on Chicago's North Side where he lived until his death. In 1997, Caryl and I were given permission to visit his room right before much of its contents were moved to The American Folk Art Museum in NYC and The Center for Intuitive and Outsider Art in Chicago.

My *Devotion* (A Black Sparrow Book published in 2004 by David R Godine, Jaffrey, N.H.

"Across the Bering Strait": Mary Ann Unger (1945–1999) was a powerful sculptor best known for her large-scale works evoking the body, bandaging, flesh and bone. Photos of her installation "Across the Bering Strait" are in *Sulfur #40* (with an essay on Unger by Carla Harryman). Unger's website is www.maryannunger.com

"Blue Zone": Ann Mikolowski (1940–1999) was a central figure in Detroit's Cass Corridor art movement. Her paintings and watercolors range from expansive, open vistas of water and sky, to tiny, realistic portraits of artists and friends. Along with her husband, Ken, she was editor, publisher, and printer of the Alternative Press broadsides and postcards for over 30 years. Her paintings have appeared on the covers of books by such writers as Helen Adam, Robert Creeley, Faye Kicknosway, William Stafford, and Adrienne Rich.

"Shopping": The quotation is from Tillie Olson's poem "I Want You Women Up North to Know," published in 1934.

"The Hybrid is the Engine of Anima Display": Although this astonishing engraving is difficult to "read," once spotted, the figure of the young woman seated inside the dancing hybrid is clearly there. While I have looked at it briefly on visits to Les Trois Frères, I have studied it in the Abbé Breuil's drawings of the engraved panels of the cave in *Les Caverns du Volp*.

An Alchemist with One Eye on Fire (Black Widow Press, Boston, 2006)

"Pause": Some implications of being "fully born" are explored in two other poems in *Anticline*: "Placenta" (included in this collection) and "Fully Born."

"An Enigmatic Signifier": This poem makes use of material to be found in Jean LaPlanche's *Seduction, Translation, Drives,* in particular the chapter "The Drive and Its Object-source: its fate in the transference."

"Samperi's Diagram": The poet Frank Samperi's (1933–1991) major work is a trilogy made up of *The Prefiguration, Quadrifarium,* and *Lumen Gloriae,* all published by Mushinsha-Grossman, in 1971 and 1973. Station Hill brought out a selected poems by Samperi, *Spiritual Necessity,* edited by John Martone, in 2003. I knew Frank both in NYC and in Kyoto, and published his *Crystals* as a Caterpillar Book (1967) as well as some of his poems in *Caterpillar* magazine. Samperi is a unique figure in American poetry, whose force field gravitated almost totally around Dante.

"For Gustaf Sobin": The poet, essayist, translator, and novelist Gustaf Sobin (1935–2005) moved to the French Provence in the 1960s, finding his true home there near the poet René Char, whom he later translated. Caryl and I last visited Gustaf in the summer of 2004. He took us to Char's birthplace, his last home, and to his tomb which Gustaf tended conscientiously for years, clipping and watering the bushes that semi-encircle it.

"Iraqi Morgue": The source for this poem is "The Face of War," an album containing photos taken on November 19, 2004, by the American military, of dead men in Fallujah. This album is to be found on Dahr Jamail's Iraq Dispatches site: www.dahrjamailiraq.com

"Combined Object": This poem draws on materials from Abyss by C.P Idyll, the paintings of Henri Michaux, and David Ball's translations in *Darkness Moves: An Henri Michaux Anthology, 1927–1984.*
There are some cuts and revisions in the version presented here.

◇

Archaic Design (Black Widow Press, Boston, 2007).

"The Assault": My initial response to the 9/11 assaults, as a citizen reader/investigator, was to start making myself more aware of what we might have done to others, beyond our borders, to instigate such an action. I read William Blum's *Killing Hope* and then his *Rogue State*. Gore Vidal in an *Observer* article alerted me to the possibility that the official version of what happened on 9/11 was bogus. Vidal referred the reader to Nafeeze Mosaddeq Ahmed's 2002 *The War on Freedom* which I then read and checked his information against Paul Thompson's *The Complete 9/11 Time Line*. I have not found any official response that convincingly contradicts Vidal, Ahmed or Thompson. The compressed time line data in the first part of my piece is mainly taken from Ahmed's book. The lyric outrage in part II is all my own (other than when factual), and participates in the tradition of the sirventes. Robert Duncan's poem, "Uprising," which condemns President Johnson for the carpet-bombing of Vietnam, hovers over "The Assault," a predecessor ghost.

I sent my piece (completed at the end of 2002) to editor Katrina Vanden Heuvel at *The Nation*, a weekly whose politics I respect. Vanden Heuvel wrote back that *The Nation* had covered all the points my poem raised. Since at the time I was reading *The Nation* weekly, I knew this was not true. In fact, *The Nation*, to my knowledge, had not published a single article disputing the official version of 9/11. So I wrote Vanden Heuvel back, asking her to point out to me where the information in my poem had been discussed. Her response was to ask me not to write to her anymore. So I sent "The Assault" to Lewis Lapham at *Harper's Magazine*. Lapham wrote me that it was an interesting imitation of Archibald MacLeish and e.e.cummings but not for them. The poem was ultimately published by Dale Smith on the *Possum Pouch* blog, by Nathaniel Mackey in *Hambone,* and in a French translation by Auxeméry in *Momentum* (Paris).

In recent years, additional information contesting the official story about 9/11 has come to light: much of this information is summed up by David Ray Griffin in *The New Pearl Harbor* and by Eric Hufschmid in *Painful Questions: An Analysis of the September 11th Attack*. The most pertinent information, at the point this note was written in 2013, confirms that a form of controlled demolition was used to destroy the twin towers and building 7 and that the Pentagon was either struck by a missile or, according to Barbara Honegger in her Seattle lecture "Behind the Smoke Curtain," attacked by "pre-placed-inside-the-building explosives." Cobbled together roughly a year after 9/11, my poem will no longer be news to those readers who have reflected on any of the materials I mention above. However, in the light of no new official investigation to take place (and thus replace the completely unsatisfactory 9/11 Commission report), I have decided to let this piece stand as it is, as the testimony of a poet's immediate response to and investigation of the event that remains the basis for our invasion of Afghanistan and Iraq and the horrendous destruction of life in those two countries as well as the death of thousands of the American soldiers sent there.

My other piece on 9/11, included in this collection, is "Minor Drag."

◇

Reciprocal Distillations (Hot Whiskey Press, Boulder CO, 2007

"Witchery": Notes that I made in the Chicago Art Institute in February 2004 (the material out of which this poem was formed) may be found on pp. 308–310 in *The Price of Experience*.

"Chauvet: Left Wall of End Chamber": James O'Hern and I visited the Chauvet Cave with guide Jean-Marie Chauvet (one of the cave's three 1994 discoverers) on January 8, 1994. My gratitude to Dominique Baffier for arranging our visit. Excellent color photographs of the wall with the lions addressed in my poem may be found in *Chauvet Cave / The Art of Earliest Times*.

"The Beheading": I am indebted to Peter Robb's rethinking of Caravaggio's life and art in M / *The Man who Became Caravaggio*, as well as to Catherine Puglisi's excellent *Caravaggio*, with its detailed investigation of "The Beheading of Saint John the Baptist," and to Leo Bersani and Ulysse Dutoit's *Caravaggio's Secrets*. I am also in debt to Dominic Cutajar, not only for his essay, "Caravaggio in Malta," but also for asking the Oratory guards in Valletta's Co-Cathedral in May 2002 to turn off the two alarm systems so that Caryl and I, along with our friends James Heller Levinson and Victoria Ganim, could almost touch the 12x17 foot "Beheading" with our noses.

"Monumental": Through March and April, in 2005, I worked on a piece for the public memorial program for the painter Leon Golub, who had died at 82 in August, 2004, at Cooper Union's Great Hall, in NYC. Golub is one of the greatest of American painters, and his painterly trackings of our horrendous overseas government involvements in torture and murder, throughout the 60s, 70s, 80s, and 90s, are acts of courageous witnessing. The last 25 years of Golub's paintings are the closest thing we have in America to Goya's "black period" and *The Disasters of War*. No wonder no major museum in the New York City area has ever given him a retrospective; his moral acuity cuts like acid through the evasion and lies that have become our public policy.

◇

Anticline (Black Widow Press, Boston, 2010).

"The Tjurunga": I was first alerted to the *tjurunga* (or *churinga*) by Robert Duncan in 1967 via his essay, "Rites of Participation" (from *The H.D. Book*) which appeared in *Caterpillar* #1 and 2. Duncan quoted Geza Róheim ("The *tjurunga*, which symbolizes both the male and female genital organ, the primal scene and combined parent concept, the father and the mother, separation and reunion… represents both the path and the goal"), and then commented: "This *tjurunga* we begin to see not as the secret identity of the Aranda initiate but as our own Freudian identity, the conglomerate consciousness of the mind we share with Róheim… the simple *tjurunga* now appears to be no longer simple but the complex mobile that S. Giedion in *Mechanization Takes Command* saw as embodying our contemporary experience: 'the whole construction is aerial and hovering as the net of an insect'—a suspended system, so contrived that 'a draft of air or push of a hand will change the state of equilibrium and the interrelations of suspended elements… forming unpredictable, ever-changing constellations and so imparting to them the aspect of space-time.'"

Reading Barry Hill's *Broken Song / T.G.H. Strehlow and Aboriginal Possession* recently brought back and refocused Duncan's words.

In Vol. 13 of *The Collected Works*, Jung writes: "*Churingas* may be boulders, or oblong stones artificially shaped and decorated, or oblong, flattened pieces of wood ornamented in the same way. They are used as cult instruments. The Australians and the Melanesians maintain that *churingas* come from the totem ancestor, that they are relics of his body or his activity, and are full of *arunquiltha* or mana. They are united with the ancestor's soul and the spirits of all those who afterwards possess them… In order to 'charge' them, they are buried among the graves so that they can soak up the mana of the dead."

In my poem I propose a kind of complex mobile made up of the authors, artists, mythological figures and acts, whose shifting combinations undermined and reoriented my life during my poetic apprenticeship in Kyoto. At a remove now of some 50 years I see these forces as a kind of GPS constantly "recalculating" as they closed and opened door after door.

In the thick of breakthroughs often interpreted by my confused mind as obstructions in Kyoto, I was able to complete only one poem that struck me as true to my situation and destiny as a poet: "The Book of Yorunomado." With bookends in mind, I see this poem and "The Tjurunga" as the "soul end" supports holding the rest of my poetry in place. Thinking back to Vallejo pointing at my gut in 1963 and indicating that I was to commit seppuku, I was struck by the following quotation from James Hillman's *Animal Presences*: "The theological message of the Siva-Ganesha, father-son pattern can be summarized in this way: submit that you may be saved, be destroyed that you may be made whole. The sacrificial violence is not the tragic conclusion but the necessary beginning of a passage into a new order… the God who breaks you makes you, destruction and creating ultimately spring from the same source."

"Hmmm": I drew upon some of Dennis J. McKenna's amazing observations while under the influence of hoasca. His account of his experience is to be found in *Ayahuasca Reader/Encounters with the Amazon's Sacred Vine*, ed. by Luis Eduardo Luna and Steven F. White.

"Octavio's Labyrinth": About one-third of the lines in this poem are from Eliot Weinberger's excellent translations of Octavio Paz's poetry in *The Collected Poems of Octavio Paz*.

"The Left Food of King Ramesses I": Information on tent caterpillars comes from *The Tent Caterpillars* by Terrence D. Fitzgerald.

"Poem to Help Will Alexander Fight Cancer": This poem was written to be read at a benefit poetry reading for Will Alexander that I helped organize at Skylight Books in Los Angeles, on January 13, 2008.

"Eternity at Domme": Whenever Caryl and I led tours to the prehistoric painted caves in southwestern France, we always visited the town of Domme, a bastide crowning a hill overlooking the Dordogne River. All of us would stand, we thought, at the same spot that Henry Miller did in the late 1930s when, during a visit to the Dordogne on his way to Greece, he made a marvelous statement about the region in ancient times (see *Juniper Fuse*, pp. 243–244 for the quotation). In 2007, standing at this spot overlooking the Dordogne River slowly meandering far below, a mass of contrasting ideas and feelings from my decades of cave research kaleidoscopically locked into focus. Suddenly I had realized my life.

"Zürn Heads": The German artist Unica Zürn (1916–1970) appears to have begun to draw after becoming the companion of Hans Bellmer (1902–1975), in Paris, in 1953, undoubtedly stimulated by Bellmer's darkly erotic and meticulous art. While in Paris she had contact with some of the Surrealists, like Breton and Matta, and is said to have been introduced to mescaline by Henri Michaux (who she referred to as "The Jasmine Man" in one of her several books). In *Sulfur #29*, Renée Riese Hubert edited a 40 page section on Zürn's texts and drawings. Zürn committed suicide in 1970, via defenestration, out of the couple's Paris apartment. For a fine collection of her drawings, see *Unica Zürn/Bilder, 1953–1970*, Verlag Brinkmann und Bose, Berlin, 1998. In *Reciprocal Distillations* and *Archaic Design*, there are two other poems on Zürn and her art.

"Munch Dissolves": I hear the word "Munch" in the title of this poem as an adjective. I have been brooding about Edvard Munch for many years. There is a draft of the "scream" section, which ends this poem, entitled "During Munch," in *Mistress Spirit*, 1989. I was recharged by Munch while viewing his MOMA retrospective in 2006. I highly recommend Sue Prideaux's *Edvard Munch / Behind the Scream*.

"Goya Black": See Robert Hughes' *Goya* for a thoughtful commentary on the Black Paintings which are to be found on the 3rd floor of the Prado Museum in Madrid.

"Ode to Nancy Spero": Nancy Spero (1926–2009) engaged the life and mind of Antonin Artaud in two major projects: "Artaud paintings" (1969–1970), and "Codex Artaud" (1971–1972). I see Nancy's Artaud projects as catalysts for her images of feminine release, taken from many cultures and times (including Greek dildo dancers and Irish Sheela-na-gigs), that proliferate throughout her art of the 1980s and 1990s. See my paper "Nancy Meets the Mômo" posted on the English *International Times* literary blog.

"Xibalbá": The name of the Maya underworld, and the site of much of the action in the *Popol Vuh*. For the past several years I have been looking at painted Maya ceramics, the polychrome vessels often found in the tombs of the Maya elite. Justin Kerr's roll-out photos have enabled us to view these wrap-around paintings as a single "strip," which, with their glyphs, evoke, for me, 20th century American comic strips, with the glyphs playing the role of our speech balloons. Many of the identities and doings of the gods, heroes, hybrids, and animals on these ceramics will probably remain obscure. For me, they are the finest display of New World aboriginal imagination. Michael Coe's many books, especially *The Art of the Maya Scribe* and *Lords of the Underworld* are indispensable guides to this Maya realm.

"Max Ernst During the Rain": My interest in Ernst was fired by his 2004 retrospective at The Metropolitan Museum in NYC. I then made use of two books on Ernst to help generate this poem: John Russell's *Max Ernst: Life & Work*, and Werner Spies' *Max Ernst / A Retrospective*.
   For a few paintings by Sultan Muhammed and Aqa Mirak, see *A King's Book of Kings/The Shah-nameh of Shah Tahmasp*.

"In Deep Sleep Dorothea Tanning Receives & Accepts the Awakened Clouds Above Her": In the George Braziller *Dorothea Tanning*, I am particular indebted to Jean Christophe Bailly's essay, "Image Redux: The Art of Dorothea Tanning." Tanning's memoir *Birthday* is a marvelous and moving evocation of her 34 years with Max Ernst.

"Pollock Pouring": this poem is based on some 20 pages of notes written while standing before Pollock's 1949 #1 (in the Museum of Contemporary Art, Los Angeles).

Clayton Eshleman was born in Indianapolis, Indiana, June 1, 1935. He has a B.A. in Philosophy and an M.A.T. in English Literature from Indiana University. He has lived in Mexico, Japan, Taiwan, Korea, Peru, France, Czechoslovakia, and Hungary. He is presently Professor Emeritus, English Department, Eastern Michigan University. Since 1986 he has lived in Ypsilanti, Michigan with his wife Caryl who over the past forty years has been the primary reader and editor of his poetry and prose. His first collection of poetry, *Mexico & North,* was published in Kyoto, 1962. From 1968 to 2004, Black Sparrow Press brought out thirteen collections of his poetry. In 2006, Black Widow Press became his main publisher and with *Clayton Eshleman/The Essential Poetry 1960–2015* has brought out seven collections of his poetry, prose, and translations, including in 2008 *The Grindstone of Rapport/A Clayton Eshleman Reader.* Wesleyan University Press has published five of his books, including *Juniper Fuse: Upper Paleolithic Imagination & the Construction of the Underworld* (2003), the first study of the Ice Age cave art by a poet. Two book-length poems, *An Anatomy of the Night* and *The Jointure,* were published by BlazeVOX in 2011 and 2012. Eshleman has published fourteen collections of translations, including *Watchfiends & Rack Screams* by Antonin Artaud (Exact Change, 1995), *The Complete Poetry of César Vallejo* (University of California Press, 2007) and *Solar Throat Slashed* by Aimé Césaire, cotranslated with A. James Arnold (Wesleyan University Press, 2011). He also founded and edited two of the most important innovative poetry journals of the later part of the 20th century: *Caterpillar* (20 issues, 1967–1973) and *Sulfur* (46 issues, 1981–2000). Among his recognitions and awards are a Guggenheim Fellowship in Poetry, The National Book Award in Translation, two grants from the NEA, two grants from the NEH, two Landon Translation Prizes from the Academy of American Poets, and a Rockefeller Study Center residency in Bellagio, Italy. Forthcoming publications include *A Sulfur Anthology* (Wesleyan University Press, 2015), *Penetralia* (Black Widow Press, 2016), and *The Complete Poetry of Aimé Césaire,* cotranslated with A. James Arnold (Wesleyan, 2016).

Clayton and Caryl Eshleman, 2011

Stuart Kendall is a writer, editor, and translator working at the intersections of poetics, visual culture, and design. His books include *Gilgamesh, The Ends of Art and Design, Georges Bataille,* and many other edited or translated volumes. Black Widow Press also published his edited volume, *Clayton Eshleman: The Whole Art,* in 2014. He lives in Oakland, California, where he teaches at the California College of the Arts.

TITLES FROM BLACK WIDOW PRESS
TRANSLATION SERIES

A Life of Poems, Poems of a Life
by Anna de Noailles. Translated by Norman
R. Shapiro. Introduction by Catherine Perry.

Approximate Man and Other Writings
by Tristan Tzara. Translated and edited
by Mary Ann Caws.

Art Poétique by Guillevic.
Translated by Maureen Smith.

The Big Game by Benjamin Péret.
Translated with an introduction by Marilyn Kallet.

Boris Vian Invents Boris Vian: A Boris Vian Reader.
Edited and translated by Julia Older.

Capital of Pain by Paul Eluard.
Translated by Mary Ann Caws, Patricia Terry, and
Nancy Kline.

Chanson Dada: Selected Poems by Tristan Tzara.
Translated with an introduction and essay by
Lee Harwood.

*Essential Poems and Writings of Joyce Mansour:
A Bilingual Anthology.* Translated with an
introduction by Serge Gavronsky.

Essential Poems and Prose of Jules Laforgue.
Translated and edited by Patricia Terry.

*Essential Poems and Writings of Robert Desnos:
A Bilingual Anthology.* Edited with an introduction
and essay by Mary Ann Caws.

EyeSeas (Les Ziaux) by Raymond Queneau.
Translated with an introduction by
Daniela Hurezanu and Stephen Kessler.

Fables in a Modern Key by Pierre Coran.
Edited and translated by Norman R. Shapiro.
Full-color illustrations by Olga Pastuchiv.

*Forbidden Pleasures: New Selected Poems
[1924–1949]* by Luis Cernuda.
Translated by Stephen Kessler.

Furor and Mystery & Other Writings by René Char.
Edited and translated by Mary Ann Caws and
Nancy Kline.

Guarding the Air: Selected Poems of Gunnar Harding.
Translated and edited by Roger Greenwald.

The Inventor of Love & Other Writings
by Gherasim Luca. Translated by Julian & Laura
Semilian. Introduction by Andrei Codrescu.
Essay by Petre Răileanu.

Jules Supervielle: Selected Prose and Poetry.
Translated by Nancy Kline and Patricia Terry.

La Fontaine's Bawdy by Jean de La Fontaine.
Translated with an introduction by
Norman R. Shapiro.

Last Love Poems of Paul Eluard.
Translated with an introduction by Marilyn Kallet.

Love, Poetry (L'amour la poésie) by Paul Eluard.
Translated with an essay by Stuart Kendall.

Pierre Reverdy: Poems, Early to Late.
Translated by Mary Ann Caws and Patricia Terry.

Poems of André Breton: A Bilingual Anthology.
Translated with essays by Jean-Pierre Cauvin
and Mary Ann Caws.

Poems of A.O. Barnabooth by Valery Larbaud.
Translated by Ron Padgett and Bill Zavatsky.

Poems of Consummation by Vicente Aleixandre.
Translated by Stephen Kessler.

Préversities: A Jacques Prévert Sampler.
Translated and edited by Norman R. Shapiro.

The Sea and Other Poems by Guillevic.
Translated by Patricia Terry. Introduction by
Monique Chefdor.

To Speak, to Tell You? Poems by Sabine Sicaud.
Translated by Norman R. Shapiro. Introduction
and notes by Odile Ayral-Clause.

Forthcoming Translations

Earthlight (Clair de Terre) by André Breton.
Translated by Bill Zavatsky and Zack Rogrow.
(New and revised edition.)

*The Gentle Genius of Cécile Périn:
Selected Poems (1906–1956).*
Edited and translated by Norman R. Shapiro.

MODERN POETRY SERIES

ABC of Translation by Willis Barnstone

An Alchemist with One Eye on Fire
by Clayton Eshleman

Anticline by Clayton Eshleman

Archaic Design by Clayton Eshleman

Backscatter: New and Selected Poems
by John Olson

Barzakh (Poems 2000–2012) by Pierre Joris

The Caveat Onus by Dave Brinks

City Without People: The Katrina Poems
by Niyi Osundare

Clayton Eshleman/The Essential Poetry: 1960–2015

Concealments and Caprichos by Jerome Rothenberg

Crusader-Woman by Ruxandra Cesereanu.
Translated by Adam J. Sorkin. Introduction
by Andrei Codrescu.

Curdled Skulls: Poems of Bernard Bador.
Translated by the author with Clayton Eshleman.

Disenchanted City (La ville désenchantée)
by Chantal Bizzini. Edited by Marilyn Kallet and
J. Bradford Anderson. Translated by J. Bradford
Anderson, Darren Jackson, and Marilyn Kallet.

Endure: Poems by Bei Dao.
Translated by Clayton Eshleman and Lucas Klein.

Exile Is My Trade: A Habib Tengour Reader.
Translated by Pierre Joris.

Eye of Witness: A Jerome Rothenberg Reader.
Edited with commentaries by Heriberto Yepez
& Jerome Rothenberg.

Fire Exit by Robert Kelly

Forgiven Submarine by Ruxandra Cesereanu
and Andrei Codrescu

from stone this running by Heller Levinson

The Grindstone of Rapport:
A Clayton Eshleman Reader

Larynx Galaxy by John Olson

The Love That Moves Me by Marilyn Kallet

Memory Wing by Bill Lavender

Packing Light: New and Selected Poems
by Marilyn Kallet

The Present Tense of the World: Poems 2000–
2009 by Amina Saïd. Translated with an
introduction by Marilyn Hacker.

The Price of Experience by Clayton Eshleman

The Secret Brain: Selected Poems 1995–2012
by Dave Brinks

Signal from Draco: New and Selected Poems
by Mebane Robertson

Wrack Lariat by Heller Levinson

Forthcoming Modern Poetry Titles

An American Unconscious
by Mebane Robertson

Funny Way of Staying Alive
by Willis Barnstone

The Hexagon by Robert Kelly

Memory by Bernadette Mayer

Soraya (Sonnets) by Anis Shivani

LITERARY THEORY /
BIOGRAPHY SERIES

Barbaric Vast & Wild: A Gathering of Outside
and Subterranean Poetry (Poems for the
Millennium, v. 5) Eds: Jerome Rothenberg
and John Bloomberg-Rissman

Clayton Eshleman: The Whole Art
by Stuart Kendall

Revolution of the Mind:
The Life of André Breton
by Mark Polizzotti

WWW.BLACKWIDOWPRESS.COM